Kaplan Publishing are constantly finding nev
difference to your studies and our exciting c
offer something different to students lookin

CW00498665

This book comes with free MyKaplan online
study anytime, anywhere. **This free online ı**
separately and is included in the price of the book.

Having purchased this book, you have access to the following online study materials:

CONTENT	ACCA (including FBT, FMA, FFA)		FIA (excluding FBT, FMA, FFA)	
	Text	Kit	Text	Kit
Electronic version of the book	✓	✓	✓	✓
Knowledge checks with instant answers	✓		✓	
Material updates	✓	✓	✓	✓
Latest official ACCA exam questions*		✓		
Pocket Notes (digital copy)	✓		✓	
Study Planner	✓			
Progress Test including questions and answers	✓		✓	
Syllabus recap Videos		✓		✓
Revision Planner		✓		✓
Question Debrief and Walkthrough Videos		✓		
Mock Exam including questions and answers		✓		

* Excludes BT, MA, FA, FBT, FMA, FFA; for all other papers includes a selection of questions, as released by ACCA

How to access your online resources

Received this book as part of your Kaplan course?
If you have a MyKaplan account, your full online resources will be added automatically, in line with the information in your course confirmation email. If you've not used MyKaplan before, you'll be sent an activation email once your resources are ready.

Bought your book from Kaplan?
We'll automatically add your online resources to your MyKaplan account. If you've not used MyKaplan before, you'll be sent an activation email.

Bought your book from elsewhere?
Go to **www.mykaplan.co.uk/add-online-resources**
Enter the ISBN number found on the title page and back cover of this book.
Add the unique pass key number contained in the scratch panel below.
You may be required to enter additional information during this process to set up or confirm your account details.

This code can only be used once for the registration of this book online. This registration and your online content will expire when the examinations covered by this book have taken place. Please allow one hour from the time you submit your book details for us to process your request.

Please scratch the film to access your unique code.

Please be aware that this code is case-sensitive and you will need to include the dashes within the passcode, but not when entering the ISBN.

KAPLAN PUBLISHING

ACCA

Strategic Professional – Options

Advanced Taxation (ATX-UK) (Finance Act 2023)

EXAM KIT

For June 2024 to March 2025 examination sittings

KAPLAN PUBLISHING

British Library Cataloguing-in-Publication Data

A catalogue record for this book is available from the British Library.

Published by:

Kaplan Publishing UK

Unit 2 The Business Centre

Molly Millar's Lane

Wokingham

Berkshire

RG41 2QZ

ISBN: 978-1-83996-398-8

Printed and bound in Great Britain.

Acknowledgements

The past ACCA examination questions are the copyright of the Association of Chartered Certified Accountants. The original answers to the questions from June 1994 onwards were produced by the ACCA and have been adapted by Kaplan Publishing.

CONTENTS

Section

Versions of some questions in this Exam Kit may also be available on the ACCA Practice Platform on the ACCA website. They are a very useful reference, in particular to attempt using ACCA's exam software. However, you should be aware that ACCA will decide when those questions will be amended for syllabus changes or replaced, so they may differ slightly from the versions in this Exam Kit.

Key features in this edition

In addition to providing a wide-ranging bank of real past exam questions, we have also included in this edition:

- An analysis of all of the recently published examination questions.
- Exam specific information and advice on exam technique.
- Our recommended approach to make your revision for this particular subject as effective as possible.

  This includes step by step guidance on how best to use our Kaplan material (study text, pocket notes and exam kit) at this stage in your studies.
- An increased number of enhanced tutorial answers packed with specific key answer tips, technical tutorial notes and exam technique tips from our experienced tutors.
- Complementary online resources including full tutor debriefs and question assistance to point you in the right direction when you get stuck.

You will find a wealth of other resources to help you with your studies on the following sites:

www.mykaplan.co.uk

www.accaglobal.com/gb/en/student.html

Quality and accuracy are of the utmost importance to us so if you spot an error in any of our products, please send an email to mykaplanreporting@kaplan.com with full details, or follow the link to the feedback form in MyKaplan.

Our Quality Co-ordinator will work with our technical team to verify the error and take action to ensure it is corrected in future editions.

INDEX TO QUESTIONS AND ANSWERS

INTRODUCTION

The style of the ATX exam questions has changed over the years and significant changes have had to be made to questions in light of the legislative changes in recent Finance Acts.

Accordingly, many of the old ACCA questions within this kit have been adapted to reflect the new style of exam and the new rules. Therefore, some questions may not be worth 50 or 25 marks. If changed in any way from the original version, this is indicated in the end column of the index below with the mark *(A)*.

Also included are the marking schemes for past ACCA real examination questions to assist you in understanding where marks are earned and the amount of time to spend on particular tasks. Note that if a question has been changed from the original version, it will have also been necessary to change the original ACCA marking scheme. Therefore, if a question is marked as adapted (A) you should assume that this also applies to the marking scheme.

Note that the majority of the questions within the kit are past ACCA exam questions, the more recent questions are labelled as such in the index.

KEY TO THE INDEX

ANSWER ENHANCEMENTS

We have added the following enhancements to the answers in this exam kit:

Key answer tips

All answers include key answer tips to help your understanding of each question.

Tutorial note

All answers include more tutorial notes to explain some of the technical points in more detail.

Tutor's top tips

For selected questions, we 'walk through the answer' giving guidance on how to approach the questions with helpful 'tips from a top tutor', together with technical tutor notes.

These answers are indicated with the 'footsteps' icon in the index.

ONLINE ENHANCEMENTS

Answer debrief

For selected questions, we recommend that they are to be completed in full exam conditions (i.e. properly timed in a closed book environment).

In addition to the examining team's technical answer, enhanced with key answer tips and tutorial notes in this exam kit, online you can find an answer debrief by a top tutor that:

- works through the question in full
- explains key elements of the answer
- ensures that the easy marks are obtained as quickly as possible.

These questions are indicated with the 'video' icon in the index.

Answer debriefs will be available on MyKaplan at:

www.mykaplan.co.uk

SECTION A QUESTIONS

TAXATION OF INDIVIDUALS

Page number

		Question	Answer	Past exam (Adapted)
1	Gail and Brad	1	165	*Jun 13 and Mar/Jun 16 (A)*
2	Ziti	6	177	*Jun 14 (A)*
3	Jonny	9	193	*Sept/Dec 15 (A)*
4	Ray, Shanira and Kelly	12	202	*Mar/Jun 16 (A)*
5	Pippin	16	214	*Mar/Jun 17 (A)*
6	Maia	19	225	*Mar/Jun 19 (A)*
7	Joe and Fiona	23	234	*Mar/Jun 21 (A)*
8	Olma and Hogan	27	245	*Mar/Jun 22 (A)*
9	Hiromi	30	256	*Mar/Jun 23 (A)*

TAXATION OF CORPORATE BUSINESSES

SECTION B QUESTIONS

TAXATION OF INDIVIDUALS

TAXATION OF CORPORATE BUSINESSES

ANALYSIS OF PAST EXAMS

The table below summarises the key topics that have been tested in recent examinations.

Key:

Q The question references are to the number of the question in this edition of the exam kit.

✓ Refers to questions which have not been included in the kit due to similarity to other recent questions.

	Sept/Dec 2020	Mar/Jun 2021	Sep/Dec 2021	Mar/Jun 2022	Sep/Dec 2022	Mar/Jun 2023
IHT						
Lifetime gifts	✓	Q7	✓	Q8, Q56	Q63	
Death estate						
Diminution in value					Q63	
BPR/APR			✓		Q63	Q45
Gift with reservation		Q27				
Quick succession relief						
Consequences of lifetime giving		Q7				Q45
Overseas aspects	✓	Q7		Q8		
Trusts			✓			
CGT						
Basic computations			Q51	✓		Q9, Q45
Leases		Q62		Q69		
Shares	✓					
Reorganisations						
Capital gains tax reliefs:						
Incorporation relief	✓					Q9
Rollover relief	✓		Q20		Q21, Q32	
BADR			Q36		Q32	
Gift holdover relief			✓			Q45
PRR/letting relief		Q27				
Planning						
Overseas aspects	✓	Q7	✓	✓		
Income Tax						
Personal tax computations		Q7	Q20	✓	Q63	Q45
Redundancy payments						
Share options and share incentives		Q27		Q8		
Employment benefits	✓	Q62	Q20			
Employed v self employed						
Property business profits						
Overseas aspects of income	✓	Q7	✓, Q51	✓		
NICs	✓	Q62	Q20			

	Sept/Dec 2020	Mar/Jun 2021	Sep/Dec 2021	Mar/Jun 2022	Sep/Dec 2022	Mar/Jun 2023
Self-employed Income						
– Capital allowances		Q7			Q32	
– Trading losses	✓		Q36	Q8		Q9
– Partnerships						
Badges of trade						
Self-assessment						Q9
Employee v partner						
Corporation Tax						
Anti-avoidance – trading losses						
Loss relief				Q69		
Loan relationships						
Research and development			Q36			
Intangible assets		Q7				Q70
Transfer pricing			Q20			
Close companies	✓	Q62			Q32	
Purchase of own shares				Q8		
Personal service company			Q51			
Groups			Q20	Q69	Q21	
Consortium relief	✓					
Capital gains implications including rollover		Q62	Q20	Q69	Q21	
Pre-entry cap loss						
Substantial shareholding exemption						
Overseas Aspects	✓		Q20		Q21	Q70
Extraction of profits (salary vs. dividend)						Q9
Liquidation		Q7				
Administration	✓					
Sole trade v company						
Financial planning						
Investments				Q56		
Pensions						
EIS/SEIS/VCT				Q56		
Stamp Duty/SDLT					Q21	
VAT						
Registration/deregistration	✓			Q8		
Schemes						
Partial exemption						
Capital goods scheme						
Groups			Q20			
Land and buildings	✓	Q7			Q21, Q32	
Transfer of going concern						
Overseas aspects			Q20			Q70
Ethical issues	✓	Q7		Q8	Q21	Q9

EXAM TECHNIQUE

In addition to reading the tips contained here, we recommend that you review the resources available on the ACCA Global Website before sitting the CBE. Here you will find guidance documents, videos and a link to the CBE question practice platform.

- Before the exam starts you will be given ten minutes to read the introductory page and the four pages of instructions. These will be the same for each ATX exam and therefore it is important that you familiarise yourself with these (using the ACCA practice exams) during your revision. The exam time (3 hours and 15 minutes) will start automatically at the end of the 10 minutes or earlier if actioned by you.
- We recommend that you spend **15 minutes reading the questions** at the beginning of the exam:
  - read the questions and examination requirements carefully, and
  - begin planning your answers.

  See the Exam Specific Information for advice on how to use this time for this exam.
- If 15 minutes are spent reading the exam, this leaves three hours to attempt the questions.
- There are 80 technical marks and 20 professional skills marks. Importantly, professional skills marks should be achieved as you work through the technical marks.
- **Divide the time** you spend on questions in proportion to the marks on offer:
  - one suggestion for this examination is to allocate 2.25 minutes to each mark available (180 minutes/80 marks). This gives 90 minutes for section A and 45 minutes for each section B question.
  - within that, try to allow time at the end of each question to review your answer and address any obvious issues.
  - if you plan to spend more or less time than 15 minutes reading the exam, your time allocation per mark will be different.

  Whatever happens, always keep your eye on the clock and **do not over run on any part of any question!**
- **Planning your answers:**

  When the exam starts spend a few minutes skimming through each question to get a feel for what is included. Within the background information for each question you will find brief summary bullet points outlining the topics covered, which will help you identify what is being tested. Once you have done this carry out an initial review of Section A. This will include a number of **exhibits** breaking down the scenario into relevant sections and including the detailed requirement. It will also include a list of the summarised **requirements** and an option to complete your answer in a **word processing** document and/or a **spreadsheet** document.
- You can move around and resize the windows that you open to lay the screen out in a format that suits you.
- Now copy and paste the specifics of the requirement into your answer document, perhaps highlighting in bold the different parts of the requirement and the verb used. Once complete review the exhibits in detail, highlighting and making notes as you do so (see detail later) and copy and pasting any relevant information to your answer document. These steps will help with your planning and structure but will also enable you to minimise the number of windows you have open.

  The procedure will be similar for Section B.

- **Written questions**:

  Your answer should have a clear structure, using headings and subheadings.

  Be concise. It is better to write a little about a lot of different points than a great deal about one or two points.

  For answers that are mostly written you may find the word processor most useful.

- If you **get completely stuck** with a question:
  - make a note of the question, and
  - **return to it later.**

- A date assumption will be given at the start of each question, and at the start of the requirements. You should pay careful attention to this date and the timing of events noted in the scenario in relation to it. Some events may have already happened, whereas others may be planned for the future. For events which have already occurred reliefs may still be able to be claimed, but you need to consider if the relevant claim date has already passed. For future events there could be tax planning implications that could be discussed.

- Stick to the question and **tailor your answer** to what you are asked.
  - Pay particular attention to the verbs in the question.
  - Try to apply your comments to the scenario where possible.

- If you do not understand what a question is asking, **state your assumptions**.

  Even if you do not answer in precisely the way the examining team hoped, you should be given some credit, if your assumptions are reasonable.

- You should do everything you can to make things easy for the marker.

  Make sure your answers use headings so it is easy for the marker to follow what you're doing.

- **Computations**:

  It is essential to include all your workings in your answers and ensure that they are clearly labelled.

  Although computations may be prepared using standard formats, you should always think about whether there is an easier way to arrive at the answer by working in the margin, say.

  You may find the spreadsheet function most useful for detailed computations. Although markers can see any formulae used, it is always clearer to show your working as well.

- **Reports, memos and other documents**:

  Some questions ask you to present your answer in the form of a report, a memo, a letter or other document.

  Make sure that you use the correct format – there could be easy marks to gain here.

  In the Section A question you may be asked to prepare multiple documents, e.g. a report and paragraphs to be included in a letter.

- **Scratch pad**:

  You will be able to make notes in the scratch pad to help with your planning. Please be aware that anything in the scratch pad will not be seen by the marker, and will therefore not score any marks. If you are sitting your exam via remote invigilation then you will not be permitted to use scrap paper, so the scratch pad will be the only way to carry out your planning. The scratch pad is available in the ACCA Practice Platform for you to practise using.

- **Checking:**

  Leave enough time to read through the answers, ensuring they are clear and organised, and to make any necessary changes.

EXAM SPECIFIC INFORMATION

THE EXAM

FORMAT OF THE EXAM

	Total marks	Technical marks	Professional skills marks
Section A: One compulsory question	50	40	10
There will be five marks on ethics in this question			
Section B: Two compulsory questions	50 (25 per question)	40 (20 per question)	10 (5 per question)
Overall	**100**	**80**	**20**

Total time allowed: 3 hours and 15 minutes.

Note that:

- The exam will be a computer-based examination (CBE).
- Candidates will be expected to undertake both calculation and narrative work. The questions will be scenario based and may involve consideration of more than one tax, some elements of planning and the interaction of taxes.
- Every ATX exam will include an ethical component for five marks in section A. The questions on ethics will be confined to the following areas:
  - prospective clients
  - conflicts of interest
  - disclosure of information to HM Revenue & Customs
  - money laundering
  - tax irregularities
  - tax avoidance
  - tax evasion.
- Apart from the above, any subject may be tested anywhere in the exam for any number of marks.
- The exam will not just test ATX knowledge: TX knowledge is still highly examinable, but will be tested in a more advanced way.

Remote invigilated exams

In certain geographical areas it may be possible for you to take your exam remotely. This option, which is subject to strict conditions, can offer increased flexibility and convenience under certain circumstances . Further guidance, including the detailed requirements and conditions for taking the exam by this method, is contained on ACCA's website at:

https://www.accaglobal.com/gb/en/student/exam-entry-and-administration/about-our-exams/remote-exams.html.

PASS MARK

The pass mark for all ACCA Qualification examinations is 50%.

PROFESSIONAL SKILLS MARKS

The ATX examination contains 20 professional skills marks which test 4 different professional skills. All four professional skills will be tested in Section A with communication only being tested in Section A. Details of the professional skills are set out below.

Each professional skill included in the mark scheme will either be worth one or two marks. There are no half marks for professional skills.

Communication

Section A questions will require you to respond in a particular format, or possibly more than one format, e.g. a report and paragraphs for inclusion in a letter.

Your tone and presentation should be professional and should be easy to follow. Ensure you include headings and subheadings to make sure you have covered all areas of the requirements in an organised manner.

It is important to ensure that your response is relevant to the requirement and adheres to any specific instructions given in the scenario. Make sure that the response is specific and not general.

When answering you should give thought to the response method you use, i.e. word processor versus spreadsheet. Where completing both written and numerical elements you should ensure that the two are clearly referenced between one another.

It is also important that you attempt all requirements in the question, so make sure you allocate time between the different requirements.

Analysis and evaluation

In order to score marks for this skill you need to be able to apply the tax rules to the facts of the scenario. You should expect to be asked to explain the consequences of one or more courses of action, and recommend or advise on the best approach.

Where applicable, you should give consideration to the impact of any variables in a scenario, e.g. different disposal dates. Any variables should be identified and the differences between them clearly explained in your analysis.

Scepticism

Demonstrating scepticism does not mean challenging every fact or figure presented in a scenario. Scepticism will be relevant where it is clear that there is uncertainty in the information, or there is information missing, e.g. it is not clear whether an individual has an annual exempt amount available.

Scepticism could also be demonstrated by challenging the views of others with regards to a particular course of action or opinion. The question will make it clear where challenges are expected, and you should ensure that you fully explain and justify any challenges that you make.

Commercial acumen

In order to demonstrate commercial acumen you need to be aware what advice is appropriate in given circumstances. You will be dealing with individuals and organisations with very different circumstances. Therefore, you should tailor your approach depending on the scenario and recommend courses of action that are plausible and appropriate in the circumstances.

Demonstrating commercial acumen does not mean having knowledge of tax issues beyond the scope of the syllabus. In order to demonstrate the skill you must use information within the question scenario to provide realistic and commercial solutions to problems.

It is important to take a forward-looking approach. So you should be aware of the implications a particular course of action may have in the future in order to make the right choices. This also includes being aware of time limits for claims, so that you are aware of what options are available in the given timeframe.

Commercial acumen can also be demonstrated by having a wider understanding of the purpose behind certain rules, e.g. anti-avoidance legislation.

SUGGESTED APPROACH TO THIS EXAM

The ATX examination will be 3 hours and 15 minutes long, with no separate time allocated for reading and planning. However, reading and planning are crucial elements of your examination technique and it is important that you allocate time in the examination to this.

Spend time reading the examination questions carefully. As stated earlier, we recommend that 15 minutes should be spent reading the questions.

There is no choice of questions in the exam, but there is a decision to be made regarding the order in which you should attempt the questions.

Therefore, in relation to ATX, we recommend that you take the following approach with your reading and planning:

- **Skim through the whole exam**, assessing the level of difficulty of each question.
- **Note** in the scratch pad **the amount of time you should spend on each part.** Do this for each part of every question.
- **Decide the order** in which you think you will attempt each question:

  This is a personal choice and you have time on the revision phase to try out different approaches, for example, if you sit mock exams.

  A common approach is to tackle the question you think is the easiest and you are most comfortable with first.

  Others may prefer to tackle the longest question first, or conversely leave it till last.

  Psychologists believe that you usually perform at your best on the second and third question you attempt, once you have settled into the exam, so not tackling the bigger Section A question first may be advisable.

  It is usual however that students tackle their least favourite topic and/or the most difficult question in their opinion last.

  Whatever your approach, you must make sure that you leave enough time to attempt all questions fully and be very strict with yourself in timing each question.

- **For each question** in turn, read the requirements and then the detail of the question carefully.

  Always read the requirement first as this enables you to **focus on the detail of the question with the specific task in mind**.

  Pay close attention to the verb in the requirement as this will tell you what kind of answer you need to produce.

  If the verb is 'calculate' then you will just need to produce calculations, and these may be best prepared in the spreadsheet answer space. Sometimes you will be asked for calculations with supporting explanations, so ensure you include these explanations as it may not be possible to pass the requirement without them.

  If the verb is 'explain' or 'discuss' then you only need a written answer. When explaining, always try to ensure that you identify the issue, explain why it is relevant and then what it means. For example, 'The substantial shareholding exemption applies to the disposal of shares because X Ltd has owned at least 10% of Y Ltd (a trading company) for at least 12 months out of the previous six years. Therefore, the gain on the disposal of the shares will be exempt from corporation tax.' Sometimes you may be asked to provide supporting calculations with your explanations. If this is the case, then include them where appropriate (e.g. to calculate a gain on a disposal you discussed) but remember that words should still be the main focus of your answer.

  Some questions will ask you to prepare a 'summary', which could be in reference to either calculations or written elements. Where it is written elements then keep these brief.

  Where the verb is 'state' or 'identify' then you can just list the relevant points without providing a supporting explanation. Do ensure you read the full requirement though, as sometimes this verb will be accompanied with 'explain', in which case see above.

  'Evaluate', 'recommend', 'advise' or 'conclude' means you need to compare two or more options and then decide what the best option is. You will probably have been given an indication in the scenario of what is most important to the client, e.g. which option creates the most after-tax cash, so this will help you to decide which option to choose. When asked to evaluate it is always important that you do so as there will always be marks for a reasoned recommendation, even if it does not match what is in the model answer.

  For computational questions:

  Highlight key numbers/information and key words in the question, or use the scratch pad or answer space to make notes to yourself to remember key points in your answer. Remember that any notes made in the scratch pad will not be seen by the marker and so will not score marks.

  For written questions:

  Take notice of the format required (e.g. letter, memo, notes) and identify the recipient of the answer. You need to do this to judge the level of sophistication required in your answer and whether the use of a formal reply or informal bullet points would be satisfactory.

  Plan your beginning, middle and end and the key areas to be addressed and your use of titles and sub-titles to enhance your answer.

For all questions:

Spot the easy marks to be gained in a question and parts which can be performed independently of the rest of the question. For example, tax payment dates, ethical issues, laying out the answer in the correct format etc.

Make sure that you do these parts first when you tackle the question.

Don't go overboard in terms of planning time on any one question – you need a good measure of the whole exam and a plan for all of the questions at the end of the 15 minutes.

By covering all questions, you can often help yourself as you may find that facts in one question may remind you of things you should put into your answer relating to a different question.

Copy the requirements into the answer space so that you ensure you answer all parts.

- With your plan of attack in mind, **start answering your chosen question** with your plan to hand, as soon as you are ready to start.

Always keep your eye on the clock and do not over run on any part of any question!

DETAILED SYLLABUS

The detailed syllabus and study guide written by the ACCA can be found at:

www.accaglobal.com/gb/en/student.html

KAPLAN'S RECOMMENDED REVISION APPROACH

QUESTION PRACTICE IS THE KEY TO SUCCESS

Success in professional examinations relies upon you acquiring a firm grasp of the required knowledge at the tuition phase. In order to be able to do the questions, knowledge is essential.

However, the difference between success and failure often hinges on your exam technique on the day and making the most of the revision phase of your studies.

The **Kaplan study text** is the starting point, designed to provide the underpinning knowledge to tackle all questions. However, in the revision phase, poring over text books is not the answer.

Kaplan online knowledge checks help you consolidate your knowledge and understanding and are a useful tool to check whether you can remember key topic areas.

Kaplan pocket notes are designed to help you quickly revise a topic area, however you then need to practise questions. There is a need to progress to full exam standard questions as soon as possible, and to tie your exam technique and technical knowledge together.

The importance of question practice cannot be over-emphasised.

The recommended approach below is designed by expert tutors in the field, in conjunction with their knowledge of the examining team and their recent real exams.

The approach taken for the applied skills level exams is to revise by topic area. However, with the strategic professional exams, a multi topic approach is required to answer the scenario-based questions.

It is very important that you familiarise yourself with the layout and functionality of the exam. You can do this by practising past exam questions which have been released in the ACCA practice platform. This enables you to attempt the questions in the real exam format and then self-mark them using detailed marking guides. More information on the practice platform and how to access it can be found at the following link:

https://www.accaglobal.com/gb/en/student/exam-support-resources/professional-exams-study-resources/cbe-platform-support.html

You can also find practice questions on the ACCA Study Hub. Many of these questions feature in our exam kit, but may have been updated by ACCA in different ways so you should not aim to compare the two.

You need to practise as many questions as possible in the time you have left.

OUR AIM

Our aim is to get you to the stage where you can attempt exam standard questions confidently, to time, in a closed book environment, with no supplementary help (i.e. to simulate the real examination experience).

Practising your exam technique on real past examination questions, in timed conditions, is also vitally important for you to assess your progress and identify areas of weakness that may need more attention in the final run up to the examination.

In order to achieve this, we recognise that initially you may feel the need to practise some questions with open book help and exceed the required time.

The approach below shows you which questions you should use to build up to coping with exam standard question practice, and references to the sources of information available should you need to revisit a topic area in more detail.

Remember that in the real examination, all you have to do is:

- attempt all questions required by the exam
- only spend the allotted time on each question, and
- get them at least 50% right!

Try and practise this approach on every question you attempt from now to the real exam.

EXAMINER COMMENTS

We have included the examiner's comments to the specific new syllabus examination questions in this kit for you to see the main pitfalls that students fall into with regard to technical content.

However, too many times in the general section of the report, the examiner comments that students had failed due to:

- 'misallocation of time'
- 'running out of time' and
- showing signs of 'spending too much time on an earlier question and clearly rushing the answer to a subsequent question'.

Good exam technique is vital.

STRATEGIC PROFESSIONAL CBE

We advise consulting the ACCA Global website for additional CBE revision resources. On the ACCA website there is a CBE demonstration. It is **ESSENTIAL** that you attempt this before your real CBE. You will become familiar with how to move around the CBE screens and the way that questions are formatted, increasing your confidence and speed in the actual exam.

Be sure you understand how to use the **software** before you start the exam. If in doubt, ask the assessment centre staff to explain it to you.

Questions are **displayed on the screen** and answers are entered using keyboard and mouse.

For additional support with your studies please also refer to the ACCA Global website.

THE KAPLAN ATX REVISION PLAN

Stage 1: Assess areas of strengths and weaknesses

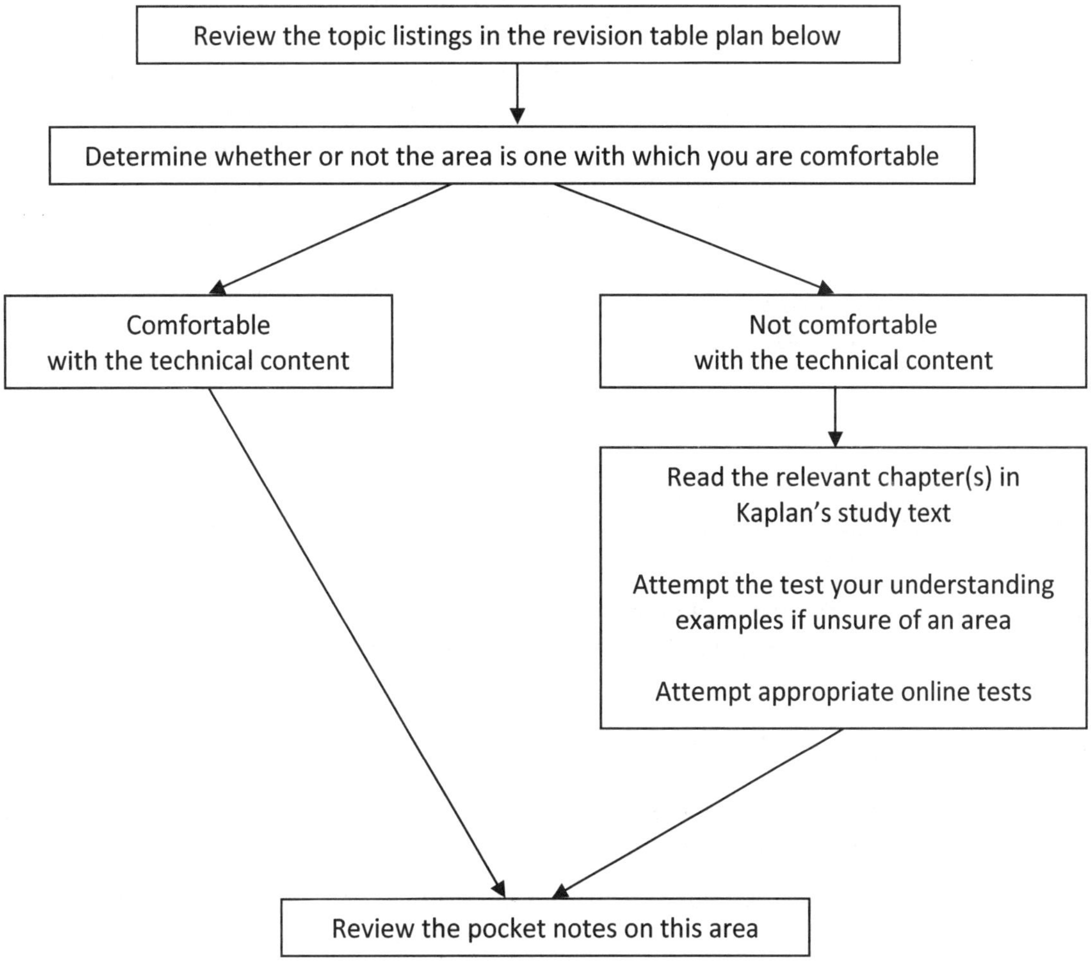

Stage 2: Practise questions

Follow the order of revision of topics as recommended in the revision table plan below and attempt the questions in the order suggested.

Try to avoid referring to text books and notes and the model answer until you have completed your attempt.

Try to answer the question in the allotted time.

Review your attempt with the model answer and assess how much of the answer you achieved in the allocated exam time.

Fill in the self-assessment box below and decide on your best course of action.

Comfortable with question attempt

↓

Only revisit when comfortable with questions on all topic areas

Not comfortable with question attempts

↓

Focus on these areas by:

- Reworking Test Your Understanding examples in Kaplan's Study Text
- Revisiting the technical content from Kaplan's pocket notes
- Working any remaining questions on that area in the exam kit
- Reattempting an exam standard question in that area, on a timed, closed book basis

Note that:

The 'footsteps questions' give guidance on exam techniques and how you should have approached the question.

The 'answer debrief' questions have an online debrief where a top tutor works through the question in full, explains key elements of the answer and how to gain marks.

Stage 3: Final pre-exam revision

We recommend that you **attempt at least one three hours and fifteen-minute mock examination** containing a set of previously unseen exam standard questions.

It is important that you get a feel for the breadth of coverage of a real exam without advance knowledge of the topic areas covered – just as you will expect to see on the real exam day.

Ideally this mock should be sat in timed, closed book, real exam conditions and could be

- a mock examination offered by your tuition provider, and/or
- a practise exam released on the ACCA practice platform.

KAPLAN'S DETAILED REVISION PLAN

Very few of the recent ATX exam questions focus on just one area of tax.

This is especially true of the big scenario questions, which often test several different areas.

This revision plan aims to lead you through a selection of the best questions, broadly grouped by the areas covered, and will ensure that you revise all of the key topics.

It is especially important that you practise the more recent questions, as the examining team has its own particular style.

Familiarisation with this style of questions will help to make sure that you are as well-prepared as possible for the real exam.

Topic	Study Text Chapter	Pocket notes Chapter	Questions to attempt	Tutor guidance	Date attempted	Self-assessment
Corporation tax	Corporation tax is often an area that students struggle with, but in recent exams has regularly formed the basis of one of the compulsory scenario questions. For this reason, it would be a good idea to start by revising corporation tax to ensure that you have enough time to cover it thoroughly.					
Losses, anti-avoidance re trading losses c/f; Losses and gains groups; Substantial shareholding exemption; Pre-entry capital losses; Capital loss restriction; Rollover relief; VAT: Land and buildings and overseas aspects; VAT registration, Temporary non-residence; Spouse tax planning; Ethics	3 4 2 4 9 26, 27 20 14	1 2 1 2 6 3, 18 14 10	Q11 Dilip Group and Emma Q16 Heyer Ltd Group and Dee	The corporation tax scenario questions often involve a group of companies; VAT is a regular feature too. Use your Kaplan pocket notes to make sure that you are happy with all the different group definitions and implications before attempting these questions. You must also learn the reliefs available for the various types of losses, as it is easy to get these confused. Rollover relief is the only capital gains relief available to companies, making it a highly examinable area. VAT on land and buildings is a favourite area, and regularly features in questions. Don't worry if you find these questions hard – the scenario questions will get easier with practice. There are walkthrough answers to help you if you get stuck. Note that stamp duty and ethics often represent easy marks in this type of question.		

Topic	**Study Text Chapter**	**Pocket notes Chapter**	**Questions to attempt**	**Tutor guidance**	**Date attempted**	**Self-assessment**
Substantial shareholding exemption; Degrouping charges; Transfer pricing; Loan relationships; Intangible fixed assets	2 4 2 2 2	1 2 1 1 1	Q68 Kitz Ltd	Another excellent question. Having attempted the previous two questions, you should start to find these easier as you become familiar with the style of question and the areas that are frequently tested.		
Sale of shares versus sale of assets; Substantial shareholding exemption; Degrouping charges; Stamp duty land tax; VAT: Transfer of going concern; Employment income; Ethics	4 2 4 6 26 17 14	2 1 2 7 18 12 10	Q18 Grand Ltd Group	This big scenario question covers disposal of a subsidiary through sale of its shares or assets. Look at the mark allocations here to gauge how much you need to write. Transfer of going concern is something that is often tested with a transfer of trade and assets, so ensure you learn the conditions and be prepared to apply them to the scenario. The question has some easy marks for stamp duty land tax and ethics, so ensure you allocate your time so that you can pick these up.		

Topic	Study Text Chapter	Pocket notes Chapter	Questions to attempt	Tutor guidance	Date attempted	Self-assessment
Further issues: Research and development; Intangibles; Consortium relief; VAT on services; partial exemption; Ethics; Controlled foreign companies	 2 2 4 26,27 14 5	 1 1 2 18 3	Q17 Mita and Snowdon, Q15 Waverley and Set Ltd Group (c) – (f)	Before attempting Q17, use your Kaplan pocket notes to make sure that you learn the rules governing the following: – enhanced relief available to companies for R&D expenditure, – intangible fixed assets, and – partial exemption for VAT There are also marks here again for group loss reliefs and ethics. Then attempt parts (c) to (f) of Q15, which is another big scenario question covering many of the same areas. Revise controlled foreign companies before attempting this one.		
Test question			Q14 Hahn Ltd Group	Now try attempting this question under exam conditions. If you spend 15 minutes reading and planning at the start of the exam, you have 2.25 minutes per mark, so 112 minutes in total.		

Topic	Study Text Chapter	Pocket notes Chapter	Questions to attempt	Tutor guidance	Date attempted	Self-assessment
The Capital taxes	The key capital taxes are capital gains tax and inheritance tax. Inheritance tax often features as part of both a compulsory question and an optional question, often linked with capital gains tax.					
Inheritance tax basics; Income tax basics; Trusts	10–12 16 13	8 11 9	Q38 Alex	Q38 is a good question to start with, covering the basic calculations and includes a straightforward income tax computation in part (a), and a written section on trusts. Trusts often feature as a small written section.		
Inheritance tax: further computations; Business property relief (BPR); Admin	 10–11 11 12	 8 8 8	Q39 Kepler	This question includes popular complications: the diminution in value principle and BPR. BPR features in nearly every exam, so you must learn the conditions in detail. Also use your Kaplan pocket notes to make sure that you learn the payment dates for inheritance tax, particularly payment by instalment.		

Topic	Study Text Chapter	Pocket notes Chapter	Questions to attempt	Tutor guidance	Date attempted	Self-assessment
Inheritance tax versus capital gains tax; Agricultural property relief; BPR; Gift holdover relief, Private residence relief; Planning	12 11 11 9 9 12	8 8 8 6 6 15	Q37 Joan Ark Q45 Anya (a) and (b) Q42 Cada	The examining team often test both the inheritance tax and capital gains tax implications of lifetime gifts, and there are many questions on this area. Q37 is not in current exam style, but is a great question as it covers most of the calculations and reliefs available for both IHT and CGT. Before attempting this question, make sure that you revise the CGT reliefs thoroughly, and try not to get IHT and CGT confused! Note that part (ii) of this question, on the advantages of lifetime gifts, is very general. You will probably have to apply this knowledge in an exam question, and just pick out the points which are relevant. Have a go at Q45 (a) and (b), a real past exam question from section B of the exam. This question covers IHT and CGT with reliefs. Then try Q42, another section B question.		
Test question			Q41 Pescara	Try answering this one under exam conditions.		

Topic	Study Text Chapter	Pocket notes Chapter	Questions to attempt	Tutor guidance	Date attempted	Self-assessment
Income tax	Income tax is not likely to be tested on its own at ATX, but will often feature as part of a bigger question. For many of the questions set at this level, the examining team will not require you to do a whole income tax computation, but rather to start part way through. For example, you may have to calculate just the tax on some extra income, working in the margin. Be prepared to write about employment benefits as well as doing calculations.					
Employment income; Private residence relief; Letting relief; Pensions; Share options	17 9 19 17	12 6 13 12	Q26 Demeter	This question is split into four requirements which are all independent of one another and can be attempted in any order. The first three requirements all cover TX knowledge, so you should find these straight forward if you have revised this well. Be careful in parts (b) and (c) as you need to ensure you have both explanations and calculations in order to score well. Part (c)(ii) covers share option plans. As this is one of the few new areas of employment income at ATX it is frequently tested.		
Company share option plan; Share incentive plan; Private residence relief; Letting relief; Gift with reservation	17 17 9 12	12 12 6 8	Q27 Yacon Ltd and Daikon	The first part of this question covers two tax-advantaged share schemes: the CSOP and SIP. Share schemes are frequently tested, as they are not examined at TX. The last part of the question covers another topic that often features in the ATX exam: gifts with reservation of benefit for inheritance tax. Make sure that you are able to identify these and explain the consequences.		

Topic	Study Text Chapter	Pocket notes Chapter	Questions to attempt	Tutor guidance	Date attempted	Self-assessment
Personal financial planning	You may be asked to advise on suitable investment products in the exam, particularly tax efficient forms of investment. Again, this is not likely to form the basis of a whole question, but will generally be combined with other areas.					
Self-employment Income tax and NIC; Badges of trade; Voluntary VAT registration; Enterprise investment scheme and EIS reinvestment relief	21 21 26 18	16 16 18 10	Q31 Tomas and Ines	This question is made up of four parts which focus on self-employment aspects, VAT and the enterprise investment scheme (EIS). Use your Kaplan pocket notes to revise the conditions for EIS before attempting this question – you need a good knowledge of the rules.		
Pensions	19	13	Q53 Stella and Maris	This question tests all aspects of pensions and so is a good one to practise to get back up to speed. Although pensions were covered at TX, they still feature quite often at ATX.		
Test question			Q3 Jonny	Try attempting this question to exam time.		
Overseas aspects of personal tax	Overseas aspects for individuals are very popular in the exam, often appearing in section B questions but also sometimes in the section A scenario questions. Before attempting these questions, use your Kaplan pocket notes to revise the definitions of residence and domicile, and make sure that you can explain how a person's status affects the way they are taxed.					
Overseas aspects: Residence tests; Remittance basis	20 20	14 14	Q48 Juanita and Buraco (b)	This is a good test of your knowledge of the rules regarding the residence tests and remittance basis, which regularly feature in the exam.		

Topic	Study Text Chapter	Pocket notes Chapter	Questions to attempt	Tutor guidance	Date attempted	Self-assessment
Capital gains tax: overseas aspects	20	14	Q50 Max	This is a great question to revise the temporary absence rules for CGT, with IHT and CGT for lifetime gifts too. It contains a both words and numbers, and you must apply the rules to the scenario to score well.		
Income tax overseas aspects	20	14	Q7 Joe and Fiona (d)	Part (d) of this question covers the remittance basis for income tax. This is often tested, so make sure that you learn the rules.		
Test question			Q46 Mirtoon	Try attempting this excellent question, covering various aspects of overseas personal tax, to exam time.		
Business scenarios	There are lots of business scenarios for the examining team to test, and because of the many aspects of tax that apply, these often feature as big section A questions. Much of the knowledge required is basic TX knowledge, but you must make sure you keep this knowledge up to date.					
Commencement of trade with basic income tax; NICs; IHT re lifetime gift; Property income; EIS relief; Ethics	21 10 18 18 14	16 8 11 10 10	Q5 Pippin	This is a scenario involving calculating the additional finance needed for an individual to start a business as a sole trader. There are many easy marks available for basic knowledge – the hard part is finding the relevant information and structuring your answer.		
Sole trader cessation; TOGC; IHT impact of date of death; VCT and EIS; Ethics	22 26 10 18 14	16 18 8 10 10	Q2 Ziti	This question tests cessation of trade for a sole trader with alternative cessation dates. It also looks at the transfer of going concern rules for VAT, which are a popular topic in the exam so ensure you learn the rules around these. There is also some IHT as well as tax efficient investments and ethics.		

Topic	Study Text Chapter	Pocket notes Chapter	Questions to attempt	Tutor guidance	Date attempted	Self-assessment
Test question			Q4 Ray, Shanira and Kelly	This is a good question on changing business scenarios, which also tests VAT registration, husband and wife planning and some overseas aspects!		
Incorporation; CGT: Incorporation relief; Incorporation loss relief; Business asset disposal relief	22 22 22 9	16 16 16 6	Q34 Enid (a) and (b)	Incorporation is a popular scenario as there are many different tax implications. This question cover some of these areas, particularly the CGT aspects with some planning points.		
Test question			Q15 Waverley and Set Ltd Group (a) – (b)	Try attempting this question to exam time.		
Qualifying interest payments; Partnerships; Redundancy; Income tax computation	16 23 17 16	11 16 12 11	Q28 Amy and Bex	This section B question is mainly made up of areas which are within the TX syllabus, such as partnership profit allocation. Redundancy payments are very common in the exam so make sure you revise these before attempting this question.		
Test question			Q9 Hiromi	Try attempting this question to exam time.		

Topic	Study Text Chapter	Pocket notes Chapter	Questions to attempt	Tutor guidance	Date attempted	Self-assessment
Family companies and planning scenarios	The following are also common scenarios that you need to be familiar with, although areas such as IR35, purchase of own shares and liquidations tend to only come up every few sittings in the exam.					
Business structure: unincorporated versus company; Loss reliefs; R&D relief; VAT registration	21, 2 3 2 26	16, 1 1 1 18	Q33 Desiree	Before attempting this question, you may want to use your Kaplan pocket notes to revise loss reliefs for individuals. There is also a requirement around R&D which is a popular topic in the ATX exam. Ensure you are happy with the relief available.		
Extraction of funds from a company	24	17	Q34 Enid (c)	Extraction of funds from a company is an area you should be familiar with. Practise this question to see how this topic could be tested in the exam.		
IR35	24	17	Q52 Monisha and Horner (b)	You may want to revisit the test your understandings covering the calculation of deemed direct payments under IR35 before attempting this question.		
Purchase of own shares	24	17	Q60 Traiste Ltd	Make sure you learn the conditions for purchase of own shares before you do this question. Part (c) illustrates another way that the examining team can test extraction of funds from a company.		
Close companies; VAT: Partial exemption	24 26	17 18	Q57 Nocturne Ltd	Close companies are a fairly regular feature in the exam. Make sure that you know the definition and the tax consequences. This question also covers VAT for partially exempt businesses, which is another area that you need to be happy with.		

Topic	Study Text Chapter	Pocket notes Chapter	Questions to attempt	Tutor guidance	Date attempted	Self-assessment
Liquidations	8, 24	5, 17	Q7 Joe and Fiona (a)	Liquidations are not tested regularly, but are fairly straightforward and mainly involve consideration of the difference in tax treatment between dividends and capital gains.		

Note that not all of the questions are referred to in the programme above.

We have recommended an approach to build up from the basic to exam standard questions where possible.

The remaining questions are available in the kit for extra practice for those who require more questions on some areas.

TAX RATES AND ALLOWANCES

Throughout this exam kit:

1 **You should assume that the tax rates and allowances for the tax year 2023/24 and for the financial year to 31 March 2024 will continue to apply for the foreseeable future unless you are instructed otherwise.**

2 **Calculations and workings need only to be made to the nearest £.**

3 **All apportionments should be made to the nearest month.**

4 **All workings should be shown.**

Income tax

		Normal rates	Dividend rates
Basic rate	£1 – £37,700	20%	8.75%
Higher rate	£37,701 – £125,140	40%	33.75%
Additional rate	£125,141 and over	45%	39.35%

Savings income nil rate band	– Basic rate taxpayers	£1,000
	– Higher rate taxpayers	£500
Dividend nil rate band		£1,000

A starting rate of 0% applies to savings income where it falls within the first £5,000 of taxable income.

Personal allowance

Personal allowance	£12,570
Transferable amount	£1,260
Income limit	£100,000

Where adjusted net income is £125,140 or more, the personal allowance is reduced to zero.

Residence status

Days in UK	Previously resident	Not previously resident
Less than 16	Automatically not resident	Automatically not resident
16 to 45	Resident if 4 UK ties (or more)	Automatically not resident
46 to 90	Resident if 3 UK ties (or more)	Resident if 4 UK ties
91 to 120	Resident if 2 UK ties (or more)	Resident if 3 UK ties (or more)
121 to 182	Resident if 1 UK tie (or more)	Resident if 2 UK ties (or more)
183 or more	Automatically resident	Automatically resident

Remittance basis charge

UK resident for:	Charge
Seven out of the last nine years	£30,000
12 out of the last 14 years	£60,000

Car benefit percentage

The relevant base level of CO_2 emissions is 55 grams per kilometre.

The percentage rates applying to petrol cars (and diesel cars meeting the RDE2 standard) with CO_2 emissions up to this level are:

51 grams to 54 grams per kilometre	15%
55 grams per kilometre	16%

The percentage for electric cars with zero CO_2 emissions is 2%.

For hybrid-electric cars with CO_2 emissions between 1 and 50 grams per kilometre, the electric range of a car is relevant:

130 miles or more	2%
70 to 129 miles	5%
40 to 69 miles	8%
30 to 39 miles	12%
Less than 30 miles	14%

Car fuel benefit

The base figure for calculating the car fuel benefit is £27,800.

Company van benefits

The company van benefit scale charge is £3,960, and the van fuel benefit is £757.

A van with zero CO_2 emissions does not give rise to a benefit.

Individual savings accounts (ISAs)

The overall investment limit is £20,000.

Rent-a-room relief

The rent-a-room relief limit is £7,500.

Pension scheme limits

Annual allowance	£40,000
Minimum allowance	£4,000
Threshold income limit	£200,000
Income limit	£240,000
Lifetime allowance	£1,073,100

The maximum contribution which can qualify for tax relief without any earnings is £3,600.

Approved mileage allowances: cars

Up to 10,000 miles	45p
Over 10,000 miles	25p

Capital allowances: rates of allowance

Plant and machinery	
Main pool	18%
Special rate pool	6%
Cars	
New cars with zero CO_2 emissions	100%
Second-hand cars with zero CO_2 emissions	18%
CO_2 emissions between 1 and 50 grams per kilometre	18%
CO_2 emissions over 50 grams per kilometre	6%
Annual investment allowance	
Rate of allowance	100%
Expenditure limit	£1,000,000
Structures and buildings allowance	
Straight line allowance	3%

Cash basis accounting

Revenue limit	£150,000

Cap on income tax reliefs

Unless otherwise restricted, reliefs are capped at the higher of £50,000 or 25% of income.

Corporation tax

Financial year	2021	2022	2023
Small profits rate	N/A	N/A	19%
Main rate	19%	19%	25%
Lower limit	N/A	N/A	£50,000
Upper limit	N/A	N/A	£250,000
Standard fraction	N/A	N/A	3/200

Marginal relief

$$(\text{Upper limit} - \text{Augmented profits}) \times \text{Standard fraction} \times \frac{\text{Taxable total profits}}{\text{Augmented profits}}$$

Quarterly instalments

Profit threshold	£1,500,000

Value added tax (VAT)

Standard rate	20%
Registration limit	£85,000
Deregistration limit	£83,000

Penalties for late VAT payments

Days late	Penalty
Up to 15 days	None
16 to 30 days	2%
More than 30 days	4% plus a 4% daily penalty

Inheritance tax: nil rate bands and tax rates

Nil rate band		£325,000
Residence nil rate band		£175,000
Rate of tax on excess over nil rate band	– Lifetime rate	20%
	– Death rate	40%

Inheritance tax: taper relief

Years before death	Percentage reduction
More than 3 but less than 4 years	20%
More than 4 but less than 5 years	40%
More than 5 but less than 6 years	60%
More than 6 but less than 7 years	80%

Capital gains tax: tax rates

	Normal rates	Residential property
Lower rate	10%	18%
Higher rate	20%	28%
Annual exempt amount		£6,000

Capital gains tax: business asset disposal relief and investors' relief

Lifetime limit – business asset disposal relief	£1,000,000
investors' relief	£10,000,000
Rate of tax	10%

National insurance contributions

Class 1 Employee	£1 – £12,570 per year	Nil
	£12,571 – £50,270 per year	12%
	£50,271 and above per year	2%
Class 1 Employer	£1 – £9,100 per year	Nil
	£9,101 and above per year	13.8%
	Employment allowance	£5,000
Class 1A		13.8%
Class 2	£3.45 per week	
	Lower profits limit	£12,570
Class 4	£1 – £12,570 per year	Nil
	£12,571 – £50,270 per year	9%
	£50,271 and above per year	2%

Rates of interest (assumed)

Official rate of interest	2.25%
Rate of interest on underpaid tax	6.50%
Rate of interest on overpaid tax	3.00%

Standard penalties for errors

Taxpayer behaviour	Maximum penalty	Minimum penalty – unprompted disclosure	Minimum penalty – prompted disclosure
Deliberate and concealed	100%	30%	50%
Deliberate but not concealed	70%	20%	35%
Careless	30%	0%	15%

Stamp duty land tax on non-residential properties

Up to £150,000	0%
£150,001 – £250,000	2%
£250,001 and above	5%

Stamp duty

Shares	0.5%

TIME LIMITS AND ELECTION DATES

Income tax

Election/claim	Time limit	For 2023/24
Agree the amount of trading losses to carry forward	4 years from the end of the tax year in which the loss arose	5 April 2028
Current and prior year set-off of trading losses against total income (and chargeable gains)	12 months from 31 January following the end of the tax year in which the loss arose	31 January 2026
Three year carry back of trading losses in the opening years	12 months from 31 January following the end of the tax year in which the loss arose	31 January 2026
Three year carry back of terminal trading losses in the closing years	4 years from the end of the last tax year of trading	5 April 2028
Set-off of loss on the disposal of unquoted trading company shares against income	12 months from 31 January following the end of the tax year in which the loss arose	31 January 2026
Transfer of assets eligible for capital allowances between connected parties at TWDV	2 years from the date of sale	

National Insurance Contributions

Election/claim	Time limit	For 2023/24
Class 1 primary and secondary – pay days	17 days after the end of each tax month under PAYE system (14 days if not paid electronically)	22nd of each month
Class 1 A NIC – pay day	22 July following end of tax year (19 July if not paid electronically)	22 July 2024
Class 2 NICs – pay days	Paid under self-assessment with balancing payment	31 January 2025
Class 4 NICs – pay days	Paid under self-assessment with income tax	

Capital gains tax

Election/claim	Time limit	For 2023/24
Replacement of business asset relief for individuals (Rollover relief)	4 years from the end of the tax year: – in which the disposal occurred or – the replacement asset was acquired whichever is later	5 April 2028 for 2023/24 sale or acquisition (if later event)
Holdover relief of gain on the gift of a business asset (Gift holdover relief)	4 years from the end of the tax year in which the disposal occurred	5 April 2028
Disapplication of incorporation relief	2 years from the 31 January following the end of the tax year in which the business is transferred If sell all shares by 5 April following tax year of incorporation: Time limit 12 months earlier than normal claim date	31 January 2027 31 January 2026
EIS reinvestment relief	5 years from 31 January following the end of the tax year in which the disposal occurred	31 January 2030
Business assets disposal relief and investors' relief	12 months from 31 January following the end of the tax year in which the disposal occurred	31 January 2026
Determination of private residence	2 years from the acquisition of the second property	

Self-assessment – individuals

Election/claim	Time limit	For 2023/24
Pay days for income tax and class 4 NIC	1st instalment: 31 January in the tax year 2nd instalment: 31 July following the end of tax year Balancing payment: 31 January following the end of tax year	 31 January 2024 31 July 2024 31 January 2025
Pay day for CGT (not UK residential property) and class 2 NIC	31 January following the end of tax year	31 January 2025
Pay day for CGT on UK residential property disposals	Within 60 days of the disposal	

Self-assessment – individuals

Election/claim	**Time limit**	**For 2023/24**
Filing dates If notice to file issued by 31 October following end of tax year	Paper return: 31 October following end of tax year Electronic return: 31 January following end of tax year	 31 October 2024 31 January 2025
If notice to file issued after 31 October following end of tax year	3 months from the date of issue of the notice to file	
Retention of records Business records Personal records	 5 years from 31 January following end of the tax year 12 months from 31 January following end of the tax year	 31 January 2030 31 January 2026
HMRC right of repair	9 months from date the return was filed	
Taxpayers right to amend a return	12 months from 31 January following end of the tax year	31 January 2026
Error or mistake claim	4 years from the end of the tax year	5 April 2028
HMRC can open an enquiry	12 months from submission of the return	
HMRC can raise a discovery assessment – No careless or deliberate behaviour – Tax lost due to careless behaviour – Tax lost due to deliberate behaviour	 4 years from the end of the tax year 6 years from the end of the tax year 20 years from the end of the tax year	 5 April 2028 5 April 2030 5 April 2044
Taxpayers right of appeal against an assessment	30 days from the assessment – appeal in writing	

Inheritance tax

Election/claim	Time limit	For 2023/24
Lifetime IHT on CLTs – pay day	Gift before 1 October in tax year: Following 30 April Gift on/after 1 October in tax year: 6 months after the end of the month of the gift	30 April 2024
Death IHT: on lifetime gifts within seven years of death (CLTs and PETs) and on the estate value	6 months after the end of the month of death	
Deed of variation	2 years from the date of death – in writing	
Transfer of unused nil rate band to spouse or civil partner	2 years from the date of the second death	

Corporation tax

Election/claim	Time limit
Replacement of business asset relief for companies (Rollover relief)	4 years from the end of the accounting period: – in which the disposal occurred or – the replacement asset was acquired whichever is later
Set-off of brought forward losses against total profits (income and gains)	2 years from the end of the accounting period in which the loss is relieved
Current year set-off of trading losses against total profits (income and gains), and 12 month carry back of trading losses against total profits (income and gains)	2 years from the end of the accounting period in which the loss arose
Surrender of current period and brought forward losses to other group companies (group relief and consortium relief)	2 years after the claimant company's accounting period
Election for transfer of capital gain or loss to another company within the gains group	2 years from the end of the accounting period in which the disposal occurred by the company actually making the disposal

Self-assessment – companies

Election/claim	Time limit
Pay day for small and medium companies	9 months and one day after the end of the accounting period
Pay day for large companies	Instalments due on 14th day of: – Seventh, Tenth, Thirteenth, and Sixteenth month **after the start** of the accounting period
Filing dates	Later of: – 12 months from the end of the accounting period – 3 months form the issue of a notice to deliver a corporation tax return
Companies error or mistake claim	4 years from the end of the accounting period
HMRC can open an enquiry	12 months from the actual submission of the return
Retention of records	6 years from the end of the accounting period

Value added tax

Election/claim	Time limit
Compulsory registration Historic test: – Notify HMRC – Charge VAT Future test: – Notify HMRC – Charge VAT	 30 days from end of the month in which the threshold was exceeded Beginning of the month, one month after the month in which the threshold was exceeded 30 days from the date it is anticipated that the threshold will be exceeded the date it is anticipated that the threshold will be exceeded (i.e. the beginning of the 30-day period)
Compulsory deregistration	30 days from cessation
Filing of VAT return and payment of VAT	End of month following the return period

Section 1

PRACTICE QUESTIONS – SECTION A

TAXATION OF INDIVIDUALS

1 GAIL AND BRAD (ADAPTED) *Walk in the footsteps of a top tutor*

You should assume that today's date is 1 June 2024.

Your manager has had a meeting with Gail and her father Brad, both of whom are clients of your firm. Gail owns the whole of the ordinary share capital of Aero Ltd.

Advice is required in respect of:

– the corporation tax issues in relation to disposals of a building and some shares,

– the extraction of funds from a company as either a bonus or a dividend,

– the consequences of non-disclosure of income, and

– the inheritance tax consequences of lifetime gifts.

The following **exhibits** provide information relevant to the question:

1 Gail – extract from a memorandum prepared by your manager

2 Schedule prepared by Mill, a junior member of your firm's tax department

3 Brad – extract from a memorandum prepared by your manager

4 Work to be carried out – email from your manager

This information should be used to answer the question **requirements**.

Exhibit 1 – Gail

> **Extract from a memorandum prepared by your manager – dated 1 June 2024**
>
> **Gail – background**
>
> Gail was born in 1976 and is resident and domiciled in the UK. She owns the whole of the ordinary share capital of Aero Ltd (A Ltd) and works full-time as a director of the company. A Ltd owns the whole of the ordinary share capital of Zephyr Ltd (Z Ltd). A Ltd and Z Ltd are both UK resident trading companies. A Ltd and Z Ltd both pay corporation tax at the main rate.

Historical transactions in respect of A Ltd and Z Ltd – all transactions took place at market value

1 January 2016	A Ltd acquired the whole of the ordinary share capital of Z Ltd for £180,000.
1 October 2020	A Ltd sold a building (the Simpson Building) to Z Ltd for £110,000. A Ltd had purchased this building for £75,000 on 1 December 2012.
1 March 2022	A Ltd sold a brand to Z Ltd for £170,000, its market value at the time was £230,000. A Ltd had purchased this brand for £115,000 on 1 June 2018.

Proposed transactions – all transactions will take place at market value

Gail intends to raise a substantial sum of money by carrying out the following transactions:

1	24 June 2024	Z Ltd will sell the Simpson Building to an unrelated purchaser for £140,000. Rollover relief will not be claimed in respect of this disposal. Z Ltd will pay a dividend to A Ltd equal to the post-tax proceeds of this sale.
2	1 July 2024	A Ltd will sell the whole of the ordinary share capital of Z Ltd for £250,000.
3	15 July 2024	All of the cash realised by A Ltd as a result of transactions 1 and 2 will be paid to Gail in the form of either a dividend or a bonus.

Non-disclosure of income

Gail has realised that she has not declared some of her income in respect of the tax year 2019/20. As a result of this, her income tax liability for that tax year was understated. I have already explained the interest and penalties which may be charged in respect of this error.

Exhibit 2 – Schedule prepared by Mill

Cash which will be available to pay to Gail as a result of the proposed transactions 1 and 2

	£
Sale of the Simpson Building by Zephyr Ltd	
Sale proceeds	140,000
Less: Cost	(110,000)
Indexation allowance (October 2020 to June 2024)	
£110,000 × 0.105	(11,550)
Chargeable gain	18,450
Less: Corporation tax payable by Zephyr Ltd at 25%	(4,613)
Dividend of post-tax proceeds paid to Aero Ltd	13,837
Less: Corporation tax payable by Aero Ltd at 25%	(3,459)
Cash available in respect of the sale of the Simpson Building	10,378
Sale proceeds in respect of Zephyr Ltd	250,000
Total cash available for Gail	260,378

Notes

1 I do not think there will be a chargeable gain on the sale of Zephyr Ltd due to the substantial shareholding exemption.

2 I think there will be a degrouping charge in respect of the brand but I do not know how to compute it.

Mill

Exhibit 3 – Brad

Extract from a memorandum prepared by your manager – dated 1 June 2024

Brad – background

Gail's father Brad is 70 years old and is married to Laura. He has always been UK domiciled.

Inheritance tax planning

Brad's estate is worth approximately £5 million. He has not made any lifetime gifts and, in his will, he intends to leave half of his estate to his daughter, Gail, and the other half to his wife, Laura. I pointed out that it may be advantageous to make a lifetime gift to Gail. Brad agreed to consider giving Gail 1,500 of his shares in Omnium Ltd and has asked for a general summary of the inheritance tax advantages of making lifetime gifts to individuals.

Omnium Ltd is an unquoted company. Brad was given his shares in the company by his wife on 1 January 2020. The ownership of the share capital of Omnium Ltd is set out below.

	Shares
Laura (Brad's wife)	4,500
Brad	3,000
Vic (Laura's brother)	1,500
Christine (friend of Laura)	1,000
	10,000

The current estimated value of a share in Omnium Ltd is set out below.

Shareholding	Value per share £
Up to 25%	190
26% to 50%	205
51% to 60%	240
61% to 74%	255
75% to 80%	290
More than 80%	300

Exhibit 4 – Work to be carried out

Email from your manager – dated 1 June 2024

Please prepare briefing notes to address the following:

(a) Schedule prepared by Mill (Exhibits 1 and 2)

I can confirm that there are no computational errors in the schedule but I suspect that Mill will have made a few technical errors.

Please identify and explain any errors in the schedule, explain whether or not the notes to the schedule are or are not correct, and calculate the correct amount of total cash available to pay to Gail.

The following movements in the Retail Prices Index should be used, where necessary.

December 2012 to December 2017	0.127
January 2016 to December 2017	0.075

(11 marks)

(b) Payment to Gail (Exhibit 1)

Calculate the additional tax and national insurance contributions due, as reduced by any corporation tax savings, if all of the cash realised by A Ltd as a result of the proposed transactions 1 and 2 is paid to Gail in the form of:

(i) a bonus

(ii) a dividend.

Gail's annual income tax liability in respect of her annual salary of £85,000 from A Ltd is £21,432. This will be her only source of income in the tax year 2024/25 other than any payments received from A Ltd as outlined above. **(9 marks)**

(c) Non-disclosure of income (Exhibit 1)

State the other matters which need to be considered, by us and by Gail, in relation to the disclosure of the error to HM Revenue and Customs (HMRC). **(5 marks)**

(d) Inheritance tax (Exhibit 3)

(i) Explain the inheritance tax advantages of making lifetime gifts to individuals, in general. **(7 marks)**

(ii) In respect of the possible gift of 1,500 shares in Omnium Ltd to Gail:

– calculate the fall in value of Brad's estate which will result from the gift

– provide a detailed explanation of whether or not business property relief would be available in respect of the gift and, on the assumption that it would be available, the manner in which it would be calculated

– state briefly any other tax issues arising from the gift, which will need to be considered at a later date. **(8 marks)**

Tax manager

Required:

You should assume that today's date is 1 June 2024.

Respond to the instructions in the email from your manager.

Note: The split of the mark allocation is shown in Exhibit 4 – Work to be carried out.

(40 marks)

Professional marks will be awarded for the demonstration of skill in communication, analysis and evaluation, scepticism and commercial acumen in your answer (10 marks)

(Total: 50 marks)

2 ZITI (ADAPTED) *Walk in the footsteps of a top tutor*

You should assume that today's date is 1 June 2024.

Your manager has received a letter from Ziti. Ziti owns and runs an unincorporated business which was given to him by his father, Ravi.

In addition to some ethical considerations which have been raised by your manager, Ziti requires advice in respect of:

- the net proceeds after income tax and capital gains tax from the disposal of his unincorporated business under two alternative methods,
- the value added tax (VAT) implications of the cessation of trade and disposal of assets,
- the potential inheritance payable on the gift of the business to Ziti in the event of Ravi's death, and
- the income tax implications of an investment in enterprise investment scheme (EIS) or venture capital trust (VCT) shares.

The following **exhibits** provide information relevant to the question:

1 Ziti – extract from letter

2 Appendix attached to letter from Ziti

3 Work to be carried out – email from manager

This information should be used to answer the question **requirements**.

Exhibit 1 – Ziti

Extract from a letter from Ziti

I have decided that, due to my father's serious illness, I want to be able to look after him on a full-time basis. Accordingly, I am going to sell my business and use the proceeds to buy a house nearer to where he lives and some shares.

My father started the business in 2009 when he purchased the building referred to in the business assets below. He gave the business (consisting of the goodwill, the building and the equipment) to me on 1 July 2020 and we submitted a joint claim for gift holdover relief, such that no capital gains tax was payable. I have no sources of income other than this business.

I have identified two possible methods of disposal.

(i) My preferred approach would be to close the business down. I would do this by selling the building and the equipment on 31 March 2025 at which point I would cease trading.

(ii) My father would like to see the business carry on after I sell it. For this to occur, I would have to continue trading until 31 March 2026 and then sell the business to my sister who would continue to operate it. I will charge my sister market value for all of the assets except the building, which I will sell to her for £300,000. My sister is not willing to make a gift holdover relief claim.

I attach an appendix setting out the information you requested in relation to the business. In order to keep a steady income stream I have plans to purchase a rental property which I will let out from 6 April 2025. The annual taxable rental income will be £52,000.

Sadly, I have been told that my father is unlikely to live for more than three years. Please let me know whether his death could result in an inheritance tax liability for me in respect of the gift of the business.

My father's only lifetime gift, apart from the business given to me, was of quoted shares to a discretionary (relevant property) trust on 1 May 2016. The shares had a market value of £190,000 at the date of the gift and did not qualify for business property relief.

Exhibit 2 – Appendix

Appendix attached to letter from Ziti

Business assets (all figures exclude value added tax (VAT))

	Goodwill	**Building**	**Equipment**
	£	£	£
Original cost of the business assets	0	60,000	18,000
Market value at the time of my father's gift on 1 July 2020	40,000	300,000	9,000
Expected market value as at 31 March 2025	40,000	330,000	10,000
Expected market value as at 31 March 2026	45,000	350,000	10,000

Financial position of the business

From 1 April 2024, it can be assumed that the business generates trading profits of £5,000 per month. Trading profits will increase to £6,000 per month from 1 April 2025. The only tax adjustment required to these figures is in respect of capital allowances.

The tax written down value of the main pool as at 31 March 2024 was £Nil. I purchased business equipment for £6,000 on 1 May 2024. There have been no disposals of equipment since 31 March 2024. I am happy to make any elections which will be beneficial from a tax perspective.

Tax-efficient investments

After selling the business I plan to use some of the sale proceeds to buy some shares, which I hope will save me some income tax as well as generating a small amount of income. I may consider investing in enterprise investment scheme (EIS) shares but am aware of the high level of risk involved. However, I understand that venture capital trusts (VCTs) have a lower level of risk.

Please let me have a comparison of the income tax implications of these two forms of investment on the assumption that I will invest £25,000 in the tax year 2026/27. I plan to keep the shares for at least five years.

Payment from HMRC

I have recently received £5,000 into my bank account from HMRC. I do not know what it relates to, but it is their error so I am going to keep the money.

Additional background information

- Ravi and I are both resident and domiciled in the UK.
- All of the equipment is movable and no item has a cost or market value of more than £6,000.
- The business is registered for VAT.
- No election has been made in respect of the building in relation to VAT.

Exhibit 3 – Work to be carried out

Extract from an email from your manager

Please prepare notes, which we can use in a meeting with Ziti, which address the following issues:

(a) Sale of the business (Exhibits 1 and 2)

(i) Calculations to enable Ziti to compare the financial implications of the two possible methods of disposal. You will need to calculate:

– Ziti's taxable trading profits from 1 April 2024 onwards and the income tax thereon, and

– any capital gains tax (CGT) payable.

You should include:

– explanations of the availability of any CGT reliefs

– a summary of the post-tax cash position, and

– any necessary assumptions. **(17 marks)**

(ii) Explanations of whether or not VAT would need to be charged on either or both of the alternative disposals. **(5 marks)**

(b) Inheritance tax (Exhibits 1 and 2)

Calculations of the amount of inheritance tax which would be payable by Ziti for all possible dates of his father's death between 2 June 2024 and 30 June 2027. You should include an explanation of the availability of any inheritance tax reliefs.

When calculating these potential inheritance tax liabilities, you should assume that Ziti will sell the business on 31 March 2025.

The best way for you to approach this is to identify the particular dates on which the inheritance tax liability will change. **(9 marks)**

(c) Tax-efficient investments (Exhibit 2)

A comparison of the income tax implications for Ziti of investing £25,000 in either EIS shares or VCT shares in the tax year 2026/27, as requested. **(4 marks)**

(d) HMRC error (Exhibit 2)

The issues arising and the actions we should take as a result of Ziti's plans for the HMRC payment. **(5 marks)**

Tax manager

Required:

You should assume that today's date is 1 June 2024.

Respond to the instructions in the email from your manager.

Note: The split of the mark allocation is shown in Exhibit 3 – Work to be carried out.

(40 marks)

Professional marks will be awarded for the demonstration of skill in communication, analysis and evaluation, scepticism and commercial acumen in your answer. (10 marks)

(Total: 50 marks)

3 JONNY (ADAPTED) *Walk in the footsteps of a top tutor*

You should assume that today's date is 1 September 2024.

Your manager has had a meeting with Jonny who is establishing a new business. Jonny will use an inheritance he received following the death of his mother to finance this new venture.

We have been asked to advise Jonny on:

- the income after tax from the new business, including consideration of the tax relief available for trading losses,
- the employment status of salesmen to be hired by Jonny, including consideration of the personal service company legislation, and
- the value of the inheritance to be received by Jonny after deducting any inheritance tax due.

There are also some ethical issues to consider.

The following **exhibits** provide information relevant to the question:

1 Unincorporated business – Jonny's income and plans for the new business

2 Inheritance tax payable – draft calculation

3 Work to be carried out – email from manager

This information should be used to answer the question **requirements**.

Exhibit 1 – Unincorporated business

Jonny's recent employment income

Jonny worked full-time for many years until 30 June 2022 earning a salary of £6,000 per calendar month. From 1 July 2022, he worked part-time earning a salary of £2,000 per calendar month until he ceased employment on 31 March 2024.

Plans for the new business

Jonny's new business will begin trading on 1 November 2024.

Two budgets have been prepared for Jonny's business based on customer demand being either strong or weak. You should assume that no tax adjustments are required to Jonny's budgeted profit/loss figures for the first two tax years.

	Strong demand	**Weak demand**
	£	£
Budgeted taxable trading profit/(loss):		
2024/25	9,200	(15,200)
2025/26	30,000	18,000
Aggregate budgeted net profit of the first two tax years	39,200	2,800

Jonny does not have any other sources of income or any taxable gains in any of the relevant tax years.

Salesmen

Jonny is proposing to enter into the following contractual arrangements with two part-time salesmen:

- They will work on Tuesday and Wednesday mornings each week.
- They will be paid a fee of £300 for each new sales contract obtained. No other payments will be made.
- They will use their own cars.
- Jonny will lend each of them a laptop computer.
- The salesmen intend to set up companies through which to operate after the first two months.

Jonny is concerned that the relationships may be caught by the personal service company legislation, and that he may have reporting requirements to fulfil.

Exhibit 2 – Inheritance tax payable

Jonny's mother died on 31 July 2024. She left the whole of her estate, with the exception of a gift to charity, to Jonny.

I attach a computation of the inheritance tax due; this was prepared by a junior member of staff and has not yet been reviewed. I can confirm, however, that all of the arithmetic, dates and valuations are correct. In addition, there were no other lifetime gifts, and none of the assets qualified for business property relief.

Computation – Inheritance tax payable on the death of Jonny's mother

Mother's lifetime gift		£
1 June 2020 – Gift of cash to Jonny		30,000

Mother's chargeable estate at death on 31 July 2024

	£	£
Freehold property – Mother's main residence		530,000
UK quoted shares		400,000
Chattels – furniture, paintings and jewellery	40,000	
Less: Items individually worth less than £6,000	(25,000)	
		15,000
Cash		20,000
		965,000
Less: Gift to charity		(70,000)
Annual exemption		(3,000)
Chargeable estate		892,000
Less: Nil rate band	325,000	
Gift in the seven years prior to death (£30,000 – £6,000)	(24,000)	
		(301,000)
		591,000
Inheritance tax (£591,000 × 40%)		236,400

Exhibit 3 – Work to be carried out

Extract from an email from your manager

Please prepare a memorandum for Jonny's client file addressing the following issues:

(a) Unincorporated business (Exhibit 1)

(i) Jonny's post-tax income

Jonny has asked for an approximation of his post-tax income position for the first two tax years. I want you to prepare calculations in order to complete the following table, assuming that any available trading loss reliefs will be claimed in the most beneficial manner.

You should include explanations of the options available to relieve the loss, clearly identifying the method which will maximise the tax saved (you do not need to consider carrying the loss forward).

Table to be completed

	Strong demand	**Weak demand**
	£	£
Aggregate budgeted net profit of the first two tax years	39,200	2,800
Aggregate income tax (payable)/refundable in respect of the profit/loss for the first two tax years	?	?
Budgeted post-tax income	?	?

Include a brief explanation as to why these calculations are only an approximation of Jonny's budgeted post-tax income. **(12 marks)**

(ii) Salesmen

Explain which of the proposed contractual arrangements with the salesmen indicate that they would be self-employed and state any changes which should be made to the other arrangements in order to maximise the likelihood of the salesmen being treated as self-employed.

In the event that the arrangements are treated as employment, explain how, if at all, the personal service company legislation would apply to Jonny's business and the salesmen. **(14 marks)**

(iii) New contracts for the business

Jonny is hoping to obtain contracts with local educational establishments and has asked us to help. One of our clients is a college and an ex-client of ours provided services to a number of schools and colleges. Accordingly, we have knowledge and experience in this area.

Explain the extent to which it is acceptable for us to use the knowledge we have gained in respect of our existing client and ex-client to assist Jonny.

(5 marks)

(b) Jonny's inheritance from his mother (Exhibit 2)

I want you to review the inheritance tax computation and identify any errors. You should explain each of the errors you find and calculate the value of the inheritance which Jonny will receive after inheritance tax has been paid. **(9 marks)**

Tax manager

Required:

You should assume that today's date is 1 September 2024.

Respond to the instructions in the email from your manager.

Note: The split of the mark allocation is shown in Exhibit 3 – Work to be carried out.

(40 marks)

Professional marks will be awarded for the demonstration of skill in communication, analysis and evaluation, scepticism and commercial acumen in your answer. (10 marks)

(Total: 50 marks)

4 RAY, SHANIRA AND KELLY (ADAPTED) *Walk in the footsteps of a top tutor*

You should assume that today's date is 1 July 2024.

Your manager has received schedules of information from Ray and Shanira and an email from Ray's niece Kelly in connection with their personal tax affairs. Ray and Shanira have been clients for some time, and Kelly has just appointed us to replace her existing tax adviser.

Advice is required in respect of the following issues:

– the income tax and national insurance payments to be made in respect of Ray's new unincorporated business,

– voluntary registration for value added tax (VAT) and the recovery of input VAT,

– the capital gains tax and inheritance tax implications of gifts to be made either before or after Ray and Shanira's marriage, and

– the income tax treatment of overseas rental income for a non-UK domiciled individual.

There are also some ethical issues to consider.

The following **exhibits** provide information relevant to the question:

1 Ray – schedule of information

2 Shanira – schedule of information

3 Kelly – email received

4 Work to be carried out – email from manager

This information should be used to answer the question **requirements**.

Exhibit 1 – Ray

Schedule of information received from Ray

I was born in 1965. I am resident and domiciled in the UK. Shanira and I are getting married on 17 September 2024.

Ray – unincorporated business

I was employed part-time until 31 March 2024. The annual salary in respect of my part-time job was £15,000. The whole of my income tax liability has always been settled via tax deducted at source.

I began trading on 1 June 2024. I purchased a computer on 3 June 2024, which is used both in the business and personally. I am not registered for the purposes of value added tax (VAT).

You have advised me that my taxable trading profits are calculated using the accruals basis, rather than the cash basis.

You have already informed me that my budgeted taxable trading profit, and my income tax liability in respect of all of my income will be:

Tax year	**Taxable trading profit**	**Income tax liability**
2024/25	£46,000	£6,686
2025/26	£66,000	£13,832

What tax payments will I be required to make between 1 July 2024 and 31 March 2027?

Exhibit 2 – Shanira

Schedule of information received from Shanira

I was born in 1968. I am resident and domiciled in the UK. Ray and I are getting married on 17 September 2024.

Gifts from Shanira to Ray

On 1 February 2024, I gave Ray a house situated in the country of Heliosa. We have only ever used this house for our holidays. The house was valued at £360,000 at the time of this gift. I purchased the house on 1 September 2007 for £280,000.

I will make the following further gifts to Ray between now and the end of the calendar year 2024:

– **Painting**

  I purchased this painting at auction for £15,000 on 1 March 2020. It is a painting which we both love and would never sell. However, I obviously paid too much for it, as its current market value is only £7,000.

– **Shares in Solaris plc**

  I will give Ray the whole of my holding of 7,400 ordinary shares in Solaris plc. The current market value is £9.20 per share.

  I acquired these shares on 1 October 2022 when Solaris plc purchased the whole of the ordinary share capital of Beem plc. This takeover was a genuine commercial transaction.

At the time of the takeover:

– I owned 3,700 ordinary shares in Beem plc, which I had purchased on 1 June 2016 for £12,960.

– In addition to the shares in Solaris plc, I also received £14,800 in cash from Solaris plc.

– An ordinary share in Solaris plc was worth £8.40 on 1 October 2022.

Additional information from your manager

– Shanira is a higher rate taxpayer.

– The gift of the house to Ray on 1 February 2024 was Shanira's first lifetime gift.

– You should use the current market values of the painting and the shares in Solaris plc in order to calculate the chargeable gains arising on these gifts.

– Neither gift holdover relief nor business asset disposal relief will be available in respect of the proposed gift of the shares in Solaris plc.

– Shanira has not made any other chargeable disposals since 5 April 2023.

– There is capital gains tax in the country of Heliosa but no inheritance tax.

– There is no double tax treaty between Heliosa and the UK.

Exhibit 3 – Kelly

Extract from an email from Kelly

I was born in 1991. I have always been domiciled in the country of Falgar. I was resident in the UK from 6 April 2001 until I moved to Falgar on 1 February 2022.

However, I have not been happy since I moved to Falgar. Consequently, I have decided to return to the UK on 1 May 2025, at which point I will resume UK residency.

Rental income in the country of Falgar

I will keep my house in Falgar, so that I can return to it at some future time. In the meantime, from 1 May 2025 I will rent it out.

My understanding of the UK tax position in relation to this rental income is as follows:

– provided I do not bring the rental income into the UK, it will not be subject to UK income tax

– if I do bring the income into the UK, I will then have to pay UK income tax upon it.

Please explain whether or not my understanding is correct.

I have also been contacted by a tax advisor who told me about some sophisticated tax planning I can do to reduce my UK tax liability which I would like to use going forwards. The advisor tells me that the scheme is a tax planning scheme rather than involving tax avoidance or evasion. I don't really understand the difference between the three, can you explain this please?

Additional information from your manager

Taxation in Falgar

– You should assume that Kelly will be a higher rate taxpayer.

– Income tax is charged at 26% on all income arising in Falgar.

– There is no capital gains tax or inheritance tax.

– There is no double tax treaty between the UK and Falgar.

Exhibit 4 – Work to be carried out

Extract from an email from your manager

Please carry out the following work:

Prepare a memorandum for the client files which addresses the following issues in respect of Ray and Shanira:

(a) Ray – unincorporated business (Exhibit 1)

– Calculations of the income tax and national insurance contribution payments to be made between 1 July 2024 and 31 March 2027 and the dates on which they will be payable.

– Ray has told me that he does not intend to withdraw all of the profits of the business. Instead, he will either increase his inventory levels or acquire additional equipment, and he has asked how this will affect his taxable income. **(11 marks)**

– Ray is incurring input tax and is considering registering voluntarily for VAT. Set out the information we need in order to advise him on whether or not voluntary registration is possible and/or financially beneficial and explain why the information is needed.

– An explanation of whether or not Ray can recover the input tax in respect of the computer purchased on 3 June 2024 if he registers for VAT. **(5 marks)**

(b) Gifts from Shanira to Ray (Exhibit 2)

– A calculation of the capital gains tax payable in respect of the gift of the house in Heliosa based on the currently available information, together with any further information required to finalise the liability, and the due date of payment.

– An explanation, with supporting calculations, of when the further gifts should be made to Ray. The objective here is to maximise Ray's capital gains tax base cost without creating a capital gains tax liability for Shanira. In order to achieve this objective, you should consider dividing the proposed gift of the shares into two gifts to be given on different days. **(10 marks)**

– The maximum possible inheritance tax liability which could arise in respect of the proposed gifts to Ray of the painting and the shares, if Shanira were to follow our advice in respect of their timing, together with the circumstances in which this liability would occur. **(5 marks)**

With regards to our new potential client Kelly:

(c) Kelly's rental income in the country of Falgar (Exhibit 3)

Please draft a response we can include in an email to Kelly which provides the explanation requested in her email. **(4 marks)**

(d) Kelly's tax planning scheme (Exhibit 3)

Please explain the difference between tax planning, tax avoidance and tax evasion, and explain the actions we should take with regards to the scheme that Kelly has been offered. **(5 marks)**

Tax manager

Required:

You should assume that today's date is 1 July 2024.

Respond to the instructions in the email from your manager.

Note: The split of the mark allocation is shown in Exhibit 4 – Work to be carried out.

(40 marks)

Professional marks will be awarded for the demonstration of skill in communication, analysis and evaluation, scepticism and commercial acumen in your answer. (10 marks)

(Total: 50 marks)

5 PIPPIN (ADAPTED) *Walk in the footsteps of a top tutor*

You should assume that today's date is 1 June 2024.

Your manager has had a meeting with Pippin, an established client of your firm who is resident and domiciled in the UK.

In addition to some ethical considerations which have been raised by your manager, Pippin would like some advice in respect of the following:

– the cash position for his new business, including the calculation of income tax and national insurance contributions and the tax relief available for trading losses,

– the capital gains tax consequences of a sale of shares that qualified for enterprise investment scheme (EIS) relief,

– the inheritance consequences of a gift of cash, and

– the income tax treatment of renting out a property.

The following **exhibits** provide information relevant to the question:

1 Commencement of 'Pinova' business – meeting notes from your manager

2 Cash receipt and cottage – notes from telephone conversation with Pippin

3 Work to be carried out – email from manager

This information should be used to answer the question **requirements**.

Exhibit 1 – Commencement of 'Pinova' business

Meeting notes from your manager – dated 1 June 2024

Pippin intends to start a new unincorporated business, 'Pinova', on 1 August 2024. He has identified two alternative strategies: strategy A and strategy B.

The budgeted tax-adjusted profit/(loss) of the two strategies are set out below. These figures are before the adjustments necessary in respect of the equipment purchases and employment costs (see below).

	Strategy A		**Strategy B**	
	Period ending 31 March 2025	**Year ending 31 March 2026 and future years**	**Period ending 31 March 2025**	**Year ending 31 March 2026 and future years**
	£	£	£	£
Profit/(loss)	13,000	60,000	(10,000)	135,000

Equipment purchases and employment costs

The above profit/loss figures need to be adjusted in respect of the following:

- Both strategies will require Pippin to purchase equipment in August 2024 for £8,000.
- Strategy B will require two employees from 1 April 2025. Pippin will pay each of them a gross salary of £2,500 per month. He will also pay them £0.50 per business mile for driving their own cars. He expects each of them to drive 250 business miles per month.
- Strategy A will not require any employees.

Pippin will claim the maximum capital allowances available to him. He will also claim opening years' loss relief in respect of the trading loss arising under strategy B.

Cessation of previous business

Pippin's previous unincorporated business ceased trading on 31 December 2023. The taxable profits of the business for its final three tax years were:

	£
2021/22	82,000
2022/23	78,000
2023/24	14,000

Pippin had no other taxable income during these three years.

Shares in Akero Ltd

Pippin owns 16,000 shares in Akero Ltd which have a current market value of £4.50 per share. Pippin subscribed £16,000 for these shares on 4 January 2022. Pippin obtained income tax relief of £4,800 (£16,000 × 30%) under the enterprise investment scheme (EIS) in the tax year 2021/22. He also claimed EIS deferral relief in that year of £16,000 in relation to a chargeable gain on the sale of a painting.

Pippin is considering selling 5,000 of his Akero Ltd shares in order to fund his personal expenditure during the start-up phase of the Pinova business.

Exhibit 2 – Cash receipt and cottage

Notes from a telephone conversation between your manager and Pippin

Receipt of £75,000

Pippin's aunt, Esme, died on 31 January 2024.

On 1 September 2018, Esme's father (Pippin's grandfather) died leaving the whole of his estate to Esme. However, on 1 January 2019 Pippin received £75,000 but cannot remember whether the money came from Esme or from his grandfather's estate.

On 1 November 2018, Esme had transferred cash of £375,000 to a trust for the benefit of her children.

Cottage in Cornwall

Pippin owns a cottage in Cornwall which he uses for family holidays. He is now thinking about renting out the cottage to long term tenants, but does not understand the tax implications of doing this.

The cottage can be rented out for £1,500 a month, received in advance on the first day of the month. Pippin would incur annual letting agent's fees of £1,800 as well as annual insurance costs of £580.

Pippin has a mortgage on the cottage with interest of £2,000 payable each year.

Exhibit 3 – Work to be carried out

Extract from an email from your manager – dated 1 June 2024

Please prepare a memorandum for the client files which addresses the following issues:

(i) Additional funds required for the 20-month period from 1 August 2024 to 31 March 2026 (Exhibit 1)

Pippin's taxable income will consist of the profits of the Pinova business and, for the tax year 2025/26 onwards, he expects to receive dividend income of £500 per year. His personal expenditure is £4,000 per month.

For the purposes of these calculations you should ignore any potential rental income from Pippin's cottage in Cornwall.

I want you to complete the table below to calculate the additional funds which Pippin would require during the first 20 months of the business under each of the two strategies (A and B) after putting aside sufficient funds to settle his tax liabilities for the tax years 2024/25 and 2025/26. You should then evaluate the two strategies by reference to the results of your calculations.

Pippin and I calculated his total **pre-tax** cash receipts; you do not need to check them. The only adjustment required to these pre-tax cash receipts is the cost of employing the two employees.

	Strategy A	**Strategy B**
	£	£
Total pre-tax cash receipts for the 20-month period	61,000	114,500
Cost of employing the two employees	0	( )
Pippin's total income tax and national insurance contribution liabilities for the tax years 2024/25 and 2025/26	( )	( )
Personal expenditure (£4,000 × 20)	(80,000)	(80,000)
Additional funds required		

(20 marks)

(ii) Sale of shares in Akero Ltd (Exhibit 1)

Explain the tax liabilities which would result if Pippin were to sell 5,000 of his Akero Ltd shares in the tax year 2024/25. **(7 marks)**

(iii) Receipt of £75,000 (Exhibit 2)

Explain, with supporting calculations, the inheritance tax implications for Pippin of the receipt of the £75,000. **(5 marks)**

(iv) Cottage in Cornwall (Exhibit 2)

Explain the income tax treatment for Pippin of the rental income to be received and expenses incurred in relation to the cottage.

This explanation should not include any calculations. **(3 marks)**

(v) Disclosure of property income

Pippin has questioned how HMRC would know about his new source of property income if he decides to rent out his cottage in Cornwall, and whether he would really need to disclose it.

I want you to list the matters which need to be considered, by us, as tax advisers to Pippin, and by Pippin, in relation to the disclosure or non-disclosure of this information to HM Revenue and Customs (HMRC). **(5 marks)**

Tax manager

Required:

You should assume that today's date is 1 June 2024.

Respond to the instructions in the email from your manager.

Note: The split of the mark allocation is shown in Exhibit 3 – Work to be carried out.

(40 marks)

Professional marks will be awarded for the demonstration of skill in communication, analysis and evaluation, scepticism and commercial acumen in your answer. (10 marks)

(Total: 50 marks)

6 MAIA (ADAPTED) *Walk in the footsteps of a top tutor*

You should assume that today's date is 1 June 2024.

Your manager has had a meeting with Maia, a client of your firm, who wants to provide some financial assistance to her nephew, Josh.

Advice is required in respect of:

– Josh's post-tax income and additional cash needed

– the capital gains tax and inheritance tax implications for Maia of the proposed gifts to Josh, and

– the income tax treatment of trust income received by Sarika, Josh's girlfriend.

There are also some ethical issues to consider.

The following **exhibits** provide information relevant to the question:

1 Maia and Josh – extracts from a memorandum prepared by your manager

2 Sarika – trust income

3 Work to be carried out – email from manager

This information should be used to answer the question **requirements**.

Exhibit 1 – Maia and Josh

Extracts from a memorandum prepared by your manager

Maia

Maia is 63 years old and has significant personal wealth. She has taxable income of approximately £120,000 each year, much of which she is able to save. She uses her capital gains tax annual exempt amount and her inheritance tax annual exemption every year. She is resident and domiciled in the UK.

Maia has agreed to provide financial assistance to her nephew, Josh.

Josh – financial position

Josh recently left university and, on 6 April 2024, he started working for NL Ltd, an unquoted company. He earns an annual gross salary of £25,200. Since 6 April 2024, NL Ltd has provided Josh with the use of a mobile telephone (market value of £650) and a home cinema system (market value of £1,700).

On 1 June 2024, NL Ltd issued 200 £1 ordinary shares to Josh. This share issue was not made as part of a tax advantaged share scheme. Josh paid £300 for these shares, which had a market value of £2,100 at that time. The shares are not readily convertible assets and Josh does not intend to sell them until 1 April 2028.

Josh currently receives dividend income of £420 each year. He is resident and domiciled in the UK.

Josh estimates that from 6 April 2024 he needs £2,500 per month to pay his rent and living expenses. Maia has asked us to calculate how much cash Josh will need for the tax years 2024/25 and 2025/26, over and above his post-tax income from all sources.

Providing financial assistance to Josh – alternative strategies

Maia is considering three alternative strategies to provide financial assistance to Josh.

(i) Gift of investment property on 1 July 2024

This investment property is currently worth £370,000.

Maia purchased the property for £130,000 on 1 July 2013. Since its acquisition, this property has been rented out for taxable net rental income of £1,100 per month. It is a residential building, but I do not know whether or not it has been rented out as furnished holiday accommodation.

Under this strategy, Josh would continue to rent out the property on the same basis from 1 July 2024 onwards.

(ii) Gift of shares in Far Ltd on 1 July 2024

These shares are worth £420,000. They represent the whole of Maia's shareholding in the company and constitute 14% of the company's issued ordinary share capital.

Maia's father gave the shares to Maia on 1 November 2023 when they were worth £375,000. That gift resulted in a chargeable gain of £225,000 of which £140,000 was held over via a gift holdover relief claim.

Far Ltd is an unquoted trading company. It owns chargeable non-business assets which represent 16% of its total chargeable assets.

(iii) Monthly cash gifts commencing on 1 July 2024

Maia would simply make a cash gift to Josh of £1,000 each month commencing on 1 July 2024.

Exhibit 2 – Sarika

Trust created for the benefit of Josh's girlfriend

Maia informed me that Josh's girlfriend, Sarika, has recently become the beneficiary of a trust and wants some tax advice regarding the income tax treatment of the trust income.

The trust was created by a gift consisting of a number of minority holdings of quoted shares valued at £260,000 in total on 1 June 2023.

Sarika received income from the trust for the first time in March 2024. Sarika's only other income is an annual salary of approximately £35,000.

Maia did not have any further information on the trust and Sarika is not currently a client of ours, so we will need to ensure we follow the correct procedures before we do any work for her.

Exhibit 3 – Work to be carried out

Extract from the email from your manager

Please prepare a memorandum for the client files consisting of the work set out below.

(a) Josh – additional cash requirement (Exhibit 1)

Calculate the total additional cash required by Josh, over and above his income from all sources, for the tax years 2024/25 and 2025/26, after deducting tax and national insurance contributions (NIC).

In order to prepare the calculations efficiently, you should think about how Josh's taxable income in 2025/26 will differ from that in 2024/25. There is no need to provide any narrative explanation of your calculations. **(9 marks)**

(b) Providing financial assistance to Josh – alternative strategies (Exhibit 1)

In respect of each of the three alternative strategies set out in my memorandum, explain:

- The increase in Josh's post-tax income for the 21-month period ending 5 April 2026.

  You should ONLY consider the post-tax income to be received by Josh in relation to strategies (i) and (iii) and NOT strategy (ii).

  There is no need to consider the capital values of any of the strategies as, in the short term, Josh will not realise any of this value.

- The capital gains tax liabilities FOR MAIA ONLY on the assumption that those reliefs which are available will be claimed.

– The inheritance tax implications for Maia and Josh including consideration of the availability of business property relief.

As I noted in my memorandum, I do not know whether the investment property qualifies as furnished holiday accommodation or not. You should explain the liabilities for both possibilities regarding this property. You SHOULD NOT provide a definition of furnished holiday accommodation.

You should cover:

(i) Gift of investment property. **(12 marks)**

(ii) Gift of shares in Far Ltd. **(7 marks)**

(iii) Monthly cash gifts. **(3 marks)**

(c) Trust created for the benefit of Josh's girlfriend (Exhibit 2)

A summary of the tax treatment of the income received by Josh's girlfriend, Sarika, as beneficiary, depending on the nature of the trust.

I understand that the only income of the trust is dividend income. **(4 marks)**

(d) Procedures we should follow before we agree to become Sarika's tax advisers (Exhibit 2)

A summary of the procedures we should follow before we agree to become Sarika's tax advisers. **(5 marks)**

Tax manager

Required:

You should assume that today's date is 1 June 2024.

Respond to the instructions in the email from your manager.

Note: The split of the mark allocation is shown in Exhibit 3 – Work to be carried out.

(40 marks)

Professional marks will be awarded for the demonstration of skill in communication, analysis and evaluation, scepticism and commercial acumen in your answer. (10 marks)

(Total: 50 marks)

Required:

You should assume that today's date is 5 December 2024.

Respond to the instructions in the email from your manager.

Note: The split of the mark allocation is shown in Exhibit 3 – Work to be carried out.

(40 marks)

Professional marks will be awarded for the demonstration of skill in communication, analysis and evaluation, scepticism and commercial acumen in your answer. (10 marks)

(Total: 50 marks

7 JOE AND FIONA (ADAPTED) *Walk in the footsteps of a top tutor*

You should assume that today's date is 1 June 2024.

You are an ACCA student working for a firm of accountants. Joe Sands, the finance director of VNL Ltd, has had a meeting with your manager to discuss the liquidation of the company and Joe's future plans in terms of starting his own unincorporated business. In addition, Joe has asked whether your firm will be able to advise his mother, Fiona, who is returning to the UK after living overseas for several years.

Advice is required in respect of the following issues:

- the consequences of VNL Ltd disposing of certain plant and machinery, intangible assets and the timing of a dividend payment,
- the ability of Joe to recover value added tax (VAT) on certain initial costs associated with his new business, and
- the basis of taxation which will apply to Fiona on her return to the UK and her projected income tax liability.

There are also some ethical issues to be considered if the firm is to accept Fiona as a new client.

The following **exhibits** provide information relevant to the question:

1 VNL Ltd

2 Joe's future business plans

3 Fiona (Joe's mother)

4 Work to be carried out – email from manager

This information should be used to answer the question **requirements**.

Exhibit 1 – VNL Ltd

Summary of points discussed in a meeting on 1 June 2024 and subsequent follow-up telephone conversation

Background

Joe advised me that the company's shareholders have decided to liquidate the company. A liquidator is to be appointed on 1 August 2024. The company has already sold certain items of plant and machinery and will dispose of some intangible fixed assets and make certain payments to its shareholders.

Sale of plant and machinery

Joe explained that VNL Ltd has recently disposed of two items of plant and machinery, but he was unsure of how to deal with them in the corporation tax computation.

The first disposal was of an item of machinery that was sold for £70,000 on 1 March 2024. It had been purchased for £200,000 and VNL Ltd claimed the 130% super deduction on the whole cost of this machinery.

The second disposal was of a lighting system. The system was originally purchased for £80,000 and VNL Ltd claimed the 50% first year allowance (FYA) on the full amount. The system was sold on 10 March 2024 for £20,000.

Sale of intangible fixed assets

On 1 September 2021, VNL Ltd purchased the trade and assets of a business from an unrelated company. The assets included goodwill and a brand name, as detailed below. These assets will be sold on 31 July 2024.

	Goodwill	Brand name
	£	£
Sale proceeds	75,000	47,000
Cost	95,000	36,000
Amortisation since acquisition	19,000	5,760

Further advice – payments to the shareholders

An interim payment will be made to the shareholders followed by a final payment at the conclusion of the liquidation which will take place in February 2025. Joe has been asked to consider the possibility of making the interim payment prior to the appointment of the liquidator.

Additional information

There are some further details which you will require and I have obtained these from the client file for you. These are as follows:

– VNL Ltd is a trading company. It has always made significant trading profits, such that it pays corporation tax at the main rate, and will be profitable in its final accounting period. It prepares accounts to 31 March each year.

– The amortisation of the goodwill was not a tax deductible expense for VNL Ltd.

– No election was made to write off the cost of the brand name at the 4% rate.

– The company's shareholders are all individuals, some of whom are employed by VNL Ltd, and include both basic rate and higher rate taxpayers.

– The shares in VNL Ltd were subscribed for prior to 17 March 2016, such that investors' relief will not be available in respect of any disposal.

Exhibit 2 – Joe's future business plans

Points discussed in meeting on 1 June 2024

Background

Joe confirmed his intention to start trading as an unincorporated trader on 1 November 2024.

Costs already incurred

Since 1 October 2023, Joe has been purchasing consultancy services every month in respect of the design and manufacture of the product the new business will be selling.

Business premises

A building for use as the business premises has been identified. It is a commercial property unit, which was constructed in 2007. Joe has agreed a price with the vendor of £190,000 plus value added tax (VAT). He intends to lease a third of the building to an unrelated business until his trading activities have grown sufficiently to require the use of the whole building.

Joe confirmed that his trading activity will be standard-rated for VAT purposes.

Exhibit 3 – Fiona (Joe's mother)

Points discussed in meeting on 1 June 2024

Background

Joe provided the following background on his mother's situation.

Fiona is 74 years old and in poor health. She has lived in the country of Parella since 1992. She will move to the UK on 1 August 2024 and acquire a home there.

Fiona's domicile and residence status

Based on the facts provided by Joe, I have already established that, as a result of moving to the UK:

- Fiona will become UK resident on 1 August 2024 under the split year basis.
- Fiona will also be UK resident in the tax year 2025/26.
- Fiona is domiciled in Parella. However, once she becomes UK resident, Fiona will be deemed domiciled in the UK for the purposes of income tax and capital gains tax (CGT) because she was born in the UK with a UK domicile of origin.

Property and interest income

Fiona's anticipated income for the tax year 2025/26, the year after she moves to the UK, is set out below.

	£
Property income	
Properties situated in the UK	26,000
Properties situation in Parella	31,000
Interest income	
UK bank interest	1,700
Parellian bank interest	1,200

The income arising in Parella is stated gross of Parellian tax. Fiona will remit all of the rental income in respect of the properties situated in Parella to the UK. The interest arising on the Parellian bank accounts will be retained in Parella.

The rate of income tax in Parella is 18% and there is no double tax treaty between the UK and Parella.

Exhibit 4 – Work to be carried out

Manager's email

To: Tax Senior

From: Tax Manager

Subject: Meeting with Joe Sands (VNL Ltd)

Date: 1 June 2024

Hi

I need you to prepare some notes in preparation for an internal team meeting to discuss the various points which Joe has raised. They should address the following issues:

(a) Liquidation of VNL Ltd (Exhibit 1)

(i) Sales of plant and machinery

Explain, with supporting calculations, the corporation tax implications for VNL Ltd of the disposals of the plant and machinery in the year ended 31 March 2024. **(5 marks)**

(ii) Sale of intangible fixed assets

Calculate the post-tax proceeds for VNL Ltd as a result of the sale of the intangible fixed assets. **(4 marks)**

(iii) Timing of payments to shareholders

Explain the tax rates, taking into account any reliefs which may be available, which the shareholders will pay on the amounts received from VNL Ltd, depending on when the payment is made. **(9 marks)**

(b) Unincorporated business (Exhibit 2)

Explain whether or not Joe will be able to recover the related input tax for value added tax (VAT) purposes in respect of the consultancy costs already incurred and the planned purchase of the business premises. **(7 marks)**

(c) Becoming Fiona's tax advisers (Exhibit 3)

Explain the actions which we should carry out before we become Fiona's tax advisers. I have already obtained her address and proof of her identity. **(5 marks)**

(d) Taxation of overseas income (Exhibit 3)

– Explain why the remittance basis will be available to Fiona in the tax year 2025/26 and whether or not she will be subject to the remittance basis charge.

– Calculate Fiona's income tax liability for the tax year 2025/26 based on her anticipated income figures. **(10 marks)**

The notes which you prepare will subsequently be distributed to all team members within our firm, so please do present them in a way which will be suitable for circulation.

Tax Manager

Required:

You should assume that today's date is 1 June 2024.

Respond to the instructions in the email from your manager.

Note: The split of the mark allocation is shown in Exhibit 4 – Work to be carried out.

(40 marks)

Professional marks will be awarded for demonstration of skill in communication, analysis and evaluation, scepticism and commercial acumen in your answer. (10 marks)

(Total: 50 marks)

8 OLMA AND HOGAN (ADAPTED) *Walk in the footsteps of a top tutor*

You should assume that today's date is 1 February 2025.

Your manager has had a meeting with Olma, a new client of your firm. Olma has recently ceased employment and started a new unincorporated business. Her brother, Hogan, is an existing client and requires some advice.

The work to be carried out is in respect of:

- a company purchase of own shares
- voluntary registration for the purposes of value added tax (VAT)
- the reliefs available in respect of a trading loss Olma is expecting to make
- a receipt of shares by Hogan from a share incentive plan (SIP), and
- a gift made by Hogan to a discretionary trust.

There are also some ethical issues to be considered.

The following **exhibits** provide information relevant to the question:

1 Olma

2 Hogan

3 Work to be carried out – email from manager

This information should be used to answer the question **requirements**.

Exhibit 1 – Olma

Extract from a memorandum prepared by your manager

In view of the changes to her financial affairs, Olma has appointed us to replace her existing tax advisers.

Background

On 1 November 2017, Olma purchased 2,000 of the 10,000 issued ordinary shares of BG Ltd (an unquoted company) for £40,000 and, on the same day, began working as a restaurant manager for the company. BG Ltd owns and operates a number of restaurants.

- Olma worked for BG Ltd from 1 November 2017 until 30 September 2024.
- However, she took unpaid leave for personal reasons from 1 September 2021 until 31 August 2022.

– On 30 September 2024, Olma ceased her employment with BG Ltd in order to start an unincorporated cafe business.

Olma has always been resident in the UK for tax purposes. From 1 November 2017 to 30 September 2024, her only source of income was her salary from BG Ltd of £6,700 per month. Since 1 October 2024, her only income has been trading income from her cafe which began trading on 1 January 2025.

Sale of shares in BG Ltd

Following disagreements with the other shareholders of BG Ltd in relation to the future direction of the business, Olma decided to leave the company and to sell her shares. Olma sold all 2,000 of her shares back to BG Ltd on 15 October 2024 for £150,000 via a company purchase of own shares. Olma will claim business asset disposal relief in respect of the chargeable gain arising on this sale.

Olma's cafe business

Voluntary registration for the purposes of value added tax (VAT)

Budgeted revenue figures indicate that Olma will be required to register for VAT with effect from 1 September 2025. However, depending on the financial implications, Olma is considering registering voluntarily at an earlier date. This is in order to give the impression that the cafe is more established than it is in reality.

All of the supplies made by Olma's cafe business are standard-rated for the purposes of VAT.

On 1 December 2024, Olma purchased furniture and equipment for use in the cafe for £8,000 excluding VAT. The principal recurring costs incurred by the cafe are employment costs, food and rent in respect of the business premises. The purchases of food are zero-rated and the rent is exempt for the purposes of VAT.

Loss planning

Olma is expecting to make a tax adjusted trading loss of £29,000 in the tax year 2024/25, her first tax year of trading, and requires advice on the reliefs available.

Introduction of Hogan as a partner

Olma has been considering asking her brother, Hogan, to become a partner in her new business in the future and assumes that there should be no problem with this as he is already one of our clients.

Exhibit 2 – Hogan

Email extract from Hogan: dated 1 February 2025

For the last 30 years I have been living in the country of Baltera.

Moving to the UK

I have entered into an employment contract with VPR plc, a UK based company. I will move to the UK to commence employment on 1 August 2025.

Employment contract with VPR plc

The contract is for a minimum period of four years.

Under the contract I will earn a salary of £16,500 per month.

In addition, I will become a member of the company's tax-advantaged share incentive plan (SIP). On 1 May each year, this SIP will award me free shares in the company. The value of these shares will be between £1,500 and £2,500 each year, depending on the performance of the company. I have been told that the receipt of these shares, together with any dividends declared in respect of them, will not give rise to a tax liability in the UK.

Trust

I am planning to create a UK discretionary trust for the benefit of my two nieces. On 1 July 2026, I will give £380,000 in cash to the trust. This cash will be transferred to the trustees from my bank deposit account in Baltera and I will pay any inheritance tax due in respect of this gift personally. I have not made any previous lifetime gifts.

Additional information from your manager

Hogan

– Hogan was born in the UK and has a UK domicile of origin. He is currently neither domiciled nor deemed domiciled in the UK in respect of all taxes, but you should bear in mind that his domicile status may change over time.

– The split year basis applies to Hogan in the tax year 2025/26. You ARE NOT required to provide an explanation as to why this is the case.

– Hogan will be UK resident in the tax year 2026/27.

Tax system in the country of Baltera

– There is no inheritance tax (IHT) in Baltera.

Exhibit 3 – Work to be carried out

Extract from an email from your manager

Please prepare a memorandum for the client file consisting of the work set out below.

(a) Sale of shares in BG Ltd (Exhibit 1)

This sale qualified as a capital disposal, such that it gave rise to a chargeable gain rather than to taxable income.

Olma's shareholding in BG Ltd was clearly substantially reduced as a result of the sale of all of her shares and she is not connected to the company. I can also confirm that the sale was not carried out as part of a scheme to avoid tax.

– Outline the other conditions which must have been satisfied, such that Olma's sale of her shares gave rise to a chargeable gain. **(5 marks)**

(b) Cafe business (Exhibit 1)

(i) Voluntary registration for the purposes of value added tax (VAT)

Olma and I have already discussed the administration aspects of VAT, including the various schemes and the penalty regime.

– Explain the additional matters we should draw to Olma's attention in order to help her understand the financial advantage(s) and/or disadvantage(s) of registering voluntarily prior to 1 September 2024. **(8 marks)**

(ii) Loss planning

– Explain, with supporting calculations, how Olma's trading loss could be offset her income and/or chargeable gains, on the assumption that she does not wish to carry the trading loss forward.

– Conclude on the most beneficial way of relieving the loss and the tax which would be saved as a result.

You should ignore national insurance contributions and VAT. **(12 marks)**

(iii) Introduction of Hogan as a partner

– Explain any issues that would arise for our firm if Hogan enters into a partnership with Olma and any actions the firm should take.

(5 marks)

(c) Award of free shares from VPR plc's share incentive plan (SIP) (Exhibit 2)

– State the conditions which must be satisfied IN THE FUTURE in order for there to be no income tax payable by Hogan in respect of the value of the shares awarded to him and the dividends paid in respect of them. **(3 marks)**

(d) Gift of £380,000 to a discretionary trust on 1 July 2026 (Exhibit 2)

– Explain by reference to Hogan's domicile why this proposed gift will give rise to a UK IHT liability.

– Calculate the amount of IHT which will be payable by Hogan. **(7 marks)**

Required:

You should assume that today's date is 1 February 2025.

Respond to the instructions in the email from your manager.

Note: The split of the mark allocation is shown in Exhibit 3 – Work to be carried out.

(40 marks)

Professional marks will be awarded for demonstration of skill in communication, analysis and evaluation, scepticism and commercial acumen in your answer. (10 marks)

(Total: 50 marks)

9 HIROMI (ADAPTED) *Walk in the footsteps of a top tutor*

You should assume that today's date is 1 September 2024.

You are an ACCA student working for a firm of accountants. Your manager has asked for your assistance in drafting notes in preparation for a meeting with Hiromi in relation to her personal tax affairs.

In addition to some ethical considerations which have been raised by your manager, advice is required in respect of:

– the capital gains tax payable on the sale of a property and the sale of business assets,

– the availability of incorporation relief,

– the reliefs available in respect of a trading loss of a sole trader,

– the tax implications of the payment and receipt of a dividend, and

– the records to be kept by a company.

The following **exhibits** provide information relevant to the question:

1 Hiromi's income and chargeable gains

2 Sale of unincorporated business

3 Work to be carried out

Exhibit 1 – Hiromi's income and chargeable gains

Extract from a memorandum from your manager (dated 1 September 2024) recording matters discussed in a meeting with Hiromi

Hiromi recently became a client of our firm. Her sources of income and chargeable gains for recent tax years are summarised below.

Sources of income

Hiromi has been in business as a sole trader since 2015. On 31 December 2024, Hiromi will incorporate her business by selling all of its assets to a newly formed company called HKR Ltd. The details of this transaction are set out in the schedule from Hiromi (Exhibit 2).

Hiromi's tax adjusted trading results for her final two tax years of trading are set out below.

	£
2024/25 (budgeted) – loss	(44,500)
2023/24 – profit	8,000

Hiromi's only other source of income in recent years was a house which she rented out until she sold it on 28 February 2024 (see below). Hiromi's assessable property income for the final two tax years in which she owned the property is:

	£
2022/23	19,400
2023/24	15,500

Chargeable gains

Hiromi's only disposal in recent years was of her rental property on 28 February 2024. Hiromi sold this house for £265,000. She had inherited it from her uncle on 1 March 2012 when it had a market value of £221,500. Hiromi's uncle had purchased the house for £135,000 on 1 September 2005. Hiromi had never lived in the property.

Income tax refund

Hiromi has received an unexpected refund of income tax from HM Revenue and Customs (HMRC) in respect of the tax year 2020/21.

Exhibit 2 – Sale of unincorporated business

Schedule from Hiromi dated 1 September 2024

Sale of the assets of my business to HKR Ltd

I will sell all of the assets of my business to HKR Ltd for their market values on 31 December 2024. Details of the assets to be sold are set out below.

	Goodwill	Building	Current assets	Total
Market value	£4,000	£290,000	£21,000	£315,000
Cost	£4,000	£118,000	N/A	
Chargeable gain	0	£172,000	N/A	£172,000

I will receive 50,000 ordinary £1 shares in HKR Ltd (the whole of the company's issued share capital). The value of these shares will be £255,000, representing 81% of the total consideration. The remainder of the consideration will be left on loan account and will be paid to me in the future.

I will not make any further capital disposals in the tax year 2024/25.

Looking to the future

I expect the turnover of the business to increase considerably in 2025 and 2026. As a result, HKR Ltd will be able to pay me a salary of £5,500 per month, beginning on 6 April 2025. I will also be paid a dividend of £7,000 each year. The first dividend will be paid on 1 November 2026. HKR Ltd will pay corporation tax at the main rate.

Finally, I require advice on the record keeping requirements which will apply to HKR Ltd in relation to its business activities.

Exhibit 3 – Work to be carried out

Extract from email from manager dated 1 September 2024

I need you to prepare some notes for internal use prior to our meeting with Hiromi. The notes should be set out in a manner which will make it easy for us to refer to them during our discussions and should address the following issues:

(a) Refund of income tax (Exhibit 1)

Summarise the actions which our firm should take, including the matters which we should bring to Hiromi's attention in relation to the refund she has received.

(5 marks)

(b) Chargeable gains (Exhibits 1 and 2)

When carrying out this work in respect of Hiromi's chargeable gains you should ignore any relief which may be available to her in respect of her trading loss.

- Calculate the capital gains tax (CGT) payable by Hiromi as a result of the sale of the rental property on 28 February 2024.
- In respect of the proposed sale of Hiromi's business assets to HKR Ltd on 31 December 2024:
  - Explain whether or not each of the three conditions for incorporation relief will be satisfied; and

– On the assumption that incorporation relief WILL be available, and that all available reliefs will be claimed where necessary, calculate the CGT which will be payable by Hiromi as a result of the sale of her business assets.

(12 marks)

(c) Trading loss (Exhibits 1 and 2)

For the purposes of this part (c) you should IGNORE terminal loss relief and national insurance contributions.

(i) State how Hiromi's budgeted trading loss for the tax year 2024/25 can be relieved. **(4 marks)**

(ii) Using the loss for the tax year 2024/25:

1 Explain, with supporting calculations, the tax savings which would result from the following two alternatives:

– relieving the loss as soon as possible assuming that NO relief is claimed in respect of the tax year 2024/25;

– relieving the loss in the future.

2 Set out the matters we should draw to Hiromi's attention in order to help her decide on how to relieve the loss. **(11 marks)**

(d) When HKR Ltd owns the business (Exhibit 2)

– Explain with supporting calculations, the tax implications for HKR Ltd and Hiromi of HKR Ltd paying a dividend of £7,000 in the tax year 2026/27.

– State the matters you would draw to Hiromi's attention in relation to the requirement for HKR Ltd to maintain and retain the records relating to its business activities. **(8 marks)**

Required:

You should assume that today's date is 1 September 2024.

Respond to the instructions in the email from your manager.

Note: the split of the mark allocation is shown in Exhibit 3 – Work to be carried out.

(40 marks)

Professional marks will be awarded for the demonstration of skill in communication, analysis and evaluation, scepticism and commercial acumen in your answer. (10 marks)

(Total: 50 marks)

TAXATION OF CORPORATE BUSINESSES

10 DRENCH, PAPRIKASH, HAIL LTD AND RAIN LTD (ADAPTED)

Walk in the footsteps of a top tutor

You should assume that today's date is 1 December 2024.

Your manager has sent you a schedule of information received from a client, named Drench, who is the managing director of Hail Ltd. Hail Ltd is a UK resident trading company with an accounting reference date of 30 June and Drench owns the whole of the company's ordinary share capital. Your manager would also like you to do some work in respect of a potential gift to be made by Paprikash, Drench's uncle.

In addition to some ethical issues raised by your manager, advice is required in respect of the following issues:

- the acquisition of a subsidiary, either by Drench personally or by Hail Ltd, with potential trading losses,
- the tax implications of Drench taking a loan from Hail Ltd,
- the advantages of the value added tax (VAT) cash accounting scheme and the ability to be able to recover VAT on initial costs, and
- the inheritance tax implications of a gift to be made either during lifetime or on death.

The following **exhibits** provide information relevant to the question:

1 Drench

2 Paprikash (Drench's uncle)

3 Work to be carried out – email from manager

This information should be used to answer the question **requirements**.

Exhibit 1 – Drench

Schedule of information from Drench

Acquisition of Rain Ltd

I intend to buy 100% of the ordinary share capital of Rain Ltd, a UK resident trading company, on 1 January 2025. I will either purchase the shares personally or Hail Ltd will acquire Rain Ltd as a 100% subsidiary.

Rain Ltd is one of two companies currently wholly-owned by Flake Ltd. All three of the companies in the Flake Ltd group are trading companies. Following its acquisition Rain Ltd will change its accounting reference date from 30 September to 30 June such that it will prepare accounts for the nine months ending 30 June 2025.

Budgeted results of Rain Ltd

The budgeted financial results of Rain Ltd for the nine months ending 30 June 2025 are set out below. The results depend on whether or not the company acquires new contracts in 2025. All of the company's sales are standard-rated for the purposes of value added tax (VAT). The chargeable gain is in respect of the disposal of a 0.3% shareholding in a quoted company.

	Nine months ending 30 June 2025	
	Without the new contracts	**With the new contracts**
	£	£
Sales revenue (exclusive of VAT)	380,000	1,425,000
Tax adjusted (loss)/profit	(110,000)	285,000
Chargeable gain	50,750	50,750

Other relevant information

In the year ended 30 September 2024 Rain Ltd realised a tax adjusted trading loss of £27,000 and had no other income or chargeable gains. The trading loss was surrendered as group relief to companies within the Flake Ltd group.

Rain Ltd's main asset is a building which is currently worth £340,000. The building was purchased from Mist Ltd, the other 100% subsidiary of Flake Ltd, on 1 July 2021 for its book value of £248,000. The market value of the building at that time was £260,000. Mist Ltd had purchased the building on 1 January 2012 for £170,000.

Hail Ltd is budgeted to realise taxable total profits in the year ending 30 June 2025 of £100,000.

Neither Rain Ltd nor Hail Ltd will receive any dividends during their accounting periods ending 30 June 2025.

Exhibit 2 – Paprikash (Drench's uncle)

Schedule of information from your manager

Uncle's property in the country of Chilaca

Paprikash (Drench's uncle) owns a property in the country of Chilaca that he uses for holidays. It has always been intended that the property would be left to Drench in his uncle's will. However, Paprikash has recently agreed to give the property to Drench now, if to do so would make sense from a tax point of view. Paprikash may still wish to use the property occasionally in the future.

The property is currently worth £600,000. However, due to the economic situation in the country of Chilaca, it is possible that this figure could either rise or fall over the next few years.

Paprikash is domiciled in the UK. He is in poor health and is not expected to live for more than a further five years. His total assets, including the property in the country of Chilaca, are worth £2 million.

Paprikash makes gifts on 1 May each year in order to use his inheritance tax annual exemption. His only other gift in the last seven years was to a trust on 1 December 2023. The gift consisted of a number of minority holdings of quoted shares valued at £290,000 in total. The trust is for the benefit of Drench's daughter, Piri. It can be assumed that Paprikash will not make any further lifetime gifts.

There is no capital gains tax or inheritance tax in the country of Chilaca.

Exhibit 3 – Work to be carried out

Email from your manager

I want you to prepare the following:

(a) A memorandum for the client file that explains the following matters, providing supporting calculations where relevant:

(i) Acquisition of Rain Ltd (Exhibit 1)

A comparison of the tax implications of:

– Drench acquiring Rain Ltd personally, and

– Hail Ltd acquiring Rain Ltd.

Drench is aware of the general implications of forming a group. Accordingly, your comparison should focus on the following specific issues.

On the assumption that Rain Ltd DOES NOT obtain the new contracts:

– The manner in which the loss for the nine months ending 30 June 2025 should be relieved in order to maximise the tax relief obtained; the tax relief should be quantified where possible. Take care when identifying the rates of corporation tax payable by Rain Ltd and Hail Ltd, as I suspect that the situation is not totally straightforward.

  Drench wants the loss to be used as soon as possible and only to be carried forward as a last resort.

– The tax implications of Hail Ltd making a payment to Rain Ltd in respect of any group relief losses surrendered.

On the assumption that Rain Ltd DOES obtain the new contracts

– The corporation tax liability of Rain Ltd for the nine months ending 30 June 2025.

– The date by when Rain Ltd will need to pay its corporation tax liability for the period in order to avoid interest charges.

The tax treatment of Rain Ltd's building, including:

– any potential tax liabilities that may arise on the acquisition of Rain Ltd, and

– the base cost of the building for the purposes of calculating the chargeable gain or loss arising on the future disposal by Rain Ltd.

(15 marks)

(ii) Loan from Hail Ltd to Drench and VAT cash accounting scheme (Exhibit 1)

– The tax implications for Hail Ltd of Drench borrowing £18,000 from the company on 1 February 2025. The loan will be interest-free and will be repaid by Drench on 1 February 2031.

– The advantages of the VAT cash accounting scheme and whether it will be possible for Rain Ltd to operate the scheme. **(8 marks)**

The following indexation factor should be used where necessary.

January 2012 to December 2017	0.168

(b) Meeting notes for a meeting with Drench including:

Uncle's property in the country of Chilaca (Exhibit 2)

Calculations of the inheritance tax liability that will become due in respect of the property in the country of Chilaca depending on whether the property is gifted to Drench on 1 February 2025 or via his uncle's will.

You should assume the following:

– His uncle, Paprikash, will die on either 30 June 2027 or 30 June 2029.

– The property will be worth £600,000 on 1 February 2025.

– Three possible values of the property at the date of Paprikash's death: £450,000, £600,000 and £900,000.

  You should calculate the inheritance tax for each of the 12 possible situations on the property only, assuming that Paprikash does not use the property after the date of the gift.

  You should start by calculating the tax on a lifetime gift with Paprikash's death on 30 June 2027. When calculating the tax on the gift via Paprikash's will, you should assume that any available nil rate band is deductible from the property.

– Conclusions drawn from the calculations.

– Any other issues that we should draw to Drench's attention. **(12 marks)**

(c) A briefing note to me

Our firm will be assisting Rain Ltd to obtain the new contracts. We have experience in this area as we used to have a client that successfully applied for government building contracts. The client moved to a rival firm at the end of 2022.

To what extent is it acceptable for us to use the knowledge we gained in respect of our ex-client to assist Rain Ltd? **(5 marks)**

Tax manager

Required:

You should assume that today's date is 1 December 2024.

Respond to the instructions in the email from your manager.

Note: The split of the mark allocation is shown in the Exhibit 3 – Work to be carried out.

(40 marks)

Professional marks will be awarded for demonstration of skill in communication, analysis and evaluation, scepticism and commercial acumen in your answer. (10 marks)

(Total: 50 marks)

11 DILIP GROUP AND EMMA (ADAPTED) *Walk in the footsteps of a top tutor*

You should assume that today's date is 1 December 2024.

Your manager has had a meeting with Dilip, a new client, and a telephone conversation with his mother Emma, a longstanding client.

Advice is required in respect of the following issues:

– the relief for the trading losses of one of Dilip's companies, Shank Ltd

– the chargeable gains/allowable losses, VAT and stamp duty land tax implications of the disposal of four buildings

– the VAT implications of supplying goods to overseas customers, and

– the disposal of shares by Emma either before or after her return to the UK.

There are also some ethical issues to be considered around a tax planning scheme offered to Emma.

The following **exhibits** provide information relevant to the question:

1 Dilip group corporate matters

2 Emma (Dilip's mother)

3 Work to be carried out – email from manager

This information should be used to answer the question **requirements**.

Exhibit 1 – Dilip group corporate matters

Summary of matters discussed at meeting with Dilip on 30 November 2024 and subsequent follow-up telephone conversation

Background

Dilip wants us to advise him on the sale of Shank Ltd, one of his companies, and on the sale of a number of buildings.

Dilip owns the Hock Ltd group of companies and Knuckle Ltd as set out below. The dates in brackets are the dates on which the companies were purchased. Neither Dilip nor his companies have any interests in any other companies.

All five companies are UK resident trading companies with a 31 March accounting reference date. All of the companies, with the exception of Shank Ltd, are profitable.

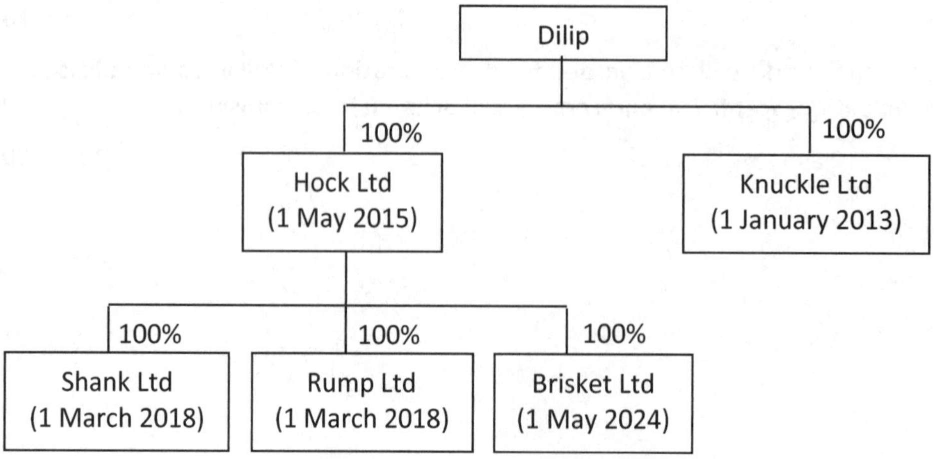

Sale of Shank Ltd

Shank Ltd has made trading losses for a number of years and, despite surrendering the maximum possible losses to group companies, it has trading losses to carry forward as at 31 March 2024 of £35,000. Shank Ltd is expected to make a further trading loss of £19,000 in the year ending 31 March 2025 and has no other sources of income.

Dilip is of the opinion that the company will only become profitable following significant financial investment, which the group cannot afford, together with fundamental changes to its commercial operations.

Accordingly, Hock Ltd entered into a contract on 1 November 2024 to sell the whole of the ordinary share capital of Shank Ltd to Raymond Ltd (an independent third party) on 1 February 2025 for £270,000; an amount that is considerably less than the group paid for it.

Sales of buildings

The following buildings are to be sold during the year ending 31 March 2025, with the exception of the Monk building which was sold on 1 March 2024. Rollover relief will not be claimed in respect of any of the gains arising.

	Gar building	**Cray building**	**Monk building**	**Sword building**
Owned by:	Shank Ltd	Rump Ltd	Brisket Ltd	Knuckle Ltd
Cost:	£210,000	£24 million	£380,000	See below
Indexation allowance factors:	0.350	0.250	N/A	0.089
Date of sale:	1 January 2025	1 February 2025	1 March 2024	1 February 2025
Purchaser:	Hock Ltd	Quail plc	Hare plc	Pheasant plc
Estimated proceeds:	£370,000	£42 million	£290,000	£460,000

On 30 June 2014 Knuckle Ltd sold its original premises, the Pilot building, for £270,000 resulting in a chargeable gain of £60,000. On 1 January 2015 it purchased the Sword building for £255,000 and claimed rollover relief in respect of the gain on the Pilot building.

Rump Ltd has capital losses brought forward as at 1 April 2024 of £10 million.

Additional information

I have just had a further conversation with Dilip. He informed me that:

- Brisket Ltd acquired the Monk building on 1 January 2020.
- Quail plc, Hare plc and Pheasant plc are all unrelated to Dilip and his companies.
- None of the companies will make any other chargeable gains or allowable losses in the year ending 31 March 2025.
- Knuckle Ltd has identified a number of potential overseas customers and expects to begin selling its products to them in 2025. At the moment, all of Knuckle Ltd's supplies are standard-rated for the purposes of value added tax (VAT).

Exhibit 2 – Emma (Dilip's mother)

Summary of points discussed on 1 December 2024

Background

Emma is 74 years old and has always been domiciled in the country of Alman. She was resident in the UK from 6 April 2001 until she moved to Alman on 1 February 2022. Emma will return to the UK on 1 May 2025 and resume UK residency.

Emma is a higher rate taxpayer.

Sale of shares in Barb plc

Emma is going to sell her 2% holding in Barb plc, which she has owned as an investment since 1 December 2020. She could sell the shares now, in which case she would realise a chargeable gain of £330,000. Alternatively, if she waits until she is back in the UK, she would be able to increase the selling price by £60,000.

She plans to sell the shares now, for the lower price, as she believes this will mean that no UK capital gains tax will be due.

Tax planning scheme

Emma has recently been approached by a firm of tax advisors who have offered her the chance to use their tax planning scheme. The scheme involves carrying out a series of complicated disposals in order to avoid paying capital gains tax and inheritance tax on Emma's chargeable assets.

Emma is very wealthy and so is intrigued by the idea of avoiding large capital tax liabilities, but would like our opinion on whether she should proceed with the scheme.

Additional information

There is no capital gains tax in the country of Alman.

Exhibit 3 – Work to be carried out

Email from your manager

(a) Dilip Group corporate matters (Exhibit 1)

I want you to draft a report for Dilip dealing with the matters set out below.

(i) Sale of Shank Ltd

– The alternative ways in which the company's trading losses can be relieved. I want some precise detail here so please try to consider all of the possibilities and any anti-avoidance legislation that may restrict the use of the losses.

– The tax treatment of the loss arising on the sale of Shank Ltd.

– An explanation of the upper and lower limits for all of the companies for the purposes of calculating the rate of corporation tax for the year ending 31 March 2025. **(12 marks)**

(ii) Sales of buildings

On the assumption that the three future building sales go ahead as planned:

– Calculations of the chargeable gain/allowable loss arising on the sale of each of the four buildings.

– The alternative ways in which any capital losses arising can be relieved, including the capital loss brought forward in Rump Ltd. I need a detailed explanation of the options available together with any restrictions that will apply.

– The need to charge VAT on the sales of the buildings.

– The stamp duty land tax implications of the sales of the buildings. **(13 marks)**

(iii) Potential sales by Knuckle Ltd to overseas customers

– The VAT implications. **(2 marks)**

(b) Sale of shares in Barb plc by Emma (Exhibit 2)

Prepare a file note explaining whether Emma should sell her shares in Barb plc now, or wait until after she returns to the UK on 1 May 2025. **(8 marks)**

(c) Tax planning scheme (Exhibit 2)

Explain the ethical issues surrounding the tax planning scheme and set out the actions our firm should take. **(5 marks)**

Tax manager

Required:

You should assume that today's date is 1 December 2024.

Respond to the instructions in the email from your manager.

Note: The split of the mark allocation is shown in Exhibit 3 – Work to be carried out.

(40 marks)

Professional marks will be awarded for demonstration of skill in communication, analysis and evaluation, scepticism and commercial acumen in your answer. (10 marks)

(Total: 50 marks)

12 JANUS PLC GROUP (ADAPTED) ***Walk in the footsteps of a top tutor***

You should assume that today's date is 1 June 2024.

Your manager has had a meeting with Aliona, the Group Finance Director of the Janus plc group of companies.

In addition to some ethical considerations raised by your manager, advice is required in respect of the following issues:

- the use of the trading loss of Janus plc,
- the corporation tax and value added tax (VAT) implications of the disposal of various assets,
- the VAT implications of the purchase of services from overseas,
- the corporation tax treatment of a future disposal of shares, and
- the acquisition of a subsidiary which trades through an overseas permanent establishment.

The following **exhibits** provide information relevant to the question:

1 Janus plc group

2 Work to be carried out – email from manager

This information should be used to answer the question **requirements**.

Exhibit 1 – Janus plc group

Memorandum recording matters discussed at the meeting with Aliona

To The files

From Tax manager

Date 1 June 2024

Subject Janus plc group

Aliona has recently been appointed the Group Finance Director of the Janus plc group. She has asked for advice on the use of the trading loss of Janus plc for the year ended 31 March 2024 and on a number of other matters.

The Janus plc group of companies

The group structure indicating the trading loss of Janus plc and the taxable total profits of each of the other group companies for the year ended 31 March 2024 is set out below. All of the companies are UK resident trading companies.

Janus plc purchased Seb Ltd, together with its subsidiary, Viola Ltd, on 1 December 2023 from Vincent. Vincent has never owned any other companies. There have not been any other changes to the group structure in recent years.

The minority holdings in Castor Ltd and Pollux Ltd are owned by UK resident individuals. The minority holding in Duet Ltd is owned by Bi plc, a UK resident company, such that Duet Ltd is a consortium company.

The group policy is for an amount equal to the corporation tax saved to be paid for any losses transferred between group companies.

Each of the companies is separately registered for the purposes of value added tax (VAT).

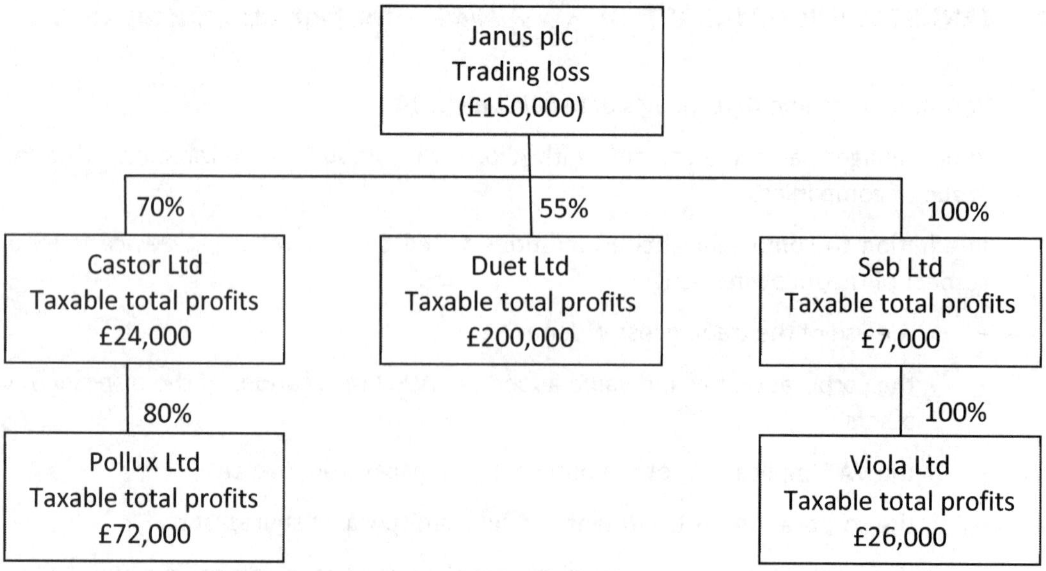

Additional information in respect of Janus plc

- Janus plc made a chargeable gain of £4,500 in the year ended 31 March 2024.
- Janus plc had taxable total profits in the year ended 31 March 2023 of £35,000 and did not make any charitable donations in the year.

Assets to be sold

(i) Pollux Ltd is to sell its administrative premises, 'P HQ', to Janus plc on 1 July 2024 for their market value of £285,000. Pollux Ltd acquired these premises from Castor Ltd on 1 March 2021 for their market value of £240,000.

(ii) Viola Ltd is to sell a warehouse to an unrelated company on 1 August 2024 for £350,000 plus VAT of £70,000. Viola Ltd acquired this warehouse on 1 February 2023 for £320,000 plus VAT of £64,000.

Aliona understands that the input tax relating to the warehouse should be recovered in accordance with the capital goods scheme because Viola Ltd is a partially exempt company, but suspects that the calculations may not have been done correctly.

The relevant VAT recovery percentages for Viola Ltd are:

Year ended 31 March 2023	70%
Year ended 31 March 2024	55%
Period from 1 April 2024 to 1 August 2024	50%

(iii) Castor Ltd is to sell patent rights to an unrelated company on 1 September 2024 for £41,000. Castor Ltd acquired these patent rights for use in its trade on 1 September 2020 for £45,000. The patent rights are being written off in Castor Ltd's accounts on a straight-line basis over a ten-year period.

Investment in Kupple Inc

Janus plc intends to purchase 15% of the ordinary share capital of Kupple Inc on 1 October 2024. Kupple Inc is a profitable trading company, resident in the country of Halven. Kupple Inc will provide consultancy services to Janus plc. This is intended to be a short-term commercial investment; Janus plc will sell the shares at some point in the next two years.

Acquisition of Ryb Ltd

On 1 May 2025, Janus plc will purchase the whole of the ordinary share capital of Ryb Ltd. For the purposes of UK tax, Ryb Ltd is resident in the UK. Ryb Ltd trades through a permanent establishment (PE) in the country of Tirona.

Ryb Ltd's budgeted taxable trading profit for the year ending 31 March 2026, all of which relates to its activities in Tirona, is £75,000. This is before any deductions for the purchase of a newly constructed office in Tirona costing £300,000 (including £80,000 for land) on 1 May 2025. The office will be brought into use in the trade immediately.

Ryb Ltd has no other source of taxable income and is not expected to make any chargeable gains during the year.

Once we are confident of the profitability of the PE in Tirona, it is intended that Ryb Ltd will establish PEs in two other countries.

Additional information in respect of Ryb Ltd

- Ryb Ltd has not made an election to exempt the profits of its overseas permanent establishment (PE) from UK tax.
- The rate of corporation tax in the country of Tirona is 14%. Other than that, the tax system in Tirona is the same as that in the UK. There is no double tax treaty between the UK and Tirona.

Exhibit 2 – Work to be carried out

Extracts from the email from your manager – dated 1 June 2024

Please prepare a file note covering the following:

(a) Use of the trading loss of Janus plc (Exhibit 1)

(i) Explain the alternative ways in which the loss can be relieved, on the assumption that it is not to be carried forward.

(ii) Advise how the loss should be relieved in order to maximise the corporation tax saved. You should include a summary showing the rate(s) of tax at which relief for the loss will be obtained. **(11 marks)**

(b) Assets to be sold (Exhibit 1)

(i) Explain how the chargeable gain on the disposal of P HQ will be calculated and state any further information required from Aliona to enable us to carry out this calculation. **(4 marks)**

(ii) Calculate the input tax recoverable from/repayable to HM Revenue and Customs in respect of the warehouse for each of the three years ending 31 March 2025, on the assumption that the sale of the warehouse goes ahead as planned. **(3 marks)**

(iii) Explain, with supporting calculations, the corporation tax implications of the sale of the patent rights. **(3 marks)**

(c) Investment in Kupple Inc (Exhibit 1)

(i) Explain the VAT implications for Janus plc of purchasing consultancy services from Kupple Inc. **(2 marks)**

(ii) Explain the corporation tax treatment of any profit or loss arising on the eventual sale of the shares in Kupple Inc. **(4 marks)**

(d) Ryb Ltd (Exhibit 1)

(i) Explain why the profits of Ryb Ltd are subject to UK corporation tax.

Calculate Ryb Ltd's expected UK corporation tax liability for the year ending 31 March 2026 based on the information available.

(ii) Discuss the advantages and disadvantages of Ryb Ltd making an election to exempt the profits of its PE in Tirona from UK tax. **(8 marks)**

(e) Use of information from previous clients

We have previously had a client who operated through an overseas PE. Explain the extent to which we can use the knowledge gained from the previous client when advising Janus plc. **(5 marks)**

Required:

You should assume that today's date is 1 June 2024.

Respond to the instructions in the email from your manager.

Note: The split of the mark allocation is shown in Exhibit 2 – Work to be carried out.

(40 marks)

Professional marks will be awarded for demonstration of skill in communication, analysis and evaluation, scepticism and commercial acumen in your answer. (10 marks)

(Total: 50 marks)

13 SPRINT LTD AND IRON LTD (ADAPTED) *Walk in the footsteps of a top tutor*

You should assume that today's date is 1 September 2024.

Your manager has received a letter from Christina. Christina is the managing director of Sprint Ltd and owns the whole of that company's ordinary share capital. Sprint Ltd is a client of your firm.

In addition to some ethical considerations which have been raised by your manager, advice is required in respect of:

- corporation tax for a long period of account,
- the tax implications of Iron Ltd being owned by either Christina personally or by Sprint Ltd,
- registration for value added tax (VAT), and
- the relief available for the trading losses of Olympic Ltd, which is wholly owned by Sprint Ltd.

The following **exhibits** provide information relevant to the question:

1 Sprint Ltd and Iron Ltd – extract from the letter from Christina

2 Work to be carried out – email from manager

This information should be used to answer the question **requirements**.

Exhibit 1 – Sprint Ltd and Iron Ltd

Extract from the letter from Christina

I intend to purchase the whole of the ordinary share capital of Iron Ltd on 1 November 2024. My company, Sprint Ltd, purchases components from Iron Ltd, so the two companies will fit together well. I hope to increase the value of Iron Ltd over the next three to five years and then to sell it at a profit.

I need your advice on the following matters.

Corporation tax payable

Iron Ltd has not been managed particularly well. It has had significant bad debts and, as a result, needs more cash. To help determine its financial requirements, I need to know how much corporation tax Iron Ltd will have to pay in respect of its results for the 16-month period ending 30 June 2025. Iron Ltd's tax adjusted trading income for this period is budgeted to be only £30,000. In fact, if we discover further problems, it is quite possible that Iron Ltd will make a trading loss for this period; but please base your calculations on the budgeted profit figure of £30,000.

Iron Ltd has no income other than trading income. Following the acquisition, Iron Ltd will sell a small industrial building for £160,000 and an item of fixed machinery for £13,700 on 1 December 2024. The industrial building and the item of fixed machinery were both purchased second-hand on 1 June 2019 for £100,000 and £13,500 respectively. At that time, rollover relief of £31,800 was claimed against the acquisition of the industrial building and £3,200 against the acquisition of the item of fixed machinery.

Ownership of Iron Ltd

I need to decide whether I should purchase the shares in Iron Ltd personally or whether the shares should be purchased by Sprint Ltd. I will be the managing director of Iron Ltd regardless of who purchases the shares.

My preference would be to own Iron Ltd personally. However, I would be interested to learn of any advantages to the company being owned by Sprint Ltd. When Iron Ltd is eventually sold, I intend to use the proceeds to purchase a holiday home in Italy. **Value added tax (VAT)**

Iron Ltd is not registered for the purposes of VAT. The current management of the company has told me that the level of bad debts is keeping the company's cash receipts in a 12-month period below the registration limit of £85,000. However, I suspect that when I have the opportunity to look at the figures in more detail, it will become apparent that the company should be registered.

Sprint Ltd rental income

Sprint Ltd has recently started renting out some of its surplus office space for £1,000 a month. As the amount is quite small I do not plan on disclosing this to HMRC, since it is immaterial.

Olympic Ltd

Sprint Ltd owns the whole of the ordinary share capital of Olympic Ltd. Both these companies are profitable and have an accounting reference date of 30 June. Both companies are registered for the purposes of VAT.

Sprint Ltd, Olympic Ltd and Iron Ltd are all UK resident trading companies.

Additional information

1 Sprint Ltd will sell a warehouse on 1 February 2025. This will result in a capital loss of £18,000.

2 Iron Ltd currently has an accounting reference date of 28 February. Following its acquisition, however, its next set of accounts will be for the 16 months ending 30 June 2025.

3 Iron Ltd currently has no associated companies.

Exhibit 2 – Work to be carried out

Extract from an email from your manager

Please carry out the work set out below.

I would like you to prepare briefing notes covering the following issues. There will be quite a few points to draw to Christina's attention, so keep each one fairly brief.

(a) Iron Ltd – Corporation tax payable (Exhibit 1)

Assuming the entire ordinary share capital of Iron Ltd is purchased by Christina personally on 1 November 2024, calculate the corporation tax payable by Iron Ltd in respect of the 16-month period ending 30 June 2025, and state when this tax will be due for payment. **(11 marks)**

(b) Ownership of Iron Ltd (Exhibit 1)

Explain the tax matters which Christina needs to be aware of in order to decide whether the ordinary share capital of Iron Ltd should be purchased by herself, personally, or by Sprint Ltd. You should assume that Iron Ltd will be required to register for VAT. You should consider the tax implications of both:

- the ownership of Iron Ltd, and
- the eventual sale of Iron Ltd (by either Christina or Sprint Ltd).

You should recognise that, regardless of who purchases and subsequently sells Iron Ltd, Christina intends to use the proceeds for personal purposes and that she is a higher rate taxpayer with a substantial amount of investment income. **(12 marks)**

(c) VAT registration (Exhibit 1)

Set out the matters which Christina should be aware of in relation to the need for Iron Ltd to register for VAT and the implications for that company of registering late. **(3 marks)**

(d) Olympic Ltd – Project Whistle (Exhibit 1)

Olympic Ltd will commence Project Whistle in 2025. As part of the project, Olympic Ltd will engage in scientific research, some of which will qualify for the additional 86% tax deduction available in respect of qualifying research and development expenditure. Due to the significant costs involved, Olympic Ltd is expected to make a trading loss in the year ending 30 June 2026.

Please explain:

- how any trading loss made by Olympic Ltd in the year ending 30 June 2026 can be relieved.
- the factors to consider when choosing between the available reliefs. **(9 marks)**

(e) Sprint Ltd rental income (Exhibit 1)

Explain the matters we should draw to Christina's attention with regards to the non-disclosure of the rental income in Sprint Ltd and any actions our firm should take. **(5 marks)**

Tax manager

Required:

You should assume that today's date is 1 September 2024.

Respond to the instructions in the email from your manager.

Note: The split of the mark allocation is shown in Exhibit 2 – Work to be carried out.

(40 marks)

Professional marks will be awarded for demonstration of skill in communication, analysis and evaluation, scepticism and commercial acumen in your answer. **(10 marks)**

(Total: 50 marks)

14 HAHN LTD GROUP (ADAPTED) *Walk in the footsteps of a top tutor*

You should assume that today's date is 1 October 2024.

Your manager has had a meeting with Helga, the finance director of Hahn Ltd, and her brother, Johannes. Both Hahn Ltd and Johannes are clients of your firm.

The work to be carried out is in respect of:

– the availability of rollover relief within the Hahn Ltd group,

– the relief for Frit Ltd's trading loss within the group,

– the due dates for payment of corporation tax by the Hahn Ltd group companies,

– group VAT registration issues, and

– the capital gains tax payable by Johannes and an explanation of his temporary non-UK residence status.

There are also some ethical issues that have been raised by your manager.

The following **exhibits** provide information relevant to the question:

1 Hahn Ltd group

2 Johannes

3 Work to be carried out – email from manager

This information should be used to answer the question **requirements**.

Exhibit 1 – Hahn Ltd group

Extracts from a memorandum prepared by your manager – dated 1 October 2024

Hahn Ltd group structure

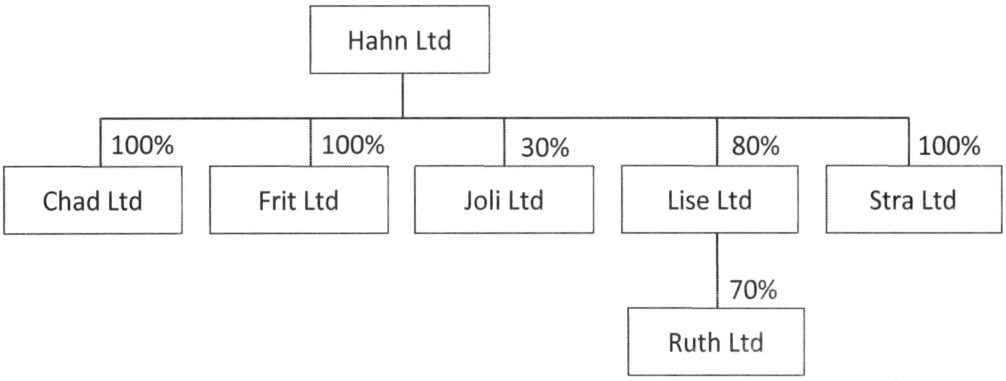

Notes

1 All of the companies are UK resident trading companies with an accounting reference date of 31 March.

2 All of the companies are registered for the purposes of value added tax (VAT).

3 With the exception of Chad Ltd, all of the companies have been members of the Hahn Ltd group for many years.

4 Hahn Ltd purchased Chad Ltd from Zeno Ltd on 1 September 2024. Prior to its disposal to Hahn Ltd, Zeno Ltd had owned Chad Ltd, and six other wholly-owned subsidiaries, for many years.

5 Joli Ltd is not a consortium company.

Budgeted results for the year ending 31 March 2025

	Hahn Ltd	**Chad Ltd**	**Frit Ltd**	**Joli Ltd**	**Lise Ltd**	**Ruth Ltd**	**Stra Ltd**
	£000	£000	£000	£000	£000	£000	£000
Tax adjusted trading profit/(loss)	280	675	(540)	410	375	320	58
Chargeable gains	–	–	65	–	–	–	–
Trading loss brought forward	–	–	–	–	–	–	(48)
Capital loss brought forward	–	–	(31)	–	–	–	–
Assets purchased which qualify for rollover relief	–	–	14	–	–	6	10

Notes

1 The budgeted results include £94,000 of sales made by Hahn Ltd to Stra Ltd. The arm's length price of these sales would be £104,000. Both of these figures are exclusive of VAT. No tax adjustments have been made in respect of these sales. The Hahn Ltd group is a large group for the purposes of the transfer pricing rules.

2 Frit Ltd's chargeable gain will be in respect of the sale of a building to an unconnected third party for £125,000. The building is a qualifying business asset for the purposes of rollover relief.

3 None of the companies will receive any dividends other than from associated companies in the year ending 31 March 2025.

4 Frit Ltd will not be able to carry its loss back to the year ended 31 March 2024.

5 All of the companies, with the exception of Frit Ltd and Stra Ltd, were required to pay their corporation tax liabilities for the year ended 31 March 2024 by instalments.

VAT

– The Hahn Ltd group is considering registering as a VAT group. Frit Ltd makes some exempt supplies, such that it is a partially exempt company. The other six companies all make standard-rated supplies only. Stra Ltd uses both the annual accounting scheme and the cash accounting scheme.

– On 1 September 2024, Chad Ltd received a refund of VAT from HM Revenue and Customs (HMRC). The company has not been able to identify any reason for this refund.

Exhibit 2 – Johannes

Extracts from a memorandum prepared by your manager – dated 1 October 2024

Background

Johannes had lived in the UK for the whole of his life until he moved with his wife to the country of Keirinia on 1 January 2021. He returned to live permanently in the UK on 30 April 2024. Whilst living in Keirinia, Johannes was non-UK resident and he is now resident in the UK. He has always been domiciled in the UK.

Johannes has significant investment income and has been a higher rate taxpayer for many years.

Capital gains

Whilst living in the country of Keirinia, Johannes sold various assets as set out below. He has not made any other disposals since 5 April 2020.

Asset	Date of sale	Proceeds	Date of purchase	Cost
		£		£
Quoted shares	1 December 2020	18,900	1 October 2019	14,000
Painting	1 June 2023	36,000	1 March 2019	15,000
Antique bed	1 March 2024	9,400	1 May 2021	7,300
Car	1 April 2024	11,000	1 February 2021	8,500

I explained that, although Johannes was non-UK resident whilst living in Keirinia, these disposals may still be subject to UK capital gains tax because he will be regarded as only temporarily non-UK resident.

There is no capital gains tax in the country of Keirinia.

Exhibit 3 – Work to be carried out

Email from your manager – dated 1 October 2024

Please prepare a memorandum for the client files which addresses the following issues:

(a) (i) Chargeable gain of Frit Ltd (Exhibit 1)

Calculate the additional amount which would need to be spent on assets qualifying for rollover relief, such that the unrelieved gain would be fully covered by Frit Ltd's brought forward capital loss. **(3 marks)**

(ii) Relieving the trading loss of Frit Ltd (Exhibit 1)

– Prepare explanations, together with supporting calculations, to show how the trading loss of Frit Ltd should be allocated between the companies in the group. The group's priority is its cash flow position and the need to minimise the corporation tax payable by instalments.

When preparing these calculations, you should assume that the whole of the chargeable gain of Frit Ltd will be relieved by rollover relief.

– Prepare a schedule setting out the amounts of corporation tax payable by Hahn Ltd, and the companies it controls (i.e. not Joli Ltd) in respect of the year ending 31 March 2025, together with the related payment dates. **(19 marks)**

(b) Group registration for the purposes of value added tax (VAT) (Exhibit 1)

By reference to the specific information in my memorandum only, set out the matters which will need to be considered when deciding which of the companies should be included in a group registration. **(5 marks)**

(c) Chad Ltd – refund of VAT (Exhibit 1)

Prepare a summary of the actions which we should take, and any matters of which Chad Ltd should be aware, in respect of the refund of VAT. **(5 marks)**

In preparation for my next meeting with Johannes, please prepare notes covering the following:

(d) Capital gains tax (Exhibit 2)

An explanation, with supporting calculations, of the UK capital gains tax liability in respect of the disposals made by Johannes whilst living in the country of Keirinia.

Your explanation should include the precise reasons for Johannes being regarded as only temporarily non-UK resident and a statement of when the tax was/will be payable. **(8 marks)**

Tax manager

Required:

You should assume that today's date is 1 October 2024.

Respond to the instructions in the email from your manager.

Note: The split of the mark allocation is shown in Exhibit 3 – Work to be carried out.

(40 marks)

Professional marks will be awarded for demonstration of skill in communication, analysis and evaluation, scepticism and commercial acumen in your answer. (10 marks)

(Total: 50 marks)

15 WAVERLEY AND SET LTD GROUP (ADAPTED) *Walk in the footsteps of a top tutor*

You should assume that today's date is 1 September 2024.

Your manager has been advising a client, Waverley, on his plans to sell his business.

Your manager has also been advising the Set Ltd group on various corporate tax issues.

In addition to some ethical considerations which have been raised by your manager, advice is required in respect of:

– the capital gains tax implications of the sale of Waverley's business, including incorporation relief and overseas aspects,

– Waverley's residence status,

– the disposal of integral features, relief for capital losses and trading losses within the Set Ltd group and payment of corporation tax by instalments,

– the value added tax (VAT) implications of transactions with overseas businesses, and

– the exemptions from the controlled foreign company (CFC) charge.

The following **exhibits** provide information relevant to the question:

1 Waverley

2 Set Ltd group

3 Work to be carried out – email from manager

This information should be used to answer the question **requirements**.

Exhibit 1 – Waverley

Background information from your manager

Waverley was born in the UK to UK domiciled parents in 1984. He divorced his wife in 2022. His three children, all of whom are under 18, live with his ex-wife in the UK.

Waverley began trading as a sole trader on 1 March 2016. We are advising him on the sale of his unincorporated business with the objective of minimising his capital gains tax liability. It has been concluded that it will be very difficult to sell the business as an unincorporated entity, so Waverley is going to sell the business to a newly-formed company which he owns, Roller Ltd. Waverley will then sell his shares in Roller Ltd.

Waverley has decided to emigrate to the country of Surferia. He wants to make a fresh start and has heard from friends that moving abroad could be advantageous from the point of view of UK tax. He will move to Surferia on 5 April 2025.

Waverley wants to see his children regularly and is also an enthusiastic member of an amateur football team in the UK. As a result, he intends to spend as many days as possible in the UK in the tax year 2025/26. He will continue to work for Roller Ltd until the company is sold and it is also possible that the purchaser of Roller Ltd will ask Waverley to do further work for the company whilst he is in the UK.

Waverley will sell his home in the UK in March 2025. The house is Waverley's private residence, such that there will be no capital gains tax in respect of its disposal. Once the house has been sold, whenever Waverley is in the UK he will stay in a hotel, as he does not have any other UK property available for his use. When he is not in the UK, he will live in a new house which he plans to buy in Surferia.

Unincorporated business

Waverley will cease trading as a sole trader on 15 January 2025 when he sells his unincorporated business to Roller Ltd. Roller Ltd will be wholly-owned by Waverley.

The assets of the unincorporated business are expected to be worth £540,000 on 15 January 2025. They will be sold at market value to Roller Ltd in exchange for 270,000 £1 ordinary shares in the company. This will result in chargeable gains, before incorporation relief, of £140,000 on the business premises and £50,000 in respect of goodwill.

The shares in Roller Ltd will be sold for £600,000 at some point during the six months following Waverley's emigration to Surferia on 5 April 2025.

Residence status

Waverley has always been resident and domiciled in the UK, but it is likely to be beneficial for him to be non-UK resident for the tax year 2025/26.

Notes on the tax system in the country of Surferia

- Individuals who are resident in Surferia are subject to capital gains tax on disposals of worldwide assets at the rate of 12%. There is no annual exempt amount.
- For the purposes of capital gains tax in Surferia, Waverley's chargeable gains will be the same as they would be in the UK.
- The payment date for capital gains tax in Surferia is the same as the payment date for capital gains tax in the UK.
- There is no inheritance tax in Surferia.
- There is a double tax treaty between the UK and Surferia.

Exhibit 2 – Set Ltd group

Background information from your manager

The finance director of the Set Ltd group of companies has become seriously ill and Delia, who is standing in for him, requires explanations of a number of matters. Extracts from an email from Delia are set out below.

Set Ltd has three wholly owned subsidiaries, Ghost Ltd, Steam Ltd and Wagon Ltd, and also owns shares in a number of other companies. Set Ltd and all of its wholly owned subsidiaries are resident in the UK.

You should assume that all of the UK resident companies in the Set Ltd group, including Ghost Ltd, pay corporation tax in instalments every year and will continue to do so, regardless of any loss relief planning entered into.

Extracts from an email from Delia – dated 1 September 2024

Ghost Ltd – corporation tax payments

I'm working on the corporation tax instalment payments which Ghost Ltd will be required to pay in the period from now until 31 March 2025.

Set Ltd acquired the whole of the ordinary share capital of Ghost Ltd on 1 September 2024. Ghost Ltd had always prepared accounts to 31 July but following its acquisition has changed its accounting reference date to 31 March in line with all of the other companies in the Set Ltd group.

The finalised corporation tax liability of Ghost Ltd for the year ended 31 July 2024 was £597,500. I am now estimating the company's liability for the eight-month period ending 31 March 2025 so that I can determine the instalment payments required.

As part of this work, I need to know how to deal with the disposal of some integral features by Ghost Ltd, which were sold in August 2024 for £315,000. Ghost Ltd originally purchased the integral features for £1,100,000 and claimed £1,000,000 annual investment allowance and the 50% first year allowance on the remaining £100,000.

I also need to know if the company's corporation tax liability can be reduced in respect of the following:

– Steam Ltd will sell a building on 1 November 2024, which is expected to result in a loss.

– Wagon Ltd has a trading loss brought forward as at 1 April 2024 of £31,500. It is expected to make a further trading loss in the year ending 31 March 2025.

Wagon Ltd – value added tax (VAT)

Wagon Ltd intends to purchase manufacturing components from Line Co. Line Co is a company resident in the country of Terminusa. There is no VAT in Terminusa.

Wagon Ltd is also planning to sell goods to Signal Co. Signal Co is resident in France. Signal Co is a small company which is not required to be registered for VAT in France.

Neither Line Co nor Signal Co has any links with the Set Ltd group.

I would like to know the VAT implications of these transactions.

Dee Co and En Co – controlled foreign company (CFC) charge

Set Ltd owns shares in two CFCs: Dee Co and En Co. Both of these companies have chargeable profits for the purposes of the CFC legislation. Estimates of the relevant financial information in respect of the year ending 31 March 2025 are as follows:

	Dee Co	**En Co**
Percentage of ordinary share capital owned by Set Ltd	21%	37%
	£	£
Non-trading income	0	65,000
Operating expenditure	8,100,000	3,200,000
Accounting profit	1,100,000	280,000
Taxable total profit	1,300,000	350,000

I can see from my files that the only exemptions from a CFC charge requiring consideration are the low profits exemption and the low profit margin exemption.

I need to know whether Set Ltd will be subject to a CFC charge in respect of either Dee Co or En Co.

Exhibit 3 – Work to be carried out

Email from your manager – dated 1 September 2024

Please prepare notes addressing the following issues:

(a) Waverley – unincorporated business (Exhibit 1)

- State the conditions which must be satisfied in order for incorporation relief to be available on the sale of the unincorporated business to Roller Ltd.
- Explain whether Waverley will qualify for business asset disposal relief on the disposal of the shares in Roller Ltd.
- Prepare calculations of Waverley's total capital gains tax liability, in the UK and in the country of Surferia, in respect of both the sale of the unincorporated business to Roller Ltd in the tax year 2024/25 (if any) and the sale of the Roller Ltd shares in the tax year 2025/26. In respect of the sale of the Roller Ltd shares, you should consider two possible situations: first where Waverley is resident only in the UK at the time of the sale, and second where he is resident only in Surferia at the time of the sale. You should not consider the rules concerning individuals who are temporarily non-UK resident.

  You should assume that Waverley will be a higher rate taxpayer in the tax years 2024/25 and 2025/26 (if UK resident) and that he realises sufficient additional chargeable gains every year to use his annual exempt amount. **(10 marks)**

(b) Waverley – residence status (Exhibit 1)

Explain the maximum number of days which Waverley will be able to spend in the UK in the tax year 2025/26 without being UK resident. I have already concluded that for the tax year 2025/26, Waverley will be neither automatically resident overseas nor automatically resident in the UK. **(6 marks)**

(c) Ghost Ltd – corporation tax payments (Exhibit 2)

Explain:

- how the disposal of the integral features should be dealt with in the period ending 31 March 2025.
- how Ghost Ltd could make use of the losses of Steam Ltd and Wagon Ltd in the period ending 31 March 2025.
- the payments of corporation tax which will need to be made by Ghost Ltd in the period starting today, 1 September 2024, and ending on 31 March 2025. For the purpose of this explanation, please assume that Ghost Ltd's corporation tax liability for the eight-month period ending 31 March 2025 is £460,000. **(11 marks)**

(d) Wagon Ltd – value added tax (VAT) (Exhibit 2)

Explain the VAT implications of the transactions to be carried out by Wagon Ltd. **(4 marks)**

(e) Dee Co and En Co – controlled foreign company (CFC) charge (Exhibit 2)

Explain whether Set Ltd will be subject to a CFC charge in respect of either Dee Co or En Co. **(4 marks)**

> **(f) Knowledge gained from previous clients (Exhibit 2)**
>
> Our firm has advised previous clients on VAT issues for overseas transactions. Explain to what extent we can use the knowledge gained from previous clients to assist us in providing the advice for Wagon Ltd. **(5 marks)**
>
> **Tax manager**

Required:

You should assume that today's date is 1 September 2024.

Respond to the instructions in the email from your manager.

Note: The split of the mark allocation is shown in Exhibit 3 – Work to be carried out.

(40 marks)

Professional marks will be awarded for demonstration of skill in communication, analysis and evaluation, scepticism and commercial acumen in your answer. (10 marks)

(Total: 50 marks)

16 HEYER LTD GROUP AND DEE (ADAPTED) *Walk in the footsteps of a top tutor*

You should assume that today's date is 1 June 2024.

Your manager has asked you to take charge of some work in connection with the Heyer Ltd group of companies, and for Dee, the finance director of Heyer Ltd.

The work to be carried out is in respect of:

- group planning within the Heyer Ltd capital gains group,
- the transfer of trade and assets within the group,
- the issues to be considered in relation to the understatement of corporation tax by the group,
- the income tax savings for various investment options,
- the inheritance tax implications of a gift to a non-domiciled spouse, and
- the capital gains tax saving from the gift of part of a property prior to sale.

The following **exhibits** provide information relevant to the question:

1 Heyer Ltd group

2 Dee and Cam

3 Work to be carried out – email from manager

This information should be used to answer the question **requirements**.

Exhibit 1 – Heyer Ltd group

Schedule of information from the client files

Group structure

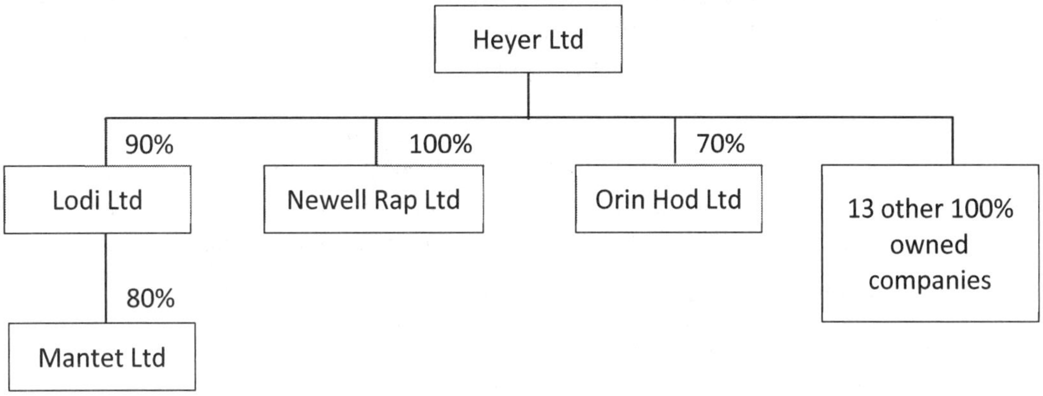

General information

– All of the companies are resident in the UK and have an accounting reference date of 31 December each year.

– The figures given below of taxable total profits (TTP) take account of all possible rollover relief claims.

– None of the companies has received any dividend income from non-group companies.

– All of the companies pay corporation tax at the main rate.

Specific information

Mantet Ltd

– Mantet Ltd has TTP of between £40,000 and £50,000 every year.

Newell Rap Ltd

– Heyer Ltd acquired Newell Rap Ltd on 1 May 2023.

– Newell Rap Ltd has a capital loss brought forward as at 1 January 2024 of £94,000. This loss arose on a sale of land on 1 February 2021.

Orin Hod Ltd

– The TTP of Orin Hod Ltd exceeds £200,000 every year.

– In the year ending 31 December 2024 Orin Hod Ltd will make chargeable gains of £86,000.

Other 100% owned companies

– Each of these companies has TTP of more than £130,000 every year.

– Four of them will have substantial chargeable gains in the year ending 31 December 2024.

– Five of them will have capital losses in the year ending 31 December 2024.

Group restructuring

– It is intended that the trade and assets of five group companies (Newell Rap Ltd and four of the other 100% owned companies) will be sold to Lodi Ltd at some point in January 2025.

– The assets of the five companies, including the business premises, machinery and equipment will be sold to Lodi Ltd for their market value.

– The tax written down value of the main pool of each of the five companies immediately prior to the sale will be zero.

Exhibit 2 – Dee and Cam

Schedule from Dee – dated 1 June 2024

I am resident and domiciled in the UK. My husband, Cam, moved to the UK in January 2019 and we married in June 2020. Cam is resident in the UK but domiciled in the country of Riviera. I have a 16-year-old son, Oder, who is resident and domiciled in the UK.

My father's London house

My father died on 1 January 2024 and I inherited his London house. The house had a value for probate purposes of £390,000, but is now worth £450,000. My father purchased the house for £130,000 in 1990. I intend to sell the house as soon as possible.

Investment plan in respect of the proceeds from the sale of the London house

I plan to invest the £450,000 proceeds as follows:

- £300,000, purchase of UK shares, and
- £150,000, cash deposit in the UK.

Alternative investment plan

It has been suggested to me by a friend (who is a tax adviser) that I should consider an alternative investment plan, which would result in a lower income tax liability for me and my family.

Under my friend's suggestion I would give £150,000 of the sales proceeds from the London house to Cam, leaving me with £300,000. We would then each invest two-thirds of our respective funds in shares with the remaining third left on cash deposit.

I would like to know what the income tax saving would be if I followed my friend's advice rather than my original plan.

Gift to Oder

I am also considering making a cash gift to Oder of £20,000 out of my existing funds (i.e. not from the proceeds from the sale of the London house). Oder would place this amount on cash deposit.

Our annual income

I set out below our current annual income.

The bank interest and dividends are in respect of cash deposits and shares all of which are held within ISAs. We invest the maximum possible amount into ISAs on 1 May each year.

Oder has no income. None of us have made any previous chargeable gains.

	Dee	**Cam**
	£	£
Annual income		
Employment income	170,000	18,000
Bank interest (within ISA)	1,500	1,200
Dividends (within ISA)	2,500	1,800

Thank you

Dee

Exhibit 3 – Work to be carried out

Email from your manager – dated 1 June 2024

Please prepare some notes and guidance in preparation for an internal team meeting to cover the following:

(a) Group planning (Exhibit 1)

The group's objective is to minimise the corporation tax payable in instalments by group companies in respect of the year ended 31 December 2024.

I have asked Cox, our tax assistant, to carry out this work and I have provided him with the details of the companies' budgeted results for 2024. There is no group relief available within the group.

Cox has not done this type of work before and he has had very little experience of capital gains groups, so I want you to prepare some guidance for him. The guidance should consist of explanations of:

– the circumstances in which a member of the Heyer Ltd group would be required to pay corporation tax in instalments, assuming that the profits threshold should be divided by 18
– which companies are members of a capital gains group
– how Cox should determine the amount of chargeable gains and capital losses to transfer between the group companies in order to achieve the group's objective, and
– the relevance to the group's objective of the **specific information** provided in the schedule of information. **(11 marks)**

(b) Group restructuring (Exhibit 1)

Identify, with reasons, the implications of the proposed group restructuring in relation to chargeable gains, stamp duty land tax and capital allowances, and what will happen to any capital losses belonging to the five companies whose trade and assets are transferred. **(4 marks)**

(c) Disclosure of transfer pricing (Exhibit 1)

It has been realised by the management of Heyer Ltd that transfer pricing adjustments should have been made in respect of the year ended 31 December 2020 for three of the companies in the group. The corporation tax liability of the group was understated as a result of this non-disclosure.

I have already explained the interest and penalties which may be charged in respect of this. I want you to list the other matters which need to be considered, by us, as tax advisers to the group, and by the management of the group, in relation to the disclosure or non-disclosure of this information to HM Revenue and Customs (HMRC). **(5 marks)**

(d) Minimising income tax on investment income (Exhibit 2)

When carrying out this work you should assume:

1 The shares purchased will yield a 4% return per annum and the cash deposits will yield a 1% return per annum.

2 The whole of the £450,000 will be available to invest, i.e. Dee will pay any capital gains tax due in respect of the sale of the London house out of her existing funds.

3 None of the investments will consist of either enterprise investment scheme (EIS) shares or venture capital trust (VCT) shares.

– Calculations of the income tax saving which would be achieved in a complete tax year if Dee were to follow her friend's advice and give £150,000 of the proceeds from the sale of the London house to Cam in accordance with the alternative investment plan.

  To do this efficiently, you should just calculate the additional tax payable by Dee and Cam on the income generated by the inherited funds, rather than preparing complete income tax computations.

  To save you some time, I have already calculated that if Dee invested the whole of the £450,000 herself, she would incur an additional income tax liability in respect of the bank interest and dividend income for a complete tax year of £5,004.

– It seems to me that the total income tax liability of Dee and Cam could be reduced further whilst still retaining the fundamentals of Dee's alternative investment plan. Dee would still give Cam £150,000 but, rather than each of them investing 2/3 of their funds in shares and leaving the remainder on cash deposit, the total investment of £300,000 in shares and £150,000 in cash deposits would be split between them in a different way.

  Set out the factors which are relevant to obtaining a more income tax-efficient split of the total investment. You should only consider the income tax positions of Dee and Cam and the nature of the proposed investments. I do not require you to produce calculations of any potential tax savings.

– The matters to be considered in relation to income tax in respect of the proposed gift of £20,000 to Oder. **(11 marks)**

(e) Gift to Cam (Exhibit 2)

– By reference to Cam's domicile status, explain why Dee's proposed gift of £150,000 to Cam could result in an inheritance tax liability and how this potential liability might be avoided.

  You should note that Dee gave Cam a half interest in her home on 1 August 2020. The value of this gift was £600,000.

– Calculations in order to show the capital gains tax saving which would be achieved if Dee were to give Cam a one-third interest in the London house prior to its sale (as opposed to cash of £150,000 following its sale). **(9 marks)**

Tax manager

Required:

You should assume that today's date is 1 June 2024.

Respond to the instructions in the email from your manager.

Note: The split of the mark allocation is shown in Exhibit 3 – Work to be carried out.

(40 marks)

Professional marks will be awarded for demonstration of skill in communication, analysis and evaluation, scepticism and commercial acumen in your answer. **(10 marks)**

(Total: 50 marks)

17 MITA AND SNOWDON (ADAPTED) *Walk in the footsteps of a top tutor*

You should assume that today's date is 1 March 2025.

Your manager has received a letter from Mita, the owner and managing director of Porth Ltd. Both Mita and Porth Ltd are clients of your firm. Your manager has also had a meeting with one of Mita's brothers, Snowdon, a potential new client.

Advice is required in respect of the following issues:

- the capital gains tax liability in respect of a sale of shares in Porth Ltd,
- the corporation tax treatment of research and development expenditure and the purchase of an intangible asset by Quod Ltd,
- the relief available for the trading loss of Quod Ltd,
- the value added tax (VAT) implications of purchasing overseas services, and
- the tax implications for Snowdon of expanding his business by taking on an employee or paying a sub-contractor.

There are also some ethical issues to be considered if the firm is to accept Snowdon as a new client.

The following **exhibits** provide information relevant to the question:

1. Porth Ltd and Quod Ltd – extracts from the letter from Mita, together with some additional information provided by your manager
2. Snowdon – extracts from a memorandum prepared by your manager
3. Work to be carried out – email from manager

This information should be used to answer the question **requirements**.

Exhibit 1 – Porth Ltd and Quod Ltd

Extracts from the letter from Mita – dated 1 March 2025

Sale of 4,000 ordinary shares in Porth Ltd

On 1 May 2025, I am going to sell 4,000 shares in Porth Ltd to my brother, Ned. I note from the work you have already done that the current market value of these shares is £260,000. However, because I am keen to get Ned involved, I have agreed a price of £200,000. Ned, who is UK resident, will sign the claim for capital gains tax gift holdover relief in respect of this sale.

Joint venture – Quod Ltd

On 1 April 2025, I shall incorporate a new company, Quod Ltd. On that day, Quod Ltd will register for value added tax (VAT) and begin to trade. It will develop a range of products over the next few years.

The planned ownership of the ordinary share capital of Quod Ltd is as follows:

Porth Ltd	60%
Either Mr Berm or Mr Berm's company, BJB Ltd	30%
CX Ltd	10%

Porth Ltd, BJB Ltd and CX Ltd are UK resident companies. Mr Berm is resident in the UK.

Quod Ltd – financial information

I have calculated Quod Ltd's budgeted tax adjusted trading loss for the year ending 31 March 2026 to be £44,000.

When calculating the loss, I deducted the whole of the costs attributable to scientific research amounting to £102,000 (note 1). I also deducted £1,000 in respect of the Cloque brand (note 2), as it will be amortised over a period of 35 years.

Note 1: Scientific research costs

	£
Equipment and computer hardware	27,500
Materials	21,000
Rent	17,400
Electricity and water	6,600
Staff costs	29,500
	102,000

– The rent is an appropriate allocation of the rent payable for Quod Ltd's premises for the year.

– All of the staff costs relate to employees of Quod Ltd with the exception of £7,000 paid to an external contractor provided by an unconnected company.

Note 2: Purchase of the Cloque brand

On 1 April 2025, Quod Ltd will purchase the Cloque brand for £35,000. Advice will then be required on how to develop this brand through the use of social media. It is intended that Quod Ltd will purchase this advice from a company based outside the UK (in a country where the rate of VAT is 9%) rather than as a standard-rated supply from a VAT registered supplier based in the UK.

Additional information provided by your manager

Porth Ltd

- Mita owns the whole of the ordinary share capital of Porth Ltd, which is an unquoted trading company.
- Mita began trading as an unincorporated business on 1 June 2017. On 1 April 2020, when the assets of her business were worth £120,000, she incorporated her business by selling all of the assets to Porth Ltd in exchange for 10,000 ordinary shares. This sale resulted in total chargeable gains of £37,400, all of which were relieved by incorporation relief.
- Porth Ltd has an accounting reference date of 31 March each year. It does not own any assets other than those which are used in its trade.

Quod Ltd

- Quod Ltd will be a small enterprise for the purposes of the additional tax relief available for expenditure on research and development.
- I have already established that the research to be carried out by Quod Ltd will qualify for this relief.
- Quod Ltd WILL NOT surrender any part of the loss in return for a cash refund from HM Revenue and Customs (HMRC).

Exhibit 2 – Snowdon

Extracts from the memorandum prepared by your manager – dated 1 March 2025

Mita's other brother, Snowdon, is resident and domiciled in the UK. He requires advice in respect of his unincorporated business, 'Siabod', which he started on 1 July 2016, as well as on the tax implications of a gift Mita is planning to make to him.

We have already obtained proof of identity and address for Snowdon, and have contacted his previous advisers to ensure there are no issues with taking him on as a client. The relevant anti-money laundering checks have also been completed.

Siabod business

Budgeted figures relating to the unexpanded Siabod business for the year ending 31 March 2026 are:

	£
Turnover	255,000
Tax adjusted trading profit	85,000
Income tax on £85,000 using current rates	21,432
Class 4 national insurance contributions on £85,000 using current rates	4,088

The Siabod business is partially exempt for the purposes of value added tax (VAT). Snowdon's budgeted input tax for the unexpanded business for the year ending 31 March 2026 was £18,000. He would have been able to recover the whole of this amount because the business would have been below the de minimis limits.

Since the above figures were prepared, Snowdon has decided to expand the Siabod business and increase its budgeted turnover for the year ending 31 March 2026 from £255,000 to £435,000. In order to carry out this expansion, Snowdon will adopt either strategy A or strategy B. Whichever strategy is adopted, the partial exemption percentage of the business will continue to be 76% (recoverable).

Strategy A

Under this strategy Snowdon will recruit an additional employee with an annual salary of £48,000.

Strategy B

Under this strategy Snowdon will appoint a sub-contractor, Tor Ltd, which will carry out the work required for the expansion. Tor Ltd will charge fees of £90,000 plus VAT each year.

Budgeted costs of expanding the business

	Strategy A	**Strategy B**
	£	£
Salary of additional employee	48,000	N/A
Other expenditure relating to the expansion, net of VAT at 20%:		
Overheads	38,000	N/A
Advertising	2,000	2,000
Fees payable to Tor Ltd, net of VAT at 20%	N/A	90,000

Additional information

– Prior to the expansion of the Siabod business, Snowdon's liability to employer's class 1 national insurance contributions for the year exceeded £5,000.

– Apart from the profits of the Siabod business, Snowdon's only income is £740 of bank interest each year.

Exhibit 3 – Work to be carried out

Extracts from the email from your manager – dated 1 March 2025

Please prepare briefing notes to cover the following work:

(a) Sale of 4,000 shares in Porth Ltd on 1 May 2025 (Exhibit 1)

– Calculate Mita's capital gains tax (CGT) liability in respect of this proposed sale to Ned assuming all available reliefs will be claimed.

Mita is resident in the UK. You should assume she will be a higher rate taxpayer in the tax year 2025/26 and that the CGT annual exempt amount WILL NOT be available to her. **(4 marks)**

(b) Quod Ltd (Exhibit 1)

– Explain the tax deduction which will be available to Quod Ltd in respect of the scientific research costs of £102,000 to be incurred in the year ending 31 March 2026.

– Explain the tax treatment of the proposed purchase of the Cloque brand (an intangible fixed asset) for £35,000.

– Calculate the amended budgeted tax adjusted trading loss for Quod Ltd for the year ending 31 March 2026 taking into account the explanations requested above.

– Explain how much of Quod Ltd's amended budgeted trading loss will be available for use by Porth Ltd.

– Explain the value added tax (VAT) implications of Quod Ltd purchasing advice from the overseas supplier, rather than the one based in the UK. **(15 marks)**

(c) Expansion of the Siabod business (Exhibit 2)

– Prepare calculations to show which of the two strategies is the most financially advantageous for Snowdon, i.e. the one which is expected to generate the most additional tax adjusted trading profit for the year ending 31 March 2026.

– Calculate the additional budgeted post-tax income for the tax year 2025/26 which is expected to be generated by the most financially advantageous strategy. **(16 marks)**

(d) Matters to consider before we agree to become Snowdon's tax advisers

Explain any matters in relation to the information provided that we should consider before we agree to become Snowdon's tax advisers. **(5 marks)**

Tax manager

Required:

You should assume that today's date is 1 March 2025.

Respond to the instructions in the email from your manager.

Note: The split of the mark allocation is shown in Exhibit 3 – Work to be carried out.

(40 marks)

Professional marks will be awarded for demonstration of skill in communication, analysis and evaluation, scepticism and commercial acumen in your answer. (10 marks)

(Total: 50 marks)

18 GRAND LTD GROUP (ADAPTED) *Walk in the footsteps of a top tutor*

You should assume that today's date is 1 September 2024.

Your manager has had a meeting with Bryce, the managing director of Grand Ltd, and his daughter Monina, who is the finance director.

In addition to some ethical considerations which have been raised by your manager in connection with a tax saving plan, advice is required in respect of:

– the sale of either the shares or the trade and assets of Colca Ltd, a Grand Ltd group company, and

– the calculation of net income for two alternative employment packages for Monina.

The following **exhibits** provide information relevant to the question:

1 Grand Ltd group

2 Monina

3 Work to be carried out – email from manager

This information should be used to answer the question **requirements**.

Exhibit 1 – Grand Ltd group

Schedule of information dated 1 September 2024

Background

Grand Ltd has two wholly owned subsidiaries, Colca Ltd and Sautso Ltd, and also owns shares in a number of other companies. All of the group companies are UK resident trading companies, with an accounting reference date of 31 March. All supplies made by the group are subject to value added tax (VAT) at the standard rate. Sautso Ltd has been a member of the Grand Ltd group for many years. Grand Ltd and its subsidiaries all pay corporation tax at the main rate.

Sale of Colca Ltd

Grand Ltd purchased the whole of the ordinary share capital of Colca Ltd for £800,000 on 1 November 2017. The value of Colca Ltd has fallen and the company is to be sold on 1 December 2024. Two separate offers have been received: offer A and offer B.

Offer A – in respect of a sale of the company's shares

– The purchaser will pay £730,000 for the whole of the ordinary share capital of Colca Ltd. This amount will be reduced by any tax liabilities payable by Colca Ltd arising as a result of the company being sold.

Offer B – in respect of a sale of the company's trade and assets

– The purchaser will pay £695,000 for the trade and assets of Colca Ltd.

Colca Ltd – expected asset values on 1 December 2024

	£
Oribi building	410,000
Atuel building	230,000
Items of machinery	25,000
Net current assets (at cost)	30,000
	695,000

There is further information in respect of these assets set out below.

The value of Colca Ltd's goodwill is negligible and should be ignored for the purposes of this work.

Colca Ltd – details of assets

Colca Ltd uses both the Oribi and Atuel buildings in its trade.

	Oribi building	**Atuel building**	**Machinery**
Date of purchase	1 February 2018	1 April 2022	N/A
Purchase cost	£320,000 (note 1)	£255,000 (note 2)	(note 3)
Value added tax option to tax made?	No	No	N/A

Notes

1 On 1 December 2017, Colca Ltd sold a machine for £74,000 resulting in a chargeable gain of £17,000. This gain was rolled over against the purchase of the Oribi building.

2 Colca Ltd purchased the Atuel building from Sautso Ltd for £255,000, its market value at that time. As Colca Ltd and Sautso Ltd are both 100% subsidiaries of Grand Ltd, the transfer of the building took place at no gain, no loss.

Sautso Ltd had purchased the Atuel building, new and unused, for £340,000 on 1 January 2022. Structures and buildings allowances have not been claimed by Sautso Ltd or Colca Ltd.

3 All of the items of machinery are movable. The sale of the machinery will give rise to a balancing charge of £12,100.

Most of the items of machinery are worth less than their original cost. However, a small number of items are particularly specialised, such that their current market value exceeds their original cost.

Exhibit 2 – Monina

Schedule of information dated 1 September 2024

Background

Monina is a higher rate taxpayer earning £60,000 per year and currently has no other income. Monina currently lives and works in Birmingham.

Working in Manchester

Grand Ltd has recently acquired the Manchester operations of the group from a third party. As a result of this, Monina is going to be based in Manchester from 1 October 2024 for a period of at least five years. She will be paid an additional £15,000 per year during this period.

Monina does not want to relocate her family to Manchester for personal reasons. She has been offered the use of a furnished flat in Manchester belonging to Grand Ltd to live in during the week. She will drive home each weekend.

Details of the company's flat are set out below.

	£
Current market value	560,000
Purchase price (1 June 2020)	517,000
Annual value	9,605
Monthly contribution required from Monina	200

Alternatively, if she does not live in the flat, Grand Ltd will pay her a mileage allowance of 50 pence per mile to cover the cost of travelling to Manchester every Monday and returning home every Friday. During the week, whilst she is in Manchester, Monina will stay with her aunt, paying her rent of £325 per month.

Monina estimates that she will drive 9,200 miles per year travelling to Manchester each week and that she will spend £1,400 per year on petrol. There would also be additional depreciation in respect of her car of approximately £1,500 per year. Grand Ltd has a policy of not providing its employees with company cars.

Monina expects to be better off due to the increase in her salary. She wants to know how much better off she will be depending on whether she lives in the company flat or receives the mileage allowance and stays with her aunt.

Exhibit 3 – Work to be carried out

Extract from an email from your manager – dated 1 September 2024

Please carry out the following work.

(a) Grand Ltd group of companies (Exhibit 1)

Please prepare a memorandum for the client file.

Note: When calculating the post-tax proceeds in respect of the two offers, you should assume that tax relief at the rate of 25% will be obtained in respect of any allowable capital losses.

Note: The following indexation factor should be used, where necessary.

November 2017 to December 2017	0.008

The memorandum should cover the following:

(i) Offer A – in respect of a sale of the company's shares

– An explanation of whether or not tax relief will be available in respect of the capital loss arising on the sale of the shares.

– An explanation of the tax implications of Colca Ltd leaving the Grand Ltd group whilst still owning the Atuel building. This explanation should not include any calculations.

– A calculation of the expected post-tax proceeds. **(8 marks)**

(ii) Offer B – in respect of a sale of the company's trade and assets

– A calculation of the expected post-tax proceeds. For this purpose, you should ignore any chargeable gains or allowable losses arising on the sale of the items of machinery.

– In relation to the sale of the items of machinery, an explanation as to whether or not they will result in chargeable gains or allowable capital losses and of the availability of rollover relief.

– An explanation of the companies to which Colca Ltd can transfer any capital losses arising on the assets sold. **(10 marks)**

(iii) Offer B – value added tax (VAT)

– In respect of offer B: an explanation as to whether or not Colca Ltd should charge VAT on the sale of its buildings and/or its machinery.

(7 marks)

(b) Monina (Exhibit 2)

I want you to prepare notes for a meeting that we will both attend with Monina. You will be leading the meeting.

Set out the information so that it is easy for you to find what you need as we go through the various issues. Include the briefest possible notes where the numbers are not self-explanatory.

The meeting notes need to include:

Working in Manchester

– Calculations showing how much better (or worse) off Monina will be under each of the alternatives as compared to her current position. If she is worse off under either of the alternatives, include a calculation of the amount of salary she would have to be paid, in addition to the £15,000, so that she is not out of pocket.

– An explanation of the tax treatment for the recipients of the mileage allowance to be paid to Monina and the rent to be paid to her aunt.

– Any further information required and the effect it could have on the calculations you have prepared. **(10 marks)**

(c) Tax evasion and tax avoidance

Bryce and Monina (who is very knowledgeable in the field of capital allowances) have drawn up a plan which they claim will enable a company to claim a tax deduction of 180% of the cost of new machinery. The plan is complicated in that it involves the creation of a new, wholly-owned subsidiary and a series of contracts involving the leasing and sub-leasing of the machinery between the two companies.

I have not looked at the plan in detail because, even if it would appear to have the intended tax effect, I am sure that it would fall within the general anti-abuse rule (GAAR).

Please prepare notes which:

– Distinguish between tax evasion and tax avoidance and state the purpose of the GAAR.

– Explain why the GAAR is likely to apply to this particular plan. **(5 marks)**

Tax manager

Required:

You should assume that today's date is 1 September 2024.

Respond to the instructions in the email from your manager.

Note: The split of the mark allocation is shown in Exhibit 3 – Work to be carried out.

(40 marks)

Professional marks will be awarded for demonstration of skill in communication, analysis and evaluation, scepticism and commercial acumen in your answer. (10 marks)

(Total: 50 marks)

19 PLAD LTD AND QUIL LTD (ADAPTED) *Walk in the footsteps of a top tutor*

You should assume that today's date is 1 March 2024.

Your manager has sent you a schedule prepared by Claire Falkner concerning her company, Plad Ltd, and a new company, Quil Ltd, which she intends to incorporate on 1 April 2024. He has also sent you a schedule of information about Laura Falkner, Claire's aunt.

You are required to carry out some work in respect of:

- the tax advantages of Quil Ltd being a wholly-owned subsidiary of Plad Ltd, including consideration of group relief and double tax relief,
- group registration for value added tax (VAT),
- the implications of Plad Ltd failing to report a chargeable gain, and
- the inheritance tax and capital gains tax implications of a gift of shares to be made by Laura.

The following **exhibits** provide information relevant to the question:

1 Plad Ltd and Quil Ltd – schedule from Claire Falkner

2 Gift of shares by Laura

3 Work to be carried out – email from manager

This information should be used to answer the question **requirements**.

Exhibit 1 – Plad Ltd and Quil Ltd

Schedule from Claire Falkner – dated 1 March 2024

Plad Ltd

I have owned the whole of the ordinary share capital of Plad Ltd since 2009. Plad Ltd trades mainly in the UK and is a UK resident company. It purchases components from third parties to be assembled into finished products. It also has a permanent establishment in the country of Chekka. The profits realised in Chekka are subject to 14% Chekkan business tax. There is no double tax treaty between the UK and the country of Chekka.

The budgeted taxable profits of Plad Ltd for the year ending 31 March 2025 are set out below. Plad Ltd's profitability is very stable, so please assume that the figures for the following year will be the same.

	£
Trading profit in the UK	58,000
Trading profit in the country of Chekka (before deduction of 14% Chekkan tax)	270,000
Taxable total profits	328,000

Quil Ltd

Quil Ltd will be incorporated, registered for value added tax (VAT) and commence trading on 1 April 2024. It will trade in the UK and be a UK resident company.

From a commercial standpoint, my intention was to own Quil Ltd personally. However, if there is a sufficient tax advantage, I will consider establishing the company as a wholly-owned subsidiary of Plad Ltd.

The first two years of budgeted results of Quil Ltd are set out below. The trading profit/(loss) figures are before the deduction of capital allowances, but have otherwise been adjusted for the purposes of corporation tax. The chargeable gain will not qualify for rollover relief.

Year ending 31 March 2025 – trading loss	£(120,000)		
Year ending 31 March 2026 – trading profit	£162,000	Chargeable gain	£16,000

On 1 April 2024, Quil Ltd will purchase the following capital assets:

New machinery and equipment	£160,000 (excluding VAT)
Newly constructed building used for manufacturing and storage	£600,000 (excluding VAT)

Construction of the building will begin on 1 April 2024. Quil Ltd will start using the building in its trade from 1 January 2025.

The cost of the building includes £230,000 in respect of thermal insulation and air-cooling equipment in order to create the appropriate conditions for manufacturing. The cost also includes £150,000 in respect of land.

Value added tax (VAT)

I would like the two companies to register as a group for VAT purposes (to avoid the need to charge VAT on intra group supplies and to generally reduce administration) and for the group to continue to use the annual accounting scheme currently used by Plad Ltd. I appreciate this would mean that the two companies would be jointly and severally liable for the group's VAT liability.

Plad Ltd – unreported chargeable gain

I have just discovered that a chargeable gain of £21,600 realised by Plad Ltd in the year ended 31 March 2020 was omitted from its corporation tax return. However, because the gain arose in respect of the sale of land, it was reported for the purposes of stamp duty land tax. Accordingly, I assume we do not need to do anything and that HM Revenue and Customs (HMRC) will contact us about this at some point.

Exhibit 2 – Gift of shares by Laura

Schedule of information regarding Laura Falkner – dated 1 March 2024

Background

Laura is 74 years old and married to Bill. The couple have two adult children: a son, Edward, and a daughter, Lily.

Edward has spent most of the last few years travelling in Asia, although Laura hopes that her proposed gift of shares will persuade him to return to the UK.

Laura is a higher rate taxpayer.

Vyc Ltd

Vyc Ltd is an unquoted manufacturing company, which is registered in the UK. It does not own any assets other than those which are used in its trade.

The shareholders in Vyc Ltd are set out below. The shareholdings have not changed for many years.

	Number of shares
Laura	35,000
Bill (Laura's husband)	19,000
Lily (Laura's daughter)	10,000
Charlotte (Laura's sister)	20,000
Louis (Charlotte's husband)	16,000
	100,000

You should use the following values for an ordinary share in Vyc Ltd when carrying out this work.

Shareholding	**Value per share**
	£
Up to 25%	10
26% to 50%	13
51% to 74%	19
More than 75%	22

On 1 October 2019, Laura made a cash gift to her daughter, Lily. This resulted in a transfer of value after deduction of exemptions of £280,000. This is the only gift Laura has made.

On 1 July 2024, Laura will give her son, Edward, 10,000 ordinary shares in the company. She is aware that there may be a UK inheritance tax (IHT) liability if she dies within seven years of this gift, but assumes that capital gains tax gift holdover relief will be available in respect of the gift.

Exhibit 3 – Work to be carried out

Extract from an email from your manager – dated 1 March 2024

Please prepare notes in preparation for meetings that I will be having with Claire and Laura, to cover the following:

(a) Group relief (Exhibit 1)

In order to help Claire make her decision on the ownership of Quil Ltd, advise her of the tax advantage of Quil Ltd being a wholly-owned subsidiary of Plad Ltd, such that the two companies form a group relief group. You should carry out this work in three stages:

(i) Explain, with supporting calculations, the maximum amount of group relief which Plad Ltd would need to receive for the year ending 31 March 2025 such that none of its double tax relief in respect of the Chekkan tax would be wasted and its UK corporation tax payable would be £Nil. You should assume the rate of corporation tax is 25% for all accounting periods.

(ii) Prepare calculations of the corporation tax liabilities of the two companies for the two years ending 31 March 2026. Your calculations should be on the basis that the trading loss of Quil Ltd will be used as soon as possible whilst restricting the amount of group relief in an accounting period to the maximum figure you calculated in part (i).

You SHOULD NOT provide any explanations of these calculations.

(iii) Conclude by explaining the tax advantage of Quil Ltd becoming a wholly-owned subsidiary of Plad Ltd, as opposed to being owned personally by Claire.

When carrying out this work, you should be aware of the following:

- in the year ending 31 March 2025, £200,000 of the annual investment allowance will be available to Quil Ltd, and Quil Ltd will claim the maximum capital allowances available
- neither of the two companies will be required to pay corporation tax in quarterly instalments. This will be true regardless of who owns Quil Ltd.

(18 marks)

(b) Group registration for value added tax (VAT) purposes (Exhibit 1)

Explain any additional matters of which Claire should be aware in relation to group registration for VAT purposes. Note that Claire is not a sole trader. **(3 marks)**

(c) Plad Ltd – unreported chargeable gain (Exhibit 1)

Explain the implications for Plad Ltd, and our firm, of the failure to report the chargeable gain to HM Revenue and Customs (HMRC). You SHOULD NOT address money laundering or the possibility of penalties, as I have already spoken to Claire about these matters. **(5 marks)**

(d) Laura – gift of shares in Vyc Ltd (Exhibit 2)

Explain the circumstances which would result in the maximum IHT liability on this gift and provide a calculation of the amount which would then be due.

When explaining the maximum IHT liability, you should focus on the date on which Laura's future death may occur and the availability of business property relief.

Explain whether Laura is right to assume that capital gains tax gift holdover relief will be available in respect of this gift. **(14 marks)**

Tax manager

Required:

You should assume that today's date is 1 March 2024.

Respond to the instructions in the email from your manager.

Note: The split of the mark allocation is shown in Exhibit 3 – Work to be carried out.

(40 marks)

Professional marks will be awarded for demonstration of skill in communication, analysis and evaluation, scepticism and commercial acumen in your answer. (10 marks)

(Total: 50 marks)

20 JEG LTD GROUP (ADAPTED) *Walk in the footsteps of a top tutor*

You should assume that today's date is 1 September 2024.

Your manager has received a schedule of information from Hale, the managing director of Jeg Ltd, a potential client for your firm.

Advice is required in respect of the following issues:

- the availability of rollover relief for the Jeg Ltd group,
- the application of the transfer pricing rules to transactions with Lis Co,
- the setting up of an overseas permanent establishment by Mot Ltd,
- the value added tax (VAT) implications of registering as a group and purchasing goods from overseas, and
- Hale's personal post-tax income.

There are also some ethical issues to be considered if the firm is to accept Jeg Ltd as a new client.

The following **exhibits** provide information relevant to the question:

1 Jeg Ltd group

2 Hale's financial position

3 Work to be carried out – email from manager

This information should be used to answer the question **requirements**.

Exhibit 1 – Jeg Ltd group

Schedule from Hale dated 1 September 2024

Background

On 1 August 2022, Jeg Ltd purchased the whole of the ordinary share capital of two companies: Kod Ltd and Lis Co.

On 1 July 2024, Jeg Ltd purchased the whole of the ordinary share capital of Mot Ltd.

All four companies in the Jeg Ltd group prepare accounts to 31 March each year, are budgeted to be profitable in the year ending 31 March 2025 and pay corporation tax at the main rate.

Further details of the companies are set out below, followed by a summary of recent significant transactions.

	Jeg Ltd	**Kod Ltd**	**Lis Co**	**Mot Ltd**
Country of residence	UK	UK	Silana	UK
Country of trading activity	UK	UK	Silana	Puran
Whether registered for VAT	Yes	Yes	No	No
Rate of overseas tax	N/A	N/A	11%	13%

Jeg Ltd – purchase of business

On 1 February 2024, Jeg Ltd purchased the trade and assets of a business. The only significant asset of the business was its production line, which consisted of three large items of fixed machinery. Jeg Ltd paid £290,000 for this machinery.

Kod Ltd

Kod Ltd is experiencing cash flow problems. On 30 June 2024, it sold its business premises to an unconnected party for £485,000, resulting in a chargeable gain of £247,000. This building was entirely used in Kod Ltd's trade throughout the period it was owned. Kod Ltd now trades from rented premises. On 1 August 2024, it used £120,000 of the sale proceeds to purchase eight delivery vans for use in its trade.

Lis Co

On 1 July 2024, Lis Co purchased a building situated in Silana for £170,000. This building was immediately brought into use in Lis Co's trade.

Lis Co manufactures industrial components, which it supplies to customers in Silana and in other countries. It is intended that Jeg Ltd will purchase components from Lis Co and import them for use in its own manufacturing trade.

In view of the low rate of business tax in Silana, I am considering pricing strategies which would maximise the profits of the group which are taxed there.

Mot Ltd

Mot Ltd carries on its trade in Puran where it has production and distribution facilities. It has not made any capital additions or disposals of significance since 2022.

Value added tax (VAT)

Finally, I am looking into the possibility of a group VAT registration.

Additional information provided by your manager

I expect the Jeg Ltd group to be an exciting new client for our firm. Hale has ambitious plans and, although we advise a number of corporate groups, this will give us our first experience of companies operating through permanent establishments situated overseas.

I can confirm:

- there is no double tax treaty between the UK and either the country of Silana or the country of Puran
- there are no controlled foreign companies implications for you to consider.

Exhibit 2 – Hale's financial position

Schedule from Hale dated 1 September 2024

My personal background

I was born in the UK and have always lived in the UK.

Income from employment in the tax year 2024/25

On 6 April 2024, I began working full time for Jeg Ltd. For the tax year 2024/25 my employment package will comprise the following:

- A gross annual salary of £87,800.
- Employment income benefits in respect of a car and accommodation, amounting to £26,230.
- 7,200 ordinary shares issued to me by Jeg Ltd on 1 May 2024 as an introductory 'thank you' for joining the company. I paid £14,400 for these shares, which had a market value of £23,200 at that time.

Additional information provided by your manager

– Shares in Jeg Ltd are not readily convertible assets.

– You should assume that Hale will have dividend income of £18,300 in the tax year 2024/25 in respect of her share portfolio.

Exhibit 3 – Work to be carried out

Email extract from your manager dated 1 September 2024

Please prepare a memorandum for the client file consisting of the work set out below.

(a) Becoming tax advisers to the Jeg Ltd group of companies (Exhibit 1)

Set out the information we require, and the actions we should take, before we agree to become tax advisers to the Jeg Ltd group of companies. **(5 marks)**

(b) Relieving the chargeable gain on the sale of Kod Ltd's business premises (Exhibit 1)

Explain the matters which should be brought to Hale's attention in relation to the availability of rollover relief in respect of the chargeable gain on the sale of Kod Ltd's business premises, and the way in which the relief would operate. **(10 marks)**

(c) Taxation of profits generated overseas (Exhibit 1)

Lis Co

Explain the implications, in relation to UK corporation tax payable, of Lis Co charging Jeg Ltd inflated prices for its components in order to maximise the profits of the group which are taxed in Silana. Jeg Ltd is a small enterprise for the purposes of the transfer pricing regime.

Mot Ltd

Explain:

– the rate of corporation tax which will be suffered by Mot Ltd in the UK on the profits generated by its permanent establishment in Puran; and

– the matters to consider when deciding whether or not to make an election to exempt the profits of the permanent establishment in Puran from UK tax. **(9 marks)**

(d) Value added tax (VAT) (Exhibit 1)

I have already established that Lis Co cannot be included within a group VAT registration with Jeg Ltd. With this in mind, explain:

– which of the other companies within the group could be included within a group VAT registration

– any potential disadvantages, relevant to the Jeg Ltd group of companies, of registering for VAT as a group

– the VAT implications for Jeg Ltd of purchasing components from Lis Co. **(7 marks)**

(e) Hale's financial position for the tax year 2024/25 (Exhibit 2)

Hale cannot understand why, despite receiving a substantial amount of UK source income, her annual personal expenditure of £57,600 exceeds her available post-tax income.

– Prepare calculations for the tax year 2024/25 in order to explain why Hale is in this financial position and summarise your findings. **(9 marks)**

Required:

You should assume that today's date is 1 September 2024.

Respond to the instructions in the email from your manager.

Note: The split of the mark allocation is shown in Exhibit 3 – Work to be carried out.

(40 marks)

Professional marks will be awarded for demonstration of skill in communication, analysis and evaluation, scepticism and commercial acumen in your answer. (10 marks)

(Total: 50 marks)

21 HUM LTD GROUP (ADAPTED) *Walk in the footsteps of a top tutor*

You should assume that today's date is 1 July 2024.

Your manager has received a schedule of information from Rawl, the finance director of Hum Ltd. The Hum Ltd group of companies is a client of your firm. A subsidiary of Hum Ltd will sell two buildings, which it currently uses in its trade, and will purchase a trading activity situated overseas.

The work to be carried out relates to:

– a corporation tax refund (which is thought to have been made by mistake)

– the tax implications of the proposed sale of two buildings

– the taxation of the profits generated by an overseas trading activity, and

– some planned share purchases and the use of capital losses.

The following **exhibits** provide information relevant to the question and outline what you need to do:

1 Hum Ltd group – background information

2 Schedule of information from Rawl

3 Work to be carried out – email from manager

Exhibit 1 – Hum Ltd group

Background information from the files as at 1 July 2024

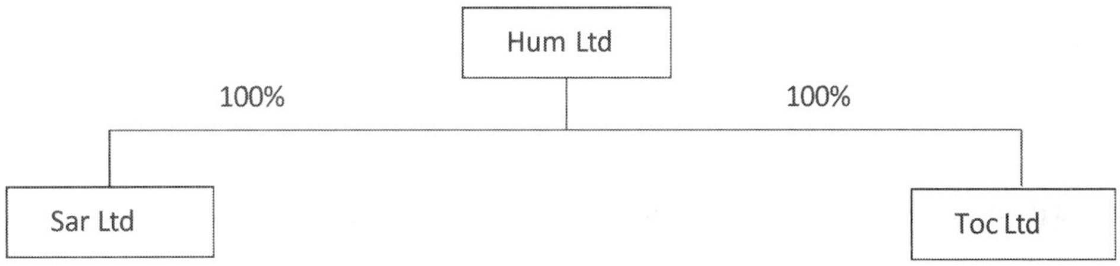

Hum Ltd has owned the whole of the ordinary share capital of Sar Ltd and Toc Ltd for many years.

– All three companies are resident in the UK for tax purposes and prepare accounts to 31 March each year.

– All three companies pay corporation tax at the main rate.

- There has only been one significant capital transaction in the last four years. On 1 February 2024, Sar Ltd purchased a building from an unconnected party for use in its trade for £90,000.
- In their ordinary trading activities, all three companies make wholly taxable supplies and are registered as a group for the purposes of value added tax (VAT).

Exhibit 2 – Schedule of information

Schedule of information from Rawl dated 1 July 2024

Background

We are aiming to develop the business of Toc Ltd and to generate cash for the group. To achieve this, we have decided on the following course of action:

Toc Ltd will sell two of the three buildings which it currently uses in its trade. It will then continue to trade in the UK from its one remaining building.

Toc Ltd will acquire a trading activity situated overseas.

Buildings to be sold by Toc Ltd

Toc Ltd will sell building 1 AND building 2 between now (1 July 2024) and 31 March 2025.

	Building 1	**Building 2**
Acquisition date	1 July 2016	1 May 2011
Cost	£290,000	£320,000
Building to be sold to	Sar Ltd	An unrelated company
Sale proceeds at market value	£440,000	£650,000

No option to tax for the purposes of value added tax (VAT) has been or will be made in respect of either of the buildings.

Acquisition of a trading activity situated overseas

Toc Ltd has identified a trading activity which is carried on, entirely in the country of Keynesia, by Qua Co. Qua Co is resident for tax purposes in Keynesia. The trade is profitable, and the profits are subject to corporation tax in Keynesia at the rate of 28%.

The purchase of this trade will take place between 1 January and 31 March 2025. Toc Ltd will acquire the trade in one of two ways.

By purchasing the whole of the ordinary share capital of Qua Co for £550,000. Qua Co would continue to trade and to be resident for tax purposes in Keynesia.

By purchasing the trading assets from Qua Co at current market value, as listed below:

Goodwill	£45,000
Building (constructed in June 2014)	£465,000
Lorries	£30,000

There is no double tax treaty between the UK and Keynesia.

Further planned share acquisitions

Hum Ltd is planning to make more capital disposals in the future that will lead to significant chargeable gains. Rawl is keen to minimise the corporation tax payable on these disposals.

Rawl has identified a company, Alpha Ltd, that Hum Ltd can buy for around £300,000. It doesn't have any business activity, but it has a brought forward capital loss of £9 million. Rawl hopes to use this loss to shelter future gains made by the group.

Rawl has also identified a different company, Beta Ltd, with a large portfolio of quoted shares which have performed very badly over recent years. The portfolio cost Beta Ltd around £5 million but the total value of the shares is estimated to have fallen to only £1 million now. As the company has no other significant assets or activity, the share capital of the company can be bought by Hum Ltd for around the current £1 million value of the share portfolio.

Exhibit 3 – Work to be carried out

Email extracts from your manager detailing work to be done – dated 1 July 2024

Please prepare a memorandum for the client file consisting of the work set out below.

(a) Hum Ltd – refund of corporation tax

Hum Ltd has received a refund of corporation tax from HM Revenue and Customs (HMRC) in respect of the year ended 31 March 2019. The company has not been able to determine why the refund was made and suspects that it may be a mistake by HMRC.

– Set out the actions which our firm should take and the matters which we should bring to Rawl's attention in relation to this refund. **(5 marks)**

(b) Sale of the two buildings (Exhibits 1 and 2)

(i) Tax implications

– Explain the chargeable gains which will arise, and the value added tax (VAT) and stamp duty land tax (SDLT) implications for the Hum Ltd group of the proposed sale of the two buildings.

You should ignore any indexation allowance and the possibility of rollover relief. **(7 marks)**

(ii) Post-tax proceeds available to the Hum Ltd group

– With reference to the conditions which need to be satisfied, explain the availability of rollover relief in respect of the chargeable gain(s) on the sale of the two buildings.

Your explanation should include consideration of both of the possible ways in which Toc Ltd might acquire the Qua Co business.

– On the basis that Toc Ltd acquires the Qua Co business in the manner which maximises the amount of gains which can be rolled over, calculate the post-tax proceeds available to the Hum Ltd group as a result of the sale of the two buildings. **(15 marks)**

(c) UK taxation of the profits generated by the Qua Co trade (Exhibits 1 and 2)

– Explain how the profits generated by the Qua Co trade in the country of Keynesia will be taxed in the UK, and the relief which will be available in respect of the cost of the trading assets, if:

(i) Toc Ltd acquires the ordinary share capital of Qua Co. You should assume that this WILL NOT result in a charge under the controlled foreign company rules.

(ii) Toc Ltd acquires Qua Co's trading assets. You should assume that Toc Ltd WILL NOT make an election to exempt the profits of the permanent establishment in Keynesia from UK corporation tax. **(6 marks)**

(d) Further planned share acquisitions (Exhibits 1 and 2)

– Explain the tax consequences of the proposed share acquisitions and whether they will achieve Rawl's objective of saving corporation tax on the planned future disposals. Detail any additional information needed.

(7 marks)

Required:

You should assume that today's date is 1 July 2024.

Respond to the instructions in the email from your manager.

Note: The split of the mark allocation is shown in Exhibit 3 – Email extracts from your manager. **(40 marks)**

Professional marks will be awarded for the demonstration of skill in communication, analysis and evaluation, scepticism and commercial acumen in your answer. (10 marks)

(Total: 50 marks)

Section 2

PRACTICE QUESTIONS – SECTION B

TAXATION OF INDIVIDUALS

EMPLOYMENT

22 MORICE AND BABEEN PLC (ADAPTED) *Walk in the footsteps of a top tutor*

You should assume that today's date is 1 April 2024.

Morice is the finance director of Babeen plc. Babeen plc is a non-close quoted trading company.

Morice wants advice in respect of:

– a proposed Save As You Earn (SAYE) share option scheme for the company's employees,

– a medical care scheme,

– payments to employees for driving their own cars on business journeys, and

– the capital gains tax implications of a sale of shares.

Proposed SAYE scheme rules:

– Employees will invest in the scheme for five years.

– The scheme will permit monthly investments of between £5 and £750.

– The scheme will be open to all employees and directors who are at least 21 years old and have worked full-time for the company for at least three years.

– The share options granted under the scheme will enable employees to purchase shares for £2.48 each.

Detailed explanations, with supporting calculations, requested by Morice:

– Whether or not each of the proposed rules will be acceptable for a SAYE scheme.

– The tax and national insurance liabilities for the employee in the illustrative example below in respect of the grant and exercise of the share options, the receipt of the bonus and the sale of the shares on the assumption that the scheme referred to meets all of the HMRC conditions.

Illustrative example – SAYE scheme that meets HMRC conditions:

- The share options will be granted on 1 January 2025 to purchase shares at £2.48 each.
- The employee will invest £250 each month for five years.
- The amount invested will be used to exercise share options.
- The share options will be exercised on 31 December 2029 and the shares will be sold on the same day.
- The employee's interest in the employing company will be less than 1%.
- A share in the employing company will be worth: £3.00 on 1 January 2025
  £4.00 on 31 December 2029

Medical care scheme:

- Babeen plc is to offer free private health insurance to its employees.
- The health insurance will cost the company £470 annually per employee.
- The insurance would cost each employee £590 if they were to purchase it personally.
- Employees who decline the offer will be able to borrow up to £12,500 from Babeen plc to pay for medical treatment.
- The loans will be interest-free and repayable over four years.

Payments to employees for driving their own cars on business journeys:

- For each mile driven – 36 pence.
- For each mile driven whilst carrying a passenger – an additional 3 pence.

Sale of shares in Wind Ltd:

- Morice subscribed for 3,500 £1 ordinary shares in Wind Ltd at par in April 2019.
- Wind Ltd is a UK manufacturing company and is not a qualifying company under the enterprise investment scheme or seed enterprise investment scheme.
- Morice sold all of his shares in Wind Ltd in August 2023 for £150,000.
- Morice is a higher rate taxpayer and has made no other disposals during the tax year 2023/24.

Required:

You should assume that today's date is 1 April 2024

(a) Prepare the DETAILED explanations, with supporting calculations, as requested by Morice in respect of the proposed SAYE scheme. (10 marks)

(b) Explain the income tax and national insurance implications for the employees of Babeen plc of:

(i) the medical care scheme (3 marks)

(ii) the payments for driving their own cars on business journeys. (4 marks)

(c) Calculate the capital gains tax payable by Morice on the sale of the Wind Ltd shares and explain the rate of tax that has been used. (3 marks)

Professional marks will be awarded for the demonstration of skill in analysis and evaluation, scepticism and commercial acumen in your answer. (5 marks)

(Total: 25 marks)

23 HYSSOP LTD (ADAPTED) *Walk in the footsteps of a top tutor*

You should assume that today's date is 1 April 2024.

Hyssop Ltd requires advice in respect of:

– the provision of assistance with home to work travel costs for Corin, who is an employee,

– the corporation tax implications of the purchase of a short lease, and

– the value added tax (VAT) implications of the sale of a warehouse.

Hyssop Ltd:

– Is a UK resident trading company.

– Prepares accounts to 31 December each year.

– Is registered for VAT.

– Leased a factory on 1 February 2024.

Corin:

– Is resident and domiciled in the UK.

– Is an employee of Hyssop Ltd, who works only at the company's head office.

– Earns an annual salary of £55,000 from Hyssop Ltd and has no other source of income.

Hyssop Ltd – assistance with home to work travel costs:

– Hyssop Ltd is considering two alternatives to provide assistance with Corin's home to work travel costs.

Alternative 1 – provision of a motorcycle:

– Hyssop Ltd will provide Corin with a leased motorcycle for travelling from home to work.

– Provision of the leased motorcycle, including fuel, will cost Hyssop Ltd £3,160 per annum. This will give rise to an annual taxable benefit of £3,160 for Corin.

– Corin will incur no additional travel or parking costs in respect of his home to work travel.

Alternative 2 – payment towards the cost of driving and provision of parking place:

– Hyssop Ltd will reimburse Corin for the cost of driving his own car to work up to an amount of £2,240 each year.

– Corin estimates that his annual cost for driving from home to work is £2,820.

– Additionally, Hyssop Ltd will pay AB Parking Ltd £920 per year for a car parking space for Corin near the head office.

Acquisition of a factory:

– Hyssop Ltd acquired a 40-year lease on a factory on 1 February 2024 for which it paid a premium of £260,000.

– The factory is used in Hyssop Ltd's trade.

Disposal of a warehouse:

– Hyssop Ltd has agreed to sell a warehouse on 31 December 2024 for £315,000, which will give rise to a chargeable gain of £16,520.

– Hyssop Ltd had purchased the warehouse when it was newly constructed on 1 January 2021 for £270,000 (excluding VAT).

– The warehouse was used by Hyssop Ltd in its trade until 31 December 2023, since when it has been rented to an unconnected party.

– Until 1 January 2024, Hyssop Ltd made only standard-rated supplies for VAT purposes.

– Hyssop Ltd has not opted to tax the warehouse for VAT purposes.

– The capital goods scheme for VAT applies to the warehouse.

Required:

You should assume that today's date is 1 April 2024

Note: You should ignore value added tax (VAT) for parts (a) and (b).

(a) **Explain, with the aid of calculations, which of the two alternatives for providing financial assistance for home to work travel is most cost efficient for:**

(i) **Corin.** **(5 marks)**

(ii) **Hyssop Ltd.** **(3 marks)**

(b) **Explain, with the aid of calculations, the corporation tax implications for Hyssop Ltd of the acquisition of the leasehold premises on 1 February 2024, in relation to the company's tax adjusted trading profits for the year ended 31 December 2024 and its ability to roll over the gain on the sale of the warehouse.** **(8 marks)**

(c) **Explain, with the aid of calculations, the VAT implications of the disposal of the warehouse on 31 December 2024.** **(4 marks)**

Professional marks will be awarded for the demonstration of skill in analysis and evaluation and commercial acumen in your answer. **(5 marks)**

(Total: 25 marks)

24 METHLEY LTD (ADAPTED) *Walk in the footsteps of a top tutor*

You should assume that today's date is 1 April 2024.

Your firm has been asked to provide advice to Methley Ltd, a close company, and Yara, a non-UK domiciled employee.

Advice is required in respect of:

– the provision of share incentives to an employee,

– the provision of either a car or an interest-free loan to an employee, and

– the income tax implications for Yara of claiming the remittance basis.

Methley Ltd:

– Is a UK resident trading company which is a close company.

Simon – share incentives:

- Simon is a director of Methley Ltd and owns 20% of its ordinary shares.
- Methley Ltd intends to provide Simon with shares worth £25,000, in the form of either free shares or share options.
- The free shares would be issued in June 2025.
- The share options would be issued under a tax advantaged company share option scheme (CSOP) in June 2025 and Simon would exercise the options in October 2029.
- In either case, Simon will sell the shares in December 2031.
- Simon is a higher rate taxpayer.

Chris:

- Is employed by Methley Ltd and owns 10% of its ordinary shares.
- Has been offered the sole use of a company car or, alternatively, a loan to enable him to purchase the same car himself.
- Receives a salary from the company of £60,000 and receives dividends of £1,000 each year.

Chris – alternative 1 – company car:

- Methley Ltd would purchase the car on 1 October 2024 for £9,600, which is £800 less than the list price.
- The car would immediately be made available to Chris exclusively for his private use.
- The car has CO_2 emissions of 76 grams per kilometre and is diesel powered. The car meets the RDE2 standard.
- Chris would contribute £700 per year towards the private use of the car. Chris pays for all of his diesel himself.
- Methley Ltd would give the car to Chris after three years, when its market value is expected to be £6,300.

Chris – alternative 2 – loan:

- Methley Ltd would provide Chris with an interest-free loan of £9,600 on 1 October 2024.
- The loan would be written off in three years' time.

Yara – non-UK domiciled employee:

- Is currently resident in the UK but domiciled in the country of Setubia.
- Became UK resident when she was employed by Methley Ltd on 6 April 2016.
- Receives an annual salary from Methley Ltd of £82,000 and has no other UK source of income.
- Receives rental income from an unfurnished residential property in Setubia.

Yara – overseas rental income:

- The gross annual rental income from the overseas property is £24,000.
- Yara only remits £10,000 of this income to the UK each year.
- Yara has previously claimed the remittance basis each tax year.

Required:

You should assume that today's date is 1 April 2024

(a) **Compare and contrast the tax implications of both the acquisition and disposal of the shares in Methley Ltd if Simon acquires the shares through a tax advantaged company share option scheme (CSOP) or, alternatively, as an award of shares.**

Note: You are not required to comment on any national insurance contributions implications. **(7 marks)**

(b) **Prepare calculations to determine which of the two proposed benefits (the company car or the loan) will result in the lower overall income tax cost for Chris. (6 marks)**

(c) **Advise Yara whether or not it would be beneficial for her to claim the remittance basis in the tax year 2023/24, and calculate the increase, if any, in her income tax liability for the tax year 2023/24 compared to that of previous years, assuming that she chooses the most tax beneficial course of action.**

Note: You are not required to consider the potential availability of double taxation relief (DTR). **(7 marks)**

Professional marks will be awarded for the demonstration of skill in analysis and evaluation and commercial acumen in your answer. (5 marks)

(Total: 25 marks)

25 DAMIANA PLC (ADAPTED) *Walk in the footsteps of a top tutor*

You should assume that today's date is 1 August 2024.

Luiza, the finance director of Damiana plc, requires advice on

- the corporation tax treatment of the company's expenditure on research and development (R&D),
- the consequences of the late filing of Damiana plc's recent corporation tax returns, and
- the tax implications for her of two alternative ways of acquiring shares in Damiana plc.

Damiana plc:

- Is a UK resident quoted trading company.

Damiana plc – R&D expenditure:

- Damiana plc is an SME (small or medium sized enterprise) for the purpose of tax relief for R&D expenditure.
- During the year ending 31 March 2025, Damiana plc will incur expenditure on qualifying R&D of £169,000. This amount includes £30,000 which will be paid to an external contractor.
- Damiana plc will have taxable total profits, before any deduction in respect of R&D expenditure, of £1,675,000 in the year ending 31 March 2025.

Damiana plc – late filing of corporation tax returns:

- Damiana plc prepared accounts for the 18-month period ended 31 March 2023.
- The corporation tax returns for this period were filed on 15 July 2024.
- All previous corporation tax returns have been filed on time.

Luiza:

- Is employed as the finance director of Damiana plc, earning a gross annual salary of £165,000.
- Has no other source of taxable income.
- Has been offered two alternative ways to acquire ordinary shares in Damiana plc.
- In either case she will sell these shares on 10 November 2027 when their market value is expected to be £32.70 per share.
- Uses her annual exempt amount for capital gains tax purposes each year.

Acquisition of Damiana plc shares – alternative 1:

- Damiana plc will transfer 5,000 ordinary shares (a 1% holding) to Luiza on 1 November 2024 for which Luiza will pay £1 per share.
- The market value of these shares on 1 November 2024 is expected to be £24.50 per share.
- Damiana plc does not expect to pay a dividend in the foreseeable future.

Acquisition of Damiana plc shares – alternative 2:

- Damiana plc will grant options over 5,000 ordinary shares to Luiza on 1 November 2024 under its newly established enterprise management incentive (EMI) scheme.
- The exercise price of these options will be £23.00 per share.
- Luiza will exercise the options on 2 November 2027.

Required:

You should assume that today's date is 1 August 2024

(a) Explain, with supporting calculations, the tax relief available for the research and development (R&D) expenditure incurred by Damiana plc in the year ending 31 March 2025, and the amount of corporation tax which will be saved as a result of claiming this relief. (5 marks)

(b) Identify the accounting periods for which corporation tax returns were required from Damiana plc in respect of the 18-month period ended 31 March 2023. State the due date(s) for filing the returns in each case, and the implications for Damiana plc in respect of their late filing. (3 marks)

(c) Explain the tax implications for Luiza if she acquires 5,000 ordinary shares in Damiana plc alternatively, (1) by means of a transfer on 1 November 2024, or (2) as a result of exercising the share options on 2 November 2027. On the assumption that she sells the shares as planned on 10 November 2027, calculate Luiza's net increase in wealth under each alternative. (12 marks)

Professional marks will be awarded for the demonstration of skill in analysis and evaluation and commercial acumen in your answer. (5 marks)

(Total: 25 marks)

26 DEMETER (ADAPTED)

You should assume that today's date is 1 January 2025.

Demeter has recently taken up a new employment and is seeking advice on:

- the income tax treatment of certain components of his remuneration package,
- the relief(s) available to reduce the chargeable gain on the sale of his house,
- the tax consequences of participating his employer's occupational pension scheme, and
- the tax implications of participating in a non-tax advantaged share option scheme.

Demeter:

- Is UK resident and domiciled.
- Commenced employment with Poseidon Ltd on 1 December 2024.
- Will have no source of income, other than from Poseidon Ltd, in all relevant future tax years.
- Has relocated to London, from Manchester, a city around 200 miles north of London, to take up this employment.

Remuneration package from Poseidon Ltd:

- Demeter will receive an annual salary of £130,000.
- On 1 December 2024, Poseidon Ltd made a one-off lump sum payment of £20,000 to Demeter as an inducement to take up employment with the company.
- Poseidon Ltd paid Demeter £5,000 towards his costs of relocating to London. The company is also paying him £1,500 each month for four months from 1 December 2024 towards renting accommodation in London until he purchases a new house on 1 April 2025.
- On 1 December 2024, Demeter was granted share options in Poseidon Ltd's non-tax advantaged share option scheme.
- From 6 April 2025, Demeter will participate in Poseidon Ltd's occupational pension scheme.

Relocation to London:

- Demeter incurred costs in relation to his relocation to London of £6,000. This amount includes estate agent fees of £2,800 in connection with the sale of his house in Manchester on 31 October 2024.
- Demeter signed a four-month lease for a flat in London from 1 December 2024 at a monthly rental of £1,700.

House in Manchester:

- Demeter purchased the house on 1 May 2011 and lived in it as his main residence.
- Demeter let the top floor of the house (comprising 30% of the total house) to tenants from 1 May 2013 to 31 October 2024. The tenants did not share Demeter's living accommodation or take meals with him.
- Demeter continued to occupy the remainder of the house as his main residence until 31 October 2024, when the entire house was sold.

- The sale gave rise to a gain, before any reliefs, of £94,000.
- Demeter did not own any other house throughout the period from 1 May 2011 to 31 October 2024.

Demeter – pension contributions:

- Demeter has made tax-allowable contributions of £40,000 (gross) to a personal pension plan for the last five tax years and will continue to do so in future tax years.
- From the tax year 2025/26, Poseidon Ltd will contribute an amount equal to 10% of Demeter's annual salary to its occupational pension scheme.
- Demeter will make no contributions to Poseidon Ltd's occupational pension scheme.

Poseidon Ltd's share option scheme:

- On 1 December 2024, Poseidon Ltd granted Demeter options over 3,000 shares in its non-tax advantaged share option scheme at a 5% discount on the market value of the shares on that date.
- The market value of Poseidon Ltd shares on 1 December 2024 was £4.20 per share.
- Demeter will exercise the options on 6 April 2030, and immediately sell the shares.
- Poseidon Ltd believes that the market value of its shares on 6 April 2030 will be £6.00 per share.

Required:

You should assume that today's date is 1 January 2025

(a) **Explain the extent to which the receipt of the £20,000 lump sum inducement payment, and the relocation package in relation to Demeter's move to London, will give rise to taxable employment income for him. (5 marks)**

(b) **Identify, and calculate, with brief explanations, the relief(s) available to Demeter to reduce the chargeable gain of £94,000 on the sale of his house in Manchester on 31 October 2024. (6 marks)**

(c) **Explain, with supporting calculations, the tax consequences for Demeter of participating in:**

(i) **Poseidon Ltd's occupational pension scheme in the tax year 2025/26. (5 marks)**

(ii) **Poseidon Ltd's non-tax advantaged share option scheme, in respect of the grant of the options on 1 December 2024 and the exercise of the options and subsequent sale of the shares on 6 April 2030. (4 marks)**

Note: Ignore national insurance contributions (NIC).

Professional marks will be awarded for the demonstration of skill in analysis and evaluation and commercial acumen in your answer. (5 marks)

(Total: 25 marks)

27 YACON LTD AND DAIKON (ADAPTED)

Answer debrief

You should assume that today's date is 1 December 2024.

Daikon, the managing director of Yacon Ltd, has requested advice on:

– the tax implications of Yacon Ltd setting up a tax advantaged share incentive scheme for its employees,

– the capital gains tax relief(s) available on the sale of his house, and

– the potential inheritance tax liability arising on the gift of an apartment.

Yacon Ltd:

– Is a UK resident, unquoted, trading company which is not part of a group.

– Is considering setting up either a company share option plan (CSOP), or a share incentive plan (SIP), both of which would be offered to selected employees.

Yacon Ltd – criteria for its tax advantaged share incentive scheme:

– Employees will be selected to join the scheme dependent on their period of employment with the company.

– If the scheme is a CSOP, each employee will be offered options to purchase shares worth up to £3,000 each year.

– Employees will exercise the options five years after being granted them.

– If the scheme is a SIP, each employee will be given free shares worth up to £3,000 each year.

– Employees will remove the shares from the plan after five years.

Daikon:

– Was gifted an apartment by his aunt, Jicama, on 5 June 2022.

– Has never lived in this apartment.

– Will sell the house he currently lives in, and move in to this apartment on 31 December 2024.

Daikon – sale of his current house:

– Daikon purchased this house on 1 July 2016, when he was employed overseas.

– Daikon did not own any other property between 1 July 2016 and 4 June 2022.

– The sale of the house on 31 December 2024 will give rise to a chargeable gain of £145,000, before any reliefs.

Daikon – occupation of his current house:

– Daikon moved in to the house on 1 January 2017, on his return to the UK.

– Daikon has occupied the house since 1 January 2017, apart from the period from 1 July 2018 to 31 December 2019, when he was, once again, employed overseas.

– Daikon resumed exclusive occupation of the house on 1 January 2020.

– Since 1 April 2020, Daikon has let the basement of the house (which comprises 25% of the property) for residential use, retaining exclusive occupation of the remaining 75% for himself.

Gift of the apartment by Jicama:

– When Jicama gifted the apartment to Daikon on 5 June 2022, it was on condition of her continuing to live in the property for the foreseeable future.

– On 12 March 2024, Jicama began living with her sister, and she removed the condition she had previously imposed on the gift from that date.

Required:

You should assume that today's date is 1 December 2024

(a) Explain whether (1) a company share option scheme (CSOP) and (2) a share incentive plan (SIP) will satisfy Yacon Ltd's criteria for a tax advantaged share incentive scheme, and the income tax implications for the employees of acquiring the shares in each case. (8 marks)

(b) Calculate, with brief explanations, the private residence relief (PRR), and letting relief), which are available to reduce the chargeable gain on Daikon's sale of his house. (7 marks)

(c) Explain the inheritance tax implications of Jicama's gift of the apartment to Daikon on 5 June 2022, if Jicama were to die in December 2027. (5 marks)

Professional marks will be awarded for the demonstration of skill in analysis and evaluation and commercial acumen in your answer. (5 marks)

(Total: 25 marks)

Calculate your allowed time, allocate the time to the separate parts..............

UNINCORPORATED BUSINESSES

28 AMY AND BEX (ADAPTED) *Walk in the footsteps of a top tutor*

You should assume that today's date is 1 March 2024.

Bex has recently left employment and entered into a business partnership with Amy. Bex requires advice in respect of:

- a loan to the partnership,
- the calculation of her share of the partnership profits, and
- the tax treatment of her redundancy payment.

Bex:

- Is resident and domiciled in the UK.
- Received an annual salary of £120,000 from her former employer, Cape Ltd.
- Was made redundant by Cape Ltd on 30 September 2023.
- Joined Amy, a sole trader, to form a partnership on 1 January 2024.
- Has no other source of income.

Amy and Bex partnership:

- Will prepare its first set of accounts for the 16-month period to 30 April 2025.
- Is expected to make a tax-adjusted profit of £255,000 (before deducting interest and capital allowances) for the period ending 30 April 2025.
- The tax written down value on its main pool at 1 January 2024 is £Nil.
- Except for the computer referred to below, no further assets will be purchased by either Amy or Bex for use in the partnership in the period ending 30 April 2025.

Profit sharing arrangements:

- The partnership's profit-sharing agreement is as follows:

	Amy	**Bex**
Annual salary	£0	£30,000
Profit sharing ratio	3	1

Bex – loans:

- In addition to her capital contribution, Bex will make a £20,000 loan to the partnership on 1 August 2024. The partnership will use this money wholly for business purposes.
- This loan will be financed by a £25,000 personal loan from Bex's bank, taken out on the same date.
- The remaining £5,000 of the bank loan will be used to purchase a computer for use in the partnership. Bex will have 20% private use of this computer.
- Both the loan from Bex to the partnership and the personal bank loan to Bex will carry interest at the rate of 5% per annum.

Bex – redundancy package from Cape Ltd:

- The package comprised a £12,000 statutory redundancy payment and an additional ex-gratia payment of £58,000.
- Bex also received three months' salary in lieu of notice. Her employment contract specified a two month notice period.

Required:

You should assume that today's date is 1 March 2024

(a) (i) Explain, with the aid of calculations, the tax deductions which will be available in respect of the loan interest payable on both the loan from Bex to the partnership and the personal bank loan to Bex. (7 marks)

(ii) In respect of the period ending 30 April 2025, show the allocation between the partners of the taxable trading profit of the partnership. (4 marks)

(b) Explain the tax implications for Bex of the receipt of the redundancy package from Cape Ltd and calculate her income tax liability and class 1 national insurance contributions (NICs) for the tax year 2023/24.

Note: For the purposes of this requirement you should assume that Bex's partnership profits assessment for the tax year 2023/24 will be £17,355. **(9 marks)**

Professional marks will be awarded for the demonstration of skill in analysis and evaluation and commercial acumen in your answer. (5 marks)

(Total: 25 marks)

29 MEG AND LAURIE (ADAPTED) *Walk in the footsteps of a top tutor*

You should assume that today's date is 1 April 2024.

Meg and her husband, Laurie, require advice regarding:

- Meg bringing her husband into her unincorporated business, either as an employee or as a partner,
- a sale of rights nil paid by Laurie, and
- the value added tax (VAT) implications of purchasing services from an overseas supplier.

Meg:

- Is 60 years old and is married to Laurie.
- Owns an unincorporated sole trader business, MT Travel.
- Has rental income of £8,600 each year in addition to any profits from MT Travel.

MT Travel:

- Was set up by Meg in 2019.
- Has accounts prepared to 31 March annually.
- Generated taxable trading profits of £1,600 for the year ended 31 March 2025.
- Currently has no employees.

MT Travel – the future:

– From 1 April 2025, Meg's husband, Laurie, will start to participate in the business.

– Meg will either:

1 employ Laurie part-time, paying him an annual salary of £12,000, the commercial rate for the work he will perform, or

2 admit Laurie into the business as a partner, sharing profits and losses in the ratio 75% to Meg, and 25% to Laurie.

– The business is expected to generate a tax-adjusted trading loss in the tax year 2025/26 of £20,000, before making any payment to Laurie.

– The business is expected to become profitable again in the tax year 2026/27 and thereafter, but profits are not expected to exceed £30,000 per year for the foreseeable future.

Laurie:

– Is 63 years old.

– Was employed for many years by Hagg Ltd, earning gross annual remuneration of £60,000, until 31 March 2024.

– Has received annual dividends of £18,000 for many years. This is currently his only source of taxable income.

Hagg Ltd rights issue:

– Laurie acquired 3,000 of the 30,000 shares in issue in Hagg Ltd in August 2018 for £60,000.

– On 31 January 2024 there was a 1 for 3 rights issue at £25 per share. The market value of the shares after the issue was £32.

– Laurie did not take up the rights issue, but instead sold his rights nil paid on 4 February 2024 for £20,000.

MT Travel – VAT:

– MT Travel is registered for the purposes of VAT.

– MT Travel currently buys standard-rated marketing services from a UK supplier, who is VAT registered.

– MT Travel can buy the same services from a supplier located in an overseas country where the rate of VAT is 12%.

Required:

(a) (i) Calculate the allowable trading loss available to each of Meg and Laurie for the tax year 2025/26 if Laurie becomes an employee or, alternatively, a partner in MT Travel on 1 April 2025. (3 marks)

(ii) Advise Meg and Laurie of the alternative ways in which their respective trading losses as calculated in (a)(i) could be used depending on whether Laurie is taken on as an employee or as a partner, and state the rate at which income tax would be saved in each case. (8 marks)

(b) Explain, with supporting calculations, the capital gains tax implications for Laurie of the sale of rights nil paid. (5 marks)

(c) Explain the value added tax (VAT) effect of MT Travel purchasing the services from the overseas supplier, rather than the UK supplier. (4 marks)

Professional marks will be awarded for the demonstration of skill in analysis and evaluation, scepticism and commercial acumen in your answer. (5 marks)

(Total: 25 marks)

30 ROD (ADAPTED)

Answer debrief

You should assume that today's date is 1 June 2024.

Rod has requested advice in relation to:

- the capital gains tax implications of selling shares he obtained through his employer's enterprise management incentive (EMI) scheme, and
- the potential income tax relief available in respect of his share of a trading loss of a partnership which he has recently joined.

Rod:

- Is resident and domiciled in the UK.
- Was employed for many years by Lumba plc, before taking early retirement on 30 June 2023.
- Joined the Thora Partnership on 1 December 2023.
- Made no disposals for capital gains tax in the tax year 2023/24, other than the sale of his shares in Lumba plc (as detailed below).

Sale of Lumba plc shares:

- In May 2019, Lumba plc granted Rod options to purchase 20,000 shares under its EMI scheme.
- The market value of a share at the date of the grant was £2.60 and the option price was £2.30 per share.
- Rod exercised all of the options on 1 June 2023, when the market value was £3.90 per share.
- Rod sold all the shares on 1 December 2023, when the market value was £4.00 per share.
- The gain is eligible for business asset disposal relief.

The Thora Partnership:

- Has been carried on for many years by two partners, Abe and Bob.
- Prepares accounts to 31 March annually.
- Admitted Rod into the partnership on 1 December 2023.
- Made a tax-adjusted trading loss of £47,000 in the year ended 31 March 2024.
- Is forecast to make a tax adjusted trading loss of £50,000 in the year ending 31 March 2025.

The Thora Partnership – profit/loss sharing arrangements:

- Before admitting Rod as a partner, Abe and Bob split the partnership profits/losses equally.
- The partnership's profit/loss sharing arrangements from 1 December 2023 are as follows:

	Abe	**Bob**	**Rod**
Annual salary	£20,000	£20,000	£0
Profit/loss sharing ratio	1	1	1

Rod's income in the tax years 2020/21 to 2023/24:

Tax year	**Employment income**	**Dividends**
	£	£
2020/21	82,000	0
2021/22	90,000	16,000
2022/23	86,000	12,000
2023/24	26,000	8,000

Required:

You should assume that today's date is 1 June 2024

(a) **Calculate Rod's after-tax proceeds from the sale of his shares in Lumba plc and explain your calculation of the base cost for the shares. (6 marks)**

(b) **(i)** **Calculate Rod's share of the tax-adjusted trading loss in the Thora Partnership for the years ended 31 March 2024 and 31 March 2025. (5 marks)**

(ii) **State how Rod is able to relieve the trading losses calculated in (b)(i) above as early as possible, and explain, with supporting calculations, the total amount of income tax saved if Rod follows this strategy. (9 marks)**

Professional marks will be awarded for the demonstration of skill in analysis and evaluation and commercial acumen in your answer. (5 marks)

(Total: 25 marks)

Calculate your allowed time, allocate the time to the separate parts..............

31 TOMAS AND INES (ADAPTED)

You should assume that today's date is 1 May 2024.

Tomas and his wife, Ines, require advice in connection with the following:

– the tax implications of commencing to trade,

– voluntary registration for value added tax (VAT) purposes and the implications of purchasing services from overseas, and

– the tax implications of selling shares in respect of which enterprise investment scheme (EIS) relief has been obtained.

Tomas:

– Is UK resident and domiciled.

– Uses his capital gains tax (CGT) annual exempt amount every year.

– Receives dividends of £1,000 every year.

Tomas – sale of sporting memorabilia:

– Tomas started selling items of sporting memorabilia from his collection during the tax year 2023/24.

– HM Revenue and Customs (HMRC) agreed that these sales should be subject to CGT in the tax year 2023/24.

– In April 2024, Tomas started purchasing and selling more items of sporting memorabilia.

– Most of the items have been owned for around two weeks before being sold.

– Some of the items Tomas purchased were in a poor state of repair, so he has been restoring them before selling them on.

– Tomas will not be required to register for value added tax (VAT) for the foreseeable future.

– Tomas will, however, consider registering voluntarily for VAT if it is financially beneficial for him to do so.

– Tomas will obtain advice on how to develop his business through the use of social media, and has been recommended a company based overseas (in a country where the rate of VAT is 9%) to complete this work.

Tomas – expected trading results from the sale of sporting memorabilia:

– Tomas estimates that his total income less expenditure for the 12 months ending 31 March 2025 will be £14,000.

– Each item of memorabilia is purchased and sold for no more than £1,000.

– All of the costs he incurs are deductible for tax purposes.

– Tomas expects his profits to increase steadily after 1 April 2025.

Ines:

– Is UK resident and domiciled.

– Is a higher rate taxpayer.

– Has made/will make no disposals for CGT purposes, other than as described below.

Ines – sale of painting:

– Ines sold a painting on 4 July 2021 for proceeds of £196,000.

– The sale gave rise to a gain of £86,000.

Ines – acquisition of shares in Tavira Ltd:

– Ines subscribed £72,000 for 20,000 shares in Tavira Ltd on 8 October 2021.

– These shares are qualifying enterprise investment scheme (EIS) shares.

– Ines elected to defer the maximum possible amount of the gain on the sale of the painting against the acquisition of these shares.

– Ines obtained EIS relief of £18,600 against her income tax liability for the tax year 2021/22.

– Ines intends to sell all of the shares in Tavira Ltd for £95,000 on 1 June 2024.

– If undertaken, this sale would qualify for business asset disposal relief.

Required:

You should assume that today's date is 1 May 2024

(a) (i) Explain, with supporting calculations, the difference in the total amount of tax payable by Tomas for the tax year 2024/25 as a result of the profit on the sales of sporting memorabilia being treated as trading income, rather than chargeable gains.

(ii) State TWO reasons why HMRC might deem that Tomas is trading for the tax year 2024/25 rather than carrying out capital transactions. (7 marks)

(b) (i) Explain TWO matters which Tomas should consider in deciding whether or not it will be financially beneficial to voluntarily register for value added tax (VAT).

(ii) Assuming Tomas DOES voluntarily register for VAT, explain the implications of purchasing advice from the overseas supplier, rather than using one based in the UK. (6 marks)

(c) Explain the tax implications for Ines of her intended sale of the Tavira Ltd shares on 1 June 2024, and calculate her after-tax proceeds from this sale. (7 marks)

Professional marks will be awarded for the demonstration of skill in analysis and evaluation and commercial acumen in your answer. (5 marks)

(Total: 25 marks)

32 YAQUI (ADAPTED)

You should assume that today's date is 1 September 2024.

Yaqui has requested advice on the following:

– the income tax and capital gains tax (CGT) implications of selling two assets following the cessation of an unincorporated business, and

– the value added tax (VAT) consequences of either selling or renting out a warehouse.

Yaqui:

– Is a higher rate taxpayer for all relevant tax years.

– Is registered for value added tax (VAT) purposes.

- Will cease trading as YP Trading on 30 September 2024.
- Will not be required to deregister for the purposes of VAT on the cessation of YP Trading as he will continue to run an existing, second, unincorporated business.

YP Trading:

- Accounts have been prepared to 30 June each year up to 30 June 2024, and the final accounts will be prepared for the three-month period to 30 September 2024.
- The business makes wholly standard rated supplies.

YP Trading – trading results:

- The budgeted tax adjusted trading profit for the three months ending 30 September 2024 is £10,000. This is BEFORE any adjustments in respect of the capital assets held on 1 July 2024.

YP Trading – capital assets:

- On 1 July 2024, these comprised a specialist fixed machine and a warehouse.
- On 1 July 2024, the brought forward written down value on the capital allowances main pool was £Nil.
- Yaqui has always claimed all available capital allowances.

Acquisition and sale of the specialist fixed machine:

- Yaqui acquired the machine on 31 March 2014 for £65,000.
- Rollover relief was claimed on this purchase to defer a chargeable gain of £11,000.
- Yaqui sold the machine on 10 July 2024 for £23,000.

Acquisition of the warehouse:

- Yaqui purchased the newly constructed warehouse from the builder on 1 October 2022 and started to use it in his business on 1 November 2022.
- The warehouse qualifies for structures and buildings allowances (SBA).
- The warehouse will continue to be wholly used in the YP Trading business until 30 September 2024.
- The warehouse cost £263,000 (exclusive of VAT) including £48,000 for the land.
- Yaqui has not opted to tax this building for VAT purposes and will not do so in the future.
- The warehouse is subject to the capital goods scheme for the purposes of VAT.

Sale of the warehouse:

- Yaqui is planning to sell the warehouse on 30 September 2024.
- The sale proceeds would be £296,000 (exclusive of VAT), which would include £55,000 for the land.

Required:

You should assume that today's date is 1 September 2024.

(a) **Explain the income tax adjustments required to the trading profit for the three-month period ending 30 September 2024 in respect of the disposal of the specialist fixed machine and the planned disposal of the warehouse. Calculate the revised adjusted trading profit.**

Note: Ignore value added tax (VAT) for this part of the question. **(4 marks)**

(b) **(i)** **Explain the capital gains tax implications for Yaqui of selling the specialist fixed machine on 10 July 2024. Your answer should include an explanation of the tax treatment of the chargeable gain of £11,000 which was deferred on the acquisition of this machine.**

Note: Ignore VAT for this part of the question.

(ii) **Explain whether or not business asset disposal relief (BADR) would be available to Yaqui if he sells the warehouse on 30 September 2024 as planned, and calculate the chargeable gain which would arise.** **(10 marks)**

(c) **Explain the VAT capital goods scheme consequences for Yaqui if:**

(i) **he sells the warehouse as planned on 30 September 2024; or, alternatively**

(ii) **he starts to rent out the warehouse to unconnected tenants from 1 October 2024.** **(6 marks)**

For guidance, part (i) is worth two marks and part (ii) is worth four marks.

Professional marks will be awarded for the demonstration of skill in analysis and evaluation and commercial acumen in your answer. **(5 marks)**

(Total: 25 marks)

CHANGING BUSINESS SCENARIOS

33 DESIREE (ADAPTED) *Walk in the footsteps of a top tutor*

You should assume that today's date is 1 June 2024.

Desiree requires advice on the following matters:

– the tax relief available for research and development expenditure,

– whether she should run her new business as an unincorporated sole trader or via a company, and

– the financial implications of registering voluntarily for value added tax (VAT).

Desiree:

– Resigned from her job with Chip plc on 30 April 2024.

– Had been employed by Chip plc on an annual salary of £90,000 since January 2021.

– Has no other income apart from bank interest of £1,000 per year.

– Intends to start a new business, to be called Duchess, on 1 September 2024.

The Duchess business:

– The business will sell pharmaceuticals.

– Market research consultants have estimated that 80% of its sales will be to commercial customers.

– The market research consultants were paid fees by Desiree in November 2023 and March 2024.

Budgeted results of the Duchess business:

– The budgeted tax-adjusted trading profit/(loss) for the first three trading periods is:

	£
Seven months ending 31 March 2025	(16,000)
Year ending 31 March 2026	22,000
Year ending 31 March 2027	44,000

– The fees paid to the market research consultants have been deducted in arriving at the loss of the first period.

– Research and development costs have not been deducted from these figures.

Duchess business research and development:

– Desiree would like to develop a revolutionary new drug to sell through the business.

– The projected costs for the seven-month period ending 31 March 2025 are as follows:

	£
Rent of laboratory	15,000
Water and electricity	3,000
Wages for Duchess employees working on research	13,000
Consumables	2,000
	33,000

Desiree's financial position:

– Desiree has not yet decided whether to run the business as an unincorporated sole trader or via a company.

– Her primary objective when deciding whether or not to operate the business via a company is the most beneficial use of the trading loss.

Registration for VAT:

– The turnover of the business is expected to exceed the VAT registration limit in January 2025.

– Desiree would consider registering for VAT earlier if it were financially advantageous to do so.

– Desiree will import some of her products from overseas, but is unsure of the VAT treatment.

Required:

You should assume that today's date is 1 June 2024

(a) (i) Explain, with supporting calculations, the tax relief available for the research and development expenditure for the following alternative structures:

- **the business is unincorporated**
- **the business is operated via a company.**

You should ignore use of the trading loss for this part of the question.

(3 marks)

(ii) Provide Desiree with a thorough and detailed explanation of the manner in which the budgeted trading loss could be used depending on whether she runs the business as an unincorporated sole trader or via a company and state which business structure would best satisfy her primary objective.

You are not required to prepare detailed calculations for part (ii) of this part of this question or to consider non-taxation issues. (10 marks)

(b) Explain in detail the financial advantages and disadvantages of Desiree registering voluntarily for VAT on 1 September 2024 and the VAT consequences of the imports, assuming she is VAT registered. (7 marks)

Professional marks will be awarded for the demonstration of skill in analysis and evaluation and commercial acumen in your answer. (5 marks)

(Total: 25 marks)

34 ENID (ADAPTED)

You should assume that today's date is 1 September 2024.

Enid requires advice on:

– the capital gains tax (CGT) and value added tax (VAT) implications of transferring her unincorporated sole trader business to a newly incorporated company, Niche Ltd, and

– the tax implications of alternative ways of extracting profits from the new company.

Enid:

– Has been in business as an unincorporated sole trader for many years.

– Receives dividends from a portfolio of investments of £500 each year.

– Has no other source of income.

– Is a higher rate taxpayer for all relevant tax years.

– Will transfer all the assets and liabilities of her business to Niche Ltd on 1 October 2024.

– Will make no other disposals for CGT purposes in the tax year 2024/25.

– Will be the only director and shareholder of Niche Ltd.

Enid's unincorporated business:

– At 1 October 2023 Enid had trading losses brought forward of £51,000.

– In the year ending 30 September 2024, Enid's business will have a taxable trading profit of £42,000, prior to the transfer to Niche Ltd.

– Is registered for the purposes of value added tax (VAT).

The assets and liabilities to be transferred to Niche Ltd:

	Cost	**Value at 1 October 2024**
	£	£
Goodwill	0	100,000
Workshop	55,000	122,000
Inventory	8,000	8,000
Liabilities	n/a	(10,000)

Consideration to be paid by Niche Ltd:

- 1,000 £1 ordinary shares in respect of 85% of the total value of the consideration for the business.
- The remainder of the consideration will be left on loan account payable by Niche Ltd to Enid.
- Enid will withdraw cash from the loan account to pay any CGT liability arising on the transfer of the business.

Niche Ltd:

- Will pay Enid a salary of £75,000 per year, and dividends of £15,000 on 31 March each year.
- Will not be regarded as a personal service company under the provisions of the IR35 legislation.
- Will have taxable total profits of approximately £200,000 each year.
- Will not receive any dividends.

Required:

You should assume that today's date is 1 September 2024

(a) **Explain how Enid can obtain relief for the trading losses of £51,000 brought forward in her unincorporated business at 6 April 2024.** **(4 marks)**

(b) **Explain why the transfer of Enid's business to Niche Ltd qualifies for incorporation relief, and, on the assumption that Enid does not elect to disapply this relief, calculate the balance on her loan account with Niche Ltd after deducting the cash to be withdrawn to pay any capital gains tax (CGT) due.** **(7 marks)**

(c) **Advise Enid of the impact on the total amount of tax payable by both herself and Niche Ltd if, instead of a dividend of £15,000, she (1) receives additional salary of £15,000, or alternatively (2) withdraws £15,000 from her loan account in the tax year 2025/26.**

Note: You should assume that there will be sufficient funds in Enid's loan account to permit this withdrawal. **(6 marks)**

(d) Advise Enid of her administrative obligations under the value added tax (VAT) legislation, arising from the transfer of her business to Niche Ltd, and whether or not she is able to transfer the VAT registration from her unincorporated business to Niche Ltd.

Note: You should assume that the transfer of a going concern rules will apply for VAT purposes, but are NOT required to discuss these rules. **(3 marks)**

Professional marks will be awarded for the demonstration of skill in analysis and evaluation, scepticism and commercial acumen in your answer. (5 marks)

(Total: 25 marks)

35 ROSA (ADAPTED)

You should assume that today's date is 1 December 2024.

Your client, Rosa, has requested advice in relation to:

– the consequences of her daughter, Siena, becoming either an employee or a partner in her unincorporated business,

– the options available to her to relieve a trading loss incurred by the business, and

– the value added tax (VAT) implications of selling a retail unit.

Rosa:

– Is 62 years old and is widowed.

– Has one daughter, Siena.

– Owns an unincorporated business, RS Trading, which she has run for many years.

– Currently has no employees in her business.

– Will bring her daughter, Siena, into the business either as an employee or a partner, on 1 April 2025.

– Has a budgeted income tax liability of £22,232, and a budgeted capital gains tax liability of £24,080 for the tax year 2024/25.

Siena:

– Will have no source of taxable income in the tax year 2025/26, other than from RS Trading.

RS Trading:

– Has an accounting date of 31 March each year.

– Has a budgeted tax adjusted trading profit of £27,000 for the year ending 31 March 2025.

– Has a budgeted trading loss of £62,000, before any payment to Siena, for the year ending 31 March 2026.

– Is registered for VAT and makes only standard-rated supplies.

RS Trading – future plans:

– Siena will become either an employee or a partner in RS Trading on 1 April 2025.

– If Siena becomes an employee, she will receive an annual salary of £22,000 which is a commercial rate for the duties she will perform.

– Alternatively, if Siena becomes a partner, the profit-sharing arrangements from 1 April 2025 will be:

	Rosa	**Siena**
Annual salary	£0	£12,000
Profit sharing ratio	80%	20%

Rosa – investment properties:

– Rosa will receive net rental income of £60,000 from a portfolio of residential properties and a retail unit in the tax year 2024/25.

– Rosa sold all the residential properties on 30 November 2024, realising total chargeable gains of £92,000.

Disposal of the retail unit:

– Rosa will sell the retail unit, which is currently being rented to tenants up to 5 April 2025, for its market value of £280,000 on 6 April 2025.

– Rosa had bought the retail unit when it was newly constructed, on 1 May 2018, for £290,000 plus VAT at 20%.

– Rosa used the retail unit in her business until 30 April 2022, since when she has let it to unconnected tenants.

– The retail unit is subject to the capital goods scheme for VAT.

– Rosa has not opted to tax the retail unit for VAT purposes.

Required:

You should assume that today's date is 1 December 2024

(a) Advise Rosa of the difference in the total amount of income tax and national insurance contributions (NICs) payable by her and Siena for the tax year 2025/26, if Siena is taken on as (i) a partner, or (ii) an employee by RS Trading on 1 April 2025. **(9 marks)**

(b) Assuming Siena is employed by RS Trading from 1 April 2025, identify and explain the relief(s) available to Rosa to relieve her trading loss of the year ending 31 March 2026, and calculate the maximum tax saving available to her as a result of claiming such relief(s) in the tax year 2024/25.

Note: You should NOT consider the possibility of Rosa carrying all, or any part, of the loss forward for relief for part (b). **(7 marks)**

(c) Explain the value added tax (VAT) implications of the disposal of the retail unit on 6 April 2025, and calculate the final VAT adjustment under the capital goods scheme. **(4 marks)**

Professional marks will be awarded for the demonstration of skill in analysis and evaluation and commercial acumen in your answer. **(5 marks)**

(Total: 25 marks)

36 SABIN AND PATAN LTD (ADAPTED)

You should assume that today's date is 1 September 2024.

Sabin, an individual, ceased to trade on 31 March 2024. Sabin subsequently sold his business premises and a specialist piece of machinery to Patan Ltd, an unconnected company, on 1 April 2024.

Advice is required on:

– the tax implications for Sabin of ceasing his loss-making unincorporated business and selling his business assets, and

– the corporation tax relief available to Patan Ltd for capital expenditure and expenditure related to its research and development activities.

Sabin:

– Has income from his business (see below), and from part-time employment (£6,000 gross per year).

– Uses his annual exempt amount for capital gains tax purposes every year.

Sabin's unincorporated business:

– Sabin commenced in business as a sole trader on 1 July 2015.

– Tax-adjusted trading profits/(losses) of the business were as follows:

Year ended 31 March 2021	Year ended 31 March 2022	Year ended 31 March 2023	Year ended 31 March 2024
£	£	£	£
44,000	32,000	21,000	(23,000)

– The terminal loss for the final 12 months of trade was £23,000.

Sabin – sale of business premises and specialist machinery to Patan Ltd on 1 April 2024:

	Date of acquisition	Cost	Sale proceeds (cash)
		£	£
Business premises	1 July 2015	86,000	114,000
Specialist machine	1 May 2020	49,000	41,000

– The business premises had been wholly occupied by Sabin's business throughout his period of ownership.

– Sabin had claimed capital allowances on the specialist machine.

Patan Ltd:

– Was incorporated and commenced trading on 1 April 2024.

– Expects to make a tax-adjusted trading loss in the year ending 31 March 2025.

– Has no other source of income or gains in this accounting period.

– Is a small or medium-sized enterprise for the purposes of research and development expenditure.

Patan Ltd – capital acquisitions and disposals:

– Patan Ltd purchased a newly-constructed factory building from a developer on 1 April 2024.

– Patan Ltd paid £142,000 for the factory, which included £56,000 for the land.

– The factory was brought into use on 1 May 2024.

Patan Ltd – expenditure on research and development activities:

– One of Patan Ltd's employees is wholly engaged in qualifying research and development activities at an annual cost to the company of £40,000.

– Patan Ltd also engages external subcontractors, provided by unconnected companies. The total cost of these will be £22,000 in the year ending 31 March 2025.

Required:

You should assume that today's date is 1 September 2024

(a) Calculate, with supporting explanations, the income tax saving for Sabin if he claims terminal loss relief ONLY for the trading loss arising in his final trading period. (7 marks)

(b) Explain the capital gains tax (CGT) implications for Sabin arising from the sale of the business premises and the specialist machine to Patan Ltd, and calculate the amount available to Sabin from the sale of these assets, after paying any CGT liability. (6 marks)

(c) Explain the tax deductions and reliefs available to Patan Ltd in the year ending 31 March 2025 in respect of (1) the acquisition of the new factory, and (2) the expenditure on research and development. (7 marks)

Professional marks will be awarded for the demonstration of skill in analysis and evaluation and commercial acumen in your answer. (5 marks)

(Total: 25 marks)

CAPITAL TAXES

37 JOAN ARK

You should assume that today's date is 1 April 2024.

Joan Ark, aged 76, has asked for your advice regarding the following gifts that she has made during the tax year 2023/24.

(a) On 13 July 2023, Joan made a gift of 250,000 ordinary shares in Orleans plc, a quoted company into a discretionary trust for the benefit of her granddaughters.

On that day, the shares were quoted at 146p – 150p, with recorded bargains of 140p, 144p, 149p and 155p.

Joan originally purchased 200,000 shares in Orleans plc during 2008 at a cost of £149,000. Joan also bought 75,000 shares on 15 August 2021 for £69,375 and has subsequently bought 10,000 shares on 21 July 2022 for £14,800.

Orleans plc has an issued share capital of 10 million ordinary shares and Joan has never been a director or employee of the company.

(b) On 15 July 2023, Joan gave 20,000 of her 40,000 ordinary shares in Rouen Ltd, an unquoted trading company, to her son Michael. Rouen Ltd has an issued share capital of 100,000 ordinary shares. Joan's husband also owns 40,000 ordinary shares in the company.

On 15 July 2023, the relevant values of Rouen Ltd's shares were as follows:

Shareholding	Value per share
	£
100%	22.30
80%	17.10
60%	14.50
40%	9.20
20%	7.90

Joan purchased her 40,000 shares in Rouen Ltd during 2010 for £96,400. Her husband works for the company but Joan does not.

(c) On 4 November 2023, Joan gave her grandson an antique vase worth £18,500 as a wedding present. Joan purchased the vase during 2008 for £14,150.

(d) On 15 January 2024, Joan gave agricultural land with an agricultural value of £175,000 to her son Charles. Joan had purchased the land during 2012 for £92,000, and it has always been let out to tenant farmers.

The most recent tenancy agreement, which started in June 2014, will soon end, and Joan has obtained planning permission to build residential accommodation on the land. The value of the land with planning permission is £300,000.

Charles owns adjoining agricultural land, and the value of this land will increase from £210,000 to £250,000 as a result of the gift.

(e) On 31 March 2024, Joan made a gift of her main residence in Wales valued at £265,000 to her daughter Catherine. However, as a condition of the gift, Joan has continued to live in the house rent free.

The house was purchased on 1 July 2002 for £67,000, and Joan occupied it as her main residence until 31 December 2006. The house was unoccupied between 1 January 2007 and 31 December 2010, and it was rented out as furnished accommodation between 1 January 2011 and 30 June 2023.

Since 1 July 2023, Joan has again occupied the house as her main residence.

Joan has not previously made any lifetime transfers of assets. She is to pay any IHT liabilities arising from the above gifts.

Required:

You should assume that today's date is 1 April 2024

(i) Advise Joan of the IHT and CGT implications arising from the gifts made during the tax year 2023/24.

Your answer should be supported by appropriate calculations, and should include an explanation of any reliefs that are available.

You should ignore the instalment option and the effect of the annual exemption for IHT purposes and the annual exempt amount for CGT purposes.

Marks for this part of the question will be allocated on the basis of:

5 marks to (a), 5 marks to (b), 3 marks to (c), 5 marks to (d), 6 marks to (e)

(24 marks)

(ii) Explain the main advantages of an individual making lifetime gifts for IHT purposes and the main factors to be considered in choosing which assets to gift. (6 marks)

Joan is a higher rate taxpayer for income tax purposes.

(Total: 30 marks)

38 ALEX (ADAPTED)

You should assume that today's date is 1 March 2024.

Alex, a widower, died on 5 February 2024. His will leaves £150,000 to charity and the remainder of his assets split in equal shares to his son, Brian and his daughter, Beatrice, who support his decision to benefit charitable causes.

The assets comprised in Alex's estate were as follows:

	Market value 5 February 2024
	£
Main residence	575,000
Building society account	15,000
NS&I investment account	55,000
NS&I savings certificates	180,000
Various chattels	40,000
Shares in Touriga Ltd	Note 1
Shares in Nacional plc	Note 2
Other quoted investments	115,000

Notes

1 Touriga Ltd is an unquoted trading company. Alex bought his 2,450 ordinary shares (representing 35% of the issued shares) in September 2021 for £8.50 per share. The shares were worth £11.00 per share at the time of his death.

2 Nacional plc is a quoted company in which Alex held 20,000 shares (representing less than 1% of the issued shares) at the time of his death. On 5 February 2024, the shares were listed ex div at 624p – 632p with marked bargains at 625p, 629p and 630p. A dividend of 18 pence per share was declared on 5 December 2023, and was received on 11 February 2024 by the executors.

Alex had made two lifetime gifts. The first was a villa in Spain. This was given to Brian in July 2018. The value at that time was £338,000. In addition, Alex settled an equal amount on a relevant property trust in March 2019. Alex agreed to pay any tax due on the gifts.

Prior to his death, Alex had the following income in the tax year 2023/24:

	£
Pension (gross – PAYE deducted at source £2,120)	10,600
Building society interest	1,600
NS&I investment account interest	870
Dividends (other than from Nacional plc (Note 2 above))	9,000

Brian, Alex's son, is aged 58, is in poor health, and is not expected to live more than a few years. His wife died ten years ago, since when he has lived alone. He owns a house, currently worth £400,000 with an £80,000 mortgage outstanding and has other assets in the form of cash investments worth £80,000, and personal belongings worth £50,000.

Consequently, Brian has no need of his inheritance from Alex and so intends to gift his share of his father's estate to his two children, Colin and Charlotte, in equal shares.

Colin, who is 20, is in his second year at university, but Brian is worried that his son will spend all of the money at once. Charlotte, who is 17, is still at school but is likely to go to university in the near future.

Again, Brian worries about the money being spent unwisely, and therefore wishes to use some form of trust to control the capital sums gifted to both his children. Brian has made no lifetime gifts to date.

Required:

You should assume that today's date is 1 March 2024

(a) Calculate the income tax (IT) payable/repayable for Alex for the tax year 2023/24. (6 marks)

(b) Explain, with supporting calculations, the inheritance tax (IHT) implications (including any additional tax due on his lifetime gifts) arising on the death of Alex, and quantify the inheritance (after tax) due to Brian and Beatrice.

Assume that Alex's wife utilised all of her nil rate bands when she died. (16 marks)

(c) (i) Explain how Brian could use a trust to maintain control of the capital he intends to gift to Colin and Charlotte following Alex's death and the inheritance tax (IHT) treatment of the trust. (5 marks)

(ii) State, giving reasons, what other inheritance tax (IHT) planning advice you would offer Brian with regard to setting up a trust for Colin and Charlotte with the assets he has inherited. (3 marks)

(Total: 30 marks)

39 KEPLER (ADAPTED)

You should assume that today's date is 1 June 2024.

Galileo is Kepler's nephew and is currently resident in the country of Astronomeria. He requires advice in respect of:

– the inheritance tax payable as a result of Kepler's death,

– the capital gains tax implications of a sale of paintings located overseas, and

– the income tax implications of the provision of employment benefits on his relocation to the UK.

Kepler:

– Died on 1 May 2024.

– Was UK resident and domiciled.

– Has two nephews; Galileo and Herschel.

– Gave his nephew, Galileo, 600 shares (a 30% holding) in Messier Ltd on 1 June 2020.

– In his will he left 1,400 shares in Messier Ltd valued at £546,000 to Galileo and the residue of his estate valued at £480,000 to Herschel.

Kepler – Lifetime gifts:

–	1 February 2019	Gave a house to Herschel valued at £311,000.
–	1 July 2019	Gave a watch costing £900 to each of his two nephews.
–	1 June 2020	Gave 600 shares in Messier Ltd to Galileo.

Messier Ltd:

- Unquoted company that transports building materials.
- Incorporated in the UK on 1 February 2011 when Kepler subscribed for 2,000 shares, the whole of its share capital.

Messier Ltd – Value of an ordinary share:

– As at	1 June 2020	1 May 2024
	£	£
As part of a 100% holding	485	570
As part of a 70% holding	310	390
As part of a 30% holding	230	260

Messier Ltd – Asset values:

– As at 1 June 2020	£
Premises	900,000
Surplus land rented to third party	480,000
Vehicles	100,000
Current assets	50,000

Galileo:

- Resident and domiciled in the country of Astronomeria where he has lived since birth.
- Lives in rented accommodation in Astronomeria.
- Intends to move to the UK from the country of Astronomeria to participate in the management of Messier Ltd.
- Will sell two paintings in order to provide funds to go towards the cost of relocating to the UK and purchasing a house here.
- Has a full-time employment contract with Messier Ltd commencing on 1 September 2024.
- Intends to stay in the UK for at least five years.

The two paintings:

- Are situated in Astronomeria and are worth approximately £20,000 each.
- Have been owned by Galileo since 1 May 2009; their cost is negligible and can be ignored.

Employment contract with Messier Ltd:

- Galileo will be paid an annual salary of £52,000.
- Messier Ltd will assist Galileo with the cost of relocating to the UK.

Required:

You should assume that today's date is 1 June 2024

(a) (i) Calculate the inheritance tax payable (if any) by Galileo in respect of:

1 the gift of shares in June 2020, and

2 the inheritance of shares in May 2024. (8 marks)

(ii) Explain why Galileo is able to pay the inheritance tax due in instalments, state when the instalments are due and identify any further issues relevant to Galileo relating to the payments. (3 marks)

(b) Prepare a reasoned explanation of how any capital gains tax arising in the UK on the sale of the paintings can be minimised. (2 marks)

(c) (i) Explain how Messier Ltd can assist Galileo with the cost of relocating to the UK and/or provide him with interest-free loan finance for this purpose without increasing his UK income tax liability. (4 marks)

(ii) State, with reasons, whether Messier Ltd can provide Galileo with accommodation in the UK without giving rise to a UK income tax liability. (3 marks)

Professional marks will be awarded for the demonstration of skill in analysis and evaluation and commercial acumen in your answer. (5 marks)

(Total: 25 marks)

40 ASH (ADAPTED) *Walk in the footsteps of a top tutor*

You should assume that today's date is 1 December 2024.

Ash requires advice in respect of:

– the availability of business asset disposal relief in respect of the assignment of a lease, and the potential capital gains tax liability,

– the requirement for his partnership to register for value added tax (VAT), and

– the reduction of his income tax payments on account.

Ash:

– Is resident in the UK.

– Had taxable income of £29,000 in the tax year 2023/24.

– Was the owner and managing director of Lava Ltd until 1 May 2023, when he resigned and sold the company.

– Is a partner in the Vulcan Partnership.

Ash – disposals of capital assets in the tax year 2023/24:

– The sale of the shares in Lava Ltd resulted in a capital gain of £235,000, which qualified for business asset disposal relief.

– Ash assigned a 37-year lease on a property for £110,000 on 1 May 2023.

– Ash sold two hectares of land on 1 October 2023 for £30,000.

– Ash sold quoted shares and made a capital loss of £16,500 on 1 November 2023.

The lease:

– The lease was previously assigned to Ash for £31,800 when it had 46 years remaining.

– The property has always been used by Lava Ltd for trading purposes.

– Lava Ltd paid Ash rent, equivalent to 40% of the market rate, in respect of the use of the property.

The sale of the two hectares of land:

– Ash purchased eight hectares of land for £27,400 on 1 June 2016.

– Ash sold six hectares of the land for £42,000 on 1 August 2019.

– The remaining two hectares of land were worth £18,000 on 1 August 2019.

Vulcan Partnership (Vulcan):

– Has a 31 March year end

– Has monthly turnover of:

Standard-rated supplies	£400
Exempt supplies	£100
Zero-rated supplies	£5,600

– Its turnover is expected to increase slightly in 2025.

– None of its customers are registered for the purposes of VAT.

– Ash expects to receive less profit from Vulcan for the tax year 2024/25 than he did in 2023/24.

Required:

You should assume that today's date is 1 December 2024

(a) **(i)** **State the conditions that must be satisfied for Ash's assignment of the lease to be an associated disposal for the purposes of business asset disposal relief.** **(3 marks)**

(ii) **Calculate Ash's capital gains tax liability for the tax year 2023/24 on the assumption that the assignment of the lease does qualify as an associated disposal and that business asset disposal relief will be claimed where possible.**

The following lease percentages should be used, where necessary.

37 years	**93.497**
46 years	**98.490**

(7 marks)

(b) **Discuss in detail whether the Vulcan Partnership may be required to register for value added tax (VAT) and the advantages and disadvantages for the business of registration.** **(7 marks)**

(c) **Set out the matters that Ash should consider when deciding whether or not to make a claim to reduce the payment on account of income tax due on 31 January 2025.** **(3 marks)**

Professional marks will be awarded for the demonstration of skill in analysis and evaluation, scepticism and commercial acumen in your answer. **(5 marks)**

(Total: 25 marks)

41 PESCARA (ADAPTED) *Walk in the footsteps of a top tutor*

You should assume that today's date is 1 December 2024.

Pescara requires advice on:

– the inheritance tax payable on death and on the gift of a property,

– the capital gains tax due on a disposal of shares, and

– the relief available in respect of the purchase of seed enterprise investment scheme shares.

Pescara and her parents:

– Pescara is a higher rate taxpayer who is resident and domiciled in the UK.

– Pescara's father, Galvez, died on 1 June 2008.

– Pescara's mother, Marina, died on 1 October 2024.

– Both Galvez and Marina were resident and domiciled in the UK.

Galvez – lifetime gifts and gifts on death:

– Galvez had not made any lifetime gifts.

– In his will, Galvez left cash of £80,000 to Pescara and a further £80,000 to Pescara's brother.

– Galvez left the remainder of his estate to his wife, Marina.

Marina – lifetime gifts and gifts on death:

– On 1 February 2019, Marina gave Pescara 375,000 shares in Sepang plc.

– Marina had made no other lifetime gifts.

Marina – gift of 375,000 shares in Sepang plc to Pescara:

–	1 January 2016	Marina purchased 375,000 shares for £420,000.
–	1 February 2017	Marina gave all of the shares to Pescara. The shares were quoted at £1.84 – £1.96 The highest and lowest marked bargains were £1.80 and £1.92.

– The shares did not qualify for business property relief or capital gains tax gift holdover relief.

– The inheritance tax nil rate band for the tax year 2008/09 was £312,000.

Acquisition of Sepang plc by Zolder plc and subsequent bonus issue:

–	1 January 2021	Zolder plc acquired the whole of the ordinary share capital of Sepang plc. Pescara received 30 pence and two ordinary shares in Zolder plc, worth £1 each, for each share in Sepang plc. The takeover was for genuine commercial reasons and not for the avoidance of tax.
–	1 July 2022	Zolder plc declared a 2 for 1 bonus issue.

Pescara's actual and intended capital transactions in the tax year 2024/25:

			£
15 November 2024	Sale	1,000,000 shares in Zolder plc	445,000
1 April 2025	Purchase	Qualifying seed enterprise investment scheme (SEIS) shares	90,000

Pescara – gift of a UK property:

– Pescara intends to give a UK property to her son on 1 October 2025.

– Pescara intends to continue to use this property, rent-free, such that this gift will be a gift with reservation.

Required:

You should assume that today's date is 1 December 2024

(a) Calculate the inheritance tax payable in respect of Marina's gift of the shares in Sepang plc, as a result of her death. (7 marks)

(b) (i) Calculate Pescara's capital gains tax liability for the tax year 2024/25 on the assumption that seed enterprise investment scheme (SEIS) relief is claimed in respect of the shares to be purchased on 1 April 2025 and that business asset disposal relief is not available. (6 marks)

(ii) State the capital gains tax implications of Pescara selling the SEIS shares at some point in the future. (3 marks)

(c) Explain how the proposed gift of the UK property will be treated for the purposes of calculating the inheritance tax due on Pescara's death. (4 marks)

Professional marks will be awarded for the demonstration of skill in analysis and evaluation, scepticism and commercial acumen in your answer. (5 marks)

(Total: 25 marks)

42 CADA (ADAPTED) *Walk in the footsteps of a top tutor*

You should assume that today's date is 1 December 2024.

Following the death of Cada, your firm has been asked to provide advice in respect of:

– the inheritance tax advantages of making lifetime gifts,

– the legacy to charity required in order to reduce the rate of inheritance tax on Cada's death,

– the capital gains tax and inheritance tax advantages of varying the terms of Cada's will, and

– capital gains tax planning in respect of Cada's shareholdings.

Cada and her family:

– Cada, who was UK domiciled, died on 20 November 2024.

– Cada is survived by two daughters: Raymer and Yang.

– Raymer has an adult son.

– Yang has no children.

Cada – Lifetime gifts and available nil rate band:

- Cada had not made any lifetime gifts since 30 November 2020.
- Cada's nil rate band available at the date of her death was £220,000.

Cada's death estate and the details of her will:

- Cada owned assets valued at £1,000,000 at the time of her death.
- Cada left her house, valued at £500,000, to Raymer.
- Cada left cash of £60,000 to a UK national charity.
- Cada left her remaining assets (including a portfolio of shares) valued at £440,000, to Yang.
- None of the remaining assets qualified for any inheritance tax reliefs.

Raymer:

- Is not an accountant, but has some knowledge of the UK tax system.
- Has made four observations regarding her mother's estate and her inheritance.

Raymer's four observations:

- 'My mother should have made additional gifts in her lifetime.'
- 'The tax rate on the chargeable estate should be less than 40% due to the gift to charity.'
- 'I do not intend to live in the house but will give it to my son on 1 July 2025.'
- 'My mother paid capital gains tax every year. However, when she died, some of her shareholdings had a value of less than cost.'

Cada's shareholdings at the time of her death:

- Quoted shares in JW plc valued at more than cost.
- Quoted shares in FR plc valued at less than cost.
- Unquoted shares in KZ Ltd valued at £Nil.

Required:

You should assume that today's date is 1 December 2024

(a) **Explain the inheritance tax advantages, other than lifetime exemptions, which could have been obtained if Cada had made additional lifetime gifts of quoted shares between 1 December 2020 and her death.** **(4 marks)**

(b) **Calculate the increase in the legacy to the charity which would be necessary in order for the reduced rate of inheritance tax to apply and quantify the reduction in the inheritance tax liability which would result.** **(5 marks)**

(c) **Explain the capital gains tax and inheritance tax advantages which could be obtained by varying the terms of Cada's will and set out the procedures required in order to achieve a tax effective variation.** **(6 marks)**

(d) **In relation to capital gains tax, explain what beneficial actions Cada could have carried out in the tax year of her death in respect of her shareholdings.** **(5 marks)**

Professional marks will be awarded for the demonstration of skill in analysis and evaluation and commercial acumen in your answer. **(5 marks)**

(Total: 25 marks)

43 ERIC (ADAPTED) *Walk in the footsteps of a top tutor*

You should assume that today's date is 1 March 2025.

Your client, Eric, and his son Zak require advice on:

- the capital gains tax implications arising from the receipt of insurance proceeds and the disposal of some shares,
- the inheritance tax reliefs available in respect of assets in Eric's estate at death, and
- the application of the personal service company (IR35) legislation to Zak.

Eric:

- Is UK resident and domiciled.
- Is a higher rate taxpayer.
- Is in ill health and is expected to die within the next few months.

Capital transactions in the tax year 2023/24:

- Eric made no disposals for capital gains tax purposes in the tax year 2023/24 other than those detailed below.
- Eric received insurance proceeds of £10,000 following damage to a valuable painting.
- Eric sold half of his shareholding in Malaga plc for £11.50 per share.

Damaged painting:

- Eric purchased the painting for £46,000 in July 2021.
- The painting was damaged in October 2023 such that immediately afterwards its value fell to £38,000.

  The insurance proceeds of £10,000 were received by Eric on 1 December 2023.
- Eric has not had the painting repaired.

Malaga plc shares:

- Malaga plc is a quoted trading company with 200,000 issued shares.
- 80% of Malaga plc's chargeable assets have always been chargeable business assets.
- Eric was given 12,000 shares in Malaga plc by his sister on 5 August 2020, when they were valued at £126,000.
- Eric's sister had purchased the shares for £96,000 on 1 March 2018.
- Gift holdover relief was claimed in respect of the gift of the shares to Eric on 5 August 2020.
- Eric paid the inheritance tax arising in respect of this gift following his sister's death on 1 September 2020.
- Eric has never worked for Malaga plc.
- Eric sold 6,000 shares in Malaga plc on 1 March 2024.

Assets owned by Eric and a previous lifetime gift:

– Eric owns farmland in the UK, which has been leased to a tenant farmer for the last ten years.

– The farmland has a market value of £420,000 and an agricultural value of £340,000.

– Eric's other assets, excluding the remaining Malaga plc shares, are valued at £408,000.

– Eric has made only one previous lifetime gift, of £60,000 cash to his son Zak on 1 July 2018.

Zak:

– Is the sole shareholder, director and employee of Yoyo Ltd, a company which provides consultancy services.

– In the year ended 31 March 2025, Yoyo Ltd's gross fee income from relevant engagements performed by Zak will be £110,000.

– All of the consultancy clients are small organisations for the purposes of the personal service company legislation.

– In the tax year 2024/25, Zak will draw a salary of £24,000 and dividends of £50,000 from Yoyo Ltd.

– Neither Yoyo Ltd nor Zak has any other source of income.

Required:

You should assume that today's date is 1 March 2025

(a) **Calculate Eric's total after-tax proceeds in respect of the two capital gains tax disposals in the tax year 2023/24.** **(6 marks)**

(b) **(i)** **On the assumption that Eric dies on 31 March 2025, advise on the availability and effect (if any), of agricultural property relief, business property relief and quick succession relief in respect of the farmland and the retained shares in Malaga plc.**

Note: You are not required to prepare calculations for this part of the question.

(6 marks)

(ii) **Explain, with the aid of calculations, the impact on the inheritance tax liability arising on Eric's death if Eric does not die until 1 August 2025.** **(3 marks)**

(c) **Calculate Zak's taxable income for the tax year 2024/25 if the personal service company (IR35) legislation were to apply to the fee income received by Yoyo Ltd.**

(5 marks)

Professional marks will be awarded for the demonstration of skill in analysis and evaluation and commercial acumen in your answer. **(5 marks)**

(Total: 25 marks)

44 LIBER (ADAPTED)

Answer debrief

You should assume that today's date is 1 September 2024.

Liber and his sister, Vesta, have requested advice on:

- the timing of the sale of shares acquired by Liber in a recent company takeover, and
- the capital gains tax and inheritance tax consequences of Vesta making a lifetime gift, rather than leaving an asset in her estate upon her death.

Liber:

- Is UK resident and domiciled.
- Has taxable income of £30,000 each year.

Liber – acquisition of ordinary shares in Mercury plc:

- Liber purchased 800 ordinary shares (a 40% holding) in Vulcan Ltd for £40,000 on 1 July 2019.
- Mercury plc acquired 100% of the ordinary share capital of Vulcan Ltd on 1 June 2024.
- In exchange for each ordinary share in Vulcan Ltd Liber received the following:
  - Four ordinary shares in Mercury plc valued at £20 per share immediately after the takeover, and
  - £15 cash.
- Mercury plc has 200,000 issued ordinary shares.
- Liber has never been a director or employee of either Vulcan Ltd or Mercury plc.
- The takeover was for *bona fide* commercial reasons and not for the avoidance of tax.

Liber – proposed transaction in Mercury plc shares:

- Liber now wishes to sell all of his shares in Mercury plc.
- He has received an offer from an unconnected person to purchase these shares on 1 January 2025 at a price of £28 per share.
- Liber would prefer to sell the shares to his nephew, Janus. However, this would delay the sale as his nephew will not have the necessary funds to purchase the shares until 1 May 2025.
- Janus has said he will also pay £28 per share.

Vesta:

- Is 66 years old and has never married or had a civil partner.
- Is in ill-health and is expected to die at some time within the tax year 2025/26.
- Has made no disposals for capital gains tax purposes in the tax year 2024/25 to date and will not make any in the tax year 2025/26.
- Has made one previous lifetime gift, of £350,000 cash, to her son, Janus, on 1 June 2024.

Vesta – investment property:

– Vesta owns an investment property, which has never been used as her private residence.

– The current market value of the property is less than the price Vesta paid for it, and its value is expected to fall further throughout the tax year 2025/26.

– Vesta is considering gifting the investment property to Janus in her lifetime, rather than leaving it to him in her estate on death.

– Janus is the sole beneficiary of Vesta's estate.

Required:

You should assume that today's date is 1 September 2024

(a) (i) Explain, with supporting calculations, the capital gains tax implications for Liber of the takeover of Vulcan Ltd by Mercury plc on 1 June 2024, and a subsequent sale of his Mercury plc shares on 1 January 2025. (8 marks)

(ii) Explain, with supporting calculations, why it would be beneficial for Liber to sell his Mercury plc shares on 1 May 2025, instead of on 1 January 2025. (4 marks)

(b) Advise Vesta whether or not there are any capital gains tax or inheritance tax advantages, for herself, or for Janus, if she were to gift the investment property to Janus on 31 December 2024, rather than leaving it to him in her estate on death. (8 marks)

Professional marks will be awarded for the demonstration of skill in analysis and evaluation and commercial acumen in your answer. (5 marks)

(Total: 25 marks)

Calculate your allowed time, allocate the time to the separate parts..............

45 ANYA

You should assume that today's date is 1 June 2024.

Anya requires advice on:

– the capital gains tax (CGT) and inheritance tax (IHT) implications of a gift of a painting,

– the CGT and IHT reliefs available on a gift of shares, and

– the impact on post-tax income of the gift of shares.

Anya:

– Is tax resident and domiciled in the UK.

– Has never been married, or in a civil partnership.

– Has one daughter, Cara, and two granddaughters, Flava and Violette, all of whom are tax resident and domiciled in the UK.

– Has made only one previous lifetime gift: on 31 March 2023, she gave Cara an investment property, valued at £390,000.

– You should assume that Anya will die on 6 September 2025.

Anya – proposed gifts:

– Anya is proposing to make the following gifts:
  – £50,000 cash to Flava on 1 July 2024.
  – A painting to Violette on 1 August 2024.
  – All of her ordinary shares in Chaski Ltd to Cara on 1 September 2024.

Proposed gift of painting:

– Anya purchased the painting on 8 July 2009 for £104,000.

– The value of the painting on 1 August 2024 will be £63,000.

Proposed gift of shares in Chaski Ltd:

– Anya acquired 100% of the ordinary shares in Chaski Ltd on 1 May 2010.

– Chaski Ltd is an unquoted trading company.

– The market values of the assets owned by Chaski Ltd at 1 September 2024 will be as follows:

	£
Land and buildings	853,000
Equipment (no item worth more than £6,000)	78,000
2% shareholding in RQ Ltd (held as an investment)	60,000
Inventory and cash	43,000
	1,034,000

Anya – income:

– Anya has gross annual taxable pension income of £65,000.

– Anya's only other source of income has been dividends from Chaski Ltd.

– Chaski Ltd paid a dividend of £40,000 in respect of its ordinary shares on 14 January 2024 and will pay a dividend of £34,000 on 13 January 2025.

Required:

You should assume that:

– **Today's date is 1 June 2024.**

– **Anya will die on 6 September 2025.**

(a) Explain the capital gains tax and inheritance tax (IHT) implications of the proposed gift of the painting to Violette on 1 August 2024. (6 marks)

(b) In relation to Anya's proposed gift of the Chaski Ltd shares to Cara on 1 September 2024:

(i) Advise on the availability to Anya of gift holdover relief, and any consequences for Cara of this relief being claimed. (5 marks)

(ii) Advise on the availability of business property relief in calculating the IHT liability on this gift as a result of Anya's death, and any additional conditions for Cara attaching to this relief. (4 marks)

(c) Calculate the reduction in Anya's post-tax income for the tax year 2024/25 as compared with the tax year 2023/24, on the assumption that she gifts all of her shares in Chaski Ltd to Cara as planned. (5 marks)

Professional marks will be awarded for the demonstration of skill in analysis and evaluation, commercial acumen and scepticism in your answer. (5 marks)

(Total: 25 marks)

MULTI TAX PERSONAL INCLUDING OVERSEAS

46 MIRTOON (ADAPTED) *Walk in the footsteps of a top tutor*

You should assume that today's date is 1 December 2024.

Mirtoon has requested advice on:

– disposals of assets and his departure from the UK,

– his liability to UK income tax and capital gains tax whilst he is living in the country of Koro, and

– reducing the potential inheritance tax liability on his death.

Mirtoon:

– Is 52 years old and divorced.

– Is self-employed.

– Has always been resident and domiciled in the UK.

Plans to move to Koro:

– Mirtoon intends to leave the UK in January 2025 in order to live in the country of Koro.

– He will continue to be UK domiciled whilst living in the country of Koro.

– He has entered into a full-time contract of employment for a fixed term of four years but he may stay in Koro for as long as ten years.

– He will buy a house in Koro and will not make any return trips to the UK whilst he is living in Koro.

Sale of house:

– Mirtoon plans to sell his house on 31 December 2024 for £730,000.

– He purchased the house for £540,000 on 1 July 2020 and has lived there ever since that date.

Sale of business assets:

– Mirtoon will cease trading on 31 December 2024.

– He will sell his business premises, a small office unit, for £120,000 on 31 December 2024.

– The office unit was purchased for £58,000 on 1 May 2015.

– Mirtoon will sell the remaining business assets, consisting of machinery and inventory, for £14,000, with no asset being sold for more than cost.

Agricultural land:

– In May 2020 Mirtoon's father gave him 230 hectares of agricultural land situated in the UK.

– A capital gain of £72,000 arose in respect of this gift and Mirtoon and his father submitted a joint claim for gift holdover relief.

– Mirtoon expects the value of the land to increase considerably in 2025 and he intends to sell it in June 2026.

Other information:

- Mirtoon does not own any buildings other than his home and his business premises.
- He will have a taxable trading profit of £5,000 in the tax year 2024/25.
- He receives bank interest in respect of UK bank deposits of £28,950 per year. He will continue to hold these bank deposits whilst living in the country of Koro.
- Mirtoon has not made any disposals for the purposes of capital gains tax in the tax year 2024/25.
- He has capital losses brought forward as at 5 April 2024 of £2,200.
- He has never made any claims in respect of business asset disposal relief.

Required:

You should assume that today's date is 1 December 2024

(a) Prepare calculations, with explanatory notes, to show the total of the following amounts:

- **The after-tax proceeds from the sale of Mirtoon's home and business assets.**
- **Any other tax liabilities arising as a result of Mirtoon's plans to leave the UK.**

Ignore income tax and national insurance contributions. (9 marks)

(b) Explain whether or not Mirtoon will be liable to UK income tax and capital gains tax whilst he is living in the country of Koro by reference to his residence and domicile status.

You should include specific reference to the capital gains tax implications of the proposed sale of the agricultural land in June 2026. Also comment on the implications of Mirtoon selling his UK home whilst he is in Koro rather than prior to his departure.

There is no double tax treaty between the UK and the country of Koro. (7 marks)

(c) Prepare a summary of the rules relating to gifts with reservation, to assist with discussions of inheritance tax with Mirtoon. (4 marks)

Professional marks will be awarded for the demonstration of skill in analysis and evaluation, scepticism and commercial acumen in your answer. (5 marks)

(Total: 25 marks)

47 SHUTTELLE (ADAPTED) *Walk in the footsteps of a top tutor*

You should assume that today's date is 1 May 2024.

Your firm has been asked to provide advice to Shuttelle and to three non-UK domiciled individuals in connection with:

– personal pension contributions, and

– the remittance basis of taxation for overseas income and gains.

Personal pension contributions:

– Shuttelle has been the production director of Din Ltd since 1 February 2011.

– Shuttelle joined a personal pension scheme on 6 April 2021.

Shuttelle's tax position for the tax year 2023/24:

– Shuttelle's only source of income is her remuneration from Din Ltd.

– Shuttelle's annual salary is £204,000. This is a substantial increase on the previous year.

– Shuttelle lived in a house owned by Din Ltd for a period of time during the tax year 2023/24.

The house provided by Din Ltd for Shuttelle's use:

– Was purchased by Din Ltd on 1 January 2011 for £500,000 and has an annual value of £7,000.

– Shuttelle lived in the house from 1 February 2011 until 30 June 2023.

– The house had a market value of £870,000 on 6 April 2023.

Contributions to Shuttelle's personal pension scheme:

– Shuttelle has made the following gross contributions:

  6 April 2021 – £9,000

  6 April 2022 – £38,000

  6 April 2023 – £120,000

– Din Ltd contributes £4,000 to the scheme in each tax year.

The remittance basis of taxation:

– Advice is to be provided to three non-UK domiciled individuals.

– Each of the three individuals is more than 18 years old.

Details of the three individuals:

Name	**Lin**	**Nan**	**Yu**
Tax year in which the individual became UK resident	2013/14	2008/09	2013/14
Tax year in which the individual ceased to be UK resident	Still resident	2021/22	Still resident
Overseas income and gains for the tax year 2023/24	£39,200	£68,300	£130,700
Overseas income and gains remitted to the UK for the tax year 2023/24	£38,500	0	£1,400

Required:

You should assume that today's date is 1 May 2024

(a) (i) Calculate Shuttelle's income tax liability for the tax year 2023/24. (8 marks)

(ii) Calculate the amount of tax relief obtained by Shuttelle as a consequence of the gross personal pension contributions of £120,000 she made on 6 April 2023.

You can assume that no reduction to the pensions annual allowance was necessary for tax years prior to 2023/24. (3 marks)

(b) (i) In respect of Lin, Nan and Yu for the tax year 2023/24:

1 explain whether or not the remittance basis is available

2 on the assumption that the remittance basis is available to ALL three individuals, state, with reasons, the remittance basis charge (if any) that they would have to pay in order for their overseas income and gains to be taxed on the remittance basis.

The following mark allocation is provided as guidance for this requirement:

1 3 marks

2 4 marks (7 marks)

(ii) Set out briefly the circumstances under which a non-UK domiciled individual born overseas would be deemed to be UK domiciled for the purposes of income tax and capital gains tax. (2 marks)

Professional marks will be awarded for the demonstration of skill in analysis and evaluation and commercial acumen in your answer. (5 marks)

(Total: 25 marks)

48 JUANITA AND BURACO (ADAPTED) *Walk in the footsteps of a top tutor*

You should assume that today's date is 1 June 2024.

Your firm has been asked to provide advice to two unrelated clients, Juanita and Buraco. Advice is required in respect of:

– the inheritance tax liability arising as a result of Juanita's husband Don's death on shares which he owned, and

– Buraco's residence status and the remittance basis.

Don:

- Died on 1 May 2024.
- Had always been UK resident and domiciled.
- Was married to Juanita, and they have one daughter, Lexi.

Lifetime gifts:

- Don made only two lifetime gifts.
- On 9 May 2019, Don gifted his overseas villa to Lexi.
- The villa was valued at £355,000 on 9 May 2019, and at £370,000 on 1 May 2024.
- On 1 March 2021, on the advice of a financial adviser, Don gifted 3,500 of his shares in Estar Ltd to Lexi.
- Prior to receiving this advice, Don had been planning to leave these shares to Lexi on his death.
- Under the terms of Don's will, Don's cousin will inherit the remaining 3,500 shares in Estar Ltd owned by Don at his death.

Estar Ltd:

- Is an investment company; no business property relief is available on the transfer of its shares.
- Before the gift on 1 March 2021, Don owned 7,000 ordinary shares in Estar Ltd.
- The remaining 3,000 ordinary shares issued by Estar Ltd are held by Juanita.
- The shares were valued as follows:

Percentage shareholding	**Value per share**	
	1 March 2021	**1 May 2024**
0%–50%	£9.00	£10.80
51%–75%	£15.00	£18.00
76%–100%	£20.00	£24.00

Buraco's links with the country of Canasta:

- Buraco is domiciled in Canasta.
- Buraco owns a home in the country of Canasta.
- Buraco's only income is in respect of investment properties in Canasta.
- Buraco frequently buys and sells properties in Canasta.

Buraco's links with the UK:

- Buraco's ex-wife and their 12-year-old daughter moved to the UK on 1 May 2023.
- Buraco first visited the UK in the tax year 2023/24 but was not UK resident in that year.
- Buraco did not own a house in the UK until he purchased one on 6 April 2024.
- Buraco expects to live in the UK house for between 100 and 150 days in the tax year 2024/25.

Required:

You should assume that today's date is 1 June 2024

(a) **Advise Juanita of the reduction in the inheritance tax liability arising on Don's death in respect of the shares in Estar Ltd as a result of Lexi having received her shares as a lifetime gift, rather than on Don's death.** **(9 marks)**

(b) **(i)** **Explain why Buraco will not satisfy any of the automatic overseas residence tests for the tax year 2024/25, and, on the assumption that he does not satisfy any of the automatic UK residence tests, explain how his residence status will be determined for that tax year.** **(8 marks)**

(ii) **On the assumption that Buraco is resident in the UK in the tax year 2024/25, state the tax implications for him of claiming the remittance basis for that year and explain whether or not there would be a remittance basis charge.** **(3 marks)**

Professional marks will be awarded for the demonstration of skill in analysis and evaluation and commercial acumen in your answer. **(5 marks)**

(Total: 25 marks)

49 CATE AND RAVI (ADAPTED) *Walk in the footsteps of a top tutor*

You should assume that today's date is 1 May 2024.

Cate and her husband, Ravi, require advice in relation to:

- the after-tax cost of taking on a part-time employee,
- the tax implications of starting to sell items via the internet, and
- the capital gains tax payable on the disposal of an overseas asset.

Cate:

- Is resident and domiciled in the UK. She is aged 48.
- Is married to Ravi.
- Runs a successful unincorporated business, D-Designs.
- Receives dividends of £30,000 each year.
- Wants to sell some second-hand books online.

D – Designs business:

- Was set up by Cate in 2016.
- Is now making a taxable profit of £90,000 per annum.
- Operates a number of dress shops and already employs six full-time staff.
- Requires an additional part-time employee.

Part time employee – proposed remuneration package:

- Salary of £12,000 per annum.
- Medical insurance costing £1,300 per annum, which would have cost the employee £1,450 per annum to purchase.

- Mileage allowance of 50 pence per mile for the 62-mile round trip required each week to redistribute stock between the shops. This will be for 48 weeks in the year.
- This employment will be the employee's only source of taxable income.

Sale of second-hand books:

- Cate inherited a collection of books from her mother in December 2022.
- Cate intends to sell these books via the internet.
- Some of the books are in a damaged state and Cate will get them rebound before selling them.

Ravi:

- Is domiciled in the country of Goland.
- Has been resident in the UK since his marriage to Cate in February 2016.
- Has UK taxable income of £126,000 in the tax year 2023/24.
- Realises chargeable gains each year from disposals of UK buy-to-let residential properties equal to the capital gains tax annual exempt amount.
- Sold an investment property (residential) in Goland in February 2024 for £130,000, realising a chargeable gain of £70,000. None of the proceeds from the sale of this property have been remitted to the UK.

Required:

You should assume that today's date is 1 May 2024

(a) Calculate the annual cost for Cate, after income tax and national insurance contributions, of D-Designs employing the part-time employee. (9 marks)

(b) Discuss whether the profit from Cate's proposed sale of books via the internet will be liable to either income tax or capital gains tax. (5 marks)

(c) Advise Ravi on the options available to him for calculating his UK capital gains tax liability for the tax year 2023/24. Provide supporting calculations of the tax payable by him in each case. (6 marks)

Professional marks will be awarded for the demonstration of skill in analysis and evaluation and commercial acumen in your answer. (5 marks)

(Total: 25 marks)

50 MAX (ADAPTED) *Walk in the footsteps of a top tutor*

You should assume that today's date is 10 May 2024.

Max ceased trading two years ago, and is now about to move overseas.

Advice is required on:

- the capital gains tax (CGT) implications of the disposal of two assets previously used in his unincorporated business, and
- the inheritance tax (IHT) implications of gifting one of them.

Max:

- Has always been UK resident and domiciled
- Is widowed and has one daughter, Fara.
- Is a higher-rate taxpayer.
- Makes disposals each year to use his annual exempt amount for capital gains tax.
- Has made one previous lifetime gift to Fara on 6 May 2021, which resulted in a gross chargeable transfer of £194,000.

Max – unincorporated business:

- Max operated as a sole trader for many years, but ceased trading on 31 May 2022.
- Max still owns office premises and a machine which had been used exclusively in his business until 31 May 2022.
- Max now wishes to dispose of these assets prior to moving overseas.

Proposed gift of the office premises:

- Max is proposing to gift the office premises to Fara on 30 June 2024.
- Max acquired the premises on 1 April 2016.
- Since 1 June 2022, the premises have been let to an unconnected company.
- The market value of the premises in June 2024 is £168,000, which exceeds the original cost.

Max – move overseas:

- Max has decided to move overseas for a period of around two and a half years commencing on 1 November 2024.
- Max does not intend to return to the UK at all during this period.
- Max will return to live permanently in the UK on 30 June 2027.
- Max is not entitled to use the split year treatment for determination of his residence status in any tax year.

Proposed sale of the machine:

- The machine was acquired on 1 August 2020 for a cost of £72,000.
- Max has received an offer of £84,000 for the immediate sale of the machine in June 2024.
- An alternative buyer has offered £90,000 for the machine, but will not be able to complete the purchase until June 2025.

Required:

You should assume that today's date is 10 May 2024

(a) In respect of the proposed gift of the office premises to Fara on 30 June 2024:

(i) Advise Max whether or not capital gains tax (CGT) gift holdover relief will be available, and if so, to what extent. (3 marks)

(ii) Advise Max of the maximum potential inheritance tax (IHT) liability, and the circumstances in which this would arise. (5 marks)

(b) Explain the effect of Max's period of living overseas on his UK residence status for all relevant tax years, and advise him of the CGT consequences of the sale of the machine (1) in June 2024, or alternatively (2) in June 2025.

Note: No calculations are required for this part. (6 marks)

(c) Explain whether or not business asset disposal relief will be available on the sale of the machine, and calculate the increase in Max's after-tax proceeds if he sells the machine in June 2025 rather than in June 2024. (6 marks)

Professional marks will be awarded for the demonstration of skill in analysis and evaluation and commercial acumen in your answer. (5 marks)

(Total: 25 marks)

51 CADEN AND AMAHLE

You should assume that today's date is 1 September 2024.

Caden is resident and domiciled in the UK and is the sole shareholder, director and employee of Mandini Ltd. Amahle, Caden's wife, receives interest income in respect of a bank deposit account in Komor.

Advice is required on:

– the capital gains tax implications of a proposed sale of antique chairs by Caden,

– the payment of the potential inheritance tax liability in respect of two lifetime gifts by Caden,

– the application of the personal service company (IR35) legislation to Caden's company, and

– the income tax implications for Amahle of receiving overseas income.

Acquisition of antique chairs:

– Caden was gifted a set of six antique chairs by his mother, Feba, on 3 March 2022.

– The chairs had a market value of £152,000 on that date.

– Feba had purchased the chairs for £106,000 on 8 August 2012.

Sale of antique chairs:

– Caden sold two of the chairs to an unconnected person for £42,000 on 10 September 2022. The four remaining chairs were valued at £93,000 on that date.

– Caden is proposing to sell the four remaining chairs to his son, Nathi, for £35,000, on 6 October 2024. These four chairs are expected to be valued at £99,000 on that date.

Caden – previous lifetime gift:

– Caden's only previous lifetime gift was of an investment property, to Nathi on 2 July 2024.

– This gift resulted in a gross chargeable transfer of £380,000.

Mandini Ltd:

– Is a personal services company for the purpose of the IR35 legislation. Its clients are private companies and qualify as small under the IR35 rules.

– Has budgeted fee income, wholly from relevant engagements, of £65,000 in the year ending 31 March 2025.

– Pays Caden a gross monthly salary of £1,500.

– Will pay Caden a dividend of £35,000 on 28 February 2025.

– Neither Caden nor Mandini Ltd has any other source of income.

Amahle:

– Is resident and domiciled in the UK.

– Earns employment income of £45,000 (gross) every year.

– Makes a contribution to a personal pension scheme of £3,000 (net) every year.

Amahle – bank account in Komor:

– On 1 January 2024, Amahle deposited £150,000 in a bank account in Komor.

– This bank account pays interest at the rate of 5% (gross) each year.

– Amahle will not remit any of this interest income to the UK.

The tax regime in Komor:

– Tax is withheld at the rate of 18% on all interest income arising in Komor.

– The UK does not have a double taxation treaty with Komor.

Required:

You should assume that today's date is 1 September 2024

(a) (i) Explain, with supporting calculations, the capital loss which will arise on the proposed sale of the antique chairs to Nathi and how this loss can be relieved. **(4 marks)**

(ii) Advise on the availability and effect of the instalment option for payment of Nathi's inheritance tax liability in respect of each of the investment property and the antique chairs, on the assumption that Caden dies on 20 March 2029.

Note: No calculations are required for part (a)(ii). **(3 marks)**

(b) Calculate Caden's taxable income for the tax year 2024/25 on the basis that the personal services company (IR35) legislation applies to the budgeted fee income receivable by Mandini Ltd in the year ending 31 March 2025. **(5 marks)**

(c) **For the tax year 2024/25, advise Amahle why the interest receivable in respect of her bank account in the country of Komor will be subject to UK income tax and explain, with supporting calculations, why this will not actually result in any UK tax payable.** **(8 marks)**

Professional marks will be awarded for the demonstration of skill in analysis and evaluation, scepticism and commercial acumen in your answer. **(5 marks)**

(Total: 25 marks)

PERSONAL FINANCE, BUSINESS FINANCE AND INVESTMENTS

52 MONISHA AND HORNER (ADAPTED) *Walk in the footsteps of a top tutor*

You should assume that today's date is 1 June 2024.

Your firm has been asked to advise two unrelated clients, Monisha and Horner.

Advice is required in relation to:

- furnished holiday accommodation,
- tax planning for a married couple, and
- the personal service company (IR35) rules.

Monisha:

- Is married to Asmat.
- Earns a salary of £80,000 per year and realises chargeable gains on residential properties of £2,300 per year.
- Owns a UK investment property, which is let to short-term tenants.

Asmat:

- Looks after the couple's children and has no income or chargeable gains.
- Expects to return to work on 6 April 2030 on an annual salary of £18,000.

The UK investment property owned by Monisha:

- The property cost £270,000 and is currently worth £300,000.
- The letting does not qualify as a commercial letting of furnished holiday accommodation.
- Annual income and expenditure

	£
Rental income	20,000
Repairs and maintenance	3,480
Council tax	1,200
Agent's fees	2,000

- The property will be sold on 5 April 2031 and is expected to create a chargeable gain of £100,000.

Proposals to reduce the couple's total tax liability:

– Monisha will give a 20% interest in the investment property to Asmat on 1 April 2025.

– The couple will ensure that, from 6 April 2025, the letting of the investment property will qualify as a commercial letting of furnished holiday accommodation.

Horner:

– Horner owns all of the shares of Otmar Ltd.

– Horner works for Otmar Ltd providing IT repair services to Florentine Ltd. This provision of services is subject to the personal service company (IR35) legislation.

– Florentine Ltd is classified as a medium or large sized organisation for the purposes of the IR35 legislation.

– Figures for Otmar Ltd for the year ending 5 April 2024 are set out below.

  Where applicable, these amounts are stated exclusive of value added tax (VAT).

	£
Income in respect of relevant engagements carried out by Horner	85,000
Costs of materials used in repairs	3,900
Horner's annual salary	50,000
Contributions paid into an occupational pension scheme in respect of Horner	2,000

Required:

You should assume that today's date is 1 June 2024

(a) (i) State the conditions which must be satisfied in order for the letting of a UK furnished property to qualify as a commercial letting of furnished holiday accommodation. (3 marks)

(ii) Calculate the total tax saving in the six tax years 2025/26 to 2030/31 if ALL of the proposals to reduce Monisha and Asmat's tax liabilities are carried out.

In respect of the second proposal, you should assume that the letting will qualify as a commercial letting of furnished holiday accommodation for the whole of the period of joint ownership and that all beneficial reliefs are claimed.

You should ignore inheritance tax. (10 marks)

(b) (i) Outline the circumstances in which the personal service company (IR35) rules apply. (3 marks)

(ii) Explain, with supporting calculations, the tax implications for Florentine Ltd of engaging Otmar Ltd. (4 marks)

Professional marks will be awarded for the demonstration of skill in analysis and evaluation and commercial acumen in your answer. (5 marks)

(Total: 25 marks)

53 STELLA AND MARIS (ADAPTED) ***Walk in the footsteps of a top tutor***

You should assume that today's date is 1 June 2024.

Your firm has been asked to provide advice to two unrelated clients, Stella and Maris, on:

- the tax implications of Stella making an increased contribution to her personal pension scheme,
- the receipt by Maris of a lump sum payment from her pension scheme, and
- the inheritance tax exemptions available on proposed lifetime gifts.

Stella:

- Is resident and domiciled in the UK.
- Received a gross salary of £203,000 in the tax year 2024/25. This was a substantial increase on the previous year.
- Does not have an occupational pension.
- Has property income from a portfolio of unfurnished properties, totalling £92,000 in the tax year 2024/25.
- Has no other source of taxable income.
- Wishes to make an increased contribution to her personal pension scheme in the tax year 2024/25.

Personal pension scheme contributions:

- Stella has contributed £40,000 (gross) to her personal pension scheme in each of the tax years 2023/24 and 2022/23 and £30,000 (gross) in each of the tax years 2021/22 and 2020/21.
- The full annual allowance (without restriction) was available for the tax years 2020/21 to 2023/24.
- Stella wishes to make an increased contribution of £90,000 (gross) in the tax year 2024/25.

Maris:

- Is resident and domiciled in the UK and is widowed.
- Has three married children and five grandchildren under the age of 12.
- Attained the age of 68 on 30 January 2024 and decided to vest some of her pension benefits on that date.
- Wishes to make regular gifts to her family in order to reduce inheritance tax on her death.

Personal pension fund:

- Maris had a money purchase pension scheme which was valued at £1,550,000 on 30 January 2024.
- Maris would like some advice on the tax implications of drawing a lump sum from this pension.

Assets and income:

- In addition to pension income and savings income totalling around £60,000, Maris receives dividends from shareholdings in quoted companies of around £45,000 each year.
- The shareholdings in quoted companies are currently valued at £980,000.
- Maris wishes to gift some of the shares or the dividend income to her children and grandchildren on their birthdays each year.
- Maris already makes gifts each year to use her annual exemption for inheritance tax purposes.

Required:

You should assume that today's date is 1 June 2024

(a) Calculate Stella's income after tax and pension contributions for the tax year 2024/25 if she does pay £90,000 (gross) into her personal pension scheme. (10 marks)

(b) (i) Explain how an amount withdrawn by Maris as a lump sum from her pension may be taxed. (4 marks)

(ii) Advise Maris of TWO relevant exemptions from inheritance tax which she will be able to use when making the birthday gifts, together with any conditions she will need to comply with in order to obtain them. (6 marks)

Professional marks will be awarded for the demonstration of skill in analysis and evaluation and commercial acumen in your answer. (5 marks)

(Total: 25 marks)

54 JESSICA (ADAPTED) ***Walk in the footsteps of a top tutor***

You should assume that today's date is 1 June 2024.

Your client, Jessica, is resident and domiciled in the UK. Jessica was made redundant on 31 March 2024 and will become a partner in the Langley Partnership on 1 July 2024. Jessica requires advice on the:

- tax liability arising on her redundancy payment,
- options available to relieve her share of a partnership trading loss, and
- the maximum contribution she can make to a personal pension scheme.

Jessica:

- Was employed by Berens Ltd up to 31 March 2024, when she was made redundant.
- Will become a partner in the Langley Partnership on 1 July 2024.
- Has never made any disposals for capital gains tax (CGT) purposes.

Jessica – income from Berens Ltd:

- Jessica received an annual salary from Berens Ltd of £145,000 each year from the tax year 2021/22.
- From 6 April 2023, Jessica was provided with a new company laptop computer, which cost Berens Ltd £850. Jessica had significant private use of this laptop computer.

Jessica – other income:

– Prior to the tax year 2023/24 Jessica had no other source of income.

– Starting from the tax year 2023/24, Jessica receives rental income of £6,000 each tax year.

Jessica – redundancy package from Berens Ltd:

– The package, received on 31 March 2024, included a statutory redundancy payment of £18,000 and an ex-gratia payment of £32,000.

– As part of the package, Berens Ltd also allowed Jessica to keep the laptop computer, which had a market value of £540 on 31 March 2024.

The Langley Partnership:

– Prior to 1 July 2024, there were two partners in the partnership – Issa and Finn.

– From 1 July 2024, the profit-sharing ratio will be: Issa 20%, Finn 40%, and Jessica 40%.

– The budgeted tax-adjusted trading (loss)/profit of the partnership is:

  – Year ending 31 March 2025 – (£160,000)

  – Year ending 31 March 2026 – £205,000.

Jessica – personal pension plan contributions:

– Jessica joined a personal pension scheme on 1 May 2024.

– She has not previously been in any pension scheme.

– She wishes to make the maximum possible contributions which will qualify for tax relief in each of the tax years 2024/25 and 2025/26.

Required:

You should assume that today's date is 1 June 2024

(a) Explain, with supporting calculations, the taxable amount of the redundancy package received from Berens Ltd on 31 March 2024, and calculate the income tax payable on it by Jessica. (5 marks)

(b) (i) Advise Jessica of the options available to her to relieve her share of the Langley Partnership loss for the year ending 31 March 2025, on the assumption that she does not wish to carry any of her share of the loss forward. (3 marks)

(ii) Determine, by reference to the amount of income tax saved in each case, which of the available loss relief options (as identified in (i) above) will result in the highest overall income tax saving for Jessica. (7 marks)

(c) Explain, with supporting calculations, the maximum amount of the contributions Jessica can pay into her pension scheme in each of the tax years 2024/25 and 2025/26 without incurring an annual allowance charge. (5 marks)

Professional marks will be awarded for the demonstration of skill in analysis and evaluation and commercial acumen in your answer. (5 marks)

(Total: 25 marks)

55 PEDRO (ADAPTED)

You should assume that today's date is 1 March 2025.

Pedro lets out a holiday cottage which he was given by his aunt. He requires advice in respect of the following:

- the inheritance tax implications of the gift of the cottage,
- furnished holiday lettings, and
- the income tax implications of making a contribution into his personal pension scheme.

Pedro:

- Was given a holiday cottage in the UK by his aunt, Marina, on 4 March 2014.
- Paid inheritance tax in respect of this gift of the holiday cottage, following Marina's death on 8 June 2024.
- Inherited a portfolio of UK unfurnished residential properties, valued at £670,000 on Marina's death.

Gift of the holiday cottage in the UK by Marina:

- Marina and Pedro agreed that she could stay in the house for two months each year, rent-free, which she did every year until her death.
- For the remainder of each year, Marina lived in her main home.

Pedro – property income:

- The cottage (which is fully furnished) has been available for rental on a commercial basis since 1 July 2024, and will have a 70% occupancy rate for the first year of letting.
- No tenant will have stayed in the cottage for more than 14 consecutive days during the first year of letting.
- The net rental income from the cottage in the tax year 2024/25 will be £14,500.
- In the tax year 2024/25, Pedro will also receive net rental income of £32,000 from the unfurnished residential properties which he inherited from Marina.

Employment income:

- Pedro has been employed by Loule Ltd since 6 April 2023.
- Pedro receives an annual gross salary of £75,000 from Loule Ltd.
- Loule Ltd has contributed £8,000 in each of the tax years 2023/24 and 2024/25 to its occupational pension scheme on behalf of Pedro.

Personal pension scheme:

- Pedro had never been a member of a pension scheme prior to taking up employment with Loule Ltd.
- Pedro wishes to start contributing to a personal pension scheme in the tax year 2024/25.
- Pedro intends to make his first contribution into the new personal pension scheme, of £85,000 (gross), on 31 March 2025.
- The annual allowance available to Pedro was not restricted in any previous tax year.
- Pedro's income tax liability for the tax year 2024/25, before taking into account the planned contribution into his personal pension scheme, is £40,332.

Required:

You should assume that today's date is 1 March 2025

(a) Explain the inheritance tax implications of the gift of the cottage to Pedro at the time the gift was made, and as a result of Marina's death. (5 marks)

(b) Explain, by reference to the relevant conditions, why the holiday cottage will qualify as a furnished holiday letting for the first 12-month period of letting. (5 marks)

(c) Calculate the reduction in Pedro's income tax liability for the tax year 2024/25 as a result of making the planned contribution of £85,000 (gross) into his personal pension scheme on 31 March 2025. Your answer should include an explanation of the amount of the personal allowance available to Pedro in this case. (10 marks)

Professional marks will be awarded for the demonstration of skill in analysis and evaluation and commercial acumen in your answer. (5 marks)

(Total: 25 marks)

56 LUIS

You should assume that today's date is 1 June 2024.

Luis has requested advice in relation to the following:

- the potential inheritance tax (IHT) payable in respect of a planned gift of an investment property
- the tax implications of the sale of qualifying enterprise investment scheme (EIS) shares, and
- the income tax implications of using the sales proceeds to repay a debt.

Luis:

- Is resident and domiciled in the UK.
- Has a son, Mario, and a daughter, Silvia.
- Has never been married or had a civil partner.
- Owns a portfolio of residential investment properties.
- Has previously been a higher rate taxpayer in all relevant tax years, with the exception of the tax year 2022/23, when he was an additional rate taxpayer.
- Prior to the tax year 2024/25, his income in every tax year entirely comprised non-savings income.

Planned gift of Ivy Cottage to Silvia:

- Luis will gift Ivy Cottage, a residential investment property, to Silvia on 31 July 2024.
- Ivy Cottage will be worth £245,000 on that date, and is expected to appreciate in value over the next few years.
- Luis has made one previous gift, of £250,000 in cash to Mario on 1 January 2021.

Sale of Yew House:

- On 1 May 2022, Luis sold Yew House, a residential investment property, for proceeds of £366,000.
- This sale gave rise to a chargeable gain of £71,000.

Acquisition of shares in Flores Ltd:

– On 1 June 2022, Luis subscribed £120,000 for 50,000 newly issued ordinary shares in Flores Ltd, a UK resident trading company.

– These shares were qualifying enterprise investment scheme (EIS) shares.

– Luis obtained EIS relief of £36,000 (£120,000 × 30%) against his income tax liability for the tax year 2022/23.

– Luis elected to defer the maximum amount of the gain on the sale of Yew House as a result of the acquisition of these shares.

Sale of shares in Flores Ltd:

– On 1 April 2024, Luis sold all of his shares in Flores Ltd to an unconnected person for £85,000, their market value on that date.

– Luis will claim the most tax-advantageous relief for any loss which arises in respect of this sale.

Luis – interest receivable and payable:

– On 6 April 2024, Luis deposited the whole of the proceeds from the sale of the Flores Ltd shares in a bank deposit account, which will pay annual interest of £850.

– Luis is considering withdrawing all the deposited funds and using the money to repay the mortgage loan outstanding on one of his residential investment properties (not Ivy Cottage).

– Interest of £1,275 per annum is currently charged on this mortgage loan.

– Luis will be a higher rate taxpayer in all tax years for the foreseeable future.

Required:

You should assume that today's date is 1 June 2024

(a) Explain the circumstances under which the maximum liability to inheritance tax (IHT) will arise in respect of Luis' planned gift of Ivy Cottage to Silvia and calculate the amount which would be payable by Silvia in this situation. (5 marks)

(b) (i) Explain the immediate income tax and capital gains tax implications of Luis' sale of his Flores Ltd shares, and

(ii) State the relief(s) available for the capital loss arising on this sale, including the rate of tax saved in respect of each relief, and advise Luis of the most tax-advantageous relief available to him. (9 marks)

(c) (i) Explain the income tax treatment for Luis of the receipt of the bank interest and payment of the mortgage loan interest, and

(ii) Calculate the after-tax net interest saving for a full tax year if he decides to repay the mortgage loan. (6 marks)

Professional marks will be awarded for the demonstration of skill in analysis and evaluation and commercial acumen in your answer. (5 marks)

(Total: 25 marks)

TAXATION OF CORPORATE BUSINESSES

FAMILY COMPANY ISSUES

57 NOCTURNE LTD (ADAPTED) *Walk in the footsteps of a top tutor*

You should assume that today's date is 1 September 2024.

Nocturne Ltd, a partially exempt company for the purposes of value added tax (VAT), requires advice on:

- the corporation tax implications of providing an asset to one of its shareholders,
- the income tax implications for another shareholder of making a loan to the company, and
- simplifying the way in which it accounts for VAT.

Nocturne Ltd:

- Is a UK resident trading company.
- Has an accounting reference date of 31 March and pays corporation tax at the rate of 19%.
- Has four shareholders, each of whom owns 25% of the company's ordinary share capital.
- Owns a laptop computer, which it purchased in October 2020 for £1,200, and which has a current market value of £150.
- Has purchased no other plant and machinery for several years and the tax written down value of its main pool at 31 March 2024 was £Nil.

Provision of a laptop computer to one of Nocturne Ltd's shareholders:

- Nocturne Ltd is considering two alternative ways of providing a laptop computer in the year ending 31 March 2025 for the personal use of one of its shareholders, Jed.
- Jed is neither a director nor an employee of Nocturne Ltd.
- Option 1: Nocturne Ltd will buy a new laptop computer for £1,800 and give it immediately to Jed.
- Option 2: Nocturne Ltd will gift its existing laptop to Jed and will purchase a brand-new replacement for use in the company for £1,800.

Loan from Siglio:

- Siglio will loan £60,000 to Nocturne Ltd on 1 October 2024 to facilitate the purchase of new equipment.
- Siglio is both a shareholder of Nocturne Ltd and the company's managing director.
- Nocturne Ltd will pay interest at a commercial rate on the loan from Siglio.
- Siglio will borrow the full amount of the loan from his bank on normal commercial terms.

VAT – partial exemption:

– Nocturne Ltd is partially exempt for the purposes of VAT.

– Nocturne Ltd's turnover for the year ended 31 March 2024 was £240,000 (VAT-exclusive).

– Nocturne Ltd's turnover for the year as a whole for VAT purposes comprised 86% taxable supplies and 14% exempt supplies.

– The input VAT suffered by Nocturne Ltd on expenditure during the year ended 31 March 2024 was:

	£
Wholly attributable to taxable supplies	7,920
Wholly attributable to exempt supplies	1,062
Unattributable	4,150

– Nocturne Ltd expects its turnover and expenditure figures to increase by approximately 25% next year.

– Siglio has heard about an annual test for computing the amount of recoverable input VAT during an accounting period and would like more information about this.

Required:

You should assume that today's date is 1 September 2024

(a) **Explain, with the aid of supporting calculations, which of the two proposed methods of providing the laptop computer to Jed would result in the lower after-tax cost for Nocturne Ltd.**

You should ignore value added tax (VAT) for part (a) of this question. **(7 marks)**

(b) **Explain the income tax implications for Siglio of providing the loan to Nocturne Ltd.** **(4 marks)**

(c) **(i)** **Determine, by reference to the de minimis tests 1 and 2, Nocturne Ltd's recoverable input VAT for the year ended 31 March 2024.** **(4 marks)**

(ii) **Advise Siglio of Nocturne Ltd's eligibility for the annual test for computing the amount of recoverable input VAT for the year ending 31 March 2025 and the potential benefits to be gained from its use.** **(5 marks)**

Professional marks will be awarded for the demonstration of skill in analysis and evaluation, scepticism and commercial acumen in your answer. **(5 marks)**

(Total: 25 marks)

58 MARIA AND GRANADA LTD (ADAPTED) *Walk in the footsteps of a top tutor*

You should assume that today's date is 1 March 2024.

Your firm has been asked to provide advice to Granada Ltd, and one of its shareholders, Maria, in relation to:

– the tax consequences of Maria selling some of her shares back to Granada Ltd, and

– the corporation tax and value added tax (VAT) implications of the recent acquisition of an unincorporated business by Granada Ltd.

Maria:

– Is resident and domiciled in the UK.

– Is a higher rate taxpayer with annual dividend income in excess of £10,000, and will remain so in the future.

– Has already realised chargeable gains of £15,000 in the tax year 2023/24.

Shares in Granada Ltd:

– Maria subscribed for 10,000 £1 ordinary shares in Granada Ltd at par in June 2014.

– Maria is one of four equal shareholders and directors of Granada Ltd.

– Maria intends to sell either 2,700 or 3,200 shares back to the company on 31 March 2024 at their current market value of £12.80 per share.

– All of the conditions for the capital treatment are satisfied, except for, potentially, the condition relating to the reduction in the level of shareholding.

Granada Ltd:

– Is a UK resident trading company which manufactures knitwear.

– Has an accounting reference date of 31 December.

– Is registered for VAT.

– Acquired the trade and assets of an unincorporated business, Starling Partners, on 1 January 2024.

Starling Partners:

– Had been trading as a partnership for many years as a wholesaler of handbags within the UK.

– Starling Partners' main assets comprise a freehold commercial building and its 'Starling' brand, which were valued on acquisition by Granada Ltd at £105,000 and £40,000 respectively.

– Is registered for VAT.

– The transfer of its trade and assets to Granada Ltd qualified as a transfer of a going concern (TOGC) for VAT purposes.

– The business is forecast to make a trading loss of £130,000 in the year ended 31 December 2024.

Granada Ltd – results and proposed expansion:

– The knitwear business is expected to continue making a taxable trading profit of around £100,000 each year.

– Granada Ltd has no non-trading income but realised a chargeable gain of £10,000 on 1 March 2024.

– Granada Ltd is considering expanding the wholesale handbag trade acquired from Starling Partners into the export market from 1 January 2025.

– Granada Ltd anticipates that this expansion will result in the wholesale handbag trade returning a profit of £15,000 in the year ended 31 December 2025.

Required:

You should assume that today's date is 1 March 2024

(a) (i) Explain, with the aid of calculations, why the capital treatment WILL NOT apply if Maria sells 2,700 of her shares back to Granada Ltd, but WILL apply if, alternatively, she sells back 3,200 shares. (4 marks)

(ii) Calculate Maria's after-tax proceeds per share if she sells:

1 2,700 shares back to Granada Ltd, and alternatively

2 3,200 shares back to Granada Ltd. (4 marks)

(b) (i) Describe the corporation tax treatment of the acquisition of the 'Starling' brand by Granada Ltd, if no charge for amortisation was required in its statement of profit or loss. (3 marks)

(ii) Discuss how Granada Ltd could obtain relief for the trading loss expected to be incurred by the trade acquired from Starling Partners, if it does not wish to carry any of the loss back. (5 marks)

(c) Explain the value added tax (VAT) implications for Granada Ltd in respect of the acquisition of the business of Starling Partners, and the additional information needed in relation to the building to fully clarify the VAT position. (4 marks)

Professional marks will be awarded for the demonstration of skill in analysis and evaluation, scepticism and commercial acumen in your answer. (5 marks)

(Total: 25 marks)

59 ACRYL LTD AND CRESCO LTD (ADAPTED) *Walk in the footsteps of a top tutor*

You should assume that today's date is 1 December 2024.

Acryl Ltd and Cresco Ltd are two unrelated companies. You have been asked to advise them on:

– the tax implications of Acryl Ltd being placed into liquidation, particularly the timing of distributions to its shareholders, and

– the relief for losses on the cessation of trade by Cresco Ltd, and its obligations in relation to value added tax (VAT).

Acryl Ltd:

– Is a UK resident trading company.

– Has always has an accounting reference date of 30 June.

– Has substantial distributable profits.

– 70% of the company's share capital is owned by Mambo Ltd.

– The remaining 30% of the share capital is owned by Mambo Ltd's managing director, Alan. Mambo Ltd and Alan both subscribed for their shares at par value on 1 March 2018.

Mambo Ltd:

– Is a UK resident trading company.

Alan:

– Will be an additional rate taxpayer in the tax year 2024/25.

– Will receive a salary from Acryl Ltd. This will be his only income in the tax year 2024/25 other than the distribution from Acryl Ltd in December 2024/March 2025.

– Will be eligible for business asset disposal relief on the disposal of his shares in Acryl Ltd.

Liquidation of Acryl Ltd:

– Winding up will commence on 1 January 2025 with the appointment of a liquidator.

– It is anticipated that the winding up will be completed on 31 March 2025, when the company will cease trading.

Alternative timing of distributions being considered by Acryl Ltd:

– Acryl Ltd is prepared to distribute the available profits to its shareholders on 31 December 2024.

– Alternatively, Acryl Ltd will delay the distribution until the completion of the winding up of the company on 31 March 2025.

Cresco Ltd:

– Is a UK resident trading company.

– Commenced trading on 1 June 2020.

– Is registered for the purposes of value added tax (VAT).

– Has made significant trading losses in recent months such that the company will need to cease trading on 31 December 2024.

Cresco Ltd – trading losses:

– Recent and anticipated results are as follows:

	Year ended 31 May 2021	Year ended 31 May 2022	Year ended 31 May 2023	Year ended 31 May 2024	Period ending 31 December 2024
	£	£	£	£	£
Trading (loss)/profit	(5,000)	17,000	8,000	(24,000)	(40,000)
Bank interest receivable	5,000	3,000	3,000	0	0

– Cresco Ltd always claims relief for trading losses as early as possible.

Required:

You should assume that today's date is 1 December 2024

(a) (i) State the corporation tax consequences arising from the commencement of Acryl Ltd's winding up on 1 January 2025. (2 marks)

(ii) Explain the tax implications for both Mambo Ltd and Alan if the distribution to be made by Acryl Ltd occurs either on 31 December 2024, or alternatively on 31 March 2025, and conclude as to which date would be preferable. (7 marks)

(b) (i) Set out, together with supporting explanations, how Cresco Ltd will claim relief for the trading losses incurred and identify the amount of trading losses which will remain unrelieved after all available loss reliefs have been claimed. (8 marks)

(ii) Advise Cresco Ltd of the value added tax (VAT) implications of the cessation of its trade. (3 marks)

Professional marks will be awarded for the demonstration of skill in analysis and evaluation and commercial acumen in your answer. (5 marks)

(Total: 25 marks)

60 TRAISTE LTD (ADAPTED) *Walk in the footsteps of a top tutor*

You should assume that today's date is 1 June 2024.

Jordi is a director and shareholder of Traiste Ltd. Jordi and his sister, Kat, have asked for your advice in connection with:

- the forthcoming redundancy of an employee,
- the sale of shares in Traiste Ltd by Kat, and
- the payment implications for Traiste Ltd of alternative ways for Jordi to extract profits from the company.

Traiste Ltd:

- Is a UK resident unquoted trading company.
- Has two shareholders, Jordi and Kat, who each own 50% of the 1,000 £1 shares in issue.

Traiste Ltd – proposed redundancy package for an employee:

- An employee, Esta, will be made redundant on 30 June 2024.
- Esta will receive statutory redundancy pay of £12,000 and an *ex-gratia* payment of £36,000 from Traiste Ltd.
- Traiste Ltd will continue to lease a car for Esta's personal use until 31 December 2024, although she has no contractual entitlement to this.
- The monthly lease payments are £420.
- The car has CO_2 emissions of 138 grams per kilometre and is petrol powered.
- The car is currently worth £10,300. Its list price when new was £18,400.

Kat:

– Is resident and domiciled in the UK.

– Is 58 years old.

– Is a director and shareholder of Traiste Ltd.

– Will receive employment income of £40,350 from Traiste Ltd and dividends from other UK companies of £500 in the tax year 2024/25.

– Has already used her annual exempt amount for capital gains tax purposes for the tax year 2024/25.

Kat – proposed sale of shares:

– Kat subscribed for her 500 shares in Traiste Ltd at par on the incorporation of the company on 1 March 2020.

– She wishes to sell all of her shares before the end of 2024, and retire from the company.

– Kat's brother, Jordi, has offered to buy these shares for £47 each. He is not prepared to sign any tax election in relation to this offer.

– Alternatively, Traiste Ltd will buy these shares for their market value of £52 each.

Jordi:

– Is resident and domiciled in the UK.

– Is 53 years old.

– Is a director and shareholder of Traiste Ltd.

– Is paid a gross annual salary of £55,000 by Traiste Ltd.

– Wishes to extract an additional cash sum of £20,000, net of all taxes, from Traiste Ltd, to be paid on 31 March 2025.

– The additional sum will be extracted as either a bonus or a dividend.

– Will not receive any other taxable income in the tax year 2024/25.

Required:

You should assume that today's date is 1 June 2024

(a) (i) **Explain briefly the income tax implications for Esta in respect of each of the three components of the proposed redundancy package.**

Note: Calculations are NOT required for this part. **(3 marks)**

(ii) **Calculate the corporation tax deductions available to Traiste Ltd in respect of the redundancy package provided to Esta.** **(4 marks)**

(b) **Explain, with reference to the after-tax proceeds in each case, why Kat should accept Jordi's offer to buy her shares in Traiste Ltd, rather than sell her shares back to Traiste Ltd.** **(8 marks)**

(c) **Explain, with supporting calculations, the amount of any payments to be made by Traiste Ltd to HM Revenue and Customs (HMRC) in respect of each of the two ways for Jordi to extract the additional £20,000 cash from the company, and state the due date of any such tax payments.** **(5 marks)**

Professional marks will be awarded for the demonstration of skill in analysis and evaluation and commercial acumen in your answer. **(5 marks)**

(Total: 25 marks)

61 DENT LTD (ADAPTED)

Answer debrief

You should assume that today's date is 1 June 2024.

Dent Ltd requires advice on:

- registering for value added tax (VAT),
- the corporation tax treatment of its expenditure on research and development (R&D) activities, and
- the after-tax cost of remuneration to be provided to a key employee.

Dent Ltd:

- Will be incorporated and start trading on 1 July 2024.
- Will undertake a research project to develop an innovative new process related to its trade.
- Will be a small enterprise for the purposes of R&D expenditure.
- Will prepare its first set of accounts to 30 June 2025.
- Will make wholly taxable supplies for VAT purposes.

Dent Ltd – budgeted income for the year ending 30 June 2025:

- The value of trading receipts in the first few months will be low; such that Dent Ltd will not be required to be compulsorily registered for VAT until 1 April 2025.
- Dent Ltd expects, however, to receive substantial fees in April to June 2025, such that it anticipates generating an overall taxable trading profit for the year ending 30 June 2025.
- Dent Ltd will pay corporation tax at the rate of 25% in the year ending 30 June 2025.
- All of Dent Ltd's customers will be registered for VAT.

Dent Ltd – budgeted R&D expenditure for the year ending 30 June 2025:

	£
Specialist equipment	110,000
Property costs	46,000
Consumables	12,000
Staff costs	185,000
	353,000

- The above figures are all exclusive of VAT, where applicable.
- The property costs entirely comprise heat, light and water expenses.
- The staff costs include a fee of £25,000 to an agency (which is VAT registered) for the provision of an unconnected external contractor's services for the year.
- The remainder of the staff costs wholly relate to amounts payable to, or on behalf of, Dent Ltd's employees, including pension contributions totalling £14,000.
- The property costs, consumables and agency fees are incurred evenly throughout the year.

Alina – design engineer:

- Alina will commence employment with Dent Ltd on 1 July 2024 to lead the R&D project.
- Alina's annual salary of £80,000 is included in the budgeted staff costs figure above.
- On 1 July 2024, Dent Ltd will additionally provide Alina with the following, none of which are included in the budgeted staff costs figure above:
  - a lump sum payment of £10,000 in recognition of her forthcoming employment
  - a computer costing £1,000, of which Alina will have use, including significant private use, for the first nine months of her employment, and
  - temporary living accommodation for the first six months of her employment (as detailed below).

Alina – provision of temporary living accommodation:

- Dent Ltd will rent a flat for Alina's use from 1 July 2024 to 31 December 2024.
- Dent Ltd will pay the rental cost of £660 per month.
- The market value of the flat is currently £225,000, and its annual value is £2,800.

Required:

You should assume that today's date is 1 June 2024

(a) **Advise Dent Ltd on the implications for the recovery of input value added tax (VAT) of registering for VAT with effect from 1 April 2025, when it will be compulsory to do so, and explain why it is beneficial for the company instead to register voluntarily with effect from 1 July 2024.**

Note: Calculations are NOT required for this part (a). **(6 marks)**

(b) **Explain the corporation tax treatment of the research and development (R&D) expenditure of £353,000 to be incurred by Dent Ltd in the year ending 30 June 2025, and, on the assumption that Dent Ltd registers voluntarily for VAT with effect from 1 July 2024, calculate the amount of the deduction which will be available in respect of this R&D expenditure for corporation tax purposes.** **(6 marks)**

(c) **State the income tax implications of the receipt of the lump sum payment for Alina, and calculate the after-tax cost for Dent Ltd in respect of the lump sum payment and provision of the computer and the temporary living accommodation to Alina in its year ending 30 June 2025.**

Note: You should ignore VAT in this part (c). **(8 marks)**

Professional marks will be awarded for the demonstration of skill in analysis and evaluation and commercial acumen in your answer. **(5 marks)**

(Total: 25 marks)

Calculate your allowed time, allocate the time to the separate parts..............

62 SAMPHIRE LTD AND KELP LTD (ADAPTED)

You should assume that today's date is 1 March 2025.

Nori, an individual, owns 75% of the ordinary shares in Samphire Ltd and the whole of the ordinary share capital of Kelp Ltd. Advice is required on:

- the cost for Samphire Ltd of gifting a computer, or, alternatively, making a loan to Nori, and
- the tax implications of Kelp Ltd replacing a factory and acquiring a new warehouse.

Nori:

- Has been a director of Samphire Ltd for many years.

Samphire Ltd:

- Is a UK resident close trading company, which prepares accounts to 31 March annually.
- Pays corporation tax at the main rate.
- Will either gift a computer to Nori on 6 April 2025, or make a loan to Nori on the same date, to allow him to purchase a computer.

Alternative 1 – Samphire Ltd gifts the computer to Nori:

- The computer was purchased by Samphire Ltd in March 2024 for £2,600 and has a current market value of £1,500.
- Samphire Ltd has purchased no other plant and machinery for several years, and the written down value of its main pool at 6 April 2025 will be £Nil.
- The sale proceeds for the purpose of capital allowances will be £Nil.
- Nori's private use of the computer has been insignificant throughout Samphire Ltd's period of ownership.

Alternative 2 – Samphire Ltd makes a loan to Nori:

- On 6 April 2025 Samphire Ltd will make an interest-free loan of £1,500 to Nori.
- Samphire Ltd will write off the loan on 6 April 2027.

Kelp Ltd – disposal of lease on Factory 1:

- Kelp Ltd is a UK resident trading company.
- Kelp Ltd was assigned a 48-year lease on a factory building ('Factory 1') on 1 November 2018, for which it paid a premium of £165,000.
- Kelp Ltd used Factory 1 in its trade until 30 April 2024, since when it has been rented to tenants who are not connected with the company.
- On 1 November 2024 Kelp Ltd sold the lease with 42 years remaining for £206,000.

Kelp Ltd – acquisition of Factory 2:

- Kelp Ltd acquired a factory building ('Factory 2') from Samphire Ltd on 1 May 2024, and immediately started to use it in its trade.
- Samphire Ltd had acquired Factory 2 for £96,000 on 5 August 2015.
- Kelp Ltd paid £138,000 for Factory 2, which was its market value on 1 May 2024.

Kelp Ltd – acquisition of warehouse:

- Kelp Ltd will acquire a warehouse from an unconnected company for £78,000 on 1 April 2025.
- Kelp Ltd will occupy 70% of this warehouse for its own trade, and will rent out the remaining 30%.

Required:

You should assume that today's date is 1 March 2025

(a) **Explain, with supporting calculations, the total additional taxes payable by Samphire Ltd:**

(i) **If Samphire Ltd gifts the computer to Nori (Alternative 1)** **(4 marks)**

(ii) **If Samphire Ltd makes a loan of £1,500 to Nori, and then writes off the loan on 6 April 2027 (Alternative 2).** **(7 marks)**

Note: ignore value added tax (VAT).

(b) (i) **Calculate the chargeable gain for Kelp Ltd on the sale of the lease on Factory 1.** **(2 marks)**

(ii) **Explain, with supporting calculations, the amount of the chargeable gain calculated in (b)(i) which will remain liable to corporation tax (if any), if Kelp Ltd claims the maximum amount of rollover relief available.** **(7 marks)**

Notes:

(1) **The following lease percentages should be used, where necessary:**

42 years 96.593

48 years 99.289

(2) **The following indexation factor should be used, where necessary:**

August 2015 to December 2017 0.070

Professional marks will be awarded for the demonstration of skill in analysis and evaluation, scepticism and commercial acumen in your answer. **(5 marks)**

(Total: 25 marks)

63 TULA (ADAPTED)

You should assume that today's date is 1 September 2024.

Your client, Tula, requires advice on the following matters:

- the income tax implications of making loans to, and being provided with assets by a close company, and
- the potential inheritance tax (IHT) liability in respect of a lifetime transfer of shares.

Tula:

- Is resident and domiciled in the UK.
- Is the sole director and shareholder of Belleza Ltd.
- Earns an annual salary of £60,000 from Belleza Ltd.
- Belleza Ltd is Tula's only source of income, so she is a higher rate taxpayer for all relevant tax years.
- Wishes to expand the trading activities of Belleza Ltd, and will partly finance this by selling some shares to her brother, Aros, and using the gross proceeds to make a personal loan to the company.
- Transferred assets worth £350,000 to a trust for the benefit of her grandchildren on 9 April 2024.

Belleza Ltd:

- Has 10,000 issued ordinary shares all of which are owned by Tula.
- Is an unquoted trading company.
- Has always been a close company.
- Pays an annual dividend of £12,000, i.e. £1.20 per share, in December each year.

Tula – sale of shares and loan to Belleza Ltd:

- Tula will sell 30% of her shares in Belleza Ltd to her brother, Aros, on 30 September 2024, for £60,000. This will represent a sale at undervalue for the purposes of inheritance tax (IHT).
- On the same date, Tula will borrow £20,000 from a bank, at an interest rate of 9% per annum.
- Tula will then lend £80,000 to Belleza Ltd on 1 October 2024, at an interest rate of 7% per annum.
- Interest on both loans will be paid monthly on the last day of each month.

Aros:

- Will not be employed by Belleza Ltd.
- Will have trading income in the tax year 2024/25 in addition to the dividend from Belleza Ltd.
- Will be a higher rate taxpayer for the tax year 2024/25.

Provision of assets to Aros by Belleza Ltd:

- From 1 October 2024, Belleza Ltd will provide Aros with the use of a new van for private purposes.
- This van will cost Belleza Ltd £25,000 and will have CO_2 emissions of 112 grams per kilometre.
- Belleza Ltd will not provide any fuel for Aros' private motoring.
- From 1 October 2024, Belleza Ltd will also loan a new computer, with a cost of £1,300, to Aros for his personal use.

Shares in Belleza Ltd:

- Tula's father subscribed for 100% of the ordinary shares in Belleza Ltd on the incorporation of the company on 1 January 2016.
- Tula inherited these shares following her father's death on 14 January 2023.

– The value of the shares in Belleza Ltd on 30 September 2024 will be as follows:

Percentage shareholding	Value per share
	£
0% – 25%	21.20
26% – 50%	29.40
51% – 75%	35.10
76% – 100%	41.80

Required:

You should assume that today's date is 1 September 2024.

(a) Explain, with supporting calculations, the income tax implications for Tula in the tax year 2024/25 in respect of:

- **the interest paid on the £20,000 loan she will take out from the bank, and**
- **the interest received on the £80,000 loan she will make to Belleza Ltd.**

(6 marks)

(b) Explain, with supporting calculations, Aros' additional income tax liability (if any) for the tax year 2024/25 as a result of the provision of the van and the computer by Belleza Ltd. (6 marks)

(c) In respect of Tula's planned sale at undervalue of Belleza Ltd shares to Aros:

(i) Explain whether or not business property relief (BPR) will be available if Tula dies within seven years of this sale.

(ii) Explain, with supporting calculations, Aros' potential liability to inheritance tax (IHT) on the assumption that Tula dies on 1 January 2030 and BPR is NOT available. (8 marks)

Professional marks will be awarded for the demonstration of skill in analysis and evaluation, scepticism and commercial acumen in your answer. (5 marks)

(Total: 25 marks)

GROUPS, CONSORTIA AND OVERSEAS COMPANY ASPECTS

64 LIZA (ADAPTED) *Walk in the footsteps of a top tutor*

You should assume that today's date is 1 June 2024.

Liza requires detailed advice on:

- the availability of rollover relief,
- capital allowances on the purchase of a building, and
- group registration for the purposes of value added tax (VAT).

Liza's business interests:

- Liza's business interests, which have not changed for many years, are set out below. Liza is not a sole trader.

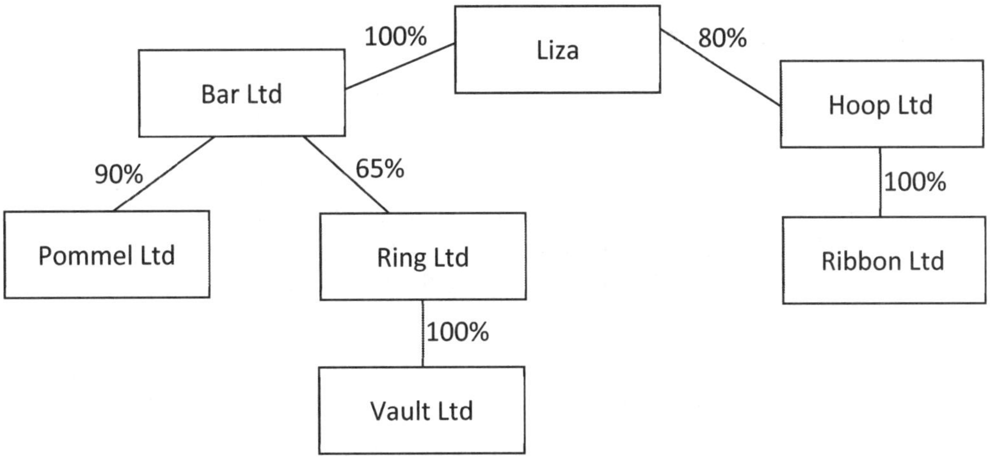

- All six companies are UK resident trading companies with a 31 March accounting reference date.
- All of the minority holdings are owned by individuals, none of whom is connected with Liza or with each other.

A building ('Building I') sold by Bar Ltd:

- Bar Ltd sold Building I on 31 May 2024 for £860,000.
- Bar Ltd had purchased the building on 1 June 2018 for £315,000 plus legal fees of £9,000.
- On 5 June 2018, Bar Ltd had carried out work on the building's roof at a cost of £38,000 in order to make the building fit for use.
- On 1 July 2023, Bar Ltd spent £14,000 repainting the building.
- Bar Ltd used Building I for trading purposes apart from the period from 1 January 2020 to 30 June 2021.
- It is intended that the chargeable gain on the sale will be rolled over to the extent that this is possible.

A replacement building ('Building II') purchased by Bar Ltd:

– Bar Ltd purchased Building II, newly constructed on 20 February 2023 and unused, for £720,000 on 1 July 2023.

– The purchase price includes £200,000 in respect of land and £150,000 in respect of electrical, water and heating systems.

– Bar Ltd brought the building into use immediately and uses two thirds of this building for trading purposes; the remaining one-third is rented out.

The trading activities of the Bar Ltd and Hoop Ltd groups of companies:

– The number of transactions between the Bar Ltd group and the Hoop Ltd group is increasing.

– Vault Ltd makes zero-rated supplies; all of the other five companies make standard-rated supplies.

Required:

You should assume that today's date is 1 June 2024

(a) (i) Calculate the chargeable gain on the sale of Building I, ignoring any potential claim for rollover relief. (3 marks)

(ii) In relation to claiming rollover relief in respect of the disposal of Building I, explain which of the companies in the Bar Ltd and Hoop Ltd groups are, and are not, able to purchase qualifying replacement assets, and state the period within which such assets must be acquired. (4 marks)

(iii) Explain, with the aid of supporting calculations, the additional amount that would need to be spent on qualifying assets in order for the maximum amount of the gain on Building I to be relieved by rollover relief. (4 marks)

Note: You should ignore Value Added Tax (VAT) when answering part (a) of this question.

(b) Explain the capital allowances that are available in respect of the acquisition of Building II. (4 marks)

(c) Explain which of the companies in the Bar Ltd and Hoop Ltd groups would be able to register as a single group for the purposes of value added tax (VAT), discuss the potential advantages of registering them as a single VAT group and the whether all companies would benefit from joining the VAT group. (5 marks)

Professional marks will be awarded for the demonstration of skill in analysis and evaluation, and commercial acumen in your answer (5 marks)

(Total: 25 marks)

65 SPETZ LTD GROUP (ADAPTED) *Walk in the footsteps of a top tutor*

You should assume that today's date is 1 December 2024.

The management of the Spetz Ltd group requires advice on:

– the value added tax (VAT) annual adjustment for a partially exempt company,

– the tax position of a company incorporated and trading overseas, and

– the penalties for late submission of VAT returns and late payment of VAT.

The Spetz Ltd group of companies:

– Spetz Ltd had 19 100% subsidiaries at 30 September 2023.

– Novak Ltd, Kraus Co and Nadal Ltd are three of the 100% subsidiaries of Spetz Ltd.

– Novak Ltd and Nadal Ltd both have a VAT year end of 30 September.

– Spetz Ltd acquired Kraus Co on 1 October 2023.

Novak Ltd – Figures for the year ended 30 September 2024:

	£
Taxable supplies (excluding VAT)	1,190,000
Exempt supplies	430,000
Input tax:	
– attributed to taxable supplies	12,200
– attributed to exempt supplies	4,900
– unattributed	16,100
– recovered on the four quarterly returns prior to the annual adjustment	23,200

Kraus Co:

– Is incorporated in, and trades through, a permanent establishment in the country of Mersano.

– Has no taxable income or chargeable gains apart from trading profits.

– Has taxable trading profits for the year ended 30 September 2024 of £520,000, all of which arose in Mersano.

– Is not a controlled foreign company.

– Has not made an election to exempt its overseas trading profits from UK tax.

The tax system in the country of Mersano:

– It can be assumed that the tax system in the country of Mersano is the same as that in the UK.

– However, the rate of corporation tax is 17%.

– There is no double tax treaty between the UK and Mersano.

Nadal Ltd VAT returns:

– Nadal Ltd has a history of submitting its VAT returns late, and has accumulated three penalty points in respect of its late returns over the last year.

– Nadal Ltd has just submitted its VAT return and VAT payment for the quarter ended 30 September 2024, 20 days late.

– The VAT payable for the quarter ended 30 September 2024 was £20,000.

Required:

You should assume that today's date is 1 December 2024

(a) **Calculate the value added tax (VAT) partial exemption annual adjustment for Novak Ltd for the year ended 30 September 2024 and state when it must be reported to HM Revenue and Customs. You should state, with reasons, whether or not each of the three de minimis tests is satisfied. (7 marks)**

(b) **(i)** **Explain how to determine whether or not Kraus Co is resident in the UK. (3 marks)**

(ii) **Explain, with supporting calculations, the UK corporation tax liability of Kraus Co for the year ended 30 September 2024 on the assumption that it is resident in the UK, and discuss the advantages and disadvantages of making an election to exempt its overseas profits from UK tax. (6 marks)**

(c) **Explain the implications for Nadal Ltd of the late submission of its VAT return and VAT payment for the quarter ended 30 September 2024. You should also explain how Nadal Ltd can reduce its penalty points to zero. (4 marks)**

Professional marks will be awarded for the demonstration of skill in analysis and evaluation, scepticism and commercial acumen in your answer (5 marks)

(Total: 25 marks)

66 KLUBB PLC (ADAPTED) *Walk in the footsteps of a top tutor*

You should assume that today's date is 1 June 2024.

Klubb plc, a client of your firm, requires advice on:

- the penalty in respect of the late filing of a corporation tax return,
- the establishment of a tax advantaged share scheme, and
- its shareholding in an overseas resident company.

Klubb plc:

- Is a UK resident trading company.
- Has been charged a penalty in respect of the late filing of corporation tax returns.
- Intends to establish a tax advantaged share plan.
- Purchased 30% of the ordinary share capital of Hartz Co from Mr Deck on 1 April 2024.

Late filing of corporation tax returns:

- Klubb plc prepared accounts for the 16-month period ended 31 March 2023.
- The corporation tax returns for this period were filed on 31 May 2024.

Tax advantaged share plan:

- The plan will be either a tax advantaged share incentive plan (SIP) or a tax advantaged company share option plan (CSOP).
- If a SIP, the shares would be held within the plan for five years.
- If a SIP, members will not be permitted to reinvest dividends in order to purchase further shares.

– If a CSOP, the options would be exercised within five years of being granted.

– In both cases it can be assumed that the plan members would sell the shares immediately after acquiring them.

Klubb plc wants the share plan to be flexible in terms of:

– The employees who can be included in the plan.

– The number or value of shares which can be acquired by each plan member.

Hartz Co:

– Is resident in the country of Suta.

– Mr Deck continues to own 25% of the company's ordinary share capital.

– Kort Co, a company resident in the country of Suta, owns the remaining 45%.

Budgeted results of Hartz Co for the year ending 31 March 2025:

– Trading profits of £330,000.

– Chargeable gains of £70,000.

– All of Hartz Co's profits have been artificially diverted from the UK.

– Hartz Co will pay corporation tax at the rate of 11% in the country of Suta.

– Hartz Co will not pay a dividend for the year ending 31 March 2025.

Required:

You should assume that today's date is 1 June 2024

(a) **State the corporation tax returns required from Klubb plc in respect of the 16-month period ended 31 March 2023 and the due dates for filing them.**

Explain the penalties which may be charged in respect of the late filing of these returns. **(4 marks)**

(b) **Compare and contrast a tax advantaged share incentive plan with a tax advantaged company share option plan in relation to:**

– **the flexibility desired by Klubb plc regarding the employees included in the plan and the number or value of shares which can be acquired by each plan member, and**

– **the income tax and capital gains tax implications of acquiring and selling the shares under each plan.** **(9 marks)**

(c) **(i)** **Explain whether or not Hartz Co will be regarded as a controlled foreign company (CFC) for the year ending 31 March 2025 and the availability or otherwise of the low profits exemption.** **(4 marks)**

(ii) **On the assumption that Hartz Co is a CFC, and that no CFC exemptions are available, calculate the budgeted CFC charge for Klubb plc based on the budgeted results of Hartz Co for the year ending 31 March 2025.** **(3 marks)**

Professional marks will be awarded for the demonstration of skill in analysis and evaluation, scepticism and commercial acumen in your answer **(5 marks)**

(Total: 25 marks)

67 ACHIOTE LTD (ADAPTED) *Walk in the footsteps of a top tutor*

Answer debrief

You should assume that today's date is 1 June 2024.

The finance director of Achiote Ltd would like your advice on:

– the tax implications of the acquisition of two intangible fixed assets,
– various transactions involving an overseas subsidiary, and
– opting to tax a commercial building.

Achiote Ltd:

– Owns 100% of the ordinary shares in Borage Ltd and 80% of the ordinary shares in Caraway Inc.
– Achiote Ltd and Borage Ltd are resident in the UK. Caraway Inc is resident in the country of Nuxabar.
– All three companies are trading companies and have an accounting reference date of 31 March.

Borage Ltd – purchase of intangible fixed assets:

– Borage Ltd purchased the goodwill of an unincorporated business for £62,000 on 1 September 2023.
– Borage Ltd will amortise this goodwill in its accounts on a straight-line basis over a five-year period.
– Borage Ltd also purchased a patent from Achiote Ltd for £45,000 on 1 January 2024.
– Achiote Ltd had purchased the patent for £38,000 on 1 January 2021.
– The patent was being amortised in Achiote Ltd's accounts on a straight-line basis over a ten-year period.
– Borage Ltd will continue to amortise the patent over the remainder of its ten-year life.

Achiote Ltd – loan to Caraway Inc:

– Achiote Ltd made a loan of £100,000 to Caraway Inc on 1 April 2023.
– The rate of interest on the loan is 6% per annum, which is 2% below the rate applicable to an equivalent loan from an unrelated party.
– There is no double tax treaty between the UK and Nuxabar.

Achiote Ltd – sale of equipment to, and proposed sale of shares in, Caraway Inc:

– Achiote Ltd acquired its 80% shareholding in Caraway Inc on 1 January 2024 for £258,000.
– Achiote Ltd is now proposing to sell an 8% shareholding in Caraway Inc to an unconnected company on 1 October 2024 for £66,000.
– An item of equipment owned by Achiote Ltd and used in its trade was sold to Caraway Inc on 1 March 2024 for its market value of £21,000.
– The item of equipment had cost Achiote Ltd £32,000 in May 2023.

Achiote Ltd – purchase and rental of a commercial building:

- Achiote Ltd has recently purchased a two-year-old commercial building from an unconnected vendor.
- The building will be rented to an unconnected company, Rye Ltd.
- Rye Ltd is a small local company, which supplies goods to Achiote Ltd but does not charge value added tax (VAT) on these sales.

Required:

You should assume that today's date is 1 June 2024

(a) Explain, with supporting calculations where appropriate, the corporation tax treatment in the year ended 31 March 2024, of the goodwill and the patent acquired by Borage Ltd. (4 marks)

(b) Explain the implications of the rate of interest charged by Achiote Ltd on the loan to Caraway Inc by reference to the transfer pricing legislation, and any action which should be taken by Achiote Ltd. (5 marks)

(c) Advise Achiote Ltd of the chargeable gains implications arising from (1) the sale of the item of equipment to Caraway Inc, and (2) its proposed sale of the shares in Caraway Inc. (5 marks)

(d) (i) On the assumption that Rye Ltd makes only taxable supplies, state TWO legitimate reasons why it might not charge value added tax (VAT) on its sales to Achiote Ltd. (2 marks)

(ii) Explain whether or not it would be financially beneficial for Achiote Ltd to opt to tax the commercial building, and the implications for Rye Ltd if it chooses to do so. (4 marks)

Professional marks will be awarded for the demonstration of skill in analysis and evaluation and commercial acumen in your answer. (5 marks)

(Total: 25 marks)

Calculate your allowed time, allocate the time to the separate parts..............

68 KITZ LTD (ADAPTED)

You should assume that today's date is 1 September 2024.

The finance director of Kitz Ltd has requested advice on the tax implications of:

- selling shares in a subsidiary company,
- making a loan to another subsidiary company, and
- selling an intangible fixed asset.

Kitz Ltd:

- Kitz Ltd owns 100% of the ordinary shares in Feld Ltd and 75% of the shares in Mayr Ltd. All three companies are UK resident trading companies.
- Kitz Ltd and Feld Ltd prepare accounts to 31 March annually.
- Both companies pay corporation tax at the main rate.

– Neither company is a small or medium-sized enterprise (SME) for the purpose of transfer pricing.

Kitz Ltd – sale of 7,500 ordinary shares (a 75% holding) in Mayr Ltd on 1 July 2024:

– Mayr Ltd is a UK resident trading company.

– The shares, which represent the whole of Kitz Ltd's shareholding, were sold to an unconnected purchaser for £790,000.

– Kitz Ltd had acquired these shares on 1 March 2017 for £455,000.

– Kitz Ltd had sold a warehouse to Mayr Ltd on 8 April 2019 for its market value on that date of £165,000.

– Kitz Ltd had purchased the warehouse on 12 May 2017 for £129,000.

– Mayr Ltd still owned the warehouse on 1 July 2024.

Kitz Ltd – loan to Feld Ltd:

– Kitz Ltd will make a loan of £450,000 to Feld Ltd on 1 April 2025.

– Feld Ltd will use the loan to purchase goodwill and office premises for use in its business, and 70% of the ordinary share capital of Durn Ltd.

– The cost of these acquisitions is as follows:

	£
Goodwill	68,000
Office premises	137,000
70% shareholding in Durn Ltd	245,000

– Kitz Ltd will charge interest at the rate of 7% per year on this loan.

– Feld Ltd has been offered a loan of £450,000 from a bank at an interest rate of 10% per annum.

– In the year ending 31 March 2026, Feld Ltd will have a trading profit of £587,000 and interest receivable of £48,100.

Kitz Ltd – proposed sale of a patent:

– Kitz Ltd will sell a patent to Durn Ltd on 3 May 2025 for £72,000.

– Kitz Ltd purchased the patent for £60,000 on 3 May 2020.

– The tax written down value of the patent on 3 May 2025 will be £30,000.

– Kitz Ltd has always used the patent in its business.

Required:

You should assume that today's date is 1 September 2024

(a) **Explain the chargeable gains implications for Kitz Ltd arising from the sale of its shares in Mayr Ltd on 1 July 2024.**

Note: No calculations are required for part (a). **(6 marks)**

(b) **Explain, with brief supporting calculations, the corporation tax implications for both Kitz Ltd and Feld Ltd in respect of the interest charged on the loan by Kitz Ltd to Feld Ltd for the year ending 31 March 2026.** **(7 marks)**

(c) **(i)** **Explain the corporation tax implications for Kitz Ltd of the sale of the patent to Durn Ltd on 3 May 2025, assuming Kitz Ltd does not make a claim for intangible fixed asset rollover relief.** **(3 marks)**

(ii) **Explain why rollover relief for intangible fixed assets will be available in respect of the sale of the patent to Durn Ltd, and, on the assumption the maximum rollover relief is claimed, calculate the impact of the claim on Kitz Ltd's corporation tax liability for the year ending 31 March 2026.** **(4 marks)**

Professional marks will be awarded for the demonstration of skill in analysis and evaluation and commercial acumen in your answer. **(5 marks)**

(Total: 25 marks)

69 FOX LTD

You should assume that today's date is 1 June 2024.

The finance director of Fox Ltd has requested advice on:

– the chargeable gains implications of the assignment (sale) of an existing lease

– the subsequent acquisition of a freehold factory; and

– the availability of group relief in respect of a trading loss.

Fox Ltd Group at 1 June 2024:

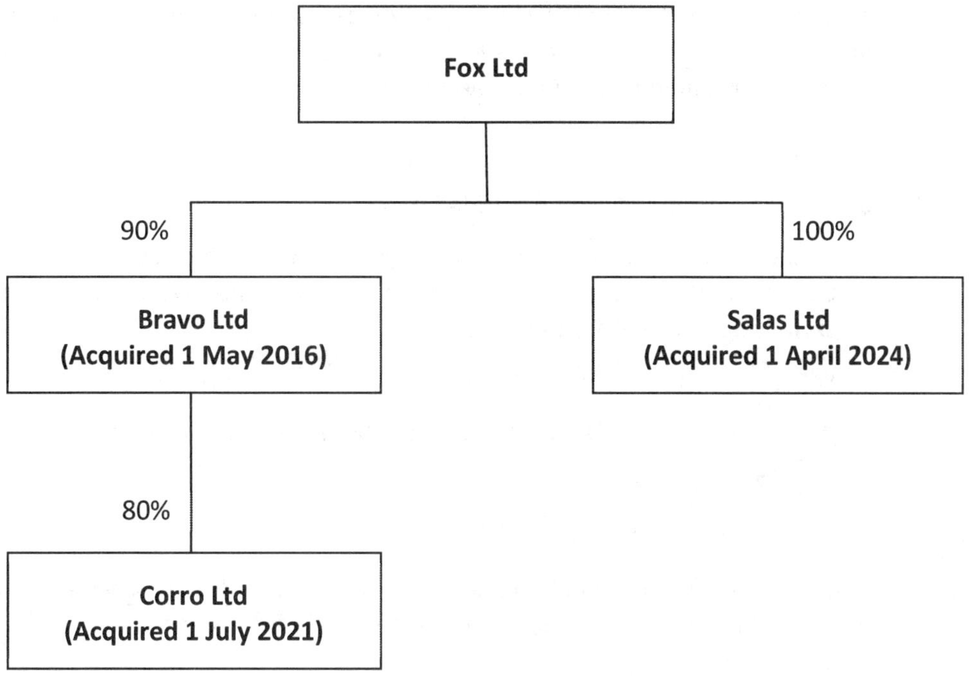

– All four companies are UK resident trading companies with a 30 June accounting reference date.

Fox Ltd – assignment of a lease and acquisition of a new freehold:

– On 1 October 2023, Fox Ltd assigned a 26-year lease on a factory to an unconnected company for £180,000.

– The lease had been acquired by Fox Ltd on 1 October 2009 for £102,000 when it had 40 years remaining.

– The leased factory was used by Fox Ltd for trading purposes throughout its period of ownership.

– Fox Ltd sold an office building on 8 March 2009 which resulted in a chargeable gain of £43,000.

– Fox Ltd claimed rollover relief in order to defer this chargeable gain following the acquisition of the lease of the factory.

– Fox Ltd plans to purchase a new freehold factory building in July 2024.

Corro Ltd:

– Acquired a warehouse on 1 July 2023 from an unconnected company for £168,000.

– Uses 70% of the building itself for trading purposes; the remaining 30% is rented out.

Salas Ltd:

– Was incorporated on 1 July 2022.

– Was wholly owned by an individual prior to joining the Fox Ltd group.

– Incurred a trading loss in the year ended 30 June 2023.

– Has no other sources of income in any accounting period.

– There are no plans to change the nature or conduct of Salas Ltd's trade.

Forecast results:

– Salas Ltd is expected to incur a tax-adjusted trading loss of £225,000 in the year ending 30 June 2024.

– Fox Ltd, Bravo Ltd and Corro Ltd will each have taxable total profits in the year ending 30 June 2024. These companies have always been profitable in the past, and will continue to be profitable in the foreseeable future.

Required:

You should assume that today's date is 1 June 2024

(a) (i) **Calculate the chargeable gain arising on the assignment of the lease on 1 October 2023 and explain the tax treatment of the deferred gain in respect of the sale of the office building.**

Notes:

(1) The following lease percentages should be used where necessary:

26 years 82.496

40 years 95.457

(2) You should ignore indexation allowance and any potential claim for rollover relief in respect of the disposal of the lease. **(4 marks)**

(ii) In relation to the chargeable gain calculated in (a)(i), explain, with supporting calculations:

- **the extent to which rollover relief will currently be available within the Fox Ltd group, and**
- **the minimum amount which Fox Ltd will need to spend on the new freehold factory, such that the full amount of the eligible gain in (a)(i) can be deferred using rollover relief. (7 marks)**

(b) Explain the group relief claims available to the Fox Ltd Group in respect of Salas Ltd's trading loss of the year ending 30 June 2024. (9 marks)

Professional marks will be awarded for the demonstration of skill in analysis and evaluation and commercial acumen in your answer. (5 marks)

(Total: 25 marks)

70 EVORA LTD

You should assume that today's date is 1 June 2024.

The finance director of Evora Ltd has requested advice on the following:

- the tax implications of acquiring two assets from an unincorporated business,
- commencing trading activities overseas, and
- the value added tax (VAT) consequences of purchasing goods and services from overseas.

Evora Ltd and Silves Ltd:

- Evora Ltd owns 100% of the ordinary shares in Silves Ltd.
- Evora Ltd and Silves Ltd are both UK tax resident trading companies.
- Both companies prepare accounts to 31 March each year.

Silves Ltd – acquisition of assets from an unincorporated business:

- On 1 April 2023, Silves Ltd acquired the following assets from an unincorporated business:

	Cost to Silves Ltd
	£
'Alte' brand	50,000
Specialist machine	30,000

- Silves Ltd is using both of these assets for the purposes of its trade.
- The 'Alte' brand will be amortised on a straight-line basis over an eight-year period.
- The specialist machine was previously used by the unincorporated business in its trade.
- Silves Ltd will adopt the most tax-efficient treatment which is available for these assets.

Evora Ltd – trading overseas:

- On 1 July 2024, Evora Ltd will start trading in the country of Salema.
- Evora Ltd has been advised that it will be advantageous for tax purposes to operate through a permanent establishment, rather than a subsidiary company incorporated and tax resident in Salema.

– The overseas operation will be loss-making for the first nine months of trading, after which it is expected to be profitable.

– Evora Ltd will take relief for the loss incurred by its operation in Salema as early as possible.

– Evora Ltd currently has no other overseas operations but plans to open additional permanent establishments overseas within the next few years.

The tax system in Salema:

– The rate of tax on the profits of permanent establishments in Salema is 28%.

– There is no double tax treaty between the UK and Salema.

Forecast trading results:

	Taxable trading profit/(loss)
	£
Evora Ltd – UK operations year ending 31 March 2025	610,000
– Salema operations period ending 31 March 2025	(240,000)
Silves Ltd year ending 31 March 2025	420,000

– Neither company has any other sources of income or gains.

Evora Ltd – value added tax (VAT):

– Evora Ltd is registered for the purposes of VAT in the UK and makes wholly taxable supplies.

– In April 2024, Evora Ltd engaged the services of a legal firm in Salema, to which it paid a fee of £3,500 in that same month.

– In May 2024, Evora Ltd purchased goods from a supplier in Salema costing £2,100 for sale in its UK operation.

Required:

You should assume that today's date is 1 June 2024.

(a) Explain the corporation tax treatment for Silves Ltd in the year ending 31 March 2024 in relation to the acquisition of each of the two assets. (6 marks)

(b) (i) Explain, by reference to the relief(s) available for the forecast trading loss, why it will be advantageous for Evora Ltd to commence trading in Salema through a permanent establishment (PE) rather than an overseas subsidiary company. You should assume for this part that Evora Ltd does not make an election to exempt the profits of its overseas PEs from UK corporation tax. (3 marks)

(b) (ii) State the tax consequences for Evora Ltd of making an election to exempt the profits of overseas PEs from UK corporation tax, and advise the company whether or not it will be beneficial to make this election on the basis of the company's current forecast results, and its future plans. (6 marks)

(c) Explain how the following items will be reported on Evora Ltd's value added tax (VAT) return for the quarter ending 30 June 2024:

- **the services purchased from the overseas legal firm; and**
- **the goods acquired from the overseas supplier.**

State how these transactions will affect the amount of VAT payable declared on this return. (5 marks)

Professional marks will be awarded for the demonstration of skill in analysis and evaluation, commercial acumen and scepticism in your answer. (5 marks)

(Total: 25 marks)

Section 3

ANSWERS TO PRACTICE QUESTIONS – SECTION A

TAXATION OF INDIVIDUALS

1 GAIL AND BRAD (ADAPTED) *Walk in the footsteps of a top tutor*

Key answer tips

This section A question comprises corporation tax groups with a particular focus on capital gains groups, the withdrawal of company profits via bonus or dividend, ethics and inheritance tax.

Part (a) requires candidates to identify errors made in a schedule prepared on group transactions including a number of asset disposals.

Part (b) is a comparison of whether it is more tax efficient to take funds out of the company via a bonus or dividend, considering the income tax, NIC and corporation tax implications.

Part (c) offers easy marks relating to the disclosure of an error and potential tax evasion. This is an area that is regularly tested and could have been attempted first as a standalone question.

Part (d) relates to IHT and is divided into two parts. The first part asks for a general explanation of the IHT advantages of making lifetime gifts. The second part concerns a particular gift of shares and requires knowledge of the valuation rules and business property relief in order to calculate a transfer of value and provide a detailed explanation of BPR. Finally, any other tax issues arising from the gift was another requirement.

In section A questions the information needed to answer the question will often be split into at least two exhibits. It is important that you read through each exhibit available in the exam to obtain all relevant information.

The highlighted words in the written sections are key phrases that markers are looking for in your letter.

Tutor's top tips

The detailed requirements and breakdown of marks are in the email from your manager.

As you come across the requirements copy them into the answer space so that you can type your answer below and ensure that it is focused on the requirements.

With questions that involve groups of companies it can be helpful to draw a group structure diagram before you start, and include on the diagram the transactions that have happened between the group companies. This will be easier than repeatedly having to refer back to the detailed information.

(a) Schedule prepared by Mill

Tutor's top tips

Any time that a company sells shares you need to think about the substantial shareholding exemption (SSE) and will always pick up marks for stating the conditions, and whether or not they have been met.

With regard to the capital gains group element of the question, remember that an intangibles degrouping charge will arise if a company leaves a group still owning an asset that it received from another gains group company on a tax neutral basis within the last six years.

The computation

– The chargeable gain on the sale of the Simpson Building is incorrect. The sale of the building on 1 October 2020 will have taken place at no gain, no loss because Aero Ltd (A Ltd) and Zephyr Ltd (Z Ltd) were in a capital gains group (A Ltd owns at least 75% of Z Ltd). Accordingly, Z Ltd's base cost in the building is the amount paid for the building by A Ltd plus indexation allowance up to December 2017 since this is earlier than the no gain, no loss transfer.

– The post-tax proceeds on the sale of the Simpson Building will be the sale proceeds (not the chargeable gain) less the related corporation tax liability.

– Dividend income received by UK companies is generally not subject to corporation tax. Accordingly, A Ltd will not have a corporation tax liability in respect of the dividend received from Z Ltd.

The notes

1 The substantial shareholding exemption is available where a company sells shares in a trading company out of a substantial shareholding (a shareholding of at least 10%) of that company's ordinary share capital. The substantial shareholding must have been owned for a continuous period of at least 12 months in the 6 years prior to the sale.

Accordingly, the SSE will be available on the sale.

2 An intangible asset (the brand) has been transferred to Z Ltd on a tax neutral basis within six years of the sale of Z Ltd. This would normally give rise to a degrouping charge in Z Ltd but this will not arise because the SSE applies to the sale of shares.

Cash available to pay to Gail as a result of transactions 1 and 2

	£	£
Sale of the Simpson Building by Z Ltd		
Sale proceeds		140,000
Less: Cost		
Cost to A Ltd	75,000	
Indexation allowance (December 2012 to December 2017) (£75,000 × 0.127)	9,525	
		(84,525)
Chargeable gain		55,475
		£
Corporation tax (£55,475 × 25%)		13,869
Dividend paid to A Ltd (£140,000 – £13,869)		126,131
Sale of Z Ltd		
Sale proceeds in respect of Z Ltd		250,000
Total cash available for Gail		376,131

Tutorial note

Indexation allowance is not permitted after December 2017. Therefore, in the above calculation no further indexation allowance is needed from the no gain, no loss transfer date to the date of eventual sale.

(b) Payment to Gail

Tutor's top tips

The computations for bonus versus dividend are fairly straightforward in each case, but don't forget to take account of the fact that a bonus but not a dividend gives rise to a corporation tax deduction, and so this needs to be factored in.

With regard to the dividend calculations, remember to apply the dividend nil rate band and then the correct dividend rates for the parts of the dividend falling into the higher rate and additional rate bands.

Payment of a bonus of £376,131 – total additional taxes

		£
Annual employment income		85,000
Bonus		376,131
Net income		461,131
Less: Personal allowance		(0)
Taxable income		461,131
	£	
	37,700 × 20%	7,540
	87,440 × 40%	34,976
	125,140	
	335,991 × 45%	151,196
	461,131	193,712
Recurring income tax liability on £85,000 of taxable income		(21,432)
Additional income tax		172,280
Additional employee's class 1 national insurance contributions (£376,131 × 2%)		7,523
Additional employer's class 1 national insurance contributions (£376,131 × 13.8%)		51,906
Reduction in A Ltd's corporation tax liability ((376,131 + £51,906) × 25%)		(107,009)
Total additional taxes where a bonus is paid		124,700

Tutorial note

The reduction in the corporation tax liability will be dependent on there being sufficient taxable profits to absorb the tax deductions.

Payment of a dividend of £376,131 – total additional taxes

	£
Annual employment income	85,000
Dividend income	376,131
Personal allowance	0
Taxable income	461,131
£	
37,700 × 20%	7,540
47,300 × 40%	18,920
85,000	
1,000 × 0%	0
39,140 × 33.75%	13,210
125,140	
335,991 × 39.35%	132,212
461,131	
	171,882
Recurring income tax liability on £85,000 of taxable income	(21,432)
Total additional taxes where a dividend is paid	150,450

There will be no national insurance contribution or corporation tax implications as a result of the payment of the dividend.

(c) Disclosure of error

Tutor's top tips

Ethical issues will always appear in section A of the ATX examination for five marks, and these can be relatively easy marks to obtain.

Write in short paragraphs and try to make sure that you have at least five separately identifiable points in your answer.

The error made by Gail must be disclosed to HM Revenue and Customs (HMRC).

Gail can inform HMRC herself or she may authorise us to do so. However, we must not disclose the error to HMRC unless we have her permission.

We cannot continue to act for Gail unless this disclosure is made.

We should ascertain how the error arose in order to determine whether there are further errors to disclose. We should inform the firm's money laundering officer of the situation.

We should notify Gail of the following consequences of not informing HMRC of her error:

– If she refuses to disclose the error, we will advise HMRC that we no longer act for her. We would not, however, give any reason for our actions.

– Non-disclosure of the error would also amount to tax evasion. This could result in criminal proceedings under both the tax and money laundering legislation.

(d) Inheritance tax

(i) The inheritance tax advantages of making lifetime gifts to individuals

Tutor's top tips

The question asks for the IHT advantages of lifetime gifts. Make sure you discuss all the issues as this part is worth seven marks.

Note that only the advantages are required, so there is no need to mention disadvantages.

A lifetime gift to an individual is a potentially exempt transfer. It will be exempt from inheritance tax if the donor survives the gift by seven years.

If the donor dies within seven years of making the gift, such that the gift is chargeable to inheritance tax, the value used will be the value at the time of the gift and not the value at the time of death. Any increase in the value of the asset will be ignored, although relief will be available if the asset falls in value following the gift.

Certain exemptions are only available in respect of lifetime gifts (i.e. they cannot be deducted from the death estate).

These exemptions are:

- the annual exemption of £3,000 each year
- gifts in consideration of marriage/civil partnership up to certain limits
- regular gifts out of income that do not affect the donor's standard of living

  the small gifts exemption of £250 per donee per tax year.

Any inheritance tax due on the donor's death will be reduced by taper relief if the donor survives the gift by more than three years.

The tax due will be reduced by 20% if the donor survives the gift by more than three but less than four years. The percentage reduction will increase by 20% for each additional year that the donor survives the gift.

(ii) In respect of the possible gift of 1,500 shares in Omnium Ltd to Gail

Tutor's top tips

There are three elements to this part of the question so make sure you attempt all parts.

The first part is a calculation of the transfer of value. For IHT, this is based on the ***fall in value*** *or* ***diminution in value*** *of Brad's estate.*

However, shares in Omnium Ltd are also owned by Brad's wife, so there is a related property calculation as part of the transfer of value.

Remember that if we are dealing with related property and shares we apportion the value of the combined ownership based on the ***number*** *of shares.*

The formula is:

A/(A+B) × combined ownership

where A is donor's number of shares and B is the related property's number of shares.

In this answer the examining team has used the short cut calculation possible for valuing shares. In the question you are given the value per share, so all you need to do is to value Brad's shares using the price per share based on the combined percentage ownership.

Fall in value of Brad's estate

Before the gift, Brad owned a 30% interest and his wife a 45% interest; therefore, the couple have a combined ownership interest of 75%.

After the gift, Brad's ownership would be 15% and therefore the combined ownership of the couple will drop to 60%.

The fall in value of Brad's estate on a gift of 1,500 shares in Omnium Ltd using the related property rules will be (see tutorial note):

	£
Value of shares held prior to the gift (3,000 × £290)	870,000
Value of shares held after the gift (1,500 × £240)	(360,000)
	510,000

Tutorial note

Using the A/(A + B) rules:

	£
Value of shares held prior to the gift:	
(7,500 × £290) × (3,000 ÷ (3,000 + 4,500))	*870,000*
Value of shares held after the gift:	
(6,000 × £240) × (1,500 ÷ (1,500 + 4,500))	*(360,000)*
	510,000

Ignoring the related property rules:

	£
Value of shares held prior to the gift (3,000 × £205)	615,000
Value of shares held after the gift (1,500 × £190)	(285,000)
	330,000

The higher fall in value of £510,000, produced by reference to related property, will be used.

Tutor's top tips

The model answer shows the transfer of value with and without using related property. Don't worry if you didn't get this point. Technically, both calculations are necessary and the higher transfer of value is the answer. However, this is almost always going to be the value used where related property is gifted.

Business property relief

Tutor's top tips

The requirement asks for a detailed explanation of whether or not BPR is available. The question does not specify what activity the company is involved in. Business property relief will not be available if the business of Omnium Ltd consists wholly or mainly of dealing in securities, stocks or shares or land and buildings or the making or holding of investments.

Business property relief will not be available if the business of Omnium Ltd consists wholly or mainly of dealing in securities, stocks or shares or land and buildings or the making or holding of investments. Accordingly, it will be necessary to determine the nature of Omnium Ltd's activities.

Brad must have owned the shares for at least two years at the time of the gift. This condition is satisfied.

Business property relief will not be available unless Gail still owns the shares at the time of Brad's death (or had died whilst owning the shares) and the shares continue to qualify for the relief.

If all of the conditions set out above are satisfied, business property relief will be available at the rate of 100%, because Omnium Ltd is an unquoted company

Tutorial note

Business property relief will only be relevant if Brad were to die within seven years of making the gift, such that the potentially exempt transfer became a chargeable transfer.

Business property relief would also be available if Gail disposed of the shares prior to Brad's death and acquired qualifying replacement property within three years of the disposal.

Other tax issues

The gift of shares will be a disposal at market value for the purposes of capital gains tax. Gift holdover relief will be available if Omnium Ltd is a trading company.

Gifts of shares are not subject to stamp duty.

Tutorial note

The question asked for a brief statement only of the other tax issues. Do not waste time writing lots of detail here.

Examiner's report

Note that this part of the question has been adapted since it was originally set.

Part (a) required candidates to review a schedule which had been prepared by a junior member of the tax department. Candidates had to identify any technical errors in the schedule and explain whether or not the notes to the schedule were correct.

There were three errors to spot and candidates did well.

The first error related to the sale of a building. The point here was that the building had been acquired from a group company at no gain, no loss, such that its base cost was the original cost to the group. The majority of candidates identified this point.

The second error was that, in calculating post-tax proceeds, the junior member had deducted the tax from the gain rather than the sales proceeds. This has been a very common error in previous sittings when candidates are asked to calculate post-tax proceeds; very few candidates identified this as an error.

The final error was that the junior member had treated a dividend from a subsidiary as being subject to corporation tax. The majority of candidates identified this error. The notes to the schedule related to degrouping charges and the substantial shareholding exemption.

Degrouping charges are not so easy to explain and candidates found it difficult to articulate precisely what had been transferred at no gain, no loss, and which company was leaving the group.

Many candidates would have benefited from stating clearly the circumstances in which a degrouping charge arises before trying to work out what would happen in relation to the particular facts of the question. This would have earned a mark and would have clarified the candidates' thinking.

Candidates' knowledge of the substantial shareholding exemption was good with many candidates scoring high marks on this aspect of the question.

Part (b) concerned the payment of a bonus or a dividend. This was more straightforward and was done quite well.

As far as the bonus was concerned, the only common error was a failure to consider the corporation tax savings, as requested by the manager in the question. Often, the candidates who missed this also failed to consider the NIC implications for the company of the method of remuneration used.

The payment of the dividend was also handled pretty well. *This part of the examiner's report has been amended following changes in tax treatment.*

The third part of the question concerned the need for the client to disclose income in respect of an earlier tax year. This was straightforward and was done well. Having said that, a minority of candidates had not prepared for this aspect of the exam and so did not attempt this part of the question. One common error was to describe the potential interest and penalties implications in great detail despite the question stating that these matters had already been explained to the client.

Part (d) of the question has been added from another past exam question. The relevant section of the examiner's report for that question is below:

In the first part of part (d) many candidates did very well but the performance of the majority was unsatisfactory.

The advantages of lifetime giving are scattered throughout the inheritance tax system with certain exemptions only being available in respect of lifetime gifts, potentially exempt transfers being exempt once the donor has lived for seven years, taper relief once the donor has lived for at least three years, and the value of a gift being frozen at the time of the gift together with the availability of relief for any fall in value of the assets gifted.

Most candidates would have known all of these rules but many did not include them all in their answers. Instead they wrote at length about some of them whilst omitting others. In particular, many candidates did not address the exemptions available in respect of lifetime giving. This is likely to be because candidates simply started writing and kept writing until they felt they had written enough. These candidates would have benefited from thinking their way through the inheritance tax system and noting each of the advantages of lifetime giving before they started writing.

The valuation, which involved fall in value together with related property, in the second part of (d) was done well with many candidates scoring full marks. A minority of candidates were not aware that it is only the spouse's property that is related whilst others failed to appreciate that it is only the donor's property that is valued (the related property is only relevant when determining the valuation).

The business property relief was done well with the majority of candidates identifying the two-year rule. Fewer candidates stated the need for the donee to continue owning the shares until the death of the donor.

Candidates did not do so well when it came to identifying other tax issues. Most candidates simply repeated the basics of the inheritance tax rules in relation to potentially exempt transfers when what was required here was consideration of capital gains tax and stamp duty.

ACCA marking scheme			
			Marks
(a)	Explanations		
	Chargeable gain on the sale of the Simpson Building		1.5
	Post-tax proceeds on the sale of the Simpson Building		1.0
	Taxation of dividend from Zephyr Ltd		1.0
	Substantial shareholding exemption		2.5
	Degrouping charge		2.0
	No non-errors identified		1.0
	Calculation		
	Chargeable gain on the sale of the Simpson Building		1.5
	Other matters		1.5
			12.0
		Maximum	11.0
(b)	Payment of bonus		
	Taxable income		1.5
	Income tax liability		1.5
	National insurance contributions		1.5
	Reduction in corporation tax		1.5
	Payment of dividend		
	Calculation		2.5
	No NIC liability or CT deduction		1.0
			9.5
		Maximum	9.0
(c)	Necessary to disclose		2.5
	Implications of failing to disclose		3.0
	Consider possibility of further errors		1.0
			6.5
		Maximum	5.0

(d)	(i)	Seven-year rule		1.0
		Valuation		2.0
		Exemptions		3.0
		Taper relief		2.0
				8.0
			Maximum	7.0
	(ii)	Fall in value		3.5
		Availability of business property relief		
		Business of Omnium Ltd		1.5
		Brad's ownership of the shares		1.0
		Circumstances on Brad's death		1.0
		Calculation of business property relief		
		Rate of relief		1.0
		Other tax matters		2.5
				10.5
			Maximum	8.0
	Professional skills marks (see below)		**Maximum**	10.0
Total				**50.0**

Professional skills marks

Communication

- General format and structure of notes (e.g. use of headings/sub-headings to make notes easy to refer to).
- Style, language and clarity (tone of notes, presentation of calculations, appropriate use of the tools, easy to follow and more than a negligible amount of content).
- Effectiveness of communication (answer is relevant, specific rather than general and focused to the requirement).
- Adherence to specific instructions made in the scenario (e.g. not checking computations in the schedule).

Analysis and evaluation

- Analysis of the information to determine the errors made in the schedule prepared by Mill in part (a).
- Use of information to perform appropriate calculations to determine the total cash available for Gail in part (a).
- Analysis of the information to determine the total additional tax payable for either a bonus or dividend in part (b).
- Use of information to determine the inheritance tax treatment of the gift of shares in Omnium Ltd in part (d).
- Demonstration of ability to consider taxes relevant to requirement (b), i.e. income tax, national insurance contributions and corporation tax.

Scepticism

- Identification that information relating to the activities of Omnium Ltd is needed to conclude whether reliefs are available in part (d)(ii).
- Recognition that BPR can be withdrawn if the shares are no longer owned at the time of Brad's death in part (d)(ii).

Commercial acumen

- Identification of relevant inheritance tax advantages of lifetime giving in part (d)(i).
- Identification of relevant tax factors for the gift of the shares besides inheritance tax in part (d)(ii).

2 ZITI (ADAPTED) *Walk in the footsteps of a top tutor*

Key answer tips

This section A question has four distinct parts:

Part (a) relates to the disposal of an unincorporated business on two alternative disposal dates (31 March 2025 and 31 March 2026). The examining team expects you to compare the after-tax sale proceeds after payment of both income tax and capital gains tax.

This is the most demanding part of the question and a methodical approach is necessary together with a sound understanding of capital allowances.

With regard to capital gains tax, Ravi (Ziti's father) gave the business to Ziti back in July 2020 and claimed full gift holdover relief, so you need to consider the impact of this on Ziti's disposal and also think about whether business asset disposal relief is available.

There are five easy marks on VAT, for a comparison of the disposal of assets following a cessation of trade and the disposal of a business as a going concern. This is commonly tested, so make sure you know the conditions.

Part (b) relates to the inheritance tax payable by Ziti if Ravi were to die any time between 2 June 2024 and 30 June 2027. This is challenging as you need to consider when the inheritance tax liability would change. As long as you realise that the two main factors affecting the IHT liability are business property relief and taper relief, you should be able to earn sufficient marks to pass this part of the question.

Part (c) looks at tax efficient investments, EIS and VCT in particular. If you have learnt the tax implications surrounding these then it should be easy to score well on this part. Keep your answer brief and to the point.

Finally, part (d) looks at ethical issues surrounding a payment received from HMRC in error. There will always be five marks on ethics in question one, so make sure you leave time to complete these well as they can be the easiest marks in the exam.

The highlighted words in the written sections are key phrases that markers are looking for.

Tutor's top tips

As is the norm for section A questions, the formal requirements that appear at the end of the question only tell you how many marks are available in total for technical and professional skills. The detailed requirements and technical mark breakdowns are all in the email from your manager.

The question has asked for meeting notes which address certain issues and you may find it useful to strike through the issues as you attempt them.

Make sure that you set out your answer in the required format. For meeting notes you need a suitable heading which will identify the subject. Use of sub-headings for each part which agree to the points in the manager's email will make your answer easier to mark.

Section A will always have professional marks for demonstrating communication skills, to cover presentation, relevant advice and quality of communication.

NOTES FOR MEETING

Prepared by Tax senior

Date 1 June 2024

Subject Ziti – various issues

(a) Sale of the business

(i) Post-tax income and sales proceeds

Income tax position

Tutor's top tips

As long as you methodically deal with each alternative disposal date, it should be easy to pass this part of the question, which is mostly based on TX knowledge.

Step 1: Find Ziti's profits for each cessation date.

Step 2: Find the income tax payable on Ziti's profits.

The key to success is recognising that the two alternative cessation dates fall into two different tax years.

If Ziti ceases to trade on 31 March 2025 then the final tax year is 2024/25, whereas if he ceases on 31 March 2026, the final tax year will be 2025/26.

Since Ziti acquires a new income source in the tax year 2025/26 this will impact the level of income tax payable on his profits.

It is also important to appreciate the effect that the capital allowances will have on the assessment of profits on cessation, based on the timing of capital additions and disposals.

Business cessation on 31 March 2025 in the tax year 2024/25

Adjusted profits for accounting period	**y/e 31.3.2025**
	£
Trading income	
(12 × £5,000)	60,000
Less: Capital allowances (£6,000 × 100% AIA)	(6,000)
Add: Balancing charge (TWDV £0 – £10,000 MV)	10,000
Adjusted trading profit	64,000

Tutor's top tips

The examining team wants you to quantify the after-tax proceeds so you have to find the income tax payable based on profits in the tax year 2024/25.

Don't worry if you have the wrong figure for taxable trading profit. As long as you calculate the income tax correctly based on your figure, you would still score full marks here.

Income tax payable	**2024/25**
	£
Taxable trading profit (above)	64,000
Less: Personal allowance	(12,570)
Taxable income	51,430
£	
37,700 × 20%	7,540
13,730 × 40%	5,492
51,430	
Income tax payable	13,032

Business disposal on 31 March 2026 in the tax year 2025/26

Adjusted profits for accounting periods	**y/e 31.3.2025**	**y/e 31.3.2026**
	£	£
Trading income		
(12 × £5,000)/(12 × £6,000)	60,000	72,000
Less: Capital allowances (£6,000 × 100% AIA)	(6,000)	
Add: Balancing charge (Note)		–
Adjusted trading profit	54,000	72,000

Assessment of profits

	£
2024/25	
Year ended 31 March 2025	54,000
2025/26	
Year ended 31 March 2026	72,000

Note: Since Ziti will be transferring the business to a connected party he can make a succession election to transfer plant and machinery at tax written down value.

Income tax payable

	2024/25	**2025/26**
	£	£
Taxable trading profit (above)	54,000	72,000
Property income		52,000
Less: Personal allowance (W1)	(12,570)	(570)
Taxable income	41,430	123,430
£ / £		
37,700 / 37,700 × 20%	7,540	7,540
3,730 / 85,730 × 40%	1,492	34,292
41,430 / 123,430		
Income tax payable	9,032	41,832
Less: Income tax in respect of property income (W2)		(8,232)
Income tax in respect of trading profits	9,032	33,600

Tutorial note

The income tax on the property income does not need to be included in order to assess the post-tax income from the business. The easiest way to strip this out is to calculate what the income tax would have been on the property income if there had been no trading profits and then deduct this from the total income tax payable.

Alternatively, the additional income tax on the trading profits could be calculated by working in the margin:

	£
Trading profit in higher rate band (£72,000 × 40%)	*28,800*
Loss of part of personal allowance (W1) (£12,000 × 40%)	*4,800*
Income tax in respect of trading profits	*33,600*

Workings

(W1) Personal allowance

	£	£
Personal allowance		12,570
Adjusted net income	124,000	
Threshold	(100,000)	
Excess	24,000	
Excess at 50%		(12,000)
		570

(W2) Income tax in respect of property income

	£
Property income	52,000
Less: Personal allowance	(12,570)
Taxable income	39,430
£	
37,700 × 20%	7,540
1,730 × 40%	692
39,430	
Income tax payable	8,232

Capital gains tax (CGT) position

Tutor's top tips

When computing the capital gain on the disposal of the business, it is necessary to deal with each asset separately. Gains will only arise on chargeable assets.

With cessation on 31 March 2025, Ziti is closing down the business so a disposal only arises on the building and the equipment, not the goodwill.

Alternatively, with the disposal on the 31 March 2026, the business is being sold as a going concern so it is necessary to consider the gain on the goodwill as well.

The question asks for explanations of the availability of any CGT reliefs as well as any necessary assumptions, so there will be marks available for these.

Sale of assets on 31 March 2025

	£
Capital gains:	
Building (£330,000 – £60,000 (W))	270,000
Equipment	0
	270,000
Less: Annual exempt amount	(6,000)
Taxable gains	264,000
CGT at 10%	26,400

No capital gains or losses will arise in respect of the equipment, as movable items (chattels) with a cost and market value of not more than £6,000 are exempt from CGT.

Working: Deemed cost of building

	£
Market value at date of gift	300,000
Less: Gain on gift held over (£300,000 – £60,000)	(240,000)
Deemed cost for Ziti	60,000

Tutorial note

The assets were originally given to Ziti by Ravi, and a gift holdover relief claim was made, which means that when Ziti now disposes of the business, his base cost will be the same as the original cost (Ravi's cost).

Sale of business on 31 March 2026

Tutor's top tips

There will now be a gain on the goodwill in addition to the gain on the building.

The market values of the assets have increased in this scenario so ensure you recalculate the gains as necessary.

	£
Capital gains:	
Goodwill	45,000
Building (£350,000 – £60,000)	290,000
Equipment	0
	335,000
Less: Annual exempt amount	(6,000)
Taxable gains	329,000
CGT at 10%	32,900

Tutorial note

The scenario stated that Ziti's sister did not agree to a gift holdover relief claim, so none of the gains could be deferred here. If she had agreed then part of the gain on the building could have been deferred since this was sold at less than market value. A gain equal to the actual proceeds less the base cost would have been left in charge.

Availability of business asset disposal relief (BADR):

BADR is available where a business which has been owned for at least two years:

- is sold; or
- ceases to be carried on and its assets are sold within three years of cessation.

Accordingly, the relief will be available in both situations.

Tutorial note

BADR may be denied on chargeable gains relating to goodwill where the goodwill is acquired by a close company and the individual making the disposal becomes a shareholder in the company.

However, in this scenario the business is being sold to an individual so the potential restriction does not apply.

Summary of post-tax cash

Tutor's top tips

When computing the after-tax proceeds consider only the cash inflows and cash outflows. This type of requirement features very regularly in the exam.

Cash inflows will consist of the trading income and sale proceeds received from the sale of the assets.

Cash outflows will consist of the capital cost of the equipment and the income tax and capital gains tax liabilities payable.

	Sale on 31 March 2025	**Sale on 31 March 2026**
	£	£
Trading income (£5,000 × 12)	60,000	
(£5,000 × 12) + (£6,000 × 12)		132,000
Equipment purchased 1 May 2024	(6,000)	(6,000)
Sale proceeds:		
Goodwill	–	45,000
Building	330,000	300,000
Equipment	10,000	10,000
Less: Income tax	(13,032)	
(£9,032 + £33,600)		(42,632)
CGT	(26,400)	(32,900)
Post-tax cash	354,568	405,468

Delaying the sale until 31 March 2026 would:

- be financially beneficial; and
- delay the payment of CGT.

Assumption:

Ziti has not used his annual exempt amount.

(ii) Value added tax (VAT)

Tutor's top tips

The VAT implications arising on a cessation of trade is an area that is regularly examined and should be an easy five marks, provided that you have revised this topic.

In both cases, Ziti is ceasing to trade and would have to deregister for VAT.

The difference between the two options is that the disposal on 31 March 2025 is not a transfer of a going concern (so output VAT would be payable) whereas the transfer on 31 March 2026 is a TOGC (so no output VAT is payable as long as certain conditions are satisfied).

Watch out for the building; remember that there are special rules for buildings. The question has confirmed that no option to tax has been made and the building is more than three years old.

Sale on 31 March 2025

VAT will need to be charged at 20% on the sale of the equipment.

The sale of the building will be an exempt supply, as it is a commercial building, more than three years old and no election has been made for it to be a taxable building.

Sale on 31 March 2026

VAT will need to be charged at 20% on the equipment and the goodwill unless the sale qualifies as a transfer of a going concern.

For the sale of the business to be regarded as a transfer of a going concern, the following conditions must be satisfied:

- The business must be a going concern.
- Ziti's sister must use the assets to carry on the same kind of business as that carried on by Ziti.
- Ziti's sister must be VAT registered or be required to be VAT registered as a result of the purchase (based on the supplies made by the purchased business in the previous 12 months).
- There should be no significant break in trading before or after the purchase of the business.

(b) Inheritance tax

Tutor's top tips

The question asked you to compute the IHT liability payable by Ziti for all possible dates based on Ravi dying between 2 June 2024 and 30 June 2027. The question did also give a hint and indicated that the best way to approach this is to identify the dates on which the IHT liability would change.

The first aspect to consider is the availability of 100% business property relief. If Ravi died while Ziti still owned the business, then 100% BPR would be available. However, if Ravi died after Ziti had sold the business then no BPR would be available.

After computing the inheritance tax liability, you then need to consider how the liability would change if Ravi was fortunate enough to survive for a longer period. For every consecutive year thereafter, the IHT liability would be reduced by 20% as a greater amount of taper relief would be available.

As with previous section A questions, it is imperative to spend a few minutes planning your approach prior to starting the question.

You should have identified four different periods.

1 2.6.2024 – 31.3.2025

During this period Ziti still owns the business so 100% BPR is available and no IHT liability would arise.

2 1.4.2025 – 30.6.2025

During this period no BPR is available as Ziti will have sold the business.

The IHT liability would be reduced by 40% taper relief as the period between the gift to Ziti and the date of Ravi's death is between 4 – 5 years.

3 1.7.2025 – 30.6.2026

Taper relief of 60% is available as the period between the gift to Ziti and the date of Ravi's death is between 5 – 6 years.

4 1.7.2026 – 30.6.2027

Taper relief of 80% is available as the period between the gift to Ziti and the date of Ravi's death is between 6 – 7 years.

The easiest way to approach the question is to compute the IHT liability based on the second period above and then reduce this liability by the increased taper relief.

Summary

Date of death	**Note**	**Liability**
		£
2 June 2024 to 31 March 2025	1	0
1 April 2025 to 30 June 2025	2	48,480
1 July 2025 to 30 June 2026	3(i)	32,320
1 July 2026 to 30 June 2027	3(ii)	16,160

Notes

1 If Ravi were to die whilst Ziti still owns the business, there would be no inheritance tax liability due to the availability of 100% business property relief on the transfer of an unincorporated business which has been owned by the transferor (Ravi) for at least two years.

2 Business property relief will not be available if Ziti does not own the business when Ravi dies, because he does not intend to reinvest all of the proceeds into replacement business property.

Taper relief will only be available once Ravi has survived the gift by at least three years.

	£	£	£
Value transferred			
(£40,000 + £300,000 + £9,000)			349,000
Less: Annual exemptions			
(2020/21 and 2019/20 b/f)			(6,000)
			343,000
Nil rate band		325,000	
GCTs in 7 years before the gift (1.7.2013 – 1.7.2020):			
Chargeable transfer	190,000		
Less: Annual exemptions			
(2016/17 and 2015/16)	(6,000)		
		(184,000)	
NRB available			(141,000)
Taxable amount			202,000

	£
Inheritance tax at 40%	80,800
Less: Taper relief (4 – 5 years) (40% × £80,800)	(32,320)
Inheritance tax payable	48,480

3 IHT liability with additional taper relief

		£
(i)	Taper relief of 60% (5 – 6 years) (IHT liability £80,800 × 40%)	32,320
(ii)	Taper relief of 80% (6 – 7 years) (IHT liability £80,800 × 20%)	16,160

(c) Tax-efficient investments

Tutor's top tips

You are asked to discuss income tax implications of investing in either EIS or VCT shares. Note that only income tax is required so don't waste time talking about CGT implications.

Think about any income tax relief available and also consider how any dividends received would be dealt with.

Income tax relief

Ziti's income tax liability in 2026/27, the tax year of investment, would be reduced by 30% of the amount invested in venture capital trust (VCT) shares, i.e. £7,500 (£25,000 × 30%).

The tax relief in respect of an investment in enterprise investment scheme (EIS) shares would be the same.

However, if Ziti invested in EIS shares, all or part of the relief could be carried back to 2025/26. There is no possibility of carry back for an investment in VCT shares.

Dividends received in respect of the investments

Dividend income in respect of VCT shares is not subject to income tax.

Dividend income in respect of EIS shares is taxable.

(d) HMRC error

We should investigate Ziti's tax affairs in order to determine whether or not there is a valid reason for the refund.

If we are unable to identify a valid reason, the receipt of the £5,000 must be disclosed to HM Revenue and Customs (HMRC) and repaid as soon as possible.

Ziti can inform HMRC himself or he may authorise us to do so. However, we must not disclose the error to HMRC unless we have his permission.

We cannot continue to act for Ziti unless this disclosure is made.

If Ziti refuses to notify HMRC and repay the money, then we must cease acting for him. We should advise HMRC that we no longer act for him, but not give any reasons why.

Non-disclosure of the error would also amount to tax evasion. This could result in criminal proceedings under both the tax and money laundering legislation.

Examiner's report

The first part of part (a) concerned the tax implications of the disposal of the business and was split into two sub-requirements. It was quite substantial and was worth 17 marks. Stronger candidates structured their answers in such a way that it was very clear which of the possible methods of disposal they were addressing and then dealt with the two methods one at a time. Weaker candidates did not spend sufficient time thinking about the facts of the question and simply dealt with a disposal without making it clear which of the possibilities they were considering.

This part of the examiner's report has been removed since the topic is no longer on the syllabus.

The trader had purchased equipment, which was then to be sold on the cessation of the business. This required knowledge of the fundamentals of capital allowances including the annual investment allowance (AIA) and the balancing charge on disposal. Most candidates identified the AIA but many then omitted to follow the story through to the disposal, such that the balancing charge was left out. In addition, weaker candidates prepared comprehensive (and time-consuming) calculations of capital allowances in order to arrive at an AIA of £6,000, when all that was required was a statement in the calculation of the trading profit that the AIA was £6,000.

The treatment of the personal allowance and the calculation of income tax was done well by the vast majority of candidates.

The capital gains tax implications of the sale of the business were straightforward and were handled reasonably well. However, one common error was to treat the sale of the business as if it were a sale of a single asset as opposed to a sale of the individual assets of the business. It is important to calculate a chargeable gain on the disposal of each individual asset and not to group assets together as a single disposal.

Many candidates concluded that the capital gains tax implications were the same regardless of which of the methods of disposal took place. However, this was not the case because there was a disposal of goodwill only where the business was sold as a going concern. This affected both the disposal proceeds of the assets and the capital gains tax arising.

Finally, candidates were required to prepare a summary.

From the point of view of the client there are many detailed issues and calculations to consider here so it is important to be able to bring matters together in a manner which is useful and informative.

The summary was worth a maximum of three marks and simply required figures from earlier calculations to be brought together in one place. In order to score the maximum marks available, candidates had to include the trading income and the proceeds from the sale of the assets together with both the income tax and the capital gains tax. It was also important to exclude any non-cash items. Very few candidates managed to score all three marks; and many candidates failed to produce any sort of summary.

The second part of part (a) was handled well by the majority of candidates with many candidates demonstrating a good knowledge of the various conditions necessary for a sale to be regarded as a transfer of a going concern.

The second part of the question concerned the basic mechanics of inheritance tax; it was done well by many candidates. The question concerned the gift of a business and the subsequent death of the donor.

Almost all candidates identified the gift of the business as a potentially exempt transfer that would become chargeable following the death of the donor within seven years. They were also competent at dealing with the annual exemptions, the nil rate band (with one exception – see below), the tax rate and taper relief.

The one area where a lot of candidates did not perform as well was when it came to business property relief (BPR). To begin with, many candidates omitted BPR altogether. BPR is a significant relief that all candidates should be aware of. It is important to slow down in the exam and make sure that you work through the tax implications of the particular situation in a logical way. So, with inheritance tax, assets need to be valued, then reliefs (including BPR) need to be considered, then exemptions, followed by the nil band, tax rate and taper relief.

Those candidates who did include BPR in their answers often failed to realise that if the business was sold by Ziti (the donee) before the death of his father (the donor), BPR would not be available because the rules require the donee to own the assets gifted at the date of the donor's death.

The point referred to above regarding the nil rate band relates to the relevance of the chargeable lifetime transfer (CLT) made by the donor of the business on 1 May 2016. It was thought by some candidates that this gift would have no effect on the nil rate band available as it was more than seven years prior to the death of the donor. However, because the CLT was made within seven years of the gift of the business on 1 July 2020, the nil rate band available when calculating the tax due in respect of the gift of the business has to be reduced by the amount of the CLT.

Parts (c) and (d) have been added to the question in order to fit the new exam format. The examiner's report relating to part (c) which was taken from a previous exam question, is included below.

The third part of the question required a comparison of the income tax implications of investing in enterprise investment scheme (EIS) or venture capital trust (VCT) shares. Overall, knowledge of these two types of investment was good, with the majority of candidates scoring at least three of the available marks. However, a significant number of candidates wasted time by apparently discussing everything they knew about these schemes, including the CGT exemption, and the general requirements on the company in order for investors to qualify. Once again, the question was very specific in stipulating that only the income tax implications were required, and careful reading of the question might have prevented these candidates from producing fairly lengthy explanations, which attracted no marks.

ACCA marking scheme

				Marks
(a)	(i)	Income tax position		
		Trading income		1.5
		Capital allowances		3.0
		Cessation on 31 March 2025		
		Income tax payable		1.0
		Cessation on 31 March 2026		
		Income tax payable		2.0
		Income tax on property income		1.0
		Capital gains tax position		
		Capital gains		3.5
		Capital gains tax		1.5
		Availability of business asset disposal relief		2.0
		Summary		3.0
		Assumption		1.0
				19.5
			Maximum	17.0
	(ii)	Sale on 31 March 2025		1.5
		Sale on 31 March 2026		
		Charge VAT unless it is a transfer of a going concern		1.0
		Conditions (one mark each, maximum three marks)		3.0
				5.5
			Maximum	5.0
(b)		Death prior to disposal of business		2.0
		Death post disposal of business		
		Value of gift		1.5
		Annual exemptions		1.0
		Business property relief		1.5
		Taper relief		1.0
		Nil rate band		1.5
		Inheritance tax liabilities		2.0
				10.5
			Maximum	9.0
(c)		EIS versus VCT investment		5.0
			Maximum	4.0
(d)		Necessary to disclose		4.0
		Implications of failing to disclose		2.0
				6.0
			Maximum	5.0
		Professional skills marks (see below)	**Maximum**	10.0
Total				**50.0**

Professional skills marks

Communication

- General format and structure of meeting notes (e.g. use of headings/sub-headings to make notes easy to refer to).
- Style, language and clarity (tone of meeting notes, presentation of calculations, appropriate use of the tools, easy to follow and more than a negligible amount of content).
- Effectiveness of communication (answer is relevant, specific rather than general and focused to the requirement).
- Adherence to specific instructions made in the scenario (e.g. identifying particular dates which would impact the IHT liability).

Analysis and evaluation

- Analysis of the information to determine appropriate calculations to perform to arrive at after tax cash in part (a)(i).
- Analysis of the information to determine the relevant income tax implications of share investments in part (c).
- Demonstration of ability to consider all taxes relevant to requirement (a)(i), i.e. income tax and capital gains tax.

Scepticism

- Identification that further information is needed on whether the annual exempt amount has been used in part (a)(i).
- Consideration of the possibility that the HMRC error is not, in fact, an error in part (d).
- Consideration of actions to take if Ziti is not willing to disclose the error in part (d).

Commercial acumen

- Recognition that a disposal of goodwill only arises on sale of the business as a going concern in part (a)(i).
- Identification of relevant capital gains tax and inheritance tax reliefs in part (a)(i) and (b).
- Demonstration of the ability to identify differing VAT treatment depending on the date of sale in part (a)(ii).
- Ability to identify differing IHT treatment depending on date of death in part (b).

3 JONNY (ADAPTED) *Walk in the footsteps of a top tutor*

Key answer tips

This question is in four separate parts, which could be answered in any order.

All of the areas covered are mainstream areas, and much of the technical knowledge tested is brought forward knowledge from TX: unincorporated businesses and trading losses, employed vs. self-employed factors, personal service companies and basic inheritance tax.

It is very important to retain your TX knowledge, as it is often tested in the ATX exam.

Remember that there will always be five marks available in section A of the exam for discussing ethical issues. These are often some of the easiest marks to obtain, as there are a limited number of different scenarios that could be examined.

The detailed information in the question would be shown as three separate exhibits in the real exam, which you would find of the left-hand side of the screen. Make sure that you access the information in each exhibit, as well as in the requirements button.

The highlighted words in the written sections are key phrases that markers are looking for in your letter.

Tutor's top tips

As is usual for section A questions, the formal requirements at the end of the question just tell you how many marks are available in total for technical and professional skills. The detailed requirements and technical mark breakdowns are all in the email from your manager.

As you read through, you may find it useful to highlight any requirements and instructions that you find. Refer back to these and cross them off as you answer the question, to ensure that you do not leave anything out.

Note that the requirement asks for a memorandum, so there will be marks available for using the correct format.

Memorandum

To The files

Prepared by Tax senior

Date 1 September 2024

Subject Jonny – new business, inheritance tax and other matters

(a) Unincorporated business

(i) Jonny's post-tax income

Tutor's top tips

Although unincorporated businesses and trading losses are TX topics, the ATX examining team has said that unincorporated businesses will be tested in every exam, so you must ensure that you can remember and apply the rules.

In order to answer this question, there are a number of steps to be undertaken:

1. *Explain the options available for relieving the loss and select the most tax efficient option.*
2. *Calculate the tax payable/saved for each of the first two tax years for both strong and weak demand.*
3. *Calculate the post-tax income.*

Options for loss relief with weak demand

The loss of £15,200 for the tax year 2024/25 can be offset against:

(i) Total income of the tax year 2024/25 and/or 2023/24.

In the tax year 2024/25, Jonny will have no taxable income.

In the tax year 2023/24, Jonny had employment income of £24,000 (12 × £2,000), such that he was a basic rate taxpayer.

Or

(ii) Total income of the tax years 2021/22, 2022/23 and 2023/24 in that order.

In the tax year 2021/22, Jonny had employment income of £72,000 (12 × £6,000), such that he had more than £15,200 of income taxable at the higher rate.

The loss should therefore be offset in the tax year 2021/22, resulting in a tax refund of £6,080 (£15,200 × 40%).

Income tax payable/refundable

	Strong demand		Weak demand	
	2024/25	2025/26	2024/25	2025/26
	£	£	£	£
Taxable trading profit	9,200	30,000	0	18,000
Less: Personal allowance	(9,200)	(12,570)	0	(12,570)
Taxable income	0	17,430	0	5,430
Income tax payable at 20%	0	3,486	0	1,086
Income tax refundable (above)			(6,080)	

Tutor's top tips

The question provides a table to be completed, so make sure that you do this. There are easy marks available for following through and calculating the post-tax income figures, regardless of whether your figures for the tax payable and tax savings are correct.

Post-tax income position

	Strong	Weak
	£	£
Aggregate budgeted net profit of the first two tax years (per email)	39,200	2,800
Aggregate income tax (payable)/refundable for the first two tax years (£6,080 – £1,086)	(3,486)	4,994
Budgeted post-tax income	35,714	7,794

These post-tax income figures are an approximation because they are based on estimates which could change.

(ii) Salesmen

Tutor's top tips

This part requires straightforward application of employed vs. self-employed factors. The key to scoring well here is to apply the factors to the scenario, not just list them all out. The requirement asks specifically for indicators of self-employment, so there is no need to discuss anything else.

Proposed contractual arrangements indicating self-employed status

– The salesmen will be paid a fee by reference to the work they do. This will enable them to earn more by working more efficiently and effectively.

– The salesmen will not be paid sick pay or holiday pay; such payments would be indicative of employed status.

– The salesmen will be required to use their own cars.

Suggested changes in order to maximise the likelihood of the salesmen being treated as self-employed

– It would be helpful if the salesmen were able to work on the days they choose rather than being required to work on specific days.

– The salesmen should be required to provide their own laptop computer rather than borrowing one from Jonny.

Tutorial note

The period for which the salesmen will work is not a relevant factor in determining their status. However, the longer they are appointed for, the more likely it is that the factors indicating employment (for example, the degree of control over the worker) will be present.

Personal service company (PSC) legislation

The anti-avoidance rules will only apply to the companies of the salesmen if each salesman owns at least 5% of the company.

The rules that will apply to the relationship depend on the size of Jonny's business.

If Jonny's business is classed as a small client, then it is up to the personal service company (i.e. the salesman) to determine whether the rules apply to it.

If Jonny's business is classed as a large client, then it will be Jonny's responsibility to determine whether the rules apply.

As Jonny has only just started his business, it is unlikely to be a large client – but Jonny should check this.

On the assumption that Jonny's business is a small client and the salesmen are, in substance, employees of the business, then a deemed employment income amount would be calculated as follows:

		£
Invoiced amount		X
Less:	Statutory 5% deduction	(X)
	Salary paid by PSC	(X)
	Employer's NICs on salary	(X)
	Pension contributions paid by PSC	(X)
	Expenses deductible if salesman was employed	(X)
Deemed employment income including employer's NICs		X
Less: Employers NICs	13.8/113.8	(X)
Deemed employment income		X

The salesmen would be liable to pay income tax and class 1 employee NICs on this amount, with the PSC paying class 1 employer's NICs.

Any amounts paid out of the deemed employment income to the salesman would not be subject to further tax.

(iii) New contracts for the business

Tutor's top tips

There are five marks available here, so try to make sure that you make five separately identifiable points in your answer.

- ACCA's Code of Ethics and Conduct includes confidentiality as one of the fundamental principles of ethics on which we should base our professional behaviour.
- Where we have acquired confidential information as a result of our professional and business relationships, we are obliged to refrain from using it to our own advantage or to the advantage of third parties.
- This principle of confidentiality applies to both ex-clients and continuing clients.
- As a result of this, we should not use any confidential information relating to our existing clients or ex-clients to assist Jonny.
- We are permitted to use the experience and expertise we have gained from advising our clients.

(b) Jonny's inheritance from his mother

Tutor's top tips

This part of the question involves correcting errors in an inheritance tax computation, which requires good basic knowledge of inheritance tax.

Take note of the information in the email from the manager: you are told that the arithmetic, dates and valuations are correct, and also that there were no other lifetime gifts and no business property relief. It is important to not waste time recalculating figures you are told are correct.

The exclusion of chattels less than £6,000 and application of the annual exemption to the death estate are common errors, so should have been easy to spot.

Even if you did not spot all of the errors, you would still score marks for following through and calculating the value of the inheritance receivable by Jonny.

Errors identified

1 Chattels (for example, furniture, paintings and jewellery) with a value of less than £6,000 are not exempt for the purposes of inheritance tax (although they are exempt for the purposes of capital gains tax).

2 The annual exemption is not available in respect of transfers on death.

3 There is a residence nil rate band of £175,000 available, as Jonny's mother's main residence was passed to him (a direct descendant) on her death.

4 The reduced rate of inheritance tax of 36% will apply. This is because:

- the chargeable estate, before deduction of the charitable donation and the residence nil rate band but after deduction of the nil rate band, is £689,000 (£619,000 (£591,000 + £25,000 + £3,000) + £70,000); and
- the gift to the charity of £70,000 is more than 10% of this amount.

Value of inheritance receivable by Jonny

	£
Chargeable estate per draft computation	892,000
No exemption for chattels valued at less than £6,000	25,000
No annual exemption	3,000
	920,000
Less: Residence nil rate band	(175,000)
Nil rate band	(301,000)
	444,000
Inheritance tax at 36%	159,840
Assets inherited by Jonny	
(£530,000 + £400,000 + £40,000 + £20,000 – £70,000)	920,000
Less: Inheritance tax payable	(159,840)
Inheritance receivable by Jonny	760,160

Examiner's report

Part (a), which was in three parts, related to a sole trader business. Part (a)(i) required candidates to calculate an individual's post- tax income for the first two tax years of trading, after considering the optimum relief for a trading loss in the first accounting period. A small number of candidates achieved full, or nearly full marks for this part but a significant minority made no or very little attempt to address this part of this question, suggesting a lack of preparation for this type of question. Unincorporated businesses are tested in every exam, and questions frequently demand consideration of basis periods and/or relief for trading losses, so question practice on these areas should always form an important part of all candidates' preparation for this exam.

Relief for trading losses is a technically demanding area, which requires accurate knowledge of what reliefs are available in which situations, and the precise rules or conditions in each case. Many candidates confined themselves to discussing just one method of loss relief, whereas careful reading of the question indicated that there were different options available and a decision was to be made regarding the optimum method of relief, thereby suggesting that more than one method of relief was available.

It appeared that many candidates would have benefited from pausing and thinking more before they started to write. It is important in a question dealing with relief for losses that a well-considered and logical approach is taken. Weaker candidates prepared detailed income tax computations for several tax years in the apparent hope that this would eventually lead to being able to determine the rate of tax paid in each year, and an ability to calculate the tax refund suggested by the question. The problem with this approach was that it was very time consuming and tended to produce redundant information as tax years were included for which it was not possible to offset the loss.

Candidates should be advised to consider first of all the tax years in which they believe loss relief is available, before launching into a series of detailed computations for which there are no marks available.

Part (a)(ii) concerned the employment status of two part-time salesmen and was done extremely well. The majority of candidates were able to identify which of the specific contractual arrangements given in the question concerning the work to be done by the salesmen indicated self-employment and any changes required to the other arrangements in order to maximise the likelihood of the salesmen being treated as self-employed. Many candidates gave the impression of being very confident with this topic, and happy to write at length about the different arrangements, giving the impression that they may well have exceeded the four marks worth of time which should have been allocated to this part. Candidates should always take note of the number of marks available for each question part and resist the temptation to elaborate unnecessarily on areas with which they are very comfortable.

Please note that this part of the question has been expanded since it was originally written to test the personal service company legislation.

Part (a)(iii) covered the ethical issue of confidentiality in relation to using knowledge and experience gained from dealing with both current and ex-clients to assist a new client. This part was done very well by the vast majority of candidates, with many scoring full marks. It was pleasing to see that most candidates related well to the specific client and the facts given in the scenario.

Part (b) of this question required candidates to identify errors in an inheritance tax computation on a death estate, and to calculate the amount to be received by the sole beneficiary of the estate, after the correct inheritance tax had been paid.

Performance on this part of the question was mixed, with a disappointing number of candidates believing that the capital gains tax exemption for chattels with a value below £6,000 also applies to inheritance tax, and that inheritance tax annual exemptions are available against assets in the death estate. These are fundamental errors which candidates at ATX should not be making. Candidates should ensure that they are able to identify and apply correctly the different exemptions available for capital gains tax and inheritance tax as these are tested on a very regular basis.

In order to calculate the correct amount of inheritance tax to be paid after correcting the errors found, the majority of candidates rewrote the entire death estate. This succeeded in gaining the relevant marks, but was probably fairly time-consuming, and candidates are encouraged to try and adopt a more efficient approach, focusing on the effect of correcting the error on the value of the chargeable estate as this would save time.

Questions at ATX frequently ask for a calculation of after-tax proceeds – here, the amount receivable by the sole beneficiary of the estate. Candidates need to think more carefully about the starting point for this type of calculation. Here, it wasn't the value of the chargeable estate, as this includes a deduction for the nil rate band.

Candidates needed to identify the actual value which would be received prior to making this deduction. Failure to identify the correct starting point is a common error.

ACCA marking scheme				
				Marks
(a)	(i)	Income tax payable or refundable		
		Strong demand		2.0
		Weak demand		2.0
		Advice on use of loss		
		Options available		3.0
		Recommendation		3.0
		Summary		1.0
		Calculation only an approximation		1.0
				12.0
	(ii)	Proposed contractual arrangements		3.0
		Suggested changes		2.0
		Personal service company legislation		
		5% of company		0.5
		Size of clients		2.5
		Conclusion for Jonny's business		1.0
		Deemed employment income		3.0
		Tax treatment		2.0
				14.0
	(iii)	One mark for each relevant point	**Maximum**	5.0
(b)	Identification of errors			5.5
	Calculations			
		Inheritance tax liability		2.0
		Inheritance receivable by Jonny		1.5
				9.0
	Professional skills marks (see below)		**Maximum**	10.0
Total				**50.0**

Professional skills marks

Communication

- General format and structure of memorandum (e.g. use of headings/sub-headings to make memorandum easy to refer to).
- Style, language and clarity (tone of memorandum, presentation of calculations, appropriate use of the tools, easy to follow and more than a negligible amount of content).
- Effectiveness of communication (answer is relevant, specific rather than general and focused to the requirement).
- Adherence to specific instructions made in the scenario (e.g. explaining the errors in part (b)).

Analysis and evaluation

- Appropriate use of the data to determine appropriate calculations to perform to arrive at post-tax income in part (a)(i).
- Demonstration of ability to consider all anti-avoidance scenarios that could be applicable.
- Use of the information to identify relevant errors in the death estate computation in part (b)
- Demonstration of ability to consider all taxes relevant to requirement (a)(ii), i.e. income tax and national insurance contributions

Scepticism

- Recognition that post-tax income figures are only an approximation in part (a)(i)
- Identification that further information is needed to determine which anti-avoidance rules apply in part (a)(ii)

Commercial acumen

- Identification of relevant loss reliefs for Jonny and the extent to which they would be beneficial in part (a)(i)
- Ability to identify appropriate changes to relationship with salesmen to avoid employment status in part (a)(ii)

4 RAY, SHANIRA AND KELLY (ADAPTED) *Walk in the footsteps of a top tutor*

Key answer tips

This section A multi-tax question covers income tax and NIC payment dates for a new sole trader, the effect of various expenditure options on levels of taxable income, VAT registration, the CGT and IHT implications of gifts between a couple before and after marriage, overseas aspects of income tax and ethics surrounding a new client. Most of the technical knowledge in the question is included in the TX syllabus and so illustrates the importance of maintaining TX knowledge.

The first section of part (a)(i) requires some basic income tax and class 2 and 4 NIC calculations (you have already been given the relevant taxable trading income and income tax liability figures) followed by an understanding of when relevant payments need to be made. As this is a new sole trader now receiving income that has not been taxed at source, you will need to consider the rules for payments on account.

The second section of part (a)(i) requires you to consider the effect that reinvesting profits in equipment or stock will have on the level of taxable profits. This is not something that would have necessarily been seen in question practice before the exam and so required some logical thinking.

Part (a)(ii) focuses on the very common exam topic of voluntary VAT registration. However, the question requires you to think a bit more specifically about when it is possible and *financially* beneficial to voluntarily register, rather than just generically noting a standard list of the pros and cons of voluntary registration.

Part (b) focuses on the IHT and CGT implications of gifts between couples who are either married or unmarried, in particular the timing of gifts before/after marriage so as to optimise the position re CGT annual exempt amounts, losses and base costs going forward. There is also a company takeover for a mixture of shares and cash to contend with. CGT and IHT are very frequently tested together and so it is important to understand the differences and interaction between the rules.

Part (c) tests the deemed domicile rules in conjunction with the remittance basis. The question clearly signposts remittance basis but you need to ask yourself if it would actually be available to Kelly based on her tax status.

Part (d) covers ethical concerns relating to tax avoidance v tax evasion.

The highlighted words in the written sections are key phrases that markers are looking for in your memorandum.

Tutor's top tips

The requirements at the end of the question serve only to highlight the number of marks available in total for technical and professional skills. The detailed requirements and technical mark breakdowns are all in the email from your manager.

Highlight the requirements as you come across them, and don't forget to keep looking back at them to make sure your answer is focused.

With the written elements in the exam you should try to get your points down as succinctly as possible which will help you make as many relevant points as possible and keep your answers focused and structured.

Memorandum

Client Ray and Shanira

Subject Various personal tax matters

Prepared by Tax senior

Date 1 July 2024

(a) Ray – unincorporated business

(i) Payments of tax and national insurance contributions

Income tax and class 4 national insurance contributions

Tutor's top tips

You are only asked to set out the payments due between 1 July 2024 and 31 March 2027, so there is no need to consider any further payments after that period.

31 January 2026	Amount payable in respect of 2024/25 (W)	£9,695
	First payment on account for 2025/26 (£9,695 × 0.5)	£4,848
31 July 2026	Second payment on account for 2025/26	£4,847
31 January 2027	Balancing payment in respect of 2025/26	
	(£17,540 – £9,695) (W)	£7,845
	First payment on account for 2026/27 (£17,540 × 0.5)	£8,770

Class 2 national insurance contributions

2024/25 £150 (£3.45 × 52 × 10/12)

Payable 31 January 2026

2025/26 £179 (£3.45 × 52)

Payable 31 January 2027

Tutorial notes

1. *Ray will not be required to make payments on account of his tax liability for the tax year 2024/25 because the whole of his tax liability for the previous year was settled via tax deducted at source.*
2. *The payment required in respect of the class 2 national insurance contributions for 2024/25 will be calculated by reference to the number of weeks in the tax year that Ray is carrying on his trade. This has been simplified to the nearest month in this answer.*

Working: Income tax and class 4 national insurance contributions payable 2024/25

	£	£
Income tax liability (per schedule)		6,686
Class 4 national insurance contributions		
(£46,000 – £12,570) × 9%		3,009
		9,695

2025/26

	£	£
Income tax liability (per schedule)		13,832
Class 4 national insurance contributions		
(£50,270 – £12,570) × 9%	3,393	
(£66,000 – £50,270) × 2%	315	
		3,708
		17,540

Effect on taxable income of increasing inventory or acquiring additional equipment

Tutor's top tips

Remember that drawings for a sole trader are not tax deductible. This means that, regardless of the level of drawings taken, a sole trader is taxed on all taxable trading profits.

You may find it easier to do the calculations in the spreadsheet part of the exam software. Here you can use formulas to do the calculations for you. Don't forget to reference through your workings to any explanations in the word processor. Ensure you use clear headings to distinguish the different parts of your answer.

Ray will be subject to income tax on his tax adjusted trading profit regardless of whether or not he withdraws the profits from the business.

However, the cost of any additional equipment will be deducted from his tax adjusted trading profit due to the availability of the 100% annual investment allowance, such that using the profits in this way will reduce Ray's taxable trading profit and thus his taxable income for the period in which the expenditure is incurred.

Conversely, because Ray's profits are calculated on the accruals basis, an increase in inventory levels will not have an immediate effect on his tax adjusted trading profit; the increase in purchases will be cancelled out by the corresponding increase in the closing level of inventory. Accordingly, using the profits in this way will not reduce Ray's taxable income for the period in which the expenditure is incurred.

An immediate tax deduction would be available for the cost of the inventory purchased if the cash basis were used instead of the accruals basis when calculating profits.

Tutorial note

Under the accruals basis, the sales in the statement of profit or loss are matched with the cost of goods actually sold, not the total purchases in the period.

However, under the cash basis, purchases can be deducted as soon as the cost is incurred.

(ii) Value added tax (VAT)

Information required in order to advise on voluntary registration

Tutor's top tips

*Note that the requirement is to set out the **information needed** to advise on whether or not voluntary VAT registration is **possible** and/or **financially beneficial** and explain **why** the information is needed.*

There are no marks for discussing any other aspects of voluntary VAT registration.

– The nature of the goods or services supplied by Ray's business.

  Ray cannot register for VAT if he is only making exempt supplies; he must be making some taxable supplies.

– The extent to which Ray's customers are registered for VAT.

  Once he is registered for VAT, Ray will have to charge VAT on his standard-rated supplies. Those customers who are not registered for VAT will be unable to recover this VAT, such that the addition of VAT would represent a price increase for them. If these customers will not bear such an increase, then Ray may well be worse off because his recovery of input tax will not be sufficient to compensate him for the output tax which he has been unable to pass on to his customers.

Input tax in respect of the computer

It is possible to recover input tax incurred in the four years prior to registering for VAT in respect of goods (whether inventory for resale or non-current assets) provided the goods are still owned at the date of registration. However, the recovery of input tax in respect of the computer will be restricted to the proportion of the time for which it is used for the purposes of the business.

(b) Gifts from Shanira to Ray

(i) Capital gains tax

Tutor's top tips

Watch out for the dates in this part of the question. The gift of the house has already happened in the tax year 2023/24.

As today's date is 1 July 2024, it is too late to make any further gifts in the tax year 2023/24. Any future gifts will arise in the tax year 2024/25 (or possibly later).

Ensure that you discuss any missing information as this demonstrates that you are applying scepticism.

House in the country of Heliosa

The chargeable gain on the gift of the house was £80,000 (£360,000 – £280,000). This will result in a UK capital gains tax (CGT) liability of £20,720 ((£80,000 – £6,000) × 28%).

The UK CGT will be reduced by double tax relief in respect of any CGT payable in Heliosa. Therefore, in order to finalise Shanira's CGT liability, we will need to confirm the amount of CGT payable in Heliosa on the sale of the house.

The UK CGT is due to be paid on 31 January 2025.

Proposed gifts

Tutor's top tips

Try not to get bogged down with all of the different options here.

The key points to identify are:

– *Gifts after the wedding will be at no gain, no loss and the base cost for the donee will be the original cost.*
– *Gifts before the wedding will be at market value, so a gain or loss will arise and the base cost for the donee will be the market value.*
– *The painting is standing at a loss, so this should be given before the wedding, and enough gains should be crystallised to use this loss.*

Before the wedding, a gift from Shanira to Ray will be treated as a disposal at market value, giving rise to either a chargeable gain or an allowable loss. After the wedding, no chargeable gain or allowable loss will arise on any assets sold or gifted by Shanira to Ray, or vice versa. Instead, the asset will be treated as having been disposed of for an amount equal to the disposer's CGT base cost.

Painting

The painting is currently worth less than its cost. Accordingly, it should be given to Ray before the wedding in order to realise the capital loss of £8,000 (£7,000 – £15,000).

Tutorial note

Although a gift of the painting prior to the wedding will result in a lower CGT base cost for Ray (£7,000 as opposed to £15,000), given that the couple wish to retain the painting rather than sell it in the future, this is not an issue.

Shares in Solaris plc

Shares given to Ray prior to the wedding will have a CGT base cost for Ray equal to their market value at the time of the gift, i.e. £9.20 per share. Shares given after the wedding will have a CGT base cost for Ray equal to Shanira's base cost, which is substantially lower. Accordingly, prior to the wedding, Shanira should give Ray the maximum number of shares which she can without giving rise to a CGT liability.

Shanira will have a capital loss in respect of the gift of the painting of £8,000. She will also have her annual exempt amount for the tax year 2024/25 of £6,000. Accordingly, she can make a chargeable gain of £14,000 without giving rise to a CGT liability.

The chargeable gain on a gift of all 7,400 shares would be:

	£
Proceeds at market value (7,400 × £9.20)	68,080
Less: Cost (W)	(10,468)
Chargeable gain	57,612
Chargeable gain per share sold (£57,612/7,400)	7.79

In order to realise a chargeable gain of £14,000, Shanira should give Ray 1,797 (£14,000/£7.79) of the shares prior to the wedding. The remaining 5,603 shares should not be gifted until after they are married.

Working

Sale proceeds in respect of the shares in Beem plc

	£
Shares in Solaris plc (7,400 × £8.40)	62,160
Cash	14,800
Total proceeds	76,960

Base cost in respect of Solaris plc shares (paper-for-paper):

£12,960 × (£62,160/£76,960) = £10,468

(ii) Inheritance tax

Tutor's top tips

Marks will be given for consistency here. As long as your answer reflects the advice you gave in part (b)(i) regarding which assets should be transferred, you should be awarded credit.

The maximum inheritance tax (IHT) liability in respect of the gift of the painting and the first tranche of shares made before the wedding will arise if Shanira were to die within three years of the gifts, such that no taper relief would be available. There would be no IHT payable in respect of the gift of shares made after the wedding, as this will be an exempt inter-spouse transfer.

There would also be IHT to pay in respect of the gift of the house in Heliosa, but this will arise regardless of whether the CGT planning is carried out or not.

	£	£	£
Painting			7,000
Shares in Solaris plc (1,797 × £9.20)			16,532
Transfer of value			23,532
Less: Annual exemption for 2024/25			(3,000)
			20,532
Nil rate band at time of death		325,000	
Less:			
Chargeable transfers in the previous seven years	360,000		
Less: Annual exemptions for 2023/24 and 2022/23	(6,000)		
		(354,000)	
Available nil rate band			(0)
			20,532
IHT at 40%			8,213

Tutorial note

A marriage exemption of £2,500 would be available if one of the gifts was made in consideration of marriage. However, the exemption would be conditional on the marriage taking place.

(c) Kelly's rental income in the country of Falgar

Tutor's top tips

The question mentioned the date Kelly first became UK resident. You should think about why you are told this; this allows you to see how many tax years she has been UK resident for and therefore if the long-term resident deemed domicile rules apply!

Remember that you are writing an extract for an email to Kelly, so the language used needs to be appropriate for a client. Avoid any abbreviations as she will not know what they mean.

The rental income arising in Falgar will be subject to income tax in the UK because you will be UK resident. This will be true regardless of whether or not you bring the money into the UK because the remittance basis will not be available to you.

The remittance basis will not be available because, although you are domiciled in Falgar, you are deemed to be domiciled in the UK for the purposes of income tax. This is because you will have been UK resident for 15 of the 20 tax years prior to the tax year in which the income arises.

However, the UK income tax due in respect of the rental income will be reduced by double tax relief. Double tax relief will be the lower of the UK tax and the Falgarian tax on the rental income, such that the effective UK rate will be 14% (40% – 26%).

(d) Kelly's tax planning scheme

Tutor's top tips

There will be five marks on ethical issues in Section A of every exam. These can be very easy marks to score, as long as you have revised the commonly tested ethical scenarios and apply your knowledge to the scenario. Make sure you leave yourself enough time to attempt these five marks well.

- Tax planning involves using the tax rules in the way which they were intended to be used in order to obtain a tax saving, e.g. using CGT reliefs.
- Tax avoidance also involves using the tax rules to obtain a tax saving, but may involve exploiting loopholes in the rules in order to apply them in a different way from that intended by the legislation.

- Tax evasion is illegal and involves not following the tax rules, e.g. hiding income or falsifying expenses.
- We should investigate the details of the scheme to determine whether it is truly a tax planning scheme, or if it is avoidance or evasion.

  If the scheme is a tax avoidance or tax evasion scheme then we should advise Kelly against using it.
- If we think that the proposed 'sophisticated tax planning' would amount to aggressive tax avoidance or tax evasion, and Kelly insists on using it, then we must resign from the engagement, as we cannot be seen to be involved with aggressive tax avoidance or tax evasion.
- If we resign from the engagement then we should inform HMRC of this, but not give the reasons for resignation.

Examiner's report

Part (a) concerned an individual who had begun trading as a sole trader. It covered his income tax and NIC position as well as aspects of VAT and was in two parts. Candidates often overcomplicated this part of the question because they did not answer the question set and they produced a lot of additional calculations and narrative.

The first part of (a) had two aspects to it. The main issue was the individual's cash flow position and when payments of tax and NIC needed to be made. The taxable profits for the tax years were provided in the question. Also, the tax liabilities were provided, so there was no need to calculate them. Instead, the question was testing candidates' abilities to identify when the taxes needed to be paid via self-assessment.

This aspect of the question was not done well. Some candidates provided answers that were not consistent with the requirement. Other candidates did not correctly apply the basic self-assessment payment dates to the facts of the question. Many candidates wasted time by providing additional answers that were not required, for example recalculating the tax liabilities. *(Part of the examiner's report has been removed as it relates to rules no longer examinable)* The timing of tax payments, particularly where an individual has commenced trading, is of considerable importance in the real world and is examined and will continue to be examined regularly.

The second aspect of this first part of (a) concerned the purchase of inventory or additional equipment as an alternative to taking drawings. Again, candidates found this to be a challenging area.

Candidates were expected to be aware that the level of drawings was irrelevant when determining the taxable profits of an unincorporated trader.

Many candidates provided incorrect responses about the tax implications of purchasing inventory. The most common was to write that this would reduce taxable profits, which of course is not the case. The purchase of additional equipment was handled reasonably well.

The second part of part (a) concerned VAT, in particular, voluntary registration. The majority of candidates were able to score reasonably well. However, a number of candidates did not pay attention to the requirements and instead wrote everything they knew about the subject as opposed to simply addressing the specific issues of the question. Finally, in respect of part (a), the recovery of pre-registration input tax was not handled particularly well because most candidates did not state that it was pre-registration input tax.

Part (b) of the question concerned capital gains tax and inheritance tax where there were to be gifts made either before or after the donor and donee got married.

Part (i), relating to capital gains tax, was challenging for many candidates. This was despite the fact that the rules being tested were fairly basic and that guidance as to how to approach the question was provided in the question.

From a capital gains tax point of view, most candidates knew that gifts prior to marriage would take place at market value, whilst those after the marriage would be at no gain, no loss. But candidates did not demonstrate that they can apply this knowledge to the question in order to come up with some advice.

They were also unclear as to the knock-on effect of these rules on the donee's base cost.

There were two things that candidates should have recognised when answering this part of the question.

The first was to recognise that the painting should be given before the wedding in order to realise the loss that was available. The second was to recognise that, in order to create a higher base cost for the shares, it was better to give them before the wedding, but only to the extent that the gains arising would be covered by the loss on the painting and the annual exempt amount. It was then simply a question of working out how many shares needed to be given in order to realise that amount of gain.

This question could not be answered well by just taking the numbers in the question and calculating some gains. Candidates needed to read the guidance from the manager in the question and then think about how to solve the problem.

The second part of (b) concerned the inheritance tax implications of the same gifts. The performance in this part was better than the rest of the question. Candidates needed to take care as regards the annual exemptions and the available nil rate band due to the earlier chargeable lifetime transfer. There was also the need to apply the spouse exemption to any gifts made after the marriage.

The following parts of the examiner's report have been added following merging of questions.

Part (c) asked candidates to explain how the client's overseas rental income would be taxed in the UK based on their domicile and residence. Many candidates decided that the client was not UK domiciled but did not realise that the client would be 'deemed UK domicile'. It is vital that candidates have an in-depth understanding of the detail of the ATX-UK tax rules; a superficial understanding of the rules is not enough to score well in this exam.

Part (d) has been added to the question since it was first published.

ACCA marking scheme				
				Marks
(a)	(i)	Class 4 national insurance contributions payable		2.0
		Class 2 national insurance contributions payable		1.5
		Payments and dates		5.0
		Non-withdrawal of profits		4.0
				12.5
			Maximum	11.0
	(ii)	Information required		4.0
		Input tax in respect of the computer		2.0
				6.0
			Maximum	5.0
(b)	(i)	House in Heliosa		
		Capital gains tax liability		1.5
		Information required – double tax relief		1.0
		Information required – other		1.0
		Due date		0.5
		Rationale re timing of proposed gifts		1.0
		Painting		2.0
		Shares in Solaris plc		
		Explanations		2.0
		Calculations		3.5
				12.5
			Maximum	10.0
	(ii)	Explanation		2.5
		Calculation		3.5
				6.0
			Maximum	5.0
(c)	Basis of taxation			3.0
	Tax rate			2.0
				5.0
				4.0
(d)	Tax planning			1.0
	Tax avoidance			1.0
	Tax evasion			1.0
	Investigate scheme			1.0
	Advise against if avoidance or evasion			1.0
	Resign			1.0
	Inform HMRC without reason			1.0
				7.0
			Maximum	5.0
	Professional skills marks (see below)		**Maximum**	10.0
Total				**50.0**

Professional skills marks

Communication

- General format and structure of memorandum (e.g. use of headings/sub-headings to make memorandum easy to refer to).
- Style, language and clarity (tone of extract of email, presentation of calculations, appropriate use of the tools, easy to follow and more than a negligible amount of content).
- Effectiveness of communication (answer is relevant, specific rather than general and focused to the requirement).
- Adherence to specific instructions made in the scenario (e.g. not including the extract for Kelly or the information about the tax planning scheme in the memorandum).

Analysis and evaluation

- Analysis of information to discuss the effect on taxable income of increasing inventory or acquiring additional equipment in part (a).
- Appropriate use of the data to determine suitable calculations to perform to quantify the capital gains tax and inheritance tax implications of the gifts to Ray in part (b).
- Use of information to determine impact of Kelly's residence status in part (c).

Scepticism

- Recognition of missing information with regards to Ray's business for VAT purposes in part (a).
- Identification that the tax in Heliosa needs to be quantified in part (b).

Commercial acumen

- Consideration that customers may not be willing to pay VAT in part (a).
- Identification that shares should be given away up to a tax-free amount for Shanira in part (b).

5 PIPPIN (ADAPTED) ***Walk in the footsteps of a top tutor***

Key answer tips

This is a Section A scenario question covering an individual setting up an unincorporated business, EIS shares, inheritance tax, property income and ethical issues.

The requirements can be answered independently, so careful thought should be given to the order in which you attempt the question. Identify the parts that you think you can answer quickly and attempt these first, leaving parts of the question that you think you will be tempted to spend too long on until last.

Make sure that you set out the question as a memorandum with an appropriate heading, set out your answer neatly and express yourself clearly in order to score the presentation marks available. You should also try to answer the question succinctly; this will save you time and help with the professional marks!

The first part of the question requires some basic level income tax and national insurance computations, but is likely to be very time pressured.

Requirement (ii) covers the sale of shares that qualified for EIS relief.

Requirement (iii) tests the IHT implications of a gift that could either be a lifetime gift or a transfer from an estate.

The fourth part of the question, part (iv), covers property income. The rules regarding finance costs for residential properties are covered here. Be careful, as the treatment of finance costs for individuals, such as Pippin, is very different from the treatment for companies.

The final requirement is your five marks on ethics. Remember for five marks you should be looking to make five separate points.

The highlighted words in the written sections are key phrases that markers are looking for in your memorandum.

(i) Memorandum

Client: Pippin

Subject: Various tax issues

Prepared by: Tax senior

Date: 1 June 2024

Tutor's top tips

In the first part of this question, you are given a table to complete, so there will be marks available for doing this, even if your figures are incorrect.

You must adopt a methodical approach and label your answer. There are two strategies to consider, and two tax years for each strategy, so make sure that you address all of these.

Once you have decided how to set out your answer, the actual calculations are relatively straightforward, basic level calculations. Don't forget the NICs, as there are easy marks available for calculating these, and all of the rates and thresholds are given in the tax tables.

Additional funds required for the 20-month period from 1 August 2024 to 31 March 2026

	Strategy A	Strategy B
	£	£
Total pre-tax cash receipts for the 20-month period	61,000	114,500
Cost of employing the two employees: (£60,000 + £3,000 + £810)	0	(63,810)
Total income tax and national insurance contribution liabilities for the tax years 2024/25 and 2025/26		
(£0 + £15,199)	(15,199)	
(£19,899 – £7,560)		(12,339)
	45,801	38,351
Personal expenditure (£4,000 × 20)	(80,000)	(80,000)
Additional funds required	34,199	41,649

Strategy A

2024/25

	£
Budgeted profit	13,000
Less: Capital allowances 100% AIA	(8,000)
Tax adjusted trading profit	5,000
Less: Personal allowance	(5,000)
Taxable income	0

Income tax:

	£
Covered by the personal allowance	0
Class 4 national insurance contributions (NICs):	
Below the lower profits limit	0
Class 2 NICs:	
Below the small profits threshold	0
Total tax and NICs	0

Tutorial note

Non-payment of class 2 NICs can affect the availability of state benefits, including the state pension.

Accordingly, it may be advisable for Pippin to pay the class 2 NICs even if his profit is below the small profits threshold.

2025/26

	£	£
Tax adjusted trading profit		60,000
Dividend income		500
Less: Personal allowance		(12,570)
Taxable income		47,930

Analysed as: Dividend income £500, non-savings income £47,430.

Income tax:

	£	£
£		
37,700 × 20% (non-savings)	7,540	
9,730 × 40% (non-savings)	3,892	
47,430		
500 × 0% (dividend nil rate band)	0	
47,930		
		11,432
Class 4 NICs:		
(£50,270 – £12,570) × 9%	3,393	
(£60,000 – £50,270) × 2%	195	
		3,588
Class 2 NICs:		
(£3.45 × 52)		179
Total tax and NICs		15,199

Strategy B

2024/25

	£
Budgeted loss	(10,000)
Less: Capital allowances 100% AIA	(8,000)
Tax adjusted trading loss	(18,000)

Claiming opening years loss relief will result in a repayment of income tax and class 4 NICs of £7,560 (£18,000 × 42%) in respect of the tax year 2021/22.

2025/26

		£	£
Budgeted profit			135,000
Less: Cost of employees			
	Salaries (£2,500 × 12 × 2)		(60,000)
	Mileage allowance (£0.50 × 250 × 12 ×2)		(3,000)
	Class 1 NICs:		
	Salary (£2,500 × 12)	30,000	
	Mileage payments ((£0.50 – £0.45) × 250 × 12)	150	
		30,150	
	(£30,150 – £9,100) × 13.8% × 2)	5,810	
	Less: Employment allowance	(5,000)	
			(810)
Tax adjusted trading profit			71,190
Income tax and NICs on profit of £60,000 (per strategy A)			15,199
Income tax and class 4 NICs on excess over £60,000			
(£71,190 – £60,000) × 42%			4,700
Total tax and NICs			19,899

Tutorial note

This answer calculates the income tax and NICs using the tax from strategy A as a base, and working in the margin to calculate the extra tax due. As Pippin is already a higher rate tax payer and his trading profit exceeds the upper threshold for national insurance, any additional income is subject to income tax at 40% and NICs at 2%.

Alternatively, you could have calculated the income tax and NICs on the tax adjusted trading profit of £71,190 from scratch. This gives the same answer and would gain the same marks in the exam, but takes considerably more time.

Evaluation of the two strategies

Tutor's top tips

You are asked to evaluate the two strategies by reference to the results of your calculations, so make sure you do this.

Even if your answer is not correct, you could still gain marks here for making some sensible comments about which strategy requires the least additional funding.

Strategy A requires less additional funding than strategy B over the 20-month period.

However, the annual profit under strategy A will only be £60,000. This will not be sufficient to generate the £48,000 (£4,000 × 12) of post-tax cash receipts required by Pippin.

The post-tax profit under Strategy B will be £51,291 (£135,000 – £63,810 – £19,899, such that there may be sufficient post-tax cash receipts for Pippin's needs.

(ii) Sale of shares in Akero Ltd

Tutor's top tips

The treatment of EIS shares is a new topic at the strategic professional level, and often features in the exam. There are lots of rules to learn, and you should make sure that you learn the key rules at least.

This question deals with the sale of shares and possible withdrawal of relief if the sale occurs within less than three years of purchase.

As you are not given the date of sale, you need to consider the possibility that the sale could happen within less than three years of purchase or after more than three years.

There are three different aspects to write about:

1 *The possible gain on the sale of the shares.*

2 *The deferred gain becoming chargeable.*

3 *The withdrawal of EIS income tax relief.*

To score well, you should write about all of these.

Capital gains tax

Chargeable gain on the sale of the shares

Pippin will realise a chargeable gain of £17,500 ((£4.50 – £1) × 5,000) if the shares are sold prior to 4 January 2025 (i.e. within three years of purchase) at their current market value.

However, if the shares are sold on or after 4 January 2025, the chargeable gain arising on the sale will be exempt.

Chargeable gain deferred in respect of the painting

Regardless of when the shares are sold, the chargeable gain which was deferred on their acquisition will become chargeable.

The chargeable gain deferred was £16,000, or £1 per share, such that, on the sale of 5,000 shares, a gain of £5,000 will become chargeable.

Capital gains tax liability

Any chargeable gains realised by Pippin in the tax year 2024/25 will be reduced by his annual exempt amount of £6,000.

Any gains not covered by the annual exempt amount will be taxed at 10%, as Pippin has no taxable income.

Income tax

If the shares are sold prior to 4 January 2025 at their current market value, there will be a withdrawal of £1,500 (5,000 × £1 × 30%) of the income tax relief originally obtained by Pippin. This is because the shares will have been sold for more than their cost.

Tutor's top tips

Even if you were not sure how to calculate the withdrawal of the income tax relief, you would still be given credit for stating that there would be a withdrawal of relief.

(iii) Receipt of £75,000

Tutor's top tips

This part of the question covers inheritance tax from the point of view of an individual who has received a gift of cash, and there are two alternatives to consider.

If Esme gave the cash to Pippin, the gift would be a potentially exempt transfer, so any tax liability would be borne by Pippin (the donee). You need to explain how much tax would be due.

However, if Pippin received the cash directly from Esme's father's death estate, the tax would be borne by the estate.

The question states that Esme's father left the whole of his estate to Esme, so the only way that Pippin could receive the cash from the estate would be if Esme changed her father's will using a deed of variation.

The tax implications for Pippin depend on whether the £75,000 was a direct gift from Esme or the result of Esme having made a tax-effective deed of variation of her father's will.

Gift from Esme

The gift would have been a potentially exempt transfer. Esme's death within seven years of the gift would result in an inheritance tax liability for Pippin as follows:

	£
Transfer	75,000
Inheritance tax at 40% (Note)	30,000
Taper relief (5 to 6 years) (£30,000 × 60%)	(18,000)
	12,000

Note: Esme's annual exemptions and her nil rate band were used by the gift on 1 November 2018.

Deed of variation

A deed of variation whereby £75,000 of Esme's inheritance was transferred to Pippin would not be treated as a gift from Esme to Pippin. Instead, the money would be regarded as having passed to Pippin via his grandfather's will. Accordingly, in these circumstances, there would be no inheritance tax implications for Pippin as a result of the death of Esme.

(iv) Cottage in Cornwall

The rental income from the cottage will be subject to income tax on a cash basis. The rent will be assessed to income tax in the tax year in which it is received and the letting agent fees and insurance will be deductible from the rental income when they are paid.

The mortgage interest is not deductible against rental income, but will be given basic rate tax relief as a deduction against Pippin's income tax liability.

Tutor's top tips

Rental income is assessed on the cash basis if gross rental receipts do not exceed £150,000 for the tax year. It is possible that Pippin could elect to be taxed on the accruals basis, but you should assume the cash basis is used unless you are told otherwise.

(v) Disclosure of property income

Tutor's top tips

There will always be five marks on ethical issues in section A of the exam, and these can be easy marks to obtain.

This requirement covers the implications of a client not disclosing information to HMRC, and is similar to requirements seen in past exams.

This information must be disclosed to HM Revenue and Customs (HMRC). We should encourage Pippin to make this disclosure when the income arises.

Pippin can inform HMRC or may authorise us to do so. However, we must not disclose the income to HMRC without permission.

We cannot continue to act for Pippin if he refuses to make this disclosure.

We should notify Pippin of the following consequences of not providing this information to HMRC:

– If he refuses to disclose the income, we will advise HMRC that we no longer act for him. We would not, however, give any reason for our actions.

– Non-disclosure of the income would also amount to tax evasion. This could result in criminal proceedings under both the tax and money laundering legislation.

We should inform our firm's money laundering officer of the situation, but not tip off Pippin.

Examiner's report

The first part concerned a plan to start a new unincorporated business. Candidates were asked to prepare a table of figures in order to determine the individual's cash position for two alternative business strategies after two years of trading. One of the strategies required the individual to take on two employees.

The technical content of this part of the question was reasonably straightforward and required candidates to:

- recognise the availability of the annual investment allowance
- determine the relief available in respect of a trading loss in the first tax year of trading
- deal with the tax implications for the employer of paying a mileage allowance to the employees
- calculate the employer's class 1 contributions in respect of the employees
- calculate the income tax, class 4 and class 2 liabilities of the individual.

Accordingly, in order to do well, candidates needed to concentrate on the detail, be brisk in their approach and avoid any unnecessary narrative. Many candidates were able to do this and there were some very high-quality answers to this part of the question.

Weaker candidates were less willing to commit themselves to the numbers and instead wrote about the tax implications in more general terms. Some candidates also let themselves down by failing to consider the individual's national insurance contributions position, such that they did not attempt quite a few of the marks on offer.

There were few technical problems with this part of the question. The one common error was the implications of the mileage allowance, with most candidates knowing there was a rule regarding the excess over 45p per mile but many thinking it related to the tax deductibility of the payments made as opposed to the class 1 contributions due.

The second part of the question required candidates to explain the tax liabilities on the sale of shares in respect of which income tax relief under the enterprise investment scheme and EIS deferral relief had been claimed.

As is so often the case, in order to score well, candidates needed to stop and think. In particular, they needed to identify the three separate implications of the sale of the shares. It was important to do this first because candidates then knew how much needed to be explained in the relatively short amount of time available.

The three implications which needed to be explained were:

- the gain which was deferred when the shares would become chargeable
- an element of the income tax relief obtained when the shares were acquired would be withdrawn
- there would be a chargeable gain on the sale of the shares themselves.

Weaker candidates identified one of these points and wrote about it at length rather than identifying all of the points which needed to be made.

The final part of the question concerned inheritance tax and was done reasonably well. Candidates were very comfortable with the basic mechanics of the tax including death within seven years of a potentially exempt transfer (PET), the nil rate band and the availability of taper relief. Weaker candidates did not always relate the facts of the question to the requirement, such that they ignored the chargeable lifetime transfer which was made prior to, but in the same tax year as, the PET. This meant that they wrote in general terms about the availability of the annual exemption and the nil rate band rather than applying the rules to the specific facts of the question.

Note that parts (iv) and (v) have been added since the question was originally set.

ACCA marking scheme			
			Marks
(i)	Completion of table		1.5
	Strategy A		
	2024/25		3.5
	2025/26		5.0
	Strategy B		
	Cost of employees		5.5
	2024/25		3.5
	2025/26		2.5
	Evaluation		2.0
			23.5
		Maximum	20.0
(ii)	Gain on shares sold		2.0
	Deferred gain		2.0
	Capital gains tax liability		1.5
	Income tax		1.5
			7.0
(iii)	PET and death within seven years		3.5
	Deed of variation		2.0
			5.5
		Maximum	5.0
(iv)	Cash basis		0.5
	Treatment of income and expenses		1.0
	Treatment of mortgage interest		1.5
			3.0
(v)	One mark per relevant point made	**Maximum**	5.0
	Professional skills marks (see below)	**Maximum**	10.0
Total			**50.0**

Professional skills marks

Communication

- General format and structure of memorandum (e.g. use of headings/sub-headings to make memorandum easy to refer to).
- Style, language and clarity (tone of memorandum, presentation of calculations, appropriate use of the tools, easy to follow and more than a negligible amount of content).
- Effectiveness of communication (answer is relevant, specific rather than general and focused to the requirement).
- Adherence to specific instructions made in the scenario (e.g. not checking the pre-tax cash receipts).

Analysis and evaluation

- Use of information to determine appropriate calculations to perform to work out additional funds required in part (i).
- Evaluation of the two strategies by reference to the figures calculated in part (i).
- Use of information to determine the appropriate tax treatment of the sale of the Akero Ltd shares in part (ii).
- Demonstration of ability to consider all taxes relevant to requirements (i) (income tax and national insurance contributions) and (ii) (income tax and capital gains tax).
- Analysis of the information to determine the inheritance tax implications of the receipt of the £75,000 in part (iii).

Scepticism

- Recognition that Strategy A may not be sustainable in the longer term, despite requiring less additional funding in part (i).
- Demonstration of an ability to challenge a client with regards to unethical behaviour in part (v).

Commercial acumen

- Calculation of tax saving for loss offset in part (i).
- Demonstration of an awareness of purpose behind the rules for EIS shares in part (ii).

6 MAIA (ADAPTED) *Walk in the footsteps of a top tutor*

Key answer tips

This question covers calculations of post-tax income, CGT and IHT implications of a variety of alternative options, as well as some trust income tax and ethics.

The first part of the question tests mostly TX knowledge, aside from the share scheme. Although this is mostly brought forward knowledge it is tested in a more advanced way as it gets you to think about post-tax income and how that has an effect on the amount of cash needed by an individual. It is important to think carefully and read the advice in the requirement before diving into the calculations.

The second part of the question may look quite overwhelming when you first read through. There is a lot to cover, but if you take an organised approach to ensure you cover each individual aspect you should be able to score well on this.

The third part of the question, part (c), covers the income tax treatment of trusts. Trusts are generally not a popular area with students, although this section is actually very straightforward if you have learnt the rules.

The final part of the question allows for some easy marks to be earned by listing out the various procedures that should be followed when appointing a new client. Ensure that you leave sufficient time to do this part well, or you may even consider doing this first.

The highlighted words in the written sections are key phrases that markers are looking for.

Memorandum

Client Maia

Subject Provision of financial assistance for Josh and advice for Sarika

Prepared by Tax senior

Date 1 June 2024

(a) Josh – additional cash requirement

Tutor's top tips

*Think carefully about what you are being asked to calculate in this part of the question. It is the **extra** cash over and above Josh's after-tax income from two tax years.*

The cash required is given in the question as this is the rent that needs to be covered for two years. You then need to find the after-tax income for the two tax years in question.

The requirement helps by telling you to think about how his income will differ in the tax year 2025/26 compared to 2024/25. The only difference is the share issue, so if you add back the tax on this to your result for the tax year 2024/25 you should get to the equivalent after tax figure for 2025/26.

2024/25	£	£
Salary	25,200	25,200
Shares in NL Ltd (£2,100 – £300)	1,800	
Home cinema (£1,700 × 20%)	340	
Mobile telephone (exempt)	0	
Employment income	27,340	
Dividend income	420	420
	27,760	
Less: Personal allowance	(12,570)	
	15,190	
		25,620
Income tax		
£14,770 (£27,340 – £12,570) × 20%	2,954	
£420 × 0% (nil rate band)	0	
		(2,954)
Class 1 national insurance contributions (NIC)		
(£25,200 – £12,570) × 12%	1,516	(1,516)
Income after tax and NIC		21,150
2025/26		
As for 2024/25		21,150
Add: Tax in respect of shares in NL Ltd (£1,800 × 20%)		360
Income after tax and NIC		21,510
Cash required (24 × £2,500)		60,000
Anticipated income (£21,150 + £21,510)		(42,660)
Additional cash required		17,340

(b) Providing financial assistance to Josh – alternative strategies

Tutor's top tips

There is a lot to do in this part of the question and it is easy to get confused. Ensure you cover all aspects by using headings to structure your answer. For each alternative strategy you should consider:

1. *The increase in post-tax income for Josh (not needed for strategy (ii))*
2. *The CGT liabilities for Maia*
3. *The IHT implication for Maia and Josh including consideration of BPR*

For both 2 and 3 you also need to consider the position whether the property qualifies as furnished holding accommodation or not. You were told not to include the definition so make sure you don't include any unnecessary detail.

(i) Gift of investment property

Increase in Josh's post-tax income

Josh would receive net rental income of £13,200 (£1,100 × 12) in a full tax year, such that he would continue to be a basic rate taxpayer. Accordingly, his additional post-tax income in the 21-month period from 1 July 2024 to 5 April 2026 would be £18,480 (£1,100 × 21 × 80%).

Capital gains tax (CGT) liabilities for Maia

Maia's gift of the building would be treated as a sale at market value for the purposes of calculating the chargeable gain. This gives rise to a gain of £240,000 (£370,000 – £130,000).

If the building IS NOT furnished holiday accommodation:

- The building would not be a business asset, such that neither gift holdover relief nor business asset disposal relief would be available.
- Maia is a higher rate taxpayer who uses her annual exempt amount every year. Accordingly, her CGT liability on the gift of the building will be £67,200 (£240,000 × 28%).

If the building IS furnished holiday accommodation:

- Gift holdover relief would be available because furnished holiday accommodation is included within the definition of business assets used in the trade. Accordingly, no CGT would be payable by Maia in respect of the gift.

Tutorial note

A claim for gift holdover relief would need to be signed by both Maia and Josh as it is a joint election. Those candidates who did not recognise the availability of gift holdover relief were given credit for explaining that business asset disposal relief would be available, such that the CGT rate applied to the gain would be 10%.

Inheritance tax (IHT) implications for Maia and Josh

If the building IS NOT furnished holiday accommodation:

- The gift would be a potentially exempt transfer, such that there would be no inheritance tax due unless Maia were to die within seven years of the gift.
- If Maia were to die within seven years of the gift, the excess of the market value of the property at the time of the gift (i.e. £370,000) over Maia's available nil rate band would be subject to IHT at 40%. This tax would be payable by Josh.
- Maia's available nil rate band would be the nil rate band for the year of death (assumed to be £325,000) less her chargeable transfers in the seven years prior to 1 July 2024.

- Taper relief would be available if Maia were to survive the gift by more than three years. This would reduce the IHT by 20% for each additional full year for which she survived the gift.

If the building IS furnished holiday accommodation:

- Since Maia will have owned the building for more than two years prior to the transfer, the gift could qualify for 100% business property relief (BPR). However, the building will only qualify as relevant business property if Maia is able to demonstrate to HM Revenue and Customs (HMRC) that it is operated as a business with substantial involvement by her (and subsequently by Josh) and additional services are provided. It should be anticipated that this treatment will be resisted by HMRC.
- Even if it does qualify for BPR, it will be necessary for Josh to still own the building (or replacement business property) and for it to still be qualifying business property at the time of Maia's death.

Tutorial note

If Josh no longer owned the property as at Maia's death, then if he had not replaced it with other qualifying business property BPR would be withdrawn and IHT would become chargeable at death. This would therefore give rise to the same consequences as if the building hadn't been furnished holiday accommodation.

(ii) Gift of shares in Far Ltd

CGT liabilities for Maia

Maia's gift of the shares would be treated as a sale at market value for the purpose of calculating the chargeable gain. Gift holdover relief would be available because Far Ltd is an unquoted trading company.

	£	£
Proceeds at market value		420,000
Less: Cost		
Market value on 1 November 2023	375,000	
Less: Gift holdover relief in respect of earlier gift	(140,000)	
		(235,000)
		185,000
Less: Gift holdover relief (£185,000 × 84% (100% – 16%))		(155,400)
Chargeable gain		29,600

Business asset disposal relief would not be available, regardless of whether or not Maia works for Far Ltd, because Maia will not have owned the shares for two years on 1 July 2024. Accordingly, as Maia is a higher rate taxpayer, her CGT liability would be £5,920 (£29,600 × 20%).

IHT implications for Maia and Josh

Business property relief would not be available because Maia will not have owned the shares for two years on 1 July 2024. Accordingly, the IHT implications would be the same as for the gift of the investment property, where it is not furnished holiday accommodation, as set out above.

(iii) Monthly cash gifts

Increase in Josh's post-tax income

There would be no income tax implications for Josh. He would therefore receive £21,000 over the 21-month period.

CGT liabilities for Maia

There would be no CGT implications for Maia because cash is an exempt asset.

IHT implications for Maia and Josh

These gifts are likely to be exempt from IHT as they would satisfy the following conditions:

- They would be part of Maia's expenditure out of her income.
- There would be a regular pattern of giving.
- They would not affect Maia's standard of living.

(c) Tax treatment of trust income received by Josh's girlfriend

Tutor's top tips

Be careful that you don't waste time here. You only need to talk about the tax treatment of the ***income*** *received from the trust by Josh's girlfriend.*

There are four marks available, so your answer needs to reflect this. Note that the question does not tell you what type of trust it is, so you need to discuss the different types of trust and the tax treatment of income received from each.

The question clearly states that the income is dividend income, so don't waste time discussing any other types of income.

The trust will be either an interest in possession trust or a discretionary trust:

- It will be an interest in possession trust if Sarika has an absolute right to the income generated by the trust assets.
- It will be a discretionary trust if the trustees have the right to accumulate the income and pay it to Sarika when they choose.

It is understood that the only income received by the trustees of the trust is dividend income.

Interest in possession trust

- The income to which Sarika is entitled must be grossed up at 100/91.25.
- The first £1,000 of dividend income will be taxed at 0% (i.e. there will be no tax).

- Where dividend income exceeds £1,000 and falls into Sarika's basic rate band (after calculating the tax on her salary) it will be taxed at 8.75%.
- The balance of the income will be taxed at 33.75%.
- There will be an 8.75% tax credit.

Discretionary trust

- The income received must be grossed up at 100/55.
- Where the income falls into Sarika's basic rate band it will be taxed at 20%.
- The balance of the income will be taxed at 40%.
- There will be a 45% tax credit.

Tutorial note

There is no £1,000 nil rate band for dividends received from a discretionary trust as the income is assessed on the beneficiary as non-savings income.

The 8.75% tax credit in respect of the dividend from the interest in possession trust and the 45% tax credit relating to the income from the discretionary trust are refundable.

(d) Procedures we should follow before we agree to become Sarika's tax advisers

– We must obtain evidence of Sarika's identity (for example, her passport) and her address.

– We must have regard to the fundamental principles of professional ethics. This requires us to consider whether becoming tax advisers to Sarika would create any threats to compliance with these principles.

– Professional competence: we must ensure that we have the skills and competence necessary to be able to deal with the matters which may arise in connection with Sarika's affairs.

  If any such threats are identified, we should not accept the appointment unless the threats can be reduced to an acceptable level via the implementation of safeguards.

– We should contact Sarika's existing tax adviser(s) (if any) in order to ensure that there has been no action by Sarika which would preclude the acceptance of the appointment on ethical grounds.

– We must carry out a review in order to satisfy ourselves that Sarika is not carrying on any activities which may be regarded as money laundering.

Examiner's report

This question concerned a wealthy aunt looking to provide financial assistance to her nephew. The aunt was considering three alternative strategies involving the gift of a property, gift of shares and a gift of cash.

The first part of the question required calculations to determine how much additional cash would be required by the nephew over a two-year period, by comparing his cash income to his cash outgoings. In order to calculate his outgoings, candidates needed to calculate his income tax and national insurance contributions. It was pleasing to see that many candidates answered this part well, with a significant number of candidates achieving almost full marks.

However, a number of candidates did not recognise that employees' national insurance contributions would not be payable on benefits-in-kind. Many candidates lost valuable time producing two full income tax computations for the two tax years instead of looking at the change that had occurred between the two years and simply calculating how this would affect income tax payable.

Despite the fact that this part of the question specifically asked candidates not to provide any narrative explanation of the calculations, many candidates spent time providing explanations for which although correct, there were no marks awarded.

The second part of the question was split into three sub-parts, asking candidates to consider three alternative strategies of gifting.

The first proposed strategy was for the aunt to gift an investment property to the nephew. The requirement asked for the capital gains tax consequence for the aunt and the inheritance tax consequences for both the aunt and the nephew of such a gift. The requirement stated that it was unclear if the property was furnished holiday accommodation or not but to explain the liabilities for both possibilities regarding the property. Many candidates failed to address both possibilities and often only addressed the possibility that the property was not a furnished holiday accommodation. Future candidates would be well advised to stop and think about the points they wish to address before they start writing.

Many candidates were able to identify that business property relief might be available when calculating inheritance tax but appeared to lack knowledge of the conditions required for this relief. A significant number of candidates gave a definition of furnished holiday accommodation when it was specifically stated in the requirement that they should not provide this definition. Again these candidates would have benefitted from spending time ensuring they fully understood the requirement and planning their answer, before beginning to write. By doing this, it is likely they would have saved themselves time in the long run and allowed themselves to earn as many of the available marks as possible.

The second proposed strategy was for the aunt to gift shares in an unquoted trading company. Many candidates were able to identify the possibility of gift holdover relief but did not restrict the gift holdover relief for chargeable non-business assets. As before, candidates were able to recognise that business reliefs such as business asset disposal relief and business property relief might be available but unfortunately did not apply the conditions for these reliefs to the facts of the question.

The third proposed strategy was for the aunt to make monthly cash gifts and it was very positive to see that many candidates scored full marks on the capital gains tax and inheritance tax implications of such cash gifts.

Marks were awarded for professional skills in this question. These marks were awarded for clear and logical explanations and calculations, for a sensible approach to solving the problems set in parts (a) and (b), for answers that were scenario specific rather than general, and for a professionally acceptable style. Generally the candidates performed reasonably well in this area.

The sections below have been inserted from previous past exam questions due to adaptation of this question to the new exam format:

The third part of the question concerned the tax treatment of income received from a trust. This was a test of knowledge, as opposed to application of knowledge, and candidates should have scored well.

However, the marks for this part were not as high as expected because candidates were not sufficiently careful in their approach. As always, the advice here is to stop and think. The question made it clear that the nature of the trust was not known and therefore candidates were expected to consider the income tax position of receipts from both an interest in possession trust and a discretionary trust. There was also the need to be specific and precise, as regards grossing up fractions and tax rates, rather than superficial and general in order to maximise the marks obtained.

The final part of the question required a summary of the procedures to be followed before agreeing to become tax advisers for the potential new client. This appeared to be a question for which most candidates were well prepared, and most scored well. Those that didn't tended to be too general in their comments, such as talking about the need to ensure adherence to ACCA's fundamental ethical principles, without identifying which of these principles is/are particularly relevant in this scenario. It is always important in an ethics requirement to relate your answer specifically to the (potential) client, and the scenario in the question.

ACCA marking scheme

			Marks
(a)	Tax year 2024/25		
	Employment income		3.0
	PA and tax liability		2.0
	National insurance contributions		1.5
	Tax year 2025/26		1.5
	Monthly cash required		2.0
			10.0
		Maximum	9.0
(b)	(i)	Income tax	2.0
		Capital gains tax	
		Taxable gain	1.0
		If the building is not furnished holiday accommodation (FHA)	1.5
		If the building is FHA	2.0
		Inheritance tax	
		If the building is not FHA	4.0
		If the building is FHA	3.0
			13.5
		Maximum	12.0
	(ii)	Capital gains tax	
		Chargeable gain	1.5
		Gift holdover relief	2.5
		Tax payable	2.5
		Inheritance tax	2.0
			8.5
		Maximum	7.0
	(iii)	Income tax	1.0
		Capital gains tax	1.0
		Inheritance tax	2.0
			4.0
		Maximum	3.0

(c)	Nature of the trust		2.0
	Tax treatment (2 × 2 marks)		4.0
			6.0
		Maximum	4.0
(d)	Identity		1.0
	Fundamental principles		2.0
	Contact existing tax advisers		1.0
	Money laundering		1.0
			5.0
	Professional skills marks (see below)	**Maximum**	10.0
Total			**50.0**

Professional skills marks

Communication

- General format and structure of memorandum (e.g. use of headings/sub-headings to make memorandum easy to refer to)
- Style, language and clarity (tone of memorandum, presentation of calculations, appropriate use of the tools, easy to follow and more than a negligible amount of content)
- Effectiveness of communication (answer is relevant, specific rather than general and focused to the requirement)
- Adherence to specific instructions made in the scenario (e.g. not providing a definition of furnished holiday accommodation).

Analysis and evaluation

- Appropriate use of the data to determine appropriate calculations to arrive at additional cash required in part (a).
- Appropriate use of the data to support discussion and draw appropriate conclusions about the capital tax implications for the holiday accommodation in part (b).
- Use of the information to analyse the tax treatment of the monthly cash gifts in part (b).
- Appropriate use of the data to support discussion of the income tax treatment of the trust income in part (c).
- Demonstration of ability to consider all taxes specified in requirement (b) (capital gains tax and inheritance tax).

Scepticism

- Discussion of both interest in possession and discretionary trusts since the scenario remains silent on the type of trust in part (c).
- Identification that money laundering should be considered when taking on a new client in part (d).

Commercial acumen

- Recognition of the availability of capital gains tax reliefs in respect of the furnished holiday accommodation in part (b).
- Demonstration of an understanding of the income tax rules for trusts in part (c).

7 JOE AND FIONA (ADAPTED) *Walk in the footsteps of a top tutor*

Key answer tips

This question covers various aspects of the ATX syllabus including liquidations, tangible and intangible asset disposals, shareholder distributions, VAT for a new unincorporated business, ethics and taxation of overseas income.

Part (a) requires consideration of the capital allowance implications of disposals of two items of plant and machinery on which enhanced capital allowances were claimed. You also need to calculate the profit or loss on the disposal of an intangible asset and show recognition of how a loss would be treated within the corporation tax computation. An in-depth knowledge of the tax implications of payments to shareholders pre and post appointment of a liquidator is required for the final part of this requirement. Consideration of CGT reliefs is also required, to reduce or defer any CGT liability.

Part (b) tests the treatment of pre-trade expenses for VAT purposes, which was seen at TX. It also covers VAT for land and buildings which is a new area at ATX and one that you should ensure you are familiar with, since it is tested often.

There will be five marks on ethical issues in section A of every ATX exam, and these can be easy marks to obtain.

Part (d) requires you to discuss why the remittance basis is available to Fiona, which requires good knowledge of the conditions and potential charges, as well as calculating her income tax liability. Make sure you split the marks and your timing between these two requirements.

The highlighted words in the written sections are key phrases that markers are looking for.

Notes for meeting

For	The files
Client	Joe Sands
Prepared by	Tax senior
Date	1 June 2024

(a) Liquidation of VNL Ltd

(i) Sales of plant and machinery

Tutor's top tips

You were not given the tax written down values of the capital allowance pools, so a full capital allowance computation is not what is required here. Explain each of the disposals in turn and then think about how you can use the figures from the scenario to illustrate what you are saying.

Machinery

A balancing charge will arise on the sale of the machinery equal to the sale proceeds of £70,000. This will increase trading profits in the year ended 31 March 2024.

Lighting system

The disposal of the lighting system will have two implications:

1. A balancing charge will arise equal to half of the sale proceeds: 50% × £20,000 = £10,000. This will increase trading profits in the year ended 31 March 2024.
2. The other half of the sale proceeds (£10,000) will be deducted from the special rate pool in the capital allowances computation. Depending on the tax written down value brought forward on the pool, this deduction will either reduce the amount that is eligible for 6% writing down allowance, or could create a further balancing charge if the balance becomes negative (although this is unlikely).

(ii) Sale of intangible fixed assets

Tutor's top tips

This requirement is focused on the calculation of the profit or loss on the disposal of two intangible assets and the post-tax proceeds. Post-tax proceeds means the disposal proceeds (not the profit) less any tax due, or plus any tax saved. This is a common requirement in the exam so you need to make sure you are ready tackle a question like this.

Make sure you read all the information given to you in the scenario to pick up on the relevant information needed to calculate the profit or loss, especially the treatment of the amortisation for tax purposes. You are told that no election has been made to write off the cost of the brand at 4%, which means that you should follow the accounting treatment instead and assume that the amortisation is allowable.

	Goodwill	Brand	
	£	£	£
Sale proceeds on 31 July 2024	75,000	47,000	122,000
Cost	(95,000)		
Tax written down value (£36,000 – £5,760)		(30,240)	
(Loss)/profit	(20,000)	16,760	
Corporation tax at 25% on profit			(4,190)
Loss relieved against total profits at 25%			5,000
Post-tax proceeds			122,810

Tutorial note

The loss on the sale of the goodwill is a non-trading debit. This loss can be offset against the total income and gains of the current accounting period.

(ii) Timing of payments to shareholders

Tutor's top tips

Liquidations are not tested regularly in the ATX exam. However, there can be some easy marks available if you are familiar with the tax treatment of distributions to shareholders both before and after the appointment of a liquidator.

Prior to the appointment of the liquidator

A payment made to the shareholders prior to the appointment of the liquidator will be subject to income tax as a dividend in the normal way.

The first £1,000 of an individual's dividend income in a tax year from all shareholdings is taxed at 0%. The excess over £1,000 will be taxed as a shareholder's top slice of income.

Any amount which falls into a shareholder's basic rate band will be subject to income tax at 8.75%. The balance of the dividend will be subject to income tax at 33.75%.

After the appointment of the liquidator

Once the liquidator has been appointed, amounts paid to shareholders will represent proceeds in respect of a part disposal of their shares for the purposes of capital gains tax (CGT).

Any amount of the chargeable gain which is not covered by the shareholder's annual exempt amount of £6,000 will be subject to CGT.

Where the disposal of the shares qualifies for business asset disposal relief, the whole of any chargeable gain (within the lifetime limit of £1,000,000) will be subject to CGT at 10% irrespective of whether the shareholders are basic rate or higher rate taxpayers.

As VNL Ltd is a trading company, business asset disposal relief will be available where:

– the shareholder had owned at least 5% of the company's ordinary share capital and been an officer or employee of the company for a period of at least two years prior to the cessation of VNL Ltd's trade, and

– the shares are disposed of within three years of the cessation of VNL Ltd's trade.

We would therefore need to establish if any individual shareholders satisfy these conditions.

Where business asset disposal relief is not available, the chargeable gain will be taxed after calculating tax on income, by reference to the income tax bands.

Any amount of the chargeable gain which falls into a shareholder's basic rate band will be subject to CGT at 10%. The balance of the chargeable gain will be subject to CGT at 20%.

Tutor's top tips

Remember in this scenario the shareholders are all individuals and therefore your focus should just be on the tax implications for individuals and not companies.

The calculations in this requirement lend themselves well to the spreadsheet functionality in the exam. Don't forget to reference through to these in the word processor.

(b) Unincorporated business

Tutor's top tips

This part of the question requires you to explain the VAT implications for pre-trade expenditure.

This is partly assumed knowledge from the TX paper, but also covers the higher-level topic of VAT on land and buildings.

Make sure that you use clear headings, so that the marker can see which cost you are addressing in your answer.

Recovery of input tax for the purposes of value added tax (VAT)

– **Consultancy services**

Joe will be able to recover input VAT in respect of services provided to him for business purposes in the six months prior to registering for VAT. This is provided that the VAT on the services would normally be recoverable, which it would be in the case of consultancy costs.

Accordingly, because Joe first incurred these costs more than six months ago, he should consider registering for VAT as soon as possible in order to recover as much of the input tax relating to the consultancy services as he can.

– **Premises**

The amount of input tax which Joe can recover will depend on whether or not he opts to tax the building for the purposes of VAT.

- If he opts to tax the building, he will be able to recover all of the input tax.
- Otherwise, he will only be able to recover two-thirds of it.

This is because the granting of the lease will be an exempt supply unless an option to tax is made in respect of the building.

The building will not be subject to the capital goods scheme because its VAT-exclusive cost will be less than £250,000.

(c) Becoming Fiona's tax advisers

Tutor's top tips

This is a standard ethical question and you need to make sure you apply the fundamental principles and address any threats to these.

There are five marks available, so try to make at least five separate points in your answer.

The actions we should carry out before we become Fiona's tax advisers:

– We must give consideration to the fundamental principles of professional ethics, for example, integrity and professional competence and due care. This requires us to consider whether becoming tax advisers to Fiona would create any threats to compliance with these principles.

If any such threats are identified, we should not accept the appointment unless the threats can be reduced to an acceptable level via the implementation of safeguards.

Fiona's move to the UK will significantly affect her tax affairs, and we must be sure that we are able to deal with the technical aspects of these matters.

– We must assure ourselves that Fiona is not involved in any form of money laundering.

- We should obtain permission from Fiona to contact her existing tax advisers in order to ensure that there is nothing in the past which would preclude us from accepting the appointment on ethical grounds.
- We should issue a letter of engagement setting out the terms of our agreement with Fiona and our agreed responsibilities.

(d) Taxation of overseas income

Tutor's top tips

This question is based on the taxation of overseas income. To tackle a tricky area such as this you need to ensure you read the scenario carefully and pick up on any hints as to whether Fiona would be entitled to the automatic remittance basis. The main conditions to look out for are:

- *Is the individual UK resident but not UK domiciled?*
- *Does she have unremitted income and gains of less than £2,000?*

You were also asked to discuss if the remittance base charge would apply; a good understanding of when this charge applies would help you to answer this part of the question.

Availability of the remittance basis

- The remittance basis is available where an individual is UK resident but not UK domiciled.
- Where an individual is UK resident and deemed domiciled in the UK, the remittance basis is only available if unremitted overseas income and gains in a tax year is less than £2,000.

  In these circumstances, the remittance basis applies automatically.
- Accordingly, for the tax year 2025/26, the amount of Fiona's taxable overseas income will be automatically calculated on the remittance basis. This is because her only unremitted overseas income will be her Parellian bank interest of £1,200.
- Fiona will not be subject to the remittance basis charge because she will qualify for the remittance basis automatically.

Fiona – income tax liability for the tax year 2025/26

Tutor's top tips

There are some easy marks here for preparing a basic income tax computation.

The only tricky part is calculating the double tax relief. In order to do this, you need to calculate the UK tax on the overseas income. This is the difference between the UK tax ***with*** *the overseas income, and the UK tax* ***without*** *the overseas income. Watch out for the impact on the savings income nil rate band!*

The calculation is best performed in the spreadsheet response option in the exam. This will enable you to use formulae to speed up workings. Remember to reference through to any workings performed in your narrative answer in the word processor.

		Working
	£	£
Property income:		
Properties in the UK	26,000	26,000
Properties in Parella	31,000	N/A
Interest income:		
UK bank interest	1,700	1,700
Parellian bank interest (unremitted)	–	–
Total income	58,700	27,700
Less: Personal allowance	(12,570)	(12,570)
Taxable income	46,130	15,130
Property income		
£37,700/£13,430 × 20%	7,540	2,686
£6,730 × 40%	2,692	
Interest income		
£500/£1,000 × 0%	0	0
£1,200 × 40%/£700 × 20%	480	140
	10,712	2,826
Double tax relief, the lower of:		
UK tax on overseas income		
£10,712 – £2,826 (W) = £7,886		
Parellian tax suffered		
£31,000 × 18% = £5,580	(5,580)	
Income tax liability	5,132	

Tutorial note

The personal allowance will be given because the remittance basis is available automatically.

Examiner's report

Part (a) concerned the liquidation of a company which had always been profitable in the past.

Part (a)(i)

This requirement has been added to the question since it was originally set.

Part (a)(ii)

The company planned to sell two intangible assets just before the liquidator was appointed and part (a)(ii) required a calculation of the post-tax proceeds of these disposals for the company.

It is important to always check the 'command' word being used in a question. In this part, it is to 'calculate'. Long explanations are therefore not required here and will not earn marks. Candidates should aim for clear labelling of figures and perhaps brief explanations of what is being done, but without wasting time on lots of narrative content.

It is also important to note that the question asks for 'post-tax proceeds'. To arrive at this figure there are distinct steps in the calculation which need to be followed. Given the facts in this scenario, it is first necessary to calculate any taxable profit or loss, then calculate any corporation tax paid or saved at the appropriate rate, and then finally calculate the proceeds less any tax paid, or plus any tax saved.

The tax treatment generally follows the accounting treatment for the sale of intangible assets which is why trading profits and losses as opposed to capital gains or losses are being calculated.

The first intangible asset sold was goodwill and candidates were told that the amortisation of this goodwill had not been a tax-deductible expense for the company. As a result, the full unamortised cost of £95,000 should be used in calculating the loss on sale i.e. £75,000 – £95,000 = £20,000 loss.

The second intangible asset sold was the brand which had been amortised. As this is an intangible asset held by a company, it should be assumed that this amortisation is tax deductible, unless told otherwise. As such, the amortised cost should be used to work out the taxable profit on the sale of the brand i.e. £47,000 less (£36,000 – £5,760) = £16,760. A number of candidates incorrectly calculated the amortisation of the brand at 4%, but the question specifically states that no election to write it off at this fixed rate had been made

Thus far only the taxable profits and losses on the disposal of these assets has been calculated. A number of candidates stopped at this point but it was important to appreciate that the requirement involved calculation of the 'post-tax proceeds' arising from these disposals.

The next stage is to therefore calculate the tax saved, or paid, at 25% on the relevant loss or profit.

Finally, this needs to be brought together to calculate the 'post-tax proceeds' arising from these transactions. The starting point for this is to go back to the actual proceeds i.e. £75,000 + £47,000 = £122,000. Then to deduct any tax paid, or add any tax saved, to the total proceeds. A common mistake made in questions of this nature is to take the profit or loss on disposal and to adjust this for the tax figure. But it should be remembered that, when looking at post-tax proceeds from the disposal of an asset, the cost itself is no longer relevant and although this does feature in the profit or loss on which the tax is based, it is the proceeds which are important, as adjusted for the tax paid or saved.

Part (a)(iii)

Part (a)(iii) of this question required an explanation of the tax rates which shareholders will pay on amounts received from the company, depending on the timing of the payment. Within the first exhibit, it was stated that there would be a final payment to shareholders at the conclusion of the liquidation but consideration was being given to making an interim payment, prior to the appointment of the liquidator.

The command word used here was 'explain'; it is important to identify this and to focus on what the requirement is actually requiring an explanation of i.e. 'tax rates'.

Many candidates were very good at dealing with the pre-liquidation payment, correctly identifying that it would be treated as a dividend and detailing the potential tax rates. The scenario had specifically stated that the shareholders would be a mix of basic and higher rate taxpayers. Some candidates merely referred to the dividend treatment but did not go on to discuss in sufficient detail the specific tax rates which would apply to these types of shareholders; therefore they did not score the marks available for this. In this context, it is important that candidates do ensure they are happy with the precise detail of a question requirement before beginning their answer. It's always worth going back to double check exactly what it is they have been asked to do, perhaps by highlighting key words in the question so that they stand out when working on the response.

Many candidates were able to identify that any final payment by a liquidator would be treated as a capital payment, but not all went on to discuss the rates of capital gains tax which the shareholders would then pay. Not only were the standard rates of capital gains tax of 10% and 20% relevant here, but also the single rate of 10% for both basic and higher rate taxpayers if business asset disposal relief were to apply.

Requirement (b) This part of the question was about Joe who was setting up in business as an unincorporated trader.

Elements of this section of the examiner's report have been removed as the respective parts of the question have been removed.

Requirement (b)

This part of the question involved an explanation of whether or not Joe could recover the input VAT on certain expenses he had incurred before starting to trade.

The expenses incurred related to two things – consultancy services and business premises.

As far as dealing with the VAT aspects of this question, a knowledge of the detailed rules and time limits for recovery of pre-registration VAT was required; namely six months prior to VAT registration for services, and four years prior to VAT registration for goods. A number of candidates demonstrated that they were aware that time limits existed, but were not sufficiently precise as to exactly what these were. A detailed, rather than purely superficial, knowledge of the tax rules is required in order to score well in this exam.

Many candidates were confused regarding the input VAT recovery on the business premises; this is a challenging area of the syllabus. Joe intended to use two thirds of the premises for his trade and to rent out the remaining one third. This meant that he could recover two thirds of the input VAT on the original cost, but given that leasing is an exempt supply for VAT purposes, would not be able to recover the remaining one third. In order to change this position, and to be able to recover the full amount including that relating to the part which was let out, Joe would need to opt to tax the building.

Requirement (c)

This part of the question tested knowledge of the actions to be taken before becoming Fiona's tax advisers.

This was a standard ethics requirement and many candidates were able to score well on this part of the question. However, when answering any ethics question dealing with aspects such as these, the need to address any threats to compliance with the fundamental principles such as integrity, professional competence and due care, should be borne in mind. If any such threats are identified, the point should be made that they can they be reduced to an acceptable level with the implementation of appropriate safeguards.

A small but significant number of candidates suggested that Fiona's address and proof of identity should be obtained, despite being specifically told in the question that this had already happened.

Before starting on an answer, it is always worth rechecking the requirement and information contained within the scenario in order to avoid wasting time on points that cannot earn marks.

A section of the examiner's report has been removed as that part of the question has been removed.

Requirement (d)

There were two subparts to this requirement.

The first asked for an explanation of why Fiona would be eligible for the remittance basis and whether or not she would be subject to the remittance basis charge.

The remittance basis is available where an individual is UK resident but not UK domiciled. Fiona's status for the tax year 2025/26 was that of resident and deemed domicile. In this case, the remittance basis is only available if unremitted overseas income and gains in any tax year is less than £2,000; in this situation it applies automatically and there is no remittance basis charge.

Some candidates appeared to know the rules but were unclear on the amount of 'unremitted' overseas income when applied to Fiona's specific circumstances. The question specifically stated that her overseas bank interest income of £1,200 would not be remitted to the UK whereas that from her overseas rental properties would be. As such, with an amount of overseas unremitted income of less than £2,000, the remittance basis automatically applies to Fiona for the relevant tax year.

The second subpart of this requirement asked for a calculation of Fiona's income tax liability for the tax year 2025/26. It's worth emphasising here once again that, if asked for a calculation, there is no need to spend time providing detailed explanations of all of the relevant numbers. As long as they are all clearly labelled, and brief explanations of any workings are given if necessary, the focus should be on doing the calculations themselves in order to earn the marks.

Many candidates were able to produce an income tax computation in response to this part of the question and showed an awareness of the fundamentals of double tax relief. Strictly, in order to calculate the UK tax suffered on the overseas income for double tax relief purposes, a calculation of the income tax liability with the overseas income included should be performed and this should then be compared with a calculation of the liability with the foreign income excluded. The difference in these two tax liabilities represents the UK tax on the overseas income, which is then compared with the foreign tax suffered. This method is demonstrated in the model answer.

ACCA marking scheme

				Marks
(a)	(i)	Machinery		1.5
		Lighting system		4.5
				6.0
			Maximum	5.0
	(ii)	Loss on sale of goodwill		1.0
		Profit on sale of brand		1.0
		Post-tax proceeds		2.0
				4.0
	(iii)	Prior to appointment		4.0
		After appointment		6.0
				10.0
			Maximum	9.0
(b)	Value added tax			
	Consultancy services			3.0
	Premises			4.0
				7.0
(c)	Fundamental principles			3.0
	Other matters			3.0
				6.0
			Maximum	5.0
(d)	Remittance basis			4.0
	Calculation of income tax liability			
		Liability before double tax relief		3.5
		Double tax relief		3.5
				11.0
			Maximum	10.0
	Professional skills marks (see below)		**Maximum**	10.0
Total				**50.0**

Professional skills marks

Communication

- General format and structure of meeting notes (e.g. use of headings/sub-headings to make meeting notes easy to refer to).
- Style, language and clarity (tone of meeting notes, presentation of calculations, appropriate use of the tools, easy to follow and more than a negligible amount of content).
- Effectiveness of communication (answer is relevant, specific rather than general and focused to the requirement).
- Adherence to specific instructions made in the scenario (e.g. not writing off the brand at 4% in part (a)(ii)).

Analysis and evaluation

- Appropriate use of information from the scenario to illustrate explanations in part (a)(I).
- Appropriate use of information to determine post-tax proceeds in part (a)(ii).
- Appropriate use of information when establishing the UK liability on the overseas income for DTR purposes in part (d).
- Consideration of relevant factors when deciding whether or not the remittance basis charge applies to Fiona in part (d).

Scepticism

- Recognition of missing information relating to the tax written down value brought forward in part (a)(i).
- Critical assessment of the potential for business asset disposal relief in part (a)(iii) and its application to the shareholders of VNL Ltd.
- Recognition of the uncertainties in relation to the option to tax in part (b).

Commercial acumen

- Recognition of there being two implications of the disposal of the lighting system in part (a)(i).
- Recognition of the importance of timing of VAT registration in order to maximise recovery of VAT on the consultancy costs in part (b).
- Effective use of information to determine the applicability of the capital goods scheme to Joe's situation in part (b).
- Recognition of the impact of the remittance basis on the subsequent computation in part (d).

8 OLMA AND HOGAN (ADAPTED) *Walk in the footsteps of a top tutor*

Key answer tips

This question covers ethics, purchase of own shares, voluntary registration for VAT, loss relief, share schemes and inheritance tax with overseas aspects.

This question contains a mix of numerical and discursive requirements. It is advisable to use the spreadsheet functionality for calculations and the word processor functionality for any discursive requirements when in the exam. Ensure you label your answer clearly so it is obvious which requirement you are answering.

Part (a) tests you on the capital route conditions for a purchase of own shares. This area is not examined often so you may not be familiar with it. However, it is only worth four marks so don't worry too much about it. Do your best and move on.

Part (b)(i) looks at voluntary registration for VAT. This is a topic that is tested fairly often, and is purely brought forward knowledge from TX. So you should be well prepared for this area.

Part (b)(ii) looks at loss relief for a sole trader. Losses almost always get tested in some form in the ATX exam, so you should be prepared to deal with this. Make sure you explain the use of the loss fully. Think: 'what, when and how'? What income is it offsetting? When is it being used? How is it being used? (i.e. is there a specific order for the offset).

Part (b)(iii) is your five marks on ethics. This is a completely standalone part to the rest of the question, so you could tackle this first to get some easy marks in the bag.

Part (c) tests the rules around SIPs. This is another area that isn't tested too often. Though again, at only three marks it is quite easy to score a pass here.

Finally, part (d) looks at inheritance tax including domicile. When considering domicile, you should always have deemed domicile in the back of your mind. Is it relevant here or not, and why?

The highlighted words in the written sections are key phrases that markers are looking for.

Memorandum

For The files

Client Olma and Hogan

Subject Cafe business and various tax issues

Prepared by Tax senior

Date 1 February 2025

(a) Sale of shares in BG Ltd

Tutor's top tips

The email from your manager mentions that the conditions around substantial reduction in shareholding, connection to the company and tax avoidance schemes have been considered. Do not waste time discussing those conditions here, as you will not gain credit for it.

The other conditions which must have been satisfied, such that Olma's sale of the shares gave rise to a chargeable gain were:

– The purchase of shares by BG Ltd was regarded as having been carried out for the benefit of its trade. This is because Olma left her employment with the company and sold all of her shares as a result of disagreements with the other shareholders over the future direction of the business.

– BG Ltd is an unquoted, trading company.

– Olma had owned the shares for at least five years.

– Olma was resident in the UK for tax purposes in 2024/25, the tax year in which the shares were sold.

(b) Cafe business

(i) Voluntary registration for the purposes of value added tax (VAT)

Tutor's top tips

There are individual expenses noted in the extract from the memorandum. You have been given this detail for a reason, so think about the VAT implications of those expenses and the impact of voluntary registration with regards to them.

Financial advantage

- Once she has registered, Olma will be able to claim recoverable input tax. However, the additional amount she will be able to claim due to registering voluntarily rather than waiting until 1 September 2025 is unlikely to be significant for the reasons set out below.
- The principal recurring costs of Olma's business are either zero-rated (food), exempt (rent) or outside the scope of VAT (employment costs), such that no input tax will be incurred in respect of them.
- Olma has incurred input tax in respect of the purchase of the furniture and equipment of £1,600 (£8,000 × 20%).

  However, there is no need for Olma to register voluntarily in order to recover this amount because, once she has registered under the compulsory registration rules, she will then be able to recover pre-registration input tax (provided she still owns the relevant items). This is due to having purchased the items in the four years prior to registration.
- Olma will also be able to recover the input tax in respect of any services purchased for business purposes in the six months prior to registration.

Financial disadvantage

- The main disadvantage of registering earlier than necessary is that it will bring forward the date on which Olma will have to start charging her customers VAT. If Olma is unable to pass on the resulting price increase to her customers, this is likely to cause her profitability to fall.

(ii) Loss planning

Reliefs available

The trading loss can be offset against Olma's total income of:

- 2024/25 (the tax year of the loss) and/or 2023/24 (the preceding year).
- 2021/22, 2022/23 and 2023/24, the three tax years prior to the tax year of the loss starting with the earliest year. This relief is available because the loss has occurred in one of the first four tax years of Olma's trade.

– Olma's total income for the relevant tax years

2024/25	(6 × £6,700)	40,200
2023/24	(12 × £6,700)	80,400
2022/23	(7 × £6,700)	46,900
2021/22	(5 × £6,700)	33,500

– The loss cannot be used to relieve Olma's chargeable gain on the sale of her shares in BG Ltd in the tax year 2024/25. This is because the loss would first have to be offset against Olma's total income for that year, and there would then be no loss remaining for offset against the chargeable gain.

Tutor's top tips

The requirement asked you to evaluate the options and conclude on the best one and the tax that would be saved, so make sure you do this! You will always gain credit for a reasoned conclusion as long as it makes sense based on your previous discussion.

Evaluation of the reliefs available

– Tax year 2024/25

Olma's taxable income (i.e. after deducting her personal allowance) will be £27,630 (£40,200 – £12,570), which is less than the basic rate band, such that she will be a basic rate taxpayer.

The whole of the chargeable gain in respect of the sale of Olma's shares in BG Ltd will be subject to capital gains tax at the rate of 10% due to the availability of business asset disposal relief. Accordingly, offsetting the trading loss against net income will not affect the amount of tax due on the chargeable gain.

– Tax year 2023/24

Olma had total income less her personal allowance of £67,830 (£80,400 – £12,570).

Of this, £30,130 (£67,830 – £37,700) was subject to income tax at 40%.

Accordingly, relieving the loss in this tax year will save income tax at 40% in respect of the whole of the loss.

– Tax year 2021/22

Olma's total income of £33,500 was less than the basic rate band, such that she was a basic rate taxpayer.

Olma should claim to offset the trading loss against her taxable income for the tax year 2023/24. This will result in a tax saving of £11,600 (£29,000 × 40%).

(iii) Introduction of Hogan as a partner

Tutor's top tips

The ethics requirement in the ATX exam will always be worth five marks, so you should be aiming to make five well explained points in order to score them all.

If our firm acts for both the partnership as well as Hogan and Olma personally, this may create a conflict of interest.

If Hogan does join the business as a partner, then we should make both Hogan and Olma aware of the potential conflict of interest.

We should obtain permission of both Olma and Hogan to continue to act for them.

We should consider whether additional safeguards could be introduced to mitigate the risk arising.

Safeguards could include using separate engagement teams for the partnership and the personal affairs of Olma and Hogan.

If it is not possible to reduce the risks to an acceptable level, then we should consider resigning from one of the engagements, i.e. either the partnership or the personal affairs of the partners.

(c) Award of free shares from VPR plc's share incentive plan (SIP)

Tutor's top tips

There are three marks available for this requirement so you should aim to make three separate points in order to achieve them all.

In order for there to be no income tax payable by Hogan in respect of the value of the shares awarded and the dividends paid in respect of them, the following conditions must be satisfied:

– the free shares must be retained within the plan for a minimum of five years;

– the dividends paid in respect of them must be used to purchase additional shares in VPR plc, and

– these additional dividend shares must be retained within the plan for a minimum of three years.

(d) Gift of £380,000 to discretionary trust on 1 July 2026

The cash is on deposit in an overseas bank account, such that it is an overseas asset.

Overseas assets are only subject to UK inheritance tax (IHT) if the donor is either domiciled or deemed domiciled in the UK.

Hogan will become deemed domiciled in the UK for the purposes of IHT from 6 April 2026. This is because:

- he was born in the UK with a UK domicile of origin;
- he will be UK resident in the tax year 2026/27, the year of the gift;
- he is UK resident in the tax year 2025/26, one of the two years prior to the year of the gift.

The gift will be a chargeable lifetime transfer because it is a gift to a trust.

The IHT liability will be:

	£
Cash transferred to trust	380,000
Less: Annual exemptions for current year and previous year	(6,000)
	374,000
Less: Nil rate band	(325,000)
	49,000
Hogan pays the tax: IHT at 25%	12,250

Tutorial note

You were told that Hogan has made no previous lifetime gifts, so he would have both the current year and previous year's annual exemptions available to offset against the gift to the trust.

Examiner's report

The first requirement has been removed since the question was originally set.

Requirement (a)

Part (a) of this question concerned the conditions which needed to be satisfied such that a particular share sale gave rise to a chargeable gain. The context of the share sale was very important here and candidates needed to look at the detail of the question before commencing their answer.

The question stated that Olma had sold her shares in BG Ltd back to the company via a company purchase of own shares. A share buy-back is a very specific tax scenario of which candidates do need to be aware. If certain conditions are met, the 'buy-back' is treated as a capital gain for the individual shareholder.

Three of the necessary conditions were already provided within the requirement, and candidates needed to outline the others.

A significant number of candidates appeared to be unaware of the relevance of the purchase of own shares scenario in this question, choosing instead to calculate the gain on the sale of shares and to list the conditions for business asset disposal relief; neither of which were required. Others provided detailed descriptions of the badges of trade, or conditions for the substantial shareholding exemption; none of which were relevant to the facts of this particular question.

Of those stronger candidates who did identify that this scenario related to a company share buy-back, many then wasted time repeating the three conditions which the question had explicitly stated had already been met. The requirement specifically asked for the 'other' conditions and there were no marks available for simply repeating the facts of the question. It is important for candidates to pick up on such signposting within questions in order that they specifically address the requirement. Highlighting of key words within a requirement may help to maintain focus and to ensure that candidates do not lose sight of what it is they are being asked to do.

The 'other' conditions that needed to be provided here were, for example, that the buy-back should be for the benefit of the company's trade, that the shareholder should be UK resident and have owned the shares for at least five years, and that the company should be unquoted and trading.

Answers to this part of the question were generally disappointing. It would appear that candidates needed to spend more time considering and understanding the context of the question, before actually starting their answers. They also needed to reflect more carefully on what information they had already been given, and what the requirement was actually asking them to do.

Requirement (b)(i)

This part of the question asked for an explanation of 'additional' matters regarding the financial advantages and disadvantages of voluntarily registering for value added tax (VAT).

A key word used here was 'additional'. The requirement explicitly stated that the administration aspects of VAT, including the various schemes and the penalty regime, had already been discussed with the client, and therefore didn't need to be addressed. However, a disappointing number of candidates needlessly wasted time by discussing these issues, with no marks being awarded for so doing. Here, once again, the words used in the requirement had been carefully chosen to signpost what was required. Candidates should pay particular attention to such wording prior to starting work on their answers, in order to ensure that they are following the instructions that they have been given and answering the question which has been set.

Despite being aware that voluntary VAT registration would potentially allow recovery of input VAT, it was good to see many candidates going on to relate this to the facts of the question and recognising that, on this occasion, the value of such recovery would be quite limited. This was due to the fact that the principal recurring costs incurred by the business were either zero-rated (food), exempt (rents) or outside the scope (employment costs) such that no input VAT would have been charged.

Of further relevance to the scenario was the fact that, prior to registering voluntarily for VAT, some furniture and other assets had been purchased for use in the business. This should have prompted candidates to discuss the recovery of pre-registration input VAT. This is possible with goods acquired in the four years before VAT registration, if still owned, and with respect to services purchased in the six months before VAT registration.

Many candidates were very good at recognising the fact that voluntary VAT registration would mean having to charge VAT on sales, which in turn would lead to an increase in prices to the customers who, on this occasion, were members of the general public and therefore not VAT registered.

Answers to this part of the question were generally strong with candidates going beyond a mere statement of the rules and making good attempts at relating their knowledge to the specific facts of the question

Requirement (b)(ii)

This requirement concerned a sole trader's opening year loss and options for relieving it; it was split into three distinct parts.

The original first part of this requirement has been removed since it is no longer examinable.

The first part required an explanation, with supporting calculations, of how the trading loss could be offset, on the assumption that the client did not wish to carry it forward.

There were several options for loss relief in this context, including current and/or prior year relief, extension against capital gains, and 'opening year' loss relief which would permit a three year carry back on a first in first out (FIFO) basis. Many candidates mistakenly thought that the trading loss could be used against gains without using the loss in the related income tax computation first. A significant number did not mention 'opening year' loss relief at all, even though this was clearly relevant since the loss arose in one of the first four years of trading. Some candidates discussed carrying forward the loss despite being specifically told in the requirement that the client did not wish to do this.

Candidates who attempted the loss relief calculations often mistakenly showed the loss being offset in the income tax computation after the personal allowance. In such instances, the loss must be used against total income before deduction of the personal allowance, which may on occasions lead to wastage of the latter.

The second part of the requirement was to conclude on the most beneficial way to relieve the loss, and to quantify the resulting tax saving. For those candidates who provided conclusions, credit was awarded based on their own workings. Many did not however go on to calculate the tax savings and therefore did not earn the marks for those calculations. Where requirements are divided into more than one sub-requirement, candidates should take time to identify all of these (possibly even by numbering each of them) to ensure that they do address all relevant parts and earn credit for correct steps.

It was apparent that those candidates who attempted their loss relief calculations in the spreadsheet platform found it easier to be able to show their workings and thus earn marks. This also appeared to make it much easier for them to work out the tax savings from the most beneficial use of the loss. Where several linked computations are involved, the functionality of the spreadsheet generally assists in the task of providing an answer which is both well laid out and easy to follow through.

Requirement (b)(iii)

This requirement has been written since the question was originally set.

The final two requirements have been added to the question since it was originally written. The relevant sections of the examiner's report from the exam they originated from are included below:

Requirement (c)

This part involved an award of free shares from a share incentive plan (SIP); candidates needed to state the conditions required in the future for there to be no income tax payable on both the shares awarded and the dividends paid in respect of them.

Many candidates demonstrated awareness of the knowledge that the shares would need to be held for a minimum of five years. However, very few discussed the conditions relating to the dividends paid in respect of the shares, namely the fact that they needed to be reinvested in plan shares which then had to be held within the plan for a minimum of three further years.

As part of their overall preparation for this exam, candidates should be aware of the extent to which such detailed knowledge of rules contained within the ATX-UK syllabus can be tested.

Requirement (d)

This part required candidates to analyse the tax consequences of making a gift of cash to a discretionary trust. The requirement was broken down into two parts; the first asking for an explanation, by reference to the client's domicile, of why the gift would give rise to UK inheritance tax (IHT) and the second, a calculation of the amount of IHT payable.

Unsurprisingly, candidates fared better on the calculative element, demonstrating good recollection of their TX-UK knowledge and being confident in the application of annual exemptions, the nil rate band, and the correct 25% tax rate.

Many of the explanations provided were however vague with the concept of deemed domicile not being sufficiently clearly understood. A number of candidates confused domicile and residence rules.

In this scenario there would be IHT on the gift if the client was either domiciled or deemed domiciled in the UK. On this occasion the conditions for deemed domicile were satisfied. This was because the client was born in the UK with a UK domicile of origin, was UK resident in the year of the gift, and had been UK resident in one of the two years prior to the year of the gift.

When an explanation is requested, there are marks available for providing this. Many candidates could improve upon their exam technique, and thus their overall marks, by focussing on, and addressing, explanatory requirements, rather than just calculative ones.

In this scenario candidates were required to prepare a memorandum for the client file in relation to a number of different tax issues.

It is important for candidates to bear in mind two key points when addressing this type of requirement. Firstly, explanations provided should be concise but comprehensive enough to be understood by anyone who is using the file. Secondly, the notes should be clearly presented in a logical, structured way, such that a user is easily able to find the information that they need.

The professional skills marks have been increased to ten marks since this question was originally set.

Professional skills

Candidates who scored well addressed all parts of the requirements, structured their answer according to the matters to be discussed (which were clearly set out in the manager's email), wrote concisely in short, clear paragraphs, and demonstrated a logical thought process when tackling each of the relevant issues.

In summary, those candidates who prepared sound answers to this question were able to do the following:

- directly address each of the tasks within the manager's email, providing concise explanations, where required;
- demonstrate a good knowledge of sole trader loss relief options; and
- tailor their knowledge intelligently to the scenario by using the facts of the question.

ACCA marking guide

				Marks
(a)	Benefit of trade			2.0
	Other points			3.0
				5.0
(b)	(i)	Input tax can be recovered		1.0
		Recoverable amounts		2.5
		Pre-registration input tax		4.0
		Charge VAT on sales		2.0
				9.5
			Maximum	8.0
	(ii)	Possible reliefs		3.5
		Identification of most beneficial relief		6.0
		Chargeable gain on sale of shares		2.0
		Income tax saving		1.0
				12.5
				12.0
	(iii)	Conflict of interest		1.0
		Inform clients		1.0
		Obtain permission		1.0
		Safeguards		1.0
		Separate teams		1.0
		Resign if can't reduce risk		1.0
				6.0
			Maximum	5.0
(c)	Conditions (1 mark each)			3.0

(d)	Overseas assets		2.0
	Deemed domiciled		3.0
	Calculation		3.0
			8.0
		Maximum	7.0
	Professional skills marks (see below)	**Maximum**	10.0
Total			**50.0**

Professional skills marks

Communication

- General format and structure of memorandum (e.g. use of headings/sub-headings to make memorandum easy to refer to).
- Style, language and clarity (tone of memorandum, presentation of calculations, appropriate use of the tools, easy to follow and more than a negligible amount of content).
- Effectiveness of communication (answer is relevant, specific rather than general and focused to the requirement).
- Adherence to specific instructions made in the scenario (e.g. not discussing administrative aspects of VAT in part (b)(i)).

Analysis and evaluation

- Analysis of information to determine which other capital route conditions have been met in respect of Olma's sale of shares to BG Ltd in part (a).
- Analysis of the data to determine the relevant loss relief options available to Olma in part (b)(ii).
- Evaluation of the loss options to determine the most appropriate option for Olma in part (b)(ii).
- Ability to consider all taxes relevant to requirement (b)(ii), i.e. income tax and capital gains tax.
- Appropriate use of the data to determine suitable calculations to perform to arrive at the inheritance tax liability for Hogan in part (d).

Scepticism

- Recognition that voluntary registration might lead to a drop in profitability in part (b)(i).
- Identification of the need to consider safeguards if a conflict of interest arises in part (b)(iii).

Commercial acumen

- Consideration of relevant advantages of voluntary VAT registration in part (b)(i).
- Demonstration of an understanding of how share incentive plans can result in no income tax payable in part (c).

9 HIROMI (ADAPTED) *Walk in the footsteps of a top tutor*

Key answer tips

This question covers ethics, capital gains tax and incorporation relief, income tax loss reliefs, the tax implications of dividend payments and rules for record keeping.

There is a mix of numerical and discursive requirements. It is advisable to use the spreadsheet functionality for calculations and the word processor functionality for any discursive requirements when in the exam. Ensure you label your answer clearly so it is obvious which requirement you are answering.

Part (a) is the ethics part of the question. This should offer five relatively easy marks.

Part (b) covers capital gains tax with incorporation relief. Incorporation relief is a new relief at the advanced level, so is tested fairly frequently in the exam.

Part (c) looks at loss reliefs for a sole trader. There are some easy marks in part (c)(i) for stating the reliefs available, then part (c)(ii) requires you to apply these to the scenario and give advice on the tax savings. Losses are tested in nearly every ATX exam, so it is important that you learn the reliefs available.

There are two separate elements to part (d). The first covers the tax implications of dividends from the point of view of both the company and the individual receiving the dividend. To score well, you need to make sure that you address both perspectives here. The second part of (d) tests your knowledge of administration and the rules for retaining records. This is brought forward knowledge from TX, so you should be well prepared for this area as long as you remember the rules.

The highlighted words in the written sections are key phrases that markers are looking for.

Notes for discussion prior to meeting

For	The files
Client	Hiromi
Subject	Various matters
Prepared by	Tax senior
Date	1 September 2024

(a) Refund of income tax

Tutor's top tips

The ethics requirement in the ATX exam will always be worth five marks, so you should be aiming to make five well explained points in order to score them all.

We should assist Hiromi in identifying whether or not there was a valid reason for the refund. If we are unable to find a valid reason, we would have to conclude that the refund was made as a result of an error on the part of HM Revenue and Customs (HMRC). In these circumstances:

– We should inform Hiromi that the amount should be repaid and that failing to do so would be a civil and/or a criminal offence.

– HMRC should be informed of their error as soon as possible in order to minimise any interest and penalties which may otherwise become payable.

– In the unlikely event that Hiromi is unwilling to return the money:

  – Hiromi's willingness to retain money which does not belong to her would require us to consider ceasing to act as her tax advisers;

  – we would then have to notify the tax authorities that we no longer act for her, although we would not provide them with any reason for our action;

  – our firm's money laundering reporting officer would also have to consider whether or not it is necessary to make a report under the money laundering rules.

(b) Chargeable gains

Tutor's top tips

Remember that gains are taxed after income, using the same tax bands. There are easy marks here for calculating the remaining basic rate band and for applying the appropriate rates of CGT to your gain.

Sale of the rental property – 2023/24 capital gains tax (CGT) payable

	£	£
Proceeds		265,000
Less: Cost (probate value)		(221,500)
Chargeable gain		43,500
Less: Annual exempt amount		(6,000)
Taxable gain		37,500
Basic rate band		37,700
Trading income	8,000	
Property income	15,500	
	23,500	
Less: Personal allowance	(12,570)	
Taxable income		(10,930)
Basic rate band remaining		26,770
CGT	£	£
£26,770 × 18%		4,819
£10,730 (£37,500 – £26,770) × 28%		3,004
		7,823

Tutorial note

The chargeable gain on the sale of the rental property will have been reported by 28 April 2024 (i.e. within 60 days of completion of the sale – February 2024 is a leap year) and a payment on account of the related CGT will have been paid at that time. However, the gain must also be included on Hiromi's 2023/24 tax return and the CGT paid in April will then be deducted from the finalised CGT liability.

Proposed sale of business assets

Incorporation relief

Tutor's top tips

CGT reliefs are tested in almost every ATX exam, so it is vital that you learn the conditions to be satisfied for each relief to be available. To score well here, you should apply the conditions to the scenario.

The following three conditions must be satisfied for the relief to be available:

(i) Hiromi's business is transferred as a going concern when it is sold to HKR Ltd.

(ii) All of the assets of Hiromi's business (other than cash) are sold to HKR Ltd.

(iii) The consideration received by Hiromi for the sale of her business includes shares in HKR Ltd.

The proposed sale will satisfy conditions (ii) and (iii).

The going concern condition will also be satisfied provided that, at the time of the sale, the business is operational and has everything it needs to carry out its business activities on a sound commercial basis. The lack of business profits in the 18 months prior to the sale does not automatically indicate that the business is not a going concern.

CGT payable

	£
Total gains:	172,000
Less: Incorporation relief (£172,000 × 81%)	(139,320)
	32,680
Less: Annual exempt amount	(6,000)
	26,680
CGT at 10% (business asset disposal relief)	2,668

(c) Trading loss

Tutor's top tips

When writing about loss reliefs it is important to be specific. Think: 'what, when and how?'. What type of income can the loss be set against? When will relief be given? How is relief given, i.e. is there a set order for relief?

(i) Trading loss for the tax year 2024/25 – reliefs available

– The trading loss can be offset against:

– the total income of:

2024/25 (the tax year of the loss), and/or

2023/24 (the preceding tax year).

– the chargeable gains of either or both of the same two years provided a claim has been made against total income for the year(s) concerned.

– the first available income (e.g. salary and/or dividends) received from HKR Ltd.

(ii) Evaluation of the reliefs available

Tutor's top tips

The requirement for this part of the question is very specific. You are told that relief will not be claimed in respect of the tax year 2024/25, so don't waste time writing about that.

Relieving the loss as soon as possible

Offsetting the trading loss against Hiromi's income in 2023/24 would use £23,500 of the loss (£8,000 + £15,500). This would result in an income tax saving of £2,186 ((£23,500 – £12,570) × 20%).

The remainder of the loss, £21,000 (£44,500 – £23,500), could then be offset against the chargeable gain on the sale of the rental property.

	£
Taxable gain (above)	37,500
Less: Remainder of trading loss	(21,000)
	16,500
CGT (all within basic rate band) £16,500 × 18%	2,970
Reduction in CGT (£7,823 – £2,970)	4,853
Income tax saving (above)	2,186
Total tax saved	7,039

Relief in the future

The trading loss could be carried forward and offset against Hiromi's employment income in 2025/26.

	Original liability	Liability after loss relief
	£	£
Employment income (£5,500 × 12)	66,000	66,000
Less: Trading loss brought forward		(44,500)
		21,500
Less: Personal allowance	(12,570)	(12,570)
	53,430	8,930
Income tax payable		
£37,700/£8,930 × 20%	7,540	1,786
£15,730 (£53,430 – £37,700) × 40%	6,292	
	13,832	1,786

Tutor's top tips

Even if your calculations are incorrect, you can still score marks for summarising the tax savings and giving advice that is consistent with your analysis.

Summary of tax savings

	£
Relieving the loss as soon as possible	7,039
Relief in the future (£13,832 – £1,786)	12,046

Matters to be drawn to Hiromi's attention

- Carrying the loss forward for offset against income derived from HKR Ltd would save additional tax of £5,007 (£12,046 – £7,039).
- However:
  - carrying the loss forward would result in the benefit of the loss relief being delayed;
  - in addition, HKR Ltd may not be as profitable as expected. This could have an effect on the salary to be paid to Hiromi, such that she would not be a higher rate taxpayer in 2025/26.
  - fortunately, the election to offset the loss against total income of 2023/24 does not need to be made until 31 January 2027, by which time we will know whether or not Hiromi is a higher rate taxpayer for 2025/26.

(d) When HKR Ltd owns the business

Tax implications of paying a dividend of £7,000 in the tax year 2026/27

Tutor's top tips

Make sure that you consider the tax implications of the dividend for both the company and Hiromi. Think about all of the possible taxes that could apply – there was a mark for stating that there would be no national insurance contributions due.

– The dividend will not be an allowable payment for the purposes of calculating HKR Ltd's taxable trading profit. Accordingly, in order to have £7,000 of post-tax profits available for distribution, HKR Ltd will have to pay corporation tax of £2,333 (£7,000 × 25/(100 – 25)).

– Hiromi will be a higher rate taxpayer due to her salary of £66,000 per year. Accordingly, she will have an income tax liability in respect of the dividend totalling £2,025, as set out below:

	£
£1,000 × 0% (nil rate band)	0
£6,000 × 33·75% (higher rate taxpayer)	2,025
	2,025

– Dividends are not liable to national insurance contributions.

Record keeping

– HKR Ltd must retain the records required to make a complete and correct corporation tax return. This will include:

  – evidence of transactions, e.g. receipts, expenses, and sales and purchases of goods;

  – supporting documents, e.g. accounts, books and contracts.

– The records must usually be retained until six years after the end of the relevant accounting period.

– HMRC may impose a penalty where insufficient records are retained. The maximum penalty is £3,000 for each accounting period.

Tax senior

Examiner's report

Requirement (a): Refund of income tax

The scenario here concerned an unexpected refund of income tax from HM Revenue and Customs (HMRC) and required a summary of the actions to be taken by the firm and matters which should be brought to the attention of their client. This was a fairly standard ethics requirement which has been tested frequently in the past.

Many candidates demonstrated a high level of familiarity with this area, and so scored full, or almost full marks. Many candidates knew the guidance on investigating the refund, informing and potentially repaying HMRC, and if the client refuses the firm should cease to act, notify HMRC, but not disclose the reason. However, the main issue for weaker candidates was in not recognising that if no valid reason for the refund can be found and the client fails to repay the amount to HMRC, the client should be informed that this would be a civil and/or criminal offence. In addition, it may be necessary for the firm to make a report under the money laundering rules.

There are a good number of past questions which have tested these ethical issues and candidates would be well advised to practise them.

We were also looking to give a scepticism professional skill mark here for appropriate application of professional judgement in relation to the client's willingness to retain the refund. Very few candidates were able to earn this mark. Going forward, candidates should be prepared to challenge the information given in the scenario if it is clear that there are uncertainties in the information provided which could affect the conclusions reached.

Requirement (b): Sale of a rental property and proposed sale of business assets: capital gains tax (CGT) implications

The first element of part (b) required candidates to calculate the CGT payable as a result of the sale of a rental property. The majority of candidates were able to score full marks on calculating the gain.

Candidates often knew they had to apply residential rates to the gain but many simply said that because the client was a basic rate taxpayer, the whole gain would be charged at 18%. Better prepared candidates went a step further and calculated how much basic rate band was remaining and then applied 18% and 28% CGT rates to the gain accordingly. This is brought forward knowledge from TX-UK and candidates should be prepared to be tested on their brought forward knowledge. Analysis and evaluation marks may be awarded for appropriate use of relevant information to determine suitable calculations and this would be an example of this.

The second element of part (b) concerned the sale of the client's business assets to a newly formed company. Candidates were first asked to explain whether or not each of the three conditions for incorporation relief would be satisfied. There was some confusion over the conditions but lots of candidates were able to pick up one or two of the marks here. Many candidates suggested that the transfer must be in exchange for consideration made up of 80% shares. In fact, the requirement is that the consideration must include some element of shares but there is no specified amount. There are a multitude of reliefs to know about for ATX-UK but the precise details are important and candidates must ensure that they are clear on which rules relate to a particular relief.

Even when candidates correctly identified that 'transfer of a going concern' was a condition, virtually nobody went on to outline the meaning of going concern. In this case the client's sole trader business had been loss-making and so there may have been uncertainty regarding whether or not the business was a going concern. In order to earn scepticism marks, candidates should be prepared to challenge the information given in the question where it is clear there is some uncertainty.

Finally in this part of the question, candidates were asked to calculate the CGT payable upon transfer of the business assets, assuming that incorporation relief would be available. It was good to see most candidates following the instruction of the requirement and attempting the incorporation relief working. Similarly, most candidates knew that the annual exempt allowance would apply and that the gain should be charged at 10% due to the availability of business asset disposal relief.

Requirement (c)(i): Sole trader's trading loss

This part of the question has been amended since it was originally set.

Part (c)(i) required candidates to state how the loss can be relieved, ignoring terminal loss relief. When it came to stating how the loss could be relieved, most candidates were able to score marks for current and prior year reliefs. Common errors were to not state the 'and/or' nature of these two reliefs, nor to state the loss would be used against total income. A reasonable number of candidates knew that the loss could also be used against gains. Candidates sometimes went on to state that the loss could be used against future business profits but should have recognised that the business was being incorporated and so the loss would have to be used against income from the company in the future.

Requirement (c)(ii): Trading loss reliefs in prior and future years

Part (c)(ii) followed on from (c)(i) by requiring candidates to explain with supporting calculations, the tax savings which would result from relieving the loss as soon as possible (with no current year relief) and relieving the loss in the future.

At ATX-UK, candidates are often required to apply rules and conditions to specific circumstances, such that a generic answer will not be sufficient to score well. It is very important to take the time to think and plan an answer to a fairly complex question like this in order to provide a comprehensive, well-structured answer. It is worth taking some time at the start of such a question part to read, and carefully consider how to approach that part. It is evident from their answers when candidates have done this, and invariably leads to a more logical, concise, and better-focused answer.

Most candidates were able to explain and calculate the income tax saving from a prior year loss relief claim, ignoring a current year loss relief claim as instructed in the question. However very few candidates then extended the prior year loss relief claim against the gain which they had calculated in part (b), even if they had identified this as a potential relief in part (c)(i). Candidates also had to relieve the loss against future income from the company and calculate the tax saving. Calculating the tax payable before and after loss relief and then taking the difference was an efficient way to present the workings for this. Candidates who tried to work 'at the margin' often chose the wrong income tax rate for the loss relief.

In order to earn professional skills marks of analysis and evaluation it was important to show a balanced appraisal of the loss relief options and by outlining the loss relief options in a methodical manner, with clarity as to which relief was being addressed.

The final requirement of part (c)(ii) was to set out matters which would help the client to decide how to relieve her loss. It was pleasing to see the majority of candidates attempting this requirement. Many candidates correctly concluded on their follow through tax savings, correctly identifying which of their reliefs gave the greater tax saving. Many also brought up the cashflow/delay issues regarding prior year or future year relief. And finally, a good number were able to point out that future profits, although predicted, were uncertain.

Effectively addressing the matters to be raised with the client regarding which loss relief to choose further enabled candidates to pick up professional skills marks as follows:

- Analysis and evaluation when addressing the advantages and/or disadvantages of a particular relief; and
- Commercial acumen when recommending which loss reliefs are practical and plausible and recognising the wider implications of the timing of any election for loss relief.

Requirement (d): Tax implications of paying a dividend and retention of business records

The first element of part (d) required candidates to explain with supporting calculations, the tax implications for the client and the newly incorporated company of paying a dividend.

It was good to see so many candidates follow the instructions to look at this from the point of view of both the company and the client. For the former, they tended to know that dividends are not allowable. For the latter they tended to score well by recognising that the client would be a higher rate taxpayer because of her future company salary and then following up with a nil rate band and 33.75% tax rate for dividends. Virtually no candidate mentioned that there would be no NIC which would have scored a mark.

A second element to part (d) was the requirement to state matters to draw to the client's attention in relation to maintaining business records. Lots of students correctly knew that the retention period for records was six years but there were also various wrong attempts of two, five and seven years. Only a few students mentioned possible penalties, and fewer still knew that there was a maximum £3,000 penalty.

As part of their overall preparation for this exam, candidates should be aware of the extent to which such detailed knowledge of rules contained within the ATX-UK syllabus can be tested. Candidates should expect tax administration issues to be tested and should not ignore these areas of the syllabus in their studies.

Professional skills marks

The analysis and evaluation, scepticism and commercial acumen skills marks tend to be given in relation to a particular question part as detailed above.

The communication skills marks tend to be given in relation to the whole answer.

Communication skills marks were broadly awarded for the following:

- General format and structure,
- Style, language and clarity,
- Effectiveness with which the information is communicated, and
- Adherence to specific instructions.

In this question scenario candidates were required to prepare notes for an internal meeting in relation to a number of different tax issues.

It is important for candidates to bear in mind two key points when addressing this type of requirement. Firstly, the explanations provided should be concise but comprehensive enough to be understood by anyone who is using the notes. Secondly, the notes should be clearly presented in a logical, structured way, such that a user is easily able to find the information that they need.

Candidates who scored well addressed all parts of the requirements, structured their answer according to the matters to be discussed (which were clearly set out in the manager's email), wrote concisely in short, clear paragraphs, and demonstrated a logical thought process when tackling each of the relevant issues.

In summary, those candidates who prepared sound answers to this question were able to do the following:

- directly address each of the tasks within the manager's email, providing concise explanations, where required;
- demonstrate a good knowledge of ethics, capital gains tax and incorporation relief, income tax loss reliefs, tax implications of dividend payments and rules for record keeping; and
- tailor their knowledge intelligently to the scenario by using the facts of the question.

ACCA marking scheme

				Marks
(a)	Investigate and inform HMRC			2.0
	Offence and penalties/interest			2.0
	Unwillingness to return the money			2.0
				6.0
			Maximum	5.0
(b)	Sale of the rental property			
	Taxable gain			1.5
	Capital gains tax liability			4.0
	Proposed sale of business assets			
	Availability of incorporation relief			5.0
	Capital gains tax liability			3.5
				14.0
			Maximum	12.0
(c)	(i)	Relief in year of loss and/or preceding year		3.0
		Relief in the future		1.5
				4.5
			Maximum	4.0
	(ii)	Relief in 2023/24		
		Against income		1.5
		Against chargeable gains		3.0
		Relief in 2025/26		
		Original liability		2.0
		Effect of offsetting loss		2.0
		Conclusions		3.0
				11.5
			Maximum	11.0
(d)	Payment of dividend			5.5
	Record keeping			3.0
				8.5
			Maximum	8.0
	Professional skills marks (see below)		**Maximum**	10.0
Total				**50.0**

Professional skills marks

Communication

– General format and structure of meeting notes (e.g. use of headings/sub-headings to make meeting notes easy to refer to).

– Style, language and clarity (tone of meeting notes, presentation of calculations, appropriate use of the tools, easy to follow and more than a negligible amount of content).

– Effectiveness of communication (answer is relevant, specific rather than general and focused to the requirement).

– Adherence to specific instructions made in the scenario.

Analysis and evaluation

– Appropriate use of relevant information to determine suitable calculations.

– Balanced appraisal of the loss relief options available.

– Demonstration of the ability to consider relevant factors when advising on the use of the trading loss.

Scepticism

– Appropriate application of professional judgement in relation to Hiromi's willingness to retain the refund.

– Critical assessment of the going concern status of Hiromi's business.

Commercial acumen

– Recommendations in respect of loss relief are practical and plausible.

– Recognition of wider implications regarding the timing of the election.

TAXATION OF CORPORATE BUSINESSES

10 DRENCH, PAPRIKASH, HAIL LTD AND RAIN LTD (ADAPTED)

Walk in the footsteps of a top tutor

Key answer tips

This is really five separate questions.

Part (a)(i) covers the acquisition of a subsidiary, with or without losses, by either an individual or a company, and is the hardest part of the question.

Part (a)(ii) is really two written questions: one on close company loans to participators and one on the cash accounting scheme for VAT. These questions should have been very straightforward if you have learnt the rules, and could be attempted before (a)(i).

Part (b) covers the popular topic of inheritance tax, but in a rather unusual way. The '12 possible situations' may put you off attempting this section, but the examining team does provide guidance on how to approach it – so if you heed their words and do not panic you should be able to score some marks.

Part (c) deals with the ethical issue of confidentiality. Again, this part is very straightforward and could be attempted before the other parts of the question, in order to gain some easy marks.

The highlighted words in the written sections are key phrases that markers are looking for.

Tutor's top tips

The formal requirements at the end of the question just tell you how many marks are available in total for technical and professional skills. The detailed requirements and technical mark breakdowns are all in the email from your manager.

(a) **MEMORANDUM**

To	The files
From	Tax assistant
Date	1 December 2024
Subject	Acquisition of Rain Ltd and other matters

(i) Acquisition of Rain Ltd

Tutor's top tips

There are four alternatives to consider here:

1 *Drench acquires Rain Ltd personally and Rain Ltd* ***does not*** *obtain the new contracts.*

2 *Drench acquires Rain Ltd personally and Rain Ltd* ***does*** *obtain the new contracts.*

3 *Hail Ltd acquires Rain Ltd and Rain Ltd* ***does not*** *obtain the new contracts.*

4 *Hail Ltd acquires Rain Ltd and Rain Ltd* ***does*** *obtain the new contracts.*

In order to score well on this part of the question, you must consider all four options. It is very important that you label your answer clearly, so that the marker can see which option you are dealing with.

Rain Ltd acquired by Drench personally

Tutor's top tips

Think carefully about the group relationships that exist here.

Drench is an individual, not a company.

Companies controlled by the same individual will be associated companies for corporation tax purposes, but they cannot form a 75% group relief group, and therefore, the companies cannot transfer losses.

Rates of corporation tax

Tutor's top tips

The examining team give you a clue here. They say to take care when identifying the rates of corporation tax payable, as 'the situation is not totally straightforward'.

If Rain Ltd is acquired by Drench personally, Rain Ltd will be associated with Hail Ltd as both companies will be under common control.

In addition, Rain Ltd will be associated with Flake Ltd and Mist Ltd for the period ending 30 June 2025, giving four associated companies in total.

As Rain Ltd prepares accounts for a nine-month period, the limits must also be time apportioned.

Rain Ltd's limits for corporation tax purposes for the nine months ending 30 June 2025 are, therefore:

Upper limit £46,875 (£250,000 × 1/4 × 9/12)

Lower limit £9,375 (£50,000 × 1/4 × 9/12)

Tutorial note

Remember that when a company joins a group or leaves a group part way through the accounting period, it is deemed to be associated for the whole of that period for the purposes of determining the relevant corporation tax rate.

This means that when a company moves from one group to another, it will be associated with the companies in both the old group and the new group for the period in which it is acquired.

Rain Ltd does not obtain the new contracts

The only option available for relief of the £110,000 trading loss will be to set it against Rain Ltd's own profits.

An amount of £50,750 can be set against total profits (i.e. the chargeable gain) for the period ending 30 June 2025.

As the profit is above the upper limit (set out above), the tax saving will be at the main rate of 25%, giving a saving of £12,688 (£50,750 × 25%).

The remaining loss of £59,250 (£110,000 – £50,750) will then be carried forward for offset against Rain Ltd's future total profits.

There is no possibility of carrying back the remaining loss, as Rain Ltd had no taxable income or gains in the previous accounting period.

Tutor's top tips

If you calculated the corporation tax limits incorrectly, you may have calculated the corporation tax saving at the main rate less marginal relief.

In that case, you would lose marks for not calculating the limits correctly, but you should still gain the marks for calculation of the corporation tax saving.

Be very specific when writing about loss reliefs. For example, just saying that the remaining loss will be carried forward is not enough. You must also state that it will be set against future total profits.

Rain Ltd does obtain the new contracts

The corporation tax liability of Rain Ltd will be as follows:

Corporation tax – nine months ending 30 June 2025

	£
Trading profit	285,000
Chargeable gain	50,750
Taxable total profits	335,750
Corporation tax at 25% (TTP exceeds the upper limit)	83,938

Corporation tax payment date

The threshold for payment of corporation tax by quarterly instalments is divided by the total number of associated companies at the end of the previous accounting period.

This will only include Rain Ltd, Flake Ltd and Mist Ltd, giving three associated companies in total.

As Rain Ltd prepares accounts for a nine-month period, the threshold must also be time apportioned.

Rain Ltd's threshold for corporation tax payment purposes for the nine months ending 30 June 2025 is, therefore £375,000 (£1,500,000 × 1/3 × 9/12).

Rain Ltd will not need to pay its corporation tax in quarterly instalments, as it does not have profits above this threshold.

The corporation tax will be due by 1 April 2026 (i.e. nine months and one day after the end of the accounting period).

Rain Ltd acquired by Hail Ltd

Tutor's top tips

Again, think carefully about the group relationships that exist here.

Hail Ltd is a company, so this time, Rain Ltd and Hail Ltd ***can*** *form a 75% group relief group, and therefore* ***can*** *transfer losses.*

Rates of corporation tax

Rain Ltd

As before, Rain Ltd will have the following limits for the nine-month period ending 30 June 2025:

Upper limit £46,875 (£250,000 × 1/4 × 9/12)

Lower limit £9,375 (£50,000 × 1/4 × 9/12)

Hail Ltd

Hail Ltd is just associated with Rain Ltd, so its limits for the year ending 30 June 2025 will be:

Upper limit £125,000 (£250,000 × 1/2)

Lower limit £25,000 (£50,000 × 1/2)

Tutorial note

There is no connection between Hail Ltd and the other companies in the Flake Ltd group; just Rain Ltd.

Rain Ltd does not obtain the new contracts

This time, there are several options for relief of the £110,000 loss, and Rain Ltd should choose the option that gives the largest tax saving.

Rain Ltd could again claim relief for the loss against its own profits, as set out above where Drench acquires Rain Ltd.

Group relief

Hail Ltd and Rain Ltd will form a 75% group relief group.

Rain Ltd could, therefore, surrender its current period loss against Hail Ltd's taxable total profits for the same period.

Losses arising before Rain Ltd is acquired by Hail Ltd cannot be surrendered against group profits arising within five years of the acquisition.

As Rain Ltd only joins the Hail Ltd group on 1 January 2025, the maximum loss available for surrender must be time apportioned as follows:

(£110,000 × 6/9) = £73,333 available

The maximum loss claimed by Hail Ltd would be restricted to its taxable total profits for the corresponding period:

(£100,000 × 6/12) = £50,000

As the available loss is more than the maximum claim, the maximum group relief would be restricted to £50,000.

Hail Ltd's profits lie between the upper and lower limits (set out above), so the surrender to Hail Ltd would save tax at the marginal rate of 26.5%, whereas set-off against Rain Ltd's profits would only save 25%.

Accordingly, in order to maximise the tax relief, the loss should be utilised as follows:

	Loss used	**Tax rate**	**Tax saved**
	£		£
Surrender to Hail Ltd	50,000	@ 26.5%	13,250
Set against Rain Ltd taxable total profits	50,750	@ 25%	12,688
	100,750		
Total tax saved			25,938

The remaining loss of £9,250 (£110,000 – £100,750) will then be carried forward for offset against Rain Ltd's future total profits.

Payment for group relief

Amounts paid for group relief are ignored for corporation tax purposes, as long as the amount paid is no more than the amount of loss surrendered.

Rain Ltd does obtain the new contracts

Rain Ltd will still have the same corporation tax limits as when acquired by Drench, so the corporation tax liability and payment date will be exactly the same as before, i.e. £83,938 due 1 April 2026. **Tax treatment of Rain Ltd's building**

Potential tax liabilities: Degrouping charge

The transfer of the building from Mist Ltd to Rain Ltd would have been at no gain, no loss, as Mist Ltd and Rain Ltd were part of a 75% gains group at the time.

Whether Rain Ltd is purchased by Drench or Hail Ltd, it will be leaving the Flake Ltd group within six years of the no gain, no loss transfer whilst still owning the building.

This will result in a degrouping charge in the nine months ending 30 June 2025 as set out below.

	£
Market value on 1 July 2021 (date of the no gain/no loss transfer)	260,000
Less: Cost to Mist Ltd	(170,000)
Less: Indexation allowance (January 2012 to December 2017) (0.168 × £170,000)	(28,560)
Degrouping charge	61,440

Tutorial note

There is no indexation allowance post December 2017.

The degrouping charge will be added to Flake Ltd's proceeds for the sale of the shares in Rain Ltd, and may increase the gain on disposal of the shares.

However, the disposal of shares will be covered by the substantial shareholding exemption, as Rain Ltd is a trading company, and Flake Ltd will have held at least 10% of the shares for at least 12 months in the six years before the disposal.

Base cost of the building

The base cost of the building for Rain Ltd will now be £260,000 as at 1 July 2021 (i.e. the market value at the date of the no gain, no loss transfer).

Tutorial note

If Rain Ltd did not leave the Flake Ltd group, the base cost of the building would be the original cost to the group of £170,000 plus indexation allowance to the earlier of the date of the transfer (1 July 2021) or December 2017.

(ii) Loan to Drench and value added tax (VAT) cash accounting scheme

Loan from Hail Ltd to Drench

Tutor's top tips

The requirement asks for the tax implications for Hail Ltd (i.e. the employer) only, so don't waste time writing at length about the implications for Drench.

However, you do need to consider the taxable benefit for Drench, as employer's class 1A national insurance contributions will be based on this.

Hail Ltd is a close company, as it is controlled by one shareholder (participator): Drench.

Accordingly, this will be a loan from a close company to a participator, and Hail Ltd must pay a tax charge to HMRC of £6,075 (33.75% × £18,000).

This tax charge should be paid with the corporation tax liability, by 1 April 2026.

When the loan is repaid by Drench, HMRC will repay the £6,075 tax charge to Hail Ltd within nine months and one day from the end of the accounting period of repayment.

Tutorial note

Watch out for close companies in the exam, as they regularly feature in questions.

A company is close if it is controlled by its directors (any number), or if it is controlled by five or fewer shareholders.

Hail Ltd must also pay employer's class 1A national insurance contributions, as the loan will give rise to a taxable employment benefit for Drench.

The benefit will be based on the official rate of interest of 2.25%, and the NICs payable will be calculated at 13.8% as follows:

(£18,000 × 2.25%) = £405 × 13.8% = £56.

The NICs will be deductible when computing the company's taxable trading profits.

Hail Ltd should include the loan on Drench's Form P11D in order to report it to HMRC.

VAT cash accounting scheme

Tutor's top tips

The cash accounting scheme for VAT is a topic that was tested at TX.

It is important that you retain your TX knowledge, as the examining team frequently tests TX topics in the ATX exam.

There are two specific aspects to write about here:

1 *The advantages of the scheme*

2 *Whether it will be possible for Rain Ltd to operate the scheme.*

Advantages

The advantages of the scheme are:

- Improved cash flow, as output VAT in respect of credit sales is only paid to HMRC when cash is received from the customer.
- Automatic relief for irrecoverable debts. If the customer does not pay, no output VAT is paid to HMRC.

Tutor's top tips

Don't just describe how the scheme works. You need to say ***why*** *it is advantageous for VAT to be accounted for when cash is received from a customer.*

Availability to Rain Ltd

A business can only join the cash accounting scheme if it has annual taxable sales revenue of no more than £1,350,000.

If Rain Ltd acquires the new contracts, it will have sales revenue of £1,425,000 for the nine months ending 30 June 2025, and so will not be able to join the scheme.

If Rain Ltd does not acquire the new contracts, it will be able to join the scheme, as long as its VAT returns and payments are up to date and it has had no convictions for VAT offences or penalties for dishonest conduct.

Tutor's top tips

Even if you could not remember the limits applicable to the scheme, you could still score marks here for knowing that there were limits, and for attempting to apply the rules to the scenario.

(b) **MEETING NOTES**

Date 1 December 2024

Subject Drench: Uncle's property in Chilaca

Inheritance tax liabilities

Tutor's top tips

This section of the question may have appeared daunting, as there are 12 possible situations to deal with. However, there are actually very few calculations needed, as a number of the situations result in the same amount of tax.

The examining team does hint at this in the question, and often they do give advice concerning the approach they want you to take with parts of questions.

Make sure that you follow this advice!

Key answer tips

Watch out for the following:

- There is no annual exemption, as Paprikash already makes gifts each year that use this.
- There is no lifetime tax, as a gift to an individual is a PET. The issue therefore revolves around charges arising as a result of death.

  In all cases, the nil rate band will be reduced by the gift in 2023, as this is less than seven years before the date of the gift/death.
- The residence nil rate band is not available as the property is not being left to a direct descendant.
- Death tax on a lifetime gift is usually based on the value of the gift at the date of gift, not at the date of death (*unless* the property falls in value), so any increases in value since the date of the gift are irrelevant for calculating death tax on a lifetime gift.
- Taper relief will be available for lifetime gifts, but only if the donor survives for at least three years.

Lifetime on 1 February 2025 – PET

Assumed Value at death (Note 1)	**Death on 30 June 2027: IHT arising: (Note 2)**		**Death on 30 June 2029: IHT arising (Note 3)**	
£		£		£
450,000	(£450,000 – £35,000) × 40% =	166,000	(£166,000 × 60%) =	99,600
600,000	(£600,000 – £35,000) × 40% =	226,000	(£226,000 × 60%) =	135,600
900,000	(£600,000 – £35,000) × 40% =	226,000	(£226,000 × 60%) =	135,600

Gift via will on 30 June 2027 or 30 June 2029 (Note 4)

Assumed Value at death (Note 1)	**Death on 30 June 2027 or 2029: IHT arising: (Note 2)**	
£		£
450,000	(£450,000 – £35,000) × 40% =	166,000
600,000	(£600,000 – £35,000) × 40% =	226,000
900,000	(£900,000 – £35,000) × 40% =	346,000

Notes

1 When Paprikash makes the gift it will be a potentially exempt transfer, thus, if the value of the property at the time of death is less than it was at the time of the gift, the inheritance tax payable will reflect the fall in value.

If the value at the time of death is higher than at the time of the gift, the 'frozen' value at the time of the gift is charged to tax at the death rates.

2 The nil rate band remaining following the gift into trust on 1 December 2023 will be:

(£325,000 – £290,000 CLT in December 2023) = £35,000.

Tutorial note

The value of the CLT on 1 December 2023 is £290,000 as:

- *the gift is a gift of a minority shareholding in quoted shares, which does not qualify for business property relief (BPR), and*
- *the annual exemptions have already been utilised.*

3 30 June 2029 would be between four and five years after the gift such that 40% taper relief would be available. Accordingly, the liability will be 60% of the liability calculated in respect of death occurring on 30 June 2027.

4 The date of death will not affect the amount of inheritance tax due.

Tutorial note

Note 4 is true, but only because it is assumed in the answer that the nil rate band does not change in the future.

In practice, the nil rate band can change in each tax year and therefore the amount of tax payable could be affected by the date of death.

Inheritance tax liabilities – conclusions

If the property is gifted on 1 February 2025, the inheritance tax due on death will never be more than the amount due if the property is transferred via Paprikash's will, even if the value of the property falls prior to the date of death.

Making a lifetime gift would turn out to be particularly beneficial if:

- The value of the property increases, as the tax would be based on the value as at 1 February 2025 rather than the value at the time of death.
- Paprikash survives the gift by more than three years such that taper relief would be available.

Tutor's top tips

Even if your calculations are not correct, you will still be able to score marks for drawing sensible conclusions.

Other issues

Tutor's top tips

The question asks for any 'other issues' that should be drawn to Drench's attention. The most obvious issue is the continuing use of the property by Paprikash, which is mentioned a couple of times in the information.

There is also the issue of capital gains tax potentially arising on lifetime gifts.

Gift with reservation

Once the property has been given to Drench, the occasional use of it by Paprikash may result in the gift being treated as a gift with reservation.

In these circumstances, the gift would be ignored for inheritance tax purposes and the property would then be included in Paprikash's death estate at its value at the time of death.

In order to ensure that the gift is effective for inheritance tax purposes Paprikash should have only minimal use of the property unless he pays Drench a market rent.

Tutorial note

HMRC guidance is that visits of up to two weeks a year without the nephew, and up to a month with the nephew, would be acceptable as 'minimal' use for these purposes. Knowledge of this guidance is not expected in the exam, but is of interest!

If the uncle pays a full commercial rent for the use of the property gifted, the gift with reservation rules will not apply. The gift will only be treated as a PET.

Capital gains tax

Lifetime gift

If Paprikash is resident in the UK in the year in which he gives the property to Drench, it will be necessary to calculate a capital gain on the gift of the property.

The gain would be the market value of the property less its cost. The gain, less any available annual exempt amount, would be taxed at 18% or 28% (residential property rates) depending on Paprikash's taxable income.

Tutorial note

If Paprikash is not resident in the UK in the year in which he gives the property to Drench, the gain will be exempt from capital gains tax (subject to the temporary residence overseas rule).

Gift on death in the will

There would be no capital gains tax if the property were given to Drench on death, via Paprikash's will.

(c) Briefing note – use of knowledge

Tutor's top tips

Ethical issues appear in every ATX exam, for five marks. It is worth learning the key principles, as these are often easy marks that can be scored very quickly.

However, you must make sure that you apply the principles to the scenario and don't just list them.

Try to make sure that you have at least five separate points in your answer, as you will probably score one mark per relevant point.

- As members of the ACCA, we must comply with the ACCA Professional Code of Ethics.
- One of the fundamental principles of this code is confidentiality.
- We must not disclose confidential information to other parties without our client's permission.
- This restriction continues to apply even if we no longer act for the client.
- Accordingly, we should not use confidential information acquired from our ex-client to assist Rain Ltd.
- However, it is acceptable to use our general experience and expertise gained from advising our ex-client.

Examiner's report

In part (a)(i) there were four possibilities to consider.

The question asked for the tax implications to be compared such that numbers should have been produced for each of the four possible situations. The question also stated that Drench was aware of the general implications of forming a group and that the comparison should focus on certain specific issues. It was important for candidates to be clear as to what they had been asked to do and also what they had been asked not to do. The answers to this question were not as good as expected.

The following general mistakes were made by many candidates:

- Many candidates did not structure their answers to this part particularly well such that it was not always clear which of the four possible situations was being addressed.
- Despite the question instructing candidates to focus on specific issues, many candidates wasted time by addressing general issues. Accordingly, a considerable amount of unnecessary information was provided in connection with groups generally and the extraction of profits from companies.
- A minority of candidates reached an initial conclusion that Rain Ltd should be acquired by Hail Ltd such that numbers were only prepared for that eventuality.

- When addressing the purchase of Rain Ltd by Drench, a minority of candidates erroneously relieved the company's losses against the income of Drench.

In addition to the general mistakes set out above, many candidates stated that the losses of Rain Ltd would have to be carried forward if the company were purchased by Drench due to the unavailability of group relief. This omitted the possibility of a current year offset against the chargeable gains in Rain Ltd. The other specific common error related to the effect of the acquisition on the accounting periods of Rain Ltd with many candidates confusing the need to time apportion losses for the purposes of group relief with the need to prepare tax computations for separate accounting periods.

Matters done well included the identification of the degrouping charge, the corporation tax payment dates and the calculations of the maximum possible group relief.

Part (a)(ii) concerned a loan from Hail Ltd to Drench and the VAT cash accounting scheme. This part was done reasonably well with many candidates demonstrating a good knowledge of the technical areas.

The question asked for the tax implications **for Hail Ltd** of the loan. Almost all candidates recognised that Hail Ltd was a close company such that a 33.75% charge would be payable to H M Revenue and Customs. However, very few candidates identified that Hail Ltd would have to pay class 1A national insurance contributions in respect of the benefit relating to the loan. This is not an obscure point and would have been known to almost all candidates. It may be candidates need to think about the requirement and identify all of the possible issues before commencing writing in order to identify as many relevant points as possible.

The majority of candidates were able to identify the advantages of using the VAT cash accounting scheme and to link the facts in the question to the scheme's limit in respect of annual taxable supplies; this part of the question was answered well.

Note that part (b) of the question has been added in from another question. The relevant section of the examiner's report for that question is included below:

Part (b) of the question concerned inheritance tax and the advantages of lifetime giving. At first sight it was a daunting question requiring the consideration of three possible property values, two dates of death and a lifetime gift or gift via will; a total of 12 possible situations. However, there was guidance from the 'manager' as to where to start together with the reassurance that 'you should find that the calculations do not take too long'.

It was very pleasing to find that the majority of candidates had no problem with this part of the question and that their knowledge of the basic mechanics of inheritance tax was sound. Candidates benefited from thinking rather than writing such that they were then able to realise that, for example, with a lifetime gift, the only difference between the two possible dates of death was the availability of taper relief. The best answers were admirably short and to the point.

The one area where candidates could have done better was in identifying the possible gift with reservation. The failure by many candidates to do this indicates, yet again, that some candidates do not take enough care in identifying all that has been asked of them.

The final part of the question concerned the ethical considerations relating to confidentiality and was done well by the majority of candidates.

ACCA marking scheme

				Marks
(a)	(i)	Rain Ltd acquired by Drench personally		
		Rain Ltd makes tax adjusted loss		
		Upper and lower limits		1.5
		Use of losses		2.5
		Rain Ltd makes tax adjusted profit		
		Corporation tax liability		1.0
		Corporation tax payment date		2.0
		Rain Ltd acquired by Hail Ltd		
		Rain Ltd makes tax adjusted loss		4.5
		Rain Ltd makes tax adjusted profit		0.5
		Rain Ltd building		
		Degrouping charge and tax treatment		3.5
		Base cost to Rain Ltd		1.0
				16.5
			Maximum	15.0
	(ii)	Loan to Drench		
		Close company loan to participator		1.0
		Payment to HMRC		2.0
		Employment income benefit		2.5
		Cash accounting scheme		
		Advantages		2.0
		Conditions		2.0
				9.5
			Maximum	8.0
(b)		Inheritance tax liabilities		
		Nil band		1.0
		Lifetime gift		
		Value at time of gift and tax rate		1.0
		Fall in value post gift		1.0
		Taper relief		1.0
		Gift via will		1.5
		Full set of outcomes		0.5
		Conclusions (1 mark each, maximum 2 marks)		2.0
		Explanatory notes (½ mark each)		2.0
		Gift with reservation		2.5
		Capital gains tax		1.5
				14.0
			Maximum	12.0
(c)		Confidentiality, 1 mark per relevant point		5.0
		Professional skills marks (see below)	**Maximum**	10.0
Total				**50.0**

Professional skills marks

Communication

- General format and structure of memorandum (e.g. use of headings/sub-headings to make memorandum easy to refer to).
- Style, language and clarity (tone of memorandum, presentation of calculations, appropriate use of the tools, easy to follow and more than a negligible amount of content).
- Effectiveness of communication (answer is relevant, specific rather than general and focused to the requirement).
- Adherence to specific instructions made in the scenario (e.g. having a separate memorandum, meeting notes and briefing note).

Analysis and evaluation

- Analysis of the information to determine the loss relief options available to the company/companies in part (a)(i)
- Use of information to determine tax saved as a result of the chosen loss relief method in part (a)(i)
- Analysis of the information to determine the appropriate corporation tax treatment of Rain Ltd's building in part (a)(i)
- Use of information to determine the tax treatment of the loan to Drench in part (a)(ii).
- Demonstration of ability to consider all taxes relevant to requirement(a)(ii), i.e. corporation tax and national insurance contributions.

Scepticism

- Recognition of the need to obtain information about previous VAT return submissions and convictions in order to identify whether Rain Ltd can use the cash accounting scheme in part (a)(ii).
- Identification of the potential for anti-avoidance rules to apply as a result of the occasional use of the property in Chilaca in part (b).

Commercial acumen

- Demonstration of ability to give relevant loss relief advice in line with the company's wishes in part (a)(i).
- Demonstration of an understanding of the rules around close company loans to participators in part (a)(ii).
- Identification of relevant factors which will cause a change in the inheritance tax liability for Drench in part (b).

11 DILIP GROUP AND EMMA (ADAPTED) *Walk in the footsteps of a top tutor*

Key answer tips

Part (a) is a typical corporation tax groups question covering: trading losses, capital gains aspects, VAT and stamp duty land tax.

The key to success is applying your knowledge to the scenario given and making sure that your answer only deals with the required issues; otherwise you are likely to run out of time.

Part (b) deals with a different individual, so be sure to keep your answer to this separate from the report for Dilip to maintain client confidentiality. This part tests the popular temporary non-residence rules. It is important to explain why the rules are applicable as well as the impact that they will have. You're asked to advise when the best time to sell the shares is, so make sure you give a reasoned recommendation to score well.

Part (c) is a totally separate stand-alone section on the professional and ethical issues to consider in relation to a tax planning scheme. Remember there will always be five marks in each exam on ethics.

There are easy marks available here, and it may therefore be a good idea to start with this part of the question just in case you run out of time on parts (a) and (b).

The highlighted words in the written sections are key phrases that markers are looking for.

Tutor's top tips

As is usual for Section A questions, the formal requirements at the end of the question just tell you how many marks are available in total for technical and professional skills. The detailed requirements and technical mark breakdowns are all in the email from your manager. Remember that in the exam the requirements you see at the end of the question in this exam kit will be on a separate button. The detailed information and requirements will be located in exhibits which you can click to view.

As you read through, highlight any requirements and instructions that you find. Copy these into the answer space to help you keep your answer focused. The requirements in this question are all in the email from the manager.

Make sure that you set out your answer to part (a) as a report, as there are marks available for this. You need to write in full sentences, but don't waste time preparing a lengthy introduction.

(a) Report

To Dilip

From Tax advisers

Date 1 December 2024

Subject Various corporate matters

(i) Sale of Shank Ltd

Use of trading losses

Tutor's top tips

There are two different trading losses to consider here:

- *The loss brought forward from the year ended 31 March 2024*
- *The current year loss for the year ended 31 March 2025.*

You will need to deal with each of these separately in your answer, and clearly label them.

The examining team asks you to consider all possibilities, so make sure that you do that. However, you must ensure that you apply your knowledge to the scenario: there is no point in spending time discussing reliefs that are not actually possible.

Loss brought forward

The loss brought forward of £35,000 can be set against future total profits within Shank Ltd. As there are no profits available in the current year, the unrelieved loss would be available for surrender as group relief along with the current year loss (see below).

Any excess loss after group relief claims would be carried forward against future total profits in Shank Ltd.

However, there is a possible restriction on the use of this loss as Shank Ltd will change its owners when it is sold to Raymond Ltd on 1 February 2025.

If there is a major change in the nature or conduct of trade within five years of this change in ownership, the loss will not be allowed to be carried forward past 1 February 2025.

A major change would include a change in products or services offered, markets or customers.

As Dilip is of the opinion that the company will only become profitable if there are fundamental changes to its commercial operations, it seems likely that the restriction will apply.

Tutor's top tips

Look for clues in the question – you are specifically asked to consider any anti-avoidance legislation that may restrict the use of the losses. This is a big hint that there is some relevant anti-avoidance legislation here!

Make sure that you apply the rules to the scenario: there will be 'fundamental changes' to the company's commercial operations.

Tutorial note

A 'change in ownership' occurs when more than 50% of the share capital in the company changes ownership. As Hock Ltd is disposing of all of the share capital in Shank Ltd, there clearly is a change in ownership.

*However, for the restriction in use of losses to apply, there must be **both** a change in ownership and a major change in the nature and conduct of trade.*

Current year loss

Tutor's top tips

Read the question carefully. The statement that Shank Ltd has surrendered the maximum possible losses to group companies applies to the losses in the past pre-31 March 2024, not the loss for the year ended 31 March 2025.

Therefore, you need to include group relief as a key option available in your answer for the use of the loss in the year ended 31 March 2025.

The loss for the year ended 31 March 2025 cannot be set against current year profits or previous year profits of Shank Ltd, as there are none available. Shank Ltd has no other source of income.

All or part of this loss and the £35,000 excess brought forward loss could be surrendered to other companies within Shank Ltd's 75% losses group. This group contains Hock Ltd, Shank Ltd, Rump Ltd and Brisket Ltd, but **not** Knuckle Ltd.

The loss available for surrender must be time apportioned, as Shank Ltd will only be part of the losses group for part of the year. For the purposes of group relief, Shank Ltd is deemed to leave the group once 'arrangements' for sale are in place. The contract for sale will represent such an 'arrangement', therefore Shank Ltd can only surrender losses up to 1 November 2024.

The maximum loss available for surrender to Hock Ltd and Rump Ltd is therefore £31,500 (7/12 × (£19,000 + £35,000)) from 1 April 2024 to 31 October 2024.

Brisket Ltd has only been part of the losses group since 1 May 2024, therefore the maximum loss available for surrender to Brisket Ltd is £27,000 (6/12 × (£19,000 + £35,000), from 1 May 2024 to 31 October 2024.

The maximum loss that can be claimed by group companies will be limited to their taxable total profits for the corresponding period.

Any remaining losses will be carried forward by Shank Ltd along with its loss incurred between 1 November 2024 and 31 January 2025, as described above.

Tutor's top tips

This part of the question is all about explaining the reliefs available, not about giving advice on which relief might be best.

There is no information given about the profits of the other group companies for you to offer such advice.

Tutorial note

The requirement is to give advice to Dilip about the options for the use of the trading losses within his group of companies, and so marks in the answer are going for advising on the loss incurred up to 31 January 2025 only, when Shank Ltd leaves the group.

There are therefore no marks for commenting on what can happen with the loss after Shank Ltd left Dilip's control.

However, were this a requirement, the loss for the year ended 31 March 2025 is actually divided into three parts:

- *1 April 2024 to 31 October 2024 (seven months loss): group relief possible within Hock Ltd group for this loss and the excess brought forward trading loss, any excess carried forward.*
- *1 November 2024 to 31 January 2025 (three months loss): can only be used within Shank Ltd and as it has no other income, will be carried forward.*

  Losses carried forward cannot be surrendered to the new group for a period of five years after the change in ownership.
- *1 February 2025 to 31 March 2025 (two months loss): can be group relieved within the new group.*

Loss on sale of Shank Ltd

The sale of Shank Ltd will be covered by the substantial shareholding exemption, as Hock Ltd is disposing of shares and has held at least 10% of the shares in Shank Ltd for 12 months in the six years before the sale, and Shank Ltd is a trading company.

Accordingly, there will be no relief for the capital loss on the disposal of the shares.

Tutorial note

You are probably aware that gains on the sale of shares are covered by the substantial shareholding exemption. However, remember that the 'exemption' means that not only are there no chargeable gains, there are no allowable losses either!

Upper and lower limits for calculation of corporation tax

Tutor's top tips

*Make sure that you read the verb in the question. You are asked to 'explain' the limits for **all** of the companies. Just calculating the limits is not enough here.*

Also, remember that not all companies will necessarily have the same limits. Check the dates carefully to see which companies have joined or left during the year, as these may be associated with old or new groups too.

Companies are associated where one company controls another, or where companies are under common control of a 'person' (i.e. an individual or a company), for all or part of an accounting period.

As the Hock Ltd group companies and Knuckle Ltd are all under the control of Dilp, they are all associated for the year ended 31 March 2025.

Accordingly, the limits for Hock Ltd, Rump Ltd and Knuckle Ltd for the purposes of determining the rate of corporation tax payable are:

Lower limit: (£50,000 ÷ 5) = £10,000

Upper limit: (£250,000 ÷ 5) = £50,000.

Shank Ltd will also be associated with its new owner, Raymond Ltd and may also be associated with other companies controlled by Raymond Ltd. Brisket Ltd will be associated with its previous owner and any other companies related to its previous owner. The limits for these companies will therefore be lower than those shown above.

The rate of corporation tax payable by each company will be found by comparing its augmented profits to these statutory limits.

Tutorial note

A company is associated if it has been a member of a group at any time in the accounting period. The upper and lower limits for Shank Ltd and Brisket Ltd will therefore be lower as they are associated with both their new and previous owners, and if applicable, other associated companies in those groups.

There is not enough information in the question, however, to specifically calculate the number of associated companies and therefore the upper and lower limits for these companies.

(ii) Sales of buildings

Gains/losses on sale

Gar building

The sale of the Gar building to Hock Ltd will be at no gain, no loss, as Shank Ltd and Hock Ltd are part of the same 75% capital gains group.

Tutor's top tips

There is no need to do a calculation here, it is enough to just state that the transfer will be at no gain, no loss and explain why.

There were no extra marks available for any calculations of the base cost of the deemed transfer.

Tutorial note

Although Shank Ltd is deemed to leave the 75% losses group on 1 November 2024, it is still part of the 75% capital gains group until the sale is completed on 1 February 2025.

Had the base cost been requested, the transfer would have occurred at the base cost of £283,500 (£210,000 + IA (£210,000 × 0.350)). The estimated proceeds given in the question are irrelevant.

There will be no degrouping charge in respect of the Gar building when Shank Ltd leaves the group. A degrouping charge only arises if the ***recipient*** *company leaves the group less than six years after a no gain, no loss transfer, with the asset acquired.*

Cray building

	£
Proceeds	42,000,000
Less: Cost	(24,000,000)
Unindexed gain	18,000,000
Less: Indexation allowance (£24,000,000 × 0.250)	(6,000,000)
Chargeable gain	12,000,000

Monk building

	£
Proceeds	290,000
Less: Cost	(380,000)
Capital loss	(90,000)

Sword building

Tutor's top tips

Be very careful here!

Before you can work out the gain on the Sword building, you need to calculate the allowable cost. There has been a rollover relief claim, but only part of the proceeds was reinvested, so only part of the gain on the Pilot building will have been rolled over.

	£
Proceeds	460,000
Less: Deemed cost (W1)	(210,000)
Unindexed gain	250,000
Less: Indexation allowance (£210,000 × 0.089)	(18,690)
Chargeable gain	231,310

Workings

(W1) Deemed cost of Sword building

	£
Original cost	255,000
Less: Rollover relief (W2)	(45,000)
Deemed cost	210,000

(W2) Rollover relief in respect of Sword building

	£
Gain on sale of the Pilot building	60,000
Less: Sale proceeds not reinvested in the Sword building (£270,000 – £255,000)	(15,000)
Rollover relief claimed	45,000

Tutorial note

The chargeable gains will arise in the company that made the disposal.

The chargeable gain arising in Knuckle Ltd's corporation tax computation cannot be moved to any other company as Knuckle Ltd is not in a capital gains group.

However, the chargeable gain arising in Rump Ltd can be moved within the capital gains group, for example to utilise capital losses brought forward.

Explaining this, however, is not mark earning as it is not specifically required in the question.

Use of capital losses

Tutor's top tips

Make sure that you provide the detailed explanations requested, and remember that capital losses are more restricted than trading losses.

The examining team is kind here, and tells you to watch out for the pre-entry loss on the Monk building. Even if you were unsure about the rules regarding pre-entry capital losses, you could still score some marks for a sensible attempt at describing its possible use.

Brought forward capital losses

Rump Ltd has brought forward capital losses which can be offset against the £12 million gain on the Cray building.

However, as the brought forward capital losses exceed £5 million, they will be subject to restriction. The amount that can be offset against the gain on the Cray building is restricted to £5 million plus 50% of the excess gains over £5 million.

The remaining capital losses continue to be carried forward against future capital gains in Rump Ltd and cannot be reallocated in the gains group.

Tutorial note

The £5 million deductions allowance is not examinable in detail, so you would not be expected to do any calculations with regards to this.

In this instance, if you were to do calculations, the amount of the gain which could be offset by the brought forward capital losses is £8.5 million (£5 million + 50% × (£12 million – £5 million)).

Remember that brought forward capital losses cannot be reallocated in a gains group, so these will be carried forwards in Rump Ltd.

Pre-entry loss

The Monk building was sold by Brisket Ltd before it joined the Hock Ltd group. Accordingly, the capital loss that arose before 1 May 2024 when Brisket Ltd joined the group is a restricted pre-entry loss.

It can only be set-off against gains on disposals made by Brisket Ltd on assets that it owned before it joined the group, or bought subsequently from unconnected persons for use in its own business.

Tutorial note

The question asks for the options available for the use of the loss only.

It does not ask for discussions re tax planning.

Therefore, no marks would be allocated to making such comments.

VAT on sale of buildings

Tutor's top tips

VAT on land and buildings and the option to tax are regularly tested in the exam. You must make sure that you learn the rules!

Inter-group transfer

Provided Hock Ltd and Shank Ltd are members of a VAT group; VAT should not be charged on the inter-group sale of the Gar building.

Other sales

VAT should only be charged on the sale of commercial buildings if:

- they are less than three years old, or
- the owner has opted to tax the building.

Stamp duty land tax

Tutor's top tips

The stamp duty rates and thresholds are given in the tax tables provided in the examination. To score marks here, you must make sure that you apply these rates to the buildings in the question.

Inter group transfer

There will be no stamp duty land tax payable on the transfer of the Gar building, as Shank Ltd and Hock Ltd are within the same 75% group.

Other sales

Stamp duty land tax will be payable at 0% on the first £150,000, then 2% on the next £100,000, then at 5% above £250,000 on the sale price of other buildings, and will be payable by the purchaser.

Tutorial note

Even though Shank Ltd leaves the 75% group within three years of the transfer of the Gar building, there is still no stamp duty land tax payable.

*Stamp duty land tax is only payable where the **transferee** company leaves the group within three years.*

(iii) Sales by Knuckle Ltd to overseas customers

VAT implications

Tutor's top tips

Consideration of the VAT implications of imports and exports is another popular area in the exam.

There are only two marks available here, so you should try to make two succinct points in your answer.

Sales to customers outside the UK are zero-rated.

The exports will not affect Knuckle Ltd's ability to reclaim input VAT, as all sales will still be taxable sales.

(b) Sale of shares in Barb plc

File note

Client: Emma

Tutor's top tips

When advising on the timing of the sale of shares it is important that you don't just consider the tax cost, but think about the impact on post-tax proceeds. The aim should be to maximise post-tax proceeds, even if this means paying a bit more tax.

For the purposes of UK CGT, Emma is a temporary non-UK resident whilst she is living in Alman. This is because:

– she was UK resident for at least four of the seven tax years immediately prior to the tax year 2021/22 (the tax year of departure), and

– on her return to the UK, she will have been absent for less than five years.

Accordingly, if Emma sells the shares now, the chargeable gain of £330,000 will still be subject to UK CGT, albeit in the tax year 2025/26 (the tax year in which she returns to the UK) as opposed to 2024/25, the tax year of sale. This rule applies because Emma owned the shares on 1 February 2022 (the date she left the UK) and will have disposed of them whilst living in Alman.

If Emma waits until she has returned to the UK, the chargeable gain will increase by £60,000 to £390,000. It will be subject to CGT in the tax year 2025/26, the tax year of disposal.

Accordingly, the chargeable gain will be subject to CGT in the tax year 2025/26 regardless of the date of sale and therefore UK CGT, at the rate of 20%, will be due on 31 January 2027.

In order to maximise her post-tax proceeds, Emma should sell the shares after she has returned to the UK. By doing so, she will realise additional post-tax proceeds of £48,000 (£60,000 × 80% (100% – 20%)).

Tutorial note

Business asset disposal relief will not be available on the sale of the shares as Emma owns less than 5% of the shares.

(c) Tax planning scheme

Tutor's top tips

There are five marks available for this section, so try to make sure that you have at least five separately identifiable points available and address each of the requirements: information needed and actions to take!

Ethical issues:

- It could be possible that the scheme is a tax avoidance scheme rather than a tax planning scheme.
- The 'series of complicated disposals' would be a signpost of a tax avoidance scheme.

Action to take:

We should investigate the scheme to determine whether it is a tax planning scheme or a tax avoidance scheme.

If it is a tax avoidance scheme we should ask if it has been notified to H M Revenue and Customs (HMRC).

If the scheme is a tax avoidance scheme then we should advise Emma to avoid it since taxpayers should not use aggressive or abusive schemes.

If Emma refuses and decides to use the scheme then we should resign from the engagement.

We should inform HMRC about our resignation, but should not give the reasons for it.

Examiner's report

Part (a) was in three parts and, on the whole, was done well by many candidates. The vast majority of candidates prepared their answer in the correct report format although a minority wasted time producing a long and unnecessary introduction.

Candidates' knowledge of the reliefs available in respect of trading losses was often very good but many let themselves down by addressing the issue in the abstract rather than in relation to the companies in the question.

This resulted in detailed explanations of reliefs that were simply not applicable (in particular the offset of losses against current and previous years' profits) such that candidates then had too little time to explain the relevant points properly.

As always, candidates benefited if they paused to allow themselves to identify the issues within the question.

There was to be a change of ownership of the loss-making company and an apparent major change in the manner in which it would carry on its activities going forward. Accordingly, it is likely that it would be unable to carry forward its losses beyond the date of the change of ownership. There were also arrangements in force for the company to be sold such that it would leave the group relief group prior to the legal transfer of the shares.

Many candidates spotted both of these points but those that did not need to think about how they would do things differently such that they would spot them in the future. Finally, a surprising number of candidates thought, incorrectly, that Knuckle Ltd was a member of the group relief group.

The capital loss on the sale of the company was not available for offset due to the substantial shareholding exemption. Somewhat surprisingly, many candidates missed this and, of those that spotted the point, many thought that whilst a gain would not be subject to tax, a loss would still be allowable.

For the final element of this part of the question candidates were asked to explain the upper and lower limits of the companies. Many candidates simply stated the number of associated companies and the consequent limits; but that was not an explanation. What was needed were the reasons for the limits being what they were including references to the companies being controlled by the same person and the effect of companies joining and leaving the group. The limits were not the same for each of the companies. Candidates needed to consider each of the companies and apply their knowledge of the rules to that company's particular circumstances.

Part (ii) concerned the planned disposal of a number of buildings. The capital gains were reasonably straightforward with just an added complication of a gain rolled over into the cost of one of the buildings.

However, many candidates missed the fact that one of the buildings would be transferred at no gain, no loss as the vendor and the purchaser were in a capital gains group. Others made errors in connection with the indexation allowance (applying the indexation factor to the unindexed gain rather than the cost) and the treatment of the held over gain. There was a sense here that some candidates had switched off in that some of the errors were very basic and were perhaps an indication of not paying sufficient attention as opposed to a lack of knowledge.

Candidates were told in the question that there was a pre-entry capital loss arising on the sale of one of the buildings. Only a small minority had a clear understanding of the manner in which the pre-entry loss could be used.

A minority of candidates wasted time on this part of the question explaining, often in some detail, how the gains and losses should be offset. This was not part of the requirements and there was insufficient information in the question to arrive at sensible conclusions. Candidates will always benefit from taking the time to read each requirement carefully and then taking care not to deviate from the tasks set.

The VAT and stamp duty land tax elements were handled well by many candidates. Those who did not do so well need to apply their knowledge to the facts as opposed to simply writing what they know. For example, the prices at which the buildings were to be sold meant that, where duty was payable, the rate would be 0%, 2% then 5%. Yet some candidates answered in the abstract and gave the various rates of duty for all possible prices that could be charged. Only a small number of candidates considered the possibility of there being a VAT group; slightly more identified that there would be no stamp duty land tax on the property transferred within the group.

Note that this part of the question has been amended since it was originally set.

Part (iii) concerned the VAT implications of selling goods overseas. There were many excellent answers to this part that, whilst being brief, often scored almost full marks. Weaker candidates either had not learned the rules or confused their terminology using the phrase 'no VAT will be charged' as opposed to 'zero-rated'; the two terms do not mean the same thing.

Note that part (b) of the question has been added in from another question. The relevant section of the examiner's report for that question is included below:

Part (b) of the question tested a knowledge and application of temporary non-UK residence rules. The client was unsure whether to sell a UK asset now whilst temporary non-UK resident or wait until they returned to the UK and sell it for substantially more proceeds. Many candidates correctly recognised that selling the asset at either time would result in a taxable gain, chargeable in the tax year of return to the UK. However, many candidates then incorrectly advised that since higher proceeds would result in a higher tax bill, the client should sell for lower proceeds to reduce their tax bill. This is very unsound, uncommercial advice. The commercial point is that the advice should be based on maximising 'post-tax proceeds' for the client. Candidates are expected to apply the detailed tax rules but also apply sound commercial judgement to their client advice.

Note that part (c) has been re-written since the question was originally set.

ACCA marking scheme

				Marks
(a)	(i)	Use of trading losses		
		Losses carried forward		3.5
		Current year loss		5.5
		Loss on sale of Shank Ltd		2.0
		Corporation tax limits		3.5
				14.5
			Maximum	12.0
	(ii)	Gar building		2.0
		Cray building		1.0
		Rump Ltd brought forward losses		2.5
		Sword building		2.5
		Monk building		
		Capital loss		0.5
		Use of pre-entry loss		2.0
		VAT		3.0
		Stamp duty land tax		2.0
				15.5
			Maximum	13.0
	(iii)	Customers situated outside the UK		1.0
		Recoverability of input tax		1.0
				2.0

(b)	Temporary non-UK resident		3.0
	Capital gains tax liability		
	Sale before returning to the UK		2.0
	Sale after returning to the UK		1.5
	Payment date		1.0
	Advice		2.5
			10.0
		Maximum	8.0
(c)	Ethical issues		2.0
	Investigate		0.5
	Notified to HMRC		1.0
	Avoid scheme		1.0
	Resign if avoidance scheme used		1.0
	Notify HMRC		0.5
	No reasons		0.5
			6.5
		Maximum	5.0
	Professional skills marks (see below)	**Maximum**	10.0
Total			**50.0**

Professional skills marks

Communication

- General format and structure of report (e.g. use of headings/sub-headings to make report easy to refer to).
- Style, language and clarity (tone of report, presentation of calculations, appropriate use of the tools, easy to follow and more than a negligible amount of content).
- Effectiveness of communication (answer is relevant, specific rather than general and focused to the requirement).
- Adherence to specific instructions made in the scenario (e.g. having a separate file note for part (b)).

Analysis and evaluation

- Analysis of the information to determine the loss relief options available to the group in part (a)(i).
- Use of information to determine which companies are associated companies for corporation tax rate limit purposes in part (a)(i).
- Analysis of the information to determine the appropriate corporation tax treatment of the building sales in part (a)(ii).
- Use of information to determine the capital gains tax treatment of the sale of the Barb plc shares for Emma in part (b).
- Demonstration of ability to consider all relevant taxes specified in the requirements, e.g. corporation tax, VAT and SDLT in in part (a)(ii).

Scepticism

- Recognition of uncertainty as to whether the loss restriction will apply to Shank Ltd (i.e. it depends whether the changes are classed as major) in part (a)(i).
- Recognition that it is not possible to specify exactly how many associated companies Brisket Ltd has without further information about the previous owner in part (a)(i).

- Critical assessment of the impact of a VAT group on the VAT treatment of the sale of the Gar building in part (a)(ii).

Commercial acumen

- Demonstration of an understanding of the restriction on loss relief where a change in ownership applies in part (a)(i).
- Demonstration of an understanding of the restriction on use of capital losses within the group in part (a)(ii).

12 JANUS PLC GROUP (ADAPTED) *Walk in the footsteps of a top tutor*

Key answer tips

This question mainly covers corporation tax groups but also examines the capital goods scheme, intangible assets (patent rights), VAT on the import of services, the substantial shareholding exemption, permanent establishments and ethics.

The groups section tests whether you understand the different types of groups that exist for corporation tax purposes. If you were not able to distinguish between the different groups you would struggle to score high marks here.

Part (d) of the question focuses on the overseas aspects of corporation tax. This is a new area at ATX, so you should be prepared for this to be tested. Make sure you are happy with the consequences of the permanent establishment (PE) exemption. This is often tested when PEs come up!

The final part of the question deals with the ethical issue of confidentiality. This part is very straightforward and could be attempted before the other parts of the question, in order to gain some easy marks.

The highlighted words in the written sections are key phrases that markers are looking for.

Tutor's top tips

Before answering the groups part of the question you should take some time to decide which companies form a group relief group and identify the consortium. It is also important to realise which companies have joined or left the group in the year as this will affect the loss claims.

Remember that Castor Ltd is not a consortium owned company because the remaining 30% is owned by individuals.

(a) Use of the trading loss of Janus plc

(i) Alternative reliefs available

Tutor's top tips

To score the marks available for explaining the reliefs you need to apply your knowledge to the facts in the scenario. Don't just list all of the possible options; be specific.

Janus plc can use the trading loss itself and/or surrender the loss as group/consortium relief. Make sure that you state clearly:

- *which profits the loss can be set against, and*
- *for which period.*

Utilising the loss themselves

Janus plc can relieve the trading loss against its chargeable gain of £4,500 in the year ended 31 March 2024. Once this current period claim has been made, the loss can then be relieved against the company's total profits of the previous accounting period of £35,000.

Group relief

Janus plc can surrender trading losses to its 75% subsidiaries. For a company to be a 75% subsidiary, Janus plc must have an effective 75% interest in the company's ordinary share capital, its distributable income and its net assets were it to be wound up. Accordingly, Janus plc is in a group relief group with Seb Ltd and Viola Ltd only (Tutorial note).

Any amount of losses can be surrendered up to the level of the group member's taxable total profits for the corresponding accounting period. Seb Ltd and Viola Ltd did not become members of the group until 1 December 2023. Accordingly, only 4/12 of each of these companies' taxable total profits can be relieved via group relief.

Tutorial note

Castor Ltd (and therefore Pollux Ltd also) is not in a group relief group with Janus plc as Janus plc owns < 75% in Castor Ltd. There is no need to mention this specifically in the answer as once the definition is given, it is sufficient to demonstrate the application of the rules by just concluding which companies are in the group relief group.

Similarly, Duet Ltd is not in a group relief group with Janus plc as Janus plc owns < 75%, but it is a consortium company as explained below.

Consortium relief

Duet Ltd is a consortium company as at least 75% of its share capital is owned by companies, each of which own at least 5%. Accordingly, £110,000 (£200,000 × 55%) of its taxable total profits can be relieved via consortium relief.

Tutorial note

The maximum consortium relief is always based on the % share of the results in the consortium company.

If the consortium company makes a loss, the members can each claim their % of that loss.

If the consortium company makes a profit (as is the case here), the members can each surrender losses against their % of the consortium company's profit.

Castor Ltd is not a consortium company as the minority interest shareholding is owned by an individual rather than a company.

(ii) Strategy in order to maximise the corporation tax saved

Tutor's top tips

Having set out the reliefs available in (a) (i) you then need to evaluate each of those reliefs in this part of the question.

Think about each in turn and consider the rate of tax saved. Remember that the maximum saving is achieved by setting losses against profits in the margin between the upper and lower limits, so your first step should be to calculate those limits.

Cash flow is not a consideration here, as the requirement specifically tells you that the loss is ***not*** *to be carried forward.*

The maximum tax saving will be achieved where losses are relieved in the companies paying corporation tax at the marginal rate. The marginal rate is charged on taxable total profits lying between the limits.

Corporation tax limits

The limits are divided by six as all five subsidiaries are controlled by, and therefore associated with, Janus plc.

In the previous year there was a single rate of corporation tax of 19%, with no upper and lower limits.

Accordingly, the limits are as follows:

Year ended 31 March 2024

Upper limit (£250,000 ÷ 6) £41,667

Lower limit (£50,000 ÷ 6) £8,333

Tutorial note

When you are counting the number of associated companies, remember that companies joining or leaving the group mid-year are included for the full period.

Strategy to maximise corporation tax saved

In the year ended 31 March 2024:

- Viola Ltd has marginal profits of £17,667 (£26,000 – £8,333)
- Duet Ltd pays tax at the main rate
- Janus plc and Seb Ltd are both paying tax at the small profits rate.

In the year ended 31 March 2023:

- Janus plc pays tax at 19%.

In order to achieve the maximum tax saving:

1. Losses should be surrendered as group relief to Viola Ltd to relieve marginal profits and achieve a tax saving of 26.5%. As stated in (i), Viola Ltd was bought on 1 December 2023 so the group relief would be restricted to just four months of profits (1 December 2023 – 31 March 2024).
2. Losses should be surrendered as consortium relief to Duet Ltd which will also achieve a tax saving of 25%. The maximum which can be surrendered to Duet Ltd is restricted to £110,000 as set out above.
3. The balance of the loss can then be used by Janus plc itself in the current period first before carrying it back for 12 months to save tax at 19%.

The trading loss of Janus plc should therefore be relieved as follows:

		Loss utilised	**Rate of tax**
		£	%
Viola Ltd (maximum = 4/12 × £26,000)		8,667	26.5
Duet Ltd (maximum = 55% × £200,000)		110,000	25.0
Janus plc:	Current year	4,500	19.0
	Prior year (remainder of loss)	26,833	19.0
Total available trading loss		150,000	

Tutor's Top Tips

You may not have come up with the same strategy as the examining team, but as long as you have a sensible solution and have prepared a summary showing the rates of tax saved, you should score the marks here.

The group relief and consortium relief claims will need to be dated the day before the claims to offset the loss against the total profits of Janus plc in order to avoid relieving the whole of the profits for the year ended 31 March 2023.

Tutorial note

*Single company loss claims are 'all or nothing' claims and cannot be restricted, so Janus Ltd must make the group/consortium relief surrenders **before** the claim to set the loss against its own profits. The order of claiming the reliefs is very important.*

(b) Assets to be sold

(i) P HQ

Tutor's Top Tips

Castor Ltd owns 80% of Pollux Ltd which is at least 75% thus the two companies are in the same capital gains group, so when Pollux Ltd acquired the building from Castor Ltd the transfer took place at no gain/no loss.

The transfer value of the building would be original cost plus indexation allowance.

However, Janus plc only owns 70% of Castor Ltd which is less than 75% so when Pollux Ltd sells the building to Janus plc the transfer must take place at market value which will result in a capital gain arising.

*The examining team has asked you to **explain** how to compute this.*

Pollux Ltd and Janus plc are not in a capital gains group as Castor Ltd is not a 75% subsidiary of Janus plc.

The sale of the building will result in a chargeable gain equal to the excess of the proceeds, £285,000, over the building's base cost.

Tutorial note

There is no degrouping charge here, as such a charge can only occur when a company leaves a capital gains group (i.e. when there is a sale of shares).

This question involved the sale of a building, not a sale of shares.

Pollux Ltd acquired the building from Castor Ltd. The two companies are in a capital gains group as Pollux Ltd is a 75% subsidiary of Castor Ltd.

Accordingly, the building would have been transferred at no gain, no loss.

The base cost of the building to Pollux Ltd is the original cost when it was acquired by Castor Ltd (assuming Castor Ltd did not acquire it via a no gain, no loss transfer), together with indexation allowance from the date the building was acquired by Castor Ltd until December 2017 (as this is earlier than the date it was sold to Pollux Ltd).

The indexation allowance reflects the movement in the retail prices index for the relevant period (rounded to three decimal places) multiplied by the relevant cost of the building.

Information required – the date the building was acquired by Castor Ltd and the price paid.

(ii) Warehouse

Tutor's top tips

A good knowledge of the capital goods scheme for VAT is required in order to answer this part of the question.

The requirement is to 'calculate', so there is no need to provide any explanation.

Year ended 31 March 2023	
£64,000 × 70%	£44,800 recoverable from HMRC
Year ended 31 March 2024	
£64,000 × 15% (70% – 55%) × 1/10	£960 repayable to HMRC
Year ended 31 March 2025	
£64,000 × 20% (70% – 50%) × 1/10	£1,280 repayable to HMRC
£64,000 × 30% (100% – 70%) × 7/10	£13,440 recoverable from HMRC

Tutorial note

The capital goods scheme is relevant where a partially exempt business buys a building for more than £250,000 (VAT-exclusive) and there is a change in the partial exemption % during the ten-year adjustment period.

Here the recoverable input VAT drops from 70% to 55% then 50%, so Viola Ltd has to pay back some of the input VAT initially reclaimed.

There is also a final adjustment in the year of disposal for the remainder of the ten-year adjustment period.

The % used for the final adjustment on the sale of the building will always be either:

- *100% taxable (if the sale of the building is subject to VAT, as it is here), or*
- *0% taxable (if the sale of the building is an exempt supply).*

(iii) Patent rights

Tutor's top tips

Patent rights are an intangible non-current asset.

For intangibles other than goodwill, the tax treatment generally follows the accounting treatment with the effect that:

- *amortisation of an intangible asset is an allowable expense (or, if preferred, a writing down allowance of 4% straight line can be claimed instead of amortisation)*
- *the taxable profit on disposal is calculated as the sale proceeds less the net book value (i.e. amortised cost) if no election has been made (or, if the election is made, the sale proceeds less the tax written down value).*

As the patent rights relate to the company's trade, both the amortisation and the profit on disposal are included in taxable trading profits.

The patent rights are an intangible non-current asset. On a disposal of the rights, the sales proceeds will be compared with the amortised cost.

	£	£
Proceeds		41,000
Cost	45,000	
Less: Amortisation (£45,000 × 10% × 4)	(18,000)	
Amortised cost		(27,000)
Profit on sale		14,000

The profit on sale will be included as part of Castor Ltd's trading income because the patent rights were purchased for the purposes of the trade.

(c) Investment in Kupple Inc

(i) Value added tax (VAT) on the import of consultancy services

Tutor's top tips

The VAT implications for purchasing consultancy services from overseas are very similar to the implications for importing goods.

The VAT treatment of imports and exports is regularly tested in the ATX exam.

When services are provided to a business, the place of supply is the place where the customer's business is established.

Accordingly, the consultancy services provided by Kupple Inc to Janus plc will be treated as being made in the UK.

Janus plc will be required to account for output tax in respect of the supply under the reverse charge procedure. It will then be able to recover the output tax as input tax in the normal way.

(ii) Sale of the shares

Tutor's top tips

Knowledge of the substantial shareholding exemption for companies – particularly the 12-month ownership requirement – is the key to success in this part.

The examining team deliberately leaves the disposal date vague, and does not say whether the shares will be sold at a profit or loss.

This means that you need to consider all possibilities:

- *Sale within 12 months at a gain*
- *Sale within 12 months at a loss*
- *Sale after more than 12 months at a gain*
- *Sale after more than 12 months at a loss.*

The tax treatment of the profit or loss on the sale of the shares will depend on when the sale occurs.

Sale within 12 months

If the shares are sold during the first 12 months of ownership, the sale will result in a chargeable gain (proceeds less cost) or an allowable loss (proceeds less cost).

An allowable loss could be offset against the chargeable gains of Janus plc or of the other companies in its chargeable gains group (Seb Ltd and Viola Ltd).

Sale after more than 12 months

However, as Janus plc will hold at least 10% of Kupple Inc's shares, once the shares have been held for 12 months, the substantial shareholding exemption will apply.

As a result of this exemption, any profit would not be taxable and any loss would not be allowable.

(d) Ryb Ltd

(i) UK corporation tax on the profits of Ryb Ltd

Ryb Ltd is subject to UK corporation tax on the profits of its permanent establishment (PE) in Tirona because a PE is not a separate legal entity and UK resident companies are subject to corporation tax on their worldwide income.

	£
Draft profits	75,000
Structures and buildings allowance (W)	(6,050)
Tax adjusted trading profits	68,950
UK corporation tax (£68,950 × 25%)	17,238
Less: Unilateral double tax relief (£68,950 × 14%)	(9,653)
UK corporation tax liability	7,585

Tutorial note

The acquisition of Ryb Ltd in the year ended 31 March 2026 would lead to there now being seven associated companies (possibly more for Ryb Ltd in the year of acquisition, as it would be associated with its previous owner and any other companies related to its previous owner). The corporation tax rate limits would therefore be a minimum of:

Upper limit: (£250,000 ÷ 7) £35,714

Lower limit: (£50,000 ÷ 7) £7,143

Accordingly, Ryb Ltd would pay tax at the main rate.

Working: Structures and buildings allowance

Structures and buildings allowance is available on the cost of the building excluding land at a rate of 3% per year. This can be claimed from the date the building is brought into use in the business.

(£300,000 – £80,000) × 3% × 11/12 = £6,050

(ii) Election to exempt the profits of the PE from UK tax

– The advantage of making such an election would be that the profits made in Tirona would not be subject to UK corporation tax.

  Based on the current rates of corporation tax in the two countries, this would save corporation tax at the rate of 11% (25% – 14%).

- However, it should be recognised that there would be no relief in the UK in the event of any losses being incurred in the trade in Tirona in the future.
- If the election is made no capital allowances can be claimed in the UK, which would mean losing the benefit of structures and buildings allowance (although allowances could still be claimed in Tirona).
- Once made, the election is irrevocable and would apply to all future overseas permanent establishments of Ryb Ltd.

  Accordingly, there would be no relief in the UK for any losses incurred in any new overseas trades operated by Ryb Ltd.

Tutor's top tips

The question mentioned plans to create more PEs in other countries. This was a clue to discuss the fact that the PE exemption would apply to future PEs as well. Make sure you consider all information given in the question and think about why you have been given it.

(e) Use of information from previous clients

- We should behave professionally when dealing with clients, which includes maintaining client confidentiality. This is one of the ethical principles set out in the ACCA's Code of Ethics and Conduct.
- Confidentiality applies not only to our current clients, but past clients as well.
- Any confidential information gained from clients cannot be used to the advantage of us or third parties.
- This means that we are unable to use any specific information from our ex-client in order to assist Janus plc.
- However, we are able to use the general experience and expertise gained from previous clients when advising Janus plc.

Examiner's report

Some candidates spent too long on part (a) and provided very detailed explanations of group relief and consortium relief; the amount of detail provided must relate to the number of marks on offer. Also, there was a tendency to repeat things, for example stating that Janus plc is in a loss group with Seb Ltd and Viola Ltd followed by a statement that it was not in a loss group with Castor Ltd. Candidates should identify the points they intend to make and then make them as concisely as possible. They will find this more efficient than making it up as they go along.

Note that this part of the question has been adapted since the question was originally set.

For part (b)(i) those candidates, who knew their stuff, slowed down, thought more and wrote less did well. This question demanded a clear understanding of the conditions necessary for a chargeable gains group to exist.

Unfortunately, many candidates thought that Janus plc and Pollux Ltd were members of a chargeable gains group; this was not the case because Janus plc does not own at least 75% of Castor Ltd. Other candidates failed to notice that Castor Ltd and Pollux Ltd were members of such a group.

The other technical problem that candidates had with this question was that many thought it included a degrouping charge. However, a degrouping charge can only occur when a company leaves a chargeable gains group, i.e. there needs to be a sale of shares, and this question involved the sale of a building. Accordingly, time spent writing about degrouping charges was wasted.

In part (b)(ii) applying the capital goods scheme to the purchase, use and subsequent sale of a building was done well by those candidates who both knew what to do and had practised applying the rules prior to the exam. Weaker candidates had a vague, confused knowledge of the rules or simply tried to describe them as opposed to apply them to the specific circumstances of the question. Very few candidates knew how to handle the adjustment following the sale of the building.

Part (b)(iii) the sale of an intangible asset and was done reasonably well by the majority of candidates.

In part (c)(i) the purchase of services from overseas to which the reverse charge applied was not answered particularly well; very few candidates had a clear understanding of the VAT treatment of the transaction.

Part (c)(ii) concerned the sale of shares in a company and was answered well. It required candidates to recognise that the substantial shareholding exemption might apply to the sale provided the conditions were satisfied. This question illustrated the need for candidates to be methodical as, if maximum marks were to be obtained, candidates needed to consider four situations; sale at a profit and sale at a loss with the substantial shareholding exemption either applying or not applying in each case.

The final two parts of the question have been added since the question was originally set.

ACCA marking scheme

			Marks
(a)	(i)	Alternative reliefs	
		Against total profits of Janus plc	1.5
		Group relief	
		Identification of group	1.5
		Amount of loss	1.0
		Consortium relief	2.0
	(ii)	Strategy	
		Relieve profits at the marginal rate	1.0
		Limits	2.0
		Advice and summary	3.5
			12.5
		Maximum	11.0

(b)	(i)	Administrative premises		
		There will be a gain on the disposal		1.5
		Indexed base cost		3.5
		Information required		0.5
				5.5
			Maximum	4.0
	(ii)	Warehouse		4.0
			Maximum	3.0
	(iii)	Patent rights		
		Calculation		1.5
		Explanation		1.5
				3.0
(c)	(i)	VAT on consultancy services		2.5
			Maximum	2.0
	(ii)	Sale of shares		4.0
(d)	(i)	UK corporation tax liability		5.0
	(ii)	Effect of making election		5.5
				10.5
			Maximum	8.0
(e)	Confidentiality: 1 mark per valid point		**Maximum**	5.0
	Professional skills marks (see below)		**Maximum**	10.0
Total				**50.0**

Professional skills marks

Communication

- General format and structure of file note (e.g. use of headings/sub-headings to make file note easy to refer to).
- Style, language and clarity (tone of file note, presentation of calculations, appropriate use of the tools, easy to follow and more than a negligible amount of content).
- Effectiveness of communication (answer is relevant, specific rather than general and focused to the requirement).
- Adherence to specific instructions made in the scenario (e.g. stating further information required from Aliona in part (b)(i)).

Analysis and evaluation

- Evaluation of the best loss relief option for Janus plc in part (a)(ii).
- Analysis of the information to determine the appropriate corporation tax treatment of the sale of P HQ in part (b)(i).
- Appropriate use of the information to determine relevant calculations to perform to illustrate the VAT implications of the sale of the warehouse in part (b)(ii).
- Appropriate use of the information to determine the corporation tax liability in respect of Ryb Ltd in part (d)(i).

Scepticism

- Identification of missing information with regards to calculating the gain on P HQ in part (b)(i).
- Critical assessment of the election to exempt overseas PEs from UK tax in part (d).

Commercial acumen

- Identification of the availability of group relief and/or consortium relief in part (a)(i).
- Identification of the availability of structures and buildings allowance for the office building purchased by Ryb Ltd in part (d)(i).
- Identification of possible disadvantages of an election to exempt overseas PEs from UK tax in part (d)(ii).

13 SPRINT LTD AND IRON LTD (ADAPTED) ***Walk in the footsteps of a top tutor***

Key answer tips

This section A question covers five separate areas: corporation tax for a long period of account, the differences between purchase of shares by an individual or by another company, registration for VAT, relief for trading losses and ethical issues.

Part (a) requires calculation of tax for a 16-month period of account, which is mainly revision of TX. Once again, this reinforces the importance of retaining basic TX knowledge.

Part (b) is a written section that requires a clear explanation of the differences between a company being held directly by an individual or as part of a corporate group. Think carefully before answering this section.

Part (c) covers registration for VAT – another TX topic that should have offered easy marks. You could have answered this part first before tackling the trickier parts of the question.

Part (d) asks for different methods in which a trading loss can be relieved and the factors to consider when choosing the method of relief. This is another commonly tested area and something you should be well prepared for.

The final part of the question is an ethical requirement looking at non-disclosure of income. This is a typical ethical scenario and so should represent some easy marks for you.

The highlighted words in the written sections are key phrases that markers are looking for.

(a) Iron Ltd – corporation tax payable for the period ending 30 June 2025

Tutor's top tips

Remember that a long accounting period must be split into the first 12 months and the balance, with two corporation tax computations prepared.

Rollover relief is often tested in corporation tax questions, so you should make sure you learn the rules. Watch out for depreciating assets, as they are treated differently for rollover relief purposes.

There are easy marks available for stating the due dates for payment of the corporation tax.

Year ending	**Year ending 28 February 2025**	**4 months ending 30 June 2025**
	£	£
Trading income		
£30,000 × 12/16	22,500	
£30,000 × 4/16		7,500
Chargeable gains (below)		
Industrial building	91,800	
Fixed machinery	200	
Crystallisation of deferred gain re sale of fixed machinery	3,200	
Taxable total profits	117,700	7,500
Corporation tax payable		
£117,700 × 25% (W1)	29,425	
£7,500 × 25%		1,875
Less: Marginal relief		
(£16,667 – £7,500) × 3/200		(138)
	29,425	1,737
Due date (W2)	1 December 2025	1 April 2026

Chargeable gains

	Industrial building	**Fixed machinery**
	£	£
Proceeds	160,000	13,700
Less: Cost (£100,000 – £31,800)	(68,200)	(13,500)
Chargeable gain	91,800	200

Tutorial note

There is no indexation allowance since the assets were both purchased after 31 December 2017.

The small gain on the machinery will be chargeable even though machinery would typically be a wasting chattel. This is because Iron Ltd will have claimed capital allowances on the machinery and so any gain arising on disposal would be chargeable, subject to the £6,000 chattel rules.

Workings

(W1) Corporation tax rate

The limits for determining the rate of corporation tax are as follows:

	Upper	Lower
Year ended 28 February 2025		
£250,000/£50,000 ÷ 3	83,333	16,667
Four months ended 30 June 2025		
(£250,000/£50,000 ÷ 3) × 4/12	27,778	5,556

Tutorial note

Iron Ltd will be associated with both Sprint Ltd and Olympic Ltd since Christina controls both Sprint Ltd and Iron Ltd, and Iron Ltd controls Olympic Ltd. Therefore, the limits for determining corporation tax rates must be shared between the three associated companies.

(W2) Due date

The threshold for payment of corporation tax by instalment is based on the number of associated companies at the end of the previous accounting period as follows:

Year ending 28 February 2025	£1,500,000
Four months ending 30 June 2025 ((£1,500,000 ÷ 3) × 4/12)	£166,667

As Iron Ltd's taxable total profits are below the threshold, quarterly instalment payments are not required.

(b) Ownership of Iron Ltd

Tutor's top tips

There are four different aspects to consider in this part of the question: ownership of shares by the company (with group implications); ownership of shares by the individual; sale of shares by the company (with substantial shareholding exemption); sale of shares by the individual (with business asset disposal relief).

A logical structure and use of headings to deal with each aspect in turn is important here.

Where possible, try to refer to facts from the scenario such as the potential trading loss in Iron Ltd. This will gain more marks than simply writing about general tax implications.

Ongoing ownership of Iron Ltd

Corporation tax

It would be advantageous for Sprint Ltd, rather than Christina, to purchase Iron Ltd for the following reasons.

– It is possible that Iron Ltd will make a trade loss for the period ending 30 June 2025. If this were to occur, a proportion of the loss could be surrendered by way of group relief to Sprint Ltd and/or Olympic Ltd and be deducted in arriving at the taxable total profits of the recipient company. Whilst all three companies remain in the group, group relief would also be available between them in respect of any losses in future periods.

– Iron Ltd will join Sprint Ltd's capital gains group on 1 November 2024. The capital loss to be made by Sprint Ltd on the sale of the warehouse could therefore be relieved against the chargeable gains to be realised by Iron Ltd on the sale of the industrial building and the fixed machinery. This would reduce the corporation tax liability of Iron Ltd by £4,500 (£29,425 – ((£117,700 – £18,000) × 25%)).

– A gain made by one of the companies in the group on the disposal of a qualifying business asset (land, buildings or fixed machinery used in the business) could be deferred if a qualifying business asset is purchased by any other company in the group during the qualifying period.

– Any future transfers of assets from one group company to another would take place on a no gain, no loss basis.

There is a possible disadvantage in Iron Ltd joining the Sprint Ltd group of companies in relation to capital allowances. The annual investment allowance will be split between the three companies if they are members of a group, whereas an additional full annual investment allowance would be available to Iron Ltd if Christina were to own Iron Ltd personally (unless Iron Ltd were to share premises or carry on activities similar to those of Sprint Ltd or Olympic Ltd).

Value added tax (VAT)

It may be beneficial for Sprint Ltd and Iron Ltd (and possibly Olympic Ltd) to register as a group for the purposes of VAT. This is because it would remove the need for Iron Ltd to charge VAT on the sales it makes to Sprint Ltd. This will, however, be possible regardless of who owns Iron Ltd because Christina will have effective control of all three companies in both situations.

Sale of Iron Ltd

Sprint Ltd owns Iron Ltd

Any chargeable gain (or loss) on the sale of the shares will be exempt due to the substantial shareholding exemption (SSE). This exemption will be available because Sprint Ltd will have owned at least 10% of the ordinary share capital of Iron Ltd for more than a year and Iron Ltd is a trading company.

Although the existence of the SSE would appear to be a significant advantage, it should be recognised that the proceeds on sale will then need to be transferred to Christina. This could be carried out via, for example, the payment of a dividend to Christina. As Christina is a higher rate taxpayer with a substantial amount of investment income, she is likely to have used her dividend nil rate band. Therefore, she would have an income tax liability of 33.75% or even 39.35% of the dividend received.

Tutorial note

Credit was also available for reference to other ways in which the proceeds of sale could be transferred to Christina, for example, via the payment of a bonus.

Christina owns Iron Ltd personally

On a sale by Christina of the shares in Iron Ltd, there will be a chargeable gain equal to the excess of the sales proceeds over the price paid for the shares. This gain, after the deduction of any annual exempt amount not used against any other gains, will be subject to capital gains tax at 10% due to the availability of business asset disposal relief (BADR).

BADR will be available because Iron Ltd is a trading company and Christina will have owned at least 5% of its shares for at least two years, and Christina will be a director of Iron Ltd.

Tutorial note

It can be seen from the marking scheme that it was not necessary to make all of the above points in order to score full marks.

(c) VAT registration

Tutor's top tips

This looks like a fairly standard section on VAT registration and penalties. The twist here was to spot that the client should be monitoring taxable sales, not cash receipts.

Iron Ltd should be monitoring the level of its taxable supplies (excluding sales of capital assets), as opposed to its cash receipts, in order to determine when it needs to register for VAT.

The implications of registering late are:

– Iron Ltd will be required to account for output tax on the sales it has made after the date on which it should have been registered. This will be a cost to Iron Ltd unless it is able to recover the VAT from its customers.

– A penalty may be charged for failing to register by the appropriate date. This penalty would be a percentage of the potential lost revenue where the percentage depends on the reason for the late registration.

– Interest may be charged in respect of the VAT paid late.

(d) Olympic Ltd – Project Whistle

Tutor's top tips

This part of the question was worth nine marks and so you should be looking to discuss several loss reliefs here in order to score well.

Loss reliefs available

A trading loss made by Olympic Ltd in the year ending 30 June 2026 can be relieved, broadly speaking, in two ways:

(i) It can be offset against the income and gains of Olympic Ltd and/or the taxable total profits of other companies in the Sprint Ltd group relief group.

- Olympic Ltd could offset the loss against its total income and gains of the loss-making accounting period, and then against its total income and gains of the previous 12 months.

- The loss could also be offset against the current period taxable total profits of Sprint Ltd and any other company which is an effective 75% subsidiary of Sprint Ltd.

- Any loss remaining will be carried forward by Olympic Ltd for relief against its future total profits, with group relief possible for any excess.

(ii) Any amount of the loss up to a maximum of 186% of the qualifying research and development expenditure can be surrendered in exchange for a cash payment of 10% of the surrendered amount.

Factors to consider when choosing between the available reliefs

Relief under (i) above will result in a minimum corporation tax saving of 19% of the loss relieved. This equates to a saving of 35.34% (186% × 19%) of the cost incurred in respect of the research and development.

Relief under (ii) above equates to a corporation tax saving of only 18.6% (186% × 10%) of the cost incurred.

Accordingly, a greater tax saving will be achieved by relieving the loss against taxable profits (under (i)) rather than surrendering it in exchange for a cash payment (under (ii)).

Tutor's top tips

The corporation tax saving will depend on which company makes use of the loss and the corporation tax rate that company pays for the relevant accounting period. You therefore need to make an assumption about the rate of corporation tax rate that will be saved. You would score equal credit if you used 25% or marginal rates.

However, if there are insufficient profits to relieve all of the trading loss, any loss remaining will have to be carried forward unless it is surrendered in exchange for the 10% cash payment.

From a cash flow point, it will be better to claim the cash payment rather than to carry the loss forward. The cash payment option is also beneficial if it transpires that Olympic Ltd or the Sprint Ltd group will not make sufficient profits in the future to relieve the losses carried forward.

(e) Sprint Ltd rental income

We should advise Sprint Ltd to disclose the additional rental income to HMRC as soon as possible, the amount of the income is irrelevant.

We should check our engagement letter to see if we have authority to disclose the income to HMRC. If we do not, then we cannot make a disclosure due to client confidentiality.

It is important to bring to Sprint Ltd's attention that it may be subject to penalties if it does not disclose the income.

If Sprint Ltd refuses to disclose the income, then we should consider resigning from the engagement.

If we resign then we should inform HMRC that we no longer act for Sprint Ltd, but not disclose why.

Non-disclosure of income is a form of tax evasion and could result in criminal prosecution. We must bring this to the attention of Christina.

We should consider whether it is necessary to make a report to the firm's money laundering reporting officer. If a report is made, we should be careful not to tip off the client.

Examiner's report

Part (a) required a calculation of the corporation tax payable for a company in respect of a 16-month set of accounts, including consideration of two asset disposals where rollover relief had been claimed previously. It was surprising, and indeed disappointing, to see that the majority of candidates calculated the corporation tax payable for the 16-month period as a whole, rather than recognising the need to split this into two separate accounting periods, the first covering the first 12 months and the second covering the remaining four months. This led to the loss of a number of what should have been easy marks. Candidates are reminded that a good level of familiarity with the TX syllabus is required for ATX; it is not enough to just focus on the new areas, candidates must ensure that they are also confident in dealing with more basic issues.

The majority of candidates recognised that the sale of the two business assets would cause the gain rolled over on the acquisition of these assets to become chargeable. However, the different treatments in respect of the depreciating asset (fixed machinery) and non-depreciating asset (building) was identified by only a small number of candidates.

Part (b) was for 12 marks and was the largest part of the question. It required a comparison of the tax implications of a company being acquired by an individual as opposed to by another company. Candidates who did well had a good knowledge of the subject, adopted a sensible, logical approach and addressed all of the issues briefly, as instructed in the question. Weaker candidates fell down in at least one of these areas.

The adoption of a logical approach in this sort of question requiring a comparison of two alternatives can save considerable confusion and avoid wasting time due to needless repetition. Candidates should pause and think before they start writing. Dealing fully with the implications of one of the alternatives first, and then the other, tended to provide a much clearer answer than those who adopted a less logical approach, apparently writing points as they occurred to them, without making it clear which alternative they were dealing with, constantly swapping between the two, and leading to a confusing answer.

Candidates should avoid repetition, including making the same point from different angles. An example in this case would be where a candidate has stated that if the company is acquired by another company, they would form a group for group relief purposes. Stating separately at a later point that if acquired by an individual there will not be a group for group relief purposes, scored no additional marks.

Part (c) concerned the often-tested area of registration for VAT, an area which the vast majority of candidates are very technically comfortable with. However, all but a handful failed to read the question in sufficient detail, and provided a very detailed account of the tests applied to determine whether compulsory registration is required, but this did not address the question and wasted a good deal of time. Where the subject coverage is very familiar it is particularly important to understand the context in which it is being tested. In this case, the key issue was recognition that monitoring the level of cash receipts is not relevant, it is the level of taxable supplies, i.e. the invoiced value of taxable sales which is relevant.

Note that part (d) of the question has been added in from another question. The relevant section of the examiner's report for that question is included below:

The fourth part of the question concerned the trading loss relief available to a company which qualifies for the additional 86% deduction available for qualifying research and development expenditure. Overall, this question part was quite well attempted, with the majority of candidates being able to explain the cashflow implications of the 'surrenderable loss' in this case, but in some instances, candidates focused entirely on this and failed to take a broad enough approach, not considering in equal detail the 'normal' loss reliefs available to a company and their implications, in order to be able to fully discuss the factors to consider when choosing between the available reliefs. The question clearly implied that more than one relief would be available, and there were nine marks *(seven in the original question)* for this requirement, so this should have prompted candidates that a broader approach was needed.

The final requirement has been added to the question since it was originally written.

ACCA marking scheme

			Marks
(a)	Trading income		1.0
	Chargeable gains		
	Industrial building		1.5
	Machinery		1.5
	Crystallisation of deferred gain		1.0
	Chargeable gains in correct period		0.5
	Corporation tax payable		2.5
	Corporation tax rate limits		1.5
	Due dates		3.5
			13.0
		Maximum	11.0
(b)	Ongoing		
	Group relief		2.0
	Relief for capital losses		2.0
	Rollover relief		1.0
	No gain, no loss transfers		1.0
	Annual investment allowance		1.0
	VAT group registration		2.0
	Sale of Iron Ltd		
	Sprint Ltd owns Iron Ltd		3.5
	Christina owns Iron Ltd		2.0
			14.5
		Maximum	12.0
(c)	Taxable supplies as monitoring basis		1.0
	Implications of late registration		2.5
			3.5
		Maximum	3.0
(d)	Loss reliefs available		
	Relief against profits		4.0
	Surrendered for cash payment		1.0
	Evaluation of the reliefs		4.0
			9.0

(e)	Disclosure		2.5
	Penalties		0.5
	Resignation		2.0
	Tax evasion		1.0
	Money laundering		1.5
			7.5
		Maximum	5.0
	Professional skills marks (see below)	**Maximum**	10.0
Total			**50.0**

Professional skills marks

Communication

- General format and structure of notes (e.g. use of headings/sub-headings to make notes easy to refer to).
- Style, language and clarity (tone of notes, presentation of calculations, appropriate use of the tools, easy to follow and more than a negligible amount of content).
- Effectiveness of communication (answer is relevant, specific rather than general and focused to the requirement).
- Adherence to specific instructions made in the scenario (e.g. explaining both implications and actions in part (e)).

Analysis and evaluation

- Use of the data to determine appropriate calculations to perform to arrive at the corporation tax payable for the period ending 30 June 2025 in part (a).
- Analysis of the information to determine the tax implications of both ownership options of Iron Ltd for Christina in part (b).
- Demonstration of ability to consider all taxes relevant to part (b), i.e. corporation tax, income tax and VAT.
- Analysis of the information to determine appropriate loss relief options for Olympic Ltd in part (d).

Scepticism

- Identification of uncertainty with regards to profit levels in Olympic Ltd to be able to quantity loss relief in part (d).
- Assumption made over corporation tax saving for the loss relief in part (d).
- Critical assessment of the attitude towards disclosure of the rental income in part (e).

Commercial acumen

- Demonstration of an understanding of how rollover relief works for depreciating assets in part (a).
- Identification that the gain on the fixed machinery will become chargeable despite the asset being a wasting chattel in part (a).
- Identification of possible advantages and disadvantages of Sprint Ltd owning Iron Ltd in part (b).

14 HAHN LTD GROUP (ADAPTED) *Walk in the footsteps of a top tutor*

Key answer tips

This is a classic Section A multi-tax question covering corporation tax groups with a mix of technical marks on corporation tax and VAT, ethical marks on HMRC errors and overseas aspects of capital gains tax.

There are five requirements, all of which can be answered independently, so careful thought should be given to the order in which you attempt the question. Identify the parts that you think you can answer quickly and attempt these first, leaving parts of the question that you think you will be tempted to spend too long on until last.

Make sure that you set out requirements (a) – (c) as a memorandum with an appropriate heading, set out your answer neatly and express yourself clearly in order to score the presentation marks available. Make sure you follow the instructions and keep the notes for requirement (d) separate.

You should also try to answer the question succinctly; this will save you time and help with the professional marks!

Requirement (a)(i) tests the common exam topic of group rollover relief. Requirement (a)(ii) tests group relief, focusing on cash flow issues.

Requirement (b) tests group VAT registration, another often tested area of the syllabus.

Requirement (c) tests the ethical implications of a client not reporting an HMRC error.

Requirement (d) requires an explanation of why an individual is only temporarily non-UK resident and calculations of the UK capital gains tax.

The payment date is also required which is an easy mark to gain, but easily forgotten and lost if you are not careful.

The highlighted words in the written sections are key phrases that markers are looking for in your memorandum.

(a) Memorandum

Client: Hahn Ltd group

Subject: Group loss planning and other matters

Prepared by: Tax senior

Date: 1 October 2024

Tutor's top tips

Group rollover relief is often tested in the exam. However, there is an unusual twist here as you are asked to calculate the amount of proceeds to reinvest to leave a specific amount of the gain chargeable after rollover relief. In order to score well here you need to have a good knowledge of how to calculate rollover relief where proceeds are only partially reinvested.

(i) Chargeable gain of Frit Ltd

The additional qualifying assets which would need to be purchased in order for the chargeable gain realised by Frit Ltd to be fully relieved by its capital losses brought forward is calculated as follows:

	£
Sales proceeds of asset sold by Frit Ltd	125,000
Less: Capital losses brought forward (Note 1)	(31,000)
Proceeds to be spent on qualifying assets	94,000
Less: Qualifying assets already purchased by group companies (£14,000 + £10,000)(Note 2)	(24,000)
Additional amount to be spent on qualifying assets	70,000

Tutorial note

1 Any amount of the proceeds from the sale of the building by Frit Ltd not reinvested in qualifying assets within the time limit will remain chargeable in year ended 31 March 2025. Therefore, in order for the chargeable gain after rollover relief to be equal to the capital loss brought forward in Frit Ltd, an amount of £31,000 should not be reinvested, such that only £34,000 of the £65,000 gain will be rolled over and the remaining £31,000 of the gain will be relieved by the capital losses brought forward.

2 The additional qualifying assets can be purchased by any member of the capital gains group. The group consists of all of the companies apart from Joli Ltd (not a 75% subsidiary of Hahn Ltd) and Ruth Ltd (not a 75% subsidiary of Lise Ltd). Therefore, the £6,000 spent on qualifying assets by Ruth Ltd cannot be utilised as reinvestment of the Frit Ltd proceeds.

(ii) Relieving the trading loss of Frit Ltd Intercompany trading

Tutor's top tips

Group relief has always been a popular topic in the exam. Now that there are three potential rates of corporation tax, groups will often look to use losses in the manner which will save the most corporation tax. However, the focus in this requirement is cash flow, and using the group losses to reduce augmented profits below the profit threshold where instalments need to be made, so that should be your main concern here.

Intra-group sales

A transfer pricing adjustment will be required in respect of the sales at undervalue from Hahn Ltd to Stra Ltd. This is because Hahn Ltd controls Stra Ltd, and the group is large for the purposes of the transfer pricing rules. Accordingly, the trading profit of Hahn Ltd must be increased by £10,000 (£104,000 – £94,000), the excess of the arm's length price over the price charged for the intra-group sales. As Stra Ltd is also within the charge to UK corporation tax, its trading profits can be reduced by the same amount.

Rationale for the allocation of the trading loss

In order to maximise the benefit to the group's cash flow position, Frit Ltd's trading loss should be surrendered to those companies paying corporation tax by quarterly instalments.

- Firstly to any company whose profits can be reduced to the payment by instalments threshold, such that instalments will no longer be required
- then to any other company with profits in excess of the payment by instalments threshold, such that their instalments will be reduced
- finally, to any other company.

The payment by instalments threshold for the Hahn Ltd group companies (excluding Chad Ltd) for the year ending 31 March 2025 is £300,000. This is the threshold of £1,500,000 divided by five (the number of associated companies as at 31 March 2024 being Hahn Ltd, Frit Ltd, Lise Ltd, Ruth Ltd and Stra Ltd).

The threshold for Chad Ltd for the year ending 31 March 2025 is £187,500. This is the threshold of £1,500,000 divided by eight (the number of associated companies in the Zeno Ltd group as at 31 March 2024, being Zeno Ltd and the companies under its control).

Tutorial note

The instalments threshold is divided by the number of associated companies as at the end of the previous accounting period. Therefore, Chad Ltd will not be included in the Hahn Ltd group for these purposes until the year ended 31 March 2026.

Allocation of the loss

	Note	£
Frit Ltd trading loss		540,000
Surrender to:		
Lise Ltd (£375,000 – £300,000)	1	(75,000)
Chad Ltd	2	(315,000)
Hahn Ltd (balance)	3, 4	150,000

Notes

1 The taxable total profits of Lise Ltd should be reduced to no more than £300,000 so that the company will not have to pay corporation tax by instalments.

2 Chad Ltd will have been a member of the group relief group for only seven months of the accounting period. Accordingly, the maximum loss which can be surrendered by Frit Ltd to Chad Ltd is £315,000, i.e. the lower of:

- Frit Ltd loss for the corresponding seven-month period of £315,000 (£540,000 × 7/12), and
- Chad Ltd profit for the corresponding seven-month period of £393,750 (£675,000 × 7/12).

This is not sufficient to reduce the taxable total profits of Chad Ltd to £187,500 but it will reduce the company's corporation tax liability and therefore the instalments due.

3 The trading profit of Stra Ltd will be £48,000 (£58,000 – £10,000 transfer pricing adjustment). Stra Ltd must assume set off of its own trading loss brought forward against its total profits, before claiming group relief. This will reduce its TTP to £Nil as Stra Ltd has no other income or gains. On this basis, no losses can be transferred from Frit Ltd to Stra Ltd.

4 Joli Ltd is not an effective 75% subsidiary of Hahn Ltd and is therefore not in the group relief group.

Ruth Ltd is neither a direct 75% subsidiary of Lise Ltd nor an effective subsidiary of Hahn Ltd and is therefore not in the group relief group.

Tutorial note

It would be equally acceptable to surrender the balance of the loss of £150,000 to Lise Ltd rather than Hahn Ltd because the corporation tax liability of both companies is due on 1 January 2026 rather than by quarterly instalments.

Although it is possible to surrender trading losses brought forward as group relief, this surrender is only available for excess losses after set off against the surrendering company's own total profits. As Stra Ltd does not have any excess trading losses brought forward, there is no possibility of surrender from Stra Ltd.

Corporation tax liabilities for the year ending 31 March 2025

	Hahn Ltd	**Chad Ltd**	**Lise Ltd**	**Ruth Ltd**
	£	£	£	£
Taxable total profit	280,000	675,000	375,000	320,000
Transfer pricing adjustment	10,000			
Group relief	(150,000)	(315,000)	(75,000)	0
	140,000	360,000	300,000	320,000
Corporation tax at 25% (W):				
Due in instalments		90,000		80,000
Due on 1 January 2026	35,000		75,000	

Frit Ltd and Stra Ltd will have no taxable total profits and therefore will not have a corporation tax liability.

Working: Corporation tax rate

The upper limit for all companies except Chad Ltd will be £41,667 (£250,000 divided by six associated companies). For Chad Ltd this limit will be even lower, as Chad Ltd will still be associated with Zeno Ltd and its subsidiaries.

Hahn Ltd, Chad Ltd, Lise Ltd and Ruth Ltd will all have profits in excess of the upper limit and therefore will be taxed at the main rate.

Tutorial note

The upper and lower limits for determining the rate of corporation tax are based on the total number of associates during the ***current*** *accounting period, including companies joining and leaving during the period. Chad Ltd would be one of 13 associated companies, as it would still be associated with Zeno Ltd and its other wholly-owned subsidiaries, as well as Hahn Ltd and its subsidiaries.*

As it is clear that all companies will have profits in excess of the reduced upper limit, there is no need to calculate the lower limit here.

Payment schedule

	£
Instalments ((90,000 + 80,000)/4):	
14 October 2024	42,500
14 January 2025	42,500
14 April 2025	42,500
14 July 2025	42,500
Nine months and one day (35,000 + 75,000):	
1 January 2026	110,000

(b) Group registration for the purposes of value added tax (VAT)

Tutor's top tips

Group VAT registration is a commonly tested topic in the exam. It is important to learn the requirements for a group of companies to form a VAT group, the consequences of doing so, and also the reasons why some companies may be better left outside of the group. However, to score well you must make sure you link your answer to the scenario.

There were some tricky marks here, testing the interaction of the cash accounting and annual accounting schemes with VAT groups. However, four out of the five marks available could be scored without mentioning these!

A group registration could be made in respect of all of the companies in the Hahn Ltd group with the exception of Joli Ltd (because this company is not controlled by Hahn Ltd). However, it is not necessary to include all of the qualifying companies within the group registration.

Sales from one company in the VAT group to another would be disregarded for the purposes of VAT. Therefore, there would be no requirement to charge VAT on the sales made by Hahn Ltd to Stra Ltd.

The annual accounting scheme is not available where companies are registered as a group. The cash accounting scheme would be available but only if the group's taxable turnover was less than £1,350,000. These matters should be considered before deciding whether or not Stra Ltd should be included in the group registration.

The inclusion of Frit Ltd in the group registration would result in the group being partially exempt. This could increase the total input tax recovered by the group, for example, if the results of the group as a whole satisfy the partial exemption de minimis limits. Alternatively, the calculation of the recoverable input tax for the group as a whole could result in a reduction in the total input tax recovered. Accordingly, further consideration is required before deciding whether or not Frit Ltd should be included in the group registration.

(c) Chad Ltd – refund of VAT

Tutor's top tips

Ethical issues will appear in every exam as part of section A for five marks. This is 10% of the marks you need to pass the exam! Provided you have revised the commonly tested ethical scenarios these marks should be relatively easy to score.

Here you needed to consider the ethical implications of a potential HMRC error. Don't forget to consider the possibility that it may not be an error!

We should investigate the VAT reporting of Chad Ltd in order to determine whether or not there is a valid reason for the refund.

If we are unable to identify a valid reason, we would have to conclude that the refund was made as a result of error on the part of HM Revenue and Customs (HMRC), in which case it should be repaid immediately. We should inform Chad Ltd that failing to return the money in these circumstances may well be a civil and/or a criminal offence.

We should also advise Chad Ltd to inform HMRC of their error as soon as possible in order to minimise any interest and penalties which may otherwise become payable.

If Chad Ltd is unwilling to return the money, we would have to consider ceasing to act as advisers to the company. We would then have to notify the tax authorities that we no longer act for Chad Ltd, although we would not provide them with any reason for our action. We should also consider whether or not it is necessary to make a report under the money laundering rules.

(d) Notes for meeting with Johannes

Capital gains tax

Tutor's top tips

The examining team frequently tests capital gains tax for an individual who leaves the UK, returns within five years, and disposes of assets whilst overseas. These are known as the temporary non-UK resident rules or temporary absence abroad rules. You are asked for an explanation of the rules as well as the calculations, so make sure you provide the explanations.

Note that the rules only apply to assets owned before the individual loses their UK resident status and as such the antique bed does not fall within the rules, as it is purchased whilst Johannes is abroad. Also note that the disposal of the car is exempt, regardless of these rules.

Johannes will be regarded as only temporarily non-UK resident whilst living in Keirinia because:

- he was absent from the UK for less than five years, and
- having always lived in the UK prior to moving to Keirinia, he was UK resident for at least four of the seven tax years immediately prior to the year of departure.

As a temporary non-UK resident, Johannes will be subject to UK capital gains tax on the assets sold whilst he was temporarily overseas, which he owned at the date of his departure from the UK.

Accordingly, the antique bed is excluded from these rules as it was both bought and sold during the period of absence.

The profit on the sale of the car is ignored as cars are exempt assets for the purposes of capital gains tax.

The shares were sold in the tax year 2020/21, before Johannes left the UK, so the gain on these shares was subject to tax in that year. However, there will have been no tax to pay as the capital gain of £4,900 (£18,900 – £14,000) was covered by the annual exempt amount for the tax year 2020/21.

The capital gains tax due on the sale of the painting is calculated as follows.

	£
Capital gain (£36,000 – £15,000)	21,000
Less: Annual exempt amount	(6,000)
Taxable gain	15,000
Capital gains tax at 20%	3,000

The gain on the sale of the painting is subject to tax in 2024/25, the tax year in which Johannes returned to the UK, and not in the year of sale.

Accordingly, the tax is due on 31 January 2026.

Examiner's report

Part (a), which was in two parts, related to a group of UK resident companies. The first of these parts required candidates to calculate the amount to be reinvested in qualifying assets in order to leave no gain on the disposal of a building chargeable to corporation tax. Most candidates made a reasonable attempt at this, but a very significant proportion also included detailed explanations to accompany their calculations, despite these clearly not being required. The fact that this question part was worth only three marks should have led candidates to realise that a lengthy discussion was not required. Accordingly, these candidates wasted time, which could have beneficially been spent elsewhere. Candidates would be advised to double check what is required by each question before making a start. The main technical error was a failure to realise that the total investment needed must equal the sale proceeds of the building, not the chargeable gain.

The second part of part (a) required candidates to relieve a trading loss within a group so as to minimise the amount of corporation tax payable by the group companies in instalments. Clearly, the majority of candidates were not aware of how this could be achieved, and therefore did not state a strategy for relieving the loss. The loss was therefore relieved in a somewhat random manner within the group. *Part of the examiner's report has been removed that relates to a topic no longer examinable.*

There were a good number of easy marks in this part for calculating the amount of corporation tax payable by each company, which most candidates achieved, but a few didn't appear to have read this part of the requirements and so failed to produce the necessary schedule. The answers to the requirement to state the due dates for payment of the instalments, where necessary, elicited a significant number of incorrect answers in relation to the starting date as many candidates thought that this was after the end of the accounting period, rather than within it. Practical issues such as due dates for payment of tax by both companies and individuals are essential knowledge within many tax planning scenarios at ATX.

Overall, group aspects of corporation tax remain a key topic at ATX and candidates should endeavour to practise a wide range of questions on these to ensure that they are confident in dealing with different aspects of this area.

Part (b) of this question related to the consideration of specific matters relating to the group of companies when deciding which companies should be included in a group registration for value added tax (VAT) purposes. Despite the requirement stating that candidates were to refer only to the specific matters within the memorandum provided, a significant number wrote in detail about the general advantages and disadvantages of registering as a group, which was not relevant, and so wasted time. However, many candidates did identify the specific issues – one of the companies being partially exempt, and another using the annual accounting scheme and the cash accounting scheme – but then discussed what this meant for the relevant companies themselves, rather than the implications of including that company within a group registration. Unfortunately, though, having identified the issues, they didn't go on to score as many marks as they could have done by answering the precise requirement.

Part (c) of this question concerned an unexpected refund of tax from HM Revenue and Customs (HMRC), and the actions to be undertaken by the firm in respect of this. This is a frequently tested area of ethics, and on the whole, candidates' performance was good, with clear explanations of the advice to be given to the client, and the consequences of the client not following this advice. Candidates generally appeared to have practised this type of question, and a good number scored full marks.

The final requirement has been added from another past exam question. The relevant examiner's report is included below:

In part (d) the majority of candidates had some knowledge of the temporary non-UK resident rules and quite a reasonable knowledge of capital gains tax generally, such that they scored reasonably well. Most candidates knew the five-year rule although a much smaller number stated the four years out of seven rule.

A minority of candidates stated a rule correctly in general terms but failed to apply it to the facts of the question. For example, some candidates stated that assets bought and sold during the period of absence were not subject to UK capital gains tax but then went on to calculate a gain in respect of the antique bed.

Other candidates failed to apply the basics. For example, a minority of candidates omitted the annual exempt amount whilst others either provided an incorrect payment date or failed to provide one at all.

When providing a payment date it is important to make it clear which tax year is being addressed. There were several possible relevant tax years in this question so stating a date without a year could not score unless the candidate explained in general terms how the date is determined (i.e. 31 January after the end of the tax year).

ACCA marking scheme				
				Marks
(a)	(i)	Calculation		3.5
				3.5
			Maximum	3.0
	(ii)	Transfer pricing		3.5
		Rationale for loss planning		2.0
		Threshold for payment by instalments		2.5
		Members of group relief group		1.0
		Allocation of loss between group companies		4.0
		Corporation tax liabilities		6.0
		Payment schedule		4.0
				23.0
			Maximum	19.0
(b)	Companies to be included			2.0
	Sales between members of the VAT group			1.0
	VAT schemes			2.0
	Frit Ltd			1.0
				6.0
			Maximum	5.0
(c)	The need to repay the tax			3.0
	Ceasing to act			3.0
				6.0
			Maximum	5.0
(d)	Conditions			2.0
	Antique bed and car			1.5
	Quoted shares			2.0
	Painting			3.5
				9.0
			Maximum	8.0
	Professional skills marks (see below)		**Maximum**	10.0
Total				**50.0**

Professional skills marks

Communication

- General format and structure of memorandum and notes (e.g. use of headings/sub-headings to make memorandum easy to refer to).
- Style, language and clarity (tone of memorandum and notes, presentation of calculations, appropriate use of the tools, easy to follow and more than a negligible amount of content)
- Effectiveness of communication (answer is relevant, specific rather than general and focused to the requirement)
- Adherence to specific instructions made in the scenario (e.g. not setting out amounts payable for Joli Ltd).

Analysis and evaluation

- Use of the data to determine appropriate calculations to establish the additional amount required to be spent on qualifying assets for rollover relief in part (a)(i).
- Analysis of the information to determine the best use of losses within the group in part (a)(ii).
- Analysis of the information to determine which companies could form a VAT group in part (b).

Scepticism

- Critical assessment of the attitude towards disclosure of the HMRC error in part (c).

Commercial acumen

- Demonstration of an understanding of how transfer pricing rules apply to the inter group transactions in part (a)(ii).
- Recognition that the inclusion of Frit Ltd in a VAT group may not be advantageous in part (b).
- Demonstration of an understanding of the temporary non-resident rules for capital gains tax in part (d).

15 WAVERLEY AND SET LTD GROUP (ADAPTED) *Walk in the footsteps of a top tutor*

Key answer tips

This 50-mark section A question tests a wide range of topics, demonstrating the need to study the whole breadth of the syllabus.

Requirement (a) tests capital gains tax, incorporation relief and the taxation of non-UK residents.

Requirement (b) tests the frequently examined topic of personal tax residence. You must make sure you tailor your answer to the scenario given here to score well.

Requirement (c) looks at the disposal of assets on which enhanced capital allowances were claimed, the use of capital and trading losses within a group as well as payment of corporation tax by instalments.

Requirement (d) looks at two different aspects of overseas VAT. There is no longer any difference between the treatment inside and outside the EU, so try not to get confused with the old rules if your earlier studies were under a different finance act.

The fifth part of the question tests knowledge of the CFC exemptions with application to two companies.

The final requirement looks at ethics surrounding whether we can use prior client knowledge to help a client. There are five easy marks to pick up here so make sure you leave enough time to do this well.

In section A questions the information needed to answer the question will usually be split over at least two exhibits. Ensure you open all exhibits and the requirements button so that you have all of the relevant information.

The highlighted words in the written sections are key phrases that markers are looking for in your answer.

(a) Waverley – unincorporated business

Incorporation relief – conditions

- Waverley's unincorporated business must be transferred to Roller Ltd as a going concern.
- All of the assets of the unincorporated business, other than cash, must be transferred.
- The whole or part of the consideration for the transfer must be the issue of shares by Roller Ltd to Waverley.

Tutor's top tips

Business asset disposal relief is tested regularly as it is an important relief for business owners.

This requirement asks you to explain whether the share disposal will qualify for the relief. You need to think about what type of company it is, the level of shareholding, Waverley's employment status and the period of ownership.

Remember that where there is an incorporation which qualifies for incorporation relief the ownership period of the unincorporated business can be combined with that of the shares when identifying if the period of ownership requirement has been met.

Business asset disposal relief (BADR)

The disposal of shares in Roller Ltd will qualify for BADR because:

- Roller Ltd is a trading company,
- Waverley owns at least 5% of the shares (he actually owns 100%),
- Waverley will be an employee of the company,
- Waverley qualifies for incorporation relief and has owned both the unincorporated business and shares for at least two years in total.

Sale of the unincorporated business to Roller Ltd and subsequent sale of Roller Ltd

> ***Tutor's top tips***
>
> *You may have found it difficult to know how to approach this part of requirement (a), given you needed to consider two residency options. The best approach to many questions testing alternative scenarios is to set your answer out in columns. This will save you considerable time compared with setting out separate computations, and make it easier for you to compare the scenarios.*

Sale of the unincorporated business to Roller Ltd (2024/25)

Country of residence of Waverley:		**UK**
	£	£
Chargeable gains arising (£140,000 + £50,000)	190,000	
Less: Incorporation relief	(190,000)	
	0	0

Sale of shares in Roller Ltd (2025/26)

Country of residence of Waverley:	**UK**		**Surferia**
	£	£	£
Proceeds	600,000		
Less: Cost (£540,000 – £190,000)	(350,000)		
Chargeable gain	250,000		
CGT in the UK at 10%		25,000	
CGT in Surferia at 12%			30,000
Total CGT		25,000	30,000

Conclusion

The tax cost on the disposal of the shares will be lower if he is resident in the UK at the time the shares are sold.

(b) Waverley – residence status

Tutor's top tips

Residence and domicile for personal tax has been a frequently tested topic in the exam in recent sittings. Each time it has been tested, it has been important for students to limit their answer to the information given in the scenario, rather than write down everything they have learnt about this topic, to keep their answer on point and to avoid running out of time.

In this question you were told that Waverley would not be automatically resident in the UK or overseas. Therefore, you should have limited your answer to discussion of the sufficient ties tests.

The number of days which Waverley can spend in the UK in the tax year 2025/26 without being UK resident will depend on the number of ties he has with the UK.

Waverley will definitely satisfy two ties:

– He was in the UK for more than 90 days in 2024/25, the previous tax year.

– In 2025/26 Waverley will have children under the age of 18 who are resident in the UK.

Waverley will also satisfy a third tie if he works in the UK for 40 days or more in the tax year 2025/26.

Waverley will not satisfy the following two ties in respect of the tax year 2025/26:

– He will not have accommodation in the UK available for his use.

– He will not be in the UK for more days than in any other country.

Accordingly, Waverley will satisfy either two or three ties.

Waverley was UK resident in the previous three tax years. Accordingly, if he works in the UK for 40 days or more, such that he satisfies three ties, he will only be able to spend up to 45 days in the UK without becoming UK resident.

If Waverley does not work in the UK for 40 days or more, he will only satisfy two ties, and will therefore be able to spend up to 90 days in the UK without becoming UK resident.

Tutorial note

The question states that Waverley will not be automatically UK resident in the tax year 2025/26. Accordingly, he must be in the UK for less than 183 days. The question also states that he will live in Surferia when he is not in the UK. Accordingly, he will spend more days in Surferia than he will in the UK.

(c) Ghost Ltd – corporation tax payments

Ghost Ltd integral features

The proportion of the sale proceeds on which the first year allowance (FYA) was claimed is: £315,000 × £100,000/£1,100,0000 = £28,636.

Half of the proceeds relating to the FYA will create a balancing charge of £14,318 (£28,636 × 50%), which will increase trading profits for the period ending 31 March 2025.

The other half of these proceeds (14,318) as well as the proceeds relating to the AIA of £286,364 (£315,000 – £28,636) will be deducted from the special rate pool in the capital allowances computation.

Depending on the tax written down value brought forward on the pool, this deduction will either reduce the amount that is eligible for 6% writing down allowance, or could create a further balancing charge if the balance becomes negative.

Tutorial note

Where the 50% FYA is claimed on the full cost of an asset then the proceeds are split equally between a deduction from the special rate pool and a balancing charge. In this scenario the AIA was claimed first, and so it is important to calculate the proportion of the proceeds that relates to the FYA.

Steam Ltd capital loss

Ghost Ltd and Steam Ltd are members of a capital gains group because Set Ltd owns at least 75% of the ordinary share capital of both companies.

Accordingly, the capital loss in respect of the disposal of the building by Steam Ltd could be transferred to Ghost Ltd. However, the loss could only be offset against chargeable gains (i.e. not trading profit or other income) realised by Ghost Ltd after it became a member of the Set Ltd capital gains group on 1 September 2024.

Wagon Ltd trading losses

Ghost Ltd and Wagon Ltd are members of a group relief group because Set Ltd owns at least 75% of the ordinary share capital of both companies. Trading losses made whilst the companies are members of the group can be transferred from one company to the other.

Ghost Ltd became a member of the Set Ltd group relief group on 1 September 2024. Its eight-month accounting period ending on 31 March 2025 will have seven months in common with the 12-month accounting period of Wagon Ltd ending on 31 March 2025. Accordingly, the maximum trading loss which can be transferred from Wagon Ltd to Ghost Ltd is the lower of:

– 7/12 of the trading loss of Wagon Ltd available for surrender (see below), and
– 7/8 of the taxable total profits of Ghost Ltd for the eight-month period ending 31 March 2025.

The trading loss of Wagon Ltd available for surrender as group relief is:

– the trading loss for the year ending 31 March 2025

– the excess trading loss brought forward, to the extent that Wagon Ltd cannot set this loss against its own total profits in the year ending 31 March 2025. If Wagon Ltd has no other income, this will be the whole of the £31,500 loss brought forward.

Tutorial note

Ghost Ltd changed ownership when it became a member of the Set Ltd group. Accordingly, if Ghost Ltd had a trading loss brought forward at the time that it joined the Set Ltd group, it would not be available to surrender this loss to the Set Ltd group for five years following the change in ownership.

However, there is no such restriction on the loss brought forward in Wagon Ltd, as Wagon Ltd has not changed its owners. This loss is available for surrender to Ghost Ltd, subject to the overlapping period adjustment set out above.

Payments of corporation tax

Tutor's top tips

Payment of corporation tax in instalments is brought forward knowledge from TX but can often be tested in ATX. You must ensure that you consider all relevant accounting periods as well as any payments already made.

In respect of the year ended 31 July 2024

14 November 2024

The final payment for this accounting period will be due. The amount due is £597,500 (the total liability for the accounting period), less all the instalment payments already made in respect of the period.

In respect of the eight-month period ended 31 March 2025

14 February 2025

The first payment for this accounting period will be due. The amount due will be 3/8 of the estimated corporation tax liability for the eight-month period, i.e. £172,500 (3/8 × £460,000).

(d) Wagon Ltd – value added tax (VAT)

Purchases from Line Co

The purchases of components will be dealt with under postponed VAT accounting. Wagon Ltd will record import VAT as output VAT on its VAT return in the VAT quarter covering the date of importation.

Provided the components are used to make taxable supplies, the VAT paid can be reclaimed by Wagon Ltd as input tax on the same VAT return.

Sales to Signal Co

The sales to Signal Co will be treated as zero-rated supplies.

Zero-rated supplies are treated as taxable supplies, so this will not impact Wagon Ltd's ability to recover input VAT.

(e) Dee Co and En Co – controlled foreign company (CFC) charge

Dee Co

No CFC charge can arise in respect of Dee Co because Set Ltd owns less than 25% of Dee Co's ordinary share capital.

En Co

Low profits exemption

The low profits exemption does not apply even though En Co has taxable total profits of less than £500,000. This is because the company's non-trading income exceeds £50,000.

Low profit margin exemption

The low profit margin exemption applies because En Co's accounting profit of £280,000 does not exceed 10% of its operating expenditure of £3,200,000.

Tutor's top tips

The question stated that the only exemptions that needed consideration were those for low profits and low profit margin. Ensure that you don't waste time going through the other exemptions as this will score no marks!

(f) Knowledge gained from previous clients

Tutor's top tips

There are five marks available here, so try to make sure that you make five separately identifiable points in your answer.

- ACCA's Code of Ethics and Conduct includes confidentiality as one of the fundamental principles of ethics on which we should base our professional behaviour.
- Where we have acquired confidential information as a result of our professional and business relationships, we cannot use it to our own advantage or to the advantage of third parties.
- This principle of confidentiality applies to both ex-clients and continuing clients.
- As a result of this, we should not use any confidential information relating to our existing clients or ex-clients to assist the Set Ltd group.

– We are, however, permitted to use the experience and expertise we have gained from advising our clients.

Examiner's report

This report has been adapted to remove elements which are no longer examinable due to changes in legislation.

Part (a) of this question required candidates to deal with various aspects of incorporating a business, including the capital gains tax implications of a disposal of shares in the new company.

The assets of the business were transferred to the company on incorporation in return for consideration comprising wholly of shares, such that the total gains on the chargeable assets were eligible for incorporation relief.

The most common error in this part of the question was failure to realise that the nominal value of the shares issued as consideration does not necessarily equal the market value of the shares. The nominal value of the shares issued is irrelevant; their market value must equal the total market value of the assets transferred where they represent the total consideration. This is a commonly tested examination point in this area, but was only picked up by a few candidates.

A logical approach was required for the final aspect of this part of the question, to calculate the capital gains tax liability arising on the subsequent disposal of shares on the alternative assumptions that the taxpayer was UK resident or overseas resident. Candidates needed to take a step back and ensure that they understood the full picture, before embarking on the calculations. This advice is also applicable more generally to Section A questions, where candidates need to stop and think about the scenario as a whole before starting to undertake the detailed work required.

Part (b) required candidates to identify the relevant 'ties' to determine the residence status, which applied to the taxpayer who has left the UK. The question clearly stated that the automatic tests for determining both UK and overseas residence were not satisfied, but a minority of candidates still discussed these rules, gaining no marks, and wasting time. However, overall this part of the question was done well, with candidates being aware of the relevant ties, and applying them to the taxpayer's situation.

The final section of the examiner's report has been removed as that part of the question has been removed.

The following parts have been added from the examiner's report of another question which these parts were taken from.

The third requirement has been adapted since the question was originally set, to include capital allowances.

The third part of the question concerned a newly acquired, wholly owned subsidiary company, and its ability to receive a capital loss or trading loss from other group companies, and, separately, the corporation tax instalments which will fall due in the next six months.

In relation to the losses, many answers were disappointingly vague, in particular not stating whether the candidate was considering the capital loss or the trading loss in their discussion, or implying that the rules were the same for both, which is not the case. Dates were given in the question, so candidates were expected to refer to these in their answers.

The identification of the amounts and due dates for payment of the company's corporation tax instalments was, surprisingly, not well done. Virtually no candidate recognised that the final instalment for payment of a company's corporation tax liability was going to be the balance of the final corporation tax liability for the year i.e. the final liability less the three instalments paid previously, which is extremely unlikely to be the same as one quarter of the final liability, as the previous instalments have been based on estimates. A good number of candidates correctly calculated the amount of the first instalment for the subsequent short accounting period, but in both cases, application of knowledge of the due dates was weak. These must be accurately stated in order to score the marks.

The fourth part of the question related to the VAT implications of importing and exporting to non-UK resident companies, neither of which are registered for VAT. Answers were very mixed; again several answers were very vague, and future candidates should take note of how this has been addressed in the model answer. In particular, with imports, candidates must be precise as to how UK VAT will be paid/accounted for on the purchases.

This part of the question has been amended to remove the VAT treatment of goods outside/within the EU following changes to legislation.

The fifth part of the question concerned the application of two specific controlled foreign company (CFC) exemptions – the low profits exemption and low profit margin exemption. Overall, knowledge of these two exemptions was good, with a significant number of candidates scoring full, or almost full marks. The most common errors were to use the wrong figures to calculate the profit margin, and to fail to recognise that for one of the companies, no CFC charge would arise due to the UK company holding less than 25% of the shares in that company. A small number of candidates wasted time by considering other exemptions from CFC status, despite being clearly instructed in the requirement to consider just these two.

There is no examiner's report for the final requirement as this has not been taken from a past exam question.

ACCA marking scheme

			Marks
(a)	Sale of business to Roller Ltd		
	Incorporation relief conditions		2.0
	Business asset disposal relief		2.0
	Sale of Roller Ltd		
	Chargeable gain on disposal		2.5
	Capital gains tax		2.0
	Conclusion		2.0
			10.5
		Maximum	10.0
(b)	Consideration of each tie		5.0
	Conclusions		2.0
			7.0
		Maximum	6.0

(c)	Ghost Ltd integral features		3.5
	Steam Ltd capital loss		2.0
	Wagon Ltd trading losses		
	Loss brought forward		1.0
	Current period loss		3.0
	Payments of corporation tax		
	In respect of the year ended 31 July 2024		2.5
	In respect of the eight-month period ended 31 March 2025		2.0
			14.0
		Maximum	11.0
(d)	Purchases from Line Co		
	Postponed VAT accounting		0.5
	Record output VAT		1.0
	Recover input VAT		1.0
	Sales to Signal Co		
	Zero-rated		1.0
	Input VAT recovery		1.0
			4.5
		Maximum	4.0
(e)	Dee Co		1.0
	En Co		3.0
			4.0
(f)	One mark for each relevant point	**Maximum**	5.0
	Professional skills marks (see below)	**Maximum**	10.0
Total			**50.0**

Professional skills marks

Communication

- General format and structure of notes (e.g. use of headings/sub-headings to make notes easy to refer to).
- Style, language and clarity (tone of notes, presentation of calculations, appropriate use of the tools, easy to follow and more than a negligible amount of content).
- Effectiveness of communication (answer is relevant, specific rather than general and focused to the requirement).
- Adherence to specific instructions made in the scenario (e.g. not discussing the automatic non-residence or residence tests in relation to Waverley in part (b)).

Analysis and evaluation

- Use of information to determine the maximum days Waverley can spend in the UK before becoming UK resident in part (b).
- Use of information to determine the capital allowance treatment of the disposal of integral features in part (c).
- Analysis of information to discuss appropriate use of losses in part (c).
- Analysis of the information to determine what corporation tax payments are due for the period in question in part (c).

- Use of information to determine which companies may be subject to a CFC charge in part (e).

Scepticism

- Recognition of missing information with regards to Waverley's employment in part (b).
- Recognition of missing information relating to the tax written down value brought forward in part (c).
- Identification that group relief will be restricted by Ghost Ltd's taxable total profits, which are not given in part (c).

Commercial acumen

- Recognition of the availability of business asset disposal relief in part (a).
- Demonstration of an awareness of purpose behind the controlled foreign companies' legislation in part (e).

16 HEYER LTD GROUP AND DEE (ADAPTED) *Walk in the footsteps of a top tutor*

Key answer tips

This 50-mark section A question tests corporation tax groups, ethical issues, and a variety of different income tax and capital tax issues.

There are five requirements that could be answered in any order, so you should think carefully about which part you answer first, in order to maximise your score in the time available.

Requirement (a) tests group planning within a capital gains group, which is an important topic in the exam.

Part (b) covers the transfer of trade and assets within a group, which is not often tested.

Requirement (c) is possibly the most straightforward part of this question, and tests the ethical implications of non-disclosure of information to HMRC.

Part (d) looks at income tax savings on different investment options. It is important to read the question carefully so that you don't do any unnecessary calculations – income tax if Dee invests all the money herself was given to you, so don't recalculate it! You need to ensure that you don't just focus on the calculations. You are also asked to explain how a more tax efficient split could be obtained as well as the consequences of a gift to a minor child. Over half the marks available are for this part.

Part (e) tests giving to a non-domiciled spouse. You need to appreciate that the usual spouse exemption will not be applicable here and explain ways to mitigate the IHT.

The highlighted words in the written sections are key phrases that markers are looking for in your answer.

(a) Group planning

> ***Tutor's top tips***
>
> *The email from your manager sets out four sub-requirements for this part of the question, so you should make sure that you address all of these.*
>
> *You could use the key words from these sub-requirements as headings in your answer, to help to give structure.*

Requirement to pay corporation tax by instalments

In respect of the year ending 31 December 2024, a company in the Heyer Ltd group will be required to pay corporation tax in instalments if its taxable total profits (TTP) exceed £83,333 (£1,500,000/18) and either:

– it had TTP of more than £83,333 in the year ended 31 December 2023, or

– its TTP for the year ended 31 December 2024 are more than £555,556 (£10,000,000/18).

> ***Tutorial note***
>
> *Companies which have a corporation tax liability of less than £10,000 are not required to pay tax in instalments. This point is not referred to in the answer as none of the companies fall within this definition.*
>
> *Strictly, the requirement to pay instalments is based on a company's augmented profits (TTP plus non-group dividends received). However, we are told in the question that no company receives any dividends from outside the group.*

The Heyer Ltd capital gains group

The Heyer Ltd capital gains group consists of Heyer Ltd, its 75% subsidiaries and their 75% subsidiaries. In addition, Heyer Ltd must have an effective interest of more than 50% in any company which it does not own directly.

Accordingly, all of the group companies are in a single capital gains group with the exception of Orin Hod Ltd.

Amount of chargeable gains and capital losses to transfer between group companies

You should aim to:

1 Reduce the TTP of as many companies as possible to £83,333, such that they are no longer required to pay corporation tax in instalments.

2 Reduce the TTP of those companies which are still required to pay corporation tax in instalments, as this will reduce the amount of each instalment.

3 The whole or part of any current period chargeable gain and/or capital loss can be transferred between companies in a capital gains group.

- Gains and losses should be transferred in order to match them against each other.
- Gains should be transferred from a company which has TTP in excess of the £83,333 threshold to a company which has TTP below the threshold.

Relevance of the specific information

Tutor's top tips

To score well in this question, it is important that you not only set out the general objectives, but also apply these to the companies in the scenario.

Companies do not need to pay by instalments if they were not large in the previous accounting period unless their augmented profits exceed £10 million. This limit is shared by associated companies and so is £555,556 for the Heyer Ltd group.

Mantet Ltd

Mantet Ltd had TTP for the year ended 31 December 2023 of less than £83,333. Accordingly, it will not be required to pay its corporation tax liability for the year ended 31 December 2024 in instalments unless its TTP for that year are more than £555,556. With this in mind, chargeable gains should be transferred to Mantet Ltd from other companies in the Heyer Ltd capital gains group provided its TTP are kept below £555,556.

Newell Rap Ltd

Newell Rap Ltd's capital losses are pre-entry capital losses because they were realised before Newell Rap Ltd was acquired by Heyer Ltd. These losses cannot be used to relieve gains on assets realised by other members of the Heyer Ltd capital gains group.

Orin Hod Ltd

Orin Hod Ltd's TTP exceed £83,333. However, it is not a member of the Heyer Ltd capital gains group because it is not a 75% subsidiary of Heyer Ltd. Accordingly, it is not possible to reduce its TTP by, for example, transferring its chargeable gains to other companies.

Other 100% owned companies

All of these companies are required to pay corporation tax in instalments.

Current period chargeable gains and capital losses realised by these companies should be transferred to other companies in the Heyer Ltd capital gains group in accordance with the guidance set out above.

(b) Group restructuring

Tutor's top tips

Even if you were not sure about the special rules that apply when there is a transfer of trade and assets between companies under 75% common control, you could have picked up some marks for explaining the implications of a transfer of assets within a 75% gains group.

Chargeable gains

Chargeable assets, including the business premises, will be transferred at no gain, no loss automatically, because all of the companies are 75% subsidiaries of Heyer Ltd. Accordingly, no chargeable gains will arise.

Stamp duty land tax (SDLT)

No SDLT will be due in respect of the sale of the business premises because Heyer Ltd owns at least 75% of the ordinary share capital of all of the companies.

Capital allowances

Machinery and equipment will be automatically transferred at tax written down value, rather than market value, because Heyer Ltd controls at least 75% of each of the companies. Accordingly, no balancing charges will arise.

Capital losses

The unused capital losses of Newell Rap Ltd, and any other company whose trade and assets will be transferred, will not be transferred to Lodi Ltd, but current period capital losses can be transferred to companies in the same capital gains group, as set out above.

(c) Disclosure of transfer pricing

Tutor's top tips

There will always be five marks on ethical issues in section A of the exam, and these can be easy marks to obtain.

This requirement covers the implications of a client not disclosing information to HMRC, and is similar to requirements seen in past exams.

It is more than 12 months since the return filing date, and therefore too late to amend the corporation tax returns. Accordingly, this information must be disclosed to HM Revenue and Customs (HMRC). We should encourage Heyer Ltd to make this disclosure.

The management of the Heyer Ltd group can inform HMRC or may authorise us to do so. However, we must not disclose the error to HMRC without permission.

We cannot continue to act for the companies unless this disclosure is made.

We should notify the group of the following consequences of not providing this information to HMRC:

– If they refuse to disclose the error, we will advise HMRC that we no longer act for them. We would not, however, give any reason for our actions.

– Non-disclosure of the error would also amount to tax evasion. This could result in criminal proceedings under both the tax and money laundering legislation.

We should inform our firm's money laundering officer of the situation.

We should ascertain how the non-disclosure occurred in order to determine whether or not there may be other matters which have been omitted from the group companies' corporation tax returns.

(d) Minimising income tax on investment income

Tutor's top tips

There is a lot to do in part (d) and it is easy to get overwhelmed by all the information.

Firstly, you need to calculate the income tax saving if Dee were to give Cam £150,000 to invest. The requirement gives you lots of guidance so ensure you follow it! You are told not to complete whole computations but just to work out the extra tax. It is clear from the income levels that Dee is an additional rate tax payer and Cam is a basic rate tax payer. You can use this information to calculate the tax just on the extra interest and dividends they will each received, rather than doing complete computations.

Gift of £150,000 to Cam – income tax saving

	£
Total income tax	
If Dee invests the whole of the £450,000	5,004
If Dee gives £150,000 to Cam (£3,205 + £263) (below)	(3,468)
Income tax saving	1,536

Dee – investing £300,000

Interest income	
(£1,000 (£300,000 × 1/3 × 1%) × 45%)	450
Dividend income	
((£8,000 (£300,000 × 2/3 × 4%) – £1,000) × 39.35%)	2,755
	3,205

Cam – investing £150,000

Interest income	
(£500 (£150,000 × 1/3 × 1%) × 0%) (savings income nil rate band)	0
Dividend income	
((£4,000 (£150,000 × 2/3 × 4%) – £1,000) × 8.75%) (dividend nil rate band)	263
	263

Tutorial note

The interest and dividends in respect of funds held within ISAs are exempt from income tax. Accordingly, they do not reduce the savings income nil rate band or the dividend nil rate band.

As Dee is an additional rate taxpayer she does not have a savings nil rate band. Cam is a basic rate taxpayer therefore will have a £1,000 savings nil rate band.

Tutor's top tips

As well as the calculations you are also asked to consider what factors would be relevant to consider in obtaining a more tax efficient split of income.

Here you should consider the fact that Cam has not utilised all of his savings income nil rate band, and he also pays tax at a much lower rate than Dee. Therefore, it may be worthwhile giving more income to him where possible.

Factors relevant to obtaining a more income tax-efficient split of the total investment

Tax allowances

Cam has £500 (£1,000 – £500) of the savings income nil rate band remaining.

Income tax rates

Even if he were to have to pay income tax on his investment income, Cam's tax rates would be considerably lower than those of Dee.

Accordingly, it makes sense for Cam's income to be maximised and Dee's income to be minimised.

Yields on the investments

The greatest change in their income levels would be achieved by Cam investing more in shares and Dee investing less in shares. This is because the yield from shares is four times the yield on cash deposits.

Tutor's top tips

The final bit of this requirement is looking at the income tax treatment of the gift of cash to a minor. The gift in itself does not create an income tax liability but the money will be placed on deposit which is going to generate interest.

Where a child is under 18 and a parental settlement results in income of over £100 per tax year this can cause a problem in that the income is taxed on the parent instead of the child. Remember that this rule only applies where the child is under 18.

Gift to Oder

The interest income in respect of Dee's proposed gift to Oder would exceed £100 (£20,000 × 1% = £200). Accordingly, until Oder is 18 years old, all of the interest income (i.e. not just the excess over £100) would be taxed as if it were Dee's income. Accordingly, no tax saving would arise.

Once Oder is 18, the interest income would be treated as his income. Oder is unlikely to be an additional rate taxpayer, such that the interest income would be taxed at a lower rate than if it were received by Dee. This would then reduce the total income tax liability of the family.

(e) Gift to Cam Inheritance tax

Tutor's top tips

In part (e) you first of all need to explain why the gift to Cam could result in an IHT liability. Remember that as Cam is a non-UK domiciled spouse so only £325,000 can be given exempt from IHT, and there has already been a gift to him. You should also discuss how the liability could be avoided. Here you may think about the election to treat Cam as UK domiciled for IHT, but also consider how Dee received the money in the first place and if anything different could be done there.

For the second part you will need two CGT computations: one for Dee disposing of the whole house herself and another where she disposes of two thirds and Cam one third. Work out the difference between the two total liabilities to find the saving.

Cam is non-UK domiciled, such that the spouse exemption, which applies to gifts between spouses, is limited to a lifetime maximum of £325,000. This limit has already been exceeded due to the gift made by Dee to Cam on 1 August 2020, which was valued at £600,000.

Accordingly, Dee's gift of £150,000 to Cam would be a potentially exempt transfer, which could give rise to an inheritance tax liability if Dee were to die within seven years of the gift.

This potential liability could be avoided in either of the following ways:

– The terms of Dee's father's will could be altered via a deed of variation; such that one-third of the London house is left directly to Cam. This would avoid the need for Dee to make a potentially exempt transfer to Cam.

– Cam could elect to be treated as UK domiciled for the purposes of inheritance tax. This would mean that all gifts from Dee would be exempt under the spouse exemption with no upper limit.

Tutorial notes

1 *The deed of variation would have to be signed by Dee and be executed within two years of Dee's father's death. It should state that it is intended to be effective for both inheritance tax and capital gains tax purposes.*

2 *The downside of Cam electing to be treated as UK domiciled would be that any non-UK assets owned by Cam would cease to be outside UK inheritance tax and so would become taxable.*

Capital gains tax (CGT) saving if Dee were to give Cam a one-third interest in the London house

	Dee	**Cam**
	£	£
Sale of the house by Dee as planned		
Chargeable gain (£450,000 – £390,000)	60,000	
Less: Annual exempt amount	(6,000)	
	54,000	
CGT at 28%	15,120	
Gift of one-third of the house to Cam		
Chargeable gain 2/3:1/3	40,000	20,000
Less: Annual exempt amount	(6,000)	(6,000)
	34,000	14,000
CGT at 28%/18%	9,520	2,520

CGT saving of £3,080 (£15,120 – (£9,520 + £2,520))

Tutorial note

The gift of one-third of the house to Cam would take place at no gain, no loss because Dee and Cam are married. As a result, the gain of £60,000 would be split between them in the ratio 2/3:1/3.

Examiner's report

The first part required candidates to prepare guidance for a tax assistant on how to minimise the corporation tax payable in instalments by the group companies by transferring chargeable gains and capital losses between them.

This was a slightly unusual requirement. It was vital that candidates spent some time thinking about how **they** would carry out the assistant's task before they started trying to explain to the assistant how to do it.

Candidates needed to think in terms of what needed to be done (objectives), and how it was to be achieved (strategies). The objectives were:

- where possible, to reduce the taxable total profits (TTP) of each company below the limit of £1,500,000 (divided by the 18 companies in the group)
- to reduce the TTP of any company required to pay tax in instalments.

These objectives can be achieved by:

- matching gains and losses in a particular company
- transferring gains from a company with TTP above the threshold to one with TTP below the threshold.

As expected, candidates found this task difficult and there was a tendency to fall back on describing the rules in general terms as opposed to trying to address the specific requirement.

The second part of the question concerned the proposal to transfer the trades and assets of five of the group companies to another of the group companies and was also challenging. The challenge here was to address all of the issues set out in the manager's email in the time available. Only four points needed to be made but there was only one mark for each point.

Having said that this was a challenging question, many candidates made a good job of it. In particular, they kept their answers brief and tried to address all of the issues raised. Weaker candidates focused on only one or two of the manager's issues which restricted the number of marks which could be obtained.

The one common technical error concerned the capital allowances treatment. The point here is that the assets would be automatically transferred at tax written down value because the companies are all under 75% common control both before and after the transfer of the trades.

The following part of the examiner's report has been removed due to that requirement being removed from the question.

The third part of the question concerned the disclosure of information to HM Revenue and Customs and was done well by the vast majority of candidates.

The final two requirements have been added from another past exam question and the relevant extracts from the examiner's report are included below:

The fourth part of the question, which was worth 11 marks, concerned proposals to minimise the overall income tax liabilities of a married couple. Performance on this question part was polarised, with a good number of candidates scoring 8+ marks, but equally, a large number scored fewer than 4 marks. Those candidates who scored well on this particular part:

- clearly spent time carefully reading and thinking about the requirements, so that they were able to adopt a structured, methodical approach to calculating the tax liabilities for each individual if the proposed strategy was followed.

- didn't waste time writing out facts from the question or suggesting alternative strategies which did not satisfy the stated requirements for the couple.

Many of those who scored low marks had attempted this question last, and appeared to have run out of time. The requirements may have appeared a little daunting in length, but those candidates who read through them carefully, and followed the very detailed guidance they contained, were rewarded with high marks. For these candidates, the standard of the calculations of the tax savings was very high, and most were able to recognise and explain the benefit of standard income tax planning measures for a married couple, such as using the savings and dividend nil rate bands, and taking advantage of the lower rate of tax paid by one of the couple. The most surprising aspect of candidates' answers related to the requirement to discuss the income tax implications of a parent providing an income-generating investment for a minor child. Not only did very few candidates recognise that the income from this investment would be taxed on the parent, but a significant number did not discuss any income tax implications at all. Despite the clear instruction in the requirement for discussion of income tax matters, an overwhelming majority of candidates (perhaps having seen the word 'gift'), discussed the inheritance tax implications, in some cases in quite some detail. Candidates are once again reminded of the importance of reading the question carefully; writing about the wrong tax clearly scores no marks.

The final part of the question related to the IHT implications of a UK domiciled spouse gifting cash from the sale of a property to their non-UK domiciled spouse, and the CGT saving from gifting a share of the property prior to sale, rather than cash following the sale. Although many candidates were not aware of the precise restriction on the spouse exemption in respect of a non-UK domiciled spouse, it was pleasing to see that the majority realised that the full spouse exemption was not likely to be available, so were able to score marks from recognising that there would only be a liability to IHT if the donor spouse died within seven years, and that a non-UK domiciled spouse is able to change their domicile on election.

In calculating the CGT saving as a result of transferring a share in the house to a spouse prior to sale, the majority of candidates adopted a full 'before and after' calculation in this case, calculating the total tax payable by the wife if she sold the house before giving her husband a share of the proceeds, with the total payable by the husband and wife together if she gave him a share of the house prior to sale. This latter strategy enabled the couple to take advantage of the husband's available annual exempt amount (AEA), and lower rate of CGT. This was an entirely reasonable approach to take in this scenario, as the calculation of the liability was quite straightforward. The main errors in this part were, firstly, not recognising that, as this was a sale of a private residence, the higher rates of CGT will apply, and secondly, focusing only on the reduction in the CGT payable by the wife, without taking in to account that there would also be a small liability for the husband in the latter strategy. A minority of candidates used a marginal approach to directly identify the amount of tax which would be saved. This proved to be very efficient if done correctly, but was quite tricky, and several candidates just provided a lot of numbers, without adequate labelling, which made it difficult to award marks in some cases.

ACCA marking scheme			
			Marks
(a)	Requirement to pay by instalments		3.5
	Definition of capital gains group		2.0
	Amount to transfer		4.0
	Specific information		
	Mantet Ltd		2.0
	Newell Rap Ltd		2.0
	Orin Hod Ltd		1.0
	Other 100% companies		0.5
			15.0
		Maximum	11.0
(b)	One mark for each relevant point (maximum of 4 marks)		4.0
(c)	The need to disclose		4.0
	Other matters		3.0
			7.0
		Maximum	5.0
(d)	Income tax saving if gift made to Cam		5.5
	Factors relevant to obtaining a more income tax-efficient split of the total investment		4.0
	Gift to Oder		3.0
			12.5
		Maximum	11.0
(e)	Inheritance tax		
	Potential liability		3.0
	Advice		3.0
	Capital gains tax		
	Dee owns the whole of the house		2.0
	Transfer of one-third of the house to Cam		2.0
			10.0
		Maximum	9.0
	Professional skills marks (see below)	**Maximum**	10.0
Total			**50.0**

Professional skills marks

Communication

- General format and structure of notes (e.g. use of headings/sub-headings to make notes easy to refer to).
- Style, language and clarity (tone of notes, presentation of calculations, appropriate use of the tools, easy to follow and more than a negligible amount of content).
- Effectiveness of communication (answer is relevant, specific rather than general and focused to the requirement).
- Adherence to specific instructions made in the scenario (e.g. not preparing complete income tax computations in part (d)).

Analysis and evaluation

- Analysis of the information to determine the most efficient use of gains and losses within the group in part (a).
- Analysis of the information to determine which group companies would be required to pay corporation tax by instalments in part (a).
- Use of the information to determine appropriate calculations to perform to arrive at the income tax saving for Dee and Cam in part (d).
- Demonstration of ability to consider all taxes relevant to requirement (e), i.e. inheritance tax and capital gains tax.

Scepticism

- Critical assessment of the attitude towards disclosure of transfer pricing in part (c).
- Critical assessment of the friend's advice in part (d).

Commercial acumen

- Identification of relevant factors to consider when deciding how to split the investment between Dee and Cam in part (d).
- Demonstrating an understanding of the anti-avoidance rules around taxation of income of minors in part (d).
- Identification of relevant tax planning opportunities with regards to the gift to Cam in part (e).

17 MITA AND SNOWDON (ADAPTED) *Walk in the footsteps of a top tutor*

Key answer tips

This question covers capital gains tax reliefs, R&D, intangibles, consortium relief, basic sole trader computations, VAT partial exemption and procedures around taking on a new client. Most of these are new areas at ATX so it should not be a surprise to see these tested.

The first part of the question looks at capital gains tax reliefs. These are commonly tested but the examining team continue to comment on the fact that candidates don't seem to know them well enough. Make sure you spend some time going over these.

Part (b) covers various areas of corporation tax and VAT. Make sure you give yourself enough time to have a go at each of the areas so you can pick up some of the easier marks.

The third part is a little bit trickier as it requires you to consider various costs involved with expanding a business including national insurance contributions and irrecoverable VAT. If you take an organised approach and consider each extra cost in turn you can score well on this part.

The final part of the question allows for some easy marks to be earned by identifying potential ethical issues when appointing a new client. Ensure that you leave sufficient time to do this part well, or even consider doing this first.

The highlighted words in the written sections are key phrases that markers are looking for in your answer.

(a) Sale of 4,000 shares in Porth Ltd on 1 May 2025

Mita – capital gains tax (CGT) liability

	£	£
Proceeds at market value		260,000
Less: Cost		
Market value of assets sold to Porth Ltd	120,000	
Less: Incorporation relief	(37,400)	
	82,600	
£82,600 × 4,000/10,000		(33,040)
		226,960
Less: Gift holdover relief (balancing figure)		(60,000)
Gain chargeable (£200,000 – £33,040)		166,960
CGT at 10% (business asset disposal relief)		16,696

Tutor's top tips

Capital gains tax reliefs are commonly tested in ATX so ensure you know the qualifying conditions for each relief as well as how they operate, so you can answer questions like the one above.

(b) Quod Ltd

Tax deduction available in respect of the scientific research costs

Tutor's top tips

Research and development expenditure is one of the new topics tested at ATX and is commonly examined. Ensure you are comfortable with how the relief works depending on the nature of the expenditure.

– The equipment and computer hardware will qualify for a 100% capital allowance as capital expenditure incurred for the purpose of research and development.

Accordingly, the total cost incurred of £102,000 will be deductible for the purposes of corporation tax.

– As Quod Ltd will be a small enterprise for research and development purposes, certain categories of revenue expenditure which are directly related to research and development activities will qualify for an additional 86% deduction when calculating the company's taxable trading income.

  This additional deduction is not available in respect of the capital expenditure or the rental costs.

  Only 65% of amounts paid to external contractors qualify for this additional deduction.

– Tax deduction available:

	£	£
Total research costs	102,000	102,000
Less:		
Equipment and computer hardware (capital)	(27,500)	
Rent	(17,400)	
Staff costs (£7,000 × 35% (100% – 65%))	(2,450)	
Amount qualifying for additional deduction	54,650	
Additional deduction (£54,650 × 86%)		46,999
Tax deduction available		148,999

Tax treatment of the purchase of the Cloque brand

– The amount of £1,000 charged to the statement of profit or loss in respect of this expenditure would be allowable for the purposes of calculating taxable trading profit.

– Alternatively, for the purpose of calculating the company's taxable trading profit, Quod Ltd could elect to write off £1,400 (£35,000 × 4%) per year, which would clearly be beneficial.

Amended tax adjusted trading loss for the year ending 31 March 2026

	£
Budgeted tax adjusted trading loss	(44,000)
Additional deduction in respect of research costs	(46,999)
Amortisation of Cloque brand (£1,400 (£35,000 × 4%) – £1,000)	(400)
Amended tax adjusted trading loss	(91,399)

Amount of trading loss available for use by Porth Ltd

– Porth Ltd will not be able to use the trading loss of Quod Ltd unless Quod Ltd is a consortium company. Quod Ltd will be a consortium company if at least 75% of its ordinary share capital is owned by companies, each of which own at least 5% but less than 75%.

– Accordingly, for consortium relief to be available, BJB Ltd must own the 30% holding rather than Mr Berm.

– The maximum amount which could be surrendered to Porth Ltd as consortium relief is £54,839 (£91,399 × 60%), reflecting Porth Ltd's holding of 60% of the ordinary share capital of Quod Ltd.

Value added tax (VAT) implications of purchasing advice from the overseas supplier

> ***Tutor's top tips***
>
> *When dealing with VAT on services it is important to ascertain whether the transaction is between two businesses (B2B) or between a business and a consumer (B2C). Make sure you clearly state which type of transaction you are dealing with and what the VAT treatment would be for the relevant party you are asked about.*

- The provision of this advice will be a business to business (B2B) service. It will be treated as supplied in the UK, because that is where Quod Ltd is established.
- Quod Ltd will be required to pay VAT at the UK standard rate of 20% to HM Revenue and Customs (HMRC) under the 'reverse charge' principle. The rate of VAT in the overseas country is irrelevant.
- The input VAT can be reclaimed on this expense in the same way as any other input tax incurred by the company.
- Accordingly, Quod Ltd's VAT position will be the same as if the services had been purchased from the UK supplier.

(c) Expansion of the Siabod business

> ***Tutor's top tips***
>
> *You are asked to calculate which strategy will generate the most additional tax adjusted trading profit. The question mentions the amount of extra turnover that will be generated and the extra costs that will be incurred, but don't forget the extra costs that are not mentioned, such as employer's national insurance and irrecoverable VAT!*

Strategy A

	£
Additional turnover (£435,000 – £255,000)	180,000
Salary	48,000
Employer's class 1 NIC ((£48,000 – £9,100) × 13.8%)	5,368
Overheads and advertising (£38,000 + £2,000)	40,000
Irrecoverable VAT (W1)	0
	93,368
Additional tax adjusted trading profit (£180,000 – £93,368)	86,632

Strategy B

	£
Additional turnover (as for strategy A)	180,000
Fee paid to Tor Ltd	90,000
Advertising	2,000
Irrecoverable VAT (W2)	8,736
	100,736
Additional tax adjusted trading profit (£180,000 – £100,736)	79,264

The most financially advantageous strategy would be strategy A.

Additional post-tax income in respect of strategy A

	£
Tax adjusted trading profit prior to expansion	85,000
Tax adjusted trading profit in respect of expansion (above)	86,632
	171,632
Interest income	740
	172,372
Personal allowance	0
	172,372

	£
Income tax on trading income	
£37,700 × 20%	7,540
(£125,140 – £37,700) × 40%	34,976
(£171,632 – £125,140) × 45%	20,921
	63,437
Income tax on interest income	
£740 × 45%	333
Class 4 NIC	
(£50,270 – £12,570) × 9%	3,393
(£171,632 – £50,270) × 2%	2,427
Total income tax and NIC	69,590
Less: Income tax and class 4 NIC on profit of £85,000 (£21,432 + £4,088)	(25,520)
Less: Income tax on interest income prior to expansion of business ((£740 – £500) × 40%)	(96)
Additional income tax and class 4 NIC in respect of expansion	43,974
Additional post-tax income (£86,632 – £43,974)	42,658

Tutorial note

Prior to expanding the business, Snowdon was a higher rate taxpayer and was therefore entitled to a savings income nil rate band of £500. Following the expansion of the business, he will be an additional rate taxpayer and will not be entitled to this allowance.

Workings

(W1) Strategy A – recoverable input tax

Partial exemption percentage	76%
	£
Total input tax (£18,000 + ((£38,000 + £2,000) × 20%))	26,000
Attributable to taxable supplies (£26,000 × 76%)	(19,760)
Attributable to exempt supplies	6,240

The VAT attributable to exempt supplies can be recovered in full as it is below the annual de minimis limit of £7,500 (£625 × 12) and is less than half of the total input tax.

(W2) Strategy B – recoverable input tax

Partial exemption percentage	76%
	£
Total input tax (£18,000 + ((£90,000 + £2,000) × 20%))	36,400
Attributable to taxable supplies (£36,400 × 76%)	(27,664)
Attributable to exempt supplies	8,736

The VAT attributable to exempt supplies cannot be recovered as it exceeds the annual de minimis limit of £7,500 (£625 × 12).

(d) Matters to consider before we agree to become Snowdon's tax advisers

– We must have regard to the fundamental principles of professional ethics. This requires us to consider whether becoming tax advisers to Snowdon would create any threats to compliance with these principles.

  If any such threats are identified, we should not accept the appointment unless the threats can be reduced to an acceptable level via the implementation of safeguards.

– Advising Snowdon on the gift to be made to him by Mita could give rise to a conflict of interest.

  This is because the course of action which would be most beneficial for Snowdon may differ to what is most beneficial for Mita, our other client. This could threaten our ability to provide objective advice to both Snowdon and Mita.

  We should therefore obtain permission of both Mita and Snowdon to act for them in this capacity.

- Professional competence: we must ensure that we have the skills and competence necessary to be able to deal with the matters which may arise in connection with Snowdon's affairs.
- We must also ensure that we maintain the confidentiality of Mita, Porth Ltd and Snowdon at all times. We should consider the use of separate engagement teams for each client in order to maintain this.

Examiner's report

This question concerned an individual's sale of shares in a recently incorporated company, various corporation tax issues in relation to a newly set up joint venture company, income tax and value added tax (VAT) issues, together with consideration of the procedures to be considered before taking on a new client. Overall, this question was not done well, which was surprising.

The first part of the question required candidates to calculate the CGT payable on the sale of shares in a newly incorporated company, in respect of which incorporation relief had been claimed. Despite the requirement being only to calculate the liability, a significant number of candidates also included explanations, which did not score marks. This was particularly noticeable among those candidates who sat computer-based exams (CBE). Many included calculations in the spreadsheet, then explained the calculations in the word processing document, which was totally unnecessary, and just wasted time. The majority of candidates omitted to deal with the previously claimed incorporation relief, despite it being clearly flagged up in the question. It was also disappointing that many candidates did not include gift holdover relief, or business asset disposal relief, both of which were relevant here. The different reliefs available to reduce, eliminate or defer capital gains are very frequently examined at ATX, and are regarded by the examining team as an extremely important part of the syllabus. It is therefore strongly recommended that candidates take time within their revision to ensure that they are familiar with the conditions required for the different reliefs, and then, precisely how they operate.

Going forward, candidates would be well advised to ensure that they practise a wide variety of questions involving capital gains tax reliefs, to improve their knowledge and application of these.

The second part of the question was worth 15 marks and comprised five tasks. In the first two tasks relating to the explanation of the tax treatment of research and development expenditure incurred by a small enterprise, and the acquisition of an intangible asset, many candidates displayed a surprising lack of technical knowledge, despite both being frequently tested areas. Fortunately, many were able to gain follow through marks in their calculation of the effect of these on the company's budgeted trading loss for the period. It was good to see that a majority of candidates recognised that the loss-making company would be a consortium company such that proportionate loss relief would be available to the parent company. Finally, in this part, the fifth task, relating to application of the reverse charge principle in respect of services received by a UK company from an overseas company again demonstrated a lack of knowledge, or of understanding of this process by very many candidates.

The final requirement of the question has now been removed and replaced with two new requirements from another past exam question. The extracts from the relevant examiner's report for those are given below:

The third part of the question concerned the appraisal of two alternative strategies being considered by the potential client in relation to expanding their unincorporated business.

This part was worth 16 marks and was wholly computational involving mainly income tax, and a few marks of VAT. It contained a considerable amount of detail relating to each of the strategies, and of the VAT implications, including possible partial exemption. Questions involving a series of detailed computations, such as this one, require careful reading, thinking and planning before starting to write, in order to produce a logical, easy to follow set of calculations. Lengthy computations such as this are challenging questions, with a number of different 'issues' embedded within them, such as the consideration of the impact of VAT, and in particular partial exemption, as there was here. Time spent in planning at the start ensures that candidates don't waste time with unnecessary calculations, which, in some cases were quite lengthy, but were irrelevant, so gained no marks. Also, candidates are able to recognise the point in the computation when specific aspects – such as partial exemption for VAT – need to be considered. It was clear where candidates had done such preparation; their computations were logically presented, and easy to mark. It cannot be stressed enough how vital it is to spend a few minutes reading, thinking and planning before starting to write an answer to these longer question parts.

The final requirement has been amended since the question was originally set.

The final part of the question required a summary of the procedures to be followed before agreeing to become tax advisers for the potential new client. This appeared to be a question for which most candidates were well prepared, and most scored well. Those that didn't tended to be too general in their comments, such as talking about the need to ensure adherence to ACCA's fundamental ethical principles, without identifying which of these principles is/are particularly relevant in this scenario. It is always important in an ethics requirement to relate your answer specifically to the (potential) client, and the scenario in the question.

ACCA marking scheme

			Marks
(a)	Chargeable gain		2.0
	Gift holdover relief		1.5
	Capital gains tax		1.0
			4.5
		Maximum	4.0
(b)	Research costs		
	Notes		4.5
	Calculation		1.5
	Amortisation of brand		2.0
	Calculation of available loss		3.0
	Consortium relief		4.0
	Value added tax		3.0
			18.0
		Maximum	15.0

(c)	Additional tax adjusted trading profit – strategy A		
	Additional turnover		0.5
	Salary, class 1 NIC and overheads		2.0
	Recoverable input tax		3.0
	Additional tax adjusted trading profit – strategy B		
	Additional turnover and fee paid to Tor Ltd		1.0
	Recoverable input tax		3.0
	Additional post-tax income		
	Taxable income		3.0
	Income tax and class 4 NIC on trading income		2.5
	Income tax on interest income		1.0
	Remainder of calculation		3.0
			19.0
		Maximum	16.0
(d)	Fundamental principles		2.0
	Conflict of interest		2.5
	Professional competence		1.0
	Confidentiality		2.0
			7.5
		Maximum	5.0
	Professional skills marks (see below)	**Maximum**	10.0
Total			**50.0**

Professional skills marks

Communication

- General format and structure of notes (e.g. use of headings/sub-headings to make notes easy to refer to).
- Style, language and clarity (tone of notes, presentation of calculations, appropriate use of the tools, easy to follow and more than a negligible amount of content).
- Effectiveness of communication (answer is relevant, specific rather than general and focused to the requirement).
- Adherence to specific instructions made in the scenario (e.g. ignoring the CGT annual exempt amount in part (a)).

Analysis and evaluation

- Use of the information to determine appropriate calculations to perform to arrive at the capital gains tax liability for the sale of the shares in Porth Ltd in part (a).
- Use of the information to determine appropriate calculations to perform to determine the tax deduction available in respect of the research and development expenditure in part (b).
- Analysis of the information to determine the loss relief implications for Porth Ltd in part (b).
- Analysis of the information to determine appropriate calculations to evaluate the most financially advantageous strategy for Snowdon's business in part (c).
- Demonstration of ability to consider all taxes relevant to part (c), i.e. income tax, national insurance contributions and VAT.

Scepticism

- Critical assessment of the use of Porth Ltd's trading loss in part (b).
- Demonstration of an understanding of the need to exercise caution when agreeing to become tax advisers for a new client in part (d).

Commercial acumen

- Identification of the availability of business asset disposal relief on the sale of the shares in Porth Ltd in part (a).
- Demonstration of an understanding of the corporation tax relief available for research and development expenditure in part (b).
- Demonstration of an understanding of how overseas supplies will impact on input VAT recovery in part (b).

18 GRAND LTD GROUP (ADAPTED) *Walk in the footsteps of a top tutor*

Key answer tips

This long section A question tests many core aspects of corporation tax along with some employment income, VAT and ethics. There is a lot of information to take on board so it is important to read through it carefully and pick out the key points.

Part (a) looks at the classic scenario of a sale of shares versus a sale of trade and assets. You need to appreciate that with a sale of shares SSE is going to be key so it is important to identify early on if this will be relevant and explain why. With the sale of trade and assets it's important to take a logical approach dealing with one asset at a time and then bring this all together at the end to see the corporation tax impact.

Part (b) covers a comparison of net income for two different employment packages. This type of question is very popular at ATX, and once you have seen one they are all very similar. The accommodation benefit is pure TX knowledge, and illustrates how important it is to retain this knowledge. However, even without this you should still be able to score a good pass here.

Part (c) is a short section dealing with tax evasion v avoidance. This is completely standalone and could be attempted first. This is often a good tactic in the exam as the ethics requirement can offer some easy marks, so ensure you get them!

The highlighted words in the written sections are key phrases that markers are looking for.

(a) Memorandum

Client Grand Ltd group

Subject Sale of Colca Ltd

Prepared by Tax senior

Date 1 September 2024

(i) Offer A – in respect of a sale of the company's shares

Tutor's top tips

This part of the question is made up of three areas.

Firstly, you must consider whether tax relief will be available for the loss on the sale of the shares. This is testing the substantial shareholding exemption. You must explain whether or not the criteria are met, and if so this means that the loss is not allowable.

You then need to go on to consider the tax implications of Colca Ltd leaving the group still owning the Atuel building. The obvious thing to discuss here is a potential degrouping charge as they are leaving the group within six years of a no gain no loss transfer. However, you should also think about whether there are any stamp tax implications.

Finally, you need to calculate post-tax proceeds.

Tax relief available in respect of the capital loss on the sale of the shares

- The capital loss on the sale of the shares will not be allowable for tax purposes due to the automatic application of the substantial shareholding exemption (SSE).
- The SSE applies because:
  - Colca Ltd is a trading company, and
  - Grand Ltd will have owned at least 10% of the ordinary share capital of Colca Ltd for at least 12 months in the six years prior to the sale of the company.

The tax implications of Colca Ltd leaving the Grand Ltd group whilst owning the Atuel building

Degrouping charge

- The sale of the Atuel building by Sautso Ltd to Colca Ltd took place at no gain, no loss because the two companies were members of a capital gains group. This resulted in a base cost in the building for Colca Ltd equal to Sautso Ltd's cost.
- Colca Ltd will leave the Grand Ltd group within six years of purchasing the building from Sautso Ltd, such that a degrouping charge will arise. Colca Ltd will be deemed to have sold the building for £255,000, its market value as at 1 April 2022.

  This deemed disposal results in a capital loss. However, this loss merely reduces Grand Ltd's proceeds for the shares in Colca Ltd. This in turn will increase the capital loss on the sale of the shares, which is exempt due to the SSE (as noted above).

Tutorial notes

1 *There was no need to calculate the capital loss in respect of the degrouping charge because it merely increases the capital loss on the sale of Colca Ltd, which is exempt under the SSE.*

2 *Colca Ltd will also be deemed to have purchased the building for £255,000, such that this will be its base cost in the building when calculating the chargeable gain or allowable loss arising on any future disposal of the building.*

Stamp duty land tax (SDLT)

– There was no SDLT liability when Colca Ltd purchased the Atuel building from Sautso Ltd because both companies were 75% subsidiaries of Grand Ltd.

– However, Colca Ltd will leave the Grand Ltd group within three years of purchasing the building, such that it will have to pay the SDLT which would have been due at the time of purchase if the group exemption had not been available.

Post-tax proceeds

	£
Sale proceeds	730,000
Less: SDLT payable by Colca Ltd in respect of the Atuel building	(2,250)
Post-tax proceeds	727,750

Working

SDLT payable by Colca Ltd in respect of the Atuel building

	£
150,000 × 0%	0
100,000 × 2%	2,000
5,000 × 5%	250
255,000	2,250

(ii) Offer B – in respect of a sale of the company's trade and assets

Tutor's top tips

The first part of this requirement asks for post-tax proceeds. You are given proceeds in the question so set up a table starting with this and slot in the tax on the various disposals as you calculate it.

You need to consider the following:

1. *Tax on any gain from the Oribi building*
2. *Tax on any balancing adjustments in capital allowances in respect of the machinery (you're told to ignore any gains or losses on this in your calculation)*
3. *Tax saved in respect of any loss on the sale of the Atuel building.*

Post-tax proceeds

	£
Sale proceeds	
Trade and assets	695,000
Tax liability/credit in respect of:	
Chargeable gain on the Oribi building (£107,000 (W1) × 25%)	(26,750)
Plant and machinery balancing charge (£12,100 × 25%)	(3,025)
Allowable loss on the Atuel building (£110,000 (W2) × 25%)	27,500
Post-tax proceeds	692,725

Workings

(W1) Sale of the Oribi building

	£
Proceeds	410,000
Less: Cost (£320,000 – £17,000)	(303,000)
Chargeable gain	107,000

Tutorial note

There is no indexation allowance in respect of the Oribi building since it was purchased after December 2017.

(W2) Sale of the Atuel building

	£
Proceeds	230,000
Less: Cost (original cost to Sautso Ltd)	(340,000)
Allowable loss	(110,000)

Tutor's top tips

Next you are asked to discuss the chargeable gains treatment of the machinery.

You are told that most of the items are worth less than their original cost, which would mean they would give rise to a capital loss. Consider what the treatment of this should be given that capital allowances have been claimed on the machinery.

There are also a small number of items worth more than their cost, so ensure you also explain the treatment of those.

You are told that the machinery is movable. Think about what this means in terms of eligibility for rollover relief.

In the final part of the requirement you need to explain which companies Colca Ltd can transfer capital losses to. This is basically asking you to discuss which companies are in a chargeable gains group with Colca Ltd. Make sure you discuss the rules that determine which companies should be included.

Chargeable gains and allowable capital losses on the sale of the machinery

- The items of machinery will not be exempt under the wasting chattels rule because they qualify for capital allowances.
- However, any item where both the cost and the proceeds are less than £6,000 will be exempt.
- In respect of the chargeable items of machinery (where the cost or the proceeds is at least £6,000):
  - An item sold at a loss will not result in an allowable capital loss. This is because Colca Ltd will have received capital allowances equal to the fall in value of the item.
  - An item sold at a profit will result in a chargeable gain. Rollover relief will not be available because the items are movable as opposed to fixed.

Transfer of capital losses to group members

- The whole or part of any capital loss can be transferred to Grand Ltd, Sautso Ltd and any other member of the Grand Ltd capital gains group.
- This group consists of Grand Ltd, its directly held 75% subsidiaries, their directly held 75% subsidiaries and so on
- Where each company is an effective 51% subsidiary of Grand Ltd.

(iii) Offer B – value added tax (VAT)

Tutor's top tips

In part (iii) you are asked to discuss VAT on the transfer of trade and assets. This is testing the transfer of a going concern (TOGC) rules. Ensure you list out the conditions for this treatment in order to score some easy marks.

Note that there are land and buildings included in the transfer. Remember that if they would be taxable at the point of the transfer then the purchaser would need to opt to tax them. Think about the situations in which a building may be taxable at the point of transfer.

Colca Ltd should not charge VAT on the sale of its business if the sale is a transfer of a going concern (TOGC). This requires all of the following conditions to be satisfied:

– the business of Colca Ltd is transferred as a going concern
– the purchaser will use the assets to carry on the same kind of business as Colca Ltd
– there is no significant break in trading
– the purchaser is VAT registered or will become registrable as a result of the purchase.

However, even where the sale of the business qualifies as a TOGC, VAT must still be charged on the sale of any building included as part of the sale if either:

– an option to tax has been made in respect of the building, or
– the building is a commercial building which is less than three years old.

No option to tax has been made in respect of either of the buildings to be sold by Colca Ltd.

However, the Atuel building is a commercial building which will be less than three years old on 1 December 2024, such that the sale of this building will be a standard-rated supply and VAT must be charged unless the purchaser opts to tax the building.

(b) **MEETING NOTES**

Date: 1 September 2024

Subject: Working in Manchester – Monina's financial position

Tutor's top tips

Monina wants to know how much better or worse off she will be compared to her current position. This means that you need to think about the additional net cash (or deficit) after taking into account any tax charges and expenses.

The information in the question states that Monina earns £60,000 per year, so it is clear that any extra taxable employment income will be subject to 40% income tax and 2% NICs.

Living in the company flat

The calculations set out below are based on the information currently available.

	£
Additional salary	15,000
Less: Income tax (£15,000 × 40%)	(6,000)
Class 1 employee's NICs (£15,000 × 2%)	(300)
Petrol and depreciation (£1,400 + £1,500) (Note 1)	(2,900)
Additional salary after income tax, NICs and motoring expenses	5,800
Less: Income tax on benefit in respect of the use of the flat (£17,150 (W) × 40%)	(6,860)
Contribution towards the flat to be made by Monina (£200 × 12)	(2,400)
Monina would be worse off by	(3,460)
Additional salary required for Monina not to be out of pocket (£3,460 ÷ 58%)	5,966

Tutor's top tips

Remember to state the additional salary needed, and remember that this will also be received net of 40% income tax and 2% NICs, so needs to be grossed up by 100/58 (or divided by 58%).

If Monina's additional salary and benefits increased her adjusted net income to more than £100,000 she would start to lose her personal allowance but that is not the case here.

Not living in the company flat

	£
Additional salary after income tax, NICs and motor expenses (as above)	5,800
Plus: Mileage allowance (9,200 × 50p)	4,600
Less: Income tax and NICs on mileage allowance (£4,600 × 42%) (Note 2)	(1,932)
Rent (£325 × 12) (Note 3)	(3,900)
Monina would be better off by	4,568

Notes

1 The depreciation is not an immediate cost but will increase the funds needed by Monina to purchase her next car.

Monina will not be able to claim a tax deduction for these costs as they relate to travelling to and from work and not to the performance of her duties.

2 The mileage allowance would be subject to tax and national insurance contributions as Monina would be travelling to and from work and not in the performance of her duties.

Manchester will not be a temporary workplace for Monina because she expects to work there for more than two years.

Tutorial note

The mileage allowance is not exempt and the approved mileage allowance of 45p per mile is irrelevant here, as the travel from home to work is private mileage, not a business trip.

If Monina had been sent to Manchester for less than two years, then the travel would represent travel from home to a temporary workplace, and would qualify as a business trip.

In this case, only the excess allowance of 5p per mile (50p – 45p) would be taxable, rather than all of it.

3 Monina's aunt will not be subject to income tax on the rent.

This is because it will be in respect of a (presumably) furnished room in her house and the rent does not exceed £7,500 per year.

Tutor's top tips

The question specifically asks for an explanation of the tax treatment of the mileage allowance and the rent paid to Monina's aunt, so make sure that you provide this.

Further information required

- The cost of the furniture provided in the flat – there will be an annual taxable benefit equal to 20% of the cost.
- Any running costs (utilities and maintenance etc.) in respect of the flat borne by Grand Ltd – there will be a taxable benefit equal to the costs incurred.
- Any capital improvements made to the property before the start of the tax year for which the benefit is being calculated.

Working: Taxable benefit in respect of the use of the flat

	£
Annual value	9,605
Additional benefit (£517,000 – £75,000) × 2.25% (Note)	9,945
	19,550
Contribution to be made by Monina (£200 × 12)	(2,400)
Accommodation benefit	17,150

Note: The cost of £517,000 will be increased by any capital improvements made to the property before the start of the tax year for which the benefit is being calculated.

Tutorial note

The current value of the property (when Monina moves in) is not relevant in this case, as the property has been owned by the employer for less than six years.

(c) Tax evasion and tax avoidance

Tutor's top tips

The final requirement offers five marks on ethical issues, specifically the quite topical area of tax evasion v avoidance. You are asked firstly to distinguish between tax evasion and avoidance which should present some easy marks.

You then need to state the purpose of the general anti-abuse rule and explain why it is likely to apply to the plan in question. Make sure you relate this back to the facts in the question to score well.

Tax evasion, tax avoidance, and the purpose of the general anti-abuse rule (GAAR)

Tax evasion is unlawful. It involves the provision of false information or the withholding of information in order to evade tax. Tax avoidance involves the use of legal methods in order to reduce the amount of tax payable.

The GAAR is intended to counteract tax advantages, obtained via what would otherwise be legal tax avoidance methods, where the arrangements can be considered to be abusive.

Why the GAAR is likely to apply to the plan drawn up by Bryce and Monina

– the tax advantage obtained would be a tax deduction in excess of the cost of the machinery

– the tax arrangements would be the formation of the subsidiary and the series of leasing contracts which are intended to obtain the tax advantage

– the arrangements are likely to be regarded as abusive because they appear to have been designed to give rise to additional tax deductions rather than for genuine commercial reasons.

Examiner's report

This question required advice on the corporation tax consequences of disposing of a wholly-owned subsidiary company by either selling all of the shares, or, alternatively, selling the trade and assets, together with the value added tax (VAT) implications if the sale of trade and assets route is chosen. There was also an ethics requirement to discuss tax evasion, tax avoidance and the purpose of the general anti-abuse rule (GAAR), and its application to a proposed plan to claim extensive capital allowances. The sale of shares versus sale of trade and assets decision is one which is regularly tested, so a well-prepared candidate should have been familiar with the main issues which they needed to discuss. Additionally, there are significant differences, practically and commercially, between selling shares in a company, and selling its trade and assets, which are reflected in the approach taken for tax purposes. If candidates are not familiar with a scenario, they should take time to think about the reality of the situation, which will often give them pointers as to the tax treatment. More generally, many candidates need to spend more time ensuring they are familiar with key areas relating to chargeable gains for companies – the substantial shareholding exemption (SSE), calculation of indexation, conditions for rollover relief and chattel exemptions in particular.

The use of subheadings, taken from the issues in the manager's email, provides a useful structure in this type of question, which all candidates should consider adopting.

The first part of the question, which was worth 8 marks, required candidates to explain whether or not tax relief would be available for a loss on the sale of the shares, the implications of the subsidiary leaving the group with a building which had recently been transferred to it by another group member, and a calculation of the after-tax proceeds. It was disappointing to see that a significant number of candidates did not mention that the SSE applied in this case, and so wasted time describing reliefs for the capital loss which were not relevant. Awareness of SSE, and when it applies is fundamental at ATX. In any question concerning a corporate disposal of shares, the candidate's first thought should be to consider the application of SSE. There will be marks for considering this, and for demonstrating knowledge of the conditions, which will allow a decision to be made as to whether or not it applies. A few candidates did consider it, but concluded that it did not, or need not, apply where there is a loss, so, again wasted time with unnecessary calculations and discussion of reliefs.

The majority of candidates recognised that the company leaving the group with an asset that had been transferred to it within the last three years would give rise to a degrouping charge (and cited the six-year time limit), but only very few also recognised that there would also be stamp duty land tax implications. A small minority of candidates confused the implications of a share sale with those of a trade and asset sale, and so included calculations of the gains/losses on the individual assets in addition to, or instead of, the shares. This confusion then continued into the second part of the question, meaning that relatively few marks were available. As stated above, a few moments spent thinking about the reality of the different scenarios should have enabled a candidate to at least set off in the right direction.

The second part of the question concerned the disposal of the trade and assets of the company, as an alternative to the sale of shares. This part was worth 10 marks *(11 marks in the original question)* and, on the whole, was done better than the sale of shares, with the majority of candidates calculating a correct, or nearly correct, gain/loss on the two buildings, and, pleasingly, identifying the balancing charge on the machinery. The most common errors in this part were to treat the whole business as a single asset, and calculate just a single gain/loss by reference to the total costs and proceeds. It was also pleasing to see that most candidates did try and address all parts of this requirement, but in a significant number of cases were let down by their lack of detailed knowledge in relation to capital gains tax exemptions and reliefs, in this case the chattels exemptions (wasting chattels and £6,000 rule), and the precise requirements for rollover relief (movable plant and machinery doesn't qualify).

The third part of the question concerned charging VAT on the sale of the building and machinery if the company decides to sell the trade and assets. This was worth 7 marks. Most candidates picked up a few marks here in relation to the buildings, and consideration of their age and the option to tax. However, very few picked up a key issue, embedded in the facts of this scenario, that transferring the trade and assets would constitute the transfer of a going concern, such that the transaction would be outside the scope of VAT, apart from, potentially, the buildings. Candidates at ATX should not rely on always been prompted in relation to the issues being tested, with a direct reference to the issue. They are encouraged to spend a little time thinking about the reality of the situation, so as to be able to identify the aspect(s) of a tax which may be relevant.

Requirement (b) has been added from another past exam question and the relevant section of that examiner's report is included below:

Part (b) concerned the implications of a change to an employee's location of work. On the whole this part of the question was done reasonably well. However, in order to score a high mark for this part it was necessary to focus on the client's financial position and calculate how much better or worse off she was going to be as a result of the change. This required candidates to think in terms of income and costs (with tax as a cost) and to recognise that costs that are not tax deductible are still costs and are therefore still relevant. This aspect of the question was not handled particularly well.

The final part of the question required candidates to distinguish between tax evasion and tax avoidance, to state the purpose of the general anti-abuse rule (GAAR), and to explain its application to the plan proposed by the client. This was clearly an area candidates were prepared for, and was generally done very well, with most candidates scoring at least four of the five available marks. A few candidates produced an exceptionally long answer, and, while they probably scored full marks, these could also have been obtained with a much more concise answer, leaving more time for other parts of the exam. It may be tempting to write at length on a topic with which a candidate is very familiar, and confident, but attention should always be paid to the maximum number of marks available.

Overall, candidates who prepared satisfactory answers to this question:

- appeared to have practised similar questions
- read the requirements very carefully
- applied their knowledge well to the scenario
- produced concise explanations and clearly laid out computations.

ACCA marking scheme

				Marks
(a)	(i)	Offer A		
		Calculation of post-tax proceeds		1.0
		Loss on the sale of the shares		3.0
		Leaving the Grand Ltd group		
		Degrouping charge		2.5
		Stamp duty land tax		3.5
				10.0
			Maximum	8.0
	(ii)	Offer B		
		Calculation of post-tax proceeds		1.5
		Oribi building chargeable gain		1.0
		Plant and machinery balancing charge		1.0
		Atuel building allowable loss		1.5
		Plant and machinery chargeable gains/allowable losses		4.0
		Capital gains group		2.0
				11.0
			Maximum	10.0
	(iii)	Transfer of a going concern		4.0
		Rules in relation to buildings		4.0
				8.0
			Maximum	7.0
(b)	Salary less tax, national insurance contributions and motoring expenses			2.0
	Living in the company flat			
		Tax on the benefit		2.0
		Contribution		0.5
		Additional salary required		1.0
	Further information required			2.0
	Staying with aunt in Manchester			
		Calculations		1.5
		Mileage allowance		1.5
		Rent paid to aunt		1.5
				12.0
			Maximum	10.0
(c)	Tax evasion, tax avoidance and the purpose of the GAAR			4.0
	Application to plan			3.0
				7.0
			Maximum	5.0
	Professional skills marks (see below)		**Maximum**	10.0
Total				**50.0**

Professional skills marks

Communication

- General format and structure of memorandum and meeting notes (e.g. use of headings/sub-headings to make memorandum easy to refer to).
- Style, language and clarity (tone of memorandum and meeting notes, presentation of calculations, appropriate use of the tools, easy to follow and more than a negligible amount of content).
- Effectiveness of communication (answer is relevant, specific rather than general and focused to the requirement).
- Adherence to specific instructions made in the scenario (e.g. not including calculations of the implications of Colca Ltd leaving the Grand Ltd group whilst still owning the Atuel building in part (a)(i)).

Analysis and evaluation

- Analysis of the information to determine the tax treatment of the capital loss arising on the Colca Ltd shares in part (a)(i).
- Use of the information to determine appropriate calculations to perform to determine the after-tax proceeds of the sale of the Colca Ltd shares in part (a)(i).
- Use of the information to determine appropriate calculations to perform to determine the after-tax proceeds of the sale of the Colca Ltd trade and assets in part (a)(ii).
- Use of the information to determine appropriate calculations to perform to arrive at the additional salary required for Monina in part (b).
- Demonstration of ability to consider all taxes relevant to part (b), i.e. income tax and national insurance contributions.

Scepticism

- Identification of further information required with regards to Monina's employment packages in part (b).
- Critical assessment of the tax plan in part (c).

Commercial acumen

- Demonstration of an understanding of the interaction of the capital allowances rules with chargeable gains rules in part (a)(ii).
- Demonstration of an understanding of the impact of transfer of going concern rules for VAT in part (a)(iii).

19 PLAD LTD AND QUIL LTD (ADAPTED) *Walk in the footsteps of a top tutor*

Key answer tips

This question covers loss relief including group relief, capital allowances, VAT groups, ethics and capital taxes.

Each of the four requirements are independent of one another so you could attempt them in any order. The ethics requirement is one where some easy marks could be earned so it may be a good idea to start with that one first.

The sub requirements in part (a) follow on from one another so you need to ensure you finish the first before moving on to the second. Time management is important here to make sure you have enough time to attempt all parts. If you need to, make up an answer for the first requirement so you can then do the second which has some easier marks in!

Part (d) looks at inheritance tax – in particular the situation that would give rise to the maximum inheritance tax liability. You will have to make some assumptions here so ensure you state your assumptions. Don't forget the extra part about gift holdover relief for capital gains tax!

The highlighted words in the written sections are key phrases that markers are looking for.

(a) Group relief

Tutor's top tips

You may find the calculation in this part of the question a little bit tricky. You can still score some easy marks by explaining the basis of what you are trying to do.

Remember that the liability in respect of the UK trading profit will not receive any DTR so this profit should be covered in full. For the overseas income the overseas tax rate is clearly lower than in the UK, so DTR will be for the overseas tax. You don't want to waste the DTR so you need an amount of group relief that will bring profits down to a level where the tax will equal that paid overseas.

(i) Maximum group relief

- The whole of Plad Ltd's UK trading profit of £58,000 should be covered by group relief. However, in order not to waste double tax relief (DTR), an amount of Plad Ltd's Chekkan profits should remain subject to corporation tax.
- The amount of Chekkan profits which should remain subject to corporation tax is £151,200 (£270,000 × 14%/25%), being the amount on which the UK corporation tax (£151,200 × 25% = £37,800) equals the whole of the Chekkan tax paid by Plad Ltd (£270,000 × 14% = £37,800).

- In this situation, the Chekkan tax suffered will be fully relieved as DTR (being the lower of the UK tax on the Chekkan income and the Chekkan tax suffered).
- Accordingly, the group relief should be the UK profits of £58,000 plus the balance of the Chekkan profits of £118,800 (£270,000 – £151,200), i.e. £176,800. With group relief of this amount, Plad Ltd's UK corporation tax liability will be fully covered by DTR, such that there will be no UK corporation tax payable.

Tutorial note

The following calculation demonstrates that where the group relief is £176,800, as calculated above, none of the DTR will be wasted and the corporation tax liability will be zero.

	£	£
Taxable total profits before group relief		328,000
Group relief		(176,800)
Taxable total profits		151,200
Corporation tax at 25%		37,800
Double tax relief – the lower of:		
UK tax on overseas profits (£151,200 × 25%)	37,800	
Overseas tax (£270,000 × 14%)	37,800	
		(37,800)
Corporation tax liability		0

Tutorial note

Whether Quil Ltd is owned by Plad Ltd or by Claire, there will be two associated companies and the limits for determining the rate of corporation tax will be divided by two. This means that the upper limit will be £125,000 (£250,000/2), and therefore corporation tax on Plad's profits will be at 25%.

However, you were told in the question to assume a corporation tax rate of 25%, so there is no need for you to calculate the limits here.

(ii) Corporation tax liabilities

Tutor's top tips

You have two companies to calculate corporation tax for in this requirement, assuming losses are used as soon as possible. Quil Ltd is the loss-making company so it would be useful to calculate its results first so you can see what the losses are. Remember that there are easy marks to be obtained for a simple capital allowances calculation.

Remember to reduce the loss by your group relief claim from part (i), it doesn't matter if this is wrong as you will get follow through marks!

The email from your manager mentions that the loss should be used as soon as possible, this means avoid carrying it forward where you can. Bear this in mind when you are using the loss.

Plad Ltd

Year ending 31 March 2025

The corporation tax liability of Plad Ltd for the first year will be £Nil, as explained above.

Year ending 31 March 2026

	£
Taxable total profit pre-group relief	328,000
Less: Group relief (W3)	(29,358)
Taxable total profit	298,642
Corporation tax at 25%	74,661
Less: DTR	
The lower of:	
UK tax on the Chekkan profits of £67,500 (£270,000 × 25%)	
Chekkan tax of £37,800	(37,800)
Corporation tax liability	36,861

Quil Ltd

	Year ending 31 March	
	2025	**2026**
	£	£
Trading profit/(loss) before capital allowances	(120,000)	162,000
Capital allowances (W1)	(230,600)	(25,308)
Structures and buildings allowances (W2)	(1,650)	(6,600)
Trading loss	(352,250)	
Trading profit	0	130,092
Chargeable gain	–	16,000
	0	146,092
Loss brought forward (W3)	–	(146,092)
Taxable total profit	0	0
Corporation tax liability	0	0

(iii) Conclusion

Tutor's top tips

Here you just need to summarise your earlier findings. There are easy marks here so don't miss out on them!

Bring in your loss figures from the earlier parts of the question and don't forget to quantify the tax benefit.

- Where the two companies are in a group relief group (as opposed to being owned personally by Claire) trading losses of £206,158 (£176,800 + £29,358) would be relieved by group relief in the two-year period rather than being carried forward.
- At the least, this is advantageous from the point of view of cash flow, as it delays total tax payments of £51,540 (£206,158 × 25%).
- In addition, if group relief were not available, such that Quil Ltd had to carry forward unused losses, there is no certainty that the losses would ever be relieved.

Tutorial note

Quil Ltd is required to use its losses brought forward against its own total profits before it can surrender losses to Plad Ltd as group relief.

Workings

(W1) Capital allowances

	Main pool	Special rate pool	Allowances
	£	£	£
Year ending 31 March 2025			
Additions qualifying for AIA	160,000	230,000	
AIA	–	(200,000)	200,000
	160,000	30,000	
WDA at 18%/6%	(28,800)	(1,800)	30,600
			230,600
TWDV carried forward	131,200	28,200	
Year ending 31 March 2026			
WDA at 18%/6%	(23,616)	(1,692)	25,308
TWDV carried forward	107,584	26,508	

(W2) Structures and buildings allowances

Year ending 31 March 2025

(£600,000 – £230,000 – £150,000) = £220,000 × 3% × 3/12 = £1,650

Year ending 31 March 2026

£220,000 × 3% = £6,600

(W3) Quil Ltd – loss memorandum

	Year ending 31 March	
	2025	**2026**
	£	£
Trading loss brought forward	0	175,450
Trading loss for the current year	352,250	
Offset against total profits of Quil Ltd	0	(146,092)
Surrender to Plad Ltd	(176,800)	(29,358)
Trading loss carried forward	175,450	0

(b) Group registration for value added tax (VAT) purposes

Tutor's top tips

When you read the schedule from Claire you will see that she already knows some of the implications of being in a VAT group. When you are drafting your answer ensure you do not cover any of these as you will not score any marks for that.

You need to focus on any aspects that Claire is not aware of.

Two companies can register as a group for the purposes of VAT provided they are established in the UK and one controls the other or they are both controlled by the same person. Accordingly, Plad Ltd and Quil Ltd will be able to register as a group regardless of whether Plad Ltd owns Quil Ltd or they are both owned personally by Claire.

Claire should be aware that the annual accounting scheme will not be available if the two companies are registered as a group.

Tutorial note

If Claire was a sole trader then she would be able to join the VAT group as well, as she is the controller of a group of companies.

(c) Plad Ltd – unreported chargeable gain

Tutor's top tips

There is always an ethics requirement in Section A for five marks and they can often be the easiest marks to achieve, so ensure you have left adequate time for this.

Ensure you cover both the implications for Plad Ltd and your firm, as requested in the email from your manager. They also noted that you shouldn't address any money laundering requirements or penalties so make sure you don't waste time discussing these.

Plad Ltd

- The company has a responsibility to report this omission to HM Revenue and Customs (HMRC) and to pay the outstanding corporation tax. It will be committing tax evasion, a criminal offence, if it fails to do so.
- HMRC will charge Plad Ltd interest on any tax which becomes payable.

Our firm

- We should investigate how this error arose and consider whether or not there are likely to be further errors.

- We will not retain a client which is engaged in deliberate tax evasion, as this poses a threat to the fundamental principles of integrity and professional behaviour. Accordingly, we could not continue to act for Plad Ltd unless the chargeable gain is disclosed to HMRC.
- If we were to cease to act for Plad Ltd, we would notify HMRC, although we would not provide them with any reason for our action.

(d) Laura – gift of shares in Vyc Ltd

Circumstances resulting in the maximum inheritance tax (IHT) liability

The maximum IHT liability will occur where both condition (i) and condition (ii), set out below, are satisfied.

(i) Laura dies by 30 September 2026, i.e. within seven years of 1 October 2019, the date on which she made the cash gift to her daughter.

Once seven years have elapsed, the gift on 1 October 2019 will no longer be accumulated in determining the nil rate band available in respect of the gift of the shares in Vyc Ltd.

Tutorial note

If Laura dies within seven years of 1 October 2019, i.e. by 30 September 2026, she will have died within three years of the gift of the shares to Edward. Accordingly, taper relief will not be available.

(ii) At the time of Laura's death, business property relief (BPR) IS NOT available.

The gift of the shares in Vyc Ltd will qualify for 100% BPR at the time of the gift because:

– Vyc Ltd is an unquoted trading company, such that the shares are relevant business property, and

– Laura has owned the shares for at least two years.

However, BPR will not be available on Laura's death if:

– the shares are no longer qualifying business property, or

– Edward has disposed of the shares prior to Laura's death, unless:

  – Edward has replaced the shares with qualifying business property, or

  – Edward has died before Laura, whilst still owning the shares (or qualifying replacement business property).

Tutorial note

The shares in Vyc Ltd are UK assets because Vyc Ltd is a UK registered company. Accordingly, a gift of the shares will be subject to UK inheritance tax regardless of Laura's domicile status.

Maximum possible IHT liability

	£	£
Transfer of value (W)		340,000
Annual exemptions:		
2024/25		(3,000)
2023/24		(3,000)
		334,000
Nil rate band	325,000	
Less: Chargeable transfer in the previous seven years	(280,000)	
		(45,000)
Taxable amount		289,000
IHT payable (£289,000 × 40%)		115,600

Working

Transfer of value by reference to related property

	£
Value of shares held prior to the gift: (35,000 × £19 (54% (35% + 19%))	665,000
Value of shares held after the gift: (25,000 × £13 (44% (25% + 19%))	(325,000)
	340,000

Assumption: The transfer of value has been calculated by reference to related property on the assumption that the fall in value would be a lower figure if related property were ignored.

Tutorial notes

1 *The value of Laura's shares is determined by reference to the shares held by her and her husband under the related property rules.*

2 *Candidates who prepared calculations both with and without reference to related property to determine which resulted in the higher figure (rather than stating an assumption) received equal credit.*

Capital gains tax (CGT)

Vyc Ltd is an unquoted trading company, such that shares in the company qualify for CGT gift holdover relief. However, for the relief to be available, it is necessary for Edward, the recipient of the gift, to be resident in the UK in the tax year in which the gift is made.

Examiner's report

The first part of the question asked candidates to explain, with supporting calculations, the maximum amount of group relief which could be transferred between two group companies, whilst preserving double tax relief in the recipient company. A number of candidates were able to produce the calculations but did not offer any explanation, thereby not achieving full marks. As previously mentioned, future candidates should focus on the 'command' words in the requirement to ensure they are answering all parts of the requirement.

Note that the next section of the question has been amended since it was originally set, to test structures and buildings allowances.

The next element in this part of the question required candidates to calculate the corporation tax liabilities of two group companies assuming the available trading loss was used as soon as possible. Most candidates answered well in respect of the capital allowances part of this question but performed less well at group relieving the loss, where many candidates appeared to lack a clear understanding of the technical rules. To succeed in the ATX-UK exam, both a detailed knowledge of the technical areas of the syllabus is required as well as the ability to apply that knowledge to a given scenario.

Many candidates were able to conclude correctly on the advantage of a particular group holding structure.

The second part of the question required candidates to advise on matters the client should be aware of in relation to group registration for VAT purposes. The client was already aware of certain issues stated in the question but needed advice on additional issues. A large number of candidates simply repeated the issues already stated in the question and were unable to discuss any additional matters, which was not an effective use of time and earned no marks.

The third part of the question concerned the ethical issues arising from an unreported chargeable gain. It was pleasing to see most candidates answering well on this issue. However, the requirement specifically asked candidates not to address money laundering or penalties and yet many candidates went on to discuss these matters, which again, was not an effective use of their valuable time and earned them no marks. Once again, these candidates would have benefitted from spending time ensuring they fully understood the requirement and planning their answer, before beginning to write.

The final section of the examiner's report relates to part of a past exam question which has been added to this question since it was originally written:

The final part of the question concerned a proposed gift of shares from the client to her son and the requirement was for an explanation of the circumstances resulting in the maximum amount of inheritance tax payable and a calculation of this amount. The two key circumstances affecting the possible inheritance tax payable were a prior gift in the last seven years and the availability of business property relief. Not all candidates were able to see the link between a prior gift in the last seven years using up nil rate band for this potential gift and missed this point completely. Most candidates recognised the relevance of business property relief but failed to recognise that this relief could be unavailable if the donee did not own the shares at the date of the donor's death.

Candidates were generally able to score marks for their calculation of inheritance tax, although they were not all clear on the rules for related property share valuations.

An extra requirement in this part of the question concerned the availability of gift holdover relief for capital gains tax purposes on the gift of the shares. Although at first it may have appeared that gift holdover relief would be available and many candidates discussed this, most candidates missed the point that the donee would need to be resident in the UK in the tax year in which the gift is made. Again this required knowledge of a detailed tax rule, applied to the circumstances of the question. Candidates with only a limited knowledge of the tax rules are left exposed by the detailed question scenarios.

ACCA marking scheme			
			Marks
(a)	Tax-efficient group relief		5.0
	Plad Ltd corporation tax liabilities		
	Year ending 31 March 2025		1.0
	Year ending 31 March 2026		3.5
	Quil Ltd corporation tax liabilities		
	Capital allowances		4.0
	Structures and buildings allowances		1.5
	Two years ending 31 March 2026		3.5
	Conclusion		2.0
			20.5
		Maximum	18.0
(b)	Conditions for group registration		2.0
	Annual accounting scheme		1.0
			3.0
(c)	Plad Ltd		2.5
	Our firm		4.0
			6.5
		Maximum	5.0
(d)	Laura's death		2.0
	Ownership of shares		5.0
	Calculation		
	Fall in value		3.5
	Inheritance tax liability		2.5
	Capital gains tax		2.0
			15.0
		Maximum	14.0
	Professional skills marks (see below)	**Maximum**	10.0
Total			**50.0**

Professional skills marks

Communication

- General format and structure of notes (e.g. use of headings/sub-headings to make notes easy to refer to).
- Style, language and clarity (tone of notes, presentation of calculations, appropriate use of the tools, easy to follow and more than a negligible amount of content).

- Effectiveness of communication (answer is relevant, specific rather than general and focused to the requirement).
- Adherence to specific instructions made in the scenario (e.g. not addressing money laundering or penalties in part (c)).

Analysis and evaluation

- Analysis of the information to determine the amount of group relief needed to avoid wasting double tax relief in part (a)(i).
- Use of the information to determine appropriate calculations to perform to arrive at the corporation tax liabilities for the two years ended 31 March 2026 in part (a)(ii).
- Analysis of the information to determine which companies may form a VAT group in part (b).
- Use of the information to determine appropriate calculations to perform to arrive at the maximum possible IHT liability in part (d).
- Demonstration of ability to consider all taxes relevant to part (d), i.e. inheritance tax and capital gains tax.

Scepticism

- Critical assessment of the unreported chargeable gain in part (c).
- Recognition of the uncertainty in relation to the valuation of the Vyc Ltd shares in part (d).

Commercial acumen

- Identification of the benefits of the selected method/methods of loss relief in part (a)(ii).
- Recognition of how the inheritance tax rules apply to a real-life scenario in order to identify the worst-case scenario in part (d).

20 JEG LTD GROUP (ADAPTED) *Walk in the footsteps of a top tutor*

Key answer tips

This question covers ethics for a new client, company gains, rollover relief, overseas aspects of corporation tax, VAT and employment income.

Part (a) is a typical ethics requirement looking at both the information required before taking on a new client and the actions to be taken. If you have revised this area you should be able to score well here.

Rollover relief is the focus of part (b). There are various acquisitions within the group, so you need to decide which (if any) qualify for rollover relief and how it will work.

Part (c) looks at overseas corporation tax issues for two companies, the first of which is dealing with transfer pricing. Decide if the rules will apply and, if so, what adjustment would be needed. The second company has an overseas permanent establishment. You need to explain the tax treatment of this, as well as the advantages and disadvantages of making an election to exempt it from UK tax.

Part (d) is all about VAT. The first part looks at eligibility to join a VAT group, and also potential disadvantages of joining a VAT group. Try to apply the eligibility criteria and disadvantages to the scenario as much as possible and don't just list them out. The second part of this requirement asks for an explanation of the VAT treatment of some imports. This should be fairly straightforward provided you have learnt the overseas VAT rules.

The final part of the question looks at the cash effect of an employment package for the managing director. You are told to prepare calculations and summarise your findings, so don't forget to do the summary otherwise you will lose easy marks.

The highlighted words in the written sections are key phrases that markers are looking for in your memorandum.

Tutor's top tips

It is important to make sure you are picking up professional skills marks as you go through the question, as well as the technical marks. Ensure your answer is in the format requested by the requirement, and that you follow any specific instructions given.

Memorandum

For	The files
Client	Jeg Ltd group
Subject	Group matters
Prepared by	Tax senior
Date	1 September 2024

(a) Becoming tax advisers to the Jeg Ltd group of companies

Tutor's top tips

The ethical requirement in the exam will always be worth five marks, so try to make five separate points in order to score a mark for each.

Information required:

– Proof of incorporation and primary business address and registered office of each company in the group.

– The group structure, directors and shareholders of the companies.

– The identities of those persons instructing the firm on behalf of the companies and those persons who are authorised to do so.

Actions to take:

– We must give consideration to the fundamental principles of professional ethics as set out in ACCA's *Professional Code of Ethics and Conduct*. This requires us to consider whether becoming tax advisers to the Jeg Ltd group would create any threats to compliance with these principles.

  In order to comply with the principle of professional competence and due care, we have an obligation to ensure that our clients receive competent, professional advice. As we have no experience of UK resident companies trading through permanent establishments situated overseas, we must obtain a thorough understanding of the relevant technical issues before we provide advice on these matters to the Jeg Ltd group of companies.

– We must assure ourselves that the companies are not involved in any form of money laundering.

– We should obtain permission to contact the group's existing tax advisers in order to ensure that there is nothing in the past which would preclude us from accepting the appointment on ethical grounds.

(b) Relieving the chargeable gain on the sale of Kod Ltd's business premises

Availability of rollover relief

All the trades carried on by members of a group of companies are treated as one trade. This means that it is possible to roll over a chargeable gain on the disposal of a business asset by one trading member of a group against the acquisition of a replacement business asset by another trading member of the group.

– For rollover relief to be available:

  – qualifying assets, i.e. land and buildings and/or fixed plant and machinery, must be purchased

  – in the four-year period commencing 1 July 2023 (one year prior to the sale of the premises)

  – by Kod Ltd or any company which was a member of the Jeg Ltd capital gains group at the time the replacement asset was purchased; and

  – the replacement assets must be either owned by a UK resident company for use in its trade or owned by a non-UK resident company and used to carry on a trade in the UK.

Tutorial note

For an asset to be eligible for rollover relief it must be used in a UK trade.

The Jeg Ltd capital gains group

– The Jeg Ltd capital gains group comprises Jeg Ltd and all of its subsidiaries, Kod Ltd, Lis Co and Mot Ltd. This is because Jeg Ltd owns at least 75% of the ordinary share capital of each of its subsidiaries.

Tutor's top tips

When explaining why companies are in certain groups it is best to quote the required percentage from the rule, rather than the actual percentage holding. i.e. 'Jeg Ltd owns at least 75%...' and not 'Jeg Ltd owns 100%....'

Review of assets acquired

- The vans purchased by Kod Ltd are not qualifying assets because they are moveable as opposed to being fixed.
- The items of machinery purchased by Jeg Ltd will, however, qualify for rollover relief because they are fixed.
- Although Lis Co is a member of the Jeg Ltd capital gains group, the building, which it purchased on 1 July 2024, is not a qualifying asset for the purposes of rollover relief. This is because Lis Co is not a UK resident company and the building is not being used to carry on a trade in the UK.

Operation of rollover relief

- If the items of machinery purchased by Jeg Ltd are the only qualifying assets purchased during the qualifying period, it will not be possible to roll over the whole of the chargeable gain on the sale of Kod Ltd's business premises. The amount of proceeds not invested in qualifying assets of £195,000 (£485,000 – £290,000) will be charged to corporation tax.
- The remainder of the chargeable gain on the sale of the business premises of £52,000 (£247,000 – £195,000) could be deferred until the earliest of the following events in relation to the machinery purchased by Jeg Ltd:
  - the sale of the machinery
  - the machinery no longer being used for the purposes of the trade
  - ten years after the date of purchase of the machinery (i.e. 31 January 2034).

If non-depreciating assets are purchased before the crystallisation of the deferred gain, the deferred gain need not be charged and can instead be rolled over against the base cost of the non-depreciating assets.

Tutorial note

Where a non-depreciating asset (e.g. a freehold building) is bought before the deferred gain crystallises, it is possible to defer the gain against the base cost of the non-depreciating asset. This can be done even if the purchase is made outside the normal reinvestment window.

(c) Taxation of profits generated overseas

Lis Co

– If components were sold by Lis Co to Jeg Ltd at an inflated price, Jeg Ltd would have lower profits and would therefore have a lower corporation tax liability than it would have done if it had purchased the components from an unrelated company. It would therefore have gained a tax advantage in the UK as a result of the artificial price.

– A transfer pricing adjustment would be required. This is because:

  – a UK tax advantage would arise on

  – a transaction between Jeg Ltd and a company which it controls, and

  – Lis Co is resident in a non-qualifying territory, i.e. a territory which does not have a double tax agreement with the UK which contains a non-discrimination article.

  Therefore, the transfer pricing regime applies despite Jeg Ltd being a small company.

– The trading profit of Jeg Ltd must be increased by the excess of the inflated price over the arm's length price. The higher profit would therefore increase Jeg Ltd's corporation tax payable.

Tutorial note

Transfer pricing is normally just applicable to transactions involving a large company. However, where a company is resident in a territory that does not have a double tax treaty with the UK, transfer pricing rules will apply regardless of size.

Mot Ltd

Rate of corporation tax in the UK on the profits of the business

– UK resident companies are subject to UK corporation tax on their worldwide income.

– The business in Puran would be a permanent establishment (PE) of Mot Ltd as opposed to being a separate legal entity.

  Accordingly, the profits of the business will be subject to UK corporation tax as part of the profits of Mot Ltd.

– The rate of corporation tax suffered in the UK on the profits generated in Puran would be 12%, i.e. UK corporation tax at 25% less double tax relief of 13%.

Election to exempt the profits of the PE from UK tax

– The advantage of making such an election would be that the profits made in Puran would not be subject to UK corporation tax.

  This would save UK corporation tax at the rate of 12% as set out above.

– However, it should be recognised that it would no longer be possible to claim capital allowances in the UK in respect of assets purchased for use in the trade carried on in Puran.

- In addition, there would be no relief in the UK in the event of any losses being incurred in the trade in Puran in the future.

- Once made, the election is irrevocable and would apply to all future overseas PEs of Mot Ltd.

  Accordingly, there would be no relief in the UK for any losses incurred in any new overseas PEs operated by Mot Ltd.

- Although Mot Ltd is part of a group, the election will not affect any other UK companies within the Jeg Ltd group as each group company can choose whether to make the election.

(d) Value added tax (VAT)

Tutor's top tips

VAT groups are tested regularly in the ATX exam, so ensure you know the rules around who can join one as well as the advantages and disadvantages of doing so.

Group VAT registration

- A company can be a member of the Jeg Ltd group VAT registration if:

  (i) it is controlled by Jeg Ltd (i.e. Jeg Ltd owns more than 50% of the company's ordinary share capital); and

  (ii) it is established in the UK (e.g. its headquarters are in the UK) or it has a fixed establishment in the UK (e.g. it has a genuine trading presence in the UK).

  Accordingly, Kod Ltd could be included within a group VAT registration, whereas Mot Ltd could not unless it satisfies (ii) above.

- Possible disadvantages

  - The members of a group VAT registration are jointly and severally liable for the group's VAT liability.

    Accordingly, the inclusion in the group of Kod Ltd must be considered particularly carefully due to its financial problems.

  - It will be necessary to obtain and collate information from the subsidiary companies in order to prepare a single VAT return, which may cause administrative difficulties.

Purchase of components from Lis Co

- Jeg Ltd would be required to account for output VAT at the standard rate on the VAT return covering the date of importation of the components.

- Jeg Ltd would be able to reclaim the VAT as input tax on the same VAT return.

(e) Hale's financial position for the tax year 2024/25

Tutor's top tips

When looking at post-tax income you need to think about the cash in less cash out. Certain elements of Hale's employment package do not represent cash. They will have an impact on her tax liability, but won't add to the amount of cash she has to spend.

Cash income after tax

	£
Salary	87,800
Dividend income	18,300
Total cash income	106,100
Income tax liability (W)	48,326
Class 1 national insurance contributions (NIC) liability (W)	5,275
Total tax	53,601
Cash income after tax (£106,100 – £53,601)	52,499

Summary of the situation

Hale's annual personal expenditure exceeds her cash income after tax by £5,101 (£57,600 – £52,499).

The tax payable by Hale in the tax year 2024/25 will be over half (£53,601/ £106,100 = 50.52%) of the income she receives in cash. This is due to the significant non-cash benefits which she receives.

Tutorial note

Credit was also available to candidates who identified that, on the assumption that Hale will not receive further shares in Jeg Ltd, her tax bill for the tax year 2025/26 will be reduced by £3,520 ((£8,800 × 40%).

Working

Income tax and class 1 NIC liability

	£
Salary	87,800
Benefits	26,230
Shares in Jeg Ltd (£23,200 – £14,400)	8,800
Employment income	122,830
Dividend income	18,300
Total income	141,130
Less: Personal allowance	(0)
Taxable income	141,130
Employment income	
£37,700 × 20%	7,540
£85,130 (£122,830 – £37,700) × 40%	34,052
Dividend income	
£1,000 × 0%	0
£1,310 (£125,140 – £122,830 – £1,000) × 33.75%	442
£15,990 (£18,300 – £1,000 – £1,310) × 39.35%	6,292
Income tax liability	48,326
£37,700 (£50,270 – £12,570) × 12%	4,524
£37,530 (£87,800 – £50,270) × 2%	751
Class 1 NIC liability	5,275

Tutorial note

The shares in Jeg Ltd are not readily convertible assets, such that they will not result in a liability to class 1 NIC.

Examiner's report

Requirement (a)

This requirement concerned the information required, and the actions to be taken, before accepting a group of companies as a client.

This was a standard ethics topic, which frequently gets tested, and many candidates were able to score well on this part of the question.

Two main issues were identified in weaker answers:

- Candidates suggested information which would have been relevant for an individual or a sole trader client, but not for a company. Candidates must be clear in terms of the status of the client they are advising when thinking about any ethical issues which may be involved.

- There was a tendency for some candidates to write out all they knew about the ethical principles, without relating their knowledge to the facts of the question. Although consideration of any threats to compliance with the fundamental principles of professional ethics will often be an integral part of an ethics question, these should be considered in the context of the particular scenario and in the light of the relevant facts which have been given. On this occasion, the company did not have any other clients who were operating overseas through permanent establishments. In view of this, it would be particularly important to ensure that the firm had the necessary professional competence in order to take on such an assignment.

Requirement (b)

Part (b) of this question required an explanation of the availability of rollover relief, and its application in respect of a qualifying asset sold by one company within the capital gains group.

It is important for candidates to always check the 'command' word(s) being used in a question, and to ensure that they note – possibly by the use of highlighting or copying and pasting – where more than one activity is required.

There were two parts to this requirement. The first part concerned the availability of rollover relief, and the second involved discussion of the way in which it would operate. Both parts needed to be addressed; it is easy to overlook the second part when immersed in the task of providing an answer to the first, so candidates should get into the habit of going back and re-reading each question requirement to ensure that it has been fully addressed.

A good starting point in any question which relates to reliefs within groups is to identify, with reasons, the qualifying group members for the purpose of the relief(s) being considered. Even on occasions where this may seem quite obvious, it should not be taken for granted that a marker knows that a candidate is aware of the underlying rules. Identification of the relevant group can often provide straightforward marks and should always be stated.

When going on to consider rollover relief it is necessary to identify the qualifying business asset(s) which has been sold – this was given in this case – and the qualifying business asset(s) which has been acquired. There were two fundamental aspects one needed to establish here: the types of assets involved (land and buildings and fixed plant and machinery) and the required time period for reinvestment (up to one year before and three years after the date of disposal of the qualifying asset).

The first exhibit provides quite a lot of information in relation to each of the group companies, and their recently acquired capital assets. Highlighting may therefore assist in order to pull out the relevant information on each of them. Time should be taken to carefully read the specific details provided about each company and each asset, noting the significance of information such as the non-UK-resident status of one of the companies (Lis Co), whether the machinery acquired is fixed or moveable (Jeg Ltd, Kod Ltd), whether an asset is wholly used in a company's trade (Kod Ltd) etc. The dates of sale and acquisition are also of importance in this context. Time should be spent reviewing and assimilating all of this detail in order to ensure that its relevance is understood when thinking about the answer.

Candidates who considered the whole scenario and adopted a logical, well thought-out approach scored well here. Those who scored less well tended to restrict their answers to various general comments about rollover relief, without considering their relevance to this particular scenario, or taking the time to develop and expand in sufficient detail on the points being made.

In relation to the second part of this question, that which dealt with the application of rollover relief, two specific aspects needed to be considered:

- Firstly, whether or not all the proceeds from the disposal of the original asset had been reinvested in one or more qualifying assets. If so, the full amount of the gain arising would be eligible to be deferred. This is however not the case here, such that the relief needs to be restricted and a gain will remain chargeable equal to the proceeds retained.
- Secondly, the way in which the relief will be obtained. This involves consideration of whether the replacement asset is a depreciating asset or a non-depreciating one. Where it is a non-depreciating (i.e. has an expected life of more than 60 years on acquisition), the gain is rolled over and deducted from the cost of the new asset. This applies to assets such as land and buildings. Where the replacement asset is a depreciating one, (which includes fixed plant and machinery and leases with 60 years or less to run), the gain is deferred until the earliest of three dates – the date of sale of the replacement asset, the date when the replacement ceases to be used in the business, and ten years from the date of its acquisition. There was on this occasion only one qualifying replacement asset – the fixed machinery purchased by Jeg Ltd. This meant that that an explanation of the deferral associated with the acquisition of a depreciating asset was required.

Candidates generally demonstrated a sound knowledge when dealing with this part of the question, but some struggled more when it came to applying their knowledge to the facts of the question and, in so doing, also failed to demonstrate the necessary professional skills. The ability to tailor and apply knowledge to specific scenarios is a key part of this exam and candidates are advised to build plenty of question practice into their revision programmes in order to become more adept and experienced at this.

Requirement (c)

Part (c) of this question involved a transfer pricing issue in relation to one group company (Lis Co), and the setting-up of an overseas permanent establishment (PE) in relation to another (Mot Ltd).

Careful reading of the entire requirement relating to Lis Co resulted in many candidates producing very comprehensive answers, which scored well. The reference to transfer pricing right at the end of the requirement provided a clear instruction as to what the first part involved. However, it was important for candidates to recognise why, on this occasion, a transfer pricing adjustment was actually going to be required. Jeg Ltd, a UK resident company, was intending to buy components from its overseas subsidiary at a price above the arm's length price; this would therefore have the impact of artificially reducing its taxable profits. We were told that Jeg Ltd was a small company; this might potentially have exempted it from the transfer pricing regime had it not been for the fact that Lis Co was resident in a non-qualifying territory (i.e. there was no double taxation agreement in place with the UK).

Most candidates seemed to be comfortable with this situation and recognised that an adjustment would be required for tax purposes. However, a fair number did not go on to develop this idea in sufficient detail by explaining the impact of such an adjustment for the UK company. This should have been relatively straightforward – the company's profits would increase as a result of the adjustment, which would then give rise to a corresponding increase in its corporation tax liability. It is vital that candidates do take the time to read and fully understand the requirement – going back and rereading it if necessary – in order to ensure that they haven't missed out on anything when preparing their answers.

The second part of this requirement related to another group company, Mot Ltd, which was setting up an overseas PE. The question specifically asked for an explanation of the rate of tax suffered in the UK on the profits which were generated overseas. The majority of candidates appeared to be very comfortable with the general UK tax treatment of an overseas PE, recognising that its profits would be taxed as part of the profits of Mot Ltd, as it was a UK resident company. However, many did not go on to specifically relate this knowledge to the rate of tax being suffered on these profits in the UK on this occasion. This required recognition of the double taxation rules, such that the tax payable in the UK at 25% would be reduced by the tax paid overseas at 13%, leading to a rate of tax payable in the UK of 12%.

Candidates were then required to explain the matters to consider when deciding whether or not to make an election to exempt the profits of the overseas PE from UK taxation. The wording of this requirement, 'whether or not', should have indicated to candidates that what was required was a consideration of both the advantages and the disadvantages of the election. Many candidates focussed exclusively on the disadvantages, overlooking the key advantage of the profits not being taxable in the UK and therefore saving UK tax. This may have seemed too obvious a point to mention but it did need to be stated since it was relevant to the final decision.

Requirement (d)

Part (d) of this question required an explanation of companies eligible to form part of a VAT group registration, and the VAT implications of purchasing goods from an overseas subsidiary.

Many answers to this part were rather vague. For all elections, across all taxes, it is necessary to have a sound understanding of the precise rules and conditions. On this occasion, a significant number of candidates were unable to accurately state and apply the rules for group VAT registration. In particular, many referred to the need for companies to be UK resident; this is incorrect for VAT purposes where, in order to meet the qualifying conditions, the company only needs to be established in the UK, or have a fixed place of business there.

A further point which was evident based on performance in this part was, once again, the need for candidates to read the requirement very carefully and ensure that effort is focused in terms of addressing the specific question, rather than wasting time on issues which would not earn marks. There were two examples of this here.

- A significant minority included Lis Co in their discussion of companies which could potentially join the VAT group even though the requirement specifically excludes Lis Co from being eligible for group membership.
- The requirement only asked for the possible disadvantages of group registration. A fair number of candidates listed all of the consequences, including the advantages. Credit could not be awarded in respect of these points and time was therefore unnecessarily wasted.

Imports and exports remain an important topic within the VAT syllabus, and candidates must ensure that they are able to apply the correct rules, particularly following changes as a result of the UK leaving the European Union.

In many cases, candidates would have benefited from more precise explanations in response to this part. On importing components, many tended to be fairly vague by saying that the UK company would suffer UK VAT, but were not sufficiently clear in terms of how or when this would arise.

The following section of the examiner's report has been added from another question which was merged with this one:

Requirement (e)

Part (e) required a calculation of an individual's income tax and NIC liabilities in order to explain and summarise their poor cashflow position. The client could not understand why her expenses (which were given) exceeded her post-tax income (which needed to be calculated).

The requirement features three key command words or phrases; candidates were asked to 'prepare calculations' in order to 'explain' the client's financial position, and then to 'summarise' their findings.

Initially, a calculation of the client's post-tax income was required. There are four things to bear in mind when addressing this part of the requirement:

1. The question asked for calculations, so time should not have been spent providing detailed explanations. Numbers should have been labelled and brief explanations of any workings provided but, in order to earn the marks available, the key focus here should have been on performance of the calculations themselves.
2. Post-tax income means gross cash income less all relevant tax deductions. Note that the requirement did not refer to 'post-income tax' income specifically, nor did it contain an instruction to ignore national insurance contributions (NIC), so these also needed to be considered given that they were relevant to the client's position in her capacity as an employee.
3. Calculation of post-tax income will require a computation of the individual's income tax liability for the tax year; this is therefore a good place to start.

4 It should be noted that the tax calculated should then have been deducted from the individual's gross cash income of the tax year, not their taxable income (which is after deduction of the personal allowance). This will include both salary and dividend income, but will exclude non-cash items such as taxable benefits. Care needed to be taken in the calculation of this figure.

It was encouraging to see that most candidates recognised the need to factor in NICs. This is something that candidates always need to be on the look-out for when considering the position of employed or self-employed taxpayers, since it is not something they will necessarily be specifically directed to. As mentioned above, a careful reading of the requirement is therefore important in this respect, just to confirm that NICs were not on this occasion being excluded, as is sometimes the case.

The final part, which required a summary of findings, involved going back to the original problem – a comparison of the client's post-tax income with her expenses for the year – and making sensible and relevant comments on the figures. An actual comparison, based on the figures already calculated, of the difference between the expenses and the post-tax income would have been useful here in order to illustrate the point and to summarise the underlying issue. However many candidates' answers didn't include such summaries, thereby missing out on the marks available for addressing this part of the requirement.

The following section of the examiner's report has been amended to reflect the new mark allocation to professional skills.

Professional skills

This question involved preparation of a memorandum for the client file covering a number of different tax issues.

Candidates should try to remember two key points when addressing this type of requirement. Firstly, explanations provided should be concise but comprehensive enough to be understood by anyone who uses the file. Secondly, the notes should be clearly presented in a logical and structured way, such that a user is able to easily find the information they need.

Candidates who scored well dealt with all parts of the requirements, structured their answer according to the matters to be addressed (which were clearly spelled out in the manager's email), wrote concisely in short, clear paragraphs, and demonstrated a logical thought process when tackling each of the relevant issues.

In summary, those candidates who prepared satisfactory answers to question 1 were able to do the following:

- directly address each of the tasks contained within the manager's email
- demonstrate a good level of knowledge of the tax rules for groups of companies, including dealing with overseas issues
- apply their knowledge intelligently to the given scenario and provide concise explanations, where required.

ACCA marking scheme

			Marks
(a)	Information required		3.0
	Actions to take		4.0
			7.0
		Maximum	5.0
(b)	Assets sold		2.0
	Capital gains group		2.0
	Assets purchased		3.0
	Operation of relief		8.0
			15.0
		Maximum	10.0
(c)	Transfer pricing		4.0
	UK rate of tax		2.5
	Election to exempt profits		4.5
			11.0
		Maximum	9.0
(d)	Group VAT registration		
	Members of the group		3.0
	Possible disadvantages		2.0
	Purchase of components from Lis Co		3.0
			8.0
		Maximum	7.0
(e)	Taxable income		3.0
	Income tax and class 1 NIC liability		4.0
	Post-tax income and summary of findings		3.5
			10.5
		Maximum	9.0
	Professional skills marks (see below)	**Maximum**	10.0
Total			**50.0**

Professional skills marks

Communication

- General format and structure of memorandum (e.g. use of headings/sub-headings to make memorandum easy to refer to).
- Style, language and clarity (clearly explained, presentation of calculations, appropriate use of the tools, easy to follow and more than a negligible amount of content).
- Effectiveness of communication (answer is relevant, specific rather than general and focused to the requirement).
- Adherence to specific instructions made in the scenario (e.g. ignoring Lis Co when discussing VAT groups in part (d)).

Analysis and evaluation

- Demonstration of reasoned judgement when considering how rollover relief will apply to the group in part (b). Clear analysis of the various purchases and their potential eligibility. Consideration also of further potential future purchases.
- Use of information to determine that the shares purchased by Hale were not readily convertible assets in part (e).
- Appropriate use of the data to determine suitable calculations for the after-tax cash Hale has available to her each year in part (e).

Scepticism

- Being prepared to challenge whether the firm is suitably qualified to advise a group of companies which includes a permanent establishment in part (a).
- Exercising an inquiring mind as to the potential for inaccurate advice given by the previous adviser in part (a).
- Effective challenge of suggestion that artificial prices could be used to manipulate where profits arise across the group to minimise the overall tax liability of the group in part (c).

Commercial acumen

- Consideration of potential future implications of making an election to exempt the profits of the PE from UK tax. Demonstrating that future implications must also be considered in part (c).
- Recognition of the potential risk to including Kod Ltd in the group VAT registration given its financial problems in part (d).
- Demonstration of a clear understanding of the difference between taxable income and cash in part (e).

21 HUM LTD GROUP (ADAPTED) *Walk in the footsteps of a top tutor*

Key answer tips

This section A question covers a variety of corporation tax topics, including gains, rollover relief, overseas aspects and capital losses.

Requirement (a) covers the popular ethical scenario of receiving a refund from HMRC. Think logically about what steps you should take here, and don't just jump straight to resigning!

Requirement (b)(i) asks for the chargeable gains, VAT and SDLT implications of two building sales. There are seven marks available here for relatively straight forward areas, so make sure you cover all aspects to score well.

Requirement (b)(ii) looks at rollover relief in the context of acquiring a new business. There are some easy marks to obtain initially just for explaining how the rules work. Of course, in order to score well on this requirement you then need to go on to apply these to the scenario.

Requirement (c) looks at the UK tax treatment of acquiring an overseas business by two different methods. It is important to cover both and use headings to make it clear which option you are addressing.

The final requirement looks at two potential business acquisitions, both of which have capital losses. It is important that you establish the difference between the capital losses in the two different companies and think about how that impacts the way in which they can be used.

The highlighted words in the written sections are key phrases that markers are looking for in your memorandum.

Memorandum

For	**The files**
Client	**Hum Ltd Group**
Subject	**Refund of corporation tax, sale of buildings, purchase of overseas trade and further planned share acquisitions**
Prepared by	**Tax senior**
Date	**1 July 2024**

(a) Hum Ltd – refund of corporation tax

We should assist Rawl in investigating whether or not there was a valid reason for the refund. If a valid reason cannot be found, we would have to conclude that the refund was made as a result of an error on the part of HM Revenue and Customs (HMRC). In these circumstances:

– We should inform Rawl that the amount should be repaid and that failing to do so would be a civil and/or a criminal offence.

– HMRC should be informed of their error as soon as possible in order to minimise any interest and penalties which may otherwise become payable.

We should inform HMRC only if our letter of engagement authorises us to do so. Otherwise, we should advise Rawl to do so.

– In the unlikely event that Rawl is unwilling to return the money, we would have to consider ceasing to act as Hum Ltd's tax advisers. We would then have to notify the tax authorities that we no longer act for the company, although we would not provide them with any reason for our action.

The firm's money laundering reporting officer would also have to consider whether or not it is necessary to make a report under the money laundering rules.

(b) Sale of the two buildings

(i) Tax implications

The chargeable gains, value added tax (VAT) and stamp duty land tax (SDLT) implications of the sale of the buildings are set out below.

Building 1

Chargeable gain:	The sale will take place at no gain, no loss, such that it will not give rise to a chargeable gain. This is because Toc Ltd and the purchaser of the building, Sar Ltd, are members of the same 75% capital gains group.
VAT	The sale will be outside the scope of VAT, such that VAT should not be charged. This is because Toc Ltd and Sar Ltd are members of a VAT group registration.
SDLT	The sale will not result in a liability to SDLT, as both Toc Ltd and Sar Ltd are 75% subsidiaries of Hum Ltd.

Building 2

Chargeable gain:	A chargeable gain of £330,000 (£650,000 – £320,000) will arise on the sale of the building.
VAT	The building will be more than three years old at the time of sale. Accordingly, the sale will be an exempt supply and VAT should not be charged.
SDLT	The sale will have no SDLT implications for Toc Ltd. SDLT will be payable by the purchaser.

Tutorial note

Toc Ltd will have owned building 2 for more than ten years at the date of its sale. Accordingly, even though the sale will be an exempt supply, there will not be a clawback of input tax under the capital goods scheme.

(ii) Post-tax proceeds available to the Hum Ltd Group

Availability of Rollover Relief

Rollover relief will be available in respect of the chargeable gain arising on the sale of building 2 because a building used for trading purposes is a qualifying business asset (QBA) for rollover relief purposes.

The relief can be claimed where replacement QBAs are purchased in the period commencing one year prior to the disposal of the asset and ending three years after the disposal. QBAs also include fixed plant and machinery.

Hum Ltd, Sar Ltd and Toc Ltd are treated as carrying on a single trade for the purposes of rollover relief because they are members of a capital gains group.

Where all of the sales proceeds are used to purchase QBAs, the whole of the gain can be rolled over. Where only part of the proceeds is so used, the amount not spent, up to a maximum of the realised chargeable gain, will be subject to corporation tax.

Qua Co

A purchase of the ordinary share capital of Qua Co would not be relevant for rollover relief, as shares are not QBAs.

If Toc Ltd were to purchase the trading assets of Qua Co, the building costing £465,000 would be a QBA for the purposes of rollover relief. Goodwill is not a QBA, and neither are lorries (as they are not fixed plant and machinery.)

Building purchased by Sar Ltd

The building purchased on 1 February 2024 for £90,000 will be a replacement QBA for the purposes of relieving the gain on the sale of building 2 provided building 2 is sold by 31 January 2025 (i.e. within the 12 months following the purchase of the factory).

Post-tax proceeds available to the Hum Ltd Group

	£	£
Proceeds from sale of building 2	650,000	650,000
Purchase of QBAs (£465,000 + £90,000)	(555,000)	
Amount of proceeds not reinvested	95,000	
Corporation tax (£95,000 × 25%)		(23,750)
Post-tax proceeds		626,250

This calculation assumes that the Hum Ltd group will make the commercial decisions, as noted above, such that the total spend on QBAs will be £555,000 (£465,000 + £90,000). The sale of building 1 has been ignored as it is to be purchased by Sar Ltd, such that it will not result in any additional cash for the group.

Tutorial notes:

1 *Although companies in a capital gains group are treated as a single trade for the purposes of rollover relief, building 1 to be purchased by Sar Ltd cannot be treated as a replacement QBA because it is to be purchased from Toc Ltd, which is in a capital gains group with Sar Ltd.*

2 *Candidates who also deducted the cost of the QBAs in arriving at the post-tax proceeds were not penalised.*

(c) UK taxation of the profits generated by the Qua Co trade

Toc Ltd acquires the ordinary share capital of Qua Co

The profits would not be subject to tax in the UK. This is because Qua Co is not a UK resident company (and there will not be a controlled foreign company charge). Any dividends received by Toc Ltd from Qua Co would be exempt income for the purposes of UK corporation tax.

Toc Ltd acquires Qua Co's trading assets

Toc Ltd is a UK tax resident company. Accordingly, the profits of a permanent establishment (PE) in Keynesia would be part of its trading profits.

Tax relief is not available in respect of either the cost or amortisation of purchased goodwill.

UK capital allowances would be available in respect of the purchase of the lorries.

UK structures and buildings allowances will not be available in respect of the building, as it was constructed prior to 29 October 2018.

Double taxation relief (DTR) would be available in the UK in respect of the corporation tax paid in Keynesia. This would be the lower of the overseas tax deducted (28%) and the UK tax on this income (25%), such that there would be no UK corporation tax liability in respect of the profits generated in Keynesia.

Tutor's top tips

The requirement mentioned that the election to exempt profits of the PE would not be made, so you would not have scored any marks for discussion of this.

(d) Potential tax saving from planned share acquisitions

Alpha Ltd

This purchase would be caught by the pre-entry capital loss restrictions. If a company enters a gains group with an already realised capital loss, that loss cannot be used to shelter gains made by other group members.

This restriction prevents the use of losses on both reallocations of gains on disposals and also gains transferred by nil gain nil loss intra group transfers.

We should advise Rawl that this purchase will not achieve his objectives.

Beta Ltd

This appears to be a tax efficient investment. As long as the shares are sold at a loss after Ilum Ltd has bought the shares, the losses should be available to shelter group gains. There are no restrictions on the use of unrealised pre-entry capital losses.

We would need to check if any of the holdings are 10% or more. If so, they will probably qualify for the substantial shareholdings exemption which would exempt any losses on those shares.

Examiner's report

Requirement (a)

The scenario here concerned an unexpected refund of corporation tax from HMRC and required discussion of the actions to be taken by the firm and their client. This was a fairly standard ethics requirement which has been tested frequently in the past.

It was important to note that candidates were expected to discuss actions to be taken by the firm and matters to be drawn to the attention of the client. It was necessary to clearly distinguish the different responsibilities.

Many candidates demonstrated a high level of familiarity with this area, and so scored full, or almost full marks. However, the main issue for weaker candidates was a lack of awareness of the firm's responsibilities in these cases, in terms of permissible contact with HM Revenue and Customs (HMRC). There were two fundamental examples of these in this question, which candidates were expected to include in their answer:

- The role of the firm is to inform the client of the need for the client to notify HMRC of an issue like this, unless the firm has authority to do so directly in the letter of engagement;
- If the firm decides they can no longer act for the client, their responsibility is to inform HMRC of this decision, but must not disclose the reason for it.

Candidates must be precise when discussing a firm's responsibilities. There are a good number of past questions which have tested these, and candidates would be well advised to practise them.

Requirement (b)(i)

Part (b)(i) concerned the proposed sales of two buildings by one of the three group companies, both of which have been used in its trade. One was a transfer to another group company, and the other was a sale to an unconnected third party. In each case the candidate was required to explain the chargeable gains, value added tax (VAT) and stamp duty land tax (SDLT) implications for the group.

It is a fundamental skill required of ATX-UK candidates to be able to recognise and accurately define a qualifying group for all relevant aspects of corporation tax. It was therefore pleasing to see that the chargeable gains implications of these sales did not prove to be a problem for most candidates, who correctly identified the existence of a gains group in respect of the transfer of building 1, such that this would be a no gain no loss transfer, and correctly calculated the gain on building 2. However, unfortunately a good number of candidates then wasted time by going on to explain the future corporation tax consequences for the receiving company of the intra-group transfer, when the question only referred to the current proposed sale. It is very important that candidates carefully read the requirements, and they restrict their answers to directly addressing these requirements.

The majority of candidates were able to state that there would be no VAT charged on the disposal in either case, but very few gave the correct reasons for this, with most just referring to the information provided in the scenario in relation to there being no option to tax in either case. This required more thought as will often be the case with property transactions for VAT. Where there is an intra-group transaction, candidates must read the information provided to ascertain whether or not the companies are all part of a single group VAT registration. This was the case here, such that the sale of building 1 to another group member was outside the scope of VAT.

In the case of building 2, the non-existence of an option to tax was relevant, but was only part of the story; candidates also needed to make reference to the fact that the building was more than three years old, such that, in the absence of the option, was exempt from VAT.

In relation to SDLT, the fact there was an intra group transfer was identified by many candidates as the reason for no SDLT on building 1, but fewer stated in relation to building 2 that there would be no SDLT for the group as this would be payable by the purchaser. This is a fundamental feature of SDLT which is often overlooked by candidates. It was noticeable that a significant number of candidates included a calculation of the SDLT payable on building 2, despite this not having been asked for (and, in fact, not relevant to the requirement).

Overall, this part was well done, but a common observation was the amount of time wasted by candidates who provided explanations and calculations which were not required. Candidates should take the time to read and re-read the requirements carefully, to ensure that they are not providing an answer beyond what is required.

Highlighting of key words within a requirement may help to maintain focus and to ensure that candidates do not lose sight of what it is they are being asked to do.

Requirement (b)(ii)

Part (b)(ii) comprised a very detailed requirement, which spelled out, step by step, what was required. Candidates who read this requirement carefully, and approached it in the stages set out, tended to produce some good, high scoring answers to this question part.

However, many candidates appeared to adopt a rather more muddled approach, which inevitably led to parts of the requirement being missed, and which often made their answers more difficult to follow. A question part which is worth 15 marks is going to require some thought and planning at the outset. It is worth taking some time at the start of such a question part to read, and carefully consider how to approach that part. It is evident from their answers when candidates have done this, and invariably leads to a more logical, concise and better-focused answer.

The first step within this part was to explain, by reference to the conditions which need to be satisfied, the availability of rollover relief in respect of the chargeable gain(s) arising on the disposal of the buildings calculated in (a)(i). In respect of the qualifying reinvestment, candidates were required to consider separately each of two possible ways of one of the group companies acquiring the trade of an overseas resident company; either purchasing the whole of the share capital, or purchasing the trading assets.

Most candidates knew the basic general rules relating to the availability of rollover relief, and were able to state the time period for reinvestment, and the types of asset which would qualify. But a generic answer was not what was required, and many didn't take their explanations far enough to address the specific facts of this question. Prime examples of this were a lack of reference to partial reinvestment, which was a feature of this scenario, and also recognition of a qualifying asset acquired by another group company. Additionally, a significant minority of candidates did not distinguish the two alternative potential reinvestments – which would have totally different consequences from a rollover relief point of view – and so produced a rather general answer in respect of reinvestment, not clearly relating to one or other, and consequently being unable to compare the two strategies. This was disappointing, and costly in terms of both technical and professional skills marks. Where two (or more) alternative options or courses of action are being considered candidates should use subheadings to clearly indicate which one they are considering.

At ATX candidates will almost invariably be required to apply rules and conditions to specific circumstances, such that a generic answer, while scoring a few marks, will not be sufficient to score well. It can not be over-emphasised how important it is to take the time to think and plan an answer to a fairly complex question like this in order to provide a comprehensive, well-structured answer.

The final step within this question part was to calculate the post-tax proceeds for the company following the disposal of the two buildings on the assumption that they adopted the acquisition strategy for the overseas trade which would maximise the availability of rollover relief. This posed something of a problem for those candidates whose answers to the availability of rollover relief were rather muddled, but those who persevered were rewarded with follow through marks where relevant. Candidates are frequently asked to calculate after-tax proceeds, or after-tax income and should remember that credit will be available here for selecting the correct figures from their previous workings so it is worth persevering.

Requirement (c)

Part (c) required a comparison of the liability to UK corporation tax of the trading profits generated overseas if the UK company (i) acquired the ordinary share capital; or (ii) acquired the trade and assets of the overseas company.

Again, with two alternatives to consider, it would have been useful for candidates to have clearly structured their answer under two separate subheadings, but this was not always done, thereby making it difficult to decide which of the alternatives was being considered to award appropriate marks. There appeared to be considerable confusion for many of the candidates as to the different rules in each case, with many not distinguishing between the alternatives.

The first step here should have been to recognise that acquisition of the ordinary share capital would mean that the overseas company would become a subsidiary company, whereas acquisition of the trade and assets would mean that it would be treated as a permanent establishment (PE), which is just an extension of the UK company. This is fundamental, and needed to be recognised and stated before going on to discuss the consequences for liability to UK taxation on the overseas profits.

There was a noticeable lack of required precision in many candidates' explanations in relation to both alternatives. In respect of the acquisition of shares many appeared not to realise that it was the fact that the subsidiary company would be overseas resident, not merely operating overseas, that determined the taxability of its profits i.e. no liability to UK tax on overseas profits for non UK-resident companies. In relation to the establishment of a PE, most recognised that in this case the profits would be taxable in the UK, but gave no explanation as to how this would be done i.e. by inclusion in the trading profit of the UK company.

Candidates are generally very confident with the operation of double taxation relief, and it was no different in the question, with many correctly explaining the operation of the relief, although not always in the right context.

The final part of the requirement was to explain the tax relief available in respect of the individual trading assets acquired. Virtually no candidate made any attempt to answer this, possibly because they had not read to the end of the requirement, and so were unable to access up to 3 marks for discussing capital allowances on plant and machinery and buildings, and the relief available for goodwill.

Requirement (d) has been added to the question since it was originally set.

Marking scheme

					Marks
(a)	Investigate and inform HMRC				2.0
	Offence and penalties/interest				2.0
	Unwillingness to return the money				2.0
					6.0
				Maximum	5.0
(b)	(i)	Building 1			
			Chargeable gain		2.0
			Value added tax		1.0
			Stamp duty land tax		1.0
		Building 2			
			Chargeable gain		1.0
			Value added tax		2.0
			Stamp duty land tax		1.0
					8.0
				Maximum	7.0
	(ii)	Rules of rollover relief			6.5
		Qua Co			3.5
		Buildings purchased by Sar Ltd			2.0
		Maximum post-tax proceeds			4.0
					16.0
				Maximum	15.0
(c)	Company resident in Keynsia				2.0
	Permanent establishment				
		Profits			2.0
		Double tax relief			4.0
					8.0
				Maximum	6.0

(d)	Alpha Ltd		
	Identify PECL issue		2.0
	Explain the impact		2.0
	Beta Ltd		
	No restriction on unrealised losses		2.0
	More information needed re SSE		2.0
			8.0
		Maximum	7.0
	Professional skills marks (see below)	**Maximum**	10.0
Total			**50.0**

Professional skills marks

Communication

- General format and structure of memorandum (e.g. use of headings/sub-headings to make memorandum easy to refer to).
- Style, language and clarity (tone of memorandum, presentation of calculations, appropriate use of the tools, easy to follow and more than a negligible amount of content).
- Effectiveness of communication (answer is relevant, specific rather than general and focused to the requirement).
- Adherence to specific instructions made in the scenario (e.g. not considering controlled foreign company rules).

Analysis and evaluation

- Use of information to perform appropriate calculations to determine the after-tax proceeds to the group in part (b)(ii).
- Demonstration of knowledge and application of rollover relief rules to the facts in the question in part (b)(ii).
- Demonstration of understanding of the difference between an overseas subsidiary and a permanent establishment in part (c).
- Demonstration of ability to consider all relevant taxes specified in requirement (b)(i), i.e. corporation tax, VAT and SDLT.

Scepticism

- Consideration of impact if client refuses to refund money to HMRC in part (a).
- Recognition of further information needed to establish whether sale of shares in Beta will create a loss in part (d).

Commercial acumen

- Recognition that intra group transfers create no additional funds for the group in part (b)(ii).
- Identification of interaction of UK and overseas tax on overall tax position in part (c).

Section 4

ANSWERS TO PRACTICE QUESTIONS – SECTION B

TAXATION OF INDIVIDUALS

EMPLOYMENT

22 MORICE AND BABEEN PLC (ADAPTED) *Walk in the footsteps of a top tutor*

Key answer tips

This question covers provision of benefits to employees and CGT with investors' relief. It is not likely to have been a popular question in the exam, as there are ten marks purely on the SAYE scheme – an area that had not been tested before in the ATX exam. However, part (b) covers some much more mainstream benefits.

Part (a) requires in-depth knowledge of the SAYE scheme conditions, which may have put off many students. However, there are six and a half marks available for applying the tax treatment of a tax advantaged share scheme to figures given in the question, so a solid pass could still have been obtained without precise knowledge of the SAYE conditions.

Part (b) on the income tax and national insurance implications of private medical insurance, beneficial loans and the use of an employee's own car for business journeys should have been straight forward. These are all TX areas.

Part (c) offers some easy marks, as long as you recognised that investors' relief would be available.

This question contains a mix of numerical and discursive requirements. It is advisable to use the spreadsheet functionality for calculations and the word processor functionality for any discursive requirements when in the exam. Ensure you label your answer clearly so it is clear which requirement you are answering.

The highlighted words in the written sections are key phrases that markers are looking for.

(a) SAYE scheme

Tutor's top tips

This part of the question is slightly unusual for a section B question as the requirement at the end of the question does not actually tell you what you need to do.

If you look back at the information in the question you will see that there are really two requirements here:

1 *Explain whether or not each of the proposed rules will be acceptable for a SAYE scheme.*

2 *Explain, with calculations, the tax and national insurance liabilities for the employee in the illustrative example.*

Whether or not the proposed rules will be acceptable for a SAYE scheme

Tutor's top tips

You need to have a good knowledge of the SAYE scheme conditions to be able to answer this part of the question, and then you need to apply these conditions to the scenario to ensure that you score a good mark.

The investment period of five years is acceptable. SAYE schemes can run for three or five years.

The minimum monthly investment of £5 is acceptable, but the maximum of £750 is not acceptable. The maximum monthly investment for a tax advantaged scheme is £500.

The scheme must be open to all employees:

- It is not acceptable to have a minimum age limit of 21.
- It is also not acceptable to exclude part time employees.
- However, it is acceptable to exclude employees who have worked for the company for less than three years.

Tutorial note

It is acceptable to exclude employees who have worked for the company for less than a qualifying period, as long as the period chosen does not exceed five years.

The share options can be granted at a discount, as long as the exercise price is no less than 80% of the market value at the date of grant. The price of £2.48 will, therefore, be acceptable, as long as the market value at 1 January 2025 is not more than £3.10 (£2.48/80%) per share.

Tutor's top tips

You are asked to explain, with calculations, the tax and national insurance liabilities for the employee in respect of:

- *grant of the share options*
- *exercise of the share options, and*
- *sale of the shares.*

Even if you did not know the conditions for the SAYE scheme, you should still be able to answer most of this part of the requirement if you knew the general tax treatment for tax advantaged share option schemes.

Note that there are three different aspects to deal with here, so make sure that you cover all of these and clearly label your answer.

Grant of share options

There is no tax liability on the grant of the share options.

Exercise of share options

There is no tax liability on the exercise of the share options.

Sale of shares

There will be a chargeable gain on the sale of the shares, which will be subject to capital gains tax.

The cost of the shares will be:

	£
Amount saved (£250 × 12 months × 5 years)	15,000
The number of shares purchased at exercise will therefore be £15,000/£2.48 per share	6,048

The gain on disposal of 6,048 shares will be as follows:

	£
Proceeds (6,048 × £4.00)	24,192
Less: Cost	(15,000)
Chargeable gain	9,192

Tutor's top tips

Don't stop here. You need to explain how the gain will be taxed, but there is no information about the tax position of the illustrative employee.

Has the employee used the annual exempt amount?

Is the employee a basic rate or a higher rate taxpayer?

You need to consider all possibilities.

This gain may be partially covered by the annual exempt amount of £6,000, if the employee has no other chargeable disposals in the tax year 2029/30 (the tax year of sale).

The rate of capital gains tax applicable to the gain after deduction of any annual exempt amount will depend on the level of the employee's taxable income:

- If the employee has taxable income of more than £37,700, then the gain will be taxed at 20%.
- If the employee has taxable income of less than £37,700, gains falling into the basic rate band will be taxed at 10% with the excess being taxed at 20%.

Business asset disposal relief will not be available as the employee will not own 5% of the company's ordinary share capital.

National insurance

There are no national insurance implications in respect of a SAYE scheme.

(b) Income tax and national insurance implications for the employees of Babeen plc

Tutor's top tips

*The benefits set out here were tested at TX. TX level knowledge is often tested at ATX, and **explaining** the tax treatment of benefits, rather than just calculating them, is a popular requirement.*

Note that you are only asked to talk about the tax implications for the employees in this question, not the employer.

(i) Medical care scheme

Private health insurance

Private health insurance is a taxable benefit.

The benefit will be the cost to the employer of £470.

Interest-free loans

As long as the amount borrowed does not exceed £10,000 at any point in the tax year, there will be no taxable benefit.

If the employee borrows more than £10,000 there will be a taxable benefit.

The benefit is calculated by multiplying the official rate of interest of 2.25% by the amount outstanding during the tax year, giving a maximum annual benefit of:

(£12,500 × 2.25%) = £281

If the amount borrowed changes during the year, there are two alternative methods of calculating the benefit:

- The average method, based on the average amount outstanding

  = (balance b/f + balance c/f) ÷ 2

- The strict method, based on the actual amounts outstanding during the year.

Either the taxpayer or HMRC can elect for the strict method.

These taxable benefits will be subject to income tax at 20% if they fall within the basic rate band or 40% if the employee is a higher rate taxpayer.

Employees do not pay national insurance contributions on private health insurance or beneficial loans.

(ii) Payments for driving their own cars

Tutor's top tips

Don't forget to refer to the tax tables given in the exam. The approved mileage allowances are provided.

However, you do need to learn the approved allowance for passengers, as this is not given.

Mileage allowance

Employees are allowed to receive a tax-free mileage allowance of 45p per mile for the first 10,000 business miles per tax year, and 25p per mile thereafter.

- If they receive less than these approved amounts, the shortfall can be deducted from taxable employment income. This means that employees of Babeen plc will be able to deduct a shortfall of 9p per mile (45p – 36p) for the first 10,000 business miles.

- If they receive more than the approved amounts, the excess will be subject to income tax.

Passenger allowance

There is a tax-free allowance of 5p per mile for carrying a passenger, so the 3p per mile paid will be tax free. However, the shortfall of 2p per mile (5p – 3p) is not tax deductible.

National insurance

As the mileage allowance is no more than 45p per mile, there will be no national insurance contributions payable. There will also be no national insurance contributions payable on the additional 3p per mile.

Tutorial note

Even if the employee drove more than 10,000 miles and had a taxable benefit in respect of the mileage allowance, there would still be no national insurance contributions payable.

However, if the employer paid more than 45p per mile, the excess would be subject to class 1 national insurance.

(c) Sale of shares in Wind Ltd

	£
Proceeds	150,000
Less: Cost (3,500 × £1)	(3,500)
Chargeable gain	146,500
Less: Annual exempt amount	(6,000)
Taxable gain	140,500
CGT (£140,500 × 10%)	14,050

The gain qualifies for investors' relief because the shares have been subscribed for in an unlisted trading company, have been owned for at least three years and Morice does not work for the company. Assuming that Morice has not already used up the £10 million lifetime limit, the gain can therefore be taxed at 10%.

Examiner's report

In order to score well in part (a) it was important for candidates to address each of the detailed rules in the question as opposed to writing generally about share option schemes. Many candidates who attempted this question were knowledgeable about Save As You Earn schemes but only a minority took a sufficiently disciplined approach to score well.

The explanation of the tax liabilities in respect of the shares acquired under the scheme was not done particularly well. Many candidates lacked precise knowledge of this area such that they did not know that no tax would be charged until the shares were sold. In addition, it needed to be recognised that the position of each employee would vary depending on whether or not they had made any other capital gains and on the level of their taxable income; very few candidates considered these matters.

The medical care scheme in part (b) was not handled particularly well in that many candidates incorrectly stated that the provision of health insurance would be an exempt benefit for the employees. However, this was not too important as it was only a minor part of the answer. The provision of an interest free loan was also not dealt with as well as might have been expected. The question stated that the loan would be 'up to £12,500' so it was necessary to point out that loans of no more than £10,000 would be exempt.

The explanation of the implications of the payments to employees for driving their own cars was handled well. The only common error was the failure to recognise that there would be no national insurance implications.

The question asked for the tax implications 'for the employees' as opposed to the tax implications generally. Accordingly, it was necessary to consider the national insurance issues for the employees (but not the employer) and there was no need to address the ability of the employer to obtain tax relief for the costs incurred.

The final section of the question was not part of the question when it was originally set.

ACCA marking scheme

				Marks
(a)	Scheme rules			
		Investment period and investment limits		1.5
		Eligible employees		1.5
		Share price		1.5
	Illustrative example			
		Grant and exercise of option		1.0
		Gain		1.5
		Capital gains tax		3.0
		National insurance contributions		1.0
				11.0
			Maximum	10.0
(b)	(i)	Health insurance		0.5
		Interest-free loan		2.5
		National insurance contributions		0.5
	(ii)	Driving on company business		
		Income tax		2.0
		National insurance contributions		1.0
		Carrying passengers		1.5
				8.0
			Maximum	7.0
(c)	Capital gain			0.5
	Annual exempt amount			0.5
	CGT liability			0.5
	Investors' relief conditions			2.0
				3.5
			Maximum	3.0
	Professional skills marks (see below)		**Maximum**	5.0
Total				**25.0**

Professional skills marks

Analysis and evaluation

- Use of information to determine appropriate calculations to perform in relation to share scheme liabilities in part (a).
- Application of SAYE conditions to scenario to determine whether the Babeen plc scheme will qualify as a SAYE scheme in part (a).
- Demonstration of ability to consider all relevant taxes specified in part (b), i.e. income tax and national insurance contributions.
- Appropriate use of the data to determine necessary calculations to perform to arrive at the capital gains tax liability in respect of the Wind Ltd shares in part (c).

Scepticism

- Assumption regarding availability of investors' relief lifetime allowance in part (c).

Commercial acumen

- Recognition of available capital gains tax reliefs in part (c).

23 HYSSOP LTD (ADAPTED) ***Walk in the footsteps of a top tutor***

Key answer tips

This question is really three separate questions covering employment benefits, payment of a lease premium by a company and the VAT capital goods scheme. As usual, there are a few twists, such as partial business use for rollover relief and the fact that the lease is a depreciating asset, but there are still enough basic marks here for you to score a pass if you missed these trickier points.

The highlighted words in the written sections are key phrases that markers are looking for.

(a) Assistance with home to work travel costs for Corin

Tutor's top tips

This part requires explanation and calculation of the cost of two alternative benefits from the point of view of the employee and the company. This type of requirement regularly appears in the ATX exam.

The key is to think about cash flows and to remember to include tax payable and tax savings.

Don't forget to consider national insurance contributions; these are payable by the employer on all benefits, but the employee only pays them on cash earnings.

You are specifically asked which is the most cost efficient for both Corin and Hyssop Ltd, so there will be marks for following through your figures and stating this.

(i) Cost to Corin

Alternative 1 – Provision of a motorcycle

Corin is a higher rate taxpayer, so will pay income tax at 40% on the annual taxable benefit.

Corin will have no national insurance liability in respect of this benefit.

The total cost of this option will be:

Income tax on benefit (£3,160 × 40%) = total cost	£1,264

Alternative 2 – Payment towards the cost of driving and provision of parking place

Provision of a parking place at or near an employee's normal place of work is an exempt benefit for income tax.

Corin will pay income tax at 40% on the cash received as reimbursement of his driving costs, together with class 1 national insurance contributions at 2%.

The total cost of this option will be:

	£
Cost of driving	2,820
Less: Amount reimbursed	(2,240)
Additional cost of driving	580
Income tax and NICs on cash received (£2,240 × 42%)	941
Total cost	1,521

The most cost-efficient option for Corin is therefore provision of the motorcycle.

Tutorial note

The approved mileage allowances are not relevant in this case as the driving costs are not related to journeys made in the course of Corin carrying out his duties of employment.

(ii) Cost to Hyssop Ltd

Alternative 1 – Provision of a motorcycle

Hyssop Ltd will have to pay class 1A national insurance contributions of 13.8% in respect of the provision of the motorcycle.

The total cost to Hyssop Ltd is therefore:

	£
Lease cost	3,160
Employer's class 1A NICs (£3,160 × 13.8%)	436
Total cost	3,596

Alternative 2 – Payment towards the cost of driving and provision of parking place

As the provision of the parking place is an exempt benefit for income tax, there will be no class 1A liability for Hyssop Ltd.

Hyssop Ltd will have a class 1 national insurance liability at 13.8% in respect of the reimbursement of driving costs.

The total cost to Hyssop Ltd is therefore:

	£
Cost of driving reimbursed	2,240
Parking cost	920
Employer's class 1 NICs (£2,240 × 13.8%)	309
Total cost	3,469

The most cost-efficient option for Hyssop Ltd is therefore the payment towards the cost of driving and provision of the parking place.

Hyssop Ltd will be able to deduct all the costs for corporation tax purposes under both options.

Tutorial note

As the amounts are deductible for corporation tax purposes under both options, there is no need to calculate the after-tax cost to Hyssop Ltd.

(b) Corporation tax implications of the acquisition of the 40-year lease

Tutor's top tips

This part tests TX knowledge of the allowable deduction for a premium paid on a short lease. You may have forgotten the formula, but could still gain marks for knowing that there is a deduction from trading profits over the life of the lease and that it should be time apportioned in the year of payment.

There are also marks here for discussing rollover relief – a very popular topic in the ATX exam, so make sure that you are able to explain and apply the rules.

Allowable deduction

As Hyssop Ltd has paid a premium on the grant of a short lease on a property which is going to be used in its trade, a deduction is available for each year of the lease in calculating Hyssop Ltd's taxable trading income.

The annual deduction is calculated as:

$$\frac{\text{Amount of premium taxed as income on the landlord}}{\text{Number of years of the lease}}$$

The amount of the premium which is taxed as income on the landlord is £57,200 ((£260,000 × (51 – 40)/50)).

The annual deduction available to Hyssop Ltd is £1,430 (£57,200/40).

As the lease was only acquired on 1 February 2024, the deduction available in the year ended 31 December 2024 is restricted to £1,311 (£1,430 × 11/12).

Tutorial note

Alternatively, the amount of premium taxed as income on the landlord could be calculated as (£260,000 – (£260,000 × (40 – 1) × 2%)) = £57,200.

Rollover relief: gain on warehouse

The factory is used in Hyssop Ltd's trade, so the lease is a qualifying business asset, and it was acquired within the 12 months before the disposal of the warehouse. Therefore, the full business use element of the gain arising may be deferred to the extent that the proceeds relating to the business use of the warehouse have been reinvested in the lease.

The warehouse will have been owned by Hyssop Ltd for four years (1 January 2021 to 31 December 2024).

The warehouse has been used by Hyssop Ltd in its trade for three years (1 January 2021 to 31 December 2023).

The proceeds relating to the business use element of the gain are £236,250 (75% × £315,000). This is less than the £260,000 premium reinvested in the acquisition of the lease, therefore the full 75% of the chargeable gain relating to the business use of the warehouse can be deferred against the acquisition of the lease. Accordingly, £12,390 (£16,520 × 75%) may be deferred.

The lease is for less than 60 years and so is a depreciating asset for capital gains purposes. Accordingly, the gain will be deferred until the earliest of:

– The date of disposal of the lease
– The date the leased factory ceases to be used in Hyssop Ltd's business
– 1 February 2034 (ten years after the acquisition of the lease).

The remaining gain of £4,130 (£16,520 × 25%), relating to the non-business use, will be included in Hyssop Ltd's corporation tax computation for the year ending 31 December 2024.

(c) Value added tax (VAT) implications of the disposal of the warehouse

Tutor's top tips

VAT for land and buildings and the capital goods scheme are popular topics in the ATX exam, so you should be prepared to answer a question on this area.

At the date of sale, the warehouse is more than three years old. Accordingly, because Hyssop Ltd has not opted to tax it, the disposal will be exempt from VAT.

As the warehouse was newly constructed when it was purchased, VAT of £54,000 (£270,000 × 20%) would have been charged and, as the warehouse was used in its standard-rated business, this would have been wholly reclaimed by Hyssop Ltd in the year ended 31 December 2021.

As the disposal is exempt from VAT, VAT will have to be repaid to HM Revenue and Customs (HMRC) because the warehouse is deemed to have 0% taxable use for the remainder of the ten-year adjustment period under the capital goods scheme. The amount of £32,400 (£54,000 × 6/10 × (100% – 0%)) will be repayable to HMRC as a result of the disposal.

Tutorial note

A further £5,400 (£54,000 × 1/10 × (100% – 0%)) will also be repayable to HMRC in respect of the year ending 31 December 2024 as the warehouse has been rented out throughout this year, with no option to tax.

Examiner's report

The first part required candidates to consider two possible ways in which an employer could provide financial assistance to an employee in respect of home to work travel and to advise on the most cost-efficient method.

Although this was, arguably, very straightforward, it was not easy to get right. As always, those candidates who thought before writing did considerably better than those who simply wrote. In particular, they recognised the importance of national insurance contributions.

Most candidates identified the income tax and corporation tax implications of the two alternatives. The one point that many missed out on was the fact that the provision of a parking space is an exempt benefit.

The problems related to the national insurance position. Some candidates missed this out completely. Others were simply not orderly enough, such that they did not earn as many marks as they could have done.

Candidates needed to recognise that the provision of a motorcycle to an employee would result in a liability to class 1A national insurance contributions for the employer but no liability to national insurance contributions for the employee. Whereas, making a payment towards an employee's driving costs would result in a liability to class 1 national insurance contributions for both the employer and the employee.

Many candidates wrote about the statutory mileage rates, but these are only relevant where payments are in respect of journeys made when carrying out employment duties, which was not the case here.

The second part of the question concerned a premium paid in respect of a lease and the availability of rollover relief. This part was not done particularly well.

There were two distinct aspects to this part of the question.

The first concerned the tax deduction available in respect of the premium paid. Most candidates were able to make a start on this but very few made it to the end. The first task was to determine the amount of the premium that would be taxed on the landlord as income. This amount was then divided by the number of years of the lease in order to determine the annual deduction. The deduction in the current period was then 11/12 of the annual deduction because the lease was entered into when there were eleven months of the accounting period remaining.

The second part of the question concerned the availability of rollover relief. Most candidates knew the basics of rollover relief. However, they did not score as well as they could have done for two reasons:

- The asset sold had not been used for the purposes of the trade for the whole of the period of ownership. As a result, although rollover relief was available, only the business-use proportion of the gain could be relieved and only that proportion of the proceeds needed to be reinvested in qualifying business assets.
- They failed to realise that the lease was a depreciating asset for the purposes of rollover relief, such that the gain would be deferred until the earliest of the date of disposal of the lease, the date the leased building ceased to be used in the business and ten years after the acquisition of the lease.

The final part of the question concerned the capital goods scheme for VAT and was not done particularly well. The capital goods scheme is not easy to explain and many candidates were unable to organise their thoughts and provide a coherent explanation of the implications of the disposal of a building.

Candidates would help themselves if they told the story from the beginning.

- The first point to make was that the input tax on the purchase of the building would have been recovered in full.
- It was then necessary to recognise that the sale of the building would be an exempt supply.
- As a result of the exempt supply, there will be deemed to be 0% taxable use of the building for the remainder of the ten-year adjustment period resulting in a repayment of VAT to HMRC.

ACCA marking scheme

				Marks
(a)	(i)	Cost of motorcycle option		1.5
		Cost of driving costs reimbursement option		3.0
		Conclusion		0.5
				5.0
	(ii)	Cost of provision of motorcycle		1.5
		Cost of driving costs reimbursement		1.0
		All costs deductible for corporation tax		0.5
		Conclusion		0.5
				3.5
			Maximum	3.0
(b)	Deduction:			
	Available against taxable trading income			1.0
	Amount			3.0
	Deferral relief available			3.0
	Date gain crystallises			2.0
				9.0
			Maximum	8.0
(c)	Disposal exempt			1.5
	Initial reclaim			1.0
	Repayment of VAT reclaimed previously y/e 31 December 2024			2.0
				4.5
			Maximum	4.0
	Professional skills marks (see below)		**Maximum**	5.0
Total				**25.0**

Professional skills marks

Analysis and evaluation

- Use of data to determine appropriate calculations to conclude on the most cost-efficient option in part (a).
- Demonstration of ability to consider all relevant taxes to the scenario in part (a), i.e. income tax, national insurance contributions and corporation tax.
- Use of data to determine the appropriate amount of rollover relief in part (b).
- Appropriate use of the data to support discussion and draw appropriate conclusions about the availability of rollover relief on the proposed sale of the warehouse in part (b).

Commercial acumen

- Recognition that rollover relief is a deferral relief in part (b).
- Recognition of impact of the capital goods scheme in part (c).

24 METHLEY LTD (ADAPTED) *Walk in the footsteps of a top tutor*

Key answer tips

This income tax focused section B question is really three separate questions about three independent taxpayers.

Requirement (a) tests the advanced level topic of share schemes, specifically the tax advantaged company share option plan.

Requirement (b) tests the income tax cost for an employee of taking a company car compared with a loan from the employer to buy the car personally.

Requirement (c) tests the remittance basis.

All of these areas are regularly tested and should not cause problems for well-prepared students. As the three requirements are independent they could have been attempted in any order. Whichever order you attempt them in, make sure you allocate enough time to each requirement.

The highlighted words in the written sections are key phrases that markers are looking for in your answer.

(a) Simon – company share option scheme (CSOP) versus an award of shares

Tutor's top tips

Share schemes are a new topic at the strategic professional level and are regularly tested, so make sure you have learnt the detail. It is important to tailor your answer to the scenario and not just write everything you know about a particular scheme.

Acquisition of the shares

Under a CSOP, there will be no charge to income tax in respect of the grant or exercise of the option given that Simon intends to exercise the option between three and ten years after the date of the grant.

There will be a charge to income tax if Simon receives free shares. Simon would have an income tax liability of £10,000 (£25,000 × 40%) in the tax year 2025/26.

Disposal of the shares

On disposal of the CSOP shares by Simon in the tax year 2031/32, any gain will be subject to capital gains tax (CGT). The gain (or loss) will be calculated by reference to the amount paid for them.

If Simon is awarded free shares worth £25,000, the disposal in the tax year 2031/32 will again be subject to CGT. However, the cost will be the market value at the date of award, i.e. £25,000. Any gains will be subject to CGT and any losses will be allowable.

Tutorial note

As Simon is a director of Methley Ltd, and will have held the shares for more than two years, any gain on disposal under both options may qualify for business asset disposal relief. This gives a 10% rate of CGT provided Methley Ltd remains a trading company and Simon has at least a 5% shareholding.

(b) Chris – provision of benefits

Tutor's top tips

Comparisons are a regular feature of the advanced taxation exam, so make sure you are ready to answer questions on the common scenarios. These include:

- *Employees: employment benefits vs. extra salary/loan*
- *Sole traders: lease an asset vs. buy an asset or take on an employee vs. take on a partner, and*
- *Small companies: take extra salary vs. take a dividend/pension contribution.*

Provision of the company car

List price of the car: £10,400 (£9,600 + £800)

Percentage to be used: 20% [16% + 1/5(75 – 55)]

Annual benefit: £2,080 (£10,400 × 20%)

The total amount taxable as employment income is therefore £10,440 (£4,140 ((£2,080 – £700) × 3) + £6,300) and the income tax cost to Chris is £4,176 (£10,440 × 40%).

Tutorial note

Remember that there is no 4% surcharge where a diesel car meets the RDE2 standard.

Provision of the loan

As the amount of the interest-free loan never exceeds £10,000, there is no taxable benefit in respect of it.

When the loan is written off, this will be treated as a distribution as Chris is a shareholder in Methley Ltd, which is a close company. Accordingly, an income tax charge of £3,240 (£9,600 × 33.75%) will arise in the year the loan is written off.

Provision of the loan will therefore result in a lower overall income tax liability for Chris.

(c) Yara – UK income tax on overseas income in the tax year 2023/24

Tutor's top tips

The remittance basis is tested frequently in the exam for a varying number of marks. It is important to tailor your answer to the scenario here and to not write everything you know about the remittance basis.

It would have been possible to answer this question by presenting full income tax computations including Yara's salary as well. However, Yara's salary is subject to UK income tax whether Yara claims the remittance basis or not, so it is quicker to 'work in the margin' and just think about the impact on Yara's overseas income given that her UK income will make her a higher rate taxpayer.

As Yara has been resident in the UK for seven tax years prior to the tax year 2023/24, she will be liable to pay a remittance basis charge of £30,000 if she continues to elect for the remittance basis.

In previous years Yara paid UK income tax of £4,000 (£10,000 × 40%) on her foreign rental income remitted to the UK. She would not have been liable to pay the remittance basis charge.

Claiming the remittance basis in the tax year 2023/24 would increase her income tax liability by £30,000 to £34,000 (£4,000 + £30,000).

However, if Yara does not claim the remittance basis in the tax year 2023/24, she will be taxed on the arising basis instead. In this case, she will pay tax on the full amount of the foreign rental income arising in the tax year of £24,000. This will result in UK income tax payable of £9,600 (£24,000 × 40%).

Yara will also be entitled to the personal allowance, which she lost in previous years when the remittance basis was claimed. As her net income will be £106,000 (£82,000 + £24,000), the personal allowance available will be restricted to £9,570 ((£12,570 – 0.5 × (£106,000 – £100,000))). This will result in an income tax saving of £3,828 (£9,570 × 40%).

Therefore, Yara's income tax on her foreign rental income on the arising basis, net of the tax saving as a result of the personal allowance, will be £5,772 (£9,600 – £3,828).

Claiming the remittance basis would not be beneficial for Yara in the tax year 2023/24. Accordingly, her income tax liability for the tax year 2023/24 in respect of her foreign rental income will increase by £1,772 (£5,772 – £4,000) compared to that payable in previous years.

Examiner's report

Part (a) of this question required candidates to compare and contrast the tax implications of an employee acquiring and disposing of shares in their company if these are acquired either through a tax advantaged company share option scheme (CSOP), or alternatively as free shares.

Most candidates demonstrated good knowledge of the tax implications of acquiring the shares through a CSOP, which has been tested many times before. Some candidates omitted to answer this part of the requirement; a significant number of those who did confused the scheme with a Share Incentive Plan (SIP), whose rules are totally different. Share incentive schemes are tested on a regular basis at ATX, so candidates should be confident with the tax implications of each, and ensure that they don't confuse the implications of the different schemes.

Note that this part of the question has been amended since it was originally set.

Part (b) of this question tested the income tax implications of two very commonly provided taxable benefits – a company car, and a beneficial loan. This is essentially brought forward knowledge from TX, but there were quite a lot of details to assimilate, and the majority of candidates did not take all of these into account. In order to provide a meaningful comparison of the income tax cost of each benefit, a candidate must ensure that all aspects of each scenario are considered. In particular, the car was to be provided for a three-year period, before being transferred to the employee, and the loan was to be made for the same three-year period, before being written off. The majority of candidates focused on the annual benefit calculation, but failed to consider that this situation would apply for three years, and then recognise the impact of the transfer/writing off. This is what essentially distinguished this as an ATX question – the ability to 'see the full picture' and advise on a holistic basis, taking into account all relevant details within a scenario. Candidates should be prepared for more questions of this style in future exams.

Part (c) dealt with the consequences of a UK resident, but non-domiciled individual claiming the remittance basis of taxation in respect of overseas income. This was clearly a question which candidates were prepared for and most scored well on this question part, recognising the need to compare the individual's income tax liability for the tax year on both an arising and a remittance basis, to determine which was lower. Almost all identified and dealt correctly with the remittance basis charge, which would be charged for the first time in the current tax year due to the individual's period of residence in the UK. However, very few actually answered the precise question set, which was to calculate the increase in the taxpayer's income tax liability in this tax year, compared with previous years, rather than just the difference between the arising and the remittance basis for the current year only. While this didn't lose the candidate many marks, it does highlight the need to read the question carefully, and ensure that the actual requirement is being addressed, rather than a requirement which the candidate is perhaps more used to seeing.

ACCA marking scheme			
			Marks
(a)	Acquisition of the shares		
	Company share option scheme		2.0
	Award of shares		2.0
	Disposal of shares		
	Company share option scheme		1.5
	Shares awarded		1.5
			7.0
(b)	Company car		3.0
	Beneficial loan		2.5
	Conclusion		0.5
			6.0
(c)	2023/24 remittance basis		3.0
	2023/24 arising basis		3.5
	Remittance basis claim not beneficial		0.5
	Increase in liability		0.5
			7.5
		Maximum	7.0
	Professional skills marks (see below)	**Maximum**	5.0
Total			**25.0**

Professional skills marks

Analysis and evaluation

- Appropriate use of data to determine tax implications relevant to the share schemes in part (a).
- Appropriate use of data to calculate income tax costs of alternative employment benefits in part (b).
- Appropriate use of data to evaluate which is the most tax efficient employment benefit in part (b).
- Appropriate use of the data to support discussion and draw appropriate conclusions about the desirability of claiming the remittance basis in part (c).

Commercial acumen

- Recognition of the impact of the close company rules on tax liabilities in part (b).
- Recognition of the consequences of claiming the remittance basis in part (c).

25 DAMIANA PLC (ADAPTED) *Walk in the footsteps of a top tutor*

Key answer tips

This question covers R&D relief for a company, corporation tax administration and share incentives for an employee.

The first part should be reasonably straightforward if you have learnt the R&D relief rules.

Part (b) tests TX level knowledge of corporation tax administration, and again should provide easy marks – provided you have retained this knowledge.

The final part of this question requires comparison of two alternative share incentives for an employee: sale of shares by the employer to the employee at less than market value versus share options issued under the enterprise management incentive (EMI) scheme. This is the trickiest part of the question, and requires some careful thought about the income tax and capital gains tax implications.

The highlighted words in the written sections are key phrases that markers are looking for in your answer.

(a) Relief for research and development (R&D) expenditure

Tutor's top tips

Remember that additional relief is available for companies incurring qualifying expenditure on R&D. You must learn the rates of relief available as these are not provided in the tax tables in the exam.

*Note the requirement to **explain** with supporting calculations. If you just prepare calculations with no explanations, you will not score full marks.*

As Damiana plc is an SME for R&D purposes, it can claim an additional deduction of 86% for its qualifying R&D expenditure. However, this additional relief is restricted in respect of the amount paid to the external contractor to 65% of the cost, i.e. £19,500 (65% × £30,000).

Accordingly, the tax saving attributable to the R&D expenditure is:

	£	£
Total R&D expenditure		169,000
Amount qualifying for additional deduction:		
Qualifying costs (£169,000 – £30,000)	139,000	
Subcontracted costs	19,500	
	158,500	
Additional deduction (£158,500 × 86%)		136,310
Total amount deductible for corporation tax		305,310
Corporation tax saving (25% × £305,310)		76,328

Tutor's top tips

You may find it easier to do the calculation for this requirement in the spreadsheet functionality in the exam. Make sure you reference through to your calculations in the word processor if you choose to answer in this way. Alternatively, you could insert a table in the word processor function, but remember there is no ability to use formulae in the word processor.

Tutorial note

As Damiana plc has augmented profits over £250,000, it will pay corporation tax at the main rate of 25%.

(b) Late filing of corporation tax returns

Tutor's top tips

Filing dates for companies and late filing penalties are key areas of corporation tax administration that you must learn.

There are two accounting periods within the 18-month period ended 31 March 2023 for which corporation tax returns should have been filed. The first is the 12 months ended 30 September 2022 and the second is the six months ended 31 March 2023.

Both returns should have been filed by 31 March 2024 (12 months after the end of the 18-month period of account).

As the returns have been filed more than three months late, each return will attract a fixed late filing penalty of £200, as previous returns have been filed on time.

Tutorial note

It has been assumed that HMRC issued notices requiring the returns to be made before 1 January 2024, so that the later three-month filing rule does not apply.

(c) Alternative 1 – transfer of shares to Luiza on 1 November 2024

Tutor's top tips

*The requirement asks you to **explain** the tax implications, so you need to provide a written answer as well as calculations.*

Note that you are asked to calculate Luiza's net increase in wealth under each alternative, which means that you should calculate the net cash that she will receive after deducting any tax due. This should provide easy marks, and you will be given credit for your method, even if the tax that you have calculated is incorrect.

As Luiza is an employee of Damiana plc, she will be treated as receiving a taxable benefit equal to the amount underpaid in respect of her shares. She is an additional rate taxpayer, so she will incur an income tax liability of £52,875 ((£24.50 – £1) × 5,000 = £117,500 × 45%) in the tax year 2024/25.

The shares are in a quoted company, so fall within the definition of 'readily convertible assets', therefore Luiza will also have a liability to class 1 national insurance contributions (NICs) of £2,350 (£117,500 × 2%).

On the sale of the shares on 10 November 2027, there will be a chargeable gain of £41,000 ((£32.70 – £24.50) × 5,000) arising in the 2027/28 tax year. As Luiza will have already used her annual exempt amount, capital gains tax will be payable on £41,000 at the rate of 20%. Business asset disposal relief will not be available as Luiza will not hold 5% of the shares in Damiana plc. The capital gains tax payable will therefore be £8,200 (£41,000 × 20%).

Luiza's net increase in wealth will be:

	£
Proceeds from sale of shares (£32.70 × 5,000)	163,500
Less: Cost of shares (£1 × 5,000)	(5,000)
Income tax	(52,875)
NICs	(2,350)
Capital gains tax	(8,200)
Net increase in wealth	95,075

Alternative 2 – Enterprise management incentive (EMI) scheme

The value of shares in the scheme on 1 November 2024 will be £122,500 (£24.50 × 5,000), which is within the £250,000 limit.

No income tax or NICs will be payable by Luiza on the granting of the options in the tax year 2024/25.

On exercise of the options on 2 November 2027, income tax and NICs will be payable on the difference between the market value at the date of grant and the exercise price of the options, i.e. £7,500 ((£24.50 – £23) × 5,000). This is the amount chargeable as it is less than the difference between the market value at the date of exercise and the exercise price. The income tax and NICs payable are therefore £3,525 (£7,500 × 47%).

As before, a chargeable gain will arise on disposal of £41,000. The gain will be charged at 10% as business asset disposal relief will be available. This is because for an EMI scheme there is no requirement for the shareholder to have a minimum 5% shareholding in the company, as long as the option was granted at least two years before the date of disposal, and the individual has worked for the company for at least two years prior to the date of disposal. The capital gains tax payable will therefore be £4,100 (£41,000 × 10%).

Luiza's net increase in wealth will be:

		£
Proceeds from sale of shares (£32.70 × 5,000)		163,500
Less:	Cost of options (£23 × 5,000)	(115,000)
	Income tax and NICs	(3,525)
	Capital gains tax	(4,100)
Net increase in wealth		40,875

Examiner's report

The first part related to the tax relief for research and development expenditure in a company. Most candidates were comfortable with the calculation of this, scoring full, or almost full, marks. However, many ignored the requirement to 'explain' the relief, and so were not able to pick up the marks for this. Candidates should ensure that they fully address all aspects of the requirements.

Note that this part of the question has been amended since it was originally set.

The second part of the question required explanation of the corporation tax return filing dates in relation to a long period of account.

Surprisingly, this was not done at all well. Most candidates recognised that the long period would be split into two accounting periods for tax purposes, but fewer were able to state the correct split of the long period. Fewer still correctly identified the filing dates, with the most common error being to state the payment dates instead.

The implications for a company in respect of late filing of returns elicited a number of answers stating that 'penalties will arise', or 'interest will be charged', but candidates must be precise as to the nature and amounts of such penalties/interest in order to gain marks in this type of question.

The final part of the question concerned the acquisition of shares by an employee, either by means of a transfer, or by exercising options in an enterprise management incentive (EMI). Although few candidates scored high marks on this question part, a good number achieved a respectable score. It appeared that many candidates ignored the last part of the requirement to calculate the taxpayer's increase in wealth under each of the alternatives, which was a shame as this should have represented relatively easy marks. It is similar to the, perhaps more familiar, requirement to calculate 'after-tax proceeds' from a transaction. In these cases, follow through marks are available as long as the candidate picks up the correct figures from their earlier calculations. The message, again, is to read the requirements of a question very carefully to ensure that what should be relatively easier marks, marks like these, are not overlooked.

ACCA marking scheme

			Marks
(a)	Explanation of treatment of R&D costs		2.5
	Calculation of tax saving		2.5
			5.0
(b)	Returns required		2.0
	Implications of late filing		2.0
			4.0
		Maximum	3.0
(c)	Alternative 1		7.0
	Alternative 2		7.0
			14.0
		Maximum	12.0
	Professional skills marks (see below)	**Maximum**	5.0
Total			**25.0**

Professional skills marks

Analysis and evaluation

- Appropriate use of the data to determine the corporation tax saving as a result of the R&D expenditure in part (a).
- Analysis of the information to determine the relevant filing dates and necessary penalty in part (b).
- Appropriate use of the data to calculate the net increase in wealth figures in part (c).
- Demonstration of ability to consider all taxes relevant to the scenario in part (c), i.e. income tax, national insurance contributions and capital gains tax.

Commercial acumen

- Ability to assess whether capital gains tax reliefs are available in part (c).

26 DEMETER (ADAPTED)

Key answer tips

Part (a) of this question looks at the treatment of a lump sum and relocation package. It is important to explain why certain amounts are taxable rather than just stating that they will be taxed.

Part (b) is testing PRR and letting relief but you may find the numbers tricky due to the fact that the property has been let out for some of the time. Remember that any time the property is occupied it will qualify for PRR but the let part won't. You also need to think about the periods of deemed occupation which you can use. Once you have reduced your gain by PRR think about the available letting relief.

Part (c) is looking at pensions. You need to explain the initial treatment of the employer contributions but you also need to consider the impact of the other contributions Demeter has already made. Think about the level of annual allowance he has and whether this could cause an issue.

Finally, part (d) is looking at share options. In this case it is a non-tax advantaged share option plan. In order to score well you need to explain the tax implications at all three stages of the option lifespan (grant, exercise and sale). Try not to get confused with the rules for tax advantaged option plans.

The highlighted words in the written sections are key phrases that markers are looking for.

(a) Receipt of the one-off lump sum inducement payment and relocation package

The one-off lump sum inducement payment of £20,000 paid on commencement of Demeter's employment is fully taxable as it wholly relates to future services to be performed by Demeter.

The total amount received by Demeter in relation to his relocation is £11,000 (£5,000 + (£1,500 × 4)). Demeter did not previously live within a reasonable daily travelling distance of his new employment, so is eligible for a maximum tax allowable amount of £8,000, provided he has spent at least this amount on qualifying expenditure.

Demeter's qualifying expenditure comprises all the costs relating to his move, including the estate agent fees on the sale of his house of £2,800, and the rent on his accommodation in London of £1,700 per month from 1 December 2024 until he purchases a new house on 1 April 2025. His total qualifying expenditure is therefore £12,800 (£6,000 + (£1,700 × 4)). This clearly exceeds £8,000, so the taxable amount of Demeter's relocation package is £3,000 (£11,000 – £8,000).

(b) Reliefs available to Demeter to reduce the chargeable gain on the sale of his house in Manchester

As the house was Demeter's only residence, private residence relief (PRR) will be available to exempt the proportion of the gain which relates to his actual or deemed occupation of the property. The relief is calculated as follows:

Demeter owned the house for 13.5 years (162 months) (1 May 2011 to 31 October 2024).

Availability of PRR:

	Exempt months	
1 May 2011 to 30 April 2013	100% occupation	24
1 May 2013 to 31 Jan 2024	70% occupation (129m × 70%)	90
1 Feb 2024 to 31 Oct 2024	Last nine months treated as 100% occupation	9
Total exempt months		123

The PRR will exempt £71,370 (£94,000 × 123/162) of the gain. The remainder of the gain, i.e. £22,630 (£94,000 × 39/162), is attributable to the let part of the property.

Letting relief provides an extension to PRR in relation to the gain arising on the part of Demeter's house which was let. The additional exemption is restricted to the lowest of:

1. The amount of the gain which is exempt under PRR (£71,370).
2. The gain attributable to the letting (£22,630).
3. £40,000.

Therefore, the letting relief available is £22,630.

(c) (i) Tax consequences for Demeter of participating in Poseidon Ltd's occupational pension scheme in 2025/26

Poseidon Ltd's contribution into its occupational pension scheme on Demeter's behalf of £13,000 (10% × £130,000) will be an exempt benefit for Demeter, so no tax liability will arise on this.

However, the contributions will count towards Demeter's annual allowance. This will remain at £40,000 as Demeter's threshold income of £90,000 (net income (£130,000) less Demeter's personal pension contributions (£40,000)) does not exceed the £200,000 threshold.

Demeter has no unused annual allowance to bring forward from earlier tax years as he has made contributions up to the maximum amount each year. As the total contributions in 2025/26 of £53,000 (£13,000 + £40,000) will exceed the annual allowance, an annual allowance charge will be payable.

Demeter's tax bands will be extended by his gross personal pension contributions, so the higher rate band will be increased to £165,140 (£125,140 + £40,000). Accordingly, as a higher rate taxpayer Demeter will pay an annual allowance charge of £5,200 (40% × £13,000 (£53,000 – £40,000)).

Tutorial note

There is no need to calculate Demeter's adjusted income as the amount of annual allowance will not be reduced regardless because his threshold income is below £200,000.

(ii) Tax consequences for Demeter of participating in Poseidon Ltd's non-tax advantaged share option scheme

No income tax will be payable by Demeter on the grant of the options on 1 December 2024.

When Demeter exercises the options on 6 April 2030, income tax will be payable on the excess of the market value of the shares at the date of exercise over the price paid by Demeter, i.e. £6,030 ((£6.00 – (£4.20 × 95%) × 3,000). The income tax payable is therefore £2,412 (£6,030 × 40%).

The exercise of the shares has no impact on Demeter's personal allowance because his adjusted net income is below £100,000. There will also be no impact on Demeter's annual allowance charge because his threshold income remains below £200,000.

As Demeter will sell the shares immediately following the exercise of the options, the shares will not have increased in value and so no chargeable gain will arise.

Examiner's report

This question concerned various matters in relation to an individual relocating to take up employment. There were four parts to the question broadly covering a relocation package, sale of a residence, pension scheme contributions and a non-tax advantaged share option scheme.

Part (a) asked candidates to consider the extent to which an inducement package and relocation expenses would be taxable. Most candidates knew that the inducement package would be taxable but were not able to explain the reason why. Similarly, most candidates knew that there was a relocation allowance of £8,000 but did not know the rules for qualifying relocation expenditure.

Part (b) required candidates to calculate and briefly explain the relief(s) available upon sale of a residence, which had been partially let to tenants. Many candidates were aware of the availability of private residence relief (PRR) in the scenario but made some mistakes in their calculations of the relief. Candidates should have known that periods of occupation are completely exempt and that the last nine months are treated as 100% occupation and therefore exempt.

Any remaining gain after private residence relief was eligible for letting relief although this proved to be a less well-known relief. Letting relief is restricted to the lowest of the following three values.

- The amount of the gain which is exempt under PRR
- The gain attributable to letting
- £40,000.

This is not a particularly tricky subject area and candidates should have been able to identify these points from the question.

Part (c)(i) considered the implications of an employer's contribution to an occupational pension scheme, when the employee is already making annual contributions to a personal pension scheme equal to the annual allowance. There was a general awareness of the rules in this area such as the £40,000 allowance but a lack of precision in relation to the detailed calculations required.

The final part of the question, part (c)(ii), concerned the tax implications of a non-tax advantaged share option scheme, from option grant through to exercise and disposal. Candidates should have been able to identify the following tax points from the facts of the question.

- No income tax payable on grant of the options
- Income tax payable on exercise of the options
- No gain on sale of the shares because it immediately follows the exercise of the options and the shares will not have increased in value.

This part was not done particularly well since candidates did not have a sufficiently precise knowledge of the rules concerning a non-tax advantaged share option plan.

ACCA marking scheme

				Marks
(a)	One-off lump sum payment			2.0
	Financial assistance with relocation			3.5
				5.5
			Maximum	5.0
(b)	Private residence relief			4.0
	Letting relief			3.0
				7.0
			Maximum	6.0
(c)	(i)	Poseidon Ltd's contributions		1.5
		Annual allowance charge		5.5
				7.0
			Maximum	5.0
	(ii)	Grant of options		1.0
		Exercise of options		2.0
		Sale of shares		1.0
		Consideration of impact on personal allowance/annual allowance charge		1.0
				5.0
			Maximum	4.0
	Professional skills marks (see below)		**Maximum**	5.0
Total				**25.0**

Professional skills marks

Analysis and evaluation

- Ability to evaluate the tax treatment of the employment package in part (a).
- Provision of at least one explanatory note in relation to the chargeable gain in part (b).
- Appropriate use of the data to calculate the reliefs available on Demeter's chargeable gain in part (b).
- Analysis of the data to determine the appropriate tax relief for pension contributions in part (c)(i).

Commercial acumen

- Ability to assess whether capital gains tax reliefs are available in part (b).

27 YACON LTD AND DAIKON (ADAPTED)

Key answer tips

This question covers provision of two alternative share schemes: CSOP and SIP, the disposal of a private residence and finally IHT on a lifetime gift.

Part (a) requires in-depth knowledge of CSOP and SIP conditions, which may have put off many students. However, there are eight marks available for applying the conditions of the two schemes and no calculations are required. Share schemes are examined fairly regularly and you need to be confident with being able to discuss and apply the conditions.

Part (b) covers the disposal of a private residence with private residence relief and letting relief. If you follow a logical, step by step approach when dealing with the reliefs available and the dates of occupation and non-occupation you should do well in this type of question. These are all TX areas.

Part (c) covers IHT in respect of a gift with reservation, with the twist that the reservation is lifted before the donor's death. In order to spot this, you need to make sure you read the information in detail to see what has happened to the apartment that was given, who it was occupied by and for how long.

(a) Company share option plan (CSOP)

Ability to select employees

In a CSOP, Yacon Ltd would be free to select employees as it wishes to participate in the scheme.

Value of options granted

Yacon Ltd can choose to award options to purchase a different number of shares to each member of a CSOP. There is no annual maximum amount, but an employee can only be granted options over shares up to a total value of £30,000, as at the date of the grant. As Yacon Ltd only proposes to grant options over shares worth up to £3,000 per year for each employee, this is well within the limits.

Holding period required and tax implications for employees

There are no tax implications for employees on the grant of the options, or on their exercise after five years as the exercise will be between three and ten years of being granted.

Share incentive plan (SIP)

Ability to select employees

Under the rules for a SIP, all employees must be offered the opportunity to participate in the plan. Yacon Ltd can specify a minimum period of employment in order to qualify, but this cannot exceed 18 months.

Value of free shares given

Yacon Ltd can give each employee free shares up to the value of £3,600 each tax year, such that the proposal to offer shares with a value of up to £3,000 to each employee each year will be acceptable. The free shares must be offered on similar terms to all employees, such that different amounts of shares can be offered to different employees, depending on their meeting certain objective criteria, such as length of service or performance targets.

Holding period required and tax implications for employees

There are no tax implications for employees when the free shares are put into the plan.

As the free shares will be held in the plan for five years, there will also be no income tax liability when they are withdrawn from the plan.

Tutorial note

The requirement only asked for the income tax implications on acquisition. It is vital to double check the precise scope of the requirement so you do not waste time on something that will not get you any marks.

(b) Daikon – reliefs available on the sale of his house

Private residence relief (PRR):

	Exempt years	Chargeable years
1 July 2016 to 31 December 2016		
Absent – no prior occupation		0.5
1 January 2017 to 30 June 2018		
Occupied	1.5	
1 July 2018 to 31 December 2019		
Absent but deemed occupation as employed overseas	1.5	
1 January 2020 to 31 March 2020		
Occupied	0.25	
1 April 2020 to 31 March 2024		
Occupied (4 years × 75%)	3	1
1 April 2024 to 31 December 2024		
Last 9 months treated as 100% occupation	0.75	
	7	1.5

PRR is £119,412 (£145,000 × 7/8.5).

Letting relief

Letting relief is available to claim where part of an individual's private residence is let out and so a proportion does not qualify for PRR. The property must be occupied by both the tenant and the owner during the let period to qualify for the relief.

The additional amount of the gain which will be exempt under letting relief is the lowest of:

1 The amount of the gain which is exempt under the PRR exemption (£119,412).

2 The gain attributable to the letting £17,059 (£145,000 × 1/8.5).

3 £40,000.

Letting relief is therefore £17,059.

(c) Inheritance tax implications of Jicama's gift of the apartment

The gift of the apartment on 5 June 2022 was a potentially exempt transfer (PET), valued at the market value of the apartment on that date. The gift was also a gift with reservation of benefit, due to the condition imposed by Jicama that she would continue to live there.

However, the reservation of benefit was lifted on 12 March 2024, when Jicama went to live with her sister. This created a further PET, which would be valued at the market value of the apartment on that date.

If Jicama dies in December 2027, this is within seven years of the date of the original gift, so both the original PET and the later deemed PET become chargeable. Taper relief would be available to reduce the liability to inheritance tax in both cases. To avoid a double tax charge, only the PET which results in a higher tax charge overall will actually be chargeable

Examiner's report

Requirement (a) – 8 marks

This requirement asked for an explanation of whether two different share schemes, a company share option plan (CSOP) and a share incentive plan (SIP), would satisfy Yacon Ltd's criteria for a tax advantaged share scheme. In addition, the income tax implications for the employees of acquiring the shares in each case needed to be explained.

Those candidates who knew the rules for share option schemes were able to apply them to the facts of the question with relative ease. Those with only a superficial understanding of the rules struggled to score well on this part. A detailed knowledge of the underlying rules is required for ATX-UK and those who don't possess this will struggle to do well on questions where this needs to be demonstrated.

A number of candidates went on to discuss the capital gains tax consequences of disposing of the shares, despite the fact that the requirement only asked for the income tax implications on acquisition. It is vital to double check the precise scope of the requirement such that time is not wasted in terms of doing something that has not been requested.

Requirement (b) – 7 marks

This requirement was to calculate, with brief explanations, the private residence relief (PRR) and potential letting relief, available to reduce the gain on the sale of a house.

It was encouraging to see that many candidates had a strong understanding of the PRR rules and were able to apply their knowledge to the facts of the question. However, common areas of confusion involved the first six-month period when the owner was working overseas; this was a chargeable period because there had been no prior period of occupation. Also it should be noted that the last nine months of ownership is always exempt, even if some of the property is rented out during that period (as long as it has been occupied as the private residence at some point in the past).

Some candidates only provided calculations, and others only explanations. The requirement did however stipulate 'a calculation, with brief explanations', so to score well a combination of the two was required.

Not all candidates were as familiar with letting relief, which is given after consideration of PRR. Those who did understand the rules were able to score the marks for knowing that it is the lower of three comparative amounts; namely £40,000, the gain already exempt under PRR and the gain attributable to the let period.

Requirement (c) – 5 marks

This part of the question related to the inheritance tax implications of a gift of an apartment, on the assumption that the donor were to die within seven years.

The facts contained within the question are that when the apartment was first gifted, the donor retained the right to continue to live in it. Many candidates correctly identified this scenario as a 'gift with reservation of benefit' and a potentially exempt transfer (PET) at the time. The question then goes on to explain that, some time later, the donor removed the condition of her right to live in the property. Not all candidates realised that the removal of this 'reservation of benefit' created a further deemed PET at the date the condition was lifted.

Since the donor then went on to die within seven years of the first PET, both PETs in theory become chargeable but tax will only be due on the one giving rise to the higher liability.

ACCA marking scheme

			Marks
(a)	Company share option plan		4.0
	Share incentive plan		5.0
			9.0
		Maximum	8.0
(b)	Private residence relief		5.5
	Letting relief		2.5
			8.0
		Maximum	7.0
(c)	Original gift 5 June 2022		2.0
	Reservation lifted		2.0
	Death in December 2027		3.0
			7.0
		Maximum	5.0
	Professional skills marks (see below)	**Maximum**	5.0
Total			**25.0**

Professional skills marks

Analysis and evaluation

- Appropriate use of the facts provided in order to reach relevant conclusions with respect to the suitability of the share plans in part (a).
- Adoption of a logical approach to prepare suitable calculations of PRR and letting relief in part (b).

Commercial acumen

- Ability to assess whether capital gains tax reliefs are available in part (b).
- Appropriate use of information to identify gift with reservation in part (c).
- Demonstration of awareness that change in Jicama's circumstances will impact the inheritance tax position in part (c).

UNINCORPORATED BUSINESSES

28 AMY AND BEX (ADAPTED) *Walk in the footsteps of a top tutor*

Key answer tips

This section B question is mostly made up of areas which are within the TX syllabus, specifically the allocation of partnership profits and also a loan made by a partner to a partnership, emphasising the importance of retaining TX knowledge. The question also includes the very commonly-tested exam topic of redundancy payments.

Part (a)(i) requires an explanation of the tax relief available for interest payable on a loan taken out by a partner which is then lent to a partnership. Both the partner and the partnership are paying interest and so the question requires an analysis of how relief is claimed from both perspectives.

Part (a)(ii) involves the allocation of partnership profits for a new business, which you should be familiar with from your TX studies.

Part (b) requires an understanding of the different rules that apply to the various elements of a typical redundancy package.

The highlighted words in the written sections are key phrases that markers are looking for.

(a) (i) Tax treatment of the interest payable

Tutor's top tips

When a partnership pays interest on a loan taken out for business purposes the interest is simply deducted from trading profits. However, when a partner takes out a loan to provide money to the partnership, the interest paid is deducted from the partner's total income rather than the partner's trading income from the partnership.

The interest payable by the partnership on the loan from Bex will be deductible in calculating the taxable trading profit of the business.

As the loan will be made on 1 August 2024, the interest payable in the period ending 30 April 2025 will be £750 (£20,000 × 5% × 9/12).

The interest payable on the loan taken out by Bex to provide the loan to the partnership will qualify for income tax relief as it is a loan for a qualifying purpose. The annual deduction from Bex's total income will be £1,000 (£20,000 × 5%), and the deduction in the tax year 2024/25 will be £667 (£1,000 × 8/12).

The purchase of a computer for use in a partnership is also a qualifying purpose for income tax relief, but the interest payable is only allowable for three years from the end of the tax year in which the loan was taken out, i.e. up to 2027/28. The allowable amount is also restricted where there is private use of the asset by the partner.

Bex will get a deduction against her total income of £133 (£5,000 × 5% × 80% × 8/12) in the tax year 2024/25 and an annual deduction of £200 (£5,000 × 5% × 80%) in each of the tax years 2025/26, 2026/27 and 2027/28.

(ii) Allocation of taxable trading profit

	£
Adjusted profit before loan interest and capital allowances	255,000
Less: Loan interest payable (from (a)(i))	(750)
Less: AIA on the computer (£5,000 × 80%)	(4,000)
Taxable trading profit	250,250

Allocation:

	Total	**Amy**	**Bex**
	£	£	£
16 months ending 30 April 2025			
Salary (£30,000 × 16/12)	40,000	0	40,000
Balance in profit sharing ratio (3:1)	210,250	157,688	52,562
Total share of profit	250,250	157,688	92,562

Tutorial note

As no other assets will be purchased by the partners in the period ending 30 April 2025, the computer equipment purchased by Bex will qualify for the annual investment allowance (AIA). This will be restricted to reflect her private use of the computer.

(b) Bex – redundancy package from Cape Ltd

Tutor's top tips

Remember that although statutory redundancy payments are always exempt from income tax, they do reduce the £30,000 tax free exemption that applies to certain qualifying discretionary (ex-gratia) lump sum payments.

The statutory redundancy pay is fully exempt from income tax and national insurance contributions. However, it reduces the £30,000 exemption available for the ex-gratia payment.

As Bex's contract entitled her to two months' pay in lieu of notice (PILON) of £20,000 (£120,000 × 2/12), this is fully taxable as earnings and is subject to income tax and class 1 employee's national insurance contributions.

The third month of PILON of £10,000 (£120,000 × 1/12) was not expected, and will therefore be taxed as a termination payment along with the ex-gratia payment.

The ex-gratia payment was not expected and so, along with the excess PILON, will attract a £30,000 exemption.

The taxable amount of the termination payment is therefore £50,000 ((£58,000 + £10,000) – (£30,000 – £12,000)). This will be subject to income tax as Bex's top slice of income, but will not be subject to national insurance contributions for Bex.

Tutorial note

Remember that for NIC purposes any ex-gratia payment and excess PILON would be exempt from employee's class 1 NICs, but the excess over £30,000 would be subject to class 1A NICs for the employer.

Bex – income tax liability 2023/24

		£
Employment income	– salary (£120,000 × 6/12)	60,000
	– PILON	20,000
Partnership profit		17,355
Taxable portion of termination payment		50,000
		147,355
Less: Personal allowance		0
Taxable income		147,355
Income tax liability:		
£		£
37,700 × 20%		7,540
87,440 × 40%		34,976
125,140		
22,215 × 45%		9,997
147,355		
Income tax liability		52,513

Class 1 employee's NICs	£
Earnings subject to NICs (£60,000 + £20,000)	80,000
(£50,270 – £12,570) × 12%	4,524
(£80,000 – £50,270) × 2%	595
	5,119

Tutorial note

As Bex's income exceeds £125,140 her personal allowance would be reduced to nil.

Examiner's report

Part (a)(i) required an explanation of the tax deductions available in respect of interest on two loans. The new partner took out a personal loan, which qualified for income tax relief in her personal tax computation, and she used this to make a loan to the partnership, which qualified for tax relief in the computation of the partnership's taxable trading profit. A good number of candidates produced rather muddled answers to this part, not making it clear which of the loans they were referring to in their explanations or supporting calculations, and therefore potentially not attracting as many marks as they could have done. The adoption of a logical approach in this sort of question requiring a discussion of two very similar issues can save considerable confusion and avoid wasting time. Candidates should pause and think before they start writing. Dealing fully with the implications of one of the loans first, and then the other, tended to provide a much clearer answer than those who adopted something of a random approach, apparently writing points as they occurred to them, without making it clear which loan they were dealing with, and leading to confusion for the reader.

In part (a)(ii) candidates were required to calculate the taxable trading profit for the first accounting period for the partnership and show the allocation between the partners. The majority of candidates correctly identified the deductions available for loan interest and capital allowances, and allocated the profit between the two partners in the profit-sharing ratio. The most common error was a failure to deal correctly with the salary paid to one of the partners, treating this as an allowable deduction from the partnership profit, rather than as part of the profit allocation.

Part (a)(iii) has been removed from the question since it tested an area no longer on the syllabus.

Part (b) required explanation of the tax treatment of various items within a redundancy package, and calculation of the taxpayer's tax liability for the year in which this was received. In the main, this was done well, with the majority of candidates appearing to be very comfortable with this topic.

ACCA marking scheme

				Marks
(a)	(i)	Interest payable by the partnership		2.0
		Interest payable by Bex		5.5
				7.5
			Maximum	7.0
	(ii)	Adjustment to profit		2.5
		Allocation of profit		2.0
				4.5
			Maximum	4.0
(b)	Taxable redundancy payment			5.0
	Calculation of income tax			4.5
	Calculation of NICs			1.5
				11.0
			Maximum	9.0
	Professional skills marks (see below)		**Maximum**	5.0
Total				**25.0**

Professional skills marks

Analysis and evaluation

- Appropriate use of the data to support discussion and draw appropriate conclusions about the availability of tax relief for the loan interest in part (a)(i).
- Consideration of both income tax and national insurance implications in part (b)
- Appropriate use of the data to determine suitable calculations to perform in order to calculate the tax liability in part (b).

Commercial acumen

- Recognition that loan has been taken out for a qualifying purpose in part (a)(i).
- Recognition that tax relief is only available for a limited time where the loan is used for plant and machinery in part (a)(i).
- Recognition that the notice period in the contract will alter the tax treatment of the PILON in part (b).

29 MEG AND LAURIE (ADAPTED) *Walk in the footsteps of a top tutor*

Key answer tips

This question covers the tax implications of taking on an employee or a partner, a sale of rights nil paid and overseas aspects of VAT.

Part (a) covers the common scenario of taking on a spouse either as an employee or as a partner, but for a loss-making business. Most of the marks in this part are for discussing the trading loss reliefs available and for providing advice on the possible tax savings.

Part (b) covers a sale of rights nil paid, which is not a very common topic in the exam. However, there are still some easy marks to pick up for basic capital gains tax computations, so do not neglect this requirement.

The final part of the question requires knowledge of the VAT implications of purchasing overseas services. Overseas aspects of VAT are tested fairly regularly in the exam.

The highlighted words in the written sections are key phrases that markers are looking for in your answer.

(a) (i) Allowable trading losses if Laurie is an employee

	£
Tax adjusted trading loss in 2025/26 before any payment to Laurie	20,000
Add: Salary paid to Laurie	12,000
Employer's NICs (Note)	0
Allowable trading loss for Meg in 2025/26	32,000

Laurie will not have an allowable trading loss in this case.

Note: Laurie's salary of £12,000 each year is an allowable expense for Meg's business. No class 1 employer's national insurance contributions (NICs) will be payable in respect of this as they will be covered by the £5,000 annual employment allowance.

Tutorial note

The NIC employment allowance is available here, even though Laurie is the only employee, as this is an unincorporated business. It is not available for a company where a director is the sole employee.

It is also not available to businesses whose employers NIC liability was £100,000 or more in the previous year. As MT Travel did not previously have any employees this rule will not be applicable here.

Allowable trading losses if Laurie is a partner

	Total	Meg	Laurie
	£	£	£
Tax-adjusted trading loss (allocated 75:25)	20,000	15,000	5,000

(ii) Loss relief available to Meg

Tutor's top tips

Trading losses for unincorporated businesses are often tested in the exam, so you must learn the rules.

The key to scoring well is to be very specific when describing the reliefs available, avoid discussing reliefs that are not relevant and apply your knowledge to the specific scenario. For example, the additional relief for losses in opening years will be available to Laurie if he commences trade as a partner, but will not be available to Meg.

In the tax year 2025/26 Meg has an allowable loss of £32,000, if Laurie is taken on as an employee, and £15,000, if Laurie becomes a partner.

Loss relief is available against Meg's total income of the tax year 2025/26 and/or 2024/25. In the tax year 2025/26 Meg's only income will be £8,600 rental income. In 2024/25 her income will include a taxable trading profit of £1,600 for the year ended 31 March 2025 in addition to the rental income of £8,600. In both these tax years her total income is covered by her personal allowance for the year, and therefore a loss relief claim will not result in any tax saving in either year.

Alternatively, the full amount of the loss can be carried forward for relief against the first available future profits from the same trade, which are expected to occur in 2026/27. The maximum rate of relief will be 20% on the amount of Meg's taxable income (all non-savings), which falls within the basic rate band.

Loss relief available to Laurie

If Laurie becomes a partner in the business, he will have an allowable trading loss of £5,000 in 2025/26. His total income in each of the tax years 2025/26 and 2024/25 is £18,000, which is wholly dividend income, so he could relieve the loss in either year resulting in tax being saved at the rate of 8.75% in respect of the dividends in excess of his personal allowance and dividend nil rate band.

As 2025/26 is the tax year of commencement of business for Laurie, he can carry back the loss against his total income of the three tax years prior to the loss-making year on a FIFO basis. Accordingly, he can offset the loss against his total income of the tax year 2022/23, when he was employed. This will result in a tax saving at the rate of 40% as the loss will be relieved against his employment income, and Laurie was a higher rate taxpayer in 2022/23.

(b) Sale of rights nil paid

The treatment of the sale of rights nil paid will depend on whether the proceeds are small or not. The proceeds of £20,000 are not small because they are greater than:

– 5% of the value of the shares on which the rights were offered (3,000 × £32 = £96,000 × 5% = £4,800), and

– £3,000.

Therefore, the sale of rights nil paid will give rise to a part disposal of the Hagg Ltd shares for Laurie and give rise to a chargeable gain.

	£
Proceeds	20,000
Less: Cost (£20,000/(£20,000 + £96,000)) × £60,000	(10,345)
Chargeable gain	9,655
Less: Annual exempt amount (Note 1)	(6,000)
Taxable gain	3,655
CGT @ 10% (Note 2)	366

Notes

1 On the assumption that Laurie has not made any other chargeable disposals in the tax year 2023/24 then his annual exempt amount may be deducted.

2 Laurie will be able to claim business asset disposal relief to obtain a 10% tax rate, provided that Hagg Ltd is a trading company. This is because he has been employed by the company and owned at least 5% of the share capital for at least two years before disposal.

Tutor's top tips

You will not always have perfect information in the ATX exam, so be prepared to make assumptions in order to draw conclusions. Ensure that you state your assumptions clearly so that credit can be awarded for them.

(c) Implications of purchasing services from the overseas supplier

Tutor's top tips

You should make sure that you know the VAT rules for imports/exports of goods, and for supply/purchase of overseas services. Be prepared to explain these rules in the exam.

As MT Travel is registered for value added tax (VAT), this is a business to business (B2B) service, so will be treated as supplied in the UK, as this is where the customer (MT Travel) is established. MT Travel must therefore pay VAT at the UK standard-rate of 20% to HM Revenue and Customs under the 'reverse charge' principle. The rate of VAT overseas is irrelevant.

Input VAT can be reclaimed on this expense in the normal way.

MT Travel's VAT position is therefore the same as if the services had been purchased from the UK supplier.

Examiner's report

Elements of this examiner's report which relate to a topic no longer on the ATX syllabus have been deleted.

This question concerned an unincorporated business which was anticipating a trading loss in a future period.

The first part of this question required a calculation of the loss available to the trader, and their spouse, on the basis that firstly, the spouse became an employee of the business, or, secondly, the spouse became a partner in the business. In general this was done well. Candidates were then required to go on and advise both taxpayers as to the reliefs available for their losses. The rules relating to trading losses are frequently examined, and while many candidates scored reasonably here, more precise answers would have scored higher marks. Candidates would do well to invest time at the revision stage of their studies to memorising the rules concerning relief for trading losses, and ensuring that they are able to recognise those rules which apply in a given scenario. In particular, they should be able to identify those which apply in certain situations only, such as the opening years of a business, which was applicable to just one of the partners here.

Those candidates who scored well on this particular part:

- adopted a structured approach to outlining the reliefs for the trading loss separately for each of the individuals, and clearly stating the rate of tax saved, as required.
- Didn't waste time considering irrelevant reliefs.

The final two requirements have been added to the question since it was originally set.

In order to gain a good mark in this type of question it is vital that candidates attempt past exam questions which are available in the question banks. Reading through model answers, while providing useful information, is often of limited help in these cases; candidates need to practise the structured approach necessary to produce a good, coherent answer.

ACCA marking scheme					
					Marks
(a)	(i)	Laurie as employee	– loss available to Meg		2.0
			– no loss available to Laurie		0.5
		Laurie as a partner	– split of loss in PSR		1.0
					3.5
				Maximum	3.0
	(ii)	Loss relief available to Meg			5.0
		Loss relief available to Laurie			4.5
					9.5
				Maximum	8.0
(b)	Proceeds not small				2.0
	Chargeable gain				2.5
	Capital gains tax				1.5
	Business asset disposal relief				1.5
					7.5
				Maximum	5.0
(c)	Reverse charge principle				3.0
	Further implications				1.5
					4.5
				Maximum	4.0
	Professional skills marks (see below)			**Maximum**	5.0
Total					**25.0**

Professional skills marks

Analysis and evaluation

- Appropriate use of the data to calculate the allowable trading losses for the partners in part (a).
- Appropriate use of the data to support discussion and draw appropriate conclusions about the loss reliefs available in part (a).
- Analysis of the information to determine whether MT Travel's VAT position will be affected by the purchase of services from overseas in part (c).

Scepticism

- Assumption made regarding availability of the annual exempt amount in part (b).
- Assumption made regarding trading status of Hagg Ltd in part (b).

Commercial acumen

- Recognition of the advantages and disadvantages of various loss relief claims in part (a).

30 ROD (ADAPTED)

Key answer tips

This question tests a mixture of new areas (EMI share options) as well as brought forward knowledge from TX (partnerships and loss relief).

Part (a) asks for a calculation of after-tax proceeds for the sale of some shares acquired via an EMI option. In order to do this, you need to think about how much would be chargeable to CGT and tax this at the appropriate rate to take away from proceeds. You were also asked to explain how the base cost is calculated for CGT so make sure you do this and not just the calculations.

Part (b) tests purely brought forward knowledge from TX. However, although this is content you have seen before, it still gets tested regularly in the ATX exam. Therefore, you need to ensure you are comfortable with loss relief for unincorporated businesses.

(a) After-tax proceeds from the sale of the Lumba plc shares

The capital gain on the sale of the Lumba plc shares is calculated as follows:

	£	£
Sale proceeds (£4.00 × 20,000)		80,000
Less: Exercise price (£2.30 × 20,000)	46,000	
Amount charged to income tax on exercise (see below)	6,000	
Base cost		(52,000)
Chargeable gain		28,000
Less: Annual exempt amount		(6,000)
Taxable gain		22,000

The capital gains tax payable is £2,200 (£22,000 × 10%).

The after-tax proceeds are £77,800 (£80,000 – £2,200).

As the options were granted at a discount to the market value at the date of grant, a charge to income tax will have arisen on 1 June 2023, when Rod exercised the options, on an amount of £6,000 (£0.30 per share × 20,000 shares), being the difference between the market value of the shares at the date of grant and the exercise price of the options (£2.60 – £2.30). This is added to the price paid for the shares (£2.30 per share) in calculating the base cost of the shares.

(b) (i) Rod's share of the tax-adjusted trading losses in the Thora Partnership for the years ended 31 March 2024 and 2025

	31 March 2024	31 March 2025
	£	£
Tax-adjusted trading loss		50,000
From 1 December 2023 to 31 March 2024		
(£47,000 × 4/12)	15,667	
Add: Salaries for Abe and Bob		
(£20,000 + £20,000)		40,000
(£20,000 + £20,000) × 4/12	13,333	
Balance of loss to be allocated in the profit/loss sharing ratio	29,000	90,000
Rod's share 1/3	9,667	30,000

Tutorial note

You were only asked to calculate Rod's share of the loss, so there was no need to show the full allocation of the loss between the partners for each period. Had you done this, you would still score full marks for this part of the question, but you would waste valuable time in the exam. The full calculations are shown below for tutorial purposes.

Alternative presentation of workings:

Y/e 31 March 2024	**Total**	**Abe**	**Bob**	**Rod**
	£	£	£	£
1 April 2023 to 30 November 2023				
Loss (£47,000 × 8/12)	(31,333)	(15,666)	(15,667)	N/A
1 December 2023 to 31 March 2024				
Salaries × 4/12	13,333	6,667	6,666	0
Balance shared 1:1:1				
(£47,000 × 4/12) + £13,333	(29,000)	(9,667)	(9,666)	(9,667)
Total	(47,000)	(18,666)	(18,667)	(9,667)

Y/e 31 March 2025	**Total**	**Abe**	**Bob**	**Rod**
	£	£	£	£
Salaries	40,000	20,000	20,000	0
Balance shared 1:1:1	(90,000)	(30,000)	(30,000)	(30,000)
Total	(50,000)	(10,000)	(10,000)	(30,000)

(ii) Tax saving available to Rod as a result of taking the earliest possible relief for his share of the trading losses of the Thora Partnership

Rod has a trading loss of £9,667 in the tax year 2023/24 and a trading loss of £30,000 in 2024/25.

The loss can be carried back and offset against Rod's total income of the three years prior to the tax year of the loss in each case, on a FIFO basis. This is the earliest possible relief available to Rod.

The loss of the tax year 2023/24 will be carried back and offset against Rod's total income of the tax year 2020/21 of £82,000, which will result in a tax saving of £3,867 (£9,667 × 40%).

The loss of the tax year 2024/25 will be carried back and offset against Rod's total income of the tax year 2021/22 of £106,000 (£90,000 + £16,000). This will result in a tax saving of £12,000 (£30,000 × 40%), as the relief will be taken against the employment income in priority to the dividends. Additionally, as Rod's total income originally exceeded £100,000, his personal allowance was restricted to £9,570 (£12,570 – ((£106,000 – £100,000)/2)). After taking loss relief, his full personal allowance will be available, generating a further tax saving of £1,200 ((£12,570 – £9,570) × 40%).

Therefore, Rod's total tax saving as a result of taking loss relief is £17,067 (£3,867 + £12,000 + £1,200).

Tutorial notes

1 *Rod is eligible to claim opening years' loss relief as the trading loss arose within the first four years of him joining the partnership.*

2 *In calculating an individual's income tax liability, losses are usually offset against non-savings income first, before savings income (if any), and then dividends. This will maximise the amount of tax relief obtained.*

Examiner's report

Please note that certain aspects of this examiner's report have been amended due to changes in the tax legislation since the question was originally set.

This question concerned various matters in relation to an individual who had been an employee of a company and had just become a partner in a partnership. There were three parts to the question, broadly covering the capital gain arising on the sale of shares awarded through an enterprise management incentive (EMI) scheme, partnership loss allocation and a partner's loss relief.

The first part of the question required a calculation of the after-tax proceeds from the sale of shares and also an explanation of the base cost of the shares. Many candidates were able to calculate the capital gains tax arising upon sale of the shares and then to calculate proceeds less tax, earning themselves many of the calculation marks. However unfortunately, many candidates appeared to lack knowledge of the detailed rules for the EMI scheme and so were unable to fully explain the base cost of the shares.

The second part of the question required candidates to allocate a trading loss between partners in a partnership and then to calculate, for a new partner who had just joined the partnership, the share of the losses available over two tax years. It was very pleasing to see that many candidates were able to earn marks for the calculations.

The third and final part of the question required candidates to state how the new partner could relieve his trading loss as early as possible and then to explain, with supporting calculations, the total amount of income tax which could be saved with this strategy. Most candidates were able to discuss a possible loss relief strategy although not all chose the loss relief strategy which would relieve the loss as early as possible. Many candidates were able to explain the subsequent tax saving and to support this with calculations. A minority of candidates recognised that claiming the loss relief would affect the amount of personal allowance available and went on to identify the tax implications of this.

ACCA marking scheme

				Marks
(a)	Calculation of chargeable gain			2.0
	Calculation of after-tax proceeds			2.0
	Explanations			3.0
				7.0
			Maximum	6.0
(b)	Calculation of Rod's share of the losses:			
	Y/e 31 March 2024 loss			3.0
	Y/e 31 March 2025 loss			2.0
				5.0
	Identification of earliest relief			3.0
	Calculation of tax saving	– 2020/21		1.5
		– 2021/22		4.0
	Total saving			1.0
				9.5
			Maximum	9.0
	Professional skills marks (see below)		**Maximum**	5.0
Total				**25.0**

Professional skills marks

Analysis and evaluation

- Appropriate use of the data to determine appropriate calculations to arrive at after tax proceeds from the sale of the Lumba plc shares in part (a).
- Appropriate use of the data to support discussion and draw appropriate conclusions about the loss reliefs available in part (b)(ii).
- Use of working in the margin to calculate tax savings for loss relief in part (b)(ii).
- Use of the information in the scenario to explain tax savings available in part (b)(ii).

Commercial acumen

- Recognition that personal allowance will be restored to the full amount with a loss carry back in part (b)(ii).

31 TOMAS AND INES (ADAPTED)

Key answer tips

This question covers some basic aspects of business tax, VAT and also the enterprise investment scheme (EIS). Much of this question could be answered with brought forward knowledge from TX. Please do not underestimate how important it is to ensure you revise this brought forward knowledge.

Part (a)(i) offers some easy marks for calculating tax on trading income. Make sure you consider all taxes that would be relevant to this income.

The second part of (a) tests the badges of trade. Make sure that you apply these to the information given in the scenario.

Next you are asked for two matters to consider when deciding whether to voluntarily register for VAT. Think about what the consequences of registration would be and what this would mean in relation to the stakeholders of the business. There is also a short section on VAT for the purchase of overseas services, which is tested fairly regularly in the ATX exam.

The final part of the questions tests the enterprise investment scheme (EIS). Here some EIS shares are being sold on which IT relief and reinvestment relief has been claimed. The key here is to consider whether the shares have been sold within three years or not. This will determine the treatment of the gain on the shares and the IT relief. You should also consider what happens to the deferred gain now that the shares have been sold.

(a) Tax treatment of the sale of sporting memorabilia

As Tomas is carrying on a trade of selling sporting memorabilia, the following liabilities will arise:

	£
Income tax	
On trading profits (£14,000 – £12,570) × 20%	286
No tax will arise on the dividends, as they are covered by the dividend nil rate band	0
National insurance contributions (NIC)	
Class 2: £3.45 × 52	179
Class 4: (£14,000 – £12,570) × 9%	129
Total tax payable	594

If the sales were treated as capital disposals, there would be no capital gains tax to pay as the memorabilia are chattels, with cost and proceeds both less than £6,000.

So the difference in the total tax which will be payable by Tomas for the tax year 2024/25 is an increase of £594.

(ii) Badges of trade

HMRC might deem Tomas to be trading because:

– Tomas is carrying out frequent transactions which is indicative of trading activity.

– The ownership period for the items is quite short.

– The items are being improved by Tomas before they are sold in order to be able to sell them for a higher price.

> ***Tutorial note***
>
> *Although three reasons have been explained here, candidates were only required to explain TWO to gain full marks.*

(b) (i) Matters to be considered by Tomas in deciding whether it is financially beneficial to register voluntarily for value added tax (VAT)

The VAT status of his suppliers. If Tomas' suppliers are VAT registered, Tomas will be charged VAT on his purchases, which he will only be able to reclaim if he is registered for VAT himself. However, if he purchases from non-VAT registered businesses, or members of the public, he will not suffer any input VAT, so there will be no financial benefit from registering.

The VAT status of his customers. If Tomas' customers are registered for VAT, they will be able to reclaim the VAT charged by Tomas on the memorabilia. However, if they are not registered, the VAT will represent an additional cost for them, which may make Tomas' prices uncompetitive, or Tomas will have to bear the burden of the VAT himself.

> ***Tutorial note***
>
> *Marks were also awarded where candidates made other sensible comments.*

(ii) VAT implications of purchasing advice from the overseas supplier

– The provision of this advice will be a business to business (B2B) service. It will be treated as supplied in the UK, because that is where Tomas' business is established.

– Tomas will be required to pay VAT at the UK standard rate of 20% to HM Revenue and Customs (HMRC) under the 'reverse charge' principle. The rate of VAT in the overseas country is irrelevant.

– The input VAT can be reclaimed on this expense in the same way as any other input tax incurred by the business.

– Accordingly, Tomas' VAT position will be the same as if the services had been purchased from a UK supplier.

(c) Sale of shares in Tavira Ltd

If the shares in Tavira Ltd are sold on 1 June 2024, Ines will have owned them for less than three years. The following consequences will therefore arise:

- A chargeable gain of £23,000 (£95,000 – £72,000) will arise on the sale; and
- The enterprise investment scheme (EIS) income tax relief obtained when the shares were acquired will be withdrawn. As the shares will be sold at a profit, the full amount of the tax credit originally given of £18,600 will be reclaimed by HM Revenue and Customs (HMRC).

In addition, the sale of the Tavira Ltd shares will result in the gain on the sale of the painting, which was deferred on the acquisition of the shares, being brought back into charge. The gain on this disposal was £86,000, but the maximum amount of the gain deferred was restricted to the qualifying expenditure of £72,000.

Ines will have a capital gains tax (CGT) liability in the tax year 2024/25, calculated as follows:

	Gain eligible for business asset disposal relief	Gain not eligible for business asset disposal relief
	£	£
Gain on Tavira Ltd shares	23,000	
Deferred gain on painting		72,000
Less: Annual exempt amount (best use)	0	(6,000)
Taxable gains	23,000	66,000

Ines' CGT liability is £15,500 ((£23,000 × 10%) + (£66,000 × 20%)).

Ines' income tax liability is £18,600.

Accordingly, Ines' after-tax proceeds from the sale of the Tavira Ltd shares is £60,900 (£95,000 – £15,500 – £18,600).

Examiner's report

Note that this is the examiner's report from the original question. Since the question was set, parts of it have been adapted.

This question concerned the taxation of profits, determination of basis periods, and voluntary registration for VAT for a new unincorporated business, and the sale of shares in respect of which enterprise investment scheme (EIS) relief had been claimed.

The first part of the question required candidates to explain the difference in the total amount of tax payable by the taxpayer due to his profits now being taxed as trading income rather than as chargeable gains. When specific taxes are not mentioned in the question, candidates need to think broadly. Although the majority of candidates correctly identified the income tax implications, very few considered that there would also be national insurance (NIC) implications as well.

In relation to the CGT implications, only a minority recognised that the items being sold constituted chattels under £6,000, and so were exempt. So, the majority of candidates were only able to score two out of a possible five marks. The question did ask for supporting calculations, but many candidates produced detailed, comprehensive income tax and CGT computations, in addition to explaining the implications. Calculations were only needed to support the explanation, and so needed to only be brief. In particular, many candidates doing the CBE explained the position in the word processing document, referring the relevant numbers, and also produced comprehensive calculations in the spreadsheet, which did not gain them any additional marks.

Part of the examiner's report has been removed as it relates to a topic that is no longer relevant due to changes in tax legislation.

Requirement (a)(ii) has been added to the question since it was originally set.

The third part of the question required candidates to explain two matters the taxpayer should consider in deciding whether it would be financially beneficial to register voluntarily for VAT. On the whole this was done well, although some candidates wasted time explaining more than two, and/or producing lengthy answers including what appeared to be all they knew about voluntary registration, without considering whether these would, in fact, have a financial impact. Candidates are encouraged to take time to read and understand the question fully before starting to write. A little more time spent reading the specific requirements here might have saved quite a bit of wasted effort in some cases.

The final part of the question tested the rules relating to the sale of shares, which qualified under the EIS scheme, being sold within three years of their acquisition. Many candidates were aware of the main principles relating to the taxation of the gain and the withdrawal of the EIS relief previously given but very few managed to get the calculation of the CGT right, particularly in relation to the treatment of the previously deferred gain, which was, admittedly quite a tricky aspect.

ACCA marking scheme

				Marks
(a)	(i)	Income tax implications		2.0
		National insurance implications		2.0
		Capital gains tax – chattels < £6,000		1.0
		Difference in tax payable		0.5
	(ii)	Badges of trade		2.0
				7.5
			Maximum	7.0
(b)	(i)	VAT status of suppliers		2.0
		VAT status of customers		2.0
	(ii)	VAT on overseas services supplied		3.0
				7.0
			Maximum	6.0
(c)	Consequences of sale			5.0
	Tax liabilities			3.0
	After-tax proceeds			0.5
				8.5
			Maximum	7.0
	Professional skills marks (see below)		**Maximum**	5.0
Total				25.0

Professional skills marks

Analysis and evaluation

- Appropriate use of information to summarise the net difference in tax cost between treating the profit as trading vs capital in part (a)(i).
- Consideration of both income tax and NIC in part (a)(i).
- Appropriate use of information to compare treatment of services provided by overseas supplier to treatment of services provided by a UK supplier in part (b).
- Recognition of more than one tax consequence of disposal of shares in part (c).
- Use of information to support discussion with respect to the implications of the sale of the Tavira Ltd shares in part (c).

Commercial acumen

- Recognition that badges of trade would determine whether Tomas is deemed to be trading or not in part (a)(ii).
- Recognition of the need to consider the impact of voluntary registration for VAT on both suppliers and customers in part (b).
- Demonstration of the ability to make the most efficient use of the annual exempt amount when providing calculations in part (c).

32 YAQUI (ADAPTED)

Key answer tips

This section B question covers capital allowances on cessation of trade (including SBA), rollover relief for depreciating assets, BADR and the capital goods scheme.

Requirement (a) asks for the income tax implications of two asset disposals. This is looking at capital allowances, so you need to think about what allowances would have been available on the assets and what needs to be done now that the business is ceasing to trade.

Requirement (b)(i) looks at the popular topic of rollover relief, but in this scenario the replacement asset was a depreciating asset. You need to appreciate that this means rollover relief will have worked differently, so think about what the implications are now.

Requirement (b)(ii) covers another popular CGT relief: BADR. You need to explain whether it would be available, as well as calculating a chargeable gain. It may be tempting just to go for the calculation here, but it is important to cover both aspects.

Requirement (c) looks at the capital goods scheme. This is one of the few areas of VAT which is new at the ATX level, and so it is important that you understand how it works, as it is tested regularly.

(a) Income tax adjustments in respect of the disposal of the specialist fixed machine and the warehouse

Specialist fixed machine

As the tax written down value of Yaqui's main pool was £Nil, the sale of the machine will have given rise to a balancing charge of £23,000. This will increase Yaqui's taxable trading profit for the period ending 30 September 2024.

Warehouse

Structures and buildings allowances (SBAs) are available on the qualifying cost of the warehouse (i.e. excluding the cost of the land). This is £215,000 (£263,000 – £48,000). An allowance of £1,613 (£215,000 × 3% × 3/12) will be available for the three-month period ending 30 September 2024, which will reduce Yaqui's taxable trading profit for this period.

The trading profit for the three-month period ending 30 September 2024 after the above adjustments will be £31,387 (£10,000 + £23,000 – £1,613).

(b) (i) Sale of the specialist fixed machine

No capital loss will arise on the sale of the specialist machine because it qualified for capital allowances.

As the specialist machine was a depreciating asset for capital gains tax purposes, the chargeable gain of £11,000 which was deferred against the purchase of this machine became chargeable on 31 March 2024, i.e. the earliest of:

- The date the machine will be sold (10 July 2024).
- The date the machine ceased to be used in Yaqui's business (10 July 2024).
- Ten years after the acquisition of the machine (31 March 2024).

This deferred gain would therefore have been chargeable to capital gains tax in the tax year 2023/24, and no chargeable gain or allowable loss will arise as a result of this sale on 10 July 2024.

Tutorial Note

1 *The specialist machine has already had relief for its fall in value through capital allowances, which means that a capital loss is not allowable since this would give relief twice.*

2 *When a depreciating asset is purchased as a replacement asset for rollover relief, no adjustment is made to the base cost of the replacement asset. Instead, the gain is frozen until one of the three crystallising events mentioned above occurs.*

(ii) Sale of the warehouse

Availability of business asset disposal relief (BADR)

BADR will be available on the sale of the warehouse because:

- The business is ceasing and the sale is within three years of the cessation of trade.
- Yaqui will have owned the business for at least two years prior to ceasing to trade.
- The warehouse will still be in business use at the date of cessation.

Tutorial Note

It is irrelevant that the warehouse was used in the YP Trading business for less than two years (1 November 2022 to 30 September 2024). When determining the availability of BADR in respect of disposals of assets used in a business which has ceased, the business must have been owned for at least two years prior to cessation, not the asset being disposed of.

Chargeable gain

	£
Sale proceeds	296,000
Add: Structures and buildings allowance (SBA) claimed (W)	12,363
	308,363
Less: Cost	(263,000)
Chargeable gain	45,363

Working: SBAs

	£
Qualifying cost for SBA (from part (a))	215,000
SBAs: Year ended 30 June 2023 (£215,000 × 3% × 8/12)	4,300
Year ended 30 June 2024 (£215,000 × 3%)	6,450
3 months ending 30 September 2024 (from part (a))	1,613
Total SBAs	12,363

Tutorial Note

When an asset on which SBA was claimed is sold, all SBA claimed up to the date of disposal must be added to the sale proceeds in the chargeable gain calculation. No balancing allowance or charge arises.

(c) Value Added Tax (VAT) consequences of the sale or rental of the warehouse

If Yaqui sells the warehouse as planned on 30 September 2024, it will be less than three years since its construction so it will be a standard rated supply. Accordingly, Yaqui must charge output VAT of £59,200 (£296,000 × 20%) on the sale. No adjustment is required for the remainder of the ten-year adjustment period for capital goods scheme purposes, as 100% taxable use is assumed for this period.

Renting out the warehouse

The sale of a new freehold commercial building is standard rated such that Yaqui will have incurred input VAT of £52,600 (£263,000 × 20%) on the purchase of the warehouse. This input tax will have been reclaimed in full on acquisition, as the warehouse was wholly used in Yaqui's business making standard rated supplies.

Renting out the warehouse from 1 October 2024 would constitute an exempt supply for VAT, as Yaqui has not opted to tax it. Accordingly, as the warehouse is within the ten-year adjustment period, an annual adjustment of £5,260 (£52,600 × 1/10 (100% – 0%)) will be required to be repaid to HMRC in respect of each of the years within this adjustment period in which it continues to be rented out.

Examiner's report

Requirement (a)

Part (a) related to the cessation of an unincorporated business.

This part related to the capital allowances implications of disposing of two assets on which allowances had been claimed.

A majority of candidates recognised that there would be a balancing charge in respect of the specialist fixed machine, and that the structures and buildings allowance (SBA) would be available in respect of the warehouse, but the calculation of this latter allowance was frequently incorrect. The most common errors related to failure to correctly calculate the qualifying cost, and/or to recognise that a time-apportioned allowance would be available as the disposal occurred in the final, 3-month accounting period.

Brief calculations were expected in this part, but the actual requirement was to 'explain' the adjustments required. Very few candidates included an explanation of these adjustments i.e. the effect they would have on the amount of the taxable trading profit.

Candidates often tend to be comfortable calculating capital allowances – which were a key topic at TX but less so if they are required to provide explanations. At ATX candidates must expect to be asked for explanations to accompany – or in some cases, replace – calculations. *The rest of requirement (a) has been removed from the question as the topic is no longer on the syllabus.*

Requirement (b)

There were two requirements within part (b) which related to the capital gains tax (CGT) implications of the asset disposals included in part (a). Performance on this part was disappointing. As in previous papers, candidates generally demonstrated a significant lack of knowledge and application skills in relation to CGT reliefs. As has been said many times before, these are an important part of the ATX-UK syllabus, and will continue to be tested on a very regular basis.

(b) (i)

The first point that was expected here was that this disposal would not give rise to an allowable capital loss as capital allowances had been claimed on the asset. Relatively few candidates stated this, despite it being a fundamental and frequently tested rule. However, even fewer identified that the fixed machine was a depreciating asset. Failure to recognise this meant that many candidates provided no explanation whatsoever, or only a very brief, incorrect one, in respect of the treatment of the deferred gain. A good number suggested that the gain would be deducted from the base cost of the machine, but as the reinvestment was in a depreciating asset, this was not the case and the deferred gain would crystallise on the earliest of three dates: the date when the machine ceased to be used in the company's trade, the date of disposal of the machine, or 10 years after its acquisition (as was the case here).

Fixed machines are very often used as examples of depreciating assets, and candidates need to remember that, as was the case here, a deferred gain can sometimes become independently chargeable, rather than being deducted from the base cost of another asset. It is important for candidates to pay attention in their studies to situations where the relief operates in this manner.

(b) (ii)

Unfortunately, the majority of candidates appeared to have very little knowledge of the BADR conditions which were relevant to this scenario and many just listed a variety of 'conditions', some of which related to other circumstances when BADR could be claimed, and some of which related to other types of relief. Irrelevant conditions score no marks; candidates must be precise and relate to the facts in the scenario.

The disposal in this case was of an asset which had been used by the individual in his business up to the date of cessation of his trade. Key conditions for BADR in this situation are that the asset was still in use at the date of cessation, and is sold within three years of cessation, but these were rarely stated. Many candidates were able to make reference to a two-year period, but were not precisely correct as to what this two-year period related to, citing ownership, or trade use of the asset, rather than the length of time the individual had run the business. The relevant two-year period is different for the different circumstances in which BADR is available (and different again for business property relief for inheritance tax purposes!). Candidates need to pay attention to this important detail.

Most candidates used the correct figures to calculate the gain (treating the land and building as a single asset), and were aware of the need to include the SBAs. They were therefore able to produce at least a reasonably accurate computation.

Requirement (c)

The key focus of this question part was the operation of the capital goods scheme (CGS) for VAT, which candidates were told applied to this warehouse. Many candidates did not even attempt this part, and it appeared that with those who did, knowledge of this scheme was sketchy, at best. Many candidates were unable to apply the rules to this situation, particularly to the potential rental of the building.

Broadly, the operation of the scheme comprises three parts:

1 The recoverability of input VAT on acquisition of the building;

2 The ten-year adjustment period, during which additional input VAT may be reclaimed/VAT may be repaid to HMRC if the proportion of taxable/exempt use changes;

3 The sale of the building during the adjustment period such that a final adjustment may be required, which will depend on whether the sale is a taxable or an exempt supply.

Candidates need to be able to deal with all three parts, as demonstrated in this question.

Those who attempted this question were usually aware that the input VAT on the warehouse would have been fully recoverable, although didn't always include the reason, i.e. that it was newly constructed so was a standard-rated supply and was used in a taxable trade.

In answering part (i) a few spotted that VAT would be chargeable on the sale of the building, with some also including the reason, namely that the sale would be a standard rated supply as the building would be less than three years old. Reference to the lack of adjustment required for CGS purposes was rare.

In answering part (ii), again a few candidates realised that letting the building would be an exempt supply and then went on to provide a calculation of the annual adjustment that would be required for the remainder of the ten-year adjustment period. However, despite being told in the scenario that the taxpayer had not opted to tax the building, and would not do so in the future, discussion of the implications of doing this seemed to form a significant part of their answer for a good number of those who responded to this question part, which just wasted time for no marks.

Explanations were required, but were frequently not provided. Candidates must pay attention to the 'command' word(s) in the requirement. Although credit was given for sensible attempts at the calculations, marks were lost by not addressing the requirement to explain the position.

The CGS for VAT is a tricky area, but is a key area of VAT at ATX-UK and is tested regularly, so candidates are advised to prepare by attempting and learning from past exam questions.

Marking scheme

				Marks
(a)	Specialist fixed machine			1.5
	Warehouse			2.5
	Adjusted trading profit			1.0
				5.0
			Maximum	4.0
(b)	(i)	Sale of specialist fixed machine		3.5
	(ii)	Business asset disposal relief availability		3.0
		Chargeable gain		2.0
		Structures and buildings allowance working		2.5
				11.0
			Maximum	10.0
(c)	Sale of warehouse			2.5
	Renting out the warehouse			4.5
				7.0
			Maximum	6.0
	Professional skills marks (see below)		**Maximum**	5.0
Total				**25.0**

Professional skills marks

Analysis and evaluation

- Consideration of the impact of the balancing charge on trade profits in part (a).
- Application of the rollover relief rules for investment in a depreciating asset in part (b)(i).
- Assessment of the availability of BADR in part (b)(ii).
- Consideration of the interaction of SBAs with the chargeable gain in part (b)(ii).

Commercial acumen

- Consideration of the impact of VAT on the decision to sell or rent property in part (c).

CHANGING BUSINESS SCENARIOS

33 DESIREE (ADAPTED) *Walk in the footsteps of a top tutor*

Key answer tips

This section B question covers the often-tested scenario of sole trader versus company, with some easy marks on voluntary VAT registration.

Part (a)(i) requires you to think about the tax relief available for research and development (R&D) expenditure for both possible business structures. R&D is one of the few new areas in trading profits in the ATX exam, and so is often tested. Ensure you learn the rules!

Part (a)(ii) requires discussion of the use of losses for a sole trader compared to a company. This is a typical textbook scenario with no tricks, and you should score well here as long as you have learnt the rules.

Part (b) requires discussion of voluntary VAT registration – a TX topic, but one which most students are likely to be happy with. There are also marks for discussing imports – a popular exam topic. The danger here is not applying the discussion to the specific scenario.

The highlighted words in the written sections are key phrases that markers are looking for.

(a) (i) Tax relief for research and development (R&D) expenditure

Tutor's top tips

Think carefully before attempting this section.

The tax relief available for research and development expenditure is different depending on whether the business is unincorporated or incorporated.

Make sure that your answer clearly explains the difference between the two.

Note that you were told to ignore the use of the trading loss for this part of the question, so do not waste time discussing this here.

Business is unincorporated

The total costs of £33,000 will be allowable trading expenses as they have been incurred wholly and exclusively for the purposes of the trade. This will increase the trading loss to £49,000 (£33,000 + £16,000).

No additional R&D relief is available.

Business is operated via a company

As above, the total costs will be allowable, but some of the costs will be eligible for an additional 86% deduction from trading profits/losses, which will increase the trading loss further.

All of the costs would be eligible for the extra deduction, with the exception of rent. The fees paid to the market research consultants would also not qualify for extra relief.

	£
Total costs	33,000
Extra 86% relief ((£33,000 – £15,000) × 86%)	15,480
Total allowable costs	48,480

The total trading loss will now be £64,480 (£48,480 + £16,000).

(ii) Advice on whether or not the business should be incorporated

Tutor's top tips

You must learn the loss reliefs available to individuals and companies, as these often feature in exam questions.

Don't write about all the loss reliefs available; just pick the ones that are relevant. For example, in this question there is no point in talking about reliefs on cessation of trade.

When writing about loss reliefs, make sure that you use very specific language. For example, don't just say 'losses can be carried forward'; say that 'losses can be carried forward against the first available future trading profits from the same trade'.

You must also apply the reliefs to the scenario.

The two key considerations for both the unincorporated business and the company are:

- *Amount of tax saved, and*
- *Timing of the relief.*

There is no point in preparing full computations of the tax saved, as the question states that detailed calculations are not required.

Business is operated via a company

If the business is operated via a company, the loss of the seven-month period ending 31 March 2025 will be carried forward for offset against future total profits of the company.

The earliest that any of the company's losses will be relieved is the year ending 31 March 2026 thus reducing the corporation tax payable on 1 January 2027.

Based on the predicted future profits, tax will be saved at the small profits rate of 19%.

However, the tax savings will only arise if the budgeted profits are achieved as the company doesn't appear to have any other income or gains. If the business does not achieve profitability the losses will be wasted.

Alternatively, if the company claims the extra 86% R&D relief, then it could surrender some of the loss for a cash payment equal to 10% of the amount surrendered.

If this option was used then the amount of the loss surrendered could not be carried forward for future use.

The maximum amount that could be surrendered would be the lower of:

- The trading loss
- 186% of the qualifying expenses.

This would obtain immediate relief for the loss, but would only save at 10% as opposed to a minimum of 19% if the loss is carried forward.

Tutorial note

Strictly speaking the trading loss available for surrender should be reduced by any potential current year claim and any actual carry back or group relief claims. Since it does not seem possible that any of these claims could be made by Duchess there is no need to mention them here.

Business is unincorporated

If the business is unincorporated, the loss can be offset against:

- The total income of the tax year of loss and/or the previous tax year
- The total income of the three tax years prior to the year of loss starting with the earliest of the three years.

This enables Desiree to obtain immediate relief for the losses.

Desiree has employment income in the tax year 2024/25 of only £7,500 (£90,000 × 1/12) together with bank interest of £1,000. All of this income will be covered by her personal allowance.

Her total income in earlier years is her salary of £90,000 and the bank interest. Accordingly, she should offset the losses against the income of the tax year 2023/24 and earlier years rather than the income of the tax year 2024/25.

The loss of the tax year 2024/25 could be offset against the total income of the tax year 2023/24 (the previous year) or 2021/22 (the first of the three years prior to 2024/25).

This will obtain full relief for the loss at a mixture of basic and higher rates of tax.

Conclusion

Desiree's primary objective is the most beneficial use of the loss.

She should therefore run the business as an unincorporated sole trader in order to obtain relief for the losses as soon as possible and obtain a higher rate of tax relief (up to 40% as opposed to 19% as a small company).

Tutor's top tips

Make sure that you state your conclusion. As long as it is consistent with your analysis, you will be given credit.

There is no loss relief cap for the relief as the trading loss is less than £50,000.

(b) Financial advantages and disadvantages of Desiree registering voluntarily for VAT

Tutor's top tips

This section of the question is mainly based on TX knowledge and is very straightforward.

You could attempt this part of the question first, just in case you run out of time on part (a).

Advantages

- Registering for VAT will enable the business to recover input tax, where possible, on expenses and capital expenditure.

  This will reduce the costs incurred by the business thus reducing its losses and its capital allowances.

- The VAT incurred on the fees paid to the market research consultants in March 2024 can be recovered as pre-registration input tax.

  The payment in November 2023 is more than six months prior to registration and therefore the input tax in relation to it cannot be recovered.

Disadvantages

- The business will have to charge its customers VAT at 20%.

  This will represent an increase in the prices charged to those customers who are unable to recover VAT (i.e. domestic customers and non-registered business customers).

  Desiree may need to consider reducing prices in order to reduce the impact of the additional VAT on these customers.

Treatment of imports

- Desiree must account for output VAT on importation.
- This can be recovered as input VAT on the same VAT return.
- As the VAT can be recovered the treatment is tax neutral.

Examiner's report

Part (a)(i) of the question has been re-written due to the original topic being removed from the syllabus.

The following requirement has also been adapted due to the above.

Part (a)(ii) required candidates to provide a 'thorough and detailed explanation' of the manner in which the losses could be used depending on the choice of business vehicle. This part of the question was done well by almost all of the candidates who attempted it. In order to maximise marks here it was necessary to be precise in terms of language used. For example, it was not sufficient to state that losses can be carried forward against future profits. Instead, candidates needed to state that losses could be carried forward for offset against future profits of *the same trade*.

There was also a requirement to state which business structure would best satisfy the client's objectives. The mark available for this was missed by those candidates who had stopped thinking and were simply writing down everything they knew about loss relief.

The other difficulty which candidates had with this part of the question was a failure to recognise that not all possible loss reliefs were available due to the particular facts of the question. Candidates should ensure that they do not write at length about matters which are irrelevant.

The final part of the question concerned the 'financial' advantages and disadvantages of registering voluntarily for VAT. Many candidates let themselves down by not reading the question carefully such that they simply listed all the advantages and disadvantages they could think of without focusing on the word financial or the particular facts surrounding the client. This meant that they missed the possibility of recovering pre-registration VAT, which was often the difference between an OK mark and a good mark.

ACCA marking scheme

				Marks
(a)	(i)	Business is unincorporated		1.0
		Business is operated via a company		2.5
				3.5
			Maximum	3.0
	(ii)	Business is operated via a company		5.5
		Business is unincorporated		
		Reliefs available		2.5
		Application to Desiree's position		3.0
		Conclusion		1.0
				12.0
			Maximum	10.0
(b)	Advantages			
		Recovery of input tax		1.5
		Pre-registration input tax		1.5
	Disadvantages			1.5
	VAT treatment of imports			3.0
				7.5
			Maximum	7.0
	Professional skills marks (see below)		**Maximum**	5.0
Total				**25.0**

Professional skills marks

Analysis and evaluation

- Use of the figures from the scenario to calculate the tax relievable amount in part (a)(i).
- Analysis of the data to determine which loss reliefs are available depending on the structure chosen in part (a)(ii).
- Analysis of the data to determine the VAT treatment of the imports in part (b).
- Demonstration of ability to consider all relevant taxes for requirement (a), i.e. income tax and corporation tax.

Commercial acumen

- Recognition that a claim against total income in the tax year 2024/25 is not beneficial due to the income being covered by the personal allowance in part (a)(ii).
- Recognition of the advantages and disadvantages of voluntary registration for VAT in part (b).

34 ENID (ADAPTED)

Key answer tips

This question looks at incorporation which is a popular topic in the exam, as well as loss relief, profit extraction and VAT.

Part (a) is looking at possible relief for brought forward losses. The key here is picking up on the special loss relief available on incorporation. Remember to make it clear what income is being offset and when in your answer to score well.

Part (b) is testing incorporation. The question asks for the balance on the loan account so you may be confused about what you need to do. However, if you read the question carefully you will see that the loan account is being used to pay the CGT so you can work out the loan account balance and then go on to calculate gains and CGT to reduce the balance by the tax payable.

In part (c) you need to discuss the tax implications for both Enid and Niche Ltd. Make sure that you address both parties in your answer – even if it's just to say that there are no tax implications!

Part (d) is looking at VAT on the transfer of the business. Note the question states NOT to discuss the TOGC rules, so ensure you don't waste time doing that. You need to think about what will happen with the registration now the sole trade business has ceased and similarly what will happen for the new company.

The highlighted words in the written sections are key phrases that markers are looking for.

(a) Reliefs available for the trading losses brought forward at 6 April 2024

Trading losses brought forward are automatically offset against the first available future profits from the same trade. Enid will therefore offset £42,000 of the trading losses brought forward against the profit of her unincorporated business prior to its transfer to Niche Ltd. £9,000 (£51,000 – £42,000) remains unrelieved.

However, as her business has been transferred to a company, Enid can relieve the remainder of the loss against her income from the company. The loss will be relieved against the first-available income from the company, earned before unearned, which will be her salary of £37,500 (£75,000 × 6/12) in the tax year 2024/25. Enid qualifies for this relief as at least 80% of the consideration for the transfer of her business will be in the form of shares. She must retain these shares until the end of 2024/25 in order to make this claim.

(b) Availability of incorporation relief and the balance on Enid's loan account

Availability of incorporation relief

Incorporation relief will be available because:

– the business will be transferred as a going concern

– all the assets will be transferred; and

– the consideration includes shares.

Amount to be withdrawn from the loan account

	£
Gain on goodwill	100,000
Gain on workshop (£122,000 – £55,000)	67,000
Total gains before relief	167,000
Less: Incorporation relief: 85% × £167,000	(141,950)
Chargeable gains	25,050

	Gain eligible for business asset disposal relief (BADR)	Gain not eligible for BADR
	£	£
Gain attributable to workshop (67/167)	10,050	
Gain attributable to goodwill (100/167)		15,000
Less: Annual exempt amount (best use)	0	(6,000)
Taxable gains	10,050	9,000

Enid's capital gains tax (CGT) liability is £2,805 ((£10,050 × 10%) + (£9,000 × 20%)).

The funds left on loan account initially will be £33,000 (15% × £220,000 (£100,000 + £122,000 + £8,000 – £10,000)).

The balance on Enid's loan account after deducting the cash to be withdrawn to pay the CGT liability will be £30,195 (£33,000 – £2,805)

> ***Tutorial note***
>
> *Goodwill is not a relevant business asset for business asset disposal relief where it is transferred by an individual to a close company, and that individual is a related party to the close company, as is the case in this scenario.*

(c) Replacement of Enid's dividend with increased salary or withdrawal from her loan account

Enid is a higher rate taxpayer. She currently receives dividends of £500 each year, so the income tax payable on the dividend of £15,000 from Niche Ltd will be £4,894 (((£1,000 – £500) × 0%) + ((£15,000 – £500) × 33.75%)).

There are no tax implications for Niche Ltd of payment of a dividend.

Neither Niche Ltd nor Enid would pay national insurance contributions (NICs) on the payment of a dividend.

1 Increased salary

Enid will pay income tax at the rate of 40% and class 1 employees' national insurance contributions (NICs) at the rate of 2% on the increased salary.

Niche Ltd will pay class 1 employer's NICs at the rate of 13.8%, but the increased salary and the NICs are deductible for corporation tax, providing a saving at the rate of 26.5% as Niche Ltd will be a marginal company.

	£	£
Amount payable by Enid:		
Income tax (£15,000 × 40%)		6,000
NIC (£15,000 × 2%)		300
		6,300
Amount payable by Niche Ltd:		
NIC (£15,000 × 13.8%)	2,070	
Corporation tax saving ((£15,000 + £2,070) × 26.5%)	(4,524)	
Net corporation tax saving	(2,454)	(2,454)
Total tax payable		3,846

Therefore, there will be a reduction in tax of £1,048 (£4,894 – £3,846) if Niche Ltd pays Enid an increased salary instead of the dividend.

2 Withdrawal of £15,000 from Enid's loan account

This will have no tax implications for either Enid or Niche Ltd.

Therefore, there will be a tax saving of £4,894.

Tutorial note

Since Niche Ltd will not receive any dividends, its taxable total profits will be equal to its augmented profits. As these are higher than £50,000 but less than £250,000 it will pay corporation tax at the marginal rate. This has an effective tax rate of 26.5% between the limits, which can be used to calculate tax savings. Note that you should not use this rate to calculate the corporation tax liability in a full corporation tax computation.

(d) The change in legal status of the business from an unincorporated business to a company means that Enid is required to cancel the business's value added tax (VAT) registration. Niche Ltd is required to register for VAT. The VAT registration number may be transferred from the business to Niche Ltd, in which case Niche Ltd will take over the rights and liabilities of the business in respect of VAT at the date of transfer.

Examiner's report

This question concerned various tax consequences of transferring an unincorporated sole trader business to a company, and the tax implications of alternative ways of extracting profit from the new company.

The first part related to the availability of loss relief for a trading loss brought forward at the start of the final accounting period in the unincorporated business. This question part was not well done, for two reasons. Firstly, the majority of candidates failed to realise that when a loss is given as being brought forward at a particular date, with no indication of the prior accounting period(s) or tax year(s) in which the loss arose, the current year/carry back reliefs against total income will not be relevant. Nor is terminal loss relief relevant, unless the loss arose in the last 12 months of trading, which was not the case here. So the only option is to carry the loss forward against the first available profits from the same trade, which here was just the profit of the final period of trading prior to incorporation. Secondly, the majority of candidates appeared to be unaware of incorporation relief, permitting the remaining loss to be carried forward against the former sole trader's income from the company. The rules relating to reliefs for trading losses for individuals are frequently examined, and candidates are expected to be precise in this sort of question. Candidates would do well to invest time at the revision stage of their studies in memorising the rules concerning relief for trading losses, and ensuring that they are able to recognise those rules which apply in a given scenario, so as not to waste time discussing reliefs which are not available.

The second part of the question focused on the CGT implications in respect of the assets transferred to the new company. It was pleasing to see that the majority of candidates knew the conditions for incorporation relief to apply, but, disappointingly, a significant number of these did not know how to apply it. More surprising, however, was the fact that relatively few candidates referred to business asset disposal relief (BADR) here. The issue of goodwill not qualifying for BADR in this situation, is, admittedly, quite a tricky one, but BADR is a very common, and frequently tested, relief available to individuals disposing of qualifying assets, so should be something that every candidate would be advised to consider, and comment on, in every situation where there is a disposal of business assets. It is important to be very familiar with the precise rules for this relief, so as to be able to ascertain whether or not it is available in any given scenario.

The third part of the question was a variation on the often-tested extraction of profits from a company, this time including withdrawal from a loan account, in addition to the more familiar dividend or salary. On the whole, this was done well, with most candidates adopting a marginal approach, and therefore being able to calculate the additional tax payable by both the individual and the company in a concise and efficient way. It is a useful skill for candidates to be able to recognise where a marginal approach will be appropriate, as in these cases it will usually prove to be much less time consuming than producing full computations, although full marks can still be obtained by a candidate who adopts this latter approach. The best way to develop this skill is, undoubtedly, question practice, in order to gain confidence in being able to identify when it is appropriate, and how to perform the marginal calculations. In relation to the withdrawal from the loan account, a significant number of candidates appeared not to have read the question properly, where it stated explicitly that there would be sufficient funds in the loan account to permit this withdrawal, and dived straight in to explaining the rules for close companies in relation to the tax charge payable on overdrawn director's loan accounts, with which they were clearly more familiar, but which unfortunately were not relevant.

The final part of the question concerned the administrative requirements in relation to deregistration for VAT by the unincorporated business, registration by the company, and the possibility of transferring the VAT registration. This was attempted well by the majority of candidates, who typically scored two out of the possible three marks.

ACCA marking guide

			Marks
(a)	Relief against future trading profit		1.5
	Relief against income from Niche Ltd		3.5
			5.0
		Maximum	4.0
(b)	Availability of incorporation relief		1.5
	Calculation of chargeable gain		2.0
	Calculation of capital gains tax liability		3.0
	Balance on loan account		2.0
			8.5
		Maximum	7.0
(c)	Tax on dividend		2.5
	Tax payable on increased salary		3.0
	Decreased total tax liability		0.5
	Tax on withdrawal from loan account		1.0
	Tax saving from loan account withdrawal		0.5
			7.5
		Maximum	6.0
(d)	Administrative requirements for VAT Total		3.0
	Professional skills marks (see below)	**Maximum**	5.0
Total			**25.0**

Professional skills marks

Analysis and evaluation

- Analysis of the data to determine which loss reliefs are available in part (a).
- Analysis of the data to determine appropriate calculations to perform to arrive at the balance on the loan account in part (b).
- Analysis of the data to determine appropriate calculations to perform to evaluate the tax saving or extra tax for alternative methods of profit extraction in part (c)
- Identification of the ability to use a marginal corporation tax rate in part (c).

Scepticism

- Acknowledgement of the need to confirm that the shares are retained until the end of 2024/25 for incorporation loss relief to be available in part (a).

Commercial acumen

- Recognition of the advantages and disadvantages of transferring VAT registration in part (d).

35 ROSA (ADAPTED)

Key answer tips

This section B question focuses on the difference in tax between taking on an employee or a partner, loss relief for individuals and the capital goods scheme for VAT.

Part (a) is a higher skills requirement that looks at the difference in income tax and national insurance between taking on someone as a partner or an employee. There are lots of calculations to do here so it is important to plan what you need to do before you get started.

In part (b) you are asked to discuss the loss relief options available to an individual. Note that she has a relatively high level of income so you should always question whether the restriction on reliefs against total income is relevant. Make sure your answer is specific to the scenario and doesn't just list out every possible loss relief.

The capital goods scheme is the focus of the final part of this question. This is a topic which is often tested in the ATX exam so you should be prepared to tackle this, and to be able to perform calculations. Note that you are only asked for the final adjustment so don't waste time discussing the annual adjustments as this will score no marks.

(a) Difference in the total amount of income tax and national insurance contributions (NICs) payable by Siena and Rosa for the tax year 2025/26 if Siena becomes (i) a partner, or (ii) an employee on 1 April 2025

(i) Siena becomes a partner

If Siena becomes a partner in RS Trading on 1 April 2025, she will be allocated £2,800 of the partnership loss of the year ending 31 March 2026 (W), such that she will have no taxable income for the tax year 2025/26. Accordingly, she will have no liability to income tax or class 2 or class 4 NIC.

Rosa will be allocated a trading loss of £59,200 in the tax year 2025/26 (W). As she will have no other source of income in that year, Rosa will have no liability to income tax or class 2 or class 4 NIC.

(ii) Siena becomes an employee

If Siena becomes an employee, on an annual salary of £22,000, she will have an income tax liability of £1,886 ((£22,000 – £12,570) × 20%), and a class 1 employee's NIC liability of £1,132 ((£22,000 – £12,570) × 12%).

In this case, RS Trading will also have a liability to class 1 employer's NIC of £1,780 ((£22,000 – £9,100) × 13.8%). As this is covered by the £5,000 employment allowance, no class 1 contributions would be payable.

Rosa will, again, have no personal liability to income tax or NIC, as she will incur a trading loss of £84,000 (£62,000 + £22,000).

Therefore, the total income tax and NIC payable by Siena and Rosa for the tax year 2025/26 will be reduced by £3,018 (£1,886 + £1,132) if Siena becomes a partner.

However, although the total tax and NIC payable by Siena and Rosa is lower if Siena becomes a partner, the amount of trading loss available for relief is higher if Siena becomes an employee (£84,000, rather than £62,000).

Working:

Allocation of RS Trading loss for the year ending 31 March 2026:

	Total	**Rosa**	**Siena**
	£	£	£
Budgeted loss	(62,000)		
Salary to Siena	(12,000)		12,000
Balance (80:20)	(74,000)	(59,200)	(14,800)
Total share of loss	(62,000)	(59,200)	(2,800)

Tutorial note

Although Rosa will have no personal liability to NIC, she can voluntarily continue to pay Class 2 contributions in order to ensure entitlement to contributions-based benefits.

(b) Loss reliefs available to Rosa in respect of the budgeted trading loss of RS Trading

Rosa will have a trading loss of £84,000 in the tax year 2025/26.

As Rosa has no other income in the tax year 2025/26, she can only carry back the loss to the tax year 2024/25 and offset the loss against her total income of that year, and then against the chargeable gains arising on the sale of the investment properties in the tax year 2024/25.

Rosa's total income in 2024/25 is £87,000 (£27,000 + £60,000). There is no restriction on the amount of loss which can be used against trading income from the same trade, but relief against the property income will be capped at the greater of £50,000 and 25% of Rosa's adjusted net income for the year, which is £21,750 (£87,000 × 25%).

Accordingly, a maximum of £50,000 can be offset against the property income. Therefore, a total of £77,000 (£27,000 + £50,000) can be offset against income leaving net income of £10,000 (£87,000 – £77,000), which will be covered by Rosa's personal allowance.

The balance of the loss of £7,000 (£84,000 – £77,000) can be relieved against the chargeable gains of £92,000 on the sale of the investment properties.

Maximum tax saving 2024/25:

	£
Income tax (No liability to income tax remains, so the whole amount is repayable)	22,232
Capital gains tax (CGT) (Working)	5,730
	27,962

Working:

CGT payable after taking loss relief:

		£
Gains remaining chargeable (£92,000 – £7,000)		85,000
Less: Annual exempt amount		(6,000)
Taxable gains		79,000
CGT:	£37,700 × 18%	6,786
	£41,300 × 28%	11,564
	£79,000	18,350

CGT saving is £5,730 (£24,080 – £18,350)

Tutorial note

Before taking loss relief, Rosa's taxable gains would all be taxed at 28% as Rosa's taxable income exceeded £37,700. After taking loss relief against Rosa's total income for the tax year 2024/25, the full amount of the basic rate band will be available to use against taxable gains.

(c) Value added tax (VAT) implications of the disposal of the retail unit

On 6 April 2025, when the retail unit is sold, it will be at least three years old. Accordingly, the sale will be exempt from VAT as Rosa has not opted to tax it.

On acquisition, the retail unit was newly constructed, so VAT of £58,000 (£290,000 × 20%) will have been charged. Rosa will have reclaimed the whole of this in the year ended 31 March 2019, as she used it in her business, making wholly standard-rated supplies.

However, as the sale of the retail unit will be an exempt disposal, for the purpose of the capital goods scheme it is deemed to have 0% taxable use for the remainder of the ten-year adjustment period. As the warehouse is sold during the eighth year of the adjustment period, there are two years of the adjustment period remaining, and therefore a final VAT adjustment of £11,600 (£58,000 × 2/10 × (100% – 0%)) will be repayable by Rosa to HM Revenue and Customs (HMRC) in respect of the sale.

Examiner's report

This question was in three main parts, concerning an unincorporated business looking to bring someone else into the business, trading losses of an unincorporated business and VAT on sale of a property.

The first part of the question required advice, based on calculations, on whether an unincorporated business owner should bring a new person into the business as an employee or as a partner. The calculations required were the total amount of income tax and national insurance contributions for each scenario. There were some excellent answers to this part of the question, dealing with each of the relevant tax liabilities in a clear and logical manner. Those candidates who did not do so well would have benefited from taking time to plan their answer before they began, thinking about which taxes affect which individual.

The second part of the question required an explanation of the loss relief available to the unincorporated trader and a calculation of the maximum tax saving available as a result of such relief. Some candidates wrote very generally about loss reliefs, without applying their knowledge to the facts of the question, which lost them marks. A significant number of candidates seemed unaware of the technical rules on restriction of income tax reliefs against total income and were unable to factor these into their calculations. A thorough understanding of the technical rules from all areas of the syllabus is a requirement to do well in this exam.

The third part of this question dealt with disposal of a retail unit which was subject to the capital goods scheme. Some candidates spent time writing everything they knew about the capital goods scheme when only the implications upon disposal were required. Only knowledge which addresses the question requirements will earn marks; candidates should not waste their time writing out tax rules if they are not asked for in the question. Even if a candidate writes lots of correct information about a particular tax topic, if it has not been asked for, it cannot earn any marks.

ACCA marking scheme

			Marks
(a)	Siena as partner		3.0
	Siena as employee		4.0
	Calculation of shares of loss		2.0
	Conclusion		2.0
			11.0
		Maximum	9.0
(b)	Availability of loss relief		2.0
	Relief against total income in 2024/25		3.5
	Tax saving		3.5
			9.0
		Maximum	7.0

(c)	Disposal exempt		1.5
	Initial reclaim		1.5
	Implications of sale		2.0
			5.0
		Maximum	4.0
	Professional skills marks (see below)	**Maximum**	5.0
Total			**25.0**

Professional skills marks

Analysis and evaluation

- Analysis of the data to determine appropriate loss reliefs available to Rosa in part (b).
- Appropriate use of the data to calculate tax savings as a result of loss reliefs in part (b).
- Demonstration of ability to consider all relevant taxes to requirement (b), i.e. income tax and capital gains tax.
- Use of information to determine appropriate VAT treatment of the retail unit disposal in part (c).

Commercial acumen

- Demonstration of an understanding of the difference in tax treatment of an employee and partner in part (a).
- Demonstration of an understanding of the purpose of the capital goods scheme rules in part (c).

36 SABIN AND PATAN LTD

Key answer tips

This question covers terminal loss relief for an unincorporated business, capital gains tax on the disposal of business assets, structures and buildings allowance (SBA) and research and development relief for a company.

In part (a) you need to identify how the trading loss can be used. When describing loss relief try to answer the questions 'what, when and how? What income will the loss offset, when will it be offset and is there a particular order in which the relief has to happen.

Part (b) looks at the capital gains tax implications of the sale of Sabin's business assets. When dealing with the disposal of business assets it is always important to think about the availability of any capital gains tax reliefs, as many of these relate to business assets. Think about whether any are relevant here.

The final part of the question looks at relief for the purchase of a building first of all. You need to be thinking about structures and buildings allowance here – how much of the cost (if any) qualifies for it, and how much can be claimed in the year? The second part looks at R&D relief for an SME. There are different costs incurred here, so think about whether there is any difference in treatment for them. You are also told that the company will be loss making, so think about the significance of this.

(a) **Income tax saving as a result of a terminal loss relief claim by Sabin**

Terminal loss relief is available for the loss of £23,000 arising in the final 12 months prior to cessation.

Sabin has no taxable trading income in 2023/24, such that he can claim terminal loss relief against his trading income of the three tax years prior to cessation on a LIFO basis, i.e. 2022/23, 2021/22, 2020/21, in that order.

Accordingly, the loss will be offset as follows:

	2020/21	**2021/22**	**2022/23**
	£	£	£
Trading income	44,000	32,000	21,000
Loss relief	Nil	(2,000)	(21,000)

Tax relief:

2022/23: Sabin's original income tax liability was £2,886 ((£21,000 + £6,000 – £12,570) × 20%). After terminal loss relief, his liability will be £Nil as his employment income (£6,000) will be covered by his personal allowance. Accordingly, the income tax saving will be £2,886.

2021/22: Sabin's original taxable income was £25,430 (£32,000 + £6,000 – £12,570). Following the terminal loss claim, this will be reduced to £23,430 (£25,430 – £2,000), such that there will be a saving of £400 (£2,000 × 20%).

The total income tax saving as a result of the terminal loss claim is therefore £3,286 (£2,886 + £400).

(b) **Capital gains tax (CGT) implications of the sale of the business premises and item of specialist machinery**

The sale of the business premises will give rise to a chargeable gain of £28,000 (£114,000 – £86,000).

No capital loss will arise on the sale of the specialist machine as capital allowances were claimed on this asset.

Tutorial note

Where capital allowances have been claimed on plant and machinery any loss arising on sale will not be an allowable capital loss. If the asset were sold at a gain, then the £6,000 chattel rules would apply.

The gain on the business premises qualifies for business asset disposal relief (BADR) because Sabin carried on the business for more than two years prior to cessation, the premises were in business use at the date of cessation, and were sold within three years of the date of cessation. CGT payable is therefore £2,800 (£28,000 × 10%). After-tax proceeds are £152,200 (£114,000 + £41,000 – £2,800).

(c) Patan Ltd

1 Tax deduction available in respect of the acquisition of the new factory

The new factory will qualify for the structures and buildings allowance (SBA) as it is a new commercial building. The cost of the land is not eligible for the allowance, so Patan Ltd may claim an annual writing down allowance of £2,580 (3% × (£142,000 – £56,000)). As Patan Ltd only brought the building in to use on 1 May 2024, the SBA available in the year ending 31 March 2025 will be £2,365 (£2,580 × 11/12).

Tutorial note

SBA can only be claimed on the cost of buildings, not land or any legal and professional fees. The allowance can be claimed from the date the building is brought into use in the business, not the date of purchase. Where applicable, the allowance should be time apportioned if it is brought into use part way through an accounting period.

2 Tax deductions available in respect of the expenditure on research and development activities

As Patan Ltd is a small or medium-sized enterprise for the purposes of obtaining tax relief for expenditure on qualifying research and development activities, the revenue expenditure which relates directly to undertaking research and development activities qualifies for an additional 86% deduction from Patan Ltd's taxable trading income. This applies to the whole of the employee cost, but only 65% of the cost of the external contractor, who is provided by an unconnected company. Accordingly, the expenditure qualifying for the additional deduction is £54,300 (£40,000 + (65% × £22,000)), and the total deduction available to Patan Ltd is £108,698 (£62,000 + 86% × £54,300).

As Patan Ltd will be a loss-making company in the year ending 31 March 2025, it can choose to claim a tax credit in respect of the qualifying research and development expenditure. The company can surrender to HM Revenue and Customs (HMRC) up to 186% of the qualifying expenditure of £54,300 in return for a tax credit of 10% of the amount surrendered.

Examiner's report

Requirement (a)

Elements of this section of the examiner's report have been amended due to changes in tax legislation.

The requirement in this part of the question was to calculate, with supporting explanations, the income tax saving for a sole trader if he claims terminal loss relief upon cessation of his loss-making business.

Generally, answers to this part of the question were disappointing. Despite the wording used in the requirement, namely to "calculate with supporting explanations" a common mistake made by many candidates was to produce only numbers and therefore miss out on the marks for providing the written explanations. Mistakes of this nature can be avoided if candidates make a point of highlighting the key words in the requirement and then subsequently go back and double check that they are doing exactly what has been required of them.

Many candidates demonstrated an understanding that the terminal loss could be carried back 36 months but made the offset against total income rather than trading profits. The best approach was to set up income tax computations (before taking account of any terminal loss) for the final four tax years of the sole trader, showing trading profits, any other sources of income, and deducting the personal allowance in order to give taxable income for all years concerned. In this scenario, there were no trading profits in the final tax year (2023/24) but there were trading profits in the previous 3 tax years (2020/21, 2021/22 and 2022/23).

The terminal loss can then be offset against the relevant trading profits of the past 36 months on a LIFO basis i.e. primarily against the trading profits of 2022/23 and then against 2021/22. There is insufficient terminal loss to use against the trading profits of 2020/21. When making the offset, it is important to remember that terminal losses of sole traders can only be carried back against the trading income of earlier years and not against any other sources of income.

Having worked out the terminal loss and shown the way in which it would be offset, it was important to remember that the requirement asked for explanatory comment, as well as calculations. So candidates needed to explain what they had done, for example by stating that the terminal loss is based on the last 12 months of trading and is then carried back against trading income of the three preceding tax years, on a LIFO basis.

To fully address the requirement, it was also necessary to calculate and explain the income tax saving as a result of the terminal loss claim. In this respect, many candidates simply took the loss used and multiplied it by the basic income tax rate of 20%. However, to answer this part accurately, consideration of the sole trader's level of income before utilisation of the terminal loss was required in order to compare it with revised levels of income once the offset had taken place. This comparison should be quite straightforward if the pre-loss and post-loss computations are set up methodically. The tax saving is then the difference in the taxable income figures (for each year involved) multiplied by the appropriate tax rate, which is 20% in this scenario.

Requirement (b)

Part (b) of this question contains two requirements. The first involves an explanation of the capital gains tax (CGT) implications of the sole trader selling his business premises and a machine to a company. The second part asks for a calculation of the amount available to the sole trader from the sale of these two assets, after paying any CGT liability.

When dealing with the first part, many candidates recognised that there would be a capital gain on the building but fewer acknowledged that there would be no capital loss on the disposal of the machine by virtue of having claimed capital allowances on the asset. It was then necessary to consider business asset disposal relief (BADR) in respect of the gain on the building. This involved a discussion of the conditions for BADR in order to consider their applicability to the relevant asset; it had been held for more than two years, was in business use at the date of cessation of the trade and was sold within three years of date of cessation. Most candidates spotted the relevance of BADR and were able to pick up some of the marks for application of the relevant conditions.

The second part of the requirement involved calculation of the 'after-tax proceeds'. Regrettably, when addressing this part, a number of candidates simply stopped at the tax liability without thinking precisely about what it was they had been asked to do. It was first necessary to calculate the CGT liability on the building – this was at 10% due to the availability of BADR. This amount then needed to be deducted from the total proceeds on the sale of both assets in order to establish the amount of after-tax proceeds. In questions of this nature, candidates should always ensure that they are clear on what it is they are being asked to calculate – whether it is an actual tax liability only or, as in this case, the after-tax proceeds. The latter involves the extra step of deducting the tax liability from proceeds received. Many candidates overlooked this final stage.

Requirement (c)

The final part of this question involves an explanation of the tax deductions and reliefs available to a company in respect of the acquisition of a new factory and expenditure incurred on research and development (R&D). Responses to this part of the question were generally good.

Although the requirement did not specifically ask for calculations, it is perfectly acceptable to provide these if they help to support the explanatory comment which had been requested.

Beginning with the factory, it was important to identify the availability of structures and buildings allowances (SBA) by virtue of its date of construction. A number of candidates were aware that SBAs were an issue, but could not explain with sufficient clarity precisely why this was the case. These allowances are available for commercial buildings constructed on, or after, 29 October 2018. It was also important to explain that the cost of land is excluded from SBAs and that the allowance is given at the rate of 3% per annum. However, on this occasion, because the building was only brought into use one month after the start of the accounting period, it needed to be pointed out that, for the accounting period concerned, the available allowance would be based on 11/12 of the full annual equivalent.

With regard to the R&D expenditure, it was important to note once again that explanations were required. Candidates were therefore expected to state how the R&D deduction works for small and medium size enterprises i.e. that a 186% deduction is available for relevant expenditure, and then to go on to apply this to the facts of the question. This involved distinguishing between the employee costs which would qualify in their entirety for the additional 86% relief and the subcontractor costs where only 65% would be eligible for the additional relief. A calculation of the total deduction could be provided in support of the explanation, as long as it didn't replace it in its entirety.

Since the company was loss-making in the period concerned, it was also necessary to go on to consider the R&D tax credit which would be available on this occasion. A significant number of candidates did not go on to think about this additional step. This involved explaining that the company would be entitled to surrender up to 186% of the R&D qualifying expenditure in return for a 10% tax credit. Again a calculation of this amount would have assisted to support the explanatory comment, as long as the calculation in itself did not become the sole focus of a candidate's answer.

ACCA marking scheme				
				Marks
(a)	Terminal loss relief – explanation			2.5
	Calculation of tax relief			4.5
				7.0
(b)	Disposal of assets			1.5
	Capital gains tax			3.5
	After-tax proceeds			1.0
				6.0
(c)	New factory			3.0
	Research and development	– deduction		3.0
		– tax credit		2.5
				8.5
			Maximum	7.0
	Professional skills marks (see below)		**Maximum**	5.0
Total				**25.0**

Professional skills marks

Analysis and evaluation

- Use of information to calculate income tax savings resulting from use of loss relief and bringing all the given information together – e.g. including the employment income in the tax saving computations in part (a).
- Identifying that business asset disposal relief was relevant in part (b).
- Appropriate use of the data to support discussion about how research and development relief would apply given that there was incomplete data as the loss was not quantified in part (c).

Commercial acumen

- Recognition of constraints and opportunities related to how loss reliefs are offset. It is simply done on a LIFO basis regardless of the wasting of personal allowances or higher potential savings to be made in other years in part (a).
- Demonstration of an understanding of the difference between cash and taxable gains in part (b).

CAPITAL TAXES

37 JOAN ARK

Key answer tips

This is a good practice question covering the IHT and CGT implications of lifetime gifts in part (a), with a written requirement on general IHT planning points in part (b).

The style of question is more like the section B questions, although it is longer than the section B questions you will see under the current exam format and has no professional skills marks. There is no mark scheme for this question as it is designed to be a revision aid and not represent the current style of the exam.

When attempting part (a), the best approach is to run through each disposal twice: once to deal with the IHT implications, then again to deal with the CGT implications.

If you try to cover both taxes at once, it is very easy to get them confused! You must also make sure that your answer is clearly labelled so that the marker knows exactly which tax and which gift you are discussing.

In a question like this, any detailed calculations should be carried out in the spreadsheet in the exam. This will enable you to set pro formas out more easily and also make use of formulae to cut down on calculation time. Don't forget to reference through to any calculations you have performed in the discursive part of your answer in the word processor.

(i) IHT and CGT implications of gifts made in the tax year 2023/24

(a) Ordinary shares in Orleans plc

IHT implications

For IHT purposes, a discretionary trust is a 'relevant property trust' and lifetime gifts into trusts are chargeable lifetime transfers.

BPR is not available as the shares are quoted and Joan does not have a controlling interest.

Tutorial note

There would be two annual exemptions available against this gift; however, the question says to ignore the effect of the annual exemption.

The shares are valued at the lower of:

- Quarter up method = 147p (146p + 1/4 × (150p –146p)) per share, or
- Average of the marked bargains = 147.5p ((140p + 155p) ÷ 2).

As Joan is to pay any IHT, the gift is a net gift and will be taxed at 25%.

	£
Transfer of value (250,000 × 147p)	367,500
Less: BPR	(0)
Exemptions	(0)
Net chargeable transfer	367,500
Less: NRB	(325,000)
Taxable amount	42,500
IHT payable (£42,500 × 25%)	10,625

The tax payable by Joan is due by 30 April 2024.

Gross gift to c/f = (£367,500 + £10,625) = £378,125

If Joan dies within seven years, before 13 July 2030, a further IHT liability may arise.

CGT implications

For CGT purposes, the shares are deemed to have been sold for their market value.

This is calculated as the mid-price = 148p ((146p + 150p) ÷ 2)

There are no acquisitions on the same day or in the next 30 days; therefore, the disposal of shares is from the share pool as follows:

	Number	**Cost**
		£
2008 – Purchase	200,000	149,000
August 2021 – Purchase	75,000	69,375
July 2022 – Purchase	10,000	14,800
	285,000	233,175
July 2023 – Gift	(250,000)	(204,539)
	35,000	28,636

The chargeable gain is calculated as follows:

	£
Market value (250,000 × 148p)	370,000
Less: Cost	(204,539)
Chargeable gain	165,461

Joan does not have a 5% interest in the company and therefore the shares are not qualifying business assets for gift holdover relief purposes.

However, Joan can elect to defer all of the gain with a gift holdover relief claim as the disposal is immediately chargeable to IHT.

Therefore, there is no capital gains tax payable.

Tutorial note

If gift holdover relief is claimed, the full gain is deferred, therefore business asset disposal (BADR) relief is not a consideration.

However, even if gift holdover relief were not claimed, BADR would not be available as Joan is not an employee and does not own a 5% interest. The gain would therefore be taxed at 20% (as Joan is a higher rate taxpayer), not 10%.

(b) Ordinary shares in Rouen Ltd

IHT implications

Joan's gift of shares in Rouen Ltd in July 2023 to her son will be a PET, calculated as follows:

	£
Value of shares held before the transfer (Note)	
40,000 × £17.10 (part of a 80% holding)	684,000
Value of shares held after the transfer	
20,000 × £14.50 (part of a 60% holding)	(290,000)
Value transferred	394,000
Less: BPR (100%) (Note)	(394,000)
Chargeable amount	0

As a PET there is no lifetime IHT payable.

If Michael still owns the shares at the date of Joan's death, 100% BPR is still available and there will be nil taxable amount.

An IHT liability will arise if Joan dies before 15 July 2030 and Michael has disposed of the shares before that date.

Tutorial note

When valuing the shares for IHT purposes, the related property provisions must be taken into account. Joan is therefore disposing of 20,000 shares out of a combined 80% holding of shares held by her husband.

Business property relief at the rate of 100% will be available as the shares are unquoted trading company shares held for at least two years.

CGT implications

A capital gain will arise as follows:

	£
MV of 20% holding (20,000 × £7.90)	158,000
Less: Cost £96,400 × (20,000/40,000)	(48,200)
Chargeable gain	109,800

Provided Joan and her son jointly elect, the gain can be held over as a gift of business assets, since Rouen Ltd is an unquoted trading company.

Therefore, there is no capital gains tax payable.

Tutorial note

If gift holdover relief is claimed, the full gain is deferred, therefore BADR is not a consideration.

However, even if gift holdover relief were not available, BADR would not be available as Joan does not work for Rouen Ltd. The gain would therefore be taxed at 20%.

Key answer tips

For IHT purposes, the diminution in the value of Joan's estate is the starting point.

For CGT purposes, the deemed proceeds are the market value of the asset gifted (i.e. a 20% holding).

Note that the diminution in value concept does not apply to CGT and the related property provisions do not apply to CGT.

(c) Antique vase

IHT implications

The gift of the vase is in consideration of marriage, and will therefore qualify for an exemption of £2,500 as it is a gift from a grandparent to grandchild.

The balance of the gift of £16,000 (£18,500 – £2,500) will be a PET made on 4 November 2023, with no tax unless Joan dies within seven years.

CGT implications

The gift of the vase is a disposal of a non-wasting chattel. The gain is calculated as £4,350 (£18,500 – £14,150).

Gift holdover relief is not available as a vase is not a qualifying business asset and there is no immediate charge to IHT.

The CGT liability due on 31 January 2025 is therefore £870 (£4,350 × 20%) (ignoring the annual exempt amount).

(d) Agricultural land

IHT implications

The gift of the agricultural land will be a PET for £300,000 on 15 January 2024 and will not become chargeable unless Joan dies within seven years.

The increase in the value of her son Charles' property is irrelevant in valuing the PET. Only the diminution in the value of Joan's estate as a result of the gift is relevant.

If the PET becomes chargeable as a result of Joan dying before 15 January 2031, agricultural property relief at the rate of 100% based on the agricultural value of £175,000 will be available. This is because the land is let out for the purposes of agriculture and has been owned for at least seven years.

However, relief will only be available if, at the date of Joan's death, Charles still owns the land and it still qualifies as agricultural property.

CGT implications

The gift of agricultural land to Charles will be valued at its open market value on the date of the gift of £300,000.

Since the land qualifies for agricultural property relief it is also eligible for gift holdover relief for CGT purposes. Joan and Charles can therefore jointly elect that the gain of £208,000 (£300,000 – £92,000) is held over as a gift of business assets.

Therefore, there is no capital gains tax payable.

Tutorial note

BPR will not be available on the remainder of the market value as Joan has rented the farm out rather than use it as her farming business.

BADR is not a consideration as the full gain is deferred with a gift holdover relief claim.

However, even if gift holdover relief were not available, BADR would not be available for the disposal of a rented property, as this is classed as an investment asset. The gain would therefore be taxed at 20%.

(e) Main residence

IHT implications

The gift of the main residence is a gift with reservation because although Joan has gifted the freehold interest, she retains an interest in the property as she has continued to live rent free in the property.

The gift will be treated as a PET for £265,000 as normal on 31 March 2024, but Joan will still be treated as beneficially entitled to the property.

If Joan continues to live in the property rent free until her death, it will be included in her estate when she dies at its market value at that date, although relief will be given should there be a double charge to IHT.

Joan could avoid these provisions by paying full consideration for the use of the property. The gift of the main residence will simply be a PET on 31 March 2024 with no gift with reservation implications.

CGT implications

The gift of the main residence is a chargeable disposal for CGT purposes and the time of the disposal is when the ownership of the asset passes to the donee.

The reservation of benefit is therefore not relevant for CGT, and a normal CGT computation is required on 31 March 2024.

	£
Deemed consideration	265,000
Less: Cost	(67,000)
	198,000
Less: PRR (W1)	(75,103)
Letting relief (W2)	(0)
Chargeable gain	122,897
Capital gains tax at 28%	34,411
Due date	30 May 2024

Tutorial note

When a UK residential property is disposed of a UK land return must be submitted and the relevant CGT paid within 60 days, rather than the usual deadline of 31st January following the end of the tax year.

Workings

(W1) Private residence relief

		Notes	Months	Exempt	Chargeable
1.7.2002 – 31.12.2006	Owner occupied		54	54	
1.1.2007 – 31.12.2010	Unoccupied	1	48	36	12
1.1.2011 – 30.6.2023	Rented out	2	150	0	150
1.7.2023 – 31.3.2024	Owner occupied		9	9	
			261	99	162

PRR = (99/261) × £198,000 = £75,103

Notes

1 Three years allowed for any reason provided the property is owner occupied at some time before and sometime after the period of absence.

2 The last nine months are always exempt. However, Joan occupies the property throughout this period anyway.

(W2) Letting relief

Letting relief is only available in respect of gains arising during periods of shared occupancy.

As Joan did not occupy any of the property while it was let out, no letting relief is available.

(ii) Main advantages in lifetime giving for IHT purposes

Possible advantages of lifetime giving include:

- Making use of lifetime IHT exemptions such as the annual exemption, small gifts exemption, marriage exemptions in reducing a taxpayer's chargeable estate at death.
- Gifts between individuals will not become liable to IHT unless the donor dies within seven years of making the gift.
- If the donor does die prematurely there may still be an IHT advantage in lifetime giving because usually:
  - The value of the asset for calculating any additional IHT arising upon death is fixed at the time the gift is made, unless the asset falls in value, in which case fall in value relief may be available.
  - The availability of taper relief (providing the donor survives at least three years) may help reduce the effective IHT rate.

Main factors to consider in choosing assets to gift

The main factors to consider include:

(i) Whether or not a significant CGT liability will arise upon making the gift.

Lifetime gifting may give rise to CGT. This therefore needs to be balanced against the fact that no CGT liability will arise upon death (i.e. if the assets are left in the estate and gifted in a will). Death results in the 'tax free' uplift of the chargeable assets included in the deceased's estate to market value.

The availability of CGT reliefs (primarily gift holdover relief for business assets or if there is an immediate charge to IHT) and CGT exemptions (e.g. annual exempt amount) to ensure there is no CGT liability on the lifetime gift is therefore relevant in selecting assets.

Some assets are completely exempt from CGT, such as cash. Giving cash during lifetime would not give rise to a CGT liability.

(ii) Whether an asset is appreciating in value.

Because any additional IHT arising as a result of death will be based on the (lower) value of the asset at the date of gift it may be advantageous to select assets that are likely to significantly appreciate in value.

Even if the value of the asset decreases, fall in value relief may be available so that lifetime giving does not result in more tax than leaving the asset in the death estate.

(iii) Whether the donor can afford to make the gift.

Whilst lifetime gifting can result in significant IHT savings this should not be at the expense of the taxpayer's ability to live comfortably, particularly in old age.

(iv) The availability of significant IHT reliefs, particularly BPR.

There may be little point in selecting an asset that already qualifies for 100% relief.

Also, if residential property is gifted in lifetime, the residence nil rate band (RNRB) will not be available. However, if property the deceased lived in is passed to direct descendants on death, a RNRB of up to £175,000 may be available.

38 ALEX (ADAPTED)

Key answer tips

This old-style section B question includes some straightforward marks for basic income tax and inheritance tax computations, with a written section on the use of trusts. There is no mark scheme for this question as it is designed to be a revision aid and not represent the current style of the exam.

There are a few tricky points in part (b) – make sure that you calculate the lifetime tax before trying to calculate the death tax on lifetime transfers, as the PET uses the nil rate band on death but does not affect the nil band when calculating the lifetime tax on the CLT.

Where shares are quoted 'ex div' you must add the dividend to the estate too. Don't forget to include the income tax from part (a) – this will be a mark for consistency, even if your figure is wrong.

Trusts are only likely to feature as part of a question in the exam, as in part (c).

(a) Income tax payable/repayable – 2023/24

	Total	Non-savings income	Savings income	Dividends
	£	£	£	£
Pension	10,600	10,600		
B.Soc interest	1,600		1,600	
NS&I interest	870		870	
Dividends – other	9,000	–		9,000
– Nacional plc (Note 1)	3,600			3,600
Total income	25,670	10,600	2,470	12,600
Less: PA (Note 2)	(12,570)	(10,600)		(1,970)
Taxable income	13,100	0	2,470	10,630

Income tax

£		£
2,470	× 0% (Savings income)	0
1,000	× 0% (Dividends)	0
9,630	× 8.75% (Dividends)	843
13,100		
Income tax liability		843
Less: Tax at source		
PAYE		(2,120)
Income tax repayable		(1,277)

Tutorial note

1 *Alex will be taxed on his income due and payable up to the date of death. He will have a full (non-apportioned) personal allowance for 2023/24, the tax year of death.*

Re-the Nacional plc dividends:

- *The dividends are declared before Alex's death and are therefore included in Alex's last income tax computation even though they are received post death.*
- *Dividends to include = (20,000 × 18p) = £3,600*

The ACCA have confirmed that this is the treatment they expect for dividends declared pre-death, received post death.

2 *The PA is always set off in the most beneficial way, and should be set against non-savings income first.*

The excess PA should not be set against Alex's savings income, as this all falls into the £5,000 starting rate band and will be taxed at 0%.

Instead, the excess PA should be set against the dividends to save tax at 8.75%, as the dividends are not fully covered by the £1,000 dividend nil rate band.

(b) Inheritance tax liability on Alex's death

Lifetime inheritance tax

July 2018 – PET

- The gift in July 2018 was a potentially exempt transfer (PET).
- No IHT is payable at the time of the gift.
- IHT only becomes payable when Alex dies within seven years.

March 2019 – CLT

- The transfer into the discretionary trust in March 2019 was a chargeable lifetime transfer (CLT).
- Lifetime IHT is due when the gift is made and additional tax is due as Alex dies within seven years of the gift.
- The value of the CLT was £338,000.
- No annual exemptions were available, as these are allocated in date order against the PET in July 2018.

- The lifetime tax on the CLT was as follows:
  (£338,000 – £325,000 nil rate band) × 25% = £3,250
- The gross chargeable transfer was therefore £341,250 (£338,000 + £3,250).

Tutorial note

1 *The question tells you that when Alex's wife died, she had utilised all of her nil rate band. As a result, only Alex's nil rate band is available.*

Had his wife not utilised her nil rate band, the proportion of unused nil rate band could be transferred to Alex on his death.

2 *Where the donor suffers the lifetime tax due, the tax rate used to calculate lifetime tax is 25% (i.e. 20/80).*

3 *All of the nil rate band is available against this lifetime gift; the PET is ignored as it is not chargeable during Alex's lifetime, although it does use the annual exemptions.*

Additional inheritance tax due at death

IHT on PET in July 2018

The PET becomes chargeable on death, as Alex died within seven years of making the gift. As there are no lifetime transfers in the previous seven years, all of the nil rate band is available.

		£
Value transferred		338,000
Less: Annual exemptions:	2018/19	(3,000)
	2017/18	(3,000)
PET		332,000
IHT due (£332,000 – £325,000) × 40%		2,800
Less: Taper relief (5 – 6 years) (60%)		(1,680)
IHT due on death		1,120

This additional tax is paid by Brian (see tutorial note).

IHT on CLT in March 2019

The PET has used up the nil rate band, so the CLT in March 2019 is fully taxable as follows:

	£
IHT due on gross gift (£341,250 × 40%)	136,500
Less: Taper relief (4 – 5 years) (40%)	(54,600)
	81,900
Less: IHT paid during lifetime	(3,250)
IHT due on death	78,650

This additional tax is paid by the trustees of the discretionary trust (see tutorial note).

Tutorial note

The additional tax on PETs and CLTs as a result of death is always paid by the donee.

Estate at death

	£	£
Main residence		575,000
Touriga shares (W1)	26,950	
Less: Business property relief	(26,950)	
		0
Nacional shares (W2)		128,800
Building society account		15,000
NS&I investment account		55,000
NS&I savings certificates		180,000
Chattels		40,000
Other quoted investments		115,000
Income tax repayment (part (a))		1,277
		1,110,077
Less: Exempt charitable legacy		(150,000)
Gross chargeable estate		960,077
Less: Residence nil rate band		(175,000)
The IHT nil rate band has already been used against gifts made in the seven years prior to death.		
Taxable estate		785,077
IHT on estate (£785,077 × 36%) (W3)		282,628

The inheritance due to each of Brian and Beatrice is £352,199 (W4).

Workings

(W1) Touriga Ltd

The total value of Touriga Ltd shares at death = (£11.00 × 2,450) = £26,950.

As these shares are unquoted trading company shares and have been held for more than two years, 100% business property relief applies.

(W2) Nacional plc

The Nacional plc shares are valued at the lower of:

(i) Quarter up method

= (624p + (632p – 624p) × 1/4) = 626p

(ii) Average of highest and lowest marked bargains

= (625p + 630p) × ½ = 627.5p

Value of 20,000 shares = (626p × 20,000) = £125,200

As the shares are quoted ex-div at the date of death, the value of the shares in the death estate needs to include the value of the next dividend (18p × 20,000 = £3,600).

The total value of the shares is therefore £128,800 (£3,600 + £125,200).

(W3) Rate of tax

	£
Taxable estate	785,077
Add: Exempt legacy to charity	150,000
Residence nil rate band	175,000
Baseline amount	1,110,077
Apply 10% test	
£1,110,077 × 10%	111,008

As the exempt charitable legacy exceeds £111,008, the estate is taxed at 36% instead of 40%.

(W4) Share of inheritance

	£
Value of estate	960,077
Value of Touriga shares	26,950
	987,027
IHT payable from estate	(282,628)
Estate value to share	704,399

Half share to each of Brian and Beatrice (£704,399 ÷ 2) = £352,199.

(c) (i) Use of a trust

Relevant property trusts

Brian has the choice of setting up an interest in possession trust or a discretionary trust.

However, regardless of the type of trust set up, if the trust is set up by Brian during his lifetime it will be a 'relevant property trust' for IHT purposes.

A relevant property trust is taxed as follows:

- Gifts into a relevant property trust are chargeable lifetime transfers (CLTs). They attract IHT at half the death rate to the extent that the cumulative lifetime transfers in the last seven years of the settlor (Brian) exceed the nil rate band (£325,000).
- The tax can be paid by the trustees out of the settled assets (i.e. borne by the trust).
- Once the assets are settled in a relevant property trust, the trust will suffer a ten-year charge (the 'principal charge').
- The charge is 6%.

- If capital assets are removed from the trust (i.e. distributed to the beneficiaries), an exit charge is also levied.

Type of trust

Given Brian's desire to retain control over the assets, it would appear that a discretionary trust would be advisable, rather than an interest in possession trust.

This is because:

- The trustees of a discretionary trust have the discretion (hence the name) over how the funds will be used.
- They can thus control the assets comprising the inheritance, while allowing Colin or Charlotte access to some or all of the income.
- It is likely that Brian himself would wish to be a trustee and he could therefore control how his children accessed the money, both the income and capital.
- In contrast, if an interest in possession trust is set up, the beneficiaries Colin and Charlotte would be legally entitled to the income generated by the trust each year and it must be paid to them.
- In the trust deed the capital must be directed to pass at a set future date or as a consequence of a future event.

(ii) Inheritance tax planning

If Brian creates a discretionary trust by making a lifetime gift of the inherited assets, this will be a CLT and will give rise to a charge to IHT with a further liability arising if Brian dies within seven years.

Therefore, Brian should be advised to pass his inheritance directly to his children by using a deed of variation to alter the disposition of Alex's estate.

Provided the deed includes a statement that the deed is effective for inheritance tax purposes, the transfer into the trust will be treated as a legacy under the will.

There will be no alteration in the tax payable on Alex's estate but Brian will not have a CLT, there will be no lifetime tax on setting up the trust and Brian will have preserved his own nil rate band for use against future lifetime gifts or the value of his own estate on death.

Tutorial note

If Brian had chosen to set up an interest in possession trust, if set up on death (under a deed of variation of Alex's will), it will be an Immediate Post Death Interest trust (IPDI) and not a 'relevant property trust'. As a result, different rules apply to the taxation of trust. These rules are beyond the scope of the ATX syllabus.

39 KEPLER (ADAPTED)

Key answer tips

This is a reasonable capital taxes question but with some complications. The calculation of inheritance tax on the lifetime gift of shares is something a well prepared student should have no problems with. You might have been puzzled when asked to calculate Galileo's inheritance tax payable on the shares he inherited on Kepler's death when there is none. The examining team did give a clue by saying tax payable (if any).

Payment by instalments is important in practice and the rules should be learnt.

You must also make sure that you are happy with the overseas aspects of personal tax, as these are very often tested in the exam.

There are some easy marks in the last sections asking for advice about employment benefits, provided you have retained this TX knowledge.

In a question like this, any detailed calculations should be carried out in the spreadsheet in the exam. This will enable you to set out pro formas more easily and also make use of formulae to cut down on calculation time. Don't forget to reference through to any calculations you have performed in the discursive part of your answer in the word processor.

(a) (i) Galileo – Inheritance tax payable

Gift of shares in June 2020

The gift of shares to Galileo was a potentially exempt transfer. It has become chargeable due to Kepler's death within seven years of the gift.

Any tax arising on a PET which becomes chargeable on death is payable by the donee (i.e. Galileo).

	£	£
Value of Kepler's holding prior to the gift to Galileo		
(2,000 × £485)		970,000
Less: Value of Kepler's holding after the gift		
(1,400 × £310)		(434,000)
Transfer of value		536,000
Less: Business property relief (W1)		(367,843)
Less: Annual exemption – 2020/21		(3,000)
– 2019/20 b/f (W2)		(1,200)
Chargeable amount		163,957
Nil rate band at death	325,000	
Gross chargeable transfers in last 7 years (W2)	(305,000)	
Nil rate band available		(20,000)
Taxable amount		143,957

	£
Inheritance tax (£143,957 × 40%)	57,583
Less: Taper relief (3 – 4 years) (£57,583 × 20%)	(11,517)
Inheritance tax payable by Galileo	46,066

Inheritance of shares in May 2024

The inheritance tax payable in respect of the shares in the death estate will be paid by the executors and borne by Herschel, the residuary legatee.

None of the tax will be payable by Galileo.

Tutorial note

As Galileo is inheriting a specific gift, he will not suffer any tax. The tax will be taken from the balance of the estate.

Workings

(W1) Business property relief

BPR at 100% is available on unquoted trading company shares held for at least two years. However, BPR is restricted if the company has excepted assets.

Excepted assets and total assets

	Total assets	**Excluding excepted assets**
	£	£
Premises	900,000	900,000
Surplus land	480,000	–
Vehicles	100,000	100,000
Current assets	50,000	50,000
	1,530,000	1,050,000
BPR (£536,000 × 100% × (£1,050,000/£1,530,000))		367,843

Tutorial note

Excepted assets are those which have not been used wholly or mainly for business in the last two years and are not likely to be required for future use in the business.

(W2) Lifetime gifts in the seven years before 1 June 2020

		1 Feb 2019	1 July 2019
		£	£
Transfer of value		311,000	1,800
(2 × £900)			
Less Annual exemptions			
–	2018/19	(3,000)	
–	2017/18 b/f	(3,000)	
–	2019/20		(1,800)
		305,000	0

- No tax is due at the time of the gifts as they are PETs.
- Both gifts fall within seven years of Kepler's death and therefore become chargeable on death.
- Therefore, the GCTs in the seven years before the gift in June 2020 are £305,000.

(ii) Payment by instalments

The inheritance tax can be paid by instalments because Messier Ltd is an unquoted company controlled by Kepler at the time of the gift and is still unquoted at the time of his death.

The tax is due in ten equal annual instalments starting on 30 November 2024.

All of the outstanding inheritance tax will become payable if Galileo sells the shares in Messier Ltd.

Tutorial note

Candidates were also given credit for stating that payment by instalments is available because the shares represent at least 10% of the company's share capital and are valued at £20,000 or more.

(b) Minimising capital gains tax on the sale of the paintings

Galileo will only become resident from the date he arrives in the UK as he will be starting to work full time in the UK for a period of one year or more and he did not have sufficient ties in the UK in order to be UK resident prior to coming to the UK. Further, the split year basis applies to him as he was not UK resident in the previous year, is UK resident in the current year and arrived in the UK part way through the current year to begin work in the UK.

Prior to that date he will not be resident such that he will not be subject to UK capital gains tax.

Galileo should sell the paintings before he leaves Astronomeria; this will avoid UK capital gains tax completely.

Tutorial note

If Galileo sells the paintings after arriving in the UK and becoming UK resident, then as a non-domiciled individual, the taxation of his gains depends on how much of them he remits to the UK.

If his unremitted gains exceed £2,000 then Galileo must choose whether to be taxed on all his gains (arising basis) but keep his entitlement to the capital gains annual exempt amount, or to be taxed only on the gains remitted to the UK (remittance basis) and lose the annual exempt amount.

If he chooses the remittance basis, then he will not have to pay the £30,000 annual charge as he has not been resident in the UK for at least seven out of the last nine tax years.

If his unremitted gains are less than £2,000, then the remittance basis of taxation applies automatically and he will be entitled to a capital gains annual exempt amount.

However, since he wants to use the proceeds of selling his paintings to help buy a house, it is likely he will bring in all the money raised from the sale and consequently will automatically be taxed on the whole of his gains. As he is not claiming the remittance basis the capital gains annual exempt amount will be available.

(c) (i) Relocation costs

Direct assistance

Messier Ltd can bear the cost of certain qualifying relocation costs of Galileo up to a maximum of £8,000 without increasing his UK income tax liability.

Qualifying costs include the legal, professional and other fees in relation to the purchase of a house, the costs of travelling to the UK and the cost of transporting his belongings. The costs must be incurred before the end of the tax year following the year of the relocation (i.e. by 5 April 2026).

Assistance in the form of a loan

Messier Ltd can provide Galileo with an interest-free loan of up to £10,000 without giving rise to any UK income tax.

(ii) Tax-free accommodation

It is not possible for Messier Ltd to provide Galileo with tax-free accommodation.

The provision of accommodation by an employer to an employee will give rise to a taxable benefit unless it is:

- necessary for the proper performance of the employee's duties (e.g. a caretaker); or
- for the better performance of the employee's duties and customary (e.g. a hotel manager); or
- part of arrangements arising out of threats to the employee's security (e.g. a government minister).

As a manager of Messier Ltd, Galileo is unable to satisfy any of the above conditions.

Examiner's report

This question concerned inheritance tax, capital gains tax and income tax together with certain implications of moving to the UK from overseas. There were five separate parts to this question, all of which had to be addressed in the time. A number of candidates failed to tailor their answers to the number of marks available and wasted time producing inappropriately long answers.

Part (a) required candidates to calculate the inheritance tax payable by the donee of a potentially exempt transfer following the death of the donor. This was done well by many candidates although a minority did not consider business property relief, which was an important element of the question. Those who did consider business property relief often failed to recognise the existence of excepted assets in the company.

Candidates were also asked to explain why the tax could be paid in instalments and to state when the instalments were due. This was not handled particularly well; many candidates did not know the circumstances in which payment by instalments is available and the payment dates given often lacked precision.

Part (b) concerned the liability to capital gains tax of an individual coming to the UK. It was only for two marks but it illustrated continued confusion on the part of many as to the treatment of someone who is not resident. Such a person is not subject to UK capital gains tax on personal investment assets and the remittance or otherwise of the proceeds is irrelevant. Candidates preparing for future exams should ensure that they fully understand the rules.

Part (c) involved the desire to assist an employee's relocation to the UK without giving rise to an income tax liability. This was done rather well with many candidates identifying the possibility of a tax-free loan and relocation assistance.

ACCA marking scheme

			Marks
(a)	(i)	Diminution in value	1.0
		Business property relief	1.5
		Annual exemptions	1.5
		Available nil band	1.5
		Inheritance tax at 40%	0.5
		Taper relief	1.0
		Tax due in respect of shares in death estate	1.0
			8.0
	(ii)	Valid reason for payment by instalments being available	1.0
		When due	1.0
		Implication of Galileo selling the shares	1.0
			3.0
(b)	Residence position		1.0
	Advice		1.0
			2.0

(c)	(i)	Relocation costs		
		Tax free with maximum		1.0
		Examples of qualifying costs (0.5 each)		1.5
		Deadline		0.5
		Interest-free loan		
		Maximum tax-free amount		1.0
				4.0
	(ii)	Provision of accommodation will be taxed		1.0
		Reasons why not exempt		2.0
				3.0
	Professional skills marks (see below)		**Maximum**	5.0
Total				**25.0**

Professional skills marks

Analysis and evaluation

- Appropriate use of the data to calculate inheritance tax payable on death in part (a)(i).
- Appropriate use of the data to calculate a restriction in business property relief in part (a)(i).
- Analysis of the information to determine the appropriate capital gains tax treatment of the paintings in part (b).

Commercial acumen

- Recognition of the availability of business property relief in part (a)(i).
- Identification that selling the Messier Ltd shares would lead to all inheritance tax becoming payable in part (a)(ii).
- Recognition of split year basis rules in part (b).
- Recognition that selling the paintings before Galileo leaves the UK will avoid capital gains tax in part (b).

40 ASH (ADAPTED) *Walk in the footsteps of a top tutor*

Key answer tips

This is a question with three independent parts which could have been attempted in any order.

The first part deals with capital gains and is a mix of straightforward marks (land part disposal) and trickier marks (lease assignment).

The second part deals with VAT registration for a business dealing with both taxable and exempt supplies but does not require any calculations.

The third part covers a tax administration issue about whether to reduce a payment on account, which tests knowledge brought forward from TX.

The highlighted words in the written sections are key phrases that markers are looking for.

(a) (i) Availability of business asset disposal relief (BADR) – lease assignment

Tutor's top tips

You may have found this part on associated disposals tough, as it is a fringe element of the ATX syllabus which is not often tested.

There are three marks available and three conditions, so one mark for each. Even if you could not remember the details of associated disposals, a few basic points relating to BADR would likely have earned you one mark out of the three available.

The following conditions must be satisfied in order for the assignment of the lease to qualify as an associated disposal such that business asset disposal relief (BADR) will be available:

- Ash's disposal of the shares in Lava Ltd must qualify for BADR
- The lease must have been owned by Ash and used for the purposes of the trade of Lava Ltd for at least two years.
- Ash must have sold the shares in Lava Ltd and the lease as part of a process of withdrawing from participating in the business of Lava Ltd.

Tutorial note

BADR is not available on an associated disposal if full commercial rent is charged for the use of the asset.

In this question, rent is charged, but not the full market rate. Therefore, BADR is available on part of the gain, but not all of the gain.

(ii) Capital gains tax liability – 2023/24

Tutor's top tips

You have already been told that the sale of shares in Lava Ltd qualified for BADR, and you can see that the land sale does not qualify as there is no mention of any business.

The best way to present the calculation of gains tax when there are gains both qualifying and non-qualifying for BADR is in two columns. The annual exempt amount and the capital loss on the sale of the quoted shares should be deducted from the non-qualifying gains first.

Even if you calculated the gain on the lease incorrectly you would still get the marks available for including it in your summary and taxing it.

It is best to perform detailed calculations like this in the spreadsheet in the exam. This will enable you to set them out more easily, and also use formulae. This can cut down on calculation time in the exam.

	BADR available	**BADR not available**
	£	£
Gain on sale of shares	235,000	
Gain on assignment of lease		
(£79,812 (W1) × 60%/40%) (Note 1)	47,887	31,925
Gain on sale of land (W2)		21,780
Loss on sale of quoted shares		(16,500)
	282,887	37,205
Less: Annual exempt amount		(6,000)
	282,887	31,205

	£
Capital gains tax (Note 2)	
Gains qualifying for BADR	
(£282,887 × 10%)	28,289
Gains not qualifying for BADR	
(£31,205 × 20%)	6,241
CGT liability	34,530

Tutorial notes

1 *BADR in respect of the lease will be restricted to 60% of the gain, due to the rent charged by Ash to Lava Ltd which is equivalent to 40% of the market rate.*

2 *Ash's taxable income is less than his basic rate band. However, the gains qualifying for BADR use up the remainder of the basic rate band first, such that all of the non-qualifying gains are taxed at 20%.*

Workings

(W1) Gain on the assignment of the lease

	£
Proceeds (for a 37-year lease)	110,000
Less: Deemed cost (£31,800 × (93.497 ÷ 98.490))	(30,188)
Chargeable gain	79,812

Tutorial note

A lease is a wasting asset whose cost depreciates in accordance with a curved line table.

	£
Proceeds	*X*
Less: Cost × (% for life left at disposal ÷ % for life left at acquisition)	*(X)*
Capital gain	*X*

(W2) Gain on the sale of the remainder land

		£	£
Proceeds			30,000
Less:	Deemed cost of the remainder		
	Original cost	27,400	
	Part disposal cost		
	£27,400 × (£42,000 ÷ (£42,000 + £18,000))	(19,180)	
			(8,220)
Chargeable gain			21,780

(b) Vulcan Partnership (Vulcan) – Value added tax (VAT) registration

Tutor's top tips

You are asked to discuss in detail whether the Vulcan Partnership may be required to register and the advantages and disadvantages of registration. This gives you three headings to structure your answer.

You must apply your knowledge to the facts of the question. You will not earn marks for listing everything you know about VAT registration.

You are not required to perform any calculations, although you may find it useful to establish the current level of annual taxable supplies.

Whether or not Vulcan may be required to register

Subject to the exceptions noted below, Vulcan will be required to register for VAT once its cumulative taxable supplies (those that are standard-rated and zero-rated) in a 12-month period exceed £85,000.

However, Vulcan will not be required to register if HM Revenue and Customs are satisfied that its total supplies for the following 12 months will be less than £83,000.

Vulcan could request to be exempt from registration because only a small proportion of its supplies are standard-rated. This exemption will be available provided it would be in a repayment position if registered.

Advantages of registration

Vulcan will be able to recover all of its input tax if the amount relating to exempt supplies is de minimis. Where Vulcan's exempt supplies are not de minimis, it will still be able to recover the majority of its input tax.

Registration will prevent third parties from knowing the size of Vulcan's business.

Disadvantages of registration

Registration will add to the amount of work required to administer the business. In addition, Vulcan may be subject to financial penalties if it fails to comply with the obligations imposed by the VAT regime.

The partnership's customers would be unable to recover any output tax charged by the partnership as they are not registered for VAT. Accordingly, the prices charged to the small proportion of customers purchasing standard-rated items would increase unless Vulcan decides to reduce its profit in respect of these sales.

(c) Payment on account on 31 January 2025

Tutor's top tips

Payments on account are regularly tested at ATX, even though they are a TX topic.

The examining team usually asks for due dates of payments on account and/or amounts payable. Here they have tested the option to reduce payments on account and the potential impact of this, demonstrating the need to review this topic thoroughly prior to your exam.

The payment on account due on 31 January 2025 is the first payment in respect of Ash's income tax payable (income tax liability as reduced by tax deducted at source) for the tax year 2024/25. The payment due is half of the income tax payable for the tax year 2023/24 unless Ash makes a claim to reduce the payment.

Ash can make a claim to reduce the payment if he expects the amount payable for the tax year 2024/25 to be less than that for 2023/24. The income tax payable for the tax year 2024/25 is likely to be less than that for 2023/24 due, principally, to Ash receiving less profit from Vulcan.

Ash will need to estimate his income tax payable for the tax year 2024/25 in order to decide whether or not to reduce the payment on account. Ash will be charged interest if the payment on account is reduced to an amount that is less than half of the final agreed amount payable for 2024/25. In addition, a penalty may be charged if Ash is fraudulent or negligent when he makes the claim to reduce the payment.

Examiner's report

Part (a)(i) required a statement of the conditions necessary for the disposal of an asset to be an associated disposal for the purposes of business asset disposal relief and was not done well. This is not an area of the syllabus that one would expect to see examined regularly and many candidates will have known immediately on reading the requirement that they did not know the answer. However, the sensible approach would then have been to write a very brief answer with some sensible comments on business asset disposal relief. It was pretty likely that this would then score one of the three marks available.

In general part (a)(ii) was done well by many candidates. There was no problem in deciding what needed to be done, so those candidates who did poorly simply did not have sufficient knowledge of the rules.

The majority of part (b) was done very well including, in particular, the advantages and disadvantages of registering for VAT. However, some candidates' answers lacked precision when it came to the circumstances where compulsory registration is required in that taxable supplies were not clearly defined and/or the 12-month period was not clearly stated. Other candidates wasted time by writing far too much on the recovery of input tax. The one area where performance was not good was the exceptions to the need to register, which were only referred to by a very small number of candidates.

Part (c) concerned an area that candidates would have been familiar with but it approached it from a slightly unusual angle: it was not done well. Candidates needed to use their common sense as much as anything else here and to recognise that the claim would need to be made before the end of the tax year. This in turn meant that the tax liability would need to be estimated and that interest would be payable if the final liability turned out to be more than the estimated liability. Making these two points would have scored two of the three marks available for this part of the question.

ACCA marking scheme				
				Marks
(a)	(i)	Conditions – 1 mark each		3.0
				——
	(ii)	Taxable capital gains		
		Assignment of lease		2.5
		Sale of land		2.0
		Other matters		1.5
		Capital gains tax		1.5
				——
				7.5
			Maximum	7.0
				——
(b)	Requirement to register			1.5
	Exceptions			2.0
	Advantages			2.0
	Disadvantages			2.0
				——
				7.5
			Maximum	7.0
				——
(c)	Context			1.5
	Circumstance in which a claim can be made			1.0
	Interest and penalties			1.5
				——
				4.0
			Maximum	3.0
				——
	Professional skills marks (see below)		**Maximum**	5.0
				——
Total				**25.0**
				——

Professional skills marks

Analysis and evaluation

- Analysis of the data to determine whether the lease assignment is an associated disposal in part (a)(i).
- Appropriate use of the data to calculate capital gains tax on the disposals in part (a)(ii).
- Recognition that BADR would be restricted in respect of the lease in part (a)(ii).
- Demonstration of understanding of the impact of VAT registration on input VAT recovery in part (b).

Scepticism

- Consideration that reducing payments on account may lead to penalties if the reduction is fraudulent in part (c).

Commercial acumen

- Recognition that registering for VAT may drive customers away from the business in part (b).

41 PESCARA (ADAPTED) *Walk in the footsteps of a top tutor*

Key answer tips

Part (a) requires the calculation of death tax on a potentially exempt transfer. It is slightly complicated in that the donor is a widow and her husband did not utilise all of his nil rate band on death, but otherwise it is straightforward.

Part (b) requires the calculation of tax due on the sale of shares which were originally acquired via a gift and had subsequently been the subject of a takeover and a bonus issue. An explanation of the treatment on the subsequent disposal of an investment in SEIS shares is also required.

Part (c) requires a straightforward explanation of the IHT payable on death in respect of a gift with reservation. However, detailed knowledge needs to be displayed, including an explanation of double charges relief to score highly on this part.

The highlighted words in the written sections are key phrases that markers are looking for.

Tutor's top tips

The calculation of death tax due on a PET which becomes chargeable on death, with careful consideration of the nil rate band available, is a classic requirement. All of this part draws on basic level tax knowledge and should provide some relatively easy marks, provided you have refreshed your basic knowledge.

(a) Marina

Inheritance tax payable in respect of the gift of the shares in Sepang plc

	£	£
Transfer of value (375,000 × £1.86) (W1)		697,500
Less: Annual exemption – 2018/19		(3,000)
– 2017/18 b/f		(3,000)
Potentially exempt transfer now chargeable		691,500
Less: Marina's NRB at death	325,000	
NRB transferred from Galvez (W2)	158,333	
NRB available		(483,333)
Taxable amount		208,167
IHT at 40%		83,267
Less: Taper relief		
(1.2.2019 – 1.10.2024) (5 – 6 years) (60%)		(49,960)
IHT payable		33,307

Workings

(W1) Value of shares in Sepang plc as at 1 February 2019

Lower of:

(i) Quarter up = (£1.84 + ((£1.96 – £1.84) × 1/4))	£1.87
(ii) Mid-market = ((£1.80 + £1.92) × 1/2)	£1.86
Therefore, value of shares used	£1.86

(W2) Nil rate band transferred from Galvez

	£
Nil rate band available in 2008/09	312,000
Legacies to Pescara and her brother (2 × £80,000)	(160,000)
Unused NRB	152,000
Unused % of current year NRB available to transfer to Marina (£325,000 × (£152,000 ÷ £312,000))	158,333

Tutorial note

Galvez had no lifetime gifts and therefore the calculation of the unused NRB just considers legacies in his will.

If there had been any CLTs or PETs in the seven years pre-death, they would have to be taken into consideration as they would also utilise some of Galvez's NRB available on death.

An alternative method of calculating Marina's NRB which is acceptable is:

- *Galvez had an unused NRB = (£152,000 ÷ £312,000) = 48.718%*
- *Marina can claim 148.718% of the current NRB = (£325,000 × 148.718%) = £483,333.*

Remember that an individual can never claim more than 200% of the current NRB.

(b) (i) Pescara

Capital gains tax liability – 2024/25

Tutor's top tips

The base cost of the original Sepang plc shares following the gift to Pescara must be established first. Then the takeover consideration received from Zolder plc, in return for the original shares in Sepang plc, must be quantified in order to allocate the base cost of the original shares to the two elements of the takeover consideration received.

The bonus issue must then be brought into the share pool of the new Zolder plc shares acquired before the gain is calculated on the disposal of some of the shares from the share pool.

	£
Proceeds: sale of 1,000,000 shares	445,000
Less: Cost (W1)	(275,362)
Chargeable gain	169,638
Less: SEIS reinvestment relief (50% × £90,000)	(45,000)
Annual exempt amount	(6,000)
Taxable gain	118,638
Capital gains tax at 20%	23,728

Tutorial note

SEIS reinvestment relief allows the exemption of gains on any asset.

The maximum amount of relief that can be claimed is the lowest of:

1 *50% of the chargeable gain = (50% × £169,638) = £84,819, or*

2 *50% of amount invested in qualifying SEIS shares (maximum 50% × £100,000)*

= (50% × £90,000) = £45,000, or

3 *Any amount up to the lower of 1 or 2.*

Therefore, any amount up to £45,000 could be claimed.

Remember that this CGT reinvestment relief is in addition to the income tax relief available which allows 50% of the cost of the investment in SEIS shares to be deducted from the income tax liability in the tax year of investment.

Workings

(W1) Base cost of 1,000,000 shares in Zolder plc

	Number	£
Original shares in Sepang plc		
Market value of gift (W2)	375,000	712,500
Exchanged for shares in Zolder plc		
Cost of new shares (W3)	750,000	619,565
Bonus issue (2:1)	1,500,000	0
	2,250,000	619,565
Cost of shares to be sold		
(1,000,000/2,250,000) × £619,565	(1,000,000)	(275,362)
Balance c/f	1,250,000	344,203

Tutorial note

1 *The base cost of shares in Sepang plc to Pescara will be the market value at the time of the gift. Remember that for CGT purposes the value of quoted shares is calculated as the mid-price, which is the average of the highest and lowest quoted prices.*

The question says that gift holdover relief is not available on these shares and therefore there will be no gain deferred against this base cost.

2 *Bonus shares are free shares to existing shareholders. The number of shares received are therefore brought into the share pool at nil cost.*

(W2) Value of shares in Sepang plc as at 1 February 2019

Mid-price = £1.90 ((£1.84 + £1.96) ÷ 2)

375,000 × £1.90 = £712,500

(W3) Takeover of Sepang plc

		MV of consideration received	Allocation of original base cost
		£	£
Cash	(375,000 × 30p)	112,500	
	(£112,500/£862,500) × £712,500		92,935
Shares	(375,000 × 2 × £1)	750,000	
	(£750,000/£862,500) × £712,500		619,565
		862,500	712,500

(ii) Pescara – Capital gains tax implications of selling the SEIS shares

Tutor's top tips

There are only three marks available here, so a short but succinct summary of the position is required.

This part could have been answered independently at the beginning to bank some easy marks first.

The treatment of the gain or loss arising on the SEIS shares depends on when they are sold.

- If they are sold within three years of their purchase, any gain arising will be chargeable and any loss will be allowable.
- If they are sold more than three years after their purchase, any gain arising will be exempt.

  If the sale results in a loss, the loss will be allowable but will be reduced by the SEIS income tax relief obtained in respect of the shares.

In addition, if the SEIS shares are sold within three years, all or part of the capital gains tax reinvestment relief will be withdrawn, depending on the number of shares sold and whether or not the sale is at arm's length.

(c) Pescara – Gift of a UK property

Tutor's top tips

This is a straightforward independent part on gifts with reservation which should produce some easy marks and could have been answered at the beginning if preferred.

The gift of a property will be a potentially exempt transfer (PET). The value of this PET will be the market value of the property at the time of the gift.

The amount which will be subject to inheritance tax in respect of this gift with reservation depends on whether or not the reservation of benefit is lifted (i.e. Pescara stops using the property rent-free, before she dies).

(i) If the reservation of benefit is lifted prior to Pescara's death, there will be a further PET equal to the value of the property at that time. This will only be chargeable if Pescara dies within the subsequent seven years.

(ii) If the reservation of benefit is still in place when Pescara dies, the value of the property at the time of her death will be included in her death estate.

In this case, the residence nil rate band will be available.

Where Pescara dies within seven years of the original PET, such that it is chargeable to inheritance tax, and either (i) or (ii) applies, the original PET or (i)/(ii) will be taxed, whichever results in the higher tax liability.

Tutorial note

1 *Where Pescara dies within seven years of the original PET, double charges relief is available.*

If the reservation has been lifted, the original PET and the deemed PET both become chargeable.

If the reservation is still in place, the original PET becomes chargeable but HMRC requires the house to be included in the estate computation at death.

Double charges relief ensures that, in either case, only the higher of these two liabilities will actually be chargeable.

2 *Pescara would be advised to stop using the property (or to start paying a market rent) if she wishes the gift to be advantageous from the point of view of inheritance tax.*

3 *Note that if Pescara was just to make incidental use of the property (such as living in the property while visiting her son) so that the benefit derived is minimal, then the GWR rules would not apply.*

Examiner's report

The majority of candidates performed well in part (a) and scored high marks. Less well-prepared candidates were unable to value the shares in Sepang plc and/or the amount of the nil rate band to be transferred from the donor's deceased husband. This was because they either did not know the rules or were unable to apply them to the facts in the question. Some candidates failed to identify that the husband's nil rate band was available for transfer.

Part (b) concerned capital gains tax and was in two parts; neither part was done particularly well. In part (i) the calculation of the base cost of the shares required a certain amount of work.

It was first necessary to realise that, due to the fact that gift holdover relief was not claimed on the original gift (the question stated that gift holdover relief was not available), the base cost of the original shares was their market value at the time of the gift. Following the takeover, this original cost had to be split between the new shares and cash received by reference to the market value of the consideration. Finally, the bonus issue increased the number of shares but had no effect on the total base cost.

A significant number of candidates lost marks here because they side-stepped the first two stages of this calculation by attributing a cost to the new shares equal to their market value at the time of the takeover. The majority of candidates had no problem with the bonus issue.

When calculating the amount subject to capital gains tax it was necessary to deduct EIS deferral relief equal to the whole of the £50,000 invested in EIS shares. Many candidates confused this relief with the relief available in respect of income tax when EIS shares are acquired. *Note: This is the examiner's comment on the original question, which has since been adapted to test SEIS reinvestment relief instead of EIS relief.*

The first problem that some candidates had in part (b)(ii) was that they answered the question by reference to income tax rather than capital gains tax. Many of those who did address capital gains tax did not score as many marks as they might have done because they were not methodical in their approach. It was important to (briefly) consider four possible situations (i.e. sale of the shares at a profit or a loss both within and after the three-year period).

Part (c) was not done particularly well as those candidates who clearly had some knowledge did not pay sufficient attention to the requirement.

The question asked how the gift would be treated for the purposes of calculating the inheritance tax due on death. This required consideration of the value to be used, whether or not the reservation was lifted prior to death and the relief available in order to avoid double taxation.

Many candidates wrote more broadly about gifts with reservation, explaining the rationale behind the rules and the actions necessary in order for the reservation to be lifted. These generalisations did not score any marks.

ACCA marking scheme				
				Marks
(a)	Value of shares			2.0
	Annual exemptions			1.0
	Nil rate band			2.5
	Inheritance tax liability			1.5
				7.0
(b)	(i)	Proceeds less cost		5.0
		SEIS reinvestment relief, annual exempt amount and liability		2.0
				7.0
			Maximum	6.0
	(ii)	Sale of SEIS shares		3.5
		Withdrawal of SEIS reinvestment relief		1.0
				4.5
			Maximum	3.0
(c)	The initial gift			1.0
	Reservation lifted within seven years			1.5
	Reservation in place at death			1.0
	Avoidance of double taxation			1.5
				5.0
			Maximum	4.0
	Professional skills marks (see below)		**Maximum**	5.0
Total				**25.0**

Professional skills marks

Analysis and evaluation

- Appropriate use of the data to calculate inheritance tax payable on death in part (a).
- Appropriate use of the data to calculate the capital gains tax liability on the shares in part (b)(i).

Scepticism

- Recognition that the implications of the sale of the SEIS shares depends on whether or not they are sold within three years in part (b)(ii).
- Recognition that the treatment of the UK property gift will depend on whether it is still held at death or not in part (c).

Commercial acumen

- Recognition of the spouse nil rate band in part (a).
- Identification that SEIS reinvestment relief is available in part (b)(i).
- Demonstration of awareness of the purpose behind the takeover rules in part (b)(i).

42 CADA (ADAPTED) *Walk in the footsteps of a top tutor*

Key answer tips

This section B question covers the very regularly tested area of CGT versus IHT, with planning points re: lifetime gifts, the reduced rate of IHT for substantial legacies to charity, deed of variation and CGT planning. It is likely to have been a very popular question, although parts of it are actually quite challenging.

Part (a) requires you to think about IHT advantages of lifetime gifts, but not the use of lifetime exemptions. The only other advantages were the freezing in value of appreciating assets, and taper relief.

Part (b) covers the reduced rate of IHT for substantial legacies to charity.

There are some easy marks in part (c) for stating the procedures for a deed of variation to be tax effective.

Part (d) is less obvious, and requires you to spot the issue that capital losses are not available at death, but can be crystallised during lifetime to save CGT, either by selling shares that have gone down in value or by making a negligible value claim for shares that are worthless.

The highlighted words in the written sections are key phrases that markers are looking for.

(a) The inheritance tax advantages of additional lifetime gifts

Tutor's top tips

Think carefully before answering this part of the question. Cada would not have survived more than seven years after these lifetime gifts, so they would not become exempt. You are specifically told not to discuss lifetime exemptions, so there will be no marks if you do.

The question also states that 'none of the remaining assets qualified for any inheritance reliefs', so there is no point in discussing business property relief either.

Also, there are no marks here for discussing CGT, as the requirement only asks for IHT advantages.

It is therefore important to cover the points regarding appreciating assets and taper relief thoroughly in order to get the four marks available.

Any additional lifetime gifts of quoted shares would have become chargeable on Cada's death on 20 November 2024.

However, the value charged to tax would have been the value of the shares at the time of the gift and not their value at the time of death.

Any increase in the value of the shares would therefore have been ignored, although relief would have been available if the shares had fallen in value following the gift.

Taper relief would have been available in respect of any gifts made in the period 1 December 2020 to 20 November 2021 (i.e. those gifts made more than three years prior to death).

This would only be relevant in respect of that amount of the gifts made which exceeded the nil rate band available of £220,000. In these circumstances, because the gift would have been made between three and four years prior to death, taper relief would have reduced the tax charged on the gift by 20%.

(b) Additional gift to charity

Tutor's top tips

It is a good idea to set out your computations before and after the additional gift to charity side by side, so that you only have to set out the headings once.

The breakdown of the estate is shown here for completeness, but you could obtain full credit by taking the total estate value of £1,000,000 straight from the question, as long as you remembered that the residence nil rate band would be available for Cada's house.

This section is only worth five marks, so is quite time pressured.

Make sure that you fully answer the question by identifying both the increase in the legacy required and the IHT saving. Even if your increased legacy is wrong, you will still score marks for calculating the tax saving based on your figures.

	Before additional gift to charity	After additional gift to charity
	£	£
House	500,000	500,000
Cash	60,000	60,000
Other assets including share portfolio	440,000	440,000
	1,000,000	1,000,000
Less: Gift to charity (W)	(60,000)	(78,000)
Gross chargeable estate	940,000	922,000
Less: Residence nil rate band	(175,000)	(175,000)
Nil rate band	(220,000)	(220,000)
Taxable estate	545,000	527,000
Inheritance tax at 40%/36%	218,000	189,720

Reduction in the inheritance tax liability (£218,000 – £189,720)	28,280
Additional gift to charity (£78,000 – £60,000)	18,000

Tutorial note

The reduced rate of 36% applies where the gift to charity is at least 10% of the individual's baseline amount.

The baseline amount consists of the assets owned at death reduced by liabilities, exemptions, reliefs, and the nil rate band but before the deduction of the charitable gift and the residence nil rate band.

An alternative method of calculating the baseline amount

= (Taxable estate plus charitable donation plus residence nil rate band)

Working: Additional charitable donation required

		£
Taxable estate		545,000
Add back:	Charitable donation	60,000
	Residence nil rate band	175,000
Baseline amount		780,000
Charitable donation required for 36% rate to apply:		
10% × baseline amount		78,000

(c) Variation of Cada's will

Tutor's top tips

Although you may have learnt some of the tax advantages of a deed of variation, such as skipping a generation, you will not score marks in this section unless you apply your knowledge to the scenario.

Potential tax advantages

(i) Gift to charity

An additional £18,000 gift to charity could be carried out via a variation of Cada's will. This would result in the tax saving set out in (b) above.

(ii) The house

There are two reasons to vary the terms of Cada's will, such that the house is left directly to Raymer's son.

Capital gains tax

Without the variation, the proposed gift of the house by Raymer to her son will result in a chargeable gain equal to the excess of the value of the house on 1 July 2025 (the date of the proposed gift) over its probate value of £500,000.

Private residence relief would not be available, as Raymer does not intend to live in the house.

Gift holdover relief would not be available as a house is not a qualifying asset for this relief.

Inheritance tax

Without the variation, the gift of the house by Raymer to her son would be a potentially exempt transfer for the purposes of inheritance tax and would become a chargeable transfer if Raymer were to die within seven years of the gift.

Procedures

- The variation of the will must be made in writing within two years of death by the person(s) who would benefit under the will (i.e. Raymer and Yang).
- It must be stated that the variation is intended to replace the terms of the will for the purposes of inheritance tax and capital gains tax.

Tutorial note

The additional gift to charity would have to come out of the legacy to Yang, since Raymer only inherited the house.

It would be beneficial for Yang to sign the deed of variation, since it will cost £18,000 in additional charitable legacies, however, it will save tax of £28,280. All the inheritance tax due on the death estate will come out of Yang's inheritance, since she is the residuary legatee. By signing the deed of variation to give an additional £18,000 to charity, Yang will actually inherit an additional £10,280 (£28,280 – £18,000).

(d) Capital gains tax – Beneficial actions in respect of shareholdings

Tutor's top tips

The key to success in this section was spotting that Cada owned shares that had fallen in value. As there is no capital gains tax on death, relief can only be obtained for these capital losses during lifetime.

There are no marks for discussing the annual exempt amount (AEA), as the question states that Cada pays capital gains tax every year, so must already be using her AEA.

Following her death, the capital gains tax base costs of Cada's shareholdings are equal to their market value as at the date of death. Accordingly, any losses which accrued up to the date of death are no longer available for relief.

Cada could have sold the shares in FR plc (valued at less than cost) prior to her death in order to realise the accrued capital losses. The capital losses could have been offset against any chargeable gains in the tax year 2024/25.

A negligible value claim could have been submitted in respect of the shares in KZ Ltd. The shares would have been treated as having been sold and reacquired at their market value, resulting in an allowable capital loss. This loss would have been available for relief against Cada's chargeable gains in the tax year 2024/25 (the year in which the claim would have been made) or in either of the two preceding tax years, provided the shares were of negligible value in those years.

Any capital losses in excess of chargeable gains in the tax year 2024/25 could have been carried back and offset against gains in the three tax years prior to death, relieving later years before earlier years.

Tutorial note

Candidates were not required to consider the possibility of a loss arising in respect of the unquoted shares being offset against the taxpayer's income.

Examiner's report

The first thing to note in part (a) was that this part of the question concerned inheritance tax and not capital gains tax. The question also stated that candidates should not consider lifetime exemptions, for example the annual exemption. Many candidates did not identify these important points and thus wrote about both of these areas rather than focussing on the question requirements.

In addition, many candidates wrote at length about business property relief. This was not relevant because business property relief is available in respect of both lifetime gifts and the death estate and thus additional lifetime gifts by the deceased would not have resulted in additional relief. Other candidates were of the opinion that lifetime gifts will reduce the value of the death estate (true) and therefore reduce the inheritance tax due on death (not necessarily true). These candidates had failed to recognise the inheritance tax due in respect of potentially exempt transfers in the seven years prior to death (which these transfers inevitably would be due to the facts of the question).

Most candidates would have benefited from reading the question more carefully (and, for example, ignoring the annual exemption) and thinking more (thus recognising that business property relief was not relevant) and then writing a shorter answer that may very well have scored more marks.

Having said that, the majority of candidates correctly identified taper relief as an advantage of lifetime gifts and many explained the concept of value freezing. However, very few candidates were able to explain fall in value relief correctly.

Part (b) required candidates to calculate the increase in the legacy to charity that would be necessary for the reduced rate of inheritance tax to apply. Candidates appeared to be well-prepared for a question on this area of the syllabus and this part was answered particularly well with the exception of a very small minority who were simply not aware of the rules regarding the 36% rate of tax.

In part (c) the tax advantages are not obscure, but they do require some thought and they are not particularly easy to explain. Candidates would have benefited from slowing down and thinking about how best to express what they wanted to say rather than writing in the hope that the necessary words would eventually appear on the page.

As always, candidates had to apply their knowledge to the facts in the question. As far as capital gains tax was concerned, many candidates knew that there was no capital gains tax on death but failed to think about the potentially undesirable implication of the proposed gift of the house and how that implication could be avoided. In respect of inheritance tax, many candidates saw that this was linked to generation skipping but mentioning the term 'generation skipping' was not in itself sufficient.

Candidates had to explain that the variation would avoid the need for Raymer to make a potentially exempt transfer and therefore removed the possibility of such a transfer being chargeable to inheritance tax in the event that Raymer died within seven years of making the gift.

The majority of candidates were able to explain the procedures necessary in order to achieve a valid variation of the terms of the will.

Many candidates were unsure of the answer to part (d) despite having sufficient knowledge to deal with it. Unfortunately, instead of calmly thinking about it, they wrote about various aspects of capital gains tax, and inheritance tax, until they ran out of time. In particular, many candidates wrote about using any unused annual exempt amount despite being told in the question that the individual paid capital gains tax every year.

The key issue here was that, because there is no capital gains tax on death, any unrealised losses in respect of shares worth less than cost are lost. Candidates simply had to point out, for example, that the quoted shares that were valued at less than cost at the time of death should have been sold prior to death in order to realise a loss that could then have been offset against chargeable gains.

ACCA marking scheme			
			Marks
(a)	Value frozen		
	Identify issue		1.0
	Relief for fall in value		1.0
	Taper relief for gifts more than three years prior to death		
	Identify issue		1.0
	Explain effect		1.5
			4.5
		Maximum	4.0
(b)	Original liability		2.5
	Additional gift to charity		2.5
	Net saving		1.0
			6.0
		Maximum	5.0
(c)	Potential tax advantages		
	Additional gift to charity		1.0
	House		3.5
	Procedures		2.0
			6.5
		Maximum	6.0

(d)	No relief for accrued losses		1.0
	Quoted shares where cost exceeds market value		1.0
	Unquoted shares		2.0
	Use of losses		2.0
			6.0
		Maximum	5.0
	Professional skills marks (see below)	**Maximum**	5.0
Total			**25.0**

Professional skills marks

Analysis and evaluation

- Appropriate use of the data to determine appropriate calculations to perform to arrive at the additional donation to charity required in part (b).
- Analysis of the information to determine the impact of using a deed of variation in part (c).
- Explanation of at least one beneficial action that Cada could have carried out in the year of death in part (d).

Commercial acumen

- Recognition of the advantages of making additional lifetime gifts in part (a).
- Recognition of the advantages of using a deed of variation in part (c).
- Recognition of relief for capital losses on death in part (d).

43 ERIC (ADAPTED) *Walk in the footsteps of a top tutor*

Key answer tips

This section B question includes aspects of CGT and IHT, which are very frequently tested together, and also tests the personal service company (IR35) rules.

Part (a) requires a calculation of the after-tax proceeds of two capital disposals, the first involving insurance proceeds received for a damaged asset and the second a sale of shares that had previously been gifted and were subject to a gift holdover relief claim.

Part (b)(i) requires written advice on the availability of some key IHT reliefs, namely agricultural property relief, business property relief and quick succession relief. Business property relief in particular is one of the most frequently tested reliefs in the exam and so detailed knowledge of the rules is essential.

Part (b)(ii) requires calculations of the IHT impact of the client living longer than expected, resulting in a PET falling more than seven years prior to death, thus leaving more nil rate band available.

Part (c) involves applying the personal service company (IR35) rules and calculations to consultancy income received. Ensure you apply the correct rules for the size of the client organisations!

The highlighted words in the written sections are key phrases that markers are looking for.

Tutor's top tips

The question includes two key, very frequently tested reliefs: CGT gift holdover relief and IHT business property relief. It is crucial to know the rules in detail to enable you to answer such questions.

Requirements (a) and (c) are best answered in the spreadsheet response option in the exam, due to the fact that they are purely computational. Requirement (b) is discursive, and so is better suited to the word processor. Make sure you clearly label your answers so it is clear to the marker which part of the question you are answering.

(a) Chargeable gains 2023/24

Tutor's top tips

Remember that the receipt of insurance proceeds for a damaged asset is treated like a normal part disposal using the A/A+B formula to calculate the proportion of the original cost to use in the gain calculation.

Effectively, it is treated as if the damaged part of the asset has been 'sold' for the insurance proceeds received (A), and the asset that is left has a remaining value (B).

Part disposal in respect of damaged painting

	£
Insurance proceeds received	10,000
Less: Cost £46,000 × £10,000/(£10,000 + £38,000)	(9,583)
Chargeable gain	417

Disposal of Malaga plc shares

	£
Sale proceeds (£11.50 × 6,000)	69,000
Less: Cost (W)	(51,000)
Chargeable gain	18,000

Total after-tax proceeds

	£
Total chargeable gains (£417 + £18,000)	18,417
Less: Annual exempt amount	(6,000)
Taxable gains	12,417
Capital gains tax payable (£12,417 × 20%)	£2,483

After-tax proceeds are £76,517 (£10,000 + £69,000 – £2,483).

Working:

5 August 2020: Gain on gift from sister (£126,000 – £96,000)	£30,000
Gain eligible for gift holdover relief (£30,000 × 80%)	£24,000
Base cost of shares for Eric (£126,000 – £24,000)	£102,000

Cost of the shares sold is £51,000 (£102,000 × 1/2).

Tutorial notes

1. *The compensation received in respect of the damaged painting cannot be deducted from the cost of the painting rather than treated as a part disposal, because it exceeds 5% of the value of the painting.*
2. *Relief would be available in computing the gain on the disposal of the Malaga plc shares for the inheritance tax paid by Eric following his sister's death on 1 September 2020. However, no inheritance tax figures were given and candidates were not expected to consider this point.*
3. *As Eric's sister owned more than 5% of the issued ordinary shares in Malaga plc, it was her personal company for the purpose of gift holdover relief. Accordingly, the proportion of the gain which was eligible for gift holdover relief was restricted to the fraction chargeable business assets/total chargeable assets.*

(b) (i) Inheritance tax reliefs available if Eric dies on 31 March 2025

Tutor's top tips

There are three reliefs to consider here, so make sure that you think about all of them for both the farmland and the Malaga plc shares.

There are marks for stating why a relief is available, and also for stating why a relief is not available; for example: BPR is not available for the farmland, as it has been held as an investment.

Farmland

Agricultural property relief will be available on the farmland, but only on its agricultural value of £340,000. It will be available at the rate of 100% as the land will have been owned by Eric for more than seven years prior to his death and occupied by a tenant farmer throughout this period.

Business property relief (BPR) will not be available on the excess of the market value over the agricultural value of the land as Eric does not farm the land himself.

Malaga plc shares

No BPR will be available in respect of these shares as they are quoted shares and Eric does not have control of the company.

Quick succession relief (QSR) will be available as a tax credit to reduce the inheritance tax payable in respect of these shares as part of Eric's death estate. This is because the shares will have been subject to inheritance tax twice within a five-year period, i.e. on the potentially exempt transfer becoming chargeable on the death of Eric's sister, and again within Eric's death estate.

QSR is calculated as:

$$\text{Inheritance tax paid on his sister's death} \times \frac{\text{net transfer}}{\text{gross transfer}} \times \text{relevant percentage}$$

The relevant percentage is 20% as the period between the date of the gift from his sister (which gave rise to the first charge to inheritance tax), and Eric's death will be 4–5 years.

(ii) Impact on inheritance tax liability if Eric does not die until 1 August 2025

The lifetime gift to Zak of £60,000 on 1 July 2018 will now be more than seven years prior to the date of death so is no longer taken into account in calculating the inheritance tax on Eric's death estate. This will mean that there is an additional £54,000 (£60,000 – (2 × £3,000 annual exemptions)) of nil rate band available to use against the death estate than there would have been if Eric had died on 31 March 2025.

As Eric's chargeable estate is worth considerably in excess of £325,000, this will result in an inheritance tax saving of £21,600 (£54,000 × 40%).

There will be no impact on the amount of QSR available as the period between the date of the gift from his sister and Eric's death will still be 4–5 years.

(c) Zak's 2024/25 taxable income

Tutor's top tips

The rules for calculating income under the personal service company legislation are different depending on the size of the client organisation involved. Always look for the size of the client in order to see which rules apply.

You are asked to calculate taxable income, not income tax payable, so don't waste time calculating the income tax due as there will be no marks for this.

	£
Yoyo Ltd fee income	110,000
Less: 5% deduction	(5,500)
	104,500
Less: Salary	(24,000)
Employer's NIC on salary ((£24,000 – £9,100) × 13.8%)	(2,056)
	78,444
Less: Employer's NIC on deemed payment 13.8/113.8 × £78,444	(9,513)
Deemed employment income	68,931

Zak – taxable income 2024/25

	£
Total income from Yoyo Ltd (£24,000 + £68,931)	92,931
Less: Personal allowance	(12,570)
Taxable income	80,361

Tutorial notes

1 *As Zak is the sole employee of Yoyo Ltd, the employment allowance of £5,000 will not be available to deduct from the employer's NIC payable.*

2 *As all the profits of Yoyo Ltd are deemed to have been paid to Zak as employment income, no further tax will arise in respect of the dividends of £50,000 paid to Zak. This is treated as exempt income to avoid a double tax charge.*

Examiner's report

Part (a) required candidates to calculate the after-tax proceeds from two capital gains tax disposals.

Questions at ATX frequently ask for a calculation of after-tax proceeds – here, the amount of proceeds remaining after the payment of capital gains tax. Candidates need to think more carefully about the starting point for this type of calculation. Failure to identify the correct starting point is a common error, with many candidates in this case deducting the tax from the taxable gain, rather than the sale proceeds, which they have used at the start of the computation.

Very few candidates proved able to calculate the capital gain arising on receipt of insurance proceeds for a damaged asset where no repair was undertaken. Similarly, many missed the implications of the previous gift holdover relief claim when calculating the gain on disposal of quoted company shares. Candidates should expect to have to deal with some of the trickier aspects of the calculation of individual gains at this level, and should therefore ensure that they practise a sufficient number of these.

The requirements for part (b)(i) stated the inheritance tax reliefs to be considered in respect of the assets in the taxpayer's estate on death. Candidates demonstrated good knowledge of the availability and operation of agricultural property relief. Business property relief, despite being examined far more frequently, was handled less well, with many candidates omitting to consider it in relation to the farmland, and believing that it is available to a minority shareholder in a quoted company. Many candidates were able to identify the ability to take quick succession relief in the given scenario, but very few were able to provide the formula for calculating it. Precise knowledge of these reliefs, when they are available, and how they are calculated is essential at ATX.

Part (b)(ii) required an explanation, with supporting calculations, of the impact on the inheritance tax arising on the taxpayer's death estate if his death occurred four months later than originally assumed. An ability to recognise the relevance of the timing of events or transactions in respect of all taxes is an important skill at ATX. The key point here was that the lifetime gift would no longer be accumulated as it was made more than seven years prior to death, thereby leaving the full nil rate band for use against the death estate. It was pleasing to see that many candidates recognised this point, providing concise explanations to score the full three marks. However, a significant number provided comprehensive calculations of the death estate, often with no explanation at all, making it difficult to demonstrate understanding of the requirement and consequently to score marks. Once again this highlights the need to read the wording of the requirement very carefully to ensure that the correct approach is taken.

Part (c) was concerned with the application of the personal service company (IR35) legislation. It was generally not well attempted by many candidates, despite having been examined in a similar way on previous occasions. It remains an important topic within the ATX syllabus.

ACCA marking scheme

				Marks
(a)	Gain on damaged painting			2.0
	Gain on shares			2.5
	After-tax proceeds			2.0
				6.5
			Maximum	6.0
(b)	(i)	Farmland – Agricultural property relief		2.0
		– Business property relief		1.0
		Shares – Business property relief		1.0
		– Quick succession relief		2.5
				6.5
			Maximum	6.0
	(ii)	Lifetime gift no longer accumulated		1.0
		Calculation of effect		2.0
		No effect on quick succession relief		1.0
				4.0
			Maximum	3.0

(c)	Yoyo Ltd – fee income less 5% deduction		1.0
	Employer's NIC on salary deducted		1.5
	Employer's NIC on deemed payment		1.0
	Taxable income		2.5
			6.0
		Maximum	5.0
	Professional skills marks (see below)	**Maximum**	5.0
Total			**25.0**

Professional skills marks

Analysis and evaluation

- Recognition that gift holdover relief needed to be restricted in respect of the Malaga plc shares in part (a).
- Appropriate use of the data to calculate the deemed employment income for Zak in part(c).

Commercial acumen

- Recognition that the holding period for APR is increased to seven years due to the farmland being rented in part (b)(i).
- Recognition of the possibility of both APR and BPR applying on the farmland in part (b)(i).
- Recognition that QSR is available due to two charges to IHT in a short time period in part (b)(i).
- Demonstration of an understanding of the personal service company legislation in part (c).

44 LIBER (ADAPTED)

Key answer tips

The first part of this question tests takeovers along with tax planning. The calculations around takeovers can sometimes be a little tricky. You need to start by looking at the base cost of the original shares and what happens to this at takeover. Consider if there are any tax implications on the takeover itself. You can then move on to deal with the subsequent sale. Remember that there are easy marks available for calculating the tax, so don't miss out on these!

The second part of part (a) looks at tax planning and the benefits of delaying the sale. Notice that if the sale is delayed it will fall into a new tax year – think about why this might be beneficial.

Part (b) looks at comparing giving in lifetime to giving at death, which is something that is often tested in ATX. Remember that you have two taxes to consider so it is worth separating your answer into two parts so that the two taxes don't get confused.

The highlighted words in the written sections are key phrases that markers are looking for.

(a) (i) Capital gains tax implications of the takeover of Vulcan Ltd on 1 June 2024 and a subsequent sale of the Mercury plc shares on 1 January 2025

Gain on the cash received in the takeover

The share-for-share exchange rules will automatically apply on the takeover of Vulcan Ltd on 1 June 2024, as this was a *bona fide* commercial transaction, and Mercury plc has acquired more than 25% of the ordinary shares in Vulcan Ltd. The shares in Mercury plc will 'stand in the shoes' of the shares in Vulcan Ltd and no gain will be chargeable in respect of these shares until they are sold. The receipt of cash is treated as a part-disposal of the Vulcan Ltd shares and a chargeable gain will arise at the date of the takeover.

The chargeable gain in respect of the cash received is £5,684 (£12,000 – £6,316 (W)).

Business asset disposal relief will not be available in respect of the gain arising on the cash consideration, as Liber was not a director or employee of Vulcan Ltd.

Gain on the sale of the Mercury plc shares

	£
Proceeds (3,200 × £28)	89,600
Less: Cost (W)	(33,684)
Chargeable gain	55,916

Business asset disposal relief will not be available on the sale of the Mercury plc shares as Liber is not a director or employee of Mercury plc, and holds less than 5% of the ordinary shares in Mercury plc.

Tutorial note

Where there is a share-for-share exchange, the two-year ownership requirement includes the holding period of the original shares.

	£
Gain on cash received on takeover	5,684
Gain on sale of shares in Mercury plc	55,916
Total chargeable gains	61,600
Less: Annual exempt amount	(6,000)
Taxable gains	55,600

Capital gains tax (CGT) payable is £10,350 (((£37,700 – £30,000) × 10%) + ((£55,600 – £7,700) × 20%)).

Working: Allocation of cost at time of takeover

	Market value	Apportioned cost
	£	£
Consideration received:		
Ordinary shares in Mercury plc		
(800 × 4 × £20)	64,000	
(£64,000/£76,000) × £40,000		33,684
Cash (800 × £15)	12,000	
(£12,000/£76,000) × £40,000		6,316
	76,000	40,000

(ii) Reasons why it is beneficial to sell the Mercury plc shares on 1 May 2025 instead of on 1 January 2025

The calculation of the gain on the sale of the Mercury plc shares will be the same, but the sale will be in the following tax year, 2025/26, so the following tax implications will arise:

The gain on the cash received on the takeover in the tax year 2024/25 will be covered by the annual exempt amount for that year and so there will be no CGT liability in the tax year 2024/25.

The whole of the 2025/26 annual exempt amount will be available to be deducted from the gain on the sale of the Mercury plc shares. This will result in a CGT liability of £9,213 in the tax year 2025/26 (W). The overall tax saving if the Mercury plc shares are sold on 1 May 2025 is therefore £1,137 (£10,350 (as in (a)(i)) – £9,213).

Tutorial note

Alternatively, delaying the sale of the shares until 1 May 2025 results in the gain on the cash received in the takeover of £5,684 being fully covered by the annual exempt amount for the tax year 2024/25 and therefore a CGT saving of £1,137 (20% × £5,684).

The tax relating to the sale of the Mercury plc shares will be due a year later on 31 January 2027, rather than 31 January 2026.

Working: CGT liability if Mercury plc shares disposed of on 1 May 2025

	£
Gain on sale of shares in Mercury plc	55,916
Less: Annual exempt amount	(6,000)
Taxable gains	49,916

CGT payable is £9,213 (((£37,700 – £30,000) × 10%) + ((£49,916 – £7,700) × 20%)).

(b) Vesta

Capital gains tax and inheritance tax advantages of gifting the investment property on 31 December 2024

Capital gains tax (CGT)

If the property remains in Vesta's estate on her death, there will be no CGT implications, such that the fall in value of the property will not give rise to an allowable loss.

If the property is gifted to Janus on 31 December 2024, an allowable loss will arise as a result of the fall in value. However, as Vesta will make no disposals for CGT purposes in the tax year 2025/26, she will not be able to relieve this loss.

Therefore, for CGT purposes, Vesta will be indifferent as to whether to gift the property to Janus in her lifetime, or to leave it to him in her estate on death.

However, Janus's base cost of the property on a future disposal is its market value at the date it is transferred to him. Accordingly, as the property is expected to be worth less at the date of Vesta's death than it is currently, it will be advantageous from Janus's point of view if Vesta gifts the property to him on 31 December 2024 as he will then have a higher base cost for CGT purposes on a future sale.

Tutorial note

As Janus and Vesta are connected persons, the CGT loss on the gift of the property to Janus on 31 December 2024 could only have been relieved against a gain arising on a later disposal by Vesta to Janus.

Inheritance tax (IHT)

If the property remains in Vesta's estate at the date of her death, it will be included at its value on death, which is expected to be lower than its current market value.

If the property is gifted to Janus on 31 December 2024, it will be a potentially exempt transfer (PET), such that there will be no immediate charge to IHT. This PET will become chargeable as a result of Vesta's death within seven years.

As the value of the property is expected to have decreased between the date of the gift and the date of death, fall in value relief will be available (assuming that Janus still owns the property, or has sold it in an arm's length transaction), so the lifetime gift will not result in any more IHT being payable on the property than if it were left to Janus in the death estate.

No annual exemptions are available as they have been used on the cash gift to Janus on 1 June 2024. No taper relief will be available as Vesta will not have survived for three years after making the gift.

Therefore, for IHT purposes, both Vesta and Janus will be indifferent between a lifetime gift and leaving the property in her estate on death.

Examiner's report

This question was in two main parts. Part (a) concerned a takeover involving cash and shares being offered in exchange for shares. Part (b) concerned advice on the capital gains tax and inheritance tax advantages of a lifetime gift rather than a death estate bequest.

When looking at the first part of the question concerning the takeover, candidates should have been able to identify the following tax issues from the facts of the question.

- At the date of the takeover, share-for-share rules automatically apply but there will be a gain on the cash element of the takeover consideration. When the new shares are eventually sold, a gain will arise on the sale.
- If the new shares are sold in the same tax year as the takeover, the gain on the cash element at takeover and the gain on the new shares will be added together and the annual exempt amount set against the total gains.
- If instead, the new shares are sold in a subsequent tax year for the same price, the gain on the new shares may be the same as calculated above but it will be offset by a new annual exempt amount. This will result in a tax saving.

Clarity of thought was critical here. Candidates needed to identify the tax implications of what had already happened and then consider the implications of the alternative sale date scenarios. Candidates should not be writing their answers immediately; they should be planning what points they need to make in their answer. Candidates who start preparing calculations in the hope that they will eventually arrive at the correct answer do not score well.

For those candidates who took a moment to consider the facts and decide on a strategy for answering the question, the calculations were not very difficult and the two possible sale alternatives could be compared, scoring high marks.

A further issue in this part of the question was whether business asset disposal relief (BADR) would be available to the individual making the share disposals. Stronger candidates understood the BADR rules but more importantly, were able to apply them to the facts of the question and decide that BADR would not be available. Weaker candidates listed the BADR rules but were not able to apply them to the scenario. A significant minority of students considered the substantial shareholding exemption which is not relevant in the scenario of an individual disposing of shares.

The second part of the question required candidates to consider the capital gains tax and inheritance tax advantages of a lifetime gift rather than a death estate bequest. Candidates may have been familiar with this as a tax planning concept but once again, the key to answering this question was in applying knowledge to the facts given in this particular question.

Candidates should have found the following tax issues arising from the facts of the question.

- A lifetime gift would result in a capital loss, not a capital gain, since the value of the asset had fallen since purchase. However the facts of the question were that the donor would not be able to use a capital loss. Since there is no capital gains tax on a death estate bequest, from a capital gains tax point of view, the donor would be indifferent between lifetime and death gifting.
- For inheritance tax purposes, a lifetime gift would be a potentially exempt transfer. However the facts of the question were that the potentially exempt transfer would become chargeable within three years, with neither taper relief nor annual exemptions available. Furthermore, fall in value relief would be available, meaning that once again the donor would be indifferent between lifetime and death gifting.

Candidates need to consider the scenario given *before* they start writing their answer and not simply state general tax rules. Each client has their own particular set of circumstances which the tax rules must be applied to. Once again, candidates would benefit from taking some thinking time to consider the scenario before they put pen to paper.

ACCA marking scheme

				Marks
(a)	(i)	Gain on cash at date of takeover		4.5
		Gain on sale of Mercury plc shares on 1 January 2025		2.5
		Capital gains tax payable		2.0
				9.0
			Maximum	8.0
	(ii)	2025/26 annual exempt amount available		1.0
		Calculation of tax saving		3.0
		Tax payable later		1.0
				5.0
			Maximum	4.0
(b)		Capital gains tax implications		4.0
		Inheritance tax implications		5.5
				9.5
			Maximum	8.0
		Professional skills marks (see below)	**Maximum**	5.0
Total				**25.0**

Professional skills marks

Analysis and evaluation

- Appropriate use of the data to calculate capital gains tax liabilities in part (a).
- Appropriate use of the data to calculate the reduction in capital gains tax if the Mercury plc share disposal is delayed in part (a)(ii).
- Analysis of the data to determine the capital tax implications of gifting the investment property in part (b).
- Demonstration of ability to consider both CGT and IHT separately in part (b).

Commercial acumen

- Consideration of the availability of BADR in part (a)(i).
- Recognition of the advantages of delaying the sale of the Mercury plc shares in part (a)(ii).
- Consideration of the availability of capital gains tax and inheritance tax exemptions and reliefs for the gift of the investment property in part (b).

45 ANYA

Key answer tips

This question covers the capital gains tax and inheritance tax aspects of a lifetime gift, CGT and IHT reliefs, and the calculation of post-tax income.

Part (a) requires explanation of the CGT and IHT implications of a lifetime gift. It is important to label your answer clearly, so that the marker can identify which tax you are addressing.

Part (b) covers gift holdover relief for CGT and business property relief for IHT. These reliefs are tested in almost every ATX exam, so you must ensure that you learn the detailed conditions. To score well here you should consider the implications for both the donor and the donee.

The final part of the question asks for a calculation of the reduction in post-tax income following the gift of shares. You could do this either by calculating post-tax income with and without the dividend received, or by working in the margin to calculate how much tax would have been due on the dividend income. Watch out for the impact on the personal allowance, as this is easy to miss.

(a) Tax implications of disposing of the painting

Capital gains tax (CGT)

This disposal will generate a capital loss of £41,000 (£63,000 – £104,000).

Violette is Anya's granddaughter, so is a connected person to Anya. Accordingly, this loss can only be relieved against gains made on any other asset disposals to Violette by Anya in the tax years 2024/25 or 2025/26 prior to her death.

Inheritance tax (IHT)

The gift of the painting will be a potentially exempt transfer (PET) for IHT, which will become chargeable as a result of Anya's death within seven years (on 6 September 2025).

No annual exemptions will be available as these will have been used against the gift of £50,000 cash to Flava on 1 July 2024. No nil rate band will be available as it will all be used against the gift of the investment property to Cara on 31 March 2023. No taper relief will be available as Anya's death occurs within three years of the gift.

Accordingly, the gift of the painting will give rise to an IHT liability of £25,200 (£63,000 × 40%), which will be payable by Violette.

(b) (i) Availability of gift holdover relief on the gift of the Chaski Ltd shares

The gift of the shares in Chaski Ltd will be eligible for gift holdover relief as Chaski Ltd is an unquoted trading company, and Cara (the donee) is tax resident in the UK. However, because Chaski Ltd is Anya's personal company (i.e. she can exercise at least 5% of the voting rights), the gift holdover relief will be restricted by reference to the shares in RQ Ltd, which are not chargeable business assets. The proportion of the gain which will be eligible for gift holdover relief will be calculated as the value of the chargeable business assets divided by the value of the total chargeable assets. Accordingly, the proportion of the gain which will qualify for relief is 93·4% (£853,000/(£853,000 + £60,000)).

Consequences for Cara of the relief being claimed

When Cara subsequently disposes of the shares, her base cost will be reduced by the amount of the gift holdover relief, such that her gain on this sale will be higher. As the gift will be liable to IHT as a result of Anya's death on 6 September 2025, the gain arising on Cara's future disposal of the shares will be reduced by the amount of IHT payable in respect of them. However, this deduction cannot be used to create a loss.

(ii) IHT reliefs available on the gift of the Chaski Ltd shares

Business property relief (BPR) will be available at the rate of 100% as Chaski Ltd is an unquoted trading company, and Anya will have held the shares for more than two years prior to the date of the gift. However, the fact that Chaski Ltd's assets include shares in RQ Ltd means that, as these shares fall within the definition of excepted assets, the relief will be restricted to the proportion: market value of business assets divided by market value of total assets. Accordingly, the relief available will be 94·2% ((£1,034,000 – £60,000)/£1,034,000) of the value of the shares.

Cara must still hold the shares (or replacement business property) at the date of Anya's death in order for BPR to be available, and the shares must still be relevant business property.

(c) Reduction in Anya's post-tax income for the tax year 2024/25

	2023/24	**2024/25**
	£	**£**
Pension income	65,000	65,000
Dividend from Chaski Ltd	40,000	–
Total income	105,000	65,000
Less: Personal allowance (Working 1)	(10,070)	(12,570)
Taxable income	94,930	52,430
Income tax: £37,700 at 20%	7,540	7,540
£17,230/£14,730 at 40%	6,892	5,892
£(40,000 – 1,000) at 33·75%	13,163	–
Total tax liability	27,595	13,432

	2023/24	**2024/25**
	£	**£**
Post-tax income: £105,000 – £27,595	77,405	
£65,000 – £13,432		51,568

Reduction in post-tax income is £25,837 (£77,405 – £51,568).

Working 1

Personal allowance restricted in 2023/24 to £10,070 (£12,570 – 1/2 × (£105,000 – £100,000)).

Tutorial note:

Alternative presentation of answer using a marginal approach:

	£
Dividend received from Chaski Ltd in 2023/24	*40,000*
Dividend receivable from Chaski Ltd in 2024/25	*–*
	———
Reduction in dividend income	*40,000*
Less: Income tax payable on dividend income in 2023/24:	
((£40,000 – £1,000) × 33·75%)	*(13,163)*
Less: Reduction in personal allowance available in 2023/24:	
(((105,000 – 100,000)/2) × 40%)	*(1,000)*
	———
Reduction in post-tax income	*25,837*
	———

Examiner's report

Requirement (a)

Part (a) related to the tax implications for the client of gifting an asset to her granddaughter.

It is quite common for CGT and IHT to be examined in this way, in relation to a single lifetime gift.

The gift will give rise to a loss for CGT purposes. The calculation of the loss was very straightforward, as there were only two figures given for this asset – the purchase price and the market value at the date of the gift. Most candidates did calculate this, and gained the 0.5 mark, and it then opened the door to go on and discuss the loss relief available to the donor. A few just stated that the painting had fallen in value, but didn't actually calculate the loss, and so were unable to score well on this part. Candidates should remember that where figures are provided to be able to calculate a chargeable gain or allowable loss in a question, they are usually required to be used for this purpose.

The key point to recognise when discussing the relief available for this loss was that the donor and donee were connected persons for CGT purposes (grandmother and granddaughter), such that relief for the loss was restricted to gains on future disposals to the same person. Candidates should learn the relationships between individuals which mean that they will be connected persons, and always note the relationship between the donor and the donee in any scenario so that they can apply this rule. In this question, there was both an analysis and evaluation mark available (for spotting the connected persons issue) and a technical mark for explaining the impact of this on the relief which would be available for the capital loss.

In general, performance was better on the IHT implications of the gift. Most candidates knew the basics – the gift was a potentially exempt transfer (PET), which would become chargeable as the donor's death would be within 7 years, and IHT would be charged at the rate of 40% – and it was pleasing to see that a good number did go on to explain why annual exemptions, the nil rate band, and taper relief wouldn't be available by reference to the facts in the question.

The command word for this requirement was to 'explain', so those candidates who provided written explanations of each of these latter three aspects – or at least two out of the three – scored well. However, there were still a number of candidates who just provided a calculation, with little to no accompanying explanation, and so were unable to score these marks. On the whole, in recent sittings, candidates' ability to address 'explain' requirements with a written answer has improved, with a majority clearly realising that if a question asks for an explanation, a calculation will not suffice, but unfortunately there are still a minority clinging to this approach, who consequently score only low marks.

Sensible use of subheadings, as candidates are so often advised to utilise, ensured that in most cases they were able to score the analysis and evaluation professional skills mark for appropriate use of information to draw separate conclusions in relation to CGT and IHT.

Requirement (b)

Part (b) once again related to the CGT and IHT implications of a proposed gift; this time it was a gift of shares in a trading company, and the requirements related specifically to the availability of two reliefs – gift holdover relief for CGT in (b)(i) and business property relief (BPR) for IHT in (b)(ii). Performance on this part was disappointing. As in previous papers, candidates generally demonstrated a significant lack of knowledge and application skills in relation to CGT reliefs – in this case gift holdover relief – but, in the main, were a bit more confident with BPR for IHT. As has been said many times before, the reliefs available for both capital taxes are an important part of the ATX-UK syllabus and will continue to be tested on a very regular basis.

Part (b)(i) initially required candidates to essentially list the conditions for gift holdover relief to apply, relating them to this scenario.

A significant number of candidates managed to identify no more than the fact that this company satisfied the condition for the shares to be in an unquoted trading company. A few went on to correctly make reference to the donee's UK tax residence status, but only a minority picked up on the existence of investments (shares in another company) among the company's assets, which meant that relief would be restricted. This meant that these candidates were unable to score the analysis and evaluation mark for recognising that relief would be restricted in this case.

The information in the scenario in relation to these investments was presented in the same way as it has been in many past exam questions, which would suggest that these candidates are not undertaking sufficient question practice in their preparation for this exam. Time and again in these examiners' reports we emphasise the need for question practice as an integral part of candidates' preparation for this exam. Among other things, this helps to familiarise candidates with the way in which information is likely to be presented to them in the exam, and for them to learn how it should be utilized in their answer.

Answers to the second part of (b)(i) relating to the consequences of a gift holdover relief claim for the recipient of the shares were generally better, with many candidates recognising that there would be an impact on her base cost, and that, overall, gift holdover relief will only enable the gain to be deferred for a time. Most therefore managed to pick up the commercial acumen mark for recognising the consequences for the donee, in that the gain would only be deferred, but fewer gained the available technical mark for specifically identifying that the gain would be deducted from the base cost of the shares for the recipient.

Virtually no candidates recognised that there would be an interaction between CGT and IHT for the recipient of the shares following the gift holdover relief claim, thereby not scoring the analysis and evaluation mark available for recognition of the potential IHT consequences.

As in previous papers, candidates on the whole dealt better with the business property relief (BPR) for IHT, than with the CGT relief. Again, citing the basic rules for BPR at the time of the gift – the company was an unquoted trading company, the donor had owned the shares for at least 2 years, and relief would be available at the rate of 100% – meant that a good number were able to score at least half of the technical marks in this section, although, once again, the investments were ignored.

However, relatively few candidates completed the explanation by considering the BPR requirements for the donee i.e. that they must still hold the shares on the donor's death, if this is within seven years of the date of the gift, in order that BPR will be available in calculating IHT as a result of the donor's death. This meant that they were unable to access the commercial acumen mark for consideration of relevant factors in relation to available reliefs and the scepticism mark for identifying that further information would be required to confirm availability of the relief.

It was noticeable that few candidates appeared to gain many professional skills marks in part (b) overall except for the reference to gift holdover relief being merely a deferral relief for CGT, as mentioned above. This was primarily due to a lack of precise enough knowledge of the two reliefs being tested, meaning that candidates were unable to demonstrate their skills in applying this knowledge. Candidates are advised to spend time learning the detailed conditions required for each of the reliefs for both CGT and IHT. Skill in identifying and applying these will continue to be rewarded with professional skills marks, in addition to technical marks for their correct applications. However, this requires a good, detailed knowledge of the reliefs in the first place.

Requirement (c)

Part (c) of this question involved the calculation and comparison of the client's post-tax income for two consecutive tax years. The vast majority of candidates were clearly more comfortable with this part of the question.

As a result of this gift, the donor would no longer receive a dividend in respect of these shares, and consequently there would be a reduction in their income tax liability. The majority of candidates recognised that the requirement to calculate the reduction in the post-tax income between two consecutive tax years could be achieved by preparing a fairly straightforward income tax computation for each year to calculate the relevant tax liability in each case, which could then be deducted from the total income for the year, and a comparison made to determine the difference.

Marks were mainly lost due to a failure to read the question properly so, for example, picking up the wrong dividend figure, or for carelessness/lack of focus which, for example, caused candidates to miss the restriction in the personal allowance. Most candidates were also able to pick up the analysis and evaluation mark for this part by at least making an attempt at a comparison of the difference in after tax income.

ACCA marking scheme

				Marks
(a)		Capital gains tax implications		2.5
		Inheritance tax implications		5.0
				7.5
			Maximum	6.0
(b)	(i)	Availability of gift holdover relief		4.0
		Consequences of claim		2.0
				6.0
			Maximum	5.0
	(ii)	Availability of business property relief		3.0
		Amount of relief		2.0
				5.0
			Maximum	4.0

(c)	Income tax liability 2023/24		3.0
	Income tax liability 2024/25		1.0
	Post-tax income		1.0
			5.0
	Professional skills marks (see below)	**Maximum**	5.0
Total			**25.0**

Profession skills marks

Analysis and evaluation

- Appropriate use of information to draw conclusions in (a).
- Appropriate use of information to determine the consequences for Cara of a gift holdover relief claim.
- Demonstration of ability to consider of relevant factors in relation to the availability of reliefs.
- Appropriate use of information to determine restrictions to the reliefs.
- Appropriate use of information to conclude on the reduction in post-tax income.

Commercial acumen

- Effective use of information to determine the relevance of the disposal to Anya's granddaughter for capital loss relief purposes.
- Recognition of the interaction between IHT and CGT in respect of a future disposal by Cara.

Scepticism

- Demonstration of the ability to identify missing information in respect of business property relief.

MULTI TAX PERSONAL INCLUDING OVERSEAS

46 MIRTOON (ADAPTED) *Walk in the footsteps of a top tutor*

Key answer tips

This was originally a section A question that has been adapted into a section B question, and so various old requirements have been removed.

There are three separate parts to this question, which could be attempted in any order. As there is a mix of numerical and discursive requirements, it is best to set out any detailed calculations in the spreadsheet response option in the exam, with discursive elements better suited to the word processor. Ensure you use headings to make it clear where each part of the question is being answered.

Part (a) requires calculation of how a disposal of assets and departure from the UK will affect an individual's financial position. Although the calculations are generally straightforward, this part is challenging due to its size and the fact that there is no indication as to how the nine marks available are split.

Part (b) covers overseas aspects of income tax and capital gains tax for an individual who is leaving the UK. This area is tested regularly, so you must ensure that you learn the complex rules that apply.

Part (c)) asks for explanation of the gifts with reservation rules relating to inheritance tax. These rules are tested regularly, so you should make sure you are familiar with them.

The highlighted words in the written sections are key phrases that markers are looking for.

(a) After-tax proceeds from sale of assets and other tax liabilities

Tutor's top tips

It is important that you answer the question here. You are asked to calculate ***the total*** *of the after-tax proceeds from the sale of the house and business assets and 'any other tax liabilities'.*

A good approach to take would be to set out a pro forma working, fill in the easy figures such as the proceeds from the sale of the house and business, and then cross reference this to separate workings for the calculation of the other missing amounts.

Even if your individual workings are wrong, you will still gain a mark for satisfying the requirement and arriving at a total.

Total net proceeds

	£
Proceeds from sale of home	730,000
Proceeds from sale of business premises	120,000
Less: Capital gains tax in respect of business premises (W1)	(6,200)
Proceeds from sale of other business assets	14,000
After-tax proceeds from sale of home and business assets	857,800
Other tax liabilities	
Capital gains tax in respect of agricultural land (W1)	(12,760)
Total net proceeds	845,040

Workings

(W1) Capital gains tax

Tutor's top tips

*Think about **all** of the gains that will arise before you calculate the capital gains tax payable.*

There will be a held over gain that crystallises when Mirtoon leaves the country.

Remember that capital losses and the annual exempt amount can be set off against the gains in the most beneficial way, in order to minimise the tax payable.

	£	£
Gains qualifying for business asset disposal relief (BADR)		
Sale of business premises (W2)	62,000	
Not qualifying for BADR		
Sale of house (Note 1)		0
Gain crystallising on agricultural land (Note 2)		72,000
Less: Annual exempt amount (Note 3)		(6,000)
Less: Capital losses brought forward (Note 3)		(2,200)
Taxable gains	62,000	63,800
Capital gains tax:		
Qualifying gains (£62,000 × 10%) (Note 4)	6,200	
Non-qualifying gains (£63,800 × 20%) (Note 5)		12,760

Explanatory notes

Tutor's top tips

Although the requirement is to 'calculate', you are asked to include explanatory notes. There will be marks available for providing these notes, so try to remember to do this.

1 Private residence relief is available to exempt the gain on the house, as it was used as Mirtoon's main residence.

2 As Mirtoon emigrates from the UK within six years of the end of the tax year in which the gift of the agricultural land was made, the held over gain from the time of the gift crystallises and is chargeable on the day before emigration (i.e. January 2025), and will be taxed in the tax year 2024/25.

Tutorial note

There is an exception to the rule regarding the emigration of the donee.

Where the donee goes overseas to take up full time employment abroad a chargeable gain will not crystallise on his departure from the UK provided:

1 he resumes his status as UK resident within three years, and

2 he has not disposed of the asset whilst abroad.

However, as Mirtoon is leaving the UK for at least four years, this exception does not apply here.

3 The capital losses and the annual exempt amount can be set off in the most tax-efficient manner. Accordingly, they will be deducted from gains that would otherwise be taxed at 20%.

4 The gain in respect of the business premises will qualify for BADR because this was an asset:

- used in a business that has now ceased, and
- was sold within three years of cessation, and
- was held for at least two years before the disposal

Accordingly, the gain will be taxed at 10%.

5 Mirtoon's basic rate band is fully used by his income and qualifying gains. Accordingly, the non-qualifying gains will all fall into the higher rate band and will be taxed at 20%.

Tutorial note

Even though Mirtoon does have some of his basic rate band remaining after deducting his taxable income, this must be set against the gains qualifying for BADR first. As these qualifying gains alone are greater than £37,700, there is clearly no basic rate band left. Had there been, any non-qualifying gains in the basic band would be taxed at 10% instead of 20%.

Tutor's top tips

Don't worry if you missed the gain crystallising on the agricultural land. In that case, you would have been given credit for setting off the capital losses and the annual exempt amount against the gain on the business premises, and you would still be given the mark for summarising the net cash position based on your figures.

(W2) Chargeable gain on sale of business premises

	£
Sale proceeds	120,000
Less: Cost	(58,000)
Chargeable gain	62,000

(b) Liability to UK income tax and capital gains tax whilst living in Koro

Tutor's top tips

Overseas aspects of income tax and capital gains tax are often tested in the exam. In order to gain a good mark in this type of question, you must ensure that you apply your knowledge to the scenario and don't just talk generally about the tax implications of residence and domicile.

You should deal with income tax and capital gains tax separately, as the rules are not the same for the two taxes.

As Mirtoon is going abroad to work full time, and is not planning to make any return trips, he will automatically be non-UK resident for the tax years that he is away.

The tax year that he leaves will be split, as he will be leaving to work full time overseas and will not spend any time in the UK after departure, having been UK resident in the previous tax year, UK resident in the current year and not UK resident in the following year.

Therefore, he will lose his residency from the date that he starts working overseas, and will regain it on the date he returns.

Income tax

As he will not be UK resident, he will not be taxed in the UK on his overseas income.

His UK income is still taxable, so he will be taxed on his UK bank interest.

Capital gains tax

Generally, Mirtoon will not be subject to UK capital gains tax if he is not resident in the UK unless he disposes of UK property.

However, as he has been resident in the UK for at least four of the seven years before leaving the UK, the temporary non-residence rules will apply.

Mirtoon must remain outside the UK for five years to avoid capital gains tax on assets owned before his departure. If he sells such an asset while he is abroad, he will be taxed on the gain in the tax year of return to the UK.

Sale of agricultural land

If he sells the agricultural land in June 2026, while he is in Koro, then the disposal will be subject to non-UK resident capital gains tax. A gain will be chargeable equal to the proceeds less the market value as at 5 April 2019.

If he returns to the UK within five years (i.e. before January 2030), a further gain will be taxed in the tax year of return. A gain will be calculated equal to proceeds less cost and then any gain already assessed to non-UK resident capital gains tax in 2026 will be deducted. However, if he returns after January 2030 there will not be a further gain taxed in the UK.

Sale of UK residential home

Tutor's top tips

The examining team have stated that only residential properties acquired after 5 April 2015 will be examined so you do not need to be aware of how to calculate a gain or loss on a property acquired before this date.

If Mirtoon sells his UK home whilst he is in Koro, the gain will not be exempt. However, only gains accruing after 5 April 2015 are chargeable and even then, only to the extent that they are not covered by private residence relief (PRR) or the annual exempt amount.

As his home was purchased after 5 April 2015, the whole gain would be chargeable to capital gains tax.

PRR will exempt any part of the gain that relates to periods of occupation.

For periods of non-residence (once Mirtoon has moved to Koro) the gain may be chargeable, although the last nine months of ownership will be covered by PRR.

If there are any further periods of non-residence, the whole tax year will be treated as a period of non-occupation and thus not exempt (i.e. any actual occupation will be ignored), unless Mirtoon has stayed in his house for a total of at least 90 nights in the tax year.

Any gain remaining after PRR and the annual exempt amount will be taxed at 18% or 28%, depending on the level of Mirtoon's UK taxable income and consequential remaining basic rate band in the normal way.

HMRC must be notified of the disposal of any UK property by a non-UK resident individual within 60 days of the conveyance of the property, even if there is no CGT liability.

(c) Gifts with reservation

Tutor's top tips

Gifts with reservation appear regularly in the ATX exam, so you should be familiar with the rules that apply here.

A 'gift with reservation of benefit' (GWR) is a lifetime gift where:

- the legal ownership of an asset is transferred, but
- the donor retains some benefit in the asset gifted.

For example, the gift of a house, but the donor continues to live in it.

Special anti-avoidance rules apply to a GWR to ensure that these gifts do not escape from an inheritance tax charge.

The gift is effectively ignored, and the asset is still included in the estate of the donor when they die.

Any tax arising is payable by the legal owner of the asset (i.e. the donee).

However, HMRC has the right to use an alternative treatment if this gives a higher overall liability on the death of the donor. This recognises the GWR as though it was a true gift at the time of the gift, and the asset is not then included in the donor's estate.

Usually including the asset in the estate gives the higher inheritance tax charge. This is because capital assets normally appreciate in value and no annual exemptions are available in the death estate.

There are some exceptions. A gift will not be treated as a gift with reservation if:

- the donor pays full consideration for the benefit retained. For example, if they pay full market rate rent for the use of a property, or
- the circumstances of the donor have changed in a way that could not be foreseen at the time of the gift. For example, if the donor moves out of the property but then later becomes ill and moves back in to be cared for by their family.

Examiner's report

Note that this part of the question has been amended since it was originally set.

In part (a), the sale of the house was handled well with almost all candidates identifying the availability of private residence relief. The crystallisation of the heldover gain in respect of the agricultural land (due to Mirtoon becoming non-resident), on the other hand, was spotted by only a small minority of candidates. However, this was an easy point to miss and it was possible to obtain a perfectly good mark without any reference to it.

A minority of candidates demonstrated a lack of precision when considering the tax due in respect of the sale of the house and business. This lack of precision included a failure to take account of the capital losses brought forward and/or the annual exempt amount.

Note that this part of the question has been amended since it was originally set.

Part (b) concerned Mirtoon's liability to income tax and capital gains tax whilst living overseas. There were some good answers to this part but also two particular areas of confusion.

The first area of confusion related to the taxation of income where an individual is not resident in the UK. It needs to be recognised that where an individual is not resident in the UK, any foreign income will not be subject to UK income tax. Where many candidates went wrong was to imagine that the remittance basis was relevant here (perhaps because Mirtoon was not resident but continued to be domiciled in the UK). This led candidates to write at length about the remittance basis thus wasting time.

The second area of confusion concerned the temporary non-resident rules. These rules relate to capital gains tax and cause gains that would otherwise not be taxable in the UK to be so taxable if the individual returns to the UK within five years of leaving. However, a minority of candidates incorrectly treated these rules as an extension of the residency rules as they relate to income tax.

The section concerning the sale of Mirtoon's UK home whilst non-UK resident is a new section added following the change in rules in FA2015.

Part (c) concerned inheritance tax and gifts with reservation. The good news was that the vast majority of candidates knew all about gifts with reservation and answered this part of the question well.

The bad news, however, was that many candidates did not restrict their answers to the above area but wrote at length about inheritance tax generally. Candidates must take care in identifying what has been asked and try to avoid addressing other areas.

The original question also contained a section on the associated operations rules which have since been removed from the ATX syllabus.

ACCA marking scheme			
			Marks
(a)	Sale of home and business premises		
	Chargeable gains		1.0
	Private residence relief		1.0
	Capital gains tax		1.0
	Agricultural land		2.5
	Total proceeds net of tax adjustments		2.0
	Explanatory notes (one mark each – maximum four marks)		4.0
			11.5
		Maximum	9.0
(b)	Status		2.5
	Income tax		1.5
	Capital gains tax		7.0
			11.0
		Maximum	7.0
(c)	Gifts with reservation		5.0
		Maximum	4.0
	Professional skills marks (see below)	**Maximum**	5.0
Total			**25.0**

Professional skills marks

Analysis and evaluation

- Use of information from the scenario to calculate total net proceeds in part (a).
- Provision of at least one explanatory note in respect of the gains calculated or reliefs used in part (a).
- Use of information from the scenario to determine Mirtoon's residence status in part (b).

Scepticism

- Recognition that the capital gains tax implications of the sale of the agricultural land will differ depending upon when Mirtoon returns to the UK in part (b).
- Identification of at least one instance where the gift with reservation of benefit rules would not apply in part (c).

Commercial acumen

- Recognition of the impact of emigration on the deferred gain in part (a).
- Recognition of the availability of BADR for the business premises in part (a).
- Recognition of relevance of the temporary non-residence rules in part (b).

47 SHUTTELLE (ADAPTED) *Walk in the footsteps of a top tutor*

Key answer tips

This section B question is divided into two distinct parts which are unrelated so could be attempted in either order.

Part (a) is a question on personal pension contributions and you are required to calculate the income tax liability of an individual who has contributed to a personal pension scheme in excess of the annual allowance. Based on your calculation, you are then required to calculate the tax relief obtained as a result of the personal pension contribution. In order to do this, you needed to determine if the annual allowance should be restricted. Note that this potential restriction has been introduced since this question was set in the ATX exam and therefore did not feature in the original question.

Part (b) is a question regarding the remittance basis for three individuals. In addition, you are required to state whether or not the remittance basis charge is applicable to the individuals and if so quantify it.

The highlighted words in the written sections are key phrases that markers are looking for.

(a) Shuttelle

Tutor's top tips

You should score some easy marks for a basic income tax computation which includes salary and an accommodation benefit.

The key was recognising that there would also be an excess pension contribution. You may not have realised that the contributions by the employer must be included in the excess pension contribution calculation. However, you would still score some marks for recognising that the excess pension contributions needed to be included as part of the tax calculation.

In order to calculate the annual allowance available, you had to consider if there was any unused relief brought forward from the previous three years and whether the annual allowance for the tax year 2023/24 needed to be restricted. Remember the annual allowance is £40,000 for the tax year 2023/24 but can be increased by any unused AA in the previous three years, starting with the earliest year first.

The personal pension contributions also extend the basic and higher rate bands.

Note that the annual allowance charge is calculated using the taxpayer's marginal rate of tax.

A numerical requirement such as this is best suited to being prepared in the spreadsheet response option in the exam. You can make use of formulae to help bring figures from workings into the main computation, and also to calculate the tax for you. Make sure your figures are clearly labelled so it is clear to the marker what you are trying to calculate.

(i) Income tax liability – 2023/24

	£
Salary	204,000
Accommodation (W1)	4,141
Net income	208,141
Less: Personal allowance (W2)	(12,570)
Taxable income (all non-savings)	195,571

£		£
157,700	× 20% (W3)	31,540
37,871	× 40%	15,148
195,571		
49,569	× 40% (Annual allowance charge) (W4)	19,828
245,140		
9,431	× 45% (Annual allowance charge) (W4) (£59,000 – £49,569)	4,244
Income tax liability		70,760

Tutorial note

The basic rate and higher rate limits are extended due to the pension contributions. Accordingly, the excess pension contributions will be taxed at 40% to the extent they fall into the higher rate band, and then 45%.

Workings

(W1) Benefit in respect of accommodation

	£
Annual value	7,000
Expensive accommodation benefit ((£500,000 – £75,000) × 2.25%)	9,563
	16,563
Benefit in 2023/24 (£16,563 × 3/12)	4,141

(W2) Personal allowance

	£
Net income	208,141
Less: Gross PPCs	(120,000)
Adjusted net income (ANI)	88,141

As ANI is < £100,000, the full personal allowance is available.

(W3) Extended basic and higher rate bands

	£	£
Current bands	37,700	125,140
Add: Gross PPCs	120,000	120,000
Revised bands	157,700	245,140

(W4) Annual allowance charge

	£
Gross contributions by Shuttelle	120,000
Gross contributions by Din Ltd	4,000
Less: Annual allowance available in 2023/24 (W5)	(65,000)
Annual allowance charge	59,000

(W5) Annual allowance available – 2023/24

	£
Brought forward from 2021/22 (£40,000 – £9,000 – £4,000)	27,000
Used in 2022/23 (£40,000 – £38,000 – £4,000)	(2,000)
Current year available in 2023/24 (W6)	40,000
	65,000

(W6) Threshold income – 2023/24

	£
Net income	208,141
Less: Gross PPCs	(120,000)
Threshold income	88,141

As Shuttelle's threshold income does not exceed £200,000 it is not necessary to calculate her adjusted income to determine if a restriction to the 2023/24 annual allowance is needed.

(ii) Total tax relief in respect of the gross personal pension contributions

Tutor's top tips

This is a comparison of the income tax liability without the pension contribution with your answer from part (i).

Don't forget

- *the tax relief at source as personal pension contributions are paid net of 20% tax, and*
- *without the PPC relief, there would be no personal allowance available.*

£		£
37,700	× 20%	7,540
87,440	× 40%	34,976
125,140		
83,001	× 45%	37,350
208,141		
Income tax liability – ignoring the gross PPCs		79,866
Income tax liability – reflecting the gross PPCs (part (i))		(70,760)
Pension contributions – tax relief at source (£120,000 × 20%)		24,000
Total tax relief in respect of pension contributions		33,106

Tutorial note

1 *When calculating the liability ignoring the pension contributions, there would be no personal allowance due to the level of the net income.*

2 *By charging tax on the excess pension contributions, relief is effectively only given for £61,000 (£120,000 – £59,000), the balance of the contributions, as set out below:*

	£
£61,000 × 45% (additional rate)	*27,450*
Tax saved in respect of personal allowance becoming available: (£12,570 × 45%)	*5,657*
Total tax relief in respect of pension contributions	*33,107*

There is a £1 difference due to rounding.

(b) The three non-UK domiciled individuals

Tutor's top tips

Overseas aspects for individuals is a commonly tested syllabus area as it is a new topic in the ATX syllabus and the rules have changed significantly in recent years, so make sure you have learnt the rules.

(i) The availability of the remittance basis and the remittance basis charge

The availability of the remittance basis

The remittance basis is available to UK resident individuals who are not domiciled in the UK.

Accordingly:

- the remittance basis is available to Lin and Yu.
- the remittance basis is not available to Nan as he is not UK resident.

The remittance basis charge

Tutor's top tips

Don't forget that if an individual is not domiciled in the UK then the level of unremitted overseas income and gains is significant.

If unremitted overseas income and gains is < £2,000 then the remittance basis is automatic, otherwise it must be claimed.

The remittance basis charge is assessed on individuals who have claimed the remittance basis (not where the remittance basis is automatically applied) and differs depending upon the length of time they have been resident in the UK.

- *Resident for 7 out of the last 9 tax years the charge is £30,000*
- *Resident for 12 out of the last 14 tax years the charge is £60,000.*

Lin has unremitted overseas income and gains of less than £2,000. Accordingly, the remittance basis will apply automatically, such that there will not be a remittance basis charge.

Nan has unremitted overseas income and gains of more than £2,000. If Nan were able to claim the remittance basis, the remittance basis charge would be £60,000 because he has been resident in the UK for 12 of the 14 tax years prior to the tax year 2023/24.

Yu has unremitted overseas income and gains of more than £2,000. The remittance basis charge would be £30,000 because Yu has been resident in the UK for 7 of the 9 tax years prior to the tax year 2023/24.

(ii) Deemed UK domicile

A non-UK domiciled individual born overseas would be deemed to be UK domiciled for the purposes of income tax and capital gains tax if:

- they were resident for 15 of the 20 tax years preceding the relevant tax year, unless
- there is no tax year beginning after 5 April 2017 in which they were UK resident.

Examiner's report

Part (a) was a tricky question to get absolutely correct, and very few candidates did so, but there were plenty of marks available to candidates who knew how to put an income tax computation together and were aware of the rules relating to the determination of the annual allowance for a particular year. On the whole candidates scored reasonably well.

In particular, most candidates handled the accommodation benefit well and knew that the tax bands needed to be extended. Many candidates were also aware that there was a three-year rule in respect of the annual allowance, although many were not absolutely clear as to how the rule worked. Many candidates missed the fact that the personal allowance would be available in full possibly because they did not pause and think at that stage of the calculation. Tax calculations should be done as a series of small steps with thought at each step, in order to ensure that important matters are not missed.

The second part of the question concerned the remittance basis and was not done particularly well. The problem here was that candidates did not have a clear set of rules. Instead, they had an awareness of a series of technical terms and time periods that were all confused. This made it very difficult to score well.

The first thing candidates had to do was to explain whether or not the remittance basis was available to each of three individuals. This required a statement of the availability of the remittance basis together with a reason. For those who did not know the rules there was a 50:50 chance as regards the availability of the remittance basis. However, the reason for its availability or non-availability caused a lot more problems.

Candidates must learn the rules and be able to apply them and state them clearly. In addition, the marks available for giving a reason are only awarded where the whole of the reason given is correct. For example, the remittance basis was available to Lin because he was UK resident but not UK domiciled. Candidates who stated this together with various time periods of residency could not score the mark for the reason as it was not clear from their answer whether it was his residence and domicile status that was relevant or the time periods.

The second thing candidates had to do was to state, with reasons, the remittance basis charge applicable to each of the individuals on the assumption that the remittance basis was available to all of them. Again, this was not done particularly well due to many candidates having a very confused knowledge of the rules. One particular area of confusion related to the automatic applicability of the remittance basis where unremitted income and gains are less than £2,000; many candidates thought the rule related to the level of remitted income and gains.

ACCA marking scheme				
				Marks
(a)	(i)	Benefit in respect of accommodation		2.0
		Personal allowance		1.0
		Tax bands		1.5
		Relevance of employer's pension contributions		1.0
		Annual allowance		3.0
		Tax on excess pension contributions		2.0
				10.5
			Maximum	8.0
	(ii)	Comparison with original liability		2.5
		Tax relief at source on pension contributions		1.0
				3.5
			Maximum	3.0
(b)	(i)	Availability of remittance basis		
		General rule		1.5
		Application of the rule to the individuals		1.5
		The remittance basis charge		
		Lin		1.0
		Nan		1.5
		Yu		1.5
				7.0
	(ii)	Deemed UK domicile		2.0
	Professional skills marks (see below)		**Maximum**	5.0
Total				**25.0**

Professional skills marks

Analysis and evaluation

- Use of the information to identify the appropriate amount of annual allowance for Shuttelle in part (a)(i).
- Appropriate use of the data to calculate the total tax relief for the personal pension contributions in part (a)(ii).
- Analysis of the information to determine whether a remittance basis charge is relevant to each individual in part (b)(i).

Commercial acumen

- Recognition of the effect of a high level of income on the annual allowance in part (a)(i).
- Identification that automatic remittance basis is available to Lin in part (b)(i).

48 JUANITA AND BURACO (ADAPTED) *Walk in the footsteps of a top tutor*

Key answer tips

This section B question covers two areas of the syllabus: inheritance tax with related property and diminution in value, and residence, including the remittance basis. These are mainly new topics at ATX level and if you had not studied these areas in detail you would struggle to gain a good mark here.

Part (a) requires a comparison between inheritance tax for a lifetime gift or a gift in the death estate. This is a common comparison to make, so you should be familiar with the differences in treatment.

Part (b)(i) requires application of the statutory residence tests. Although this is a technically challenging area, lots of help could be gained by looking at the tax rates and allowances provided in the exam and applying to the scenario.

Part (b)(ii) offers three marks for the remittance basis rules, which have been tested several times before. The main pitfall here would be spending too long explaining all the rules, rather than just answering the specific question set.

The highlighted words in the written sections are key phrases that markers are looking for.

Tutor's top tips

This is really two separate, standalone questions. You could attempt parts (a) and (b) in whichever order you like, as long as you clearly label your answer.

(a) Inheritance tax (IHT) liability on the Estar Ltd shares

Tutor's top tips

Related property is a commonly tested area of the syllabus which is new at the strategic professional level. It is tested in a tricky way here as you need to consider the impact of related property being gifted in lifetime on the IHT due on an individual's estate. However, if you have revised the topic and think carefully about how best to set out your answer before beginning to write, you should be able to score well here.

Regardless of whether the shares in Estar Ltd were gifted to Lexi in Don's lifetime or on his death, IHT will be payable at the rate of 40% because the gift of the villa in 2019 has used the full nil rate band.

However, whether the shares were gifted or not will impact on their value in Don's death estate under the related property valuation rules.

The IHT due in respect of the Estar Ltd shares on Don's death as a result of his making the lifetime gift to Lexi is £52,240 (£27,040 + £25,200) (W).

If all the shares had been retained by Don until his death, the IHT payable in respect of the shares would have been £67,200 (7,000 × £24 × 40%).

Therefore, there is a reduction in the IHT liability on the Estar Ltd shares of £14,960 (£67,200 – £52,240).

Working: Value of the lifetime gift of 3,500 shares

Related property rules apply as the shares in Estar Ltd were held by both Don and Juanita at the date of the gift.

	£
Value before the gift: 7,000 shares at £20 (70% + 30%)	140,000
Value after the gift: 3,500 shares at £15 (35% + 30%)	(52,500)
Diminution in value	87,500
Business property relief not available (as per question)	
Less: AE 2020/21	(3,000)
AE 2019/20 (used on gift of villa)	0
Gross chargeable transfer	84,500
IHT at 40%	33,800
Less: Taper relief at 20% (3 – 4 years)	(6,760)
IHT payable by Lexi	27,040

The remaining 3,500 shares held by Don at the date of his death will give rise to an IHT liability on his death of £25,200 (40% × 3,500 × £18 (35% + 30%)).

(b) (i) Residence status – 2024/25

Tutor's top tips

The requirement for this part of the question is very specific, and you will not be given credit for providing information that is not requested.

There are only two aspects of residency to discuss:

1 *The automatic overseas residence tests (i.e. automatic non-UK residence tests)*

2 *The sufficient ties tests.*

No credit was given for considering the automatic UK residence tests in detail as the question clearly states that these are not satisfied.

You must apply your knowledge to the scenario, and you will not score marks for writing about residency in general terms.

When considering the sufficient ties tests, you should discuss all possibilities. Buraco could either fall into the '91 – 120 days in the UK' bracket, or the '121 – 182 days in the UK' bracket.

Automatic overseas residence tests

Buraco will not satisfy any of the automatic overseas residence tests for the tax year 2024/25 because he will have been in the UK for 46 days or more in that tax year.

Tutorial note

The 90-day test does not apply to Buraco because he does not work full time overseas.

Residence status – 2024/25

Buraco was not UK resident for any of the three previous tax years, accordingly:

– if he is in the UK for between 100 and 120 days, he will be resident if he has three or more of the four relevant UK ties; or

– if he is in the UK for between 121 and 150 days, he will be resident if he has two or more UK ties.

Buraco does not satisfy the tie relating to work, as he does not work in the UK.

Buraco satisfies the close family tie and the accommodation tie, as he has a minor child in the UK and a house which he has stayed in during the year.

Accordingly, as he satisfies two of the ties, he will be UK resident if he is in the UK for more than 120 days.

If he is in the UK for less than 120 days, he will only be resident if he satisfies the final tie relating to time spent in the UK during either of the two previous tax years. This tie will be satisfied if Buraco spent more than 90 days in the UK during the tax year 2023/24.

(ii) Tax implications of claiming the remittance basis

Tutor's top tips

Make sure that you apply your knowledge to the scenario and set out the implications for Buraco. He has only been in the UK since 2023, so there will be no remittance basis charge.

There are just three marks available, so you should try to have three separate points in your answer.

If Buraco claims the remittance basis in the tax year 2024/25, he will only be subject to UK tax on his overseas income and overseas chargeable gains remitted to the UK.

However, Buraco would not be entitled to the income tax personal allowance or the capital gains tax annual exempt amount.

There would not be a remittance basis charge because Buraco was not resident in the UK for seven of the nine tax years prior to 2024/25.

Examiner's report

The first requirement of this question has been replaced since the original topic is no longer part of the syllabus.

Requirement (a) has been replaced with that of another past exam question, the examiner's report for which is included below.

Part (a) examined two key principles in valuing unquoted shares which are gifted in lifetime, namely related property and diminution in value (comparing the value of the shareholding before and after the gift). Both of these were relevant in respect of the gift in this case, and it was pleasing to see that a significant number of candidates identified these, but unfortunately in many cases were not then able to apply them correctly to the figures given. An earlier lifetime gift was included, so that candidates had to recognise that there would be no annual exemption to bring forward, and no nil rate band available. This is a common examination technique which candidates should be familiar with if they have practised similar past examination questions. However, a common issue here was for candidates to provide a full calculation of the inheritance tax payable in respect of this earlier gift, despite this being totally irrelevant in order to address the requirement, which was to focus on the tax payable only in respect of the shares. In some cases, this wasted a considerable amount of time for no marks. This highlights the need to read the wording of the requirement very carefully to ensure that the right approach is taken and time is not wasted on unnecessary calculations.

In part (b)(i) candidates appeared to be well-prepared for a question on this area of the syllabus with good levels of knowledge.

However, it was important for candidates to realise that this was a question that required their knowledge to be applied to the specific facts and that it was not enough to simply set down everything they knew on the topic. For example, candidates should have realised that, depending on the number of days spent in the UK (which was left imprecise in the question) the relevant number of ties was either two or three. Then, it was not sufficient to list the ties, it was necessary to state whether or not they were met by the individual concerned. It was then good exam technique to draw the various aspects of the explanation together into a form of summary or conclusion.

The other common mistake made by candidates when answering this question was to include irrelevant information in their answers. A significant number of candidates explained the automatic UK residency tests despite the wording of the requirement. Such explanations would not have scored any marks as they were irrelevant to the requirement and thus such candidates put themselves under unnecessary time pressure as a result.

Part (b)(ii), the final part of the question, concerned the remittance basis. This was answered well by many candidates. There were only two matters to note here. Firstly, some candidates' knowledge of the rules governing the remittance basis charge was somewhat imprecise. Secondly, a minority of candidates set out the rules but did not apply them to the individual concerned.

ACCA marking scheme				
				Marks
(a)	Value of shares gifted			3.0
	IHT on gifted shares			3.0
	IHT on remaining shares in the death estate			1.5
	IHT if all the shares are in the death estate			1.0
	IHT saving			0.5
				9.0
(b)	(i)	Automatic overseas residence tests		1.0
		Days and ties		2.5
		Work, family and accommodation ties		3.0
		90 days tie		1.5
		Conclusion		1.0
				9.0
			Maximum	8.0
	(ii)	UK tax on overseas income and gains		1.0
		Personal allowance and annual exempt amount		1.0
		No remittance basis charge		2.0
				4.0
			Maximum	3.0
	Professional skills marks (see below)		**Maximum**	5.0
Total				**25.0**

Professional skills marks

Analysis and evaluation

- Appropriate use of the data to support discussion and draw appropriate conclusions about the reduction in inheritance tax in part (a).
- Analysis of the information to determine appropriate calculations to perform to arrive at the reduction in inheritance tax in part (a).
- Analysis of the information to determine the residence status of Buraco in part (b)(i).
- Appropriate use of the data to determine the tax implications of claiming the remittance basis in part (b)(ii).

Commercial acumen

- Recognition that the related property rules are relevant to the valuation of the Estar Ltd shares in part (a).
- Recognition of possible consequences of a claim for the remittance basis in part (b)(ii).

49 CATE AND RAVI (ADAPTED) *Walk in the footsteps of a top tutor*

Key answer tips

This section B question is about a husband, Ravi, who is UK resident but not domiciled and his wife, Cate who is a sole trader.

Part (a) requires calculation of the cost of Cate taking on an employee, and is similar to requirements seen in previous exam questions.

In part (b) Cate is planning to sell some items she inherited and you need to consider the badges of trade in relation to this new venture.

Part (c) covers the commonly tested topic of arising versus remittance basis for a non-UK domiciled individual, but for CGT rather than income tax.

The highlighted words in parts (b) and (c) are key phrases that markers are looking for.

(a) Cate – After-tax cost of taking on the part time employee

Tutor's top tips

The first three headings from the scenario relate to this part of the question. Make sure you use all of the information given; in particular, consider why you have been provided with Cate's dividend income.

The requirement is to 'calculate', so you do not need to provide written explanations, although you should show all of your workings.

You are calculating the after-tax cost for Cate, so you do not need to consider the tax payable by the employee.

		£
Salary		12,000
Medical insurance – cost to employer		1,300
Class 1A NICs (1,300 × 13.8%)		179
Mileage allowance (£0.50 × 62 × 48 weeks)		1,488
Class 1 NICs (W1)		421
Total additional expenditure		15,388
Less:	Income tax and class 4 NIC saving (£15,388 × 42%) (Note)	(6,463)
	Income tax saving on personal allowance (£7,694 × 40%) (W2)	(3,078)
After-tax cost		5,847

Tutorial note

The additional expenditure is deductible from Cate's taxable trading profit and will save income tax and class 4 NICs.

The income tax saving is at 40% as Cate is a higher rate taxpayer. Class 4 NICs are saved at 2% as Cate's taxable trading profits are above the upper limit for class 4.

Workings

(W1) Class 1 NICs: employer's contributions

	£
Salary: (£12,000 – £9,100) × 13.8%	400
Mileage allowance: ((£0.50 – 0.45) × 62 × 48 weeks) × 13.8%	21
	421

Tutorial note

1. *Only the excess mileage allowance over 45p per mile is liable to NICs.*
2. *Medical insurance is subject to Class 1A.*
3. *The £5,000 employment allowance would already have been fully offset against the class 1 NICs payable in respect of D-Designs' existing employees.*

(W2) Personal allowance

	Before taking on employee		**After taking on employee**	
	£	£	£	£
Basic PA		12,570		12,570
Less: Abatement				
ANI (W3)	120,000		104,612	
Less: Limit	(100,000)		(100,000)	
	20,000		4,612	
50% deduction		(10,000)		(2,306)
Revised PA		2,570		10,264
Increase in PA (£10,264 – £2,570)			7,694	

Tutorial note

Before taking on the additional part time employee Cate's adjusted net income was £120,000, so her personal allowance would have been reduced to £2,570.

After taking on the employee, Cate's adjusted net income will be reduced by the total additional expenditure of £15,388. She will therefore be entitled to a reduced personal allowance for the year of £10,264.

(W3) Adjusted net income

	Before taking on employee	After taking on employee
	£	£
Trading profit	90,000	90,000
Dividends	30,000	30,000
	120,000	120,000
Less: Additional allowable expenditure	–	(15,388)
Total income = Net income = ANI	120,000	104,612

(b) Cate – Sale of second-hand books

Tutor's top tips

To score the marks here you must apply the badges of trade to the scenario.

Make sure you structure your answer with headings, and give a conclusion for an easy mark.

Badges of trade

The tax treatment of the income from the sale of the second-hand books will depend on whether or not Cate is deemed to be carrying on a trade of selling books.

If she is, the income will be treated as trading income, and subject to income tax in the same way as her taxable profits from D-Designs.

If not, then the sales will be dealt with under the capital gains tax rules.

In determining how Cate should be taxed, HMRC will make reference to the 'badges of trade', a series of factors to be considered in order to determine whether or not an individual is trading.

Factors indicating that the sale of books does not constitute a trade

- Cate has inherited the books; she did not buy them for resale.
- Selling second-hand books is not related in any way to Cate's existing business, the running of a chain of dress shops.
- The frequency of transactions; this would appear to be a one-off batch of sales.

Factors indicating that the sale of books does constitute a trade

- Having some of the books rebound may be viewed as 'supplementary work' in order to generate increased profit.
- Taking steps to find purchasers by advertising the books on the internet could indicate a trading motive.

Conclusion

Based on the above factors, it is more likely that the capital gains tax treatment will apply.

For capital gains tax purposes books are chattels so, as no individual book is likely to have a value in excess of £6,000, if the capital gains tax treatment does apply, any gains made by Cate will be exempt from tax.

Tutorial note

Marks were available for discussion of any relevant factors and for reaching a sensible conclusion.

(c) Ravi – Capital gains tax on overseas property gain

Tutor's top tips

It is more efficient to perform your workings for the two options alongside one another. This can be done easily in the spreadsheet response option in the exam.

Remember to give a conclusion as you have been asked to advise. This is best presented in the word processor, but remember to reference through to any workings in the spreadsheet.

Arising basis

Ravi is resident in the UK, so would normally be liable to pay UK capital gains tax on disposals of both his UK and overseas assets on an arising basis.

On this basis, the gain on the disposal of the overseas property is fully liable to UK capital gains tax, as his annual exempt amount for the tax year 2023/24 has already been used.

As Ravi is an additional rate taxpayer, capital gains tax will be charged at the residential property rate of 28% and the capital gains tax payable will therefore be £19,600 (W).

Double tax relief will be available against this UK capital gains tax liability for any tax suffered on the same gain in Goland.

Remittance basis

However, as Ravi is not domiciled in the UK, he should consider making a claim for the remittance basis for the taxation of his overseas gain.

As he has not remitted any of the proceeds from the sale, if he makes such a claim, there will be no gain chargeable in the UK.

However, he will lose his entitlement to the annual exempt amount, which will generate an additional capital gains tax liability of £1,680 (W) on his UK asset gains.

Additionally, as Ravi has been resident in the UK since February 2016 (at least seven out of the last nine tax years), he will be liable to pay a remittance basis charge of £30,000.

The total amount payable as a result of claiming the remittance basis would therefore be £31,680 (W).

Conclusion

A remittance basis claim will not be worthwhile for the tax year 2023/24.

Working: Capital gains tax

	Arising basis	**Remittance basis**
	£	£
Overseas gain	70,000	N/A
UK gains	6,000	6,000
Less: AEA	(6,000)	N/A
Taxable gains	70,000	6,000
Capital gains tax at 28%	19,600	1,680
Plus: Remittance basis charge	N/A	30,000
Total capital gains tax	19,600	31,680

Examiner's report

Part (a) concerned an individual, Cate, running a successful unincorporated business that required an additional part-time employee. The requirement was to calculate the annual cost of employing the part-time employee.

The first thing candidates had to do was determine all of the costs that were going to be incurred. On the whole this was done reasonably well, although some candidates confused cost with tax deductibility, and some simply prepared tax computations for Cate, which was not what they had been asked to do. In addition, many candidates failed to consider the employer national insurance contributions aspects which were a key part of the question.

Once the costs had been determined, it was simply a case of recognising that Cate was a higher rate tax payer, such that she would save income tax at 40% and class 4 national insurance contributions at 2% as a result of the increased costs. This was not tackled well by the majority of candidates who tried to do before and after calculations rather than working at the margin. In addition, many failed to consider the class 4 national insurance contribution implications altogether.

There was a more subtle point in the question in relation to the income tax personal allowance. The reduction in Cate's taxable trading income due to the costs relating to the part-time employee meant that part of her personal allowance would be reinstated, thus reducing the after-tax cost to her of taking on the new employee.

Part (b) required a discussion of the tax treatment of the profit derived from the sale of books on the internet. This required candidates to consider the badges of trade in relation to the specific transactions taking place. This part of the question was done well by many candidates. However, some candidates did not give themselves sufficient thinking time, such that they failed to realise what the question was testing.

It was important that candidates tried to reach a conclusion based on the information provided and that they thought about the capital gains tax implications as well as the income tax implications. There was no right answer as such, just a need to think about the relevant issues and to express the implications in a clear manner.

The final part of the question was arguably more challenging. It concerned the capital gains tax position of an individual, Ravi, who was resident in the UK but domiciled overseas and focussed principally on the remittance basis.

Although some candidates did reasonably well here, almost all candidates could have scored more marks if they had organised their thoughts before they began writing. There was a mark for making the point that Ravi was liable to UK capital gains tax because he was UK resident and a further mark for recognising that the remittance basis was available because he was domiciled overseas. In order to score these two marks, candidates had to make it clear that the liability to capital gains tax was due to his residence status and the remittance basis was due to his domicile status. Many candidates did not make these two points clearly, such that they only scored one of the two available marks.

Candidates were then expected to address the remittance basis charge and the loss of the annual exempt amount. This was done well by the majority of candidates.

ACCA marking scheme

			Marks
(a)	Total additional expenditure		5.0
	Income tax and class 4 NIC saving		2.0
	Saving due to personal allowance		2.5
			9.5
		Maximum	9.0
(b)	Trading income v capital gain issue		1.0
	Relevant badges of trade factors		3.0
	Any reasonable conclusion		1.0
	Chattels, so exempt CGT		1.0
			6.0
		Maximum	5.0
(c)	CGT on an arising basis as UK resident		2.0
	Optional remittance basis as not UK domiciled		1.0
	CGT effect if remittance basis used		2.0
	Remittance basis charge		1.5
	Conclusion		0.5
			7.0
		Maximum	6.0
	Professional skills marks (see below)	**Maximum**	5.0
Total			**25.0**

Professional skills marks

Analysis and evaluation

- Use of the information to determine appropriate calculations to perform to arrive at the after-tax cost for Cate in part (a).
- Demonstration of ability to consider both income tax and national insurance contributions in part (a).
- Provision of at least one factor indicating that the sale of books may or may not be a trade in part (b).
- Analysis of the information to determine whether a remittance basis claim is worthwhile for Ravi in part (c).

Commercial acumen

- Recognition that the extra costs incurred will lead to a reinstatement of some of the personal allowance in part (a).
- Identification that badges of trade must be used to determine the tax treatment of the sale of the books in part (b).
- Identification that remittance basis is available to Ravi in part (c).

50 MAX (ADAPTED) *Walk in the footsteps of a top tutor*

Key answer tips

The first two parts of this question look at the capital gains tax and inheritance tax aspects of a lifetime gift. It is important to pay attention to the dates in these parts of the question.

Part (b) covers the statutory residence tests and the temporary non-residence rules for capital gains tax. It is important that both parts of the requirement are covered and not just one!

The final part of the question asks for an explanation of the availability of business asset disposal relief together with a calculation of the increase in post-tax proceeds if a different disposal date is used. This type of higher skills requirement is commonly set in ATX and should be expected.

The highlighted words in the written sections are key phrases that markers are looking for in your answer.

(a) (i) Availability of gift holdover relief in respect of the gift of the office premises

The office premises are eligible for gift holdover relief as they were used for the purpose of Max's trade. However, as they ceased to be used in the business on 31 May 2022, the proportion of the gain to be held over is restricted to the gain on disposal × period of business use/total period of ownership. Therefore, the proportion of the gain eligible for gift holdover relief is 74/99 ((1 April 2016 – 31 May 2022)/(1 April 2016 to 30 June 2024)).

As the office premises are UK land and buildings, the relief will be available regardless of whether the donee, Fara, is UK resident.

Tutorial notes

1 *Max is disposing of the building used in his sole trader business. He hasn't used it in the trade for the whole period of ownership as his trade ceased some time before the gift to Fara. Therefore, gift holdover relief must be restricted so that only the proportion of the gain relating to business use qualifies.*

2 *Usually, gift holdover relief will only be available if the donee is UK resident. However, as UK non-residential property is still subject to capital gains tax for non-UK residents, gift holdover relief will be available here even if Fara is not UK resident.*

(ii) Maximum potential inheritance tax (IHT) liability in respect of the gift of the office premises

No IHT is payable at the time the gift is made, but a liability may arise if Max dies within seven years of making the gift.

Business property relief is not available as this is a gift of an individual asset which has been used in an unincorporated sole trader business, rather than the gift of the business itself. However, annual exemptions are available for the tax years 2024/25 and 2023/24, such that the gross chargeable value of the gift will be £162,000 (£168,000 – £3,000 – £3,000).

Max has made one prior gift, on 6 May 2021, which will use part of his nil rate band if he dies before 6 May 2028. Taper relief will be available if Max dies after 30 June 2027 (three years after the date of the gift on 30 June 2024), so the maximum potential IHT liability will arise if Max dies before this date.

The maximum potential inheritance tax liability is therefore £12,400 (£162,000 – (£325,000 – £194,000) × 40%) and will arise if Max dies on or before 30 June 2027.

(b) Effect of Max's two-and-a-half-year period overseas on his UK residence status and the capital gains tax (CGT) consequences on the sale of the machine

Tutor's top tips

It is important to consider the statutory residence tests before going into any implications for capital gains tax. Ensure that you run through the tests in order and address the ones that are not met and those that are met, and state why.

Max will leave the UK on 1 November 2024. As Max was resident in the UK for one or more of the previous three tax years, and he will spend more than 91 days in the UK in the tax year 2024/25, then he will NOT satisfy any of the automatic overseas tests.

Max WILL satisfy the first automatic UK residence test in the tax year 2024/25 as he will spend 183 days or more in the UK in that tax year.

In the tax years 2025/26 and 2026/27 Max will satisfy the first automatic overseas residence test as he will spend less than 16 days in the UK.

In the tax year 2027/28 Max's return to live permanently in the UK from 30 June 2027 means that he will not satisfy any of the automatic overseas residence tests, but will satisfy the UK residence test as he will spend 183 days or more in the UK in that tax year.

1 Sale in June 2024

As Max is resident in the UK in June 2024, the disposal will give rise to a chargeable gain in 2024/25.

2 Sale in June 2025

Disposals of assets made by non-UK resident individuals are not chargeable to CGT in the UK. However, Max will be regarded as a temporary non-resident, as his period of non-residence will be less than five years, and he has been UK resident for at least four of the seven tax years prior to the tax year of departure. Accordingly, any gains made in the period of non-residence in respect of assets held prior to Max's departure, and disposed of while he is overseas, will become chargeable in 2027/28 (the tax year of his return).

Tutorial note

Although a machine is a wasting chattel and would therefore normally be an exempt asset for capital gains purposes, the exemption does not apply if capital allowances would have been claimed on it, which is the case here. Accordingly, since cost and proceeds exceed £6,000, a gain has to be calculated.

(c) Availability of business asset disposal relief (BADR) on the sale of the machine

The sale of the machine will satisfy two of the conditions for BADR in that it was in use within Max's business at the date of cessation, and the business had been owned by Max for at least two years prior to cessation. However, the third condition that the disposal must be within three years of the date of cessation, will only be satisfied if the disposal takes place before 1 June 2025. Accordingly, if the sale takes place in June 2024, BADR will be available, but if it does not take place until June 2025, it will not.

Sale in June 2024

If the sale of the machine takes place in June 2024, this will give rise to a chargeable gain of £12,000 (£84,000 – £72,000).

As Max will be able to claim BADR in respect of this chargeable gain, the after-tax proceeds will be £82,800 (£84,000 – (£12,000 × 10%)).

Sale in June 2025

If the sale of the machine is delayed until June 2025, this will give rise to a chargeable gain of £18,000 (£90,000 – £72,000) in the tax year 2027/28.

As Max will not be able to claim BADR in respect of this chargeable gain, the after-tax proceeds will be £86,400 (£90,000 – (£18,000 × 20%)).

The increase in after-tax proceeds is therefore £3,600 (£86,400 – £82,800).

Tutorial note

Although the disposal occurs in June 2025 the gain does not become chargeable until the tax year 2027/28 under the temporary non-residence rules as this is the tax year that Max returns and becomes UK resident again.

Tutor's top tips

The final requirement asked for both explanations and calculations. It is important not to neglect the explanations.

Examiner's report

This question concerned the capital gains tax and inheritance tax implications of a lifetime gift, and also the implications of a taxpayer moving abroad on his UK residence status, and his proposed sale of a UK asset.

The first part related to the availability of gift holdover relief in respect of a commercial building which has previously been used in a business, but which is now being rented out. Most candidates who attempted this question part were able to identify the issues and score two out of the three possible marks. Very few candidates went on to quantify the proportion of the gain which would be eligible for relief. Candidates should remember that where dates or figures are given in a question, they are usually required to use these in their answer.

The second part of the question required advice on the maximum potential inheritance tax liability which could arise in respect of the gift of the commercial building. The majority of candidates produced a good computation, but only a minority provided the necessary supporting explanations to fully satisfy the requirement – in this case, the fact that taper relief is available to reduce an inheritance tax liability if the donor of the lifetime gift survives for at least three years. Where an explanation or justification is needed for including or omitting figures, candidates must provide this.

The third part of the question required explanation of the implications of an individual moving overseas for a few years on his UK residence status for each of those years, and the consequences for the timing of a proposed disposal for capital gains tax purposes. The majority of candidates appeared not to have read the question properly, and dived straight in to explaining the rules for temporary non-residence for capital gains tax purposes, with which they were clearly very familiar, but ignoring the need to first of all consider the individual's actual residence status by reference to the automatic rules for determining this. This meant that they restricted the number of marks which they were able to obtain. Candidates should ensure that they fully address all aspects of a requirement, not just what they perceive to be the key point, in order to score a high mark on a question.

The final part of the question concerned an explanation of the availability of business asset disposal relief, and the calculation of the increase in after-tax proceeds if the individual delayed selling a further business asset to a date when he would not be UK resident. Almost all candidates had identified that the temporary non-residence rules would apply, and implemented them correctly, and, it was pleasing to see, followed through the calculation to the end, quantifying the increase in after-tax proceeds, as required, and thereby scoring a high mark on this part. The main area of difficulty for this question was imprecise knowledge of the conditions for business asset disposal relief, and future candidates are reminded once again of the need to be very familiar with the precise rules in respect of all the capital gains tax reliefs.

ACCA marking scheme

				Marks
(a)	(i)	Gift holdover relief		4.0
			Maximum	3.0
	(ii)	Gross chargeable value of the gift		2.5
		Circumstances in which maximum liability arises		2.5
		Calculation of maximum liability		1.0
				6.0
			Maximum	5.0
(b)	Max's residence status			3.0
	Sale in June 2024			1.0
	Sale in June 2025			3.0
				7.0
			Maximum	6.0
(c)	Business asset disposal relief			3.0
	After-tax proceeds from sale in June 2024			1.5
	After-tax proceeds from sale in June 2025			1.5
	Increase in after-tax proceeds			0.5
				6.5
			Maximum	6.0
	Professional skills marks (see below)		**Maximum**	5.0
Total				**25.0**

Professional skills marks

Analysis and evaluation

- Use of data to determine that gift holdover relief would be restricted to the period in which the office had been used in the business in part (a)(i).
- Clear evaluation of when an IHT liability arises on a potentially exempt transfer (PET) and therefore an accurate analysis of the situation that will give rise to the biggest IHT liability in part (a)(ii).
- Clear evaluation of Max's presence in the UK and overseas and the effect that this has on his UK residency status for tax purposes in part (b).
- Application of his residency status to the proposed timing of the sale of the machine to determine the impact on CGT due in part (c).

Commercial acumen

- Recognition that the timing of the sale of the machine affects the availability of business asset disposal relief in part (c).
- Calculation of the difference in after tax proceeds for each proposed sale date in part (c).

51 CADEN AND AMAHLE (ADAPTED)

Key answer tips

This question covers part disposals and connected people for capital gains tax, payment by instalments for inheritance tax, personal service companies and overseas aspects of income tax.

Part (a)(i) looks at a part disposal to a connected person. This is all brought forward knowledge from TX so should be a fairly straightforward four marks.

Part (a)(ii) covers the instalment option for IHT. This is quite a specific part of administration, but is very important in real life and so you should ensure you learn the rules around this.

Part (b) looks at the personal service company rules. When dealing with a requirement on this it is important to establish the size of the client(s) to know which rules to apply.

The final part of the question looks at the overseas aspects of income tax. Here you first of all need to explain which basis of assessment applies to the individual and then consider the numbers involved. Tax has already been paid overseas, so be sure to take this into consideration in your calculations.

(a) (i) Capital gains tax implications of the sale of the four antique chairs

As Caden's son is a connected person to Caden, the market value of the chairs at 6 October 2024 will be used as proceeds. The capital loss on the sale will be calculated as follows:

	£
Market value of the four chairs at 6 October 2024	99,000
Less: Cost (working)	(104,711)
Allowable loss	(5,711)

Caden can relieve this loss only against gains arising on further disposals to his son in the tax year 2024/25 or future tax years.

Working:

	£
Market value of the six chairs at 3 March 2022	152,000
Less: Used on disposal of first two chairs	
$£152{,}000 \times \dfrac{£42{,}000}{£42{,}000 + £93{,}000}$	(47,289)
Cost of remaining four chairs	104,711

Tutorial note

Where a loss is made on a disposal to a connected person, that loss can only be used against future gains made on disposals to the same connected person.

(ii) Availability and effect of the instalment option for payment of inheritance tax (IHT)

Investment property

Land and buildings are qualifying assets for the instalment option for payment of IHT, so this will be available in respect of the IHT liability on the investment property, provided Nathi still owns the property on 20 March 2029, the date of his father's death.

The IHT will be payable in ten equal annual instalments, commencing on 30 September 2029. However, if Nathi sells the house within the ten-year instalment period, the outstanding liability will become payable immediately.

Antique chairs

Antique chairs are not qualifying assets for the instalment option.

Tutorial notes

1 *Instalments for IHT can only be made on land and buildings, unincorporated businesses, shares or securities where the donor has a controlling interest and some unquoted shares.*

2 *As the gift of the investment property was a potentially exempt transfer (PET) and Caden dies within seven years of the date of the gift, IHT is due on Caden's death.*

3 *Although Nathi will pay Caden £35,000 for the purchase of the antique chairs, for IHT purposes the loss to donor principle applies – i.e. the gross chargeable transfer value will be based on the diminution in the value of Caden's estate at the time of the gift. The difference between the value of the chairs and the price paid by Nathi (i.e. £64,000) will be treated as a PET on 6 October 2024 and will become chargeable to IHT on Nathi's death within seven years.*

(b) Implications of the application of the IR35 legislation for Caden

Deemed employment payment

	£
Budgeted fee income (all from relevant engagements)	65,000
Less: 5% deduction	(3,250)
	61,750
Less: Salary (£1,500 × 12)	(18,000)
Employer's NIC ((£18,000 – £9,100) × 13.8%)	(1,228)
	42,522
Less: Employer's NIC on deemed payment (£42,522 × 13.8/113.8)	(5,156)
Deemed employment payment	37,366
Total employment income (£18,000 + £37,366)	55,366
Less: Personal allowance	(12,570)
Taxable income	42,796

Tutorial notes

1 *The deemed employment payment is treated as being made on 5 April 2025 and will therefore be allowable (together with the employer's NIC) for corporation tax purposes in the year ending 31 March 2026.*

2 *As Caden is the only employee, and is also a director of Mandini Ltd, the employment allowance of £5,000 will not be available to deduct from the employer's NIC payable.*

3 *Caden can make a claim to set the deemed employment payment against the dividends of £35,000 paid in order to avoid a double tax charge. This will reduce the taxable dividend to £Nil as the deemed employment payment exceeds the dividend paid.*

(c) Interest arising on Amahle's bank account in Komor

As Amahle is resident in the UK, she will be assessed to UK income tax on her worldwide income, including the interest on the bank account in Komor. The remittance basis is not available to her because she is UK domiciled. Accordingly, she will be assessed on the full amount of interest income arising regardless of whether or not she remits it to the UK.

In the tax year 2024/25, Amahle will make a contribution of £3,000 (net), to her personal pension scheme, so her basic rate band will be extended by £3,750 (£3,000 × 100/80) to £41,450 (£37,700 + £3,750).

Amahle's taxable income of £39,930 (employment income of £45,000 and interest income on the Komor bank account of £7,500 (£150,000 × 5%) less the personal allowance of £12,570) will all fall into her basic rate band. As a basic rate taxpayer, a savings income nil rate band of £1,000 is available to Amahle, so her UK income tax liability in respect of the Komor interest will be £1,300 ((£1,000 × 0%) + (£6,500 × 20%)).

As the interest income will have already been taxed in Komor, double taxation relief (DTR) will be available. This will equal the lower of the UK tax and the overseas tax payable on this income. As the overseas tax payable of £1,350 (£7,500 × 18%) exceeds the UK tax of £1,300, the DTR will equal the UK tax liability. Accordingly, there will be no tax to pay in the UK.

Examiner's report

Requirement (a)(i)

Candidates were required to explain, with supporting calculations, the capital loss arising on the sale of four antique chairs, and how the loss could be relieved. The overall quality of responses to this part of the question was somewhat disappointing. Candidates needed to be aware of the requirement to both explain and calculate. Many went straight for the numbers without providing any form of written comment.

As far as the explanation was concerned, it is important to note that because the chairs were being sold to the individual's son, it was a connected party disposal which meant that market value should be used as the sale proceeds. Very few candidates seemed to be aware of this rule and used actual proceeds instead. In addition, since a capital loss arises on a disposal to a connected person, that loss can only be used against gains arising on future disposals to exactly the same person.

When it came to performing the calculations, there appeared to be a certain degree of confusion. The cost of the four chairs to use in the capital loss calculation requires some thought. The four chairs were originally part of a set of six chairs, which were gifted to the individual by his mother when their total market value was £152,000; this figure therefore becomes the cost figure for the six chairs to use in future disposals. Some of this original cost will then have been allocated to the earlier disposal of two of the chairs. This will have been calculated in accordance with the part disposal formula of A/(A+B), and leaving the balance of the £152,000 to be used in the capital loss calculation on the disposal of the remaining four.

Requirement (a)(ii)

This requirement involved advice on the availability and effect of the instalment option for the payment of an inheritance tax liability on certain gifts which had now become chargeable to IHT as a result of the death of the donor. Despite the requirement specifically stating that calculations were not required for this part, a significant number of candidates still provided them. It is very important for candidates to highlight such instructions in order to avoid wasting time in terms of doing things which are not required and for which credit cannot therefore be awarded.

Correct answers involved explaining that the instalment option would only be available on the property and not the chairs, and on the basis that the property was still owned at the time of the donor's death. Credit was also awarded for stating that the instalment option would involve 10 equal annual amounts, commencing 6 months from the end of the month of death. But if the property were sold by the recipient within the 10-year period, the remainder of the tax owing would become payable immediately.

Many candidates discussed inheritance tax reliefs here which were not relevant to the scenario, such as taper relief; this wasted their time and failed to earn them any marks.

Requirement (b)

This part involved the calculation of an individual's taxable income for 2023/24 on the basis that the personal services company (IR35) legislation applied to the budgeted fee income received by the company concerned.

Although the requirement was to calculate, it is still important on such occasions for the logic behind the underlying calculations to be shown. Markers need to see how answers are derived so that appropriate credit can be awarded, even if the final answer is wrong. This means that each stage of the calculations needs to be shown, with a brief narrative explanation next to each number, so that the marker can follow the candidate's method.

Part of the examiner's report has been removed as the question has been adapted to remove that element.

Requirement (c)

This part of the question related to the UK income tax liability arising on interest from an overseas bank account of an individual who was both UK resident and domiciled.

The requirement was to advise the individual why the overseas interest will be subject to UK income tax and then to explain, with supporting calculations, why this would not actually result in any UK tax payable.

With regard to the first part of the requirement, a UK resident individual is subject to UK income tax on their worldwide income, and because the individual is UK domiciled, the arising basis will always apply. Many candidates wrongly concluded that the remittance basis would be available on this occasion.

The key to answering the next part of the question, as to why no actual UK tax liability would arise on this occasion, was an understanding of how double tax relief (DTR) works. The individual's initial income tax liability will be based on all of their UK and overseas income. However, candidates then needed to explain that DTR would be available based on the lower of UK tax and overseas tax suffered on the overseas source of income. On this occasion, since the overseas tax exceeded the relevant UK liability, DTR would equal the UK liability meaning that there would be no further tax to pay in the UK. Many candidates failed to draw appropriate conclusions at this point.

Extra complexity was added to this question by including personal pension contributions, which impacted on the basic rate band when calculating the UK liability, and remembering to take advantage of the savings nil rate band which meant on this occasion, with the individual being a basic rate taxpayer, that the first £1,000 of the overseas savings income was taxed at the rate of 0%.

ACCA marking scheme				
				Marks
(a)	(i)	Calculation		2.0
		Explanation		2.5
				4.5
			Maximum	4.0
	(ii)	Availability of instalment option		1.5
		Effect		3.0
				4.5
			Maximum	3.0
(b)		Deemed employment payment		3.5
		Caden – taxable income		1.5
				5.0
(c)		Explanation of liability to UK income tax		2.5
		Explanation and calculation of UK tax		4.0
		Double tax relief		1.5
		Conclusion		1.0
				9.0
			Maximum	8.0
		Professional skills marks (see below)	**Maximum**	5.0
Total				**25.0**

Analysis and evaluation

- Analysis of the data to determine capital gains tax treatment of the chair disposal in part (a)(i).
- Analysis of the data to determine availability of instalments as a payment option for IHT in part (a)(ii).
- Evaluating that the dividend will not be taxable in addition to the deemed employment payment in part (b).
- Demonstration of a clear understanding of how individuals are taxed and how the relief for overseas taxation works, but in words rather than just a calculation performed by rote learning, in part (c).

Scepticism

- Identification that selling the house within ten years will have an impact on IHT instalments in part (a)(ii).

Commercial acumen

- Recognition of the purpose of the connected party rules for capital gains tax purposes in part (a)(i) by demonstrating an essential understanding that we look to tax the substance of a transaction, not the form, to prevent tax avoidance.
- Recognition that the instalment option for payment of IHT may be expensive but may give the beneficiary of a gift sufficient time to raise the IHT due on a PET in part (a)(ii).

- Evaluation of the IR35 rules in relation to Caden's circumstances and in particular deduction of the salary actually paid and the employer's NIC due thereon – demonstrating an understanding that the rules are designed to tax the deemed salary that would not otherwise be subject to IT and NIC, not tax the entire revenue from relevant engagements, in part (c).

PERSONAL FINANCE, BUSINESS FINANCE AND INVESTMENTS

52 MONISHA AND HORNER (ADAPTED) ***Walk in the footsteps of a top tutor***

Key answer tips

This section B question tests your knowledge of furnished holiday lettings, tax planning for married couples (and civil partners) and the IR35 rules.

The first part of (a) concerns various aspects of income tax and capital gains tax in relation to tax planning for a married couple and in particular deals with furnished holiday accommodation. This is purely TX knowledge so should be an opportunity to score well if you have refreshed your TX knowledge!

The second part of (a) was the more difficult part of the question. It required a calculation of the total tax saving on the transfer of a 20% interest in a rental property from one spouse (Monisha) to the other (Asmat) together with the property being let as furnished holiday accommodation in the future. It is necessary to think very clearly about the taxes that would be saved and the impact on the computations of both husband and wife.

Part (b) covers the personal service company (IR35) rules and required an outline of the circumstances in which the rules apply, and clear explanations were needed to score highly. Then an explanation of the tax implications for the client was required, with supporting calculations. Here you should ensure that your main focus is the explanation, and not spend too long on the numbers.

The highlighted words in the written sections are key phrases that markers are looking for.

Tutor's top tips

The definition of furnished holiday accommodation should supply easy marks provided the conditions had been learnt.

(a) Monisha

(i) Furnished holiday accommodation in the UK – conditions

- The property must be available for commercial letting to the public as holiday accommodation for at least 210 days in the tax year.

- The property must be commercially let as holiday accommodation for at least 105 days in the tax year, excluding any periods of longer-term occupation.
- There must be no more than 155 days of longer-term occupation in the tax year.

Longer term occupation occurs where there is a continuous period of occupation by the same person for more than 31 days.

(ii) The total tax saving for the six years ending 5 April 2031

Tutor's top tips

With the time allocation for this part, it is important to pause, think about which taxes are involved (i.e. income tax and capital gains tax) and then perform the calculations at the margin.

There is insufficient time to do full blown income tax computations before and after, and there is no need to do computations for multiple years as the levels of income and gains are the same for the first five years.

Once the situation is defined, the calculations are very straightforward. However, time needs to be spent making sure the requirement is fully understood before any calculations are performed to avoid time wasted doing unnecessary calculations.

Furnished holiday accommodation has several tax benefits. For income tax, the full cost of furniture is deductible (or capital allowances are available, if using the accruals basis) instead of claiming for replacement furniture relief and the income is relevant earnings for pension relief purposes. From a CGT point of view, the gain is eligible for business asset disposal relief, rollover relief and gift holdover relief.

Income tax

	£
Income tax saved in the first five tax years (£6,660 (W) × 40% × 5 years) (Note)	13,320
Income tax saved in the final tax year (£6,660 (W) × (40% – 20%))	1,332
Total income tax saved	14,652

Tutorial note

In the first five years, Monisha is a higher rate taxpayer but as Asmat has no other income his share of property income will be covered by his personal allowance (PA) and he will pay no tax on that income. The income tax saving will therefore be 40%.

Note that with or without the proposals, Asmat would not be able to transfer £1,260 of his unused PA to Monisha as she is a higher rate taxpayer. Therefore, his entire PA remains with him. Without the proposal to transfer income to him, his PA would be wasted.

In the final year (2030/31), Asmat will be earning £18,000 p.a. and therefore he will utilise his entire PA, even without the proposal, and he will be a basic rate taxpayer. The income tax saving from moving income from Monisha into his computation is therefore 20% (40% – 20%).

Working: Taxable property income

	£
Rental income	20,000
Less: Allowable expenses (£3,480 + £1,200 + £2,000)	(6,680)
Total property income	13,320
Amount subject to income tax in the hands of Asmat (£13,320 × 50%) (tutorial note)	6,660

For the first five tax years, Asmat will not have any other income, such that his share of the property income will be covered by his personal allowance.

Tutorial note

Despite the fact that Monisha gifts only a 20% interest in the investment property to Asmat, the income of a jointly held asset is automatically split equally between a married couple, regardless of their actual interests in the property.

Monisha and Asmat could elect to split the income between them in the ratio 80:20, but to do so would not be beneficial in their particular circumstances.

Accordingly, property income of £6,660 (W) will be subject to income tax in the hands of Asmat, rather than being taxed at 40% in the hands of Monisha, in each of the six tax years.

Capital gains tax

Tutor's top tips

Once the scenario is understood, this part follows on easily. However, remember that part of Monisha's annual exempt amount is still available.

Asmat will have a full annual exempt amount available and business asset disposal relief will be available if the property is treated as furnished holiday accommodation.

Inter spouse transfer

The gift of the 20% interest in the property will take place at no gain, no loss because Monisha and Asmat are married.

Capital gains tax saving on the disposal of the property

If the proposals are not carried out:

Monisha

	£
Total gain	100,000
Less: Annual exempt amount available	
(£6,000 – £2,300 other chargeable gains)	(3,700)
Taxable gain	96,300
CGT at 28%	26,964

If the proposals are carried out:

Monisha

	£	£
Share of gain (£100,000 × 80%)		80,000
Less: Annual exempt amount available		
(£6,000 – £2,300 other chargeable gains)		(3,700)
Taxable gain		76,300
Asmat		
Share of gain (£100,000 × 20%)	20,000	
Less: Annual exempt amount available	(6,000)	
Taxable gain		14,000
Total taxable gains		90,300
CGT at 10% (Business asset disposal relief)		9,030
Capital gains tax saved (£26,964 – £9,030)		17,934
Total tax saved (£14,652 + £17,934)		32,586

Tutorial note

1 *The gain on the sale of the property will be allocated between Monisha and Asmat in the ratio 80:20.*

2 *A gain on the sale of furnished holiday accommodation qualifies for business asset disposal relief.*

3 *To be advantageous for capital gains tax purposes, it was not necessary for Monisha to transfer 50% of the interest in the property to Asmat. It was only necessary to utilise Asmat's annual exempt amount. The excess gain above the annual exempt amount is taxed at 10% regardless of who it accrues to.*

(b) Horner

Tutor's top tips

Clear explanations of when the rules apply are needed to score highly on this part.

As there are only three marks available, there is no need to go into great detail about the factors used to determine an employed or self-employed type relationship.

(i) The circumstances in which the personal service company (IR35) rules apply

1. A company enters into a contract to provide services to a client.
2. The services are carried out by an individual.
3. If the services were provided under a contract between the individual and the client, the individual would be regarded as an employee of the client.
4. The individual has an interest of at least 5% in the company or an entitlement to receive payments from the company, other than salary, in respect of the services provided to the client.

In respect of condition three, when determining whether or not the individual would be regarded as an employee of the client, the rules used to distinguish between employees and the self-employed are used.

Tutorial note

It is possible for a partnership, rather than a company, to enter into the contract with the client.

(ii) Tax implications for Florentine Ltd of engaging Otmar Ltd.

Tutor's top tips

When dealing with the personal service company legislation, it is important to identify the size of the client organisation involved. This determines whether it is the responsibility of the personal service company or the client to determine whether the rules apply.

As Florentine Ltd is a medium or large sized client organisation, they must determine whether Otmar Ltd falls within the personal service company legislation.

If they determine that Otmar Ltd does fall within the legislation, then they must provide a Status Determination Statement to Horner.

Florentine Ltd will be required to deduct income tax and NIC from the deemed direct payment at the relevant rates. This payment is calculated as follows:

		£
Otmar Ltd – income from relevant engagements		85,000
Less:	Materials used to provide services	(3,900)
Deemed direct payment		81,100

Tutorial note

1 *When calculating the deemed direct payment, the cost of any materials used to carry out the services can be deducted, as well as any expenses which would normally be deductible against employment income (if any).*

2 *Horner's salary and the pension contributions are not deductible when calculating the deemed direct payment. These would only be relevant when calculating the deemed employment income where the client involved is a small organisation.*

Examiner's report

Part (a)(i) was answered very well by the majority of candidates. The only difficulty related to confusion over the meaning of 'longer term accommodation' and the maximum number of days of such occupation permitted in a tax year.

Part (a)(ii) was done poorly by many candidates who either did not have a thorough attempt at it or worked very hard but did not pause to think about how to approach the problem.

The key was to first calculate the taxable property income in order to identify the amount of taxable income that would be taxed in the hands of Asmat rather than Monisha.

It was then necessary to recognise that for the first five years under consideration, Monisha would be a higher rate taxpayer whereas Asmat's income would be covered by his personal allowance, such that no tax would be payable. Accordingly, by working at the margin, it was easy to see that for the first five years the saving would be 40% of the income transferred. In the sixth year, Asmat was expected to be employed, such that the income transferred would be taxed at 20% and the saving would therefore be 20% (40% – 20%) of the income transferred.

The problem was that very few candidates chose to work at the margin. Instead, many chose to prepare income tax computations for the two individuals before and after the transfer of the interest in the property in order to quantify the difference in the total liability. This was very time consuming. Some candidates even prepared calculations for each of the five years despite the fact that the figures were the same in each year.

Calculating tax liabilities can be very time consuming. Candidates should always stop and think about the most efficient way of approaching a set of calculations before they start writing.

The capital gains tax element of this part of the question was not handled particularly well. This was perhaps due to a shortage of time. It required candidates to recognise that an additional annual exempt amount would be available and that tax would be charged at 10%, due to the availability of business asset disposal relief, rather than at 28%. Only a minority of candidates were able to quantify the effect of these points.

The majority of candidates struggled to satisfy the requirement in part (b)(i) despite a reasonable knowledge of the rules. It was generally recognised that the rules were in place in order to prevent the avoidance of tax but there was some confusion as to exactly where tax was being avoided. Very few candidates were able to state the commercial relationship between the taxpayer, the personal service company and the client in a clear manner.

The final part of the examiner's report has been removed as it relates to part of the question which has been changed since the question was set.

ACCA marking scheme

				Marks
(a)	(i)	The conditions – one mark each		3.0
		Meaning of longer-term occupation		1.0
				——
				4.0
			Maximum	3.0
				——
	(ii)	Income tax		
		Taxable property income		1.0
		Allocated equally		1.0
		First five tax years		1.5
		Final tax year		1.0
		Capital gains tax		
		Gift of 20% interest is at no gain, no loss		1.0
		Capital gains tax if the proposals are not carried out		1.5
		Capital gains tax if the proposals are carried out		2.5
		Total saving		0.5
				——
				10.0
				——
(b)	(i)	The conditions – one mark each		3.0
		Reference to rules used to determine employer, employee relationship		1.0
				——
				4.0
			Maximum	3.0
				——
	(ii)	Responsibility is with Florentine Ltd		1.0
		Status Determination Statement		0.5
		Deduct income tax and NIC		1.0
		Deemed direct payment		1.0
		No deduction for salary and pension contributions		0.5
				——
				4.0
				——
	Professional skills marks (see below)		**Maximum**	5.0
				——
Total				**25.0**
				——

Professional skills marks

Analysis and evaluation

- Analysis of the information to determine appropriate calculations to perform to calculate tax saved if proposals are carried out in part (a)(ii).
- Use of information to determine the correct tax treatment regarding the engagement with Otmar Ltd in part (b)(ii).
- Analysis of the information to calculate the deemed direct payment in part (b)(ii).

Commercial acumen

- Demonstration of an awareness of the purpose behind the furnished holiday accommodation rules in part (a)(i).
- Identification of the availability of business assets disposal relief in part (a)(ii).
- Demonstration of an awareness of the purpose behind the personal service company rules in part (b).

53 STELLA AND MARIS (ADAPTED) *Walk in the footsteps of a top tutor*

Key answer tips

This section B question is really two separate questions which could be attempted in either order. The first covers income tax and relief for pension contributions; the second covers pension benefits and inheritance tax exemptions.

Given the heavy emphasis on pensions, this may not have been the most popular question in the exam.

Part (a) is similar to questions seen in other ATX exams and tests the pensions annual allowance charge. Note that the restriction of the annual allowance has been introduced since this question was set in the exam, so this aspect would not have needed consideration in the original question.

Part (b)(i) tests the application of the lifetime allowance for pensions, which is only tested rarely in the ATX exam.

Part (b)(ii) is a much more straightforward section covering the small gifts exemption and normal expenditure from income.

The highlighted words in the written sections are key phrases that markers are looking for.

(a) Stella – Income after tax and pension contributions 2024/25

Tutor's top tips

There are easy marks here for basic income tax computations and for calculating income after tax.

The key to scoring well was recognising that there would also be an excess pension contribution. In order to calculate the annual allowance available, you had to consider if there was any unused relief brought forward from the previous three years and also if the current year annual allowance needed to be restricted.

Remember the unrestricted annual allowance is £40,000 for the tax year 2024/25 but can be increased by any unused AA in the previous three years, starting with the earliest year first.

The personal pension contributions also extend the basic and higher rate bands.

Note that the annual allowance tax charge is calculated using the taxpayer's marginal rate of tax.

Detailed calculations such as those needed in requirement (a) are best completed in the spreadsheet response option in the exam. Formulae can be used to cut down on calculation time, but remember it is still important to label all workings.

Income tax liability

	£
Employment income	203,000
Property income	92,000
Net income	295,000
Less: Personal allowance (W1)	(0)
Taxable income (all non-savings income)	295,000

£		£
127,700	× 20% (W2)	25,540
87,440	× 40%	34,976
215,140 (W2)		
79,860	× 45%	35,937
295,000		
67,500	× 45% (annual allowance charge) (W3)	30,375
Income tax liability		126,828

Income after-tax and pension contributions

	£
Income received	295,000
Less: Income tax liability	(126,828)
Less: Pension contributions paid (W5)	(72,000)
Income after-tax and pension contributions	96,172

Tutorial note

The ATX examining team has stated that credit was also awarded to candidates who calculated the class 1 national insurance contributions on Stella's employment income.

Workings

(W1) Personal allowance

	£
Net income	295,000
Less: Gross PPCs	(90,000)
Adjusted net income (ANI)	205,000

As ANI is > £125,140, the personal allowance is reduced to £Nil.

(W2) Extended basic and higher rate bands

	£	£
Current bands	37,700	125,140
Add: Gross PPCs qualifying for tax relief	90,000	90,000
Revised bands	127,700	215,140

(W3) Annual allowance charge

	£
Annual allowance for 2024/25 (W4)	12,500
Unused annual allowance for three previous tax years:	
2021/22 (£40,000 – £30,000)	10,000
2022/23 (£40,000 – £40,000)	0
2023/24 (£40,000 – £40,000)	0
Maximum gross pension contribution in 2024/25	22,500

Annual allowance charge is £67,500 (£90,000 – £22,500).

(W4) Threshold income 2024/25

	£
Net income	295,000
Less: Gross personal pension contributions	(90,000)
Threshold income	205,000

As threshold income is > £200,000 it is necessary to calculate adjusted income to determine if a restriction to the 2024/25 annual allowance is required.

Adjusted income 2024/25

	£
Net income	295,000
Plus: Employer/employee occupational pension contributions	0
Adjusted income	295,000

As adjusted income is > £240,000 (and threshold income is > £200,000) the annual allowance must be restricted.

	£
Annual allowance 2024/25	40,000
Less: (£295,000 – £240,000) × 50%	(27,500)
Revised annual allowance	12,500

Tutorial note

The minimum annual allowance for a tax year is £4,000, but this is not relevant to Stella as her annual allowance for the tax year 2024/25 exceeds this amount

(W5) Pension contributions paid

The amount actually paid in respect of the pension contribution by Stella is £72,000 (£90,000 × 80%).

(b) (i) Maris – Maximum receivable as a lump sum

Tutor's top tips

You should be aware of the basic rule that 25% of the pension fund can be taken tax free, and you are given the lifetime allowance in the tax rates and allowances. There are easy marks for discussing and applying these.

As this requirement is discursive it lends itself better to being completed in the word processor response option in the exam. Be sure to label up each requirement clearly so that it is clear to the marker what is being answered where.

The value of Maris's pension fund exceeds the lifetime allowance of £1,073,100.

Accordingly, the maximum lump sum which she can take tax-free is restricted to £268,275 (25% × £1,073,100).

The excess of the fund over the lifetime allowance may be taken as a lump sum, subject to an income tax charge at 55% on the value of this excess.

Any withdrawals from the balance of the lifetime allowance will be treated as taxable non-savings income. As Maris is a higher rate taxpayer, these would be taxed at 40%, or possibly 45% if her total income increases above the higher rate limit of £125,140.

(ii) Inheritance tax – Lifetime exemptions available

> ***Tutor's top tips***
>
> *This section should offer easy marks as long as you write down the conditions for the exemptions to apply and refer to the information given in the question wherever possible.*
>
> *There are six marks available, so try to make six separately identifiable points in your answer.*

Small gift exemption

Maris can make exempt gifts valued at up to £250 each tax year to any number of recipients. If the total value of the gifts to any one recipient exceeds £250, the full value of the gifts will be taxable. The gifts can comprise either cash or shares.

Exemption for normal expenditure out of income

The following conditions must be satisfied for the gifts to be exempt:

– The gift is made as part of Maris's normal expenditure. As she is intending to make regular gifts to her family on their birthdays, she should be able to establish a regular pattern of giving.

– The gift is made out of income, not capital. Maris must therefore give cash, not part of her shareholdings.

– Maris is left with sufficient income to maintain her usual standard of living. As she appears to have fairly significant pension and savings income this condition should be satisfied.

There is no monetary limit on the amount of this exemption.

ACCA marking scheme

				Marks
(a)	Qualifying pension contributions			1.0
	Taxable income			2.0
	Restriction of annual allowance 2024/25			1.0
	Excess pension contribution			3.0
	Income tax liability			2.5
	Net income after-tax and pension contributions			2.0
				11.5
			Maximum	10.0
(b)	(i)	Tax free amount		1.5
		Taxed amount		2.5
				4.0
	(ii)	Small gift exemption		3.0
		Exemption for normal expenditure out of income		4.0
				7.0
			Maximum	6.0
	Professional skills marks (see below)		**Maximum**	5.0
Total				**25.0**

Professional skills marks

Analysis and evaluation

- Analysis of the information to determine appropriate calculations to perform to arrive at Stella's annual allowance in part (a).
- Use of information to determine appropriate calculations to perform to arrive at Stella's income tax liability in part (a).
- Analysis of the information to determine the appropriate tax treatment of Maris's withdrawals from her pension in part (b)(i).

Commercial acumen

- Recognition that Stella's annual allowance would be reduced in part (a).
- Demonstration of awareness of the purpose of the lifetime allowance for pensions in part (b)(i).
- Identification of the availability of relevant inheritance tax lifetime exemptions in part (b)(ii).

54 JESSICA (ADAPTED) *Walk in the footsteps of a top tutor*

Key answer tips

The first part of the question focuses on the tax treatment of a redundancy package with a small income tax calculation. This offers easy marks if you have learnt the rules.

The second part of the question is a common requirement to see in ATX of discussing loss relief options and calculating tax savings. You should ensure you are well prepared to deal with the tax saving calculations.

The final part of the question covers the maximum contribution that can be made into a pension scheme without an annual allowance charge. Care should be taken around the level of relevant earnings and also the level of annual allowance.

The highlighted words in the written sections are key phrases that markers are looking for in your answer.

(a) Income tax implications of the redundancy package

The statutory redundancy pay is fully exempt from income tax. However, it reduces the £30,000 exemption available for the ex-gratia payment.

The taxable amount of the ex-gratia payment is therefore £20,000 (£32,000 – (£30,000 – £18,000)).

The cash equivalent of the gift of the laptop computer must also be included. This is the higher of:

1 the market value at 31 March 2024, i.e. £540, and

2 the value of the laptop computer at the date it was first provided to Jessica, less the amounts subsequently taxed on her as a benefit, i.e. £680 (£850 – £170 (20% × £850))

The total taxable amount of the package is therefore £20,680 (£20,000 + £680).

The package is taxed as the top slice of Jessica's income for the tax year 2023/24, so the income tax payable on the redundancy package will be £9,306 (£20,680 × 45%).

Tutorial note

Jessica's taxable income for the tax year 2023/24 already exceeds £125,140 (salary £145,000 + rental income £6,000; no personal allowance is available). Jessica is therefore an additional rate taxpayer.

(b) (i) Reliefs available for Jessica's share of the partnership loss

The trading loss for tax purposes has arisen in the tax year 2024/25.

It can be relieved against Jessica's total income for 2024/25, the tax year of the loss, and/or 2023/24, the previous tax year.

Alternatively, because the loss has arisen in one of the first four tax years in which Jessica will be a partner, it can be relieved against her total income of the three years prior to the year of the loss starting with the earliest year (i.e. 2021/22).

(ii) Strategy for loss relief to maximise Jessica's income tax savings

Tutor's top tips

It is important to consider each of the loss relief options in turn. You should consider Jessica's income for the year to determine what rate of tax she would pay so that the tax saving can be calculated.

Jessica will join the Langley Partnership on 1 July 2024. Accordingly, her share of the partnership loss for the year ending 31 March 2025 will be £48,000 (£160,000 × 9/12 × 40%).

In the tax year 2024/25, Jessica's only source of income will be rental income of £6,000. As this will be covered by her personal allowance, relieving the loss in this year will not result in any tax saving.

In the tax year 2023/24, Jessica's taxable income before loss relief will be £171,850 (£145,000 + £6,000 + £170 + £20,680).

The loss will reduce Jessica's taxable income to £123,850 (£171,850 – £48,000), saving tax partly at the additional rate of 45% and partly at the higher rate of 40%. In addition, as Jessica's income will be reduced below £125,140 a small amount of the personal allowance will become available. As a result, the loss of £48,000 will generate a tax saving of £21,794 (W1).

If, alternatively, Jessica carries the loss back to the tax year 2021/22 it will be relieved against her total income of that year of £145,000. As the resulting total income of £97,000 (£145,000 – £48,000) is below £100,000, the full personal allowance will become available and again tax will be saved partly at 45% and partly at 40%. Accordingly, the total income tax saving will be £24,971 (W2).

Therefore, the most beneficial claim is to carry back the loss and offset it in the tax year 2021/22 as this results in the highest tax saving, of £24,971.

Workings

(W1) Tax saving for the tax year 2023/24

	£
Additional rate (£46,710 (£171,850 – £125,140) × 45%)	21,020
Higher rate (£1,290 (£48,000 – £46,710) × 40%)	516
Increase in PA	258
((£12,570 – ((£171,850 – £48,000 – £100,000) × 50%) × 40%))	
Total tax saving	21,794

(W2) Tax saving for the tax year 2021/22

	£
Additional rate (£14,860 (£140,000 – £125,140) × 45%)	6,687
Higher rate (£33,140 (£48,000 – £14,860) × 40%)	13,256
Increase in PA (£12,570 × 40%)	5,028
Total tax saving	24,971

(c) Jessica – maximum pension contributions 2024/25 and 2025/26

The maximum gross contribution which Jessica can make attracting tax relief each tax year is the higher of

1 Jessica's relevant earnings in the tax year, and

2 the basic amount of £3,600.

Jessica has no relevant earnings in the tax year 2024/25 as the Langley Partnership has made a loss in that year, and she has no other source of earned income. So the maximum contribution she can make in the tax year 2024/25 is £3,600.

In 2025/26, Jessica has relevant earnings of £82,000 (£205,000 × 40%) comprising her share of the partnership profit for the year ending 31 March 2026. Accordingly, she can make a contribution into the scheme of up to £82,000. This exceeds the annual allowance available of £40,000, but as she was a member of a pension scheme in the tax year 2024/25 she can bring forward her unused allowance from that tax year of £36,400 (£40,000 – £3,600).

Therefore, the total amount of annual allowance available is £76,400 (£40,000 + £36,400), so this is the maximum gross contribution which Jessica can make without incurring an annual allowance charge.

Tutorial note

No unused relief can be brought forward from years prior to the tax year 2024/25 as Jessica was not a member of a pension scheme until 1 May 2024.

Jessica's level of income is quite clearly low enough to ensure the full £40,000 annual allowance is available. You should not waste time doing lengthy calculations around this.

Examiner's report

This question concerned the receipt of a redundancy package on leaving employment, the reliefs available for an individual's share of a partnership trading loss, and the payment of contributions into a personal pension scheme.

The first part concerned the income tax implications of the receipt of a redundancy package comprising a statutory redundancy payment, an ex-gratia payment, and retention of a company provided laptop computer. Most candidates were clearly very comfortable with the availability of the £30,000 exemption in respect of the ex-gratia payment, and the fact that this would be reduced by the amount of the statutory redundancy payment. However, relatively few appeared to realise that the statutory redundancy pay is always exempt, irrespective of this, as this statement was rarely made. The majority of candidates included the laptop computer in their calculation, but did not know how to calculate its value, being an asset transferred to an employee who has previously been taxed on the provision of the benefit under the '20% × market value rule'. Termination payments are regularly tested at ATX, and should provide an opportunity for candidates to score well if they have practised these, and taken note of what has been required in previous model answers.

The second part of this question required candidates to state the loss reliefs available to a partner who has just joined a loss-making partnership. On the whole, candidates scored well on this part. The main issue seen was a lack of accuracy in identifying the available reliefs. The rules relating to trading losses are frequently examined, and candidates are expected to be precise in this sort of question. Candidates would do well to invest time at the revision stage of their studies memorising the rules concerning relief for trading losses, and ensuring that they are able to recognise those rules which apply in a given scenario. In particular, they should be able to identify those which apply in certain situations only, such as the opening years of a business, as here. It was disappointing to see that a number of candidates included consideration of the relief available by carrying the loss forward, when the requirement had specifically stated that the taxpayer did not want to do this. This wasted time, particularly if the candidate then went on to consider the tax savings in the next part.

The third part of the question required a calculation of the loss available to the partner, and determination of the loss relief strategy which would provide the highest income tax saving for the taxpayer.

Those candidates who scored well on this particular part:

- adopted a structured, methodical approach to considering in turn each of the reliefs for the trading loss which they had identified in the previous part, stating the taxpayer's total income in each year, and hence being able to identify the rate of tax which would be saved.
- Didn't waste time considering irrelevant reliefs.

In order to gain a good mark in this type of question it is vital that candidates attempt past exam questions. Reading through model answers, while providing useful information, is often of limited help in these cases; candidates need to practise the structured approach necessary to produce a good, coherent answer.

The final part of the question concerned an explanation and calculation of the maximum amount of contributions which could be paid into the taxpayer's personal pension scheme without incurring an annual allowance charge. The majority of candidates were aware of the £40,000 allowance and the ability to bring forward unused allowances. However, a significant number failed to relate their knowledge to the scenario, bringing forward several years' worth of unused allowance, despite the fact that the taxpayer had not previously been in any pension scheme, and spending a considerable amount of time calculating whether or not the maximum amount of allowance would be restricted, when a quick calculation would have revealed that the taxpayer's income fell well below the income limits. At the ATX level, general rules are rarely required; candidates will invariably be asked to apply rules to a given scenario, so they must ensure they have taken this into consideration at every stage of their answer, to avoid wasting time.

ACCA marking scheme

				Marks
(a)	Cash amounts received			2.5
	Laptop computer			2.0
	Calculation of income tax payable			1.5
				6.0
			Maximum	5.0
(b)	(i)	Options for relief of Jessica's share of the partnership loss		3.0
	(ii)	Share of partnership loss year ending 31 March 2025		1.0
		Relief in 2024/25		1.5
		Relief in 2023/24		3.5
		Relief in 2021/22		2.5
		Conclusion		0.5
				9.0
			Maximum	7.0
(c)	Maximum contribution 2024/25			2.5
	Maximum contribution 2025/26			4.0
				6.5
			Maximum	5.0
	Professional skills marks (see below)		**Maximum**	5.0
Total				**25.0**

Professional skills marks

Analysis and evaluation

- Recognition that the laptop would be included as part of the redundancy package and that the taxable redundancy package would be taxed as the top slice of income such that could use the marginal rate to calculate the income tax due in part (a).
- Practical application of the loss relief rules to Jessica's facts with clear understanding of how to calculate the savings without the need to do a full income tax computation in part (b).
- Clear evaluation of Jessica's earnings each year and therefore produces an accurate analysis of her ability to contribute to a personal pension scheme in part (c).

Commercial acumen

- Recognition that different loss relief options work in different ways and the need to consider all the possible options to ensure the maximum amount of tax is saved in part (b).
- Recognition that whilst the tax rules may permit carry forward of an unused annual allowance from more than one year, they also require Jessica to have been a member of a pension scheme to generate an unused allowance. As she did not join a scheme until 1 May 2024, she cannot carry forward any allowance from a year prior to the tax year 2024/25. in part (c).

55 PEDRO (ADAPTED)

Key answer tips

This question covers personal tax aspects including inheritance tax, furnished holiday lets and pensions.

In the first part of the question you are asked to explain the IHT implications of a gift which happened many years ago. Firstly, consider the treatment in lifetime, and then on death. This is worth five marks so it may not be as straight forward as it appears!

The second part of the question tests furnished holiday letting. This is an area that does not come up very often in ATX, but offers some easy marks if you have learnt the rules.

The final part of the question tests pensions. Pedro is looking to make a large pension contribution, so you should consider whether all of this would receive tax relief or if there would be an annual allowance charge. You are told about his previous pension arrangements so bear this in mind when considering the available annual allowance.

(a) Inheritance tax (IHT) implications of the gift of the holiday cottage to Pedro

The gift of the holiday cottage was a potentially exempt transfer (PET), and therefore no tax was payable in Marina's lifetime. Although Marina died more than seven years after making this gift, IHT was payable as a result of her death as the gift constituted a gift with reservation. This is because Marina continued to derive benefit from the use of the holiday cottage following the gift, and she did not pay a market rent for staying in the cottage.

As the reservation was not lifted prior to her death, the IHT payable would have been calculated as the higher of (1) the total IHT payable if the cottage was included in her death estate at its value on death, and (2) the total IHT payable, if the cottage was taxed as a PET made in March 2014. As the latter liability is £Nil, due to the date of the PET being more than seven years before Marina's death, the cottage would have been included in Marina's death estate.

As the value of her death estate exceeded the nil rate band of £325,000 (as it included a portfolio of properties valued at £670,000), IHT was payable on the estate. The IHT attributable to the cottage, being a gift with reservation, was payable by the recipient of the gift, which, in this case, was Pedro.

(b) Why the holiday cottage will qualify as a furnished holiday letting

The letting of the holiday cottage satisfies all the conditions to qualify as a furnished holiday letting:

Availability – the cottage is available continuously for commercial letting from 1 July 2024 onwards, so will meet the condition to be available for at least 210 days in the first 12-month period.

Actual letting – the cottage will have a 70% occupancy rate throughout the period it is available for letting, such that it will be let for at least 105 days in the first 12-month period.

Pattern of occupation – no tenant will stay in the cottage for more than 14 consecutive days during the first year for which it will be available for letting, so there is no possibility of the number of days of 'longer term occupation' (more than 31 consecutive days) exceeding 155 in the first 12-month period.

The cottage is situated in the UK, has been let furnished, and on a commercial basis.

(c) Reduction in Pedro's income tax liability for the tax year 2024/25 as a result of making the planned contribution of £85,000 (gross) to a personal pension scheme

Income tax liability with the pension contribution

			£
Employment income (£75,000 + £0)			75,000
Property income (£14,500 + £32,000)			46,500
Total/net income			121,500
Less: Personal allowance (see note below)			(12,570)
Taxable income			108,930
Income tax liability (W1)			
£108,930 × 20%			21,786
Add: Pension contribution additional charge (W2)			
	£13,770 × 20%	2,754	
	£7,230 × 40%	2,892	5,646
	£21,000		
Income tax liability			27,432

Payment of the pension contribution leads to a reduction of £12,900 (£40,332 – £27,432) in Pedro's income tax liability for the tax year 2024/25.

Personal allowance

The pension contributions which qualify for tax relief cannot exceed Pedro's relevant earnings for the tax year. Pedro's relevant earnings for the tax year 2024/25 are £89,500 (employment income of £75,000, plus income from furnished holiday lettings of £14,500). The whole of the £85,000 contribution is therefore eligible for tax relief.

Adjusted net income is £36,500 (£121,500 – £85,000), so there is no restriction of the personal allowance.

Workings

(W1) Increase in basic rate band

The basic rate band threshold is increased to £122,700 (£37,700 + £85,000).

(W2) Annual allowance charge

	£
Contribution by Pedro (gross)	85,000
Contribution by Loule Ltd to occupational scheme	8,000
Total contributions 2024/25	93,000
Less: Annual allowance available – 2024/25 (W3)	(40,000)
2023/24 (W4)	(32,000)
Annual allowance charge	21,000

(W3) Annual allowance available 2024/25

Threshold income

	£
Net income	121,500
Less: Personal pension contributions (gross)	(85,000)
Threshold income	36,500

As Pedro's threshold income does not exceed £200,000, the annual allowance for the tax year 2024/25 is not restricted. It is not necessary to calculate Pedro's adjusted income for the year.

(W4) Unused annual allowance brought forward

The annual allowance brought forward from the tax year 2023/24 is £32,000 (£40,000 – £8,000).

The annual allowance is not available to bring forward from the tax year 2021/22 or 2022/23 as Pedro was not a member of a pension scheme in those years.

Examiner's report

This question concerned the IHT implications of a gift with reservation, a furnished holiday letting, and a calculation of the impact on an individual's income tax liability of them making a substantial contribution to their personal pension scheme.

The first part of the question required candidates to advise the client of the IHT implications of having received a lifetime gift following the death of the donor. Most candidates recognised that the lifetime gift was a potentially exempt transfer (PET) and also a gift with reservation. Significantly fewer knew the consequences of this as a result of the death of the donor, which was disappointing.

The second part of this question related to the holiday cottage referred to in the first part, requiring candidates to explain why this cottage would qualify as a furnished holiday letting. The majority of candidates demonstrated good knowledge of these rules and applied them correctly to the information given in the question. As a result, a good number were able to score at least four of the five available marks.

The third part of this question was worth ten marks and involved a detailed income tax computation including both occupational and personal pension scheme contributions. There were few very good answers to this question part, although many managed to score half marks. Weaker candidates were clearly very confused about the rules for pension contributions relief and produced some very muddled answers. It appeared that quite a few candidates adopted a 'scattergun' approach, including parts of calculations, presumably as they occurred to them, which proved difficult to follow, and to mark, in some cases. It is important to adopt a logical approach to this sort of question, working through the income tax computation line by line, thinking through one stage at a time. Question practice, once again, is invaluable for this. Additionally, some candidates wasted time by calculating the individual's income tax liability prior to making the personal pension contribution, when this was given in the question. Others wrote a detailed explanation of some of the rules, instead of, or as well as, calculations. The only explanation required was in respect of the amount of personal allowance available to the taxpayer. Other explanations, sadly, didn't score marks.

ACCA marking scheme

			Marks
(a)	Gift treated as a PET		1.0
	Recognition of gift with reservation		2.0
	Implications of gift with reservation		3.0
			6.0
		Maximum	5.0
(b)	Availability		1.5
	Actual days let		1.5
	Pattern of occupancy		2.0
	Furnished/commercial basis/UK		1.0
			6.0
		Maximum	5.0

(c)	With pension contribution		
	Total income		2.0
	Personal allowance note		2.0
	Tax calculation		1.0
	Annual allowance charge		4.0
	Tax on annual allowance charge		1.0
	Impact on tax liability		0.5
			10.5
		Maximum	10.0
	Professional skills marks (see below)	**Maximum**	5.0
Total			**25.0**

Professional skills marks

Analysis and evaluation

- Appropriate use of relevant information to determine that there are two alternative charges to IHT in part (a).
- Demonstration of ability to consider the availability of the personal allowance in part (c).
- Adoption of a logical approach to prepare suitable calculations in part (c).

Commercial acumen

- Appropriate use of information in the question to identify gift with reservation in part (a).
- Recognition of the relevance of the property portfolio in part (a).
- Effective application of the general rules to the specific facts of the scenario in part (b).

56 LUIS (ADAPTED)

Key answer tips

This question covers inheritance tax, EIS shares and income tax treatment of interest.

Part (a) focuses on inheritance tax, but in a slightly different way, as it asks you to calculate the maximum possible inheritance tax liability. You are dealing with a lifetime gift, so you need to think about what tax would be payable when, and what circumstances could change the amount of inheritance tax.

Part (b) focuses entirely on the tax reliefs available around EIS shares. This is quite a niche area that you haven't seen before at TX, so it is important to learn the rules surrounding these shares.

In part (b)(i) you are asked to look at the income tax and capital gains tax implications of selling the shares. Make a note of how long the shares have been owned for, as this will have an impact on the relief(s) available.

Part (b)(ii) then asks you to discuss the use of the loss on the disposal of the shares. Make sure you explain what the loss can be used against, when it can be used and how much tax it could save.

The final requirement is a higher skills requirement. The technical topics being tested (interest receivable and interest paid regarding a residential rental property) are TX level subjects, but the way they are being tested is a bit more advanced. Break the requirement down and think about each bit individually first, as you can score some easy marks for explaining the tax treatment. Then think about how these fit together to calculate the net saving.

(a) Circumstances which will give rise to the maximum inheritance tax (IHT) liability

The gift of Ivy Cottage to Silvia will be a potentially exempt transfer (PET) which will become chargeable to IHT if Luis dies within seven years of making this gift i.e. before 31 July 2031.

However, the maximum IHT liability will arise if Luis dies before 31 July 2027 because:

1. This date is within three years of gifting the investment property to Silvia on 31 July 2024, such that taper relief will not be available in respect of this gift; and
2. It is within seven years of the gift of cash to Mario on 1 January 2021, such that this gift will also become chargeable as a result of Luis' death, and it will be accumulated in determining the nil rate band available in respect of the gift of Ivy Cottage to Silvia.

Maximum IHT liability

			£
Value of property at 31 July 2024			245,000
Less: Annual exemptions:	2024/25		(3,000)
	2023/24		(3,000)
			239,000
Nil rate band		325,000	
Less: Chargeable transfer in the previous seven years			
(£250,000 – £3,000 – £3,000)		(244,000)	
		81,000	
			(81,000)
Taxable amount			158,000
IHT payable (£158,000 × 40%)			63,200

(b) (i) Sale of shares in Flores Ltd

As Luis sold his Flores Ltd shares on 1 April 2024 he owned them for less than three years such that there will be a withdrawal of the income tax relief given when the shares were acquired. Enterprise investment scheme (EIS) relief was obtained on the acquisition of these shares at the rate of 30% i.e. £36,000 = (£120,000 × 30%). As the shares were sold to an unconnected party at a loss, the amount of relief withdrawn will be calculated by reference to the sale proceeds i.e. £25,500 (£85,000 × 30%).

A capital loss will arise on the sale of the shares. The allowable cost for this calculation will be reduced by the EIS relief obtained and not withdrawn.

	£
Proceeds	85,000
Less: Cost (£120,000 – (£36,000 – £25,500))	(109,500)
Allowable loss	(24,500)

In addition, this sale will result in the gain on the sale of Yew House, which was deferred on the acquisition of the Flores Ltd shares, being brought back in to charge. As the amount reinvested in qualifying shares (£120,000) exceeded the gain on disposal (£71,000), the full amount of the gain will have been deferred, as Luis elected to defer the maximum possible amount. This gain will become chargeable in the tax year 2023/24.

Tutorial note

It is possible to defer a lower amount than the maximum possible amount when using EIS reinvestment relief. This can be useful to make use of the annual exempt amount or capital losses. However, you were told that Luis deferred the maximum possible amount, so in this case that would be the full gain.

(ii) Reliefs available for the capital loss

Luis can offset the loss on disposal of his shares against the chargeable gain of £71,000 on the sale of Yew House. This would save CGT at the rate of 28%.

Alternatively, as the shares qualified for EIS relief, he can offset the loss against his total income of the tax year 2023/24 and/or 2022/23. In the tax year 2022/23 Luis was an additional rate taxpayer, so would save at least some income tax at the rate of 45%, with any balance at 40%. In the tax year 2023/24, Luis was a higher rate taxpayer, so would save at least some income tax at the rate of 40% with any balance at 20%.

Therefore, it will be tax advantageous for him to elect to offset the loss in the tax year 2022/23 against his total income.

Tutorial note

Where a disposal of either EIS or SEIS (seed enterprise investment scheme) shares give rise to a capital loss, this can be used in the normal way (i.e. against capital gains) or can be offset against total income in the tax year of the loss and/or the previous tax year.

As income tax rates are generally higher than capital gains tax rates, using the loss against income is usually the more attractive option. However, this will depend on the individual circumstances of the taxpayer.

(c) Interest received and paid

Income tax on interest received

As Luis will be a higher rate taxpayer in future tax years, a savings nil rate band of £500 will be available. Interest received in excess of £500 will be taxed at the rate of 40%.

Income tax relief on interest paid

Tax relief will be available at the basic rate of income tax (20%) in respect of the interest paid on the property mortgage loan. This will be given as a tax credit, deducted from Luis' income tax liability for the relevant tax year.

Tutorial note

Tax relief for mortgage interest on a residential property is given as a 20% tax reducer against the income tax liability. This is in contrast to mortgage interest on non-residential properties which would be deductible against property income.

	Mortgage not repaid	**Mortgage repaid**
	£	£
Interest received:	850	0
Income tax: (£850 – £500) × 40%	(140)	
Interest paid:	(1,275)	0
Tax relief on interest paid: 20% × £1,275	255	
Net interest paid	(310)	0

Therefore, the after-tax interest saving will be £310

Examiner's report

Requirement (a)

This requirement asked for an explanation of the circumstances under which the maximum liability to inheritance tax (IHT) would arise in respect of a lifetime gift, and a calculation of the amount of IHT payable in this case.

The technical content of this part was quite straightforward, and overall candidates scored well. Most were able to cite the basic rules that IHT would be chargeable if Luis died within 7 years of making the gift, and that no taper relief would be available unless he survived for at least 3 years. However, fewer stated that additionally he would need to die within 7 years of making the earlier gift, such that this would use up part of his nil rate band. This gift was frequently included in the subsequent calculation of the IHT liability, but candidates omitted to include it as part of their explanation of the circumstances under which the maximum liability would arise.

The calculative aspects of this part were generally handled well, with the main issue being the omission of annual exemptions in respect of each of the gifts.

It is however important that candidates are not only able to produce good, accurate basic IHT computations, but are also able to provide written explanations where required to address the specific slant of the requirement.

Requirement (b)

There were two requirements within part (b). The first part asked for the income tax and capital gains tax (CGT) implications of the sale of qualifying enterprise investment scheme (EIS) shares. The sale gave rise to a loss, so the second part then went on to deal with the relief available in respect of this capital loss.

The command word in the first part of the requirement was 'Explain', so although some brief calculations were useful here, the emphasis needed to be on the written explanations. The majority of candidates knew that the immediate income tax implication was that the EIS relief given previously would be withdrawn as the shares had been held for less than three years. However very few were able to go on and explain that, since the sale had resulted in a loss, the relief withdrawn would, on this occasion, be based on 30% of the sale proceeds (as opposed to 30% of the original qualifying cost).

The CGT implications were not dealt with as well. In many cases candidates simply compared cost and sale proceeds to establish the amount of the capital loss. It was apparent that many candidates were struggling with the calculation of a capital loss in this situation, and also with the consequences of having made a claim for EIS reinvestment relief to defer a gain arising on the disposal of a previous asset. CGT reliefs can be quite tricky areas of the syllabus, but one or more are examined in almost every session, so candidates would be well advised to ensure that they do take the time to study all of them in some detail. The consequence of disposing of shares in respect of which reinvestment relief has been claimed, is that the deferred gain will crystallise and become chargeable to CGT in the tax year of the share disposal.

Answers to part (ii) were, in the main, rather imprecise. Candidates referred to relief against 'income' and 'gains' but needed to be more specific in terms of their explanations. The relief was available against general income of the tax years 2023/24 and/or 2022/23, and against chargeable gains of the tax year 2023/24 only.

Candidates are strongly encouraged to practise past exam questions which include explanations of loss reliefs in order to familiarise themselves with the level of specific detail that the examining team is typically looking for. Very few candidates stated that the relief was available against general income because the shares had qualified for EIS relief. It is not a relief that is otherwise ordinarily available for capital losses.

Many candidates did not address the final two parts of this requirement. This involved a discussion of the rate of tax savings in respect of each relief. The question stated that Luis was an additional rate taxpayer in 2022/23, and a higher rate taxpayer in 2023/24, so those who attempted this were able to deduce that the income tax saving in 2022/23 would be at the rate of 45%, and in 2023/24 at the rate of 40%. The gain on the residential property would be taxed at 28%. Those who did consider rates of tax were generally then able to go on and provide sensible advice to Luis regarding the most tax-advantageous relief. The command word here was "advise" which meant that candidates had to consider and summarise the different options, and then go on to reach a conclusion. In situations such as this, there will always be credit available for a sensible conclusion/advice, based on the information the candidate has provided in their answer – it is therefore always advisable to attempt such parts, rather than leave them out completely.

Requirement (c)

This was also a two-part question. In the first part candidates were required to explain the tax treatment of both interest received on an investment, and interest payable on a residential mortgage. Most candidates had no problem with the interest received, identifying the availability of the £500 savings nil rate band, as Luis was a higher rate taxpayer in 2023/24. However, a fair number were not aware of the rules in relation to tax relief on mortgage interest, and said it was an allowable expense against income, rather than a tax reducer at the rate of 20%. The command word here was 'Explain'. It was therefore insufficient just to provide calculations, without any attempt at written explanation.

In the second part, many candidates were able to produce some form of computation, but unfortunately this did not always take into account the specific figure that was needed in order to address the requirement. The question asked for a calculation of the after-tax net interest saving from repayment of the mortgage. Candidates had to include four relevant figures here in order to derive this: the interest paid on the mortgage, which would be saved; the tax relief on the mortgage interest which would be foregone; the interest received on the investment, which would also be foregone; and the tax payable in respect of the interest received, which would be saved.

Although the requirement here was simply to 'calculate', candidates should still ensure that they do clearly label their figures. Otherwise, it is not always clear to markers what the various figures represent, particularly if there are no accompanying workings. For any figure that does have to be calculated, workings should always be provided, either on the face of the answer or embedded in the relevant cell, so that markers are able to see what has been done, and award credit accordingly.

ACCA marking guide

				Marks
(a)	PET/death within seven years			1.0
	Circumstances for maximum liability			3.0
	Calculation of amount payable			3.0
				7.0
			Maximum	5.0
(b)	(i) Withdrawal of EIS income tax relief			2.5
	Capital gains tax implications			3.5
	(ii) Offset of loss			4.5
				10.5
			Maximum	9.0
(c)	Interest received – explanation			1.0
	Interest payable – explanation			2.0
	If mortgage not repaid – calculation			2.0
	If mortgage repaid – calculation			1.0
	Saving			0.5
				6.5
			Maximum	6.0
	Professional skills marks (see below)		**Maximum**	5.0
Total				**25.0**

Professional skills marks

Analysis and evaluation

- Adoption of a logical approach to prepare suitable calculations to arrive at the maximum inheritance tax liability in respect of the gift of Ivy Cottage in part (a).
- Analysis of the information to determine implications for both income tax and capital gains tax in respect of the disposal of the Flores Ltd shares in part (b)(i).
- Analysis of the information to evaluate the best option for loss relief in part (b)(ii).
- Appropriate use of the data to determine suitable calculations to perform to arrive at the net interest received/paid by Luis in part(c)(ii).

Commercial acumen

- Identification of the factors that will increase the inheritance tax liability in respect of the gift of Ivy Cottage in part (a).
- Identification that the loss on the Flores Ltd shares can be used against total income in part (b)(ii).

TAXATION OF CORPORATE BUSINESSES

FAMILY COMPANY ISSUES

57 NOCTURNE LTD (ADAPTED) *Walk in the footsteps of a top tutor*

Key answer tips

This section B question has three separate requirements which can be attempted in any order.

The first two parts relate to Nocturne being a close company:

Part (a) is about the gift of an asset to a participator who is not an employee or a director.

Part (b) is about a loan made to the company by a participator who is also a director.

Part (c) is about the partial exemption for VAT.

The highlighted words in the written sections are key phrases that markers are looking for.

(a) Provision of a laptop computer for Jed

Tutor's top tips

Read the question carefully: you are only asked to consider the after-tax cost for the company, Nocturne Ltd, not the impact on Jed.

Option 1: Purchase of a new laptop computer

Nocturne Ltd is a close company as it is controlled by any three of its four shareholders. As Jed is not a director or employee of Nocturne Ltd, the provision of the laptop computer will not be treated as a taxable benefit, but as a distribution.

Nocturne Ltd will not be able to claim capital allowances in respect of the new laptop computer and there will be no national insurance contribution implications.

No further capital allowances are available to Nocturne Ltd in respect of the existing laptop computer as its tax written down value is already £Nil.

Option 2: Transfer of an existing laptop computer

The disposal of the laptop computer to Jed will give rise to a balancing charge in Nocturne Ltd (W). The laptop computer is an exempt asset for capital gains tax purposes, as it is a chattel which cost and is worth no more than £6,000.

The new laptop computer to be used in the business will be eligible for capital allowances. The annual investment allowance is available for 100% of the amount of the expenditure.

The corporation tax relief in the year ending 31 March 2025 due to capital allowances will be £314 (19% × £1,650 (W)).

Working: Capital allowances for year ended 31 March 2025

Balancing charge: £150

AIA: £1,800

Total allowances: £1,800 – £150 = £1,650

Summary of after-tax costs

Tutor's top tips

When considering two possible courses of action it is useful to summarise the tax implications of the two options in a table.

To calculate the after-tax costs, take account of all costs to the company and any corporation tax relief available for that expenditure.

	Option 1	**Option 2**
	£	£
Amount paid for new laptop	1,800	1,800
Less: Corporation tax saving (above)	0	(314)
After-tax cost	1,800	1,486

Conclusion

Option 2 is therefore the preferable option for Nocturne Ltd.

(b) Provision of loan finance by Siglio

Tutor's top tips

*Make sure you are clear about the situation being described in the scenario: this is a loan **from** a participator, not **to** a participator.*

Explaining how savings income is taxed on an individual and the tax relief available for eligible interest on qualifying loans draws on pure TX knowledge and should have provided easy marks.

Interest received by Siglio

Siglio will receive interest on the loan from Nocturne Ltd net of a 20% income tax deduction. It will be taxed as savings income in Siglio's income tax computation. If Siglio is a basic rate taxpayer, the first £1,000 will be taxed at 0%. If he is a higher rate taxpayer this reduces to £500 and if he is an additional taxpayer, there will be no savings income nil rate band. Any interest in excess of the nil rate band (if available) will be taxed at his marginal rate of tax, but with credit given for the tax deducted at source.

Interest paid by Siglio

As Siglio has taken out a loan to provide the loan finance to Nocturne Ltd, he will be able to obtain tax relief on the interest paid on the loan because the following conditions are satisfied:

– Nocturne Ltd is a close company, and

– Siglio owns at least 5% of the shares in Nocturne Ltd.

Also, as he is the company's managing director, it is highly likely that he works full time for Nocturne Ltd. Therefore, Siglio will be able to deduct the interest paid on the bank loan in calculating his taxable income each year.

(c) (i) Recoverable input VAT for the year ended 31 March 2024

Tutor's top tips

All input tax (including that relating wholly or partly to exempt supplies) may be recovered if a business is below the de minimis limits. There are three tests to see whether a business is de minimis; the business need only meet one of them.

Test 1

Total input tax ≤ £625 per month on average, and value of exempt supplies ≤ 50% of value of total supplies.

Test 2

Total input tax less input tax directly attributable to taxable supplies ≤ £625 per month on average, and value of exempt supplies ≤ 50% of value of total supplies.

Test 3

Input tax relating to exempt supplies ≤ £625 per month on average, and input tax relating to exempt supplies ≤ 50% of total input VAT.

In this question you are only required to consider tests 1 and 2.

Applying the de minimis tests to the annual figures provided:

Test 1

Although the value of the exempt supplies is less than 50% of the total supplies, the total input VAT of £13,132 (£7,920 + £1,062 + £4,150) is above the de minimis limit of £7,500 (£625 × 12) so test 1 is not satisfied.

Test 2

Total input VAT less input VAT directly attributed to taxable supplies is £5,212 (£13,132 – £7,920).

This is below the de minimis limit of £7,500 and the value of exempt supplies is less than 50% of the total supplies so test 2 is satisfied and all the input VAT incurred of £13,132 is reclaimable.

Tutorial note

As test 2 is satisfied and all of the input tax is reclaimable, there is no need to apportion the unattributable input VAT.

Had both tests 1 and 2 been failed, the following working would have been required in order to carry out test 3:

Recoverable input VAT for the year ended 31 March 2024:

	Total	*Recover*	*Disallow*
	£	*£*	*£*
Wholly attributable to taxable supplies	*7,920*	*7,920*	
Wholly attributable to exempt supplies	*1,062*		*1,062*
Unattributable (£4,150 × 86%/14%)	*4,150*	*3,569*	*581*
Total	*13,132*	*11,489*	*1,643*

(ii) Annual test

Tutor's top tips

This part of the question covers the annual test for partially exempt businesses, and has nothing to do with the annual accounting scheme for VAT!

Nocturne Ltd's eligibility for the annual test

The annual test allows a business to apply the de minimis tests once a year instead of for every VAT return period.

The conditions to be satisfied are:

1 The business must have been de minimis in the previous partial exemption year

2 The business will consistently apply the annual test throughout any given partial exemption year, and

3 There are reasonable grounds to expect that the input tax incurred by the business in the current partial exemption year will not exceed £1 million.

Nocturne Ltd satisfied the de minimis condition in respect of the partial exemption year ended 31 March 2024 (condition 1) and there is no reason to believe that conditions 2 and 3 will not be met in relation to the partial exemption year ending 31 March 2025.

Potential benefits to be gained from use of the annual test

The benefits for Nocturne Ltd result from a provisional recovery of all input tax during the partial exemption year ending 31 March 2025 as the company can recover the full amount of input tax suffered in each return period without performing calculations to see if the de minimis tests are satisfied each time.

This will provide a cash flow benefit and an administrative time saving. This administrative time saving is particularly useful as Nocturne Ltd's turnover and associated costs are expected to increase in the year ended 31 March 2025, such that the simplified de minimis tests 1 and 2 may not be satisfied and the more complicated de minimis test 3 might otherwise be required.

Notwithstanding these benefits, an annual adjustment will have to be performed at the end of the year using the de minimis limits for the year as a whole, which may result in the need to repay part of the VAT previously recovered in full.

Examiner's report

The first part concerned two alternative ways in which a computer was to be provided to a shareholder who was not employed by the company. Despite knowing the relevant rules, candidates did not perform as well as they could have done in this part for two reasons. Firstly, they failed to consider all of the aspects of the situation and secondly, they did not answer the question set.

Most candidates appreciated that the provision of the computer would give rise to a distribution but many failed to address the capital allowances position of the company. This was important because it differed in the two alternative situations. Similarly, many candidates failed to address the tax treatment of the loss on the transfer of the existing computer in the second alternative. Candidates will benefit if they think before they write and identify all the different aspects of the transaction. They should then address each of the aspects in a concise manner.

The failure to answer the question set related to the need to determine the after-tax cost for the company. Most candidates focused on the tax treatment for the individual, which meant that they missed out on some of the available marks.

Part (b) concerned Siglio, the company's managing director, who was going to borrow money from a bank and then lend it to the company. Many candidates provided unsatisfactory answers to this question part because they wanted the question to deal with a loan from a close company to a participator in that company – but it wasn't. It was also important to deal with the two loans separately.

The loan to the company was a normal commercial loan. The company would obtain a tax deduction for the interest paid and Siglio would pay income tax on the interest income in the normal way. It was no more complicated than that.

The loan from the bank to Siglio was more interesting in that in that it would be a qualifying loan, such that the interest paid by Siglio would be tax deductible. Some candidates were aware of this point but very few stated the detailed reasons for the tax deduction being available.

The final part of the question concerned VAT and was in two parts.

Part (i) concerned the partial exemption de minimis tests. It was a straight forward test of the rules and was done well by those candidates who knew them. As always, it was important to read the question carefully and to address the requirement and nothing more; some candidates wasted time by addressing other aspects of VAT that were not required. Candidates should recognise that VAT is tested at every sitting and that the partial exemption rules are tested regularly.

Part (ii) concerned the annual test for computing recoverable input tax and was not done well. The problem here was that the majority of candidates addressed the annual accounting scheme rather than the subject of the question. This was unfortunate and meant that very few candidates did well on this part of the question. Candidates should always try to be sure as to what the question is about; both parts of part (b) related to partial exemption.

ACCA marking scheme

				Marks
(a)	Close company			1.0
	Purchase of new computer for Jed			2.5
	Transfer of existing computer to Jed			3.5
	Conclusion			0.5
				7.5
			Maximum	7.0
(b)	Treatment of interest received			2.0
	Conditions for income tax deduction			2.5
	Conclusion re Siglio			0.5
				5.0
			Maximum	4.0
(c)	(i)	De minimis test 1		2.0
		De minimis test 2		2.0
		Conclusion		0.5
				4.5
			Maximum	4.0
	(ii)	Annual test – conditions		2.0
		– Application to Nocturne		1.0
		– Implications		3.0
				6.0
			Maximum	5.0
	Professional skills marks (see below)		**Maximum**	5.0
Total				**25.0**

Professional skills marks

Analysis and evaluation

- Analysis of the information to determine the tax treatment for Nocturne Ltd of the provision of the laptop to Jed in part (a).
- Use of the information to determine appropriate calculations to perform to arrive at the after-tax cost to Nocturne Ltd in part (a).
- Analysis of the information to determine the relevant tax treatment for interest for Siglio in part (b).

Scepticism

- Identification of uncertainty in respect of the working hours of Siglio in part (b).
- Identification of uncertainty regarding the level of expected input tax in the current partial exemption year in part (c)(ii).

Commercial acumen

- Recognition of relevant benefits of using the annual test for partial exemption in part (c)(ii).

58 MARIA AND GRANADA LTD (ADAPTED) *Walk in the footsteps of a top tutor*

Key answer tips

This section B question covers company repurchase of shares, and aspects of the corporation tax and VAT implications of a company acquiring an unincorporated business.

Part (a)(i) requires an understanding of the rules which determine whether the capital (CGT) or income (dividend) treatment will apply to a shareholder's sale of shares back to the company. However, the question focuses specifically on one of the tests required for capital treatment namely that the shareholder's holding must be 'substantially reduced'. This is a new area in ATX and so you should ensure you learn the conditions!

Part (a)(ii) requires calculations for both alternatives. These calculations should have been straightforward even if you were not able to attempt part (a)(i), as you are told in the question to apply each set of rules.

Part (b)(i) requires an explanation of the corporation tax treatment of the acquisition of a brand (i.e. an intangible asset).

Part (b)(ii) focuses on the options and rules for using any losses that the new unincorporated business makes.

Part (c) deals with the VAT implications of the acquisition and the transfer of going concern rules, including the transfer of a property. These rules are some of the most commonly tested from the VAT section of the syllabus.

This question is mostly discursive so lends itself well to the word processor in the exam.

The highlighted words in the written sections are key phrases that markers are looking for in your letter.

(a) (i) Sale of 2,700 shares back to Granada Ltd

Tutor's top tips

This part of the question only requires you to consider the substantial reduction test for a purchase of own shares.

There are no marks for writing about the other conditions that must be satisfied for the capital treatment to apply, so confine your answer to the specific requirement.

For capital gains tax treatment to apply, Maria's shareholding in Granada Ltd must be reduced to no more than 75% of her pre-sale holding.

Maria has a 25% shareholding before the sale. Therefore, after the sale her shareholding must be reduced to no more than 18.75% (75% × 25%).

The total number of shares in issue after the sale will be reduced as the shares repurchased by the company are cancelled.

Maria will hold 7,300 (10,000 – 2,700) shares out of 37,300 ((10,000 × 4) – 2,700) total shares in issue. This is a 19.6% (7,300/37,300 × 100%) holding, i.e. greater than 18.75%, so that the condition relating to the reduction in the level of shareholding will not be met.

Sale of 3,200 shares back to Granada Ltd

Maria will now hold 6,800 (10,000 – 3,200) shares out of 36,800 (40,000 – 3,200) total shares in issue. This is an 18.5% (6,800/36,800 × 100%) holding, i.e. less than 18.75%, so that the condition relating to the reduction in the level of shareholding will be met.

(ii) Sale of 2,700 shares back to Granada Ltd

Tutor's top tips

Remember that whenever an individual sells shares in a company, when dealing with the CGT implications you will need to consider whether business asset disposal relief (BADR) does/does not apply. This particular requirement asks you to 'calculate', so there is no need to provide lengthy explanations.

The income tax payable in respect of each share is £3.98 ((£12.80 – £1.00) × 33.75%). The post-tax proceeds per share are therefore £8.82 (£12.80 – £3.98).

Tutorial note

1. *As Maria does not satisfy all of the conditions for this sale to be dealt with under the capital gains tax rules, the disposal will be treated as an income distribution and Maria will have an income tax liability.*
2. *The net dividend is the difference between the sale proceeds and the amount originally subscribed.*
3. *As Maria is a higher rate taxpayer and has used her £1,000 dividend nil rate band, the rate of tax payable on dividends is 33.75%.*

Sale of 3,200 shares back to Granada Ltd

The capital gains tax payable in respect of each share is £1.18 ((£12.80 – £1.00) × 10%).

The post-tax proceeds per share are therefore £11.62 (£12.80 – £1.18).

Tutorial note

The disposal will qualify for BADR as Maria has owned at least 5% of the ordinary shares of Granada Ltd (a trading company) and has been director of the company for the two years before the disposal. The capital gain arising will therefore be taxed at 10%.

(b) (i) Acquisition of the 'Starling' brand

Tutor's top tips

Although intangibles are treated as trading assets and it is usual, therefore, to simply follow the accounting amortisation deductions for tax, the question requires you to be aware that if no amortisation charges have been made in the accounts it is possible to instead claim a straight line 4% deduction for tax purposes.

As the brand is an intangible asset which has been acquired as part of the 'Starling' trade, it will be treated as a trading asset by Granada Ltd and an allowable deduction will be available in calculating the taxable trading profit each accounting period.

Although Granada Ltd has not made any charge for amortisation in its statement of profit or loss, it may take an annual writing down allowance for tax purposes equal to 4% of the cost of the brand, on a straight-line basis. This would be £1,600 (£40,000 × 4%) per year.

If an election is made to claim the 4% writing down allowance, any accounting debits for impairment would be disallowable for tax purposes. Such an election would be irrevocable.

(ii) Relief for the expected loss from the former Starling Partners' trade

> ***Tutor's top tips***
>
> *Note that the 'major change in nature or conduct of trade' rules only apply to stop the carry forward of trading losses where there has been a change in ownership of a* ***company****, not a change in the ownership of an unincorporated business.*

As Starling Partners is an unincorporated business, Granada Ltd took over ownership of the assets and responsibility for the trade following its acquisition on 1 January 2024.

The forecast trading loss of £130,000 from Starling Partners' handbag trade could be offset against Granada Ltd's total profits for the year ending 31 December 2024, comprising the trading profit from the knitwear business of £100,000 and the chargeable gain of £10,000.

So a loss of £20,000 (£130,000 – £110,000) will be left unrelieved.

As Granada Ltd does not want to carry any of the loss back, the unrelieved loss of £20,000 will be carried forward for relief against future total profits.

Granada Ltd wishes to change the nature of the Starling Partners' trade, by starting to sell to the export market from 1 January 2025. Although this may be seen as a major change in the nature of the trade, it should not serve to prevent the loss incurred in the year ended 31 December 2024 from being carried forward. The impact of a major change in the nature or conduct of a trade in restricting loss relief is only relevant where it precedes or follows a change in ownership of a company, not the acquisition of the trade and assets from an unincorporated business.

Accordingly, based on the expected total profit, all £20,000 of the carried forward loss may be relieved in the year ending 31 December 2025, although Granada Ltd does not have to make a claim to set off the loss in that year.

(c) Value added tax (VAT) implications following the acquisition of the trade and assets of Starling Partners

For VAT purposes, the transfer of Starling Partners' trade and assets qualified as a transfer of a going concern (TOGC). Therefore, no VAT will have been charged on the transfer of the assets generally, and so there will have been no input VAT for Granada Ltd to reclaim.

However, additional information is needed in respect of the building, as its treatment will depend on its age and whether or not the option to tax has been exercised.

Age of the building: If the building was less than three years old at 1 January 2024, its sale would have been a taxable supply, chargeable to VAT at the standard rate.

Option to tax: If the building was at least three years old, its sale would have been exempt from VAT, unless Starling Partners exercised the option to tax.

If the building was less than three years old or Starling Partners had opted to tax the building, then the transfer would have been a taxable supply, chargeable to VAT at the standard-rate. In either case, to bring the transfer of the building within the TOGC regime, so that no VAT is charged, Granada Ltd must also have opted to tax the building, prior to the date of transfer. Alternatively, if Granada Ltd did not opt to tax the building, but uses the building in its business, it may obtain an input credit for the VAT charged.

Examiner's report

Part (a)(i) of this question focused on the requirement for the sale of shares by an individual shareholder to the company to result in a 'substantial reduction' in their shareholding in order to receive capital treatment on the disposal. Unfortunately, it would appear that this is an aspect of a company purchasing its own shares which many candidates are not comfortable with. A small number of candidates just reproduced the conditions to be satisfied in order to obtain capital treatment, which was not required and so scored no marks. Of those candidates who did try to answer this part of the question, the most common mistake was to forget that when a company repurchases shares from a shareholder, the shares are cancelled so that the total issued share capital of the company is reduced as a consequence.

Part (a)(ii) of this question required the calculation of after-tax proceeds on the disposal of two alternative numbers of shares from a shareholding, one of which did qualify for capital treatment and one of which didn't. This information was given in the requirements. In spite of this, a lack of technical knowledge or inadequate reading of the question meant that a significant number of candidates did not apply this and treated both disposals as giving rise to chargeable gains, rather than correctly treating one of them as a distribution. Additionally, many candidates failed to recognise that the disposal which attracted capital treatment would also qualify for business asset disposal relief. In any question regarding the disposal of shares by an individual, candidates should automatically consider the application of business asset disposal relief. This is an area where it is very important to know the precise conditions, to be able to state definitively whether or not the relief applies, and the reasons why, or why not. Candidates who went on to calculate the after-tax proceeds generally identified the correct starting point on this occasion, which was pleasing.

Part (b)(i) concerned the tax deductions available to a company on the acquisition of an intangible asset. There were very few good answers to this part of the question. Intangible assets are examined frequently at ATX, so candidates need to be aware of their tax treatment as trading assets, rather than capital assets, for companies, and the consequential tax treatment of these for corporation tax purposes.

Part (b)(ii) required candidates to explain how the company could get tax relief for a loss incurred by a recently acquired trade. Several candidates incorrectly discussed group relief here. This was not the acquisition of shares in a company, which would have created a group, but the acquisition of trade and assets from a partnership. The two situations are completely different, and candidates must take care to ensure that they read and interpret the facts in this type of question correctly. It appeared that many candidates would have benefited from pausing and thinking more before they started to write. It is important in any question dealing with relief for losses that a well-considered and logical approach is taken. Well-prepared candidates were able to identify that at least part of the trading loss would have to be carried forward.

Note that this part of the question has been adapted since it was originally set.

Part (c) required an explanation of the VAT implications of the acquisition of the business and additional information needed to fully clarify the VAT position in relation to a building. The majority of candidates were able to identify that the transaction would not be liable to VAT as it concerned the transfer of a going concern. Candidates who performed less well on this part, however, then went on to explain why the going concern rules applied, stating all the conditions, but reasons why a particular treatment applies aren't required in a discussion of the VAT implications of that treatment. The VAT rules relating to property are very frequently tested at ATX and it was good to see that the majority of candidates were aware of the main facts here in relation to the age of the building and the existence, or otherwise of an option to tax.

ACCA marking scheme

				Marks
(a)	(i)	Sale of 2,700 shares		3.5
		Sale of 3,200 shares		1.0
				4.5
			Maximum	4.0
	(ii)	Sale of 2,700 shares		2.5
		Sale of 3,200 shares		2.0
				4.5
			Maximum	4.0
(b)	(i)	Entitled to deduction		1.0
		Writing down allowance		1.0
		Impairment/consistent treatment		1.0
				3.0
	(ii)	Current year relief		2.0
		Carry forward		1.5
		No relevance of change in nature of trade		2.0
				5.5
			Maximum	5.0
(c)	General implications of going concern transfer			1.0
	Additional information			4.0
				5.0
			Maximum	4.0
	Professional skills marks (see below)		**Maximum**	5.0
Total				**25.0**

Professional skills marks

Analysis and evaluation

- Analysis of the information to determine the correct treatment of the sale of shares back to Granada Ltd in part (a)(i).
- Use of information to determine appropriate calculations to perform to arrive at the post-tax proceeds per share in part (a)(ii).
- Analysis of the information to determine the relevant VAT treatment for the acquisition of trade and assets in part (c).

Scepticism

- Recognition that additional information about the age of the building is needed in order to determine the appropriate VAT treatment in part (c).

Commercial acumen

- Recognition that the shares will be cancelled following the buy back in part (a)(i).
- Recognition that the election for a 4% writing down allowance is irrevocable in part (b)(i).
- Identification of appropriate loss relief options for Granada Ltd given its request not to carry back in part (b)(ii).

59 ACRYL LTD AND CRESCO LTD (ADAPTED) *Walk in the footsteps of a top tutor*

Key answer tips

This is a two-part company-focused section B question.

Requirement (a) tests liquidations, specifically the effect of the timing of distributions on their corporation tax and income tax treatment.

Requirement (b) tests terminal loss relief for a company.

The highlighted words in the written sections are key phrases that markers are looking for in your answer.

(a) Acryl Ltd

Tutor's top tips

Liquidations are not often tested in the exam, and this question requires precise knowledge of the tax treatment of distributions so you may have struggled here. Note however that as long as you knew that a pre-liquidation dividend was treated as an income distribution and a post-liquidation dividend as a capital distribution, there were straightforward marks available for explaining the income/capital gains tax due!

(i) Implications of the commencement of winding up

The commencement of winding up will lead to the end of an accounting period on 31 December 2024 and the commencement of a new accounting period on 1 January 2025.

Acryl Ltd will remain liable to corporation tax until the winding up is completed. Accordingly, a corporation tax computation is required for each of the two accounting periods: the first from 1 July 2024 to 31 December 2024, and the second from 1 January 2025 to 31 March 2025.

(ii) Distribution on 31 December 2024

In this case the distribution will be made prior to the commencement of winding up and therefore will be treated as an income distribution (i.e. a normal dividend) for tax purposes for both shareholders.

Mambo Ltd will not be subject to corporation tax on this dividend as companies are not subject to corporation tax on dividends.

Alan will be subject to income tax on the dividend. The first £1,000 will be subject to income tax at 0% as it is covered by the dividend nil rate band. The excess above £1,000 will be subject to income tax at 39.35% as Alan is an additional rate taxpayer.

Tutorial note

The question states that Alan's only income in the tax year 2024/25 will be a salary from Acryl Ltd. This information is included so you know that the dividend nil rate band is available to set against a distribution from Acryl Ltd that is treated as a dividend.

*Remember, the dividend nil rate band of £1,000 is available to taxpayers **regardless** of their taxable income. In contrast, the amount of savings income nil rate band available is different depending on whether the individual is a basic rate taxpayer (£1,000), a higher rate tax payer (£500) or an additional rate taxpayer (£Nil).*

Distribution on 31 March 2025

As the distribution will be made while the company is in liquidation, it will be treated as a capital receipt on disposal of the shares in Acryl Ltd for both shareholders.

Mambo Ltd should not be subject to corporation tax on the disposal as it should qualify as a disposal out of a substantial shareholding. Mambo Ltd will have held at least 10% of the shares in Acryl Ltd for more than 12 continuous months out of the six years preceding the disposal and Acryl Ltd is a trading company.

Alan will be subject to capital gains tax on any gain arising. As Alan is eligible for business asset disposal relief on the disposal of his Acryl Ltd shares, capital gains tax will be charged at 10% on the taxable gain.

Conclusion

Mambo Ltd will not be subject to corporation tax under either alternative but Alan would probably prefer 31 March 2025 as he is likely to suffer a lower rate of tax if the distribution is made on this date.

Tutorial note

It is not necessary to consider the possibility of a capital loss on receipt of the distribution on 31 March 2025. Mambo Ltd and Alan subscribed for the shares at par, so they will have a very low base cost and Acryl Ltd has substantial distributable profits.

(b) (i) Cresco Ltd – relief for trading losses

Tutor's top tips

Losses tend to appear in every exam, typically in a sole trader/partnership question or a corporation tax question, so you need to be ready for them!

In this question there were three losses to deal with which you may have found daunting. Remember to consider them in chronological order, the 2021 loss first, and then the two losses arising in the final two periods. Terminal loss relief only applies to losses generated in the final twelve months of trading, so you will need to apportion the loss for the year ended 31 May 2024.

You may find it easiest to set out the loss workings in the spreadsheet response option in the exam, with any notes produced in the word processor. Where using both response options ensure it is clear which part of your answer is in which response option.

	Year ended 31 May 2021	Year ended 31 May 2022	Year ended 31 May 2023	Year ended 31 May 2024	Period ended 31 December 2024
	£	£	£	£	£
Trading income	0	17,000	8,000	0	0
Bank interest receivable	5,000	3,000	3,000	0	0
	5,000	20,000	11,000		
Less:					
Loss for y/e 31 May 2021 (Note 1)	(5,000)				
Loss for y/e 31 May 2024 (Note 2)			(11,000)		
Loss for the 12 m/e 31 December 2024 (Note 3)		(20,000)			
	0	0	0	0	0

Losses unrelieved:

	£
Year ended 31 May 2024:	
(£24,000 – £11,000 – £10,000)	3,000
Terminal loss: (£50,000 – £20,000)	30,000
Total unrelieved:	33,000

Tutorial note

£10,000 of the trading loss in the year ended 31 May 2024 is included as part of the terminal loss and used against the profits of the year ended 31 May 2022 (see note 3 below).

Notes:

1 The trading loss for the year ended 31 May 2021 of £5,000 will have been relieved against the £5,000 of bank interest (total profits) in the year.

2 As there is no other income or gains in the year ended 31 May 2024, the trading loss of £24,000 will have been carried back and offset against the total profits in the year ended 31 May 2023 of £11,000 (£8,000 + 3,000). £13,000 of the loss remains unrelieved. However, £10,000 of this forms part of the terminal loss (see note 3).

3 As Cresco Ltd has ceased to trade on 31 December 2024, the loss of the last 12 months of trading is a terminal loss which is eligible to be carried back up to 36 months. The loss available for such relief is £50,000 (£40,000 + (£24,000 × 5/12), including the five months of loss for the period from 1 January 2024 to 31 May 2024. As there are no profits remaining in the years ended 31 May 2024 or 2023, the loss can be offset against the total profits of £20,000 (£17,000 + £3,000) in the year ended 31 May 2022.

(ii) Value added tax (VAT) implications of the cessation of trade

Tutor's top tips

VAT implications of cessation of trade is a commonly tested topic so make sure you learn the rules.

Cresco Ltd must notify HM Revenue and Customs of the cessation of its business within 30 days of ceasing to make taxable supplies.

Output tax must be accounted for on any business assets it still holds at the date of cessation of trade in respect of which input tax was previously recovered. However, there is no need to account for this output tax if it is less than £1,000.

Examiner's report

Part (a)(i) required candidates to state the corporation tax implications arising for a company as a result of the appointment of a liquidator. The commencement of winding up/appointment of a liquidator is one of the factors which will bring a company's accounting period for corporation tax purposes to an end. This was worth only two marks, but most candidates appeared to not be aware of the impact on a company's accounting periods and so scored zero on this question part.

Part (a)(ii) was a 'textbook' question requiring an explanation of the tax implications for both an individual and a corporate shareholder of a distribution being made alternatively before the commencement of liquidation or on completion of the winding up. Answers were very mixed. A good number of candidates realised that the distribution would be taxed as a dividend prior to commencement of liquidation, but as a capital receipt once liquidation had commenced, although a surprising number were not aware of this distinction. For those candidates who realised this, the majority were able to go on and correctly identify the tax implications for the individual shareholder, but, disappointingly, not for the corporate shareholder. Many candidates referred to the corporate shareholder paying corporation tax on both of these, thereby failing to recognise that dividends are not taxable on corporate shareholders, and that the substantial shareholding exemption would apply in the case of the capital receipt. These are both fundamental points which candidates at ATX need to be very familiar with, as they can be tested in a variety of different scenarios.

In part (b)(i) candidates were required to show how a company could relieve trading losses incurred in its last few periods of account. This involved consideration of loss relief in an ongoing company, in addition to the availability of terminal loss relief. It is important in any question dealing with relief for losses that a well-considered and chronological approach is taken. Precise explanations of the reliefs are required in these sorts of questions. Well-prepared candidates were able to deal correctly with the earlier losses in accounting periods prior to the final period, and were aware that, on cessation, an extended three year carry back is available, but almost all neglected to correctly calculate the loss which was available for this terminal loss relief. Nevertheless, those who adopted a sensible, logical approach scored well on this question part.

Part (b)(ii) required candidates to explain the VAT implications for the company of ceasing to trade. Many candidates were clearly confident with this situation and scored the full three marks available.

ACCA marking scheme

			Marks
(a)	(i)	Effect on accounting periods	1.0
		Two computations required	1.0
			2.0
	(ii)	Distribution 31 December 2024	3.0
		Distribution 31 March 2025	5.0
		Recommendation with reason	1.0
			9.0
		Maximum	7.0

(b)	(i)	Loss year ended 31 May 2021		0.5
		Loss year ended 31 May 2024		1.5
		Terminal loss		5.0
		Loss unrelieved		1.0
				8.0
	(ii)	Notify HMRC		1.0
		Output tax on assets held on cessation		2.0
				3.0
	Professional skills marks (see below)		**Maximum**	5.0
Total				**25.0**

Professional skills marks

Analysis and evaluation

- Use of information to determine the tax implications of winding up in part (a)(i).
- Analysis of the information to determine whether a pre or post liquidation distribution would be preferable for both shareholders in part (a)(ii).
- Use of the information from the scenario to prepare logical calculations in respect of the available loss reliefs for Cresco Ltd in part (b)(i).
- Use of the information to determine the VAT implications of the cessation of trade for Cresco Ltd in part (b)(ii).

Commercial acumen

- Recognition that the substantial shareholding exemption would be relevant to the distribution on 31 March 2025 to Mambo Ltd in part (a)(ii).
- Identification of appropriate loss relief options for Cresco Ltd given its preference to claim relief as early as possible in part (b)(i).

60 TRAISTE LTD (ADAPTED) ***Walk in the footsteps of a top tutor***

Key answer tips

This question covers the tax implications of making an employee redundant, the post-tax proceeds on a sale of shares and the extraction of profits from a company by a director shareholder.

Requirement (a) tests redundancy payments, which regularly feature in the exam.

Requirement (b) tests the sale of shares by an individual, either to another individual or back to the company.

Requirement (c) covers payment of a bonus versus a dividend, but in terms of the payments made by the company to HMRC.

These three parts could be answered in any order.

The highlighted words in the written sections are key phrases that markers are looking for in your answer.

(a) Redundancy package provided to Esta

Tutor's top tips

The car benefit received by Esta after she is made redundant is treated in the same way as the ex gratia payment.

(i) Income tax implications for Esta

The statutory redundancy pay is exempt from income tax. However, it reduces the £30,000 exemption available for ex-gratia payments.

To the extent that the ex-gratia payment exceeds the remainder of the £30,000 exemption, the excess will be charged to income tax at Esta's highest marginal rate of income tax.

The continuing use of the company car will be valued according to the normal rules for calculating the cash equivalent of this taxable benefit. It will be wholly taxable as the £30,000 exemption is initially allocated, and has already been applied, to the cash receipts.

(ii) Corporation tax deductions for Traiste Ltd

Tutor's top tips

Be careful here! The amount deductible for Traiste Ltd will not be the same as the amount taxable on Esta.

The amount deductible by Traiste Ltd in respect of the redundancy package for Esta is as follows:

	£
Statutory redundancy	12,000
Ex-gratia payment	36,000
Lease payments: ((£420 × 6) × 85%)	2,142
Class 1A national insurance contributions ((£18,000 (W1) + £2,944 (W2)) × 13.8%)	2,890
	53,032

Workings

(W1) Ex-gratia payment

Class 1A national insurance is payable on the excess of the ex-gratia payment: £36,000 – (£30,000 – £12,000) = £18,000

(W2) Car benefit

The car benefit for Esta is £2,944 (£18,400 × 32% (16% + (135 – 55)/5) × 6/12).

(b) Kat – proposed sale of shares

Tutor's top tips

The sale of shares to Jordi is a simple sale of shares to another individual, requiring a standard capital gains tax computation.

However, the sale of shares to Traiste Ltd would be a purchase of own shares, for which there are two possible tax treatments:

– *Income treatment*

– *Capital treatment (if conditions are satisfied).*

To Jordi

On the sale of the shares to Jordi, a chargeable gain will arise, calculated by reference to the market value of the shares as Kat and Jordi are connected persons. A chargeable gain of £25,500 (500 × (£52 – £1) will therefore arise on the disposal.

As Kat has held at least 5% of the shares in Traiste Ltd for at least than two years, and works for the company, business asset disposal relief applies.

As Kat has already used her annual exempt amount for the tax year 2024/25, there will be a capital gains tax liability of £2,550 (£25,500 × 10%).

Kat's after-tax proceeds will be £20,950 ((500 × £47) – £2,550).

To Traiste Ltd

As Kat wishes to sell her shares before the end of 2024, the disposal will not qualify for capital treatment as she will not have owned the shares for the requisite five years until 1 March 2025. She will therefore be taxed on the receipt as a dividend.

She will be treated as receiving a dividend of £25,500 (500 × (£52 – £1)). This will be taxed as follows:

	£
Balance of the nil rate band for dividends: £500 (£1,000 – £500) at 0%	0
Balance of the basic rate band (W): £8,920 (£9,420 – £500) at 8.75%	781
Balance of the dividend: £16,080 (£25,500 – £500 – £8,920) at 33.75%	5,427
Income tax on dividend	6,208

Working: Basic rate band remaining

	£
Employment income	40,350
Dividend	500
Less: Personal allowance	(12,570)
Taxable income	28,280
Basic rate band	(37,700)
Basic rate band remaining	9,420

Tutorial note

The dividend income taxed at the nil rate reduces the remaining basic rate band.

After-tax proceeds are £19,792 ((500 × £52) – £6,208).

The sale of the shares to Jordi will therefore be preferable as it will leave Kat with the higher after-tax proceeds.

(c) Jordi – extraction of profits

Tutor's top tips

The requirement is to explain the payments made by Traiste Ltd to HMRC in respect of the bonus or dividend, ***not*** *to calculate the tax suffered by Jordi.*

However, you still need to consider the tax suffered by Jordi on the bonus in order to work out the gross bonus paid and the amounts deducted by the company under PAYE.

Payment of bonus

Traiste Ltd will have to account for income tax and class 1 employee's and employer's national insurance contributions (NICs), under the PAYE regulations.

Jordi will suffer deduction of income tax at the rate of 40%, and employee's NICs at the rate of 2% on the gross amount of the bonus. The gross amount payable will therefore need to be £34,483 (£20,000/0.58).

The total amount payable to HM Revenue and Customs (HMRC) by Traiste Ltd will be:

	£
Income tax on £34,483 at 40%	13,793
Employee's NICs on £34,483 at 2%	690
Employer's NICs on £34,483 at 13.8%	4,759
	19,242

This is due for payment by 22 April 2025.

Payment of dividend

No payments to HMRC will be required from Traiste Ltd.

Examiner's report

The first part concerned the redundancy of an employee. This part of the question consisted of two tasks.

Candidates did not have any particular difficulties with the first task which required them to explain the income tax implications of the redundancy package. Many answers were pleasingly concise and the relevant rules were well known by the majority of candidates.

However, candidates did not fare so well with the second task which required them to calculate the corporation tax deductions in respect of the redundancy package.

The main problem was that many candidates were unable to think in terms of 'allowable cost' as opposed to 'tax'. This led to candidates identifying the employment income benefit as the cost to the company as opposed to the cost of leasing the vehicle.

The second part of the question required candidates to explain the post-tax proceeds on a sale of shares. This is a part of the syllabus which candidates tend to be familiar with, such that most candidates should be able to do well. However, although this part was done very well by some candidates it was done poorly by others. The problem was that candidates did not spend sufficient time thinking about what was going on in the question. The shareholder was either going to sell the shares to an individual or was going to sell them back to the company. This latter disposal was, of course, a purchase of own shares by the company, but this was missed by many candidates.

Other common errors included; failing to recognise that the sale to the individual would be deemed to take place at market value because the vendor and the purchaser were connected persons and failing to identify the availability of business asset disposal relief.

On the plus side, the majority of candidates handled the concept of post-tax proceeds well in that they correctly deducted the tax liability from the proceeds received.

The final part of the question concerned the extraction of profits from a company by a director shareholder. The question required candidates to explain the payments to be made by the **employing company** to HM Revenue and Customs.

Unfortunately, many candidates failed to notice this precise aspect of the requirement, such that they simply focused on the recipient individual's tax liabilities in respect of the amounts received as opposed to the amounts which would be paid by the company in respect of the payments made. As a result, many candidates did not do as well as they could have in this part.

Candidates who did well in this question:

- had a precise knowledge of the various detailed rules
- read the requirements carefully and ensured that they answered the question set.

ACCA marking scheme

				Marks
(a)	(i)	Income tax implications for Esta		4.0
			Maximum	3.0
	(ii)	Cash payments deductible		1.0
		Car lease		1.5
		Class 1A national insurance contributions		3.0
				5.5
			Maximum	4.0
(b)	Sale of shares to Jordi			4.5
	Sale of shares to Traiste Ltd			5.0
				9.5
			Maximum	8.0
(c)	Payment of bonus			4.0
	Payment of dividend			1.0
				5.0
	Professional skills marks (see below)		**Maximum**	5.0
Total				**25.0**

Professional skills marks

Analysis and evaluation

- Use of information to determine income tax implications for each element of Esta's redundancy package in part (a)(i).
- Appropriate use of the data to determine relevant calculations to perform to arrive at the deductible amount for Traiste Ltd in respect of the redundancy package in part (a)(ii).
- Analysis of the information to determine appropriate calculations to perform to arrive at the after-tax proceeds for Kat in each disposal scenario in part (b).
- Appropriate use of the data to determine relevant calculations to perform to arrive at the gross amount of bonus payable to Jordi in part (c).
- Demonstration of ability to consider all taxes relevant to part (c), i.e. income tax and national insurance contributions.

Commercial acumen

- Demonstration of an understanding of the rules around termination packages in part (a).
- Identification of the availability of business asset disposal relief for Kat in part(b).

61 DENT LTD (ADAPTED)

Key answer tips

This question is made up of three separate requirements which could be attempted in any order.

Part (a) covers VAT registration and requires you to consider the input VAT recovery implications of registering for VAT as well as explaining why voluntary registration would be beneficial. There are six marks for this requirement so you need to ensure you consider all aspects of input VAT and not just that incurred after registration.

Part (b) asks you to explain the corporation tax treatment of the R&D expenditure and calculate the allowable deduction for corporation tax purposes. There are four different costs incurred so you need to ensure you explain the treatment of each of them, as some of them may be treated differently. Once you have done this you can summarise your findings with the calculation.

In the final part of the question you need to explain the income tax treatment of a lump sum and calculate after tax employment costs for the company. In these calculations it is important that you think about any associated employer's NIC costs for the income and benefits provided, as well as what corporation tax saving will be available. Remember that Alina is working on the R&D project so some of the costs may be eligible for extra relief.

(a) Compulsory registration for value added tax (VAT) and why voluntary registration is beneficial

If Dent Ltd registers for VAT on 1 April 2025, it can make a claim to recover input tax suffered on goods and services purchased prior to registration as follows:

Input tax may be recovered on assets which have been purchased for the purpose of the business in the four years prior to registration, provided they are still held by Dent Ltd on 1 April 2025. Thus, Dent Ltd will be able to recover the VAT paid on the purchase of the specialist equipment. However, VAT will not be recoverable on the cost of the consumables which have been consumed prior to 1 April 2025.

Input tax may be recovered on the supply of services for the purpose of the business, which were supplied within the six months prior to registration. Accordingly, Dent Ltd will not be able to recover input VAT on a proportion of the property costs and the agency fees which relate to the period from 1 July 2024 to 30 September 2024.

If Dent Ltd registers for VAT on 1 July 2024, all the VAT suffered on the goods and services supplied from commencement of the business will be recoverable. Additionally, there will be a cash flow advantage for Dent Ltd as it is likely to be in a repayment position in at least the first of its VAT returns.

Although Dent Ltd will have to charge VAT on its taxable supplies from 1 July 2024, this will not be a problem for its customers, as they will all be VAT registered and therefore able to reclaim any VAT charged.

(b) Corporation tax relief available in respect of the research and development (R&D) expenditure

The expenditure on the specialist equipment qualifies for a 100% capital allowance as it is capital expenditure on an asset to be used for R&D purposes.

As Dent Ltd is a small enterprise for the purposes of R&D expenditure, an additional 86% deduction is available in calculating the company's taxable trading income in respect of qualifying revenue expenditure which is directly related to the R&D activities. In this case, this will apply to the property costs (as they comprise only heat, light and water charges), consumables and the staff costs (including the pension contributions). However, this additional relief is restricted in respect of the contractor supplied by the agency (as an unconnected third party) to 65% of the cost, i.e. £16,250 (65% × £25,000).

Therefore, the total deduction available to Dent Ltd in the year ending 30 June 2025 is £554,455 (£353,000 + (86% × (£46,000 + £12,000 + (£185,000 – £25,000 + £16,250)))).

(c) Lump sum payment and provision of computer and temporary living accommodation to Alina

Income tax implications for Alina of receiving the lump sum payment

The lump sum payment is fully taxable on Alina in the tax year 2024/25 as it relates to future services to be performed by her.

Tutorial note

This sort of lump sum payment given to induce employment is often referred to as a 'golden hello'. It is taxable when it is received as it relates to future services to be provided by the employee.

After-tax cost to Dent Ltd

Lump sum payment

	£
Amount of payment	10,000
Class 1 employer national insurance contributions (NIC) (£10,000 × 13.8%)	1,380
Pre-tax cost of lump sum payment	11,380

This is eligible for the additional 86% deduction as it is qualifying R&D expenditure, so the tax-deductible amount for Dent Ltd is £21,167 (£11,380 × 186%).

Provision of computer and temporary living accommodation

	£
Rent paid (£660 × 6)	3,960
Class 1A NICs (£4,110 (W) × 13.8%)	567
Pre-tax cost of the temporary living accommodation	4,527
Cost of computer	1,000
Pre-tax cost of the provision of computer and temporary living accommodation	5,527

The total tax-deductible amount is £26,694 (£21,167 + £4,527 + £1,000)

	£
Total pre-tax cost to Dent Ltd (£11,380 + £5,527)	16,907
Less: Corporation tax relief: (£26,694 × 25%)	(6,674)
After-tax cost	10,233

Working

	£
Taxable benefits for Alina in the tax year 2024/25:	
Computer (£1,000 × 20% × 9/12)	150
Accommodation benefit: Higher of	
(i) annual value = £1,400 (£2,800 × 6/12)	
(ii) rent paid by Dent Ltd = £3,960 (£660 × 6)	3,960
Taxable benefit	4,110

Tutorial note

1 *The provision of taxable benefits to an employee is not qualifying expenditure for the purpose of the additional 86% deduction for R&D expenditure.*

2 *Dent Ltd can claim AIA on the cost of the computer.*

Examiner's report

This question was in three main parts, dealing with VAT, research and development (R&D) expenditure and income tax and national insurance. The first part of the question asked for two VAT scenarios to be discussed. The first scenario concerned the implications of compulsory registration and the second scenario concerned the benefits of an earlier voluntary registration. Many candidates did not deal with these two scenarios separately and answered generally about VAT registration and so did not achieve all of the available marks. Some candidates gave detailed rules regarding when VAT registration would become compulsory, which was not asked for and earned no marks. A number of candidates were clear on the rules for input tax recovery on pre-registration expenditure but unfortunately did not apply the rules to the facts of the question.

The second part of the question required an explanation of the tax treatment of the R&D expenditure incurred and a calculation of the available R&D deduction relating to this expenditure. The question specifically stated that the company was a small enterprise for the purposes of R&D expenditure and yet a number of candidates discussed R&D tax relief in a large company as well as a small company. These candidates spent time providing explanations for which although correct, there were no marks awarded. Unfortunately, many candidates appeared to be unsure of the tax relief available for R&D capital expenditure but seemed to have a much better understanding of the basics of tax relief for R&D revenue expenditure.

Note that R&D relief for large companies is no longer on the ATX syllabus.

The third part of the question concerned a lump sum payment and the provision of benefits-in-kind by a company to an employee. Candidates were required to state the income tax implications of the lump sum payment for the employee and to calculate the after-tax cost for the company of providing the payment and the benefits-in-kind. Initially candidates needed to calculate the value of the lump sum payment and each benefit-in-kind and then calculate the employer's national insurance contributions. They then needed to add the actual cost of the payment and the benefits-in-kind to the employer's national insurance contributions and deduct the corporation tax saving from the total. It was pleasing to see that many candidates were able to deal well with these requirements. However, some candidates did not recognise the difference between the actual cost to the employer of providing the benefits-in-kind and the taxable value of the benefits-in-kind in the hands of the employee.

ACCA marking scheme			
			Marks
(a)	Pre-registration expenditure – goods		3.0
	Pre-registration expenditure – services		1.5
	Benefits of voluntary registration		2.5
			7.0
		Maximum	6.0
(b)	Capital expenditure – explanation		1.0
	Additional deduction for revenue expenditure – explanation		3.5
	Total deduction – calculation		2.0
			6.5
		Maximum	6.0

(c)	Income tax implications for Alina		1.0
	Pre-tax cost of lump sum payment		2.5
	Pre-tax cost of computer and living accommodation		4.0
	Total pre-tax expenditure		0.5
	Corporation tax saving		0.5
			8.5
		Maximum	8.0
	Professional skills marks (see below)	**Maximum**	5.0
Total			**25.0**

Professional skills marks

Analysis and evaluation

- Use of information to identify at least one implication of VAT registration in part (a).
- Appropriate use of the data to determine relevant calculations to perform to calculate the total deduction available to Dent Ltd in respect of the R&D expenditure in part (b).
- Appropriate use of the data to determine relevant calculations to perform to arrive at the after-tax cost of providing the benefits to Alina in part (c).
- Demonstration of ability to consider all relevant taxes in part (c), i.e. income tax, national insurance contributions and corporation tax.

Commercial acumen

- Demonstration of an understanding of the impact of VAT registration on cash flow and customers in part (a).
- Identification of restriction of reliefs for R&D expenditure in part (b).

62 SAMPHIRE LTD AND KELP LTD (ADAPTED)

Key answer tips

This question covers the provision of benefits to a director/shareholder, which incorporates assumed knowledge from the TX exam as well as dealing with the close company rules. There is also the disposal of a leased factory, which triggers a chargeable gain, and the purchase of a new factory and warehouse which enables a rollover relief claim.

Part (a) requires in-depth knowledge of the close company rules and the impact of providing either an asset or a loan to a director who is also a participator. You are told in the question that Samphire Ltd is a close company and this is a key hint in the scenario which will help you to approach this part of the question. You also need to be confident about how to establish whether a company is a close company, as this information may not always be provided in the question.

Note that for both sub-parts of part (a) you are required to explain as well as performing the calculations. This means that you should have some writing to support your figures, and you will not be able to score well without this.

Part (b) is a chargeable gains question covering the disposal of a lease on a factory and the outright purchase of a new factory and warehouse. The question is split into two sub requirements Part (b)(i) is purely computational and requires the use of lease percentages provided in the question. This is worth two marks and should be straightforward to calculate.

Part (b)(ii) requires an explanation, along with supporting calculations, of the gain left chargeable after the consideration of rollover relief. However, you need to read the scenario carefully as full rollover relief is not available. There are seven marks available for this part of the requirement; with so many marks available this is unlikely to be a straightforward rollover relief question.

(a) **(i)** **Alternative 1: Gift of a computer to Nori**

The transfer of the computer to Nori will not result in a balancing charge on the main pool, as the proceeds will be £Nil.

The transfer of the computer will also be a disposal of a chattel by Samphire Ltd, but this will be an exempt disposal as both cost and deemed proceeds are less than £6,000.

As Nori is a director of Samphire Ltd, the gift of the computer will give rise to a taxable benefit of £1,500, i.e. the market value of the computer at the date of the gift. Accordingly, there will be a class 1A national insurance contributions (NIC) liability for Samphire Ltd of £207 (£1,500 × 13.8%). Corporation tax relief of £52 (£207 × 25%) will be available in respect of this.

Therefore, the total additional taxes payable in respect of this alternative for Samphire Ltd are £155 (£207 – £52).

(ii) **Alternative 2: Make a loan to Nori**

Samphire Ltd is a close company. Accordingly, on making a loan to Nori, a participator, it must make a payment of notional tax of £506 (£1,500 × 33.75%) to HM Revenue and Customs (HMRC). This payment will be due by 1 January 2027. Following the write off of the loan (on 6 April 2027), HMRC will repay all the notional tax to Samphire Ltd, (by 1 January 2029).

Writing off the loan is treated as a distribution, so there will be no corporation tax implications for Samphire Ltd.

Although the loan is interest-free, it will not give rise to a taxable benefit for Nori. This is because the total amount of the loan will not exceed £10,000 at any time. Accordingly, Samphire Ltd will not have any liability to Class 1A NIC.

However, a liability to class 1 NIC will arise on writing off the loan on 6 April 2027, as Nori is also an employee of the company. Accordingly, Samphire Ltd will have a class 1 NIC liability of £207 (£1,500 × 13.8%) and corporation tax relief in respect of this of £52 (£207 × 25%).

Therefore, the total additional taxes payable in respect of this alternative for Samphire Ltd is also £155 (£207 – £52).

(b) (i) Gain on the sale of the lease

	£
Proceeds	206,000
Less: Cost (£165,000 × 96.593/99.289)	(160,520)
Chargeable gain	45,480

Tutorial notes

1 *This requirement was to calculate the gain on the sale of the lease of Factory 1. Technically this is an 'assignment of a short lease'. The cost figure needs to be restricted by reference to the lease percentages provided in the question but you also need to remember to apply the indexation allowance, as this is a disposal by a company.*

2 *There is no indexation allowance in respect of the lease since it was purchased after December 2017.*

(ii) Gain remaining chargeable after claiming the maximum amount of rollover relief.

Kelp Ltd owned the lease on Factory 1 for six years from 1 November 2018 to 1 November 2024. However, it did not occupy the building for trading purposes during the last six months of ownership from 1 May 2024 to 1 November 2024. Accordingly, only £41,690 (£45,480 × 5.5/6) of the gain is eligible for rollover relief.

In order to relieve the whole of this eligible gain, Kelp Ltd must reinvest £188,833 (£206,000 × 5.5/6) in qualifying business assets within the four-year period commencing one year before the disposal of Factory 1.

The factory acquired from Samphire Ltd (Factory 2) is a qualifying business asset, acquired within the year prior to the disposal of Factory 1. Kelp Ltd and Samphire Ltd are not in a gains group, as they are owned by an individual, not a company. Accordingly, the price paid by Kelp Ltd of £138,000 is its relevant acquisition cost. As Kelp Ltd will use Factory 2 wholly for trading purposes, the full amount of £138,000 is the qualifying cost for rollover relief purposes.

The warehouse to be acquired by Kelp Ltd is also a qualifying business asset, and it will be acquired within the three years following the disposal of Factory 1. However, as only 70% of the warehouse will be used by Kelp Ltd in its trade, only £54,600 (£78,000 × 70%) of its cost will be a qualifying acquisition for rollover relief purposes.

Accordingly, £192,600 (£138,000 + £54,600) has been reinvested in qualifying business assets. As this exceeds £188,833, the whole of the eligible gain of £41,690 can be deferred, leaving an immediately chargeable gain of £3,790 (£45,480 – £41,690).

Examiner's report

Requirement (a)

This part of the question concerned a UK resident close trading company which was looking to either make a gift of a computer to a director of the company or a loan to the same director to allow him to purchase the computer himself.

Requirement (a)(i)

The requirement here was to explain, with supporting calculations, the total additional taxes payable by Samphire Ltd if the company gifts the computer to the director.

It is important to focus on the requirement here and to break it down – first of all, 'explain, with supporting calculations' means providing a combination of words and numbers in the answer. Secondly, the reference to 'total' additional taxes implies that there will be more than one additional tax which is relevant and that therefore the sum of all of them should eventually be provided. Thirdly, the question refers to the total additional taxes 'payable by Samphire Ltd', and not by the director. Some candidates discussed the additional taxes payable by the latter; this did not earn credit because it was not what was required. It is always worth double checking a requirement to ensure that it is fully understood, perhaps by highlighting the key words in order to ensure that candidates are doing exactly what it is they are being asked to do.

The question stated that the written down value of the main pool, where the computer would originally have been allocated, was £Nil and that the sale proceeds for the purpose of capital allowances were also £Nil. This therefore indicated that there would be no balancing charge on the main pool as a result of the gift.

The gift of a capital asset should also lead to a consideration of the capital gains consequences for the company although on this occasion this was an exempt disposal, the cost and sale proceeds of the computer both being less than £6,000.

Since the gift of the computer was to a director of the company, this would also constitute a taxable benefit for the individual. However, it was only the tax implications for the company of making the gift which were relevant on this occasion. The provision of the asset by way of gift will mean that the company will have to pay class 1A national insurance contributions (NIC) on the taxable benefit amount, which will then be tax deductible for the company when calculating its corporation tax liability.

Thus the total additional taxes payable by the company are the class 1A NIC cost less the 25% corporation tax relief thereon.

Requirement (a)(ii)

This part of the question required an explanation, together with supporting calculations, of the total additional taxes payable by Samphire Ltd if the company were to make a £1,500 loan to the director, and then to write off that loan two years later.

Once again, it is advisable to break down the requirement and highlight the key words. Candidates were being asked to explain and give supporting calculations, so both did need to be provided here. They were asked for total additional taxes, implying once again the need to consider more than one tax, and then total them all up. And finally, they were being asked for additional taxes payable by the company, not the director, so this should be kept in mind when preparing the answer.

Many candidates correctly identified that, since this was a loan from a close company to a director who is also a shareholder, this would result in a notional tax charge being payable by the company. Several then went on to discuss what would have happened if the loan was repaid, but in doing so failed to pick up on the facts of the question where they were specifically told that the loan would be written off in two years' time.

This write-off would lead to repayment of the notional tax, meaning that the overall tax cost to the company will be £Nil.

There would however be a cashflow impact because, having paid the notional tax, the company would have to wait two years for its repayment from HMRC. The write-off of the loan itself would be classified as a distribution so there would be no corporation tax implications from the company's perspective. There were however some further consequences which needed to be considered and many candidates did not go on to think about these. These involved the national insurance cost to the company.

The loan would not give rise to a taxable benefit for the director because, although interest free, it was below the £10,000 threshold. This means there will be no class 1A NIC liability for Samphire Ltd.

However, when a loan to a director gets written off, class 1 NICs will be payable by the company on the amount of the write-off; this will then be tax deductible for the company when calculating its corporation tax liability.

Therefore, in conclusion, the total additional taxes payable by the company under this alternative scenario are the class 1 NIC cost of the write-off as reduced by the 25% corporation tax saving on that amount.

Requirement (b)

This part of the question involved a different company, Kelp Ltd, which was disposing of a lease on a building and acquiring a factory and a warehouse.

Requirement (b)(i)

This section of the examiner's report has been amended due to legislative changes made to the answer.

This requirement was to calculate the gain on the sale of the lease of Factory 1. Technically this is an 'assignment of a short lease'. The calculation of the chargeable gain involves the usual 'Sale proceeds less cost' but, in view of the wasting nature of the asset involved, the cost figure needs to be restricted by reference to the lease percentages provided in the question.

Requirement (b)(ii)

This part of the question required an explanation, with supporting calculations, of the amount of the chargeable gain calculated in part (b)(i) remaining liable to corporation tax, after taking advantage of maximum rollover relief claims

Once again, a full analysis of the requirement is important before starting to work on the answer. Explanations and calculations need to be provided. Having worked out the maximum rollover relief, it is then necessary to go to state how much of the gain will remain liable to corporation tax after the rollover relief claim has been made

Firstly, before even considering the replacement assets acquired, it is necessary to consider how much of the gain arising on the disposal of the lease on Factory 1 is eligible for rollover relief.

The question states that Factory 1 was owned for 6 years but only used for trading purposes for 5 years and 6 months, having been rented out for the final six months of ownership. Consequently, only 5.5/6 of the gain is eligible for rollover relief i.e. £45,480 × 5.5/6 = £41,690.

This also means that Kelp Ltd must reinvest 5.5/6 of the sale proceeds from Factory 1, if this gain is to be rolled over in full i.e. £206,000 × 5.5/6 = £188,833.

So to summarise, with regard to the asset being disposed of, there are two items which have to be pro-rated for non-trade use; namely the gain and the amount of sale proceeds which need to be reinvested.

Looking now at the assets in which Kelp Ltd has reinvested, these must be qualifying business assets purchased within the four-year period commencing one year before the disposal of Factory 1.

In the scenario Kelp Ltd acquires Factory 2 from Samphire Ltd. Kelp Ltd and Samphire Ltd are both owned by the same individual, Nori. Many candidates thought that this therefore meant that they were in a single gains group but this would only have been correct if they had been owned by a company, and not an individual. As such, since Factory 2 is to be wholly used for trading purposes, its full cost of £138,000 counts as qualifying expenditure for rollover relief purposes.

Kelp also acquires a second property within the relevant four-year time-frame, namely the warehouse. But this is only to be used 70% for trade purposes. Therefore, only 70% of the cost of the warehouse counts as qualifying expenditure for rollover relief purposes i.e. 70% × £78,000 = £54,600.

All of the above figures now need to be brought together in order to answer the question. The total qualifying acquisition cost of Factory 2 and the warehouse comes to £138,000 + £54,600 = £192,600. Since this amount is greater than the relevant sale proceeds from the sale of Factory 1 i.e. £188,833, it means that the whole of the eligible gain of £41,690 can be rolled over. However, it should be noted that the question actually asks for the amount of chargeable gain remaining liable to corporation tax, after a maximum rollover claim; given that £41,690 of the total gain of £45,480 is being rolled over, this leaves an amount of gain of £3,790 which is left in charge. This amount needed to be stated in order to answer the question fully

ACCA marking scheme

				Marks
(a)	(i)	Tax implications of transfer		1.5
		Class 1A national insurance contributions (NIC)		2.0
		Tax cost		1.0
				4.5
			Maximum	4.0
	(ii)	Loan to participator		4.5
		NIC implications		3.0
		Tax cost		1.0
				8.5
			Maximum	7.0
(b)	(i)	Calculation of chargeable gain		2.0
	(ii)	Gain eligible for rollover relief		1.5
		Reinvestment required		2.0
		Qualifying expenditure – factory 2		2.0
		– warehouse		1.5
		Conclusion		1.0
				8.0
			Maximum	7.0
	Professional skills marks (see below)		**Maximum**	5.0
Total				**25.0**

Professional skills marks

Analysis and evaluation

- Consideration of relevant taxes payable in part (a).
- Appropriate use of information to determine the relationship between Samphire Ltd and Kelp Ltd and its relevance in the context of part (b).
- Appropriate use of relevant information to consider the impact of non-trade use in part (b).
- Appropriate use of information to support explanation of the maximum rollover relief in part (b).

Scepticism

- Consideration of potential taxable benefits which could arise in part (a).

Commercial acumen

- Consideration of the cashflow implications of the notional tax in part (a).
- Consideration of the capital gains tax implications arising from the disposal of the computer in part (a).

63 TULA (ADAPTED)

Key answer tips

This section B question covers the income tax implications of loans, close companies and inheritance tax on a sale at undervalue.

Requirement (a) asks for the income tax implications of two loans. The first is a loan that Tula has taken out, and the second is one that she has made to a company. Think about the interest in each scenario and what the tax implications would be.

Requirement (b) covers the implications of a close company providing benefits to a shareholder. Close companies are a popular topic in the ATX exam, so ensure you know the anti-avoidance rules surrounding them and their participators.

Requirement (c) is all about inheritance tax on a sale at undervalue. Think about how you would calculate the value of the transfer if it is a sale rather than an outright gift. You also need to consider BPR here. BPR is tested frequently, so ensure you know when it applies.

(a) Income tax implications of the interest paid/received on the loans

Interest paid on the loan from the bank

Tula will be eligible for tax relief on the interest she pays on the bank loan she has taken out to partially finance the loan to Belleza Ltd. This is because:

- Belleza Ltd is a close trading company.
- The loan is to be applied wholly and exclusively for business purposes.
- Tula holds a material interest (more than 5%) in the shares of the company.

The interest paid in the tax year 2024/25 will be £900 (£20,000 × 9% × 6/12). This amount will be deductible from her total income, resulting in tax relief of £360 (£900 × 40%).

Interest received on the loan to Belleza Ltd

In the tax year 2024/25, Tula will receive gross interest income of £2,800 (£80,000 × 7% × 6/12). As she is a higher rate taxpayer, the first £500 of this interest will be taxed at 0%. The remaining £2,300 (£2,800 – £500) will be taxed at 40%, resulting in a tax liability of £920.

(b) Provision of assets to Aros

Aros will be a participator in Belleza Ltd for close company purposes. As he will not be a director or employee of the company, the amount of the taxable benefit in respect of the provision of the van and the computer will be taxed on him as a distribution.

The amount of the taxable benefit in respect of the van will be £1,980 (£3,960 × 6/12).

The taxable amount in respect of the computer will be £130 (£1,300 × 20% × 6/12), based on its value when first provided to an employee.

As Aros will also receive a dividend of £3,600 (£12,000 × 30%) from Belleza Ltd in December 2024, the dividend nil rate band will already be accounted for.

Accordingly, Aros will have an additional income tax liability in respect of the provision of these assets of £712 ((£1,980 + £130) × 33·75%).

(c) (i) Availability of business property relief (BPR)

Belleza Ltd is an unquoted trading company, so its shares are eligible for BPR.

Although Tula will not have owned the shares for two years when she sells them on 30 September, the ownership period requirement is deemed to have been satisfied because:

- The shares were eligible for BPR when Tula acquired them from her father, and
- Tula acquired the shares as a result of her father's death.

Accordingly, BPR will be available, provided Aros still retains the shares at Tula's death, and they remain relevant business property.

(ii) Potential inheritance tax (IHT) payable by Aros if BPR is not available

The annual exemptions for the tax years 2024/25 and 2023/24, and Tula's nil rate band, will have been utilised against the transfer into the trust on 9 April 2024.

Aros' maximum potential IHT liability will be calculated as follows:

	£
Value of Tula's shares before the transfer (10,000 × £41.80)	418,000
Value of Tula's shares after the transfer (7,000 × £35.10)	(245,700)
	172,300
Less: Received from Aros	(60,000)
Diminution in value	112,300
IHT (£112,300 × 40%)	44,920
Less: Taper relief (£44,920 × 60%)	(26,952)
Maximum potential IHT liability	17,968

Examiner's report

Requirement (a)

This requirement related to the income tax implications for a participator in a close company in respect of interest on loans made to and received from that company.

Candidates were told in the scenario that the company in this question was a close company. When this information is provided it will always be relevant for the answer, and candidates may find it helpful to highlight it as they are reading through the question. The relevance in this case was that the £20,000 loan from the bank was to be used for a qualifying purpose (to make a loan to a close trading company), such that the interest payable on it would qualify for income tax relief as a deduction from the taxpayer's total income.

The interest received on the £80,000 loan to the company will be taxed as savings income, subject to a savings nil rate band of £500 as the client is a higher rate taxpayer. The requirement was to focus on explanations, but supporting calculations were expected in the form of the amounts of interest payable and receivable in the tax year 2024/25, and the consequential income tax saving or additional liability

Candidates' performance on this part was generally very poor. A significant number got no further than calculating the interest paid on the £20,000 loan and the interest received on the £80,000 loan, thereby gaining none of the explanatory marks and only minimal marks for the calculations. Of those who realised that the interest paid would qualify for tax relief, most were unable to cite the reasons for this in full. Many incorrectly said it was deductible from income tax, or from trading income, rather than from total income. A fair number were also concerned that the interest rates on the two loans were different, and decided that the rate on the loan to the company needed to be amended to be the same as the rate being paid on the bank loan as this was the arm's length rate. There was no suggestion in the scenario or the requirement that the interest rates were to be questioned, so this just led to unnecessary calculations which scored no marks, and wasted time. Others netted the interest paid against the interest received, possibly erroneously applying corporation tax rules. A minority did recognise the relevance of the company being a close company in determining the tax treatment, but then often went on to explain why the company was close, which was totally irrelevant, and wasted time. If told that a company is close, candidates will not be expected to explain why this is the case unless it is specifically included in a requirement.

Requirement (b)

Aros was a participator in Belleza Ltd, but was not a director or employee. Accordingly, the taxable value of the benefits provided to him by the company (van and computer) would be taxed as a dividend. Candidates who realised this, and the fact that Aros would have already used his dividend nil rate band for 2024/25 as a result of receiving a dividend from the company, were usually able to score at least half marks on this part.

However, many candidates did not have the required detailed knowledge of the calculation of taxable benefits brought forward from TX to be able to calculate these correctly, and consequently provided incorrect values for both the van (using car benefit rules rather than the van scale charge) and the computer (stating either that it was exempt, or that the full value was chargeable).

The command word at the start of the requirement was 'explain', so although supporting calculations were also required, more emphasis needed to be given in many cases to the written explanations, which were often rather 'thin' or simply ignored.

Requirement (c)

This was a two-part question relating to a potential IHT liability in respect of a lifetime transfer. In the first part candidates were required to explain whether or not the transfer of unquoted company shares would qualify for BPR if it became chargeable as a result of Tula's death within seven years. A majority of candidates were able to state two basic conditions for BPR to apply: the two-year ownership rule and the requirement for the recipient to still own the shares at the date of the donor's death. A good number also cited that the company was unquoted, but didn't always pick up on the requirement for it to be a trading company. Most candidates were therefore able to score up to 2.5 marks (out of 5) on this part.

However, few had the required detailed knowledge in relation to the alternative to the two-year ownership rule where the shares had been inherited to be able to score the remaining marks. It was also disappointing to see that many candidates included conditions which are relevant for CGT reliefs, such as BADR or gift holdover relief. We frequently comment on this problem in these reports, and would encourage candidates to spend some time in their revision learning the relevant conditions for both CGT and IHT reliefs. The ability to distinguish these is an important skill ATX.

Part (c)(ii) required an explanation and calculation of the IHT liability which would arise in respect of these shares if the donor dies on a specific date, 1 January 2030, on the assumption that BPR is not available.

The usual table of share values was provided so that candidates could apply the diminution in value rules to the sale of the shares. The majority of candidates appeared to be confident with the application of these rules and calculated correctly the value of the transfer for IHT purposes, although some neglected to deduct the amount paid by the recipient as this was a sale at undervalue rather than a gift.

The remainder of the computation was then fairly straightforward, and many candidates went on to score well, with the odd careless error e.g. an incorrect interval between the date of the gift and her death for taper relief purposes. But some seemed to revert to 'autopilot', deducting annual exemptions and the nil rate band without considering the full details of the scenario, to establish that these would both have been fully utilised by an earlier gift. Some even produced full computations for each of the lifetime gifts – both when made and on death – thereby needlessly wasting a considerable amount of time.

Marking scheme

				Marks
(a)	Interest paid			5.0
	Interest received			2.0
	Any other sensible point			1.0
				–––
				8.0
			Maximum	6.0
				–––
(b)	Aros' status			2.5
	Van benefit			1.0
	Computer benefit			1.0
	Tax liability			1.5
				–––
				6.0
				–––
(c)	(i)	Availability of business property relief		5.0
	(ii)	Potential IHT liability		5.0
				–––
				10.0
			Maximum	8.0
				–––
	Professional skills marks (see below)		**Maximum**	5.0
				–––
Total				**25.0**
				–––

Professional skills marks

Analysis and evaluation

- Analysis of the information to determine the income tax implications of the loans made to and from Tula in part (a).
- Identification of close company implications in part (b).
- Demonstration of ability to value benefits from a company in part (b).

Scepticism

- Recognition of the requirement for BPR that the new owner retains ownership in part (c)(i).

Commercial acumen

- Identification of the impact of the percentage shareholding on IHT values in part (c)(ii).
- Recognition that the cash received from Aros reduces the transfer of value for IHT purposes in part (c)(ii).

GROUPS, CONSORTIA AND OVERSEAS COMPANY ASPECTS

64 LIZA (ADAPTED) *Walk in the footsteps of a top tutor*

Key answer tips

This section B question addresses three unrelated issues:

Part (a)(i) requires a calculation of the chargeable gain on the sale of a building and the correct treatment of expenses incurred in acquiring, enhancing and maintaining the property. This is a straightforward part of the question based on TX knowledge so should be a good opportunity to pick up marks.

Part (a)(ii) covers group rollover relief, a commonly tested syllabus area.

Part (a)(iii) is a tricky part of the question that requires you to calculate the additional expenditure required such that the chargeable gain calculated in (a)(i) can be fully deferred. The complication is that the asset owned by Bar Ltd was not used in the trade for the entire period of ownership and the new asset acquired is only partly used for trade purposes.

Part (b) tests capital allowances, which is another TX topic and is tested in a straightforward manner. SBAs are dealt with differently to capital allowances on plant and machinery, so ensure you know the differences in the rules.

Part (c) tests the rules on companies joining a VAT group and the advantages of registering companies as a single VAT group. This is a very commonly tested area in the ATX exam and usually a good opportunity to score some easier marks.

The highlighted words in the written sections are key phrases that markers are looking for.

(a) (i) Chargeable gain – Sale of Building I

Tutor's top tips

Don't forget that expenditure on an asset to make it fit for use is capital expenditure and is therefore allowable expenditure for chargeable gains purposes.

	£	£
Net sales proceeds		860,000
Less: Purchase price	315,000	
Legal fees	9,000	
Work on roof to make fit for use	38,000	
		(362,000)
Chargeable gain		498,000

Tutorial note

A deduction is available for the legal fees incurred in acquiring the building and the costs incurred shortly afterwards to make the building fit for use.

The cost of repainting the building would have been an allowable deduction in calculating the company's trading profits and would not be allowable when computing the chargeable gain.

Indexation allowance is not available since the property was purchased after December 2017.

(ii) Acquisition of qualifying assets for the purposes of rollover relief

Tutor's top tips

You need to explain which companies in the group are part of the 75% chargeable gains group and therefore can purchase replacement assets for rollover relief purposes. Don't forget to include the time limit for claiming rollover relief. This is easily missed, but an easy mark if you have learned the rule.

The assets can be purchased by companies within the Bar Ltd chargeable gains group.

A chargeable gains group consists of a principal company, Bar Ltd, its 75% subsidiaries, the 75% subsidiaries of those subsidiaries and so on.

Bar Ltd must have an effective interest of more than 50% in all of the companies in the group.

Accordingly, the only companies able to purchase qualifying replacement assets are Bar Ltd and Pommel Ltd.

Ring Ltd is not a 75% subsidiary of Bar Ltd, such that it and Vault Ltd cannot be members of the Bar Ltd chargeable gains group.

The Hoop Ltd group is a separate group.

The qualifying replacement assets must be purchased in the period from 1 June 2023 to 31 May 2027.

(iii) The additional amount that would need to be spent on qualifying assets

Tutor's top tips

Don't forget that rollover relief is only available if the asset has been used in the trade.

Bar Ltd owned the building from 1 June 2018 to 31 May 2024, a period of 72 months. The building was not used for trading purposes from 1 January 2020 to 30 June 2021, a period of 18 months.

Accordingly, the building was used for the purposes of the trade for a period of 54 (72 – 18) months, such that only 54/72 of the gain can be relieved via rollover relief.

Therefore, qualifying business assets costing £645,000 (£860,000 × 54/72) will need to be acquired in order to relieve the whole of the gain qualifying for rollover relief.

Only two-thirds of the new building is to be used for trading purposes, such that only £480,000 (£720,000 × 2/3) of its cost will be a qualifying acquisition for the purposes of rollover relief.

Accordingly, the additional amount that would need to be spent on qualifying acquisitions in order to relieve the whole of the gain that qualifies for rollover relief would be £165,000 (£645,000 – £480,000).

(b) Capital allowances available in respect of the new building

Integral features

Electrical, water and heating systems qualify for plant and machinery capital allowances on the price of £150,000.

They are classified as integral features, such that they are included in the special rate pool where a 6% writing down allowance is available.

The annual investment allowance available to the Bar Ltd group should be set against these additions in priority to those assets which qualify for the 18% writing down allowance.

Structures and buildings allowances (SBAs)

The cost of the building less the value of the land and integral features of £370,000 (£720,000 – £200,000 – £150,000) qualifies for SBAs at the rate of 3%.

SBAs can be claimed from the date the building is brought into qualifying use (1 July 2023).

The annual investment allowance is not available to offset against the £370,000 which qualifies for SBA.

Tutorial note

Qualifying use for SBAs includes use in the trade and for property letting.

(c) Group registration for the purposes of Value Added Tax (VAT)

Tutor's top tips

This section also covers material from the TX syllabus.

VAT groups are frequently tested so make sure you can demonstrate a good knowledge of VAT groups and be specific to the question.

A sole trader can be included in a VAT group if the sole trader is the controller of a group of companies. As Liza is not a sole trader she cannot be a member of the VAT group.

Note that zero-rated companies should not be included in the VAT group as they can reclaim any VAT charged by the other group companies on a monthly basis. This is a cash flow advantage to the group.

The companies able to register as a group

Two or more companies may register as a group provided they are established in the UK, or have a fixed establishment in the UK, and they are controlled by the same person. The person can be an individual, a company, or a partnership.

Accordingly, all of the companies in the Bar Ltd and Hoop Ltd groups can register as a single group for the purposes of VAT.

The potential advantages of registering as a group

The advantage of a group registration would be that there would be no need to charge VAT on the transactions between the group companies. This would reduce administration and improve the group's cash flow.

Whether companies would benefit from joining the group

Vault Ltd makes zero-rated supplies and will therefore be in a repayment position, such that it can improve its cash flow by accounting for VAT on a monthly basis. However, if it were registered as part of a VAT group, it would not be able to do this as the group, as a single entity, is very unlikely to be in a regular repayment position. Accordingly, if a group registration is to be entered into, consideration should be given to excluding Vault Ltd from that registration.

Examiner's report

Part (a)(i) was a gentle introduction to the question and was done well.

Part (a)(ii) was done well by those candidates who knew the rules for group rollover relief and who expressed themselves carefully.

This part required candidates to know three things: that rollover relief can be claimed where one company in a gains group sells a qualifying business asset and another company in the group buys one, the definition of a gains group, and the time period in which a replacement asset needs to be purchased in order for rollover relief to be available.

The majority of candidates knew the first and third points although a small minority failed to address the third point despite, probably, knowing the rule. The difficulty came in dealing with the second point and the definition of a gains group where a minority of candidates revealed a level of confusion. This stemmed from a problem in distinguishing the 75% aspect of the rule from the 51% aspect and led to some candidates concluding erroneously that Vault Ltd and Bar Ltd were in a gains group. For there to be a chargeable gains group, the direct holding between each company in the chain must be at least 75%; if it isn't, the two companies cannot be in a group regardless of the level of the indirect holding.

The final part of part (a) was the hardest part of the question and was not done particularly well.

It required candidates to know the basic rule whereby the whole of the relevant proceeds has to be spent on replacement assets in order for the maximum gain to be rolled over, whilst recognising the relevance of the non-business use of both the asset sold and the asset acquired. Almost all candidates knew the basic rule but the majority struggled to apply it in these particular circumstances.

The following part of the question has been amended to test a new syllabus area (SBAs).

Part (b) concerned the availability of capital allowances in respect of electrical, water and heating systems acquired as part of a building and was done well.

The following section of the examiner's report has been amended following adaptations made to the original question.

In the final part of the question the majority of candidates made a reasonable job of discussing the advantages of registering as a VAT group and made a series of concise points. However, the definition of a group for the purposes of VAT was not handled particularly well. In particular, a sizable minority of candidates thought that the required holding was 75% as opposed to control. In addition, many candidates did not appreciate that control could be exercised by an individual (i.e. Liza), as well as by a company, such that all of the companies in the question were able to register as a single group.

As always, a minority of candidates wrote in general terms, for example, about partial exemption, rather than addressing the specifics of the question, such that they wasted time.

ACCA marking scheme

				Marks
(a)	(i)	Chargeable gain		3.0
	(ii)	Chargeable gains group		2.0
		Identification of relevant companies		1.5
		Qualifying period		1.0
				4.5
			Maximum	4.0
	(iii)	Amount relievable via rollover relief		2.0
		Total acquisitions necessary		1.0
		Further acquisitions necessary		1.5
				4.5
			Maximum	4.0
(b)	Integral features			
		Plant and machinery as integral feature		1.0
		Special rate pool		1.0
		Use of AIA		1.0
	Structures and buildings allowances			
		Available allowances		1.0
		Date brought into qualifying use		0.5
		No AIA		0.5
				5.0
			Maximum	4.0
(c)	Ability to register as a group			2.0
	Discussion			4.0
				6.0
			Maximum	5.0
	Professional skills marks (see below)		**Maximum**	5.0
Total				**25.0**

Professional skills marks

Analysis and evaluation

- Appropriate use of information to calculate the gain in part (a)(i).
- Appropriate use of information to determine how much extra needs to be spent on qualifying assets in order to defer the maximum amount of gain on Building I in part (a)(iii).
- Appropriate use of relevant information to consider the capital allowances available in part (b).

Commercial acumen

- Recognition of the implications for rollover relief of being in a chargeable gains group in part (a)(ii).
- Consideration of the advantages of joining a VAT group in part (c).
- Identification of companies for which it may not be beneficial to join a VAT group in part (c).

65 SPETZ LTD GROUP (ADAPTED) *Walk in the footsteps of a top tutor*

Key answer tips

The section B question concerns VAT and overseas issues in relation to corporation tax, and was the least popular of the section B questions in this exam. This is probably because it requires detailed knowledge of some smaller topics in the syllabus and involved some overseas aspects!

Part (a) requires a calculation of the VAT partial exemption annual adjustment in respect of a company and should have been straightforward, although remembering all the detail of the three de minimis tests is demanding.

The first part of (b) requires an explanation of how to determine whether or not the company was resident in the UK which is worth only three marks. It is testing TX knowledge which should be easy if you have learnt the rules, but difficult if you have not.

The second part of (b) requires an explanation of the company's corporation tax liability together with the advantages and disadvantages of making an election to exempt the profits of an overseas permanent establishment (branch) from UK tax.

Part (c) has been added to the question in place of an existing requirement which was no longer examinable. This is another VAT requirement, but this time focusing on the administration side of things. It is very important to clients that they know when to submit their returns and pay the relevant liabilities in order to avoid penalties and interest. Of course, there will often be cases where the deadlines are not met, and it is important that you can advise on the consequences in these cases.

The highlighted words in the written sections are key phrases that markers are looking for.

Tutor's top tips

The first VAT requirement is a standalone part and asks for a calculation, a due date and an explanation of reasons as to whether the de minimis limits apply.

Make sure that you address all three elements of the requirement.

Note that partial exemption is regularly examined in the ATX exam.

When a business makes both taxable and exempt sales it is necessary to apportion input VAT on overheads between taxable sales and exempt sales. If the input VAT attributable to exempt sales exceeds the de minimis amount, then it cannot be claimed back.

(a) Novak Ltd

Value added tax – partial exemption annual adjustment

	Total	Recoverable	Irrecoverable
	£	£	£
Input tax			
– attributed to taxable supplies	12,200	12,200	
– attributed to exempt supplies	4,900		4,900
Unattributed input tax (W)	16,100	11,914	4,186
	33,200	24,114	9,086

To determine whether or not the £9,086 irrecoverable input VAT is in fact recoverable, the three de minimis tests must be considered:

- De minimis test 1 is not satisfied, as the total input tax (£33,200) exceeds an average of £625 per month (£625 × 12 = £7,500).
- De minimis test 2 is not satisfied, as the total input tax less that directly attributed to taxable supplies (£33,200 – £12,200 = £21,000) exceeds an average of £625 per month (£21,000 ÷ 12 = £1,750).
- De minimis test 3 is also not satisfied, as exempt input tax of £9,086 exceeds the de minimis limit of £625 per month.

Accordingly, in total for the year, only £24,114 is recoverable.

The £9,086 input VAT is not de minimis and is therefore irrecoverable.

	£
Recoverable input VAT for the year	24,114
Less: Input tax recovered on quarterly returns	(23,200)
Annual adjustment = Additional input tax recoverable	914

The annual adjustment must be made on:

- the final VAT return of the year

  (i.e. the return for the period ended 30 September 2024), or
- the first VAT return after the end of the year.

Working: Recoverable unattributed input tax

(Taxable supplies/Total supplies) × 100

= (£1,190,000 ÷ (£1,190,000 + £430,000)) × 100 = 73.4%

This is rounded up to 74%.

(b) (i) Residence status of Kraus Co

Tutor's top tips

With only three marks available, three short succinct points need to be made and applied to the scenario given.

The key point to make is that overseas incorporated companies such as Kraus Co are treated as UK resident if they are controlled and managed from the UK.

- A company is regarded as resident in the UK if it is incorporated in the UK or if its central management and control is exercised in the UK.
- Kraus Co was incorporated in the country of Mersano. Accordingly, it will only be resident in the UK if its central management and control is exercised in the UK.
- The central management and control of a company is usually regarded as being exercised in the place where the key operational and financial decisions are made (e.g. where meetings of the board of directors are held).

(ii) Kraus Co

Tutor's top tips

The calculation required is very simple as Kraus Co has no other income or gains other than trading income.

However, the majority of the marks are available for explaining the branch profits exemption and consequences.

UK resident companies are subject to corporation tax on their worldwide income, with DTR available if applicable.

As Kraus Co's profits are clearly above the upper limit for corporation tax, it will pay UK tax at the main rate.

Tutorial note

Since Kraus Co is one of 20 associated companies, the limits for determining the rate of corporation tax rate that it will pay are reduced:

Upper limit: £250,000 ÷ 20 = £12,500

Lower limit: £50,000 ÷ 20 = £2,500

In the year of acquisition, the limits could actually be divided by more than 20 if Kraus Co was previously associated with another group of companies.

However, as Kraus Co's taxable profits of £520,000 are already greater than the £250,000 limit for a single company, it is clear that it will pay tax at the main rate regardless of the number of associates.

	£
UK corporation tax (£520,000 × 25%)	130,000
Less: Unilateral double tax relief	
Lower of UK rate and overseas rate	
(£520,000 × 17%)	(88,400)
UK corporation tax liability	41,600

Tutorial note

The profits will be subject to UK tax because no election has been made to exempt the profits and losses of the overseas permanent establishment from UK corporation tax.

Note that the branch election is irrevocable and applies to all current and future overseas branches of the company. It is therefore important to carefully consider if an election will be beneficial, as once it is made overseas branch profits will not be subject to UK corporation tax, but losses of overseas branches could not be set off against UK profits and UK capital allowances would not be available in respect of the overseas branches' plant and machinery.

Election to exempt the overseas profits from UK tax

The advantage of making such an election would be that the profits made in Mersano would not be subject to UK corporation tax. Based on the current rates of corporation tax in the two countries, this would save corporation tax at the rate of 8% (25% – 17%).

When considering this election, it should be recognised that it is irrevocable and would apply to all future overseas permanent establishments of Kraus Co. Accordingly, there would be no relief in the UK for any losses incurred in the trade in Mersano in the future or for any other losses incurred in any additional overseas trades operated by Kraus Co.

(c) Nadal Ltd VAT returns

Tutor's top tips

The consequences of late filing depend on the history of the previous returns, so it is important that you pay close attention to the information in the scenario so that you can determine the implications of this late filing.

Late filing

Nadal Ltd will receive a further penalty point for the late submission of its VAT return, which means that it will reach the threshold of four penalty points. As a result, a penalty of £200 will now be due.

In order to reset its penalty points to zero, Nadal Ltd will be required to submit four consecutive VAT returns on time.

Late payment

As the VAT was paid between 16 and 30 days late, a penalty of £400 (£20,000 × 2%) will be payable.

Late payment interest will be payable at the rate of 6.5% of the underpaid VAT from the due date to the date of payment (i.e. 7 November 2024 to 27 November 2024).

Tutorial note

The due date for payment of VAT is one month and seven days from the end of the return period. For the quarter ended 30 September 2024, the due date would have been 7 November 2024, and you are told that Nadal Ltd paid 20 days after this.

Examiner's report

Part (a) was done reasonably well by those candidates who had a working knowledge of the de minimis rules. A minority of candidates had very little awareness of the rules, such that their performance was poor. Candidates who did not have a precise knowledge of the rules were able to score reasonably well provided they satisfied the requirement and attempted to address all three de minimis tests.

Part (b)(i) simply required a statement of the rules regarding country of incorporation and place of management and control but the majority of candidates were unable to state these fundamental rules.

Part (b)(ii) was done well. The majority of candidates prepared a short accurate calculation and were able to state the particular disadvantages of making such an election.

Note that the final part of this examiner's report has been deleted, as it relates to part of the question that has been removed.

Part (c) has been added to the question since it was originally set.

ACCA marking scheme

				Marks
(a)	Input tax attributed to taxable supplies and unattributed input tax			1.5
	Test 1			1.0
	Test 2			1.5
	Test 3			1.5
	Adjustment and date			1.5
				7.0
(b)	(i)	Not incorporated in the UK		1.0
		Central management and control		2.0
				3.0
	(ii)	Calculation of liability		2.5
		Taxation of worldwide profits		1.0
		Discussion of election		
		Advantage		1.5
		Disadvantages		2.0
				7.0
			Maximum	6.0
(c)	Late filing			2.0
	Late payment			2.0
				4.0
	Professional skills marks (see below)		**Maximum**	5.0
Total				**25.0**

Professional skills marks

Analysis and evaluation

- Appropriate application of information from the scenario to the de minimis tests in part (a).
- Analysis of the information to conclude on whether Novak Ltd meets any of the de minimis tests in part (a).
- Appropriate use of relevant information to determine the applicable corporation tax rate in part (b)(ii).
- Analysis of the information to determine implications of both late filing and late payment in part (c).

Scepticism

- Recognition that further information is needed about Kraus Co's central management and control in order to determine its residence status in part (b)(i).

Commercial acumen

- Identification of at least one advantage and disadvantage in relation to the election to exempt PE profits in part (b)(ii).

66 KLUBB PLC (ADAPTED) *Walk in the footsteps of a top tutor*

Key answer tips

This section B question covers three areas: corporation tax administration; a comparison of share schemes: SIP versus CSOP, and the CFC rules.

Part (a) is TX revision of filing dates for a long period of account and basic corporation tax penalties. This should offer easy marks if you remember the rules.

Part (b) tests your knowledge of the conditions for two tax advantaged share schemes, SIPs and CSOPs. Share schemes are a new topic at ATX level and are regularly tested.

Part (c) covers another new topic at the ATX level – CFCs. If you have not learnt the detailed rules you may struggle with this part of the question.

The highlighted words in the written sections are key phrases that markers are looking for.

Tutor's top tips

This is really three separate, standalone questions and you can attempt them in any order as long as you clearly label your answer.

(a) Late submission of corporation tax returns

Tutor's top tips

You are not asked to identify corporation tax payment dates or the penalties for late payment of tax, so there would be no marks for doing so.

Corporation tax returns are required for the two accounting periods within the long period of account: the 12 months ended 30 November 2022 and the four months ended 31 March 2023.

The returns should have been filed by 31 March 2024 (12 months after the end of the 16-month period of account).

There will be a late filing penalty of £100 in respect of each of the returns because they were filed within three months of the filing date.

However, this £100 penalty is increased to £500 where the returns for the two preceding accounting periods were also submitted late.

Tutorial note

It has been assumed that HM Revenue and Customs (HMRC) issued notices prior to 1 January 2024 requiring the returns to be made.

(b) Comparison of a share incentive plan (SIP) with a company share option plan (CSOP)

Tutor's top tips

This part of the question does not ask you to write everything you know about SIPs and CSOPs. The client is specifically interested in the flexibility each scheme offers and the tax implications.

You are required to compare three specific areas:

- *Employees who can/must be included in the scheme*
- *Number or value of shares which can be acquired*
- *Income tax and CGT implications of acquiring and selling shares.*

Use these as headings in your answer to help you to focus, and make sure that you clearly state which scheme you are referring to and which tax – income tax or CGT.

Employees who must be included in the plan

A CSOP is significantly more flexible than a SIP.

Klubb plc would be able to select particular employees to join a CSOP whereas, under the rules for SIPs, Klubb plc would be required to offer shares to all of its full time and part time employees, although a minimum qualifying period of employment may be specified.

The number or value of shares which can be acquired by each plan member

Again, a CSOP is more flexible than a SIP.

Klubb plc can choose to award options to purchase different numbers of shares to each member of a CSOP. The options awarded are simply at the discretion of Klubb plc. However, the award is subject to a maximum whereby a member is only allowed to hold options to purchase shares with a maximum value (at the time the options were granted) of £30,000.

Under the rules for SIPs, free shares up to a maximum value of £3,600 can be given to each member of the plan each tax year. These free shares must be awarded on similar terms to all of the plan members. This means that any variation in the number of free shares awarded must be by reference to objective criteria, for example, length of service or performance targets.

In addition, a member of a SIP can purchase partnership shares (at market value) up to a maximum value of the lower of £1,800 and 10% of salary each tax year. Klubb plc could then give the plan members up to two further free shares (known as matching shares), in respect of each partnership share purchased. This represents additional free shares with a maximum value of £3,600.

Tax implications of acquiring and selling the shares

Under the rules for SIPs, there are no income tax implications when free shares or matching shares are awarded to scheme members. Similarly, there are no income tax implications when shares are withdrawn from the plan if they have been held within the plan for five years. There will be no capital gains tax on the immediate sale of the shares because their base cost is equal to their market value at the time they are withdrawn from the SIP.

The rules for a CSOP are not as generous as those for a SIP.

There would be no tax charged on the grant and exercise of the options.

However, there would be a chargeable gain on the sale of the shares equal to the proceeds received less the amount paid for them.

Tutorial note

It was not necessary to make all of the above points in order to score full marks for this question.

(c) (i) Status of Hartz Co and availability of the low profits exemption

Tutor's top tips

The controlled foreign company rules are complex, and there are several exemptions that could apply.

However, this part of the question just requires you to know – and apply:

- *the definition, and*
- *the low profits exemption.*

There are no marks available for discussing other aspects of CFCs.

Hartz Co is a non-UK resident company.

It will be a controlled foreign company (CFC) if it is controlled by UK resident persons.

Accordingly, its status depends on the residency of Mr Deck. If he is a UK resident, Hartz Co will be a CFC.

Hartz Co is not expected to satisfy either of the conditions for the low profits exemption. This is because:

- its profits are expected to exceed £50,000, and
- although its profits are expected to be less than £500,000, it will have chargeable gains (non-trading profits) of more than £50,000.

(ii) CFC charge

	£
Chargeable profits of Hartz Co	330,000
Chargeable profits apportioned to Klubb plc (30% × £330,000)	99,000
Corporation tax at 25%	24,750
Less: Creditable tax (£330,000 × 11% × 30%)	(10,890)
CFC charge	13,860

Tutorial notes

Chargeable gains are not part of chargeable profits and thus are not included in the calculation of the CFC charge.

The CFC charge is always calculated at the main rate of 25%, regardless of the level of augmented profits.

Examiner's report

In part (a) the first thing candidates had to point out was the need to split the long period of account into two accounting periods. Unfortunately, many candidates failed to identify this point. Candidates then had to know the filing dates and the penalty rules. However, many candidates wrote about the dates on which corporation tax has to be paid as opposed to the filing dates of the returns, such that they did not answer the requirement set.

Part (b) of the question was more substantial. It was very important to identify clearly the particular areas that needed to be addressed, and to stick to them. Failure to do this could result in irrelevant parts of an answer that would score no marks, despite being technically accurate. Unfortunately, many candidates were insufficiently disciplined in their approach and regarded the question as being about the two share schemes generally as opposed to being about certain aspects of the two schemes.

Generally, candidates' knowledge of this area was good with many candidates providing satisfactory answers. The candidates who did best were those who structured their answer in a very clear manner so that it was always clear which aspect of which scheme was being addressed. This clear structure enabled candidates to keep their answers relatively brief whilst addressing all of the precise requirements of the question.

However, a minority of candidates appeared to be making up their answer as they went along, such that they were setting out each thought as it occurred to them. The problem with this approach was that some points were repeated, other points were made which were not relevant and some aspects of the requirement were omitted altogether.

Most candidates knew that under a share incentive plan, shares need to be offered to, broadly, all employees whereas, under a company share option plan, the employer can choose certain employees to join the scheme. Candidates' knowledge of the number or value of shares that could be offered under each scheme was also satisfactory notwithstanding that some candidates confused the two schemes or confused the different categories of shares that can be offered under a share incentive plan.

When it came to the tax implications of acquiring and selling the shares it was important for candidates to stick to the facts of the question. It was clear from the question how long the shares would be held for and when they would be sold. Accordingly, there was no need to address all of the different tax implications that could occur if the shares were sold at other times. Candidates who failed to realise this wasted time writing lengthy answers that were not addressing the requirements of the question.

When explaining the tax implications, stronger candidates were clear as to which scheme they were writing about and which tax (income tax or capital gains tax) they were addressing. The answers of other candidates were more confused and used the general term 'tax' as opposed to the specific tax concerned.

Part (c)(i) was done reasonably well by many candidates.

Candidates had two main problems when answering this first part of the question. First, they confused the definition of a controlled foreign company with the exemptions that are available. Secondly, there was a tendency to write about all of the available exemptions as opposed to the particular one in the question requirement; this resulted in irrelevant parts of answers.

For part (c)(ii) candidates had to remember to exclude the gains from the calculation of a CFC charge, bring in only 30% of the trading profits, and deduct an appropriate amount of creditable tax. Answers here were generally not as accurate as might have been hoped.

ACCA marking scheme

			Marks
(a)	Two accounting periods		1.0
	Filing date		1.0
	Penalty		2.0
			4.0
(b)	Employees		2.0
	Value		
	SIP		4.0
	CSOP		2.0
	Tax on realisation of value		
	SIP		2.0
	CSOP		2.0
			12.0
		Maximum	9.0

(c)	(i)	Status of Hartz Co		2.5
		Low profits exemption		2.0
				4.5
			Maximum	4.0
	(ii)	Profits apportioned		1.5
		Calculation of charge		1.5
				3.0
	Professional skills marks (see below)		**Maximum**	5.0
Total				**25.0**

Professional skills marks

Analysis and evaluation

- Analysis of information to determine relevant late filing penalties for Klubb plc in part (a).
- Demonstration of ability to consider all relevant taxes specified in part (b), i.e. income tax and capital gains tax.
- Analysis of the information to determine the availability of the low profits exemption in part (c)(i).
- Appropriate use of the information to determine relevant calculations to perform to arrive at the CFC charge in part (c)(ii).

Scepticism

- Recognition that information about Mr Deck's residency status is needed to determine whether Hartz Co will be a CFC in part (c)(i).

Commercial acumen

- Recognition that a CSOP scheme is more flexible than a SIP in part (b).
- Demonstration of an understanding of the controlled foreign company rules in part (c).

67 ACHIOTE LTD (ADAPTED) *Walk in the footsteps of a top tutor*

Key answer tips

This is a four-part company-focused section B question covering intangible fixed assets, transfer pricing, gains groups and VAT in respect of a commercial building.

The four parts could be attempted in any order. As they are mostly discursive they lend themselves well to being completed in the word processor response option in the exam. Any small calculations can be completed in tables.

The highlighted words in the written sections are key phrases that markers are looking for in your answer.

(a) Goodwill

Tutor's top tips

The intangible fixed asset rules for companies are often tested in the exam. Remember that the rules that apply to goodwill and other intangibles are not the same.

No amortisation in respect of goodwill is deductible for corporation tax purposes, so the amortisation charged in the accounts for the year ended 31 March 2024 must be added back for tax purposes.

Patent

As the patent is transferred between two members of a capital gains group, it will be transferred at a price which is tax neutral.

The written down value of the patent in Achiote Ltd at the date of its sale to Borage Ltd was £26,600 (£38,000 – (3 × 10% × £38,000)). Accordingly, this will be the deemed acquisition price for Borage Ltd.

Borage Ltd will continue to amortise the patent over the remainder of its ten-year life.

In the year ended 31 March 2024 amortisation charged in its accounts will be £950 (£26,600/7 × 3/12).

This amount is allowable for corporation tax purposes.

(b) Loan to Caraway Inc

Tutor's top tips

Exam questions often test the transfer pricing rules applicable to the sale of goods between connected companies.

The principles are the same for a loan: if the amount received by the UK company is less than the market rate, an adjustment must be made.

Note that there are five marks available for this part of the question, so you should try to write at least five separate points in your answer.

It would appear that an arm's length rate of interest on the loan would be 8% as this is the rate at which Caraway Inc could have obtained an equivalent loan from an unrelated party. As Achiote Ltd controls Caraway Inc, they are connected companies and so the transfer pricing rules apply.

The interest receivable by Achiote Ltd is £2,000 (£100,000 × 2%) less than it would be under an arm's length agreement.

This means that Achiote Ltd's non-trading loan relationship income is reduced by this amount, such that less tax is payable in the UK. Therefore, Achiote Ltd must adjust the figures within its corporation tax return to reflect the arm's length price.

As there is no double tax treaty between the UK and Nuxabar, Nuxabar will be regarded as a non-qualifying territory. As a result, the exemption which might otherwise have been available if a group is not large will not be available to the Achiote Ltd group.

Achiote Ltd can seek advance approval from HM Revenue and Customs (HMRC) in respect of any intra-group pricing arrangements, including the rate of interest to be charged on a loan.

(c) Transfer of the item of equipment and the sale of shares in Caraway Inc

Sale of item of equipment

Tutor's top tips

Think before you answer this part of the question!

An overseas resident company ***cannot*** *transfer assets at no gain, no loss within a capital gains group.*

The intra-group transfer of the item of equipment by Achiote Ltd to Caraway Inc will not be treated as a no gain, no loss transfer, because even though Achiote Ltd owns 80% of the company, such that the companies are in a capital gains group, the fact that Caraway Inc is not a UK resident company means that the asset will no longer be within the charge to UK taxation.

This is therefore a chargeable disposal for Achiote Ltd at 1 March 2024.

Although the equipment has fallen in value, no capital loss will arise as the asset qualified for capital allowances as it was used in Achiote Ltd's trade.

Sale of shares in Caraway Inc

Tutor's top tips

The substantial shareholding exemption is regularly tested in the exam, so you must learn and apply the conditions.

In this scenario, the exemption does not apply and a gain must be calculated.

The sale of the 8% holding in Caraway Inc will not be exempt from corporation tax under the substantial shareholding exemption (SSE) rules. This is because Achiote Ltd will only have held its shares in Caraway Inc for nine months prior to the proposed disposal date and so will not meet the criteria to have owned at least 10% of the shares in Caraway Inc for a continuous 12-month period out of the six years prior to disposal.

Accordingly, a chargeable gain will arise on the disposal, calculated as follows:

	£
Disposal proceeds	66,000
Less: Cost (£258,000 × 8/80)	(25,800)
Chargeable gain	40,200

There will be no indexation allowance, as the shares were acquired after December 2017.

Tutorial note

The equipment is not exempt as a wasting asset as it qualified for capital allowances due to being used in a business.

(d) (i) Reasons why Rye Ltd might not charge value added tax (VAT) on its sales to Achiote Ltd

Tutor's top tips

Read the question carefully: the first part of this requirement concerns Rye Ltd, a company that supplies goods to Achiote Ltd. It is not about the commercial building.

Rye Ltd is a small company, and its taxable supplies may not yet have reached the registration threshold.

Rye Ltd's taxable supplies have reached the registration threshold, but its supplies to Achiote Ltd are zero-rated.

(ii) Option to tax the commercial building

Tutor's top tips

VAT on land and buildings and the implications of opting to tax often feature in the exam, so you should be prepared to answer questions on these rules.

As the building purchased by Achiote Ltd was less than three years old, and a commercial building, it would have been a standard-rated supply. So Achiote Ltd will have incurred a significant amount of input value added tax (VAT) in relation to this expenditure.

For this reason, it will be financially beneficial (at least in the short term), for Achiote Ltd to opt to tax the building in order to be able to reclaim this tax.

This will also enable Achiote Ltd to recover the input tax in respect of the building's running costs.

However, VAT must then be added to the rent charged by Achiote Ltd to Rye Ltd. The impact of this on Rye Ltd will depend on its size and the nature of its supplies.

- If its taxable supplies are currently below the registration limit, Rye Ltd could voluntarily register for VAT purposes and reclaim the input VAT charged on the rent payments.
- If Rye Ltd's taxable supplies have reached the registration threshold, but its supplies are wholly or partially zero-rated, provided it has registered for VAT purposes, the input VAT charged on the rent payments will, again, be reclaimable, and may lead to a (higher) repayment of VAT from HMRC.

Tutorial note

In order to determine whether or not opting to tax the commercial building would be commercially beneficial, longer term implications, such as the impact on the building's future marketability, would also need to be considered. Credit was also available for candidates who made reference to partial exemption.

Examiner's report

The first part required an explanation of the corporation tax implications of acquiring goodwill and a patent. The goodwill was a minor point and was handled well by the majority of candidates. The patent, however, was not handled so well. Many candidates treated it as a standard asset as opposed to being part of the intangible assets regime. As a result, the inter-group transfer was treated as a no gain, no loss transfer as opposed to a tax neutral transfer. This, in turn, caused problems when calculating the tax deductions available in the future.

The second part concerned transfer pricing. This part was not done particularly well because many candidates did not identify sufficient mark-scoring points.

It was important to start the explanation at the beginning by identifying why the transfer pricing rules applied. This required a reference to the fact that one of the companies controlled the other and the lack of an arms' length price. Many candidates did not do this but simply took it for granted that the regime applied.

Once the relevance of the rules had been established, candidates should then have explained the effect of the rules by reference to the need to increase the company's taxable profit and the amount of the increase. It was this part which most candidates focused on.

It was then necessary to consider any other relevant matters including the availability of the exemption where a group is not large and the possibility of obtaining advance approval of the arrangements from HM Revenue and Customs.

The third part concerned the chargeable gains implications of the sale of an item of equipment and of some shares. Candidates needed to concentrate and take care in order to score well.

The equipment was being transferred between two companies in a chargeable gains group. However, the company acquiring the property was not resident in the UK, such that the no gain/no loss treatment would not apply to the transaction. In addition, due to the availability of capital allowances, the loss arising on the disposal would not be available.

When dealing with the sale of the shares, it was important to recognise that the substantial shareholder exemption would not be available because the vendor would not have owned the shares for a 12-month period in the six years prior to the sale.

The final part concerned various aspects of VAT.

The aspects of this part relating to the option to tax a commercial building were generally handled well. However, candidates found the other aspect of this part more difficult.

Candidates were asked to suggest reasons why a company which made taxable supplies did not charge VAT on sales made to an unconnected party. Stronger candidates stopped for a moment to gather their thoughts and then wrote about the registration limit and/or the making of zero-rated supplies. Weaker candidates simply wrote about registration in general and often lengthy terms. Candidates need to be in a rhythm throughout the exam of reading, thinking and then writing.

ACCA marking scheme

				Marks
(a)	Goodwill			1.0
	Patent			4.0
				5.0
			Maximum	4.0
(b)	Transfer pricing	– reason why it applies		1.0
		– implications and action		5.0
				6.0
			Maximum	5.0
(c)	Transfer of equipment			2.5
	Sale of shares			3.5
				6.0
			Maximum	5.0
(d)	(i)	Reasons why VAT is not charged		2.0
	(ii)	Beneficial due to input VAT incurred		1.5
		Implications of option to tax for Rye Ltd		3.0
				4.5
			Maximum	4.0
	Professional skills marks (see below)		**Maximum**	5.0
Total				**25.0**

Professional skills marks

Analysis and evaluation

- Appropriate use of information to determine the tax treatment of the intangible fixed assets in part (a).
- Appropriate use of information to determine the corporation tax treatment of both the equipment and shares in Caraway Inc in part (c).
- Analysis of the information to evaluate whether it will be beneficial to opt to tax the building purchased by Achiote Ltd in part (d)(ii).

Commercial acumen

- Demonstration of an understanding of the transfer pricing rules by application to the loan to Caraway Inc in part (b).
- Identification of the option to seek approval from HMRC for transfer prices in part (b).
- Demonstration of an understanding of the substantial shareholding exemption by application to the shares in Caraway Inc in part (c).

68 KITZ LTD (ADAPTED)

Key answer tips

This corporation tax focused section B question looks at degrouping charges, transfer pricing and intangible fixed assets.

In part (a) you are asked to explain the chargeable gains implications arising from a sale of shares. You are told that an asset has been transferred to the company being sold several years ago, so should consider the possibility of a degrouping charge. Note that the question states no calculations are needed so ensure you don't waste time preparing any.

Part (b) asks for the corporation tax implications of a loan from both the perspective of the lender and the borrower – make sure you cover both to score well. You're told about how much the borrower was offered by a bank and at what interest rate, so think about why you're being told this. Could there be transfer pricing issues?

The final part of the question looks at intangible fixed assets and the associated rollover relief. Here you need to think about the information from other parts of the question – remember what Feld Ltd was going to use the loan for. You should always be prepared to join information together from different parts of the question, it won't always be kept in discrete parts.

(a) Chargeable gains implications for Kitz Ltd arising from the sale of the shares in Mayr Ltd on 1 July 2024

The sale of the 75% shareholding in Mayr Ltd on 1 July 2024 will be exempt from corporation tax under the substantial shareholding exemption (SSE). This is because Kitz Ltd owned more than 10% of the shares in Mayr Ltd for a continuous 12-month period out of the six years prior to sale, and Mayr Ltd is a trading company.

The sale of the warehouse to Mayr Ltd on 8 April 2019 was originally a no gain no loss transfer, because Kitz Ltd and Mayr Ltd were in a capital gains group, as Kitz Ltd owned 75% of Mayr Ltd. As Mayr Ltd left the group within six years of this transfer, still owning the warehouse, a degrouping charge will arise. This is added to the consideration received by Kitz Ltd on the sale of the Mayr Ltd shares. However, the SSE, which applies to sale of the shares, will also apply to the degrouping charge, such that this will also be exempt.

(b) Corporation tax implications of the interest charged on the loan by Kitz Ltd to Feld Ltd for the year ending 31 March 2026

Tutorial note

There are clues in the question that transfer pricing could be applicable here. Though this is often tested involving an overseas company the rules can still apply to transactions between two UK companies, as is the case here.

Feld Ltd has been offered an interest rate of 10% per annum from a bank (which is an unrelated party), so this would appear to be an arm's length rate of interest.

As Kitz Ltd controls Feld Ltd, they are connected companies for the purpose of transfer pricing. No exemption is available as the companies are not small or medium-sized enterprises (SMEs).

As the interest receivable by Kitz Ltd is 7% per annum, i.e. lower than the arm's length rate, Kitz Ltd must make a transfer pricing adjustment, and include interest receivable in its corporation tax computation calculated at the rate of 10%. This will be an addition of £13,500 (£450,000 × (10% – 7%)) for the year ending 31 March 2026. Interest receivable of £45,000 (£450,000 × 10%) will be included as non-trading loan relationship (NTLR) income.

As Feld Ltd is also within the charge to UK corporation tax, it can make a claim to amend its computation to an arm's length basis, and deduct a total of £45,000 in respect of the interest payable on the loan.

The interest payable in respect of the proportion of the loan used to acquire assets for use in Feld Ltd's business will be deducted from trading income; the interest payable in respect of the proportion of the loan used to acquire shares in Durn Ltd will be deducted from NTLR income.

Accordingly, for the year ending 31 March 2026, £20,500 (£45,000 × 205/450) is deductible from Feld Ltd's trading income of £587,000, and £24,500 (£45,000 × 245/450) is deductible from its NTLR income of £48,100.

(c) (i) Corporation tax implications for Kitz Ltd of the sale of the patent to Durn Ltd

Durn Ltd will not be in a capital gains group with Kitz Ltd and Feld Ltd, as Feld Ltd will not have the minimum 75% holding in Durn Ltd which is required for this. Accordingly, the sale of the patent, which is an intangible asset, will give rise to a trading profit for Kitz Ltd, equal to the excess of the sale proceeds over the tax written down value of the patent at the date of sale. The profit on sale of the patent will therefore be £42,000 (£72,000 – £30,000). This will be included in Kitz Ltd's taxable trading profit for the year ending 31 March 2026.

(ii) Impact on Kitz Ltd's corporation tax liability for the year ending 31 March 2026 if the maximum rollover relief claim is made

As Feld Ltd is a UK resident, wholly owned subsidiary of Kitz Ltd, the two companies are in a capital gains group.

Feld Ltd will acquire an intangible fixed asset (goodwill of an unincorporated business) on 1 April 2025, which is within the 12 months prior to the sale of the patent by Kitz Ltd.

Accordingly, rollover relief will be available for part of the profit on the sale of the patent to be deferred against the cost of the goodwill. As the cost of the goodwill is less than the sale proceeds for the patent, the maximum profit which can be deferred is restricted to the excess of the amount invested in the goodwill over the original cost of the patent.

Therefore, the maximum profit which can be deferred is £8,000 (£68,000 – £60,000).

This would lead to a reduction in Kitz Ltd's corporation tax liability of £2,000 (£8,000 × 25%).

Tutorial note

Where intangibles rollover relief is claimed a gain should be left chargeable equal to the proceeds not reinvested (£72,000 – £68,000 = £4,000) plus any amortisation claimed on the old asset (£60,000 – £30,000 = £30,000).

Examiner's report

This question was in three main parts, dealing with a company selling shares in a subsidiary, transfer pricing and the sale of an intangible fixed asset.

The first part of the question asked for an explanation of the implications of a sale of shares in a subsidiary and many candidates were able to identify the availability of the substantial shareholding exemption and the associated conditions for this exemption. However, a substantial number of candidates missed the further point regarding a degrouping charge arising, despite clues in the question pointing towards this. Candidates should practise as many questions as they can before sitting the ATX-UK exam so that they become accustomed to picking up relevant information given in exam questions.

This question part specifically asked for no calculations and yet a significant number of candidates gave calculations. Even if candidates' workings were correct, there were no marks awarded for calculations when they have been specifically asked not to provide them. Once again, the candidates are wasting their limited exam time and earning no marks. Candidates should read the requirement carefully and only answer what is being asked for.

The second part of the question dealt with the transfer pricing consequences for two group companies making an intra-group loan at an interest rate below market rate. This part of the question was generally very poorly answered. Many candidates were not aware of the most basic elements of the transfer pricing rules and very few could apply the rules to the facts of the question. The ATX-UK exams will seek to examine all areas of the syllabus and candidates need to have a solid understanding of all aspects of the syllabus.

The third part of the question dealt with the sale of an intangible fixed asset (IFA) and subsequent rollover relief. It was clear that very few candidates understood the detailed IFA rules and even less understood the IFA rollover relief and this part of the question was very poorly answered. Once again, candidates should be aware that any part of the syllabus can be tested and given that all questions are compulsory, candidates should aim to be prepared to answer questions on any topic.

ACCA marking scheme

				Marks
(a)	Availability of substantial shareholding exemption			3.0
	Implications re degrouping charge			4.0
				7.0
			Maximum	6.0
(b)	Implications for Kitz Ltd			4.0
	Implications for Feld Ltd			3.5
				7.5
			Maximum	7.0
(c)	(i)	Implications of the sale of the patent		2.5
		Calculation of trading profit		1.0
				3.5
			Maximum	3.0
	(ii)	Reason for availability of rollover relief		2.0
		Maximum rollover relief available		2.5
		Calculation of reduction in corporation tax liability		0.5
				5.0
			Maximum	4.0
	Professional skills marks (see below)		**Maximum**	5.0
Total				**25.0**

Professional skills marks

Analysis and evaluation

- Appropriate use of information to determine the corporation tax treatment of the sale of the shares in Mayr Ltd in part (a).
- Evaluation of the actual adjustments required to the taxable total profits of both Kitz Ltd and Feld Ltd by analysing the data available in part (b).
- Appropriate use of information to determine the corporation tax treatment of the sale of the patent in part (c)(i).

Commercial acumen

- Demonstration of an understanding of the substantial shareholding exemption by application to the sale of the Mayr Ltd shares in part (a).
- Recognition that the interest rate offered by the bank is an arm's length transaction and supports the purpose of the transfer pricing rules to prevent the avoidance of tax in part (b).
- Recognition that the acquisition of the goodwill by Feld Ltd enables Kitz Ltd to rollover the gain on disposal of its intangible fixed asset in part (c)(ii).

69 FOX LTD (ADAPTED)

Key answer tips

This question covers assignment of a lease, rollover relief and group relief.

Part (a)(i) firstly looks at the assignment of a lease. This is an area that is not frequently examined, but the calculation is fairly straight forward if you remember the rules. The other thing to consider in this requirement is the deferred gain. Will there be any impact with regards to that now that the lease has been disposed of?

Part (a)(ii) tests group rollover relief. You first of all need to establish which group companies, if any, will be able to take part in a group rollover relief claim. Once you have done this you then need to consider group acquisitions and the extent to which they would be qualifying assets for rollover relief. This information, together with the information from part (a)(i) should help you to work out how much still needs to be spent to rollover the maximum amount.

Part (b) looks at loss relief for companies. There is a group in this scenario, so it may be tempting to dive straight into talking about group relief. However, you will score easy marks for discussing how the loss making company could use its own losses first, and also for identifying which companies are in a group relief group and why.

(a) (i) Chargeable gain on the assignment of the lease

	£
Proceeds	180,000
Less: Cost (£102,000 × 82.496/95.457)	(88,151)
	91,849

Tax treatment of the deferred gain

On acquisition the lease had less than 60 years remaining so was a depreciating asset for capital gains tax purposes. Accordingly, the gain on the factory building of £43,000 was deferred until the earliest of:

– The date the lease ceased to be used in Fox Ltd's business

– The date of disposal of the lease

– 1 October 2019 (ten years after the acquisition of the lease).

Therefore, the deferred gain became chargeable on 1 October 2019 and not on the assignment of the lease of the factory. Accordingly, the chargeable gain on disposal of the lease is just £91,849.

(ii) Rollover relief available

As Fox Ltd acquired at least 75% of the ordinary shares in Salas Ltd on 1 April 2024, Salas Ltd became a member of a capital gains group with Fox Ltd, Bravo Ltd and Corro Ltd from that date. Corro Ltd is a member of the capital gains group as Bravo Ltd's holding in Corro Ltd is at least 75%, and Fox Ltd's effective holding in Corro Ltd is more than 50% (90% × 80% = 72%).

Qualifying assets acquired from outside the group by any of the members of the capital gains group within the period from 2 October 2022 to 1 October 2026 may be eligible assets for the purposes of a rollover relief claim. Qualifying assets include land and buildings, and items of fixed plant and machinery.

Tutorial note

Rollover relief can be claimed on a group wide basis by members of a chargeable gains group. This means that one group member can sell a qualifying asset, but the acquisition of a qualifying asset by another group member will still be eligible for rollover relief.

The whole of the gain on the disposal of the lease is eligible for relief as the leased factory was wholly used in Fox Ltd's trade. Therefore, £180,000 needs to be reinvested in qualifying business assets.

Corro Ltd acquired a warehouse on 1 July 2023 for £168,000. This is a qualifying business asset, acquired within the qualifying reinvestment period, but as only 70% of the building will be used for trading purposes, only £117,600 (£168,000 × 70%) of its cost will be a qualifying acquisition for rollover relief purposes.

Tutorial note

An asset only qualifies for rollover relief to the extent that it is used in a trade. Where a new asset is purchased we must multiply the acquisition cost by the percentage of the asset that will be used in the trade to find the qualifying cost for rollover relief purposes.

Accordingly, £62,400 (£180,000 – £117,600) of the proceeds from the disposal of the lease currently have not been reinvested, so this is the minimum amount that Fox Ltd must spend on acquiring the new freehold factory in order that the full amount of the eligible gain on the disposal of the lease can be deferred.

(b) Group relief in respect of Salas Ltd's trading loss of the year ending 30 June 2024

As Fox Ltd acquired at least 75% of the ordinary shares in Salas Ltd on 1 April 2024, Salas Ltd became a member of a group for group relief purposes with Fox Ltd and Bravo Ltd from that date. Corro Ltd is not a member of the group for group relief purposes as Fox Ltd's effective holding in Corro Ltd is only 72%

Tutorial note

In order to be a member of a group relief group a direct holding of at least 75% is required, and effective holdings must also be at least 75%.

Pre-acquisition loss

Salas Ltd has no other sources of income in any accounting period, and generated a trading loss in the previous accounting period (which was its first accounting period), so there is no possibility of taking current period or carry back relief in Salas Ltd. Therefore, the amount of the pre-acquisition loss available for group relief will be £168,750 (£225,000 × 9/12).

This pre-acquisition loss will not be eligible for group relief against the total profits of Fox Ltd or Bravo Ltd until after five years from the end of the accounting period in which the change in ownership occurred i.e. 30 June 2029, and then only to the extent that Salas Ltd has not been able to relieve it against its own taxable total profits.

Post-acquisition loss

The loss of the three months ending 30 June 2024 of £56,250 (£225,000 × 3/12) is a post-acquisition loss. This loss may be surrendered to Fox Ltd and/or Bravo Ltd for relief against these companies' taxable total profits of the corresponding period. The amount of the loss surrendered cannot exceed the companies' taxable total profits for the corresponding period. Any remaining loss can be carried forward for group relief in future accounting periods. In future periods the loss must be relieved as far as possible by Salas Ltd against its own taxable total profits before any remaining loss can be surrendered.

Examiner's report

Requirement (a)(i)

This requirement involved the calculation of a chargeable gain arising on the assignment of a lease and an explanation of the tax treatment of a deferred gain.

The lease in the question had 26 years left to run (i.e. a short lease) which meant that candidates needed to consider two things in relation to its disposal:

1. The fact that it was a wasting asset. Lease percentages were provided to enable candidates to restrict the cost figure in the computation of the gain.
2. The fact that it was a depreciating asset (life of less than 60 years) for the purposes of rollover relief (ROR). This meant that, as the gain on the disposal of a previous asset had been deferred by virtue of investing in the lease, the deferred gain would not have been deducted from the base cost of the lease, but would crystallise on the earliest of three dates: the date of disposal of the lease, the date when the lease ceased to be used in the company's trade, or 10 years after its acquisition. In this scenario the gain would have already crystallised as the leasehold premises had been owned for more than 10 years.

Most candidates prepared a computation of the gain, but mistakes were frequently made. Candidates generally realised that they needed to use the lease percentages provided, but in many cases applied them incorrectly, or applied them to the gain, rather than the cost.

Failure to recognise that the lease was a depreciating asset meant that many candidates provided no explanation whatsoever, or only a very brief incorrect one, with regard to the treatment of the deferred gain. Candidates need to remember that, as was the case here, a deferred gain can sometimes become independently chargeable, rather than being deducted from the base cost of another asset. It is important for candidates to pay attention in their studies to situations where the relief operates in this manner.

Requirement (a)(ii)

There were two requirements within part (a)(ii). Candidates were required to provide an explanation, with supporting calculations of:

1 The ROR currently available within the Fox Ltd group in respect of the gain on the lease calculated in (a)(i); and then

2 The minimum amount to be spent on a proposed new qualifying asset such that the full amount of the eligible gain could be rolled over.

Picking up on the reference to the 'group' in the first part, many candidates commenced with an explanation of which companies were members of Fox Ltd's gains group. This was a good place to start. It was encouraging to see that candidates generally appeared to have learnt the definitions of both gains groups and group relief groups, and were able to apply their knowledge to a given scenario. The ability to do this is fundamental at this level. It was then necessary to explain, and calculate, the amount of ROR currently available. A methodical approach was useful here:

1 What were the requirements for ROR, and were they satisfied in this scenario?

Yes, Fox Ltd sold a qualifying asset, and Corro Ltd acquired a qualifying asset, within the required time period of four years commencing one year before the date of disposal.

2 To what extent was the gain eligible for relief?

The full gain was eligible as the leasehold premises were wholly used in Fox Ltd's trade throughout its ownership of the property.

3 To what extent were the proceeds on disposal invested in a qualifying asset(s)?

Corro Ltd had acquired a warehouse, which was a qualifying asset, but was going to use it only 70% for trading purposes. The qualifying expenditure therefore had to be restricted to 70%. The amount of the proceeds retained constituted the gain which would be immediately chargeable, and the remainder of the gain was the amount which was eligible for ROR.

Very few candidates adopted such a methodical approach. A majority spotted that the warehouse acquired by Corro Ltd would be a qualifying asset but didn't say why. Also, many picked up on the 70% trade use, but then applied this to the gain on the lease, rather than the cost of the replacement. Very few went on to consider the retained proceeds, and consequently the amount of ROR available, which was what they were specifically asked to do.

As a result of not completing the workings for the first part, many candidates were not then able to go on and get the mark for part (ii) by identifying the balance of the proceeds to be spent on the proposed new factory building. For those who did, the most common mistake was to deduct the amount spent by Corro Ltd from the gain, rather than the proceeds.

Requirement (b)

This requirement related to a trading loss incurred by a new group member, Salas Ltd, in the accounting period in which it joined the group. Again, many candidates started, quite sensibly, by identifying the qualifying group for group relief purposes. Once again, this reinforces the necessity to learn these rules, and to be able to explain them and correctly apply them to a specific scenario.

The next step was to recognise that, as the company had joined the group part way through its accounting period, the loss had to be time apportioned into the pre-acquisition and post-acquisition elements, and then each part of the loss discussed separately. This step was key, however, many candidates missed it, suggesting that they had not taken enough time to read the question carefully. Dates are frequently provided in questions, and it is critical that candidates take the time to appreciate their relevance and any wider implications.

In respect of the pre-acquisition loss, group relief would potentially be available, but only after five years had elapsed, and then only to the extent that Salas Ltd had been unable to relieve this loss itself.

As for the post-acquisition loss, group relief was available in the corresponding accounting period for the other group companies, but only to the extent of their taxable total profits for this period. Any remaining loss could then be carried forward for group relief in the future.

Candidates need to be more accurate when discussing loss reliefs. Imprecise comments such as 'companies can take relief against their current profits' are not sufficient; candidates are expected to refer to 'taxable total profits' of the 'corresponding accounting period'.

Additionally, candidates should read the requirements very carefully to ensure that their answer is directed at what is specifically being asked. In this case, some candidates discussed the criteria for optimum relief within a group (surrendering the loss to a company which pays its corporation tax in instalments), or mentioned the possibility of consortium relief; neither of these points were relevant here. This wasted time and scored no marks.

ACCA marking guide

				Marks
(a)	(i)	Gain on lease		1.5
		Explanation re deferred gain		4.0
				5.5
			Maximum	4.0
	(ii)	Existence of gains group		2.0
		Extent to which rollover relief is available		4.5
		Minimum amount to be spent on lease		2.0
				8.5
			Maximum	7.0
(b)	Qualifying group			1.0
	Pre-acquisition loss			4.5
	Post-acquisition loss			4.5
				10.0
			Maximum	9.0
	Professional skills marks (see below)		**Maximum**	5.0
Total				**25.0**

Professional skills marks

Analysis and evaluation

- Analysis of information to determine the appropriate treatment of the deferred gain in part (a)(i).
- Assessment of the availability of group rollover relief in part (a)(ii).
- Appropriate use of the data to determine what calculations to perform to conclude on the amount to be spent on the new freehold factory in part (a)(ii).
- Evaluation of the loss options available for Salas Ltd's losses in part (b).

Commercial acumen

- Identification that partial business use of a new asset would restrict rollover relief in part (a)(ii).
- Demonstration of an understanding of how group relief works where there is a new group member in part (b).

70 EVORA LTD

Key answer tips

This is a three-part company-focused section B question covering intangible and tangible fixed assets, branch versus subsidiary and overseas aspects of VAT.

The three parts could be attempted in any order. As they are mostly discursive they lend themselves well to being completed in the word processor response option in the exam.

Part (a) requires an explanation of the corporation tax treatment of the purchase of a brand (i.e. an intangible asset) and a machine. You should note the number of marks available here as this gives an indication of how much detail you should provide. To score well you need to discuss the alternative tax treatments of the purchase of the intangible asset and consider the limit to the annual investment allowance for capital allowances.

Part (b)(i) asks you to explain the advantages of trading through an overseas permanent establishment (branch) compared to a subsidiary, focusing on the relief for losses. There is no point in writing about any other aspects of branch versus subsidiary, as this will waste valuable time and score no extra marks.

Part (b)(ii) then goes on to ask about the consequences of making an election to exempt the profits of an overseas permanent establishment from UK tax. The key here is to consider what will happen once the business is profitable, not just the consequences while it is loss-making, and to apply the rules to the information in the scenario.

The final part of the question covers the VAT implications of purchasing goods and services from overseas. Overseas aspects of VAT are tested regularly in the ATX exam, so you need to make sure that you are happy with the rules.

(a) Corporation tax implications of the acquisition of the assets of the unincorporated business

'Alte' brand

The amortisation charged in Silves Ltd's accounts will be an allowable deduction for corporation tax purposes. In the year ended 31 March 2024, the charge will be £6,250 (£50,000/8). An alternative treatment would be to claim an annual writing down allowance for tax purposes equal to 4% of the cost of the brand, on a straight-line basis, but clearly this would be less tax efficient for Silves Ltd.

Specialist machine

The acquisition of the machine is qualifying expenditure for the purpose of the 100% annual investment allowance (AIA). However, the AIA is limited to £1m in a 12-month accounting period, and this limit applies to a group of related (> 50%) companies, so if the total qualifying assets acquired by the two companies exceed this limit, they may need to choose how to allocate the AIA between them in the most tax-efficient way.

(b) (i) Tax advantage for Evora Ltd of commencing to trade through a permanent establishment (PE)

A PE does not constitute a separate legal entity, unlike a subsidiary company. Therefore, as the PE will incur a trading loss in the first nine months of trading, this can be offset against Evora Ltd's UK trading profit for the year ending 31 March 2025, thereby obtaining immediate tax relief for the losses.

However, trading losses incurred by a non-UK tax resident subsidiary company would not be available for relief in the UK, so loss relief would be delayed.

(ii) Election to exempt the profits of overseas PEs from UK corporation tax

Tax consequences

- Trading profits generated in overseas PEs will not be liable to UK corporation tax.
- No relief will be available in the UK in respect of trading losses incurred in overseas PEs.
- No capital allowances can be claimed in the UK in respect of assets acquired for use in overseas PEs.
- The election is irrevocable.
- The election will apply to all future overseas PEs established by Evora Ltd.

Advice to Evora Ltd

There is clearly no advantage in Evora Ltd making this election at this point, as the PE in Salema will generate losses in its first nine months of trading, which, without making the election, can be relieved in the UK.

When the PE in Salema subsequently becomes profitable (after the first nine-month period), there will be no UK corporation tax liability in respect of these profits due to the availability of double taxation relief (DTR). This is because the rate of tax charged on profits in Salema is higher than the rate charged in the UK. So there is still no advantage to making the election at this point.

In addition, the election would prevent UK capital allowances being available in respect of expenditure on capital assets used in any overseas PEs, and no loss relief would be available in respect of any future trading losses incurred by any overseas PEs, including those which are yet to be set up.

Therefore, making this election would not appear to be beneficial for Evora Ltd.

(c) Value added tax (VAT)

Overseas legal fees

The legal services provided to Evora Ltd will be regarded as being supplied in the UK, as this is Evora Ltd's place of business. Accordingly, Evora Ltd will be required to account for output tax in its VAT return for the quarter ending 30 June 2024. It can then recover this amount as input tax on the same VAT return. Therefore, this expense will not impact on the amount of VAT payable by Evora Ltd for this quarter.

Import of goods

On the assumption that Evora Ltd uses postponed accounting in respect of the import of goods from overseas suppliers, these goods will be reported on Evora Ltd's VAT return for the quarter ending 30 June 2024 in the same way as the legal services supplied (above). Therefore this expense will also not impact on the amount of VAT payable by Evora Ltd for this VAT quarter.

Examiner's report

Requirement (a)

This question part asked for an explanation of the corporation tax treatment in relation to the acquisition of two assets, one being a brand and the other a machine.

Some candidates scored full marks on the treatment of the brand, knowing that amortisation was allowed and that there was an alternative '4%' treatment, correctly concluding which one may be more advantageous. However, many candidates incorrectly discussed giving capital allowances on the brand.

Candidates generally knew that the machine would be eligible for capital allowances. Of those that correctly identified that the machine would be eligible for the annual investment allowance (AIA), not all went on to discuss the annual £1m limit for the AIA and there were virtually no references to this limit applying to the group.

In order to score an analysis and evaluation skills mark in this part, candidates needed to use relevant information to determine suitable calculations. By doing this, candidates are showing that they not only know the rules but that they can apply them to the facts of the question.

In order to score a scepticism mark here, we were looking for candidates to challenge the uncertainty in the question of whether the annual investment allowance had been used by the group to any extent. In future questions, candidates should be looking to challenge uncertain information in the facts of the question to earn scepticism marks.

Requirement (b)(i)

This part asked for an explanation of why it would be advantageous to trade through a permanent establishment (PE) rather than an overseas subsidiary company, with reference to the relief available for a loss in the overseas entity.

The majority of candidates were able to score at least two out of three marks on this part for recognising that, with an overseas PE, the loss could be used by the UK company but this was not the case if the loss arose in an overseas subsidiary. Some candidates lost out on a mark by only describing the consequence with a PE and not going on to describe the consequence with an overseas subsidiary. We were also looking for candidates to describe that a permanent establishment was not a separate legal entity but only a minority made this additional point.

A number of students wasted time discussing the treatment of profits in each of the two overseas entities which had not been asked for and so wasted time and earned no marks.

Candidates should take the time to read and re-read the requirements carefully, to ensure that they are not providing an answer beyond what is required. Highlighting key words within a requirement may help to maintain focus and to ensure that candidates do not lose sight of what it is they are being asked to do.

Requirement (b)(ii)

Part (b)(ii) asked candidates to state the tax consequences of making an election to exempt the profits of overseas PEs from UK corporation tax and further, to advise the company whether or not it will be beneficial to make this election (given the facts in the question).

A good number of candidates were able to state the consequences and scored well for doing this.

When candidates came to give advice, many knew that the election was not worthwhile while the overseas PE was loss-making. However, the facts of the question detailed that the overseas tax rate on PEs was higher than the UK tax rate and that there was no double tax treaty between the UK and the overseas jurisdiction. There was lots of confusion about the meaning of this. Some candidates wrongly thought that in the absence of a treaty there would be no double tax relief (DTR). Some candidates mistakenly thought that by making the election the loss would remain in the overseas PE to be used to save tax at the overseas (higher) tax rate and that this would be beneficial. Only a minority of candidates correctly recognised that with a higher overseas tax rate, DTR would be equal to the UK tax charged on any future profits, so overall there would be no UK tax charged on overseas profits anyway (so no need to make the election to exempt profits). Many candidates just ignored the possibility of profits despite them being detailed in the question.

In order to recommend effectively, candidates needed to have assessed all aspects of the scenario i.e. current losses, future profits and plans for future PEs. Candidates needed to consider all the facts presented to them in the scenario and address them in their answers.

Another issue with this part of the question was that a number of candidates thought that they were still answering a question about PE versus overseas subsidiary company (as had been asked in part (b)(i)) instead of the PE election and so earned few or no marks. Candidates should read and re-read the given requirement to ensure that they are clear on what they are being asked to do before they begin their answers.

In order to earn analysis and evaluation and commercial acumen marks for this part of the question, candidates needed to demonstrate that they had considered all the relevant factors relating to the election, such as losses, future profits and plans for future PEs. They needed to use appropriate information to draw conclusions, based on a balanced appraisal of the information and considering the possible consequences of an election.

Requirement (c)

This part asked candidates to explain how each of services and goods, both purchased from an overseas supplier, would be reported on a VAT return for a particular quarter.

Candidates fell into broadly three camps for this part. There were those who just didn't know any rules regarding VAT on goods and services from overseas and so earned no marks. They wasted time discussing zero-rated and exempt goods and services and partial exemption rules. The next group of candidates did have some understanding of the VAT rules but discussed the rules generally and did *not* discuss them in the context of what would be reported on a VAT return and so could only earn limited marks. The third group of candidates applied the rules to the context of submission of the VAT return and were able to score well.

In order to score well at ATX-UK, candidates need to be able to do more than state generic rules. They must be able to apply the rules to the facts of the question and what is being asked of them.

ACCA marking scheme

				Marks
(a)	Brand			4.0
	Machine			3.5
				7.5
			Maximum	6.0
(b)	(i)	Permanent establishment		2.0
		Subsidiary company		2.0
				4.0
			Maximum	3.0
	(ii)	Consequences of election		3.0
		Advice		4.5
				7.5
			Maximum	6.0
(c)	Value added tax (VAT) on overseas legal fees			3.0
	VAT on imported goods			2.0
				5.0
	Professional skills marks (see below)		**Maximum**	5.0
Total				**25.0**

Professional skills marks

Analysis and evaluation

– Appropriate use of relevant information to determine suitable calculations.

– Demonstration of the ability to consider all relevant factors in relation to the election.

– Balanced appraisal of information to make a recommendation in respect of the election.

– Appropriate use of information to draw conclusions.

Commercial acumen

– Recognition of possible consequences of making the election.

Scepticism

– Demonstration of the ability to identify missing information in respect of the annual investment allowance.

Section 5

SPECIMEN EXAM QUESTIONS

SECTION A

This question is compulsory and MUST be attempted

1 REP LTD AND FREYA (ADAPTED) *Walk in the footsteps of a top tutor*

You should assume that today's date is 1 September 2024.

You are an ACCA student working for a firm of accountants. Your manager, Sheila Hughes, has asked for your assistance in drafting notes in preparation for an internal meeting to discuss issues raised by Lamar, who is the majority shareholder and managing director of REP Ltd, and his wife, Freya. Both Lamar and Freya are clients of your firm.

In addition to some ethical considerations which have been raised by your manager, advice is required in respect of:

- the corporation tax issues in relation to a proposed purchase of shares by REP Ltd in an overseas company
- the value added tax (VAT) implications of the purchase of an investment property
- the income tax consequences of ceasing to trade, and
- the inheritance tax consequences of a gift of shares to a trust.

The following **exhibits** provide information relevant to the question:

1 REP Ltd – note of a conversation between Lamar and your manager

2 Personal tax affairs – email from Freya

3 Work to be carried out – email from manager

This information should be used to answer the question **requirements**.

Exhibit 1 – REP Ltd

Note of a telephone conversation between Lamar and Sheila Hughes (tax manager) on 1 September 2024

1 Potential investment in JAY Ltd

The directors of REP Ltd are in discussion with the management of CRO Ltd (an unconnected company) regarding the establishment of a new company, JAY Ltd. Both REP Ltd and CRO Ltd are UK resident companies which prepare accounts to 31 March each year.

JAY Ltd would commence trading on 1 April 2025 and carry on its business activities in the country of Garia, where it would manufacture computer components.

Business profits generated in Garia are subject to 13% business tax in that country. There is no double tax treaty between the UK and Garia.

Size of investment

CRO Ltd is proposing that REP Ltd would own 30% of the ordinary share capital of JAY Ltd, with CRO Ltd owning the remaining 70%. However, Lamar and his fellow directors regard this potential investment as somewhat risky, such that if they decide to proceed, they may prefer to own just 20% of JAY Ltd rather than 30%. If REP Ltd owns 20% then CRO Ltd would increase its holding to 80%.

JAY Ltd will have no source of taxable income, other than its trading profits, and will not make any chargeable gains during the year ending 31 March 2026.

JAY Ltd's tax adjusted trading profit for the year ending 31 March 2026 is budgeted to be £135,000, all of which will relate to its activities in Garia. However, there is the possibility that it will be loss making in either that year, or in future years.

Additional information

REP Ltd has not been involved in a joint venture of this nature before and has no experience of carrying on business outside the UK. Lamar told me that he had been provided with the following additional relevant information:

(i) It has not yet been determined whether JAY Ltd will be resident in the UK or in Garia.

(ii) If JAY Ltd is resident in the UK, it will be carrying on its business through a permanent establishment in Garia and will consider making an election to exempt its overseas trading profits from UK tax.

(iii) Confirmation has been received that if JAY Ltd is resident in Garia, this will not result in a charge under the controlled foreign company (CFC) rules.

2 Purchase of investment property

The directors are considering the purchase by REP Ltd of a new, unused commercial building, situated in the UK, for £200,000 plus 20% value added tax (VAT). REP Ltd would then grant a 20-year lease of this building to one of a number of different businesses they are currently in discussions with.

The directors are keen to recover the VAT charged by the vendor on the sale of this building. Lamar told me that one of his friends had suggested that they could do this by opting to tax the building before granting the lease, and that this would have no effect on their tenant or any potential future purchaser.

Exhibit 2 – Personal tax affairs

Email extract from Freya dated 1 September 2024

Cessation of my business

I am intending to cease my unincorporated consultancy business on 31 March 2025. I began trading in 2016 and have always prepared accounts to 31 March each year. My business is my only source of income.

– I will prepare a set of accounts for the year ended 31 March 2025. The budgeted tax adjusted profit for this period, before deduction of capital allowances, is £94,000.

– The only capital asset within my business is a car which has always been used 65% for business purposes. I will withdraw this car from the business on 31 March 2025 when it will have a market value of £11,100, which is less than its original cost. The tax written down value of this car as at 31 March 2024 was £8,700.

Proposed gift of shares to trust

– I established a discretionary trust for the benefit of my nieces and nephews on 1 August 2014.

– I own shares in Dexil Ltd and on 1 November 2024, I am planning to give 20,000 of these shares to the trust. After I have made the gift, I will still own 60,000 shares (60% of the company).

  You have already advised me that these shares are not relevant business property for the purposes of business property relief, due to the investment activities of Dexil Ltd. Accordingly, I am aware that the gift on 1 November 2024 may result in an inheritance tax (IHT) liability. If I decide to make the gift, I will pay any IHT due and I need to know by when such amount would fall due.

– I have made the following gifts in the past:

		£
1 August 2014	Cash to trustees on the creation of the trust	120,000
1 February 2020	Cash to brother	35,000
1 May 2020	Additional cash to trustees	170,000
1 July 2024	Cash to sister	45,000

– None of these gifts has resulted in an IHT liability.

Additional information provided by your manager

These are the Dexil Ltd share valuations you should use:

Shareholding	Up to 25%	26% to 50%	51% to 74%	75% or more
Value per share	£8	£11	£17	£24

Freya currently owns 80% of the ordinary share capital of Dexil Ltd. The remaining shares in the company are owned by individuals who have no connection with Freya.

Exhibit 3 – Work to be carried out

To: Tax Assistant

From: Sheila Hughes, Tax Manager

Subject: Lamar

Date: 1 September 2024

Hi

I need you to prepare some notes in preparation for an internal meeting with the rest of the engagement team. The notes should be set out in a manner which will make it easy for you to refer to them during the meeting and should address the following issues:

(a) Knowledge obtained from advising other clients

We have many existing clients which trade from permanent establishments situated overseas, and a few years ago we had a client with a presence in the country of Garia.

– Identify the points which should be made in order to explain the extent to which REP Ltd can benefit from the knowledge our firm has gained from advising other clients. **(5 marks)**

(b) Investment in JAY Ltd by REP Ltd (Exhibit 1)

(i) Residency of JAY Ltd

– Explanations of the relevance of the country of residency of JAY Ltd in relation to:

  – the amount of corporation tax payable in the UK and Garia in respect of its profits; and

  – the relief available to REP Ltd if JAY Ltd's business in Garia were to make a trading loss.

Before you start, take some time to identify the different possibilities which need to be addressed, recognising that it is not yet known what percentage of JAY Ltd will be owned by REP Ltd. **(10 marks)**

(ii) Election to exempt the profits of JAY Ltd's overseas permanent establishment from UK tax

– List the implications of JAY Ltd making this election. **(3 marks)**

(iii) Controlled foreign company (CFC) rules

I can confirm that a CFC charge will not arise if JAY Ltd is resident in Garia. However, I want to provide Lamar with:

– an explanation of the purpose of the CFC rules and the charge which can be levied under them. **(3 marks)**

(c) Purchase of investment property by REP Ltd (Exhibit 1)

– Explain how opting to tax the building would enable REP Ltd to recover the value added tax (VAT) charged by the vendor, and

– Explain whether or not the advice from Lamar's friend is correct.

There is no need for you to consider partial exemption or the capital goods scheme.

(5 marks)

(d) Personal tax affairs (Exhibit 2)

(i) Cessation of Freya's business on 31 March 2025

– A calculation of Freya's estimated liability to income tax and class 4 national insurance contributions in respect of her final tax year of trading. **(6 marks)**

(ii) Proposed gift of shares to trust on 1 November 2024

– A calculation of the inheritance tax which would be payable by Freya if she were to give 20,000 shares in Dexil Ltd to the trust on 1 November 2024, as planned. Your calculation should indicate the availability or otherwise of all relevant annual exemptions.

– The payment date, together with a brief explanation of how it has been determined. **(8 marks)**

I look forward to seeing your notes.

Sheila

Required:

You should assume that today's date is 1 September 2024.

Respond to the instructions in the email from your manager.

Note: The split of the mark allocation is shown in Exhibit 3 – Work to be carried out.

(40 marks)

Professional marks will be awarded for the demonstration of skill in communication, analysis and evaluation, scepticism and commercial acumen in your answer. **(10 marks)**

(Total: 50 marks)

SECTION B

BOTH questions are compulsory and MUST be attempted

2 AMELIA (ADAPTED)

You should assume that today's date is 1 September 2024.

Amelia is a sole trader. She is seeking advice in respect of:

– the tax reliefs available for a loss incurred by her business,

– the income tax and capital gains tax implications of replacing a warehouse, and

– deregistration for value added tax (VAT) purposes.

Amelia:

– Has owned her unincorporated business, AS Trading, for many years.

– Has savings income of £6,000 each year.

– Had rental income of £11,600 from a UK residential property in the tax year 2023/24.

– Has no rental income in the tax year 2024/25 as the letting ceased on 31 March 2024.

– Sold this property on 30 April 2024.

AS Trading – tax adjusted trading profit/(loss):

	£
Year ended 31 March 2024	30,000
Year ending 31 March 2025 (forecast)	(14,000)

Amelia – recent capital disposals:

– Amelia's capital disposals are as follows:

Asset	**Date of disposal**	**(loss)/gain**
Painting	1 June 2023	(10,700)
UK rental property	30 April 2024	45,000
Shares in Swartz Ltd	16 August 2024	28,000

– All of these disposals were made to unconnected persons.

– Amelia had never lived in the UK rental property.

– Swartz Ltd is an unquoted trading company.

– Amelia sold the whole of her 3% shareholding in Swartz Ltd. She had acquired the shares in 2022.

Proposed sale of Warehouse 1:

– Amelia acquired Warehouse 1 on 1 August 2018 for £86,000.

– Amelia will sell Warehouse 1 on 1 August 2025 for its expected market value at that date of £118,000.

– AS Trading occupies three out of the four floors of Warehouse 1.

– The remaining floor has been rented to tenants throughout Amelia's ownership of the building.

Proposed purchase of Warehouse 2:

- Amelia will purchase this warehouse on 1 June 2025. Structures and buildings allowance is not available in respect of the warehouse.
- She will also acquire a forklift truck for use in the warehouse, on 1 June 2025.
- Amelia will pay £83,000 for Warehouse 2, and will pay £23,000 for the forklift truck.
- Amelia will start to use the whole of Warehouse 2 in her business from 1 August 2025.

AS Trading – taxable turnover for value added tax (VAT) purposes:

	£
Year ended 31 March 2024	92,000
Year ending 31 March 2025 (forecast)	65,000
Year ending 31 March 2026 (forecast)	79,000

- Amelia expects that the taxable turnover of the business will continue to increase gradually in the next few years.
- AS Trading makes wholly standard-rated supplies.
- Amelia wishes to apply for voluntary deregistration for VAT purposes on 31 March 2025.

Required:

You should assume that today's date is 1 September 2024.

(a) (i) State the reliefs available to Amelia in respect of her trading loss of the year ending 31 March 2025, on the assumption that Amelia does not wish to carry forward any of the loss. (3 marks)

(ii) Explain, with supporting calculations, how much tax would be saved for each of the reliefs identified in requirement (a)(i). (8 marks)

(b) Explain, with supporting calculations, the capital gains tax and income tax implications for Amelia of the proposed sale of Warehouse 1, and the acquisition of Warehouse 2 and the forklift truck. (6 marks)

(c) Explain why Amelia can apply to voluntarily deregister for value added tax (VAT) purposes on 31 March 2025, from what date her VAT registration would be cancelled, and the immediate consequences for her of deregistering. (3 marks)

Professional marks will be awarded for the demonstration of skill in analysis and evaluation and commercial acumen in your answer. (5 marks)

(Total: 25 marks)

3 DORIAN

You should assume that today's date is 1 January 2025.

You have been asked to provide advice to Dorian, the managing director of Taupe Ltd, in relation to:

– Taupe Ltd's status as a close company,

– the provision by the company of employment benefits to Dorian, and

– the late filing of the company's corporation tax return.

Dorian and Taupe Ltd

Taupe Ltd:

– Is a UK resident trading company, and is also a close company.

– Has six directors, Dorian and five other, unrelated, individuals.

– Has an accounting reference date of 30 April each year.

– Always pays all amounts due to HM Revenue and Customs (HMRC) by the due date.

– Is not a large company for the purpose of being required to pay its corporation tax liability in instalments.

Taupe Ltd – shareholders:

– The shares in Taupe Ltd are held as follows:

	Percentage of issued ordinary shares
Dorian	5%
The other five directors (each holding 5%)	25%
Basil (Dorian's father)	23%
Other, unrelated, shareholders (each holding less than 2%)	47%
	100%

Dorian:

– Has an annual salary of £78,000 from Taupe Ltd.

– Was provided with an interest-free loan of £7,500 from Taupe Ltd on 6 April 2023. Notional tax was payable on this loan by Taupe Ltd.

– Is due to repay this loan on 30 June 2026, but may repay it earlier, on 30 April 2026.

– Has no other income.

– Works full time at Taupe Ltd's office in London.

Taupe Ltd – assistance with Dorian's home to work travel costs:

– Taupe Ltd is considering two alternatives to assist Dorian with the costs of his daily travel from home to work for the tax year 2025/26.

Alternative 1:

- On 6 April 2025, Taupe Ltd will make an interest-free loan to Dorian of £4,800, equal to the cost of his annual travel season ticket.
- Taupe Ltd will write off this loan on 5 April 2026.
- Dorian will incur no additional travel costs under this alternative.

Alternative 2:

- Taupe Ltd will pay Dorian a mileage allowance for driving his own car to work, amounting to £3,600 for the year ending 5 April 2026.
- Taupe Ltd will pay an unconnected company an annual fee of £1,200 for a car parking space for Dorian near the company's London office.
- Dorian has estimated that his current annual cost of driving from home to work is £5,220, including £1,320 for parking.

Taupe Ltd – late filing of corporation tax returns:

- Taupe Ltd filed its corporation tax return for the year ended 30 April 2023 on 29 August 2024.
- HMRC issued a notice requiring the filing of this return on 8 June 2023.
- Taupe Ltd had filed its corporation tax return for the year ended 30 April 2022 on 6 July 2023.
- All previous corporation tax returns had been filed on time.

Required:

You should assume that today's date is 1 January 2025.

(a) Explain why Taupe Ltd is classed as a close company. (4 marks)

(b) Explain, with supporting calculations, the tax implications for both Dorian and Taupe Ltd, if Dorian repays the £7,500 loan on 30 April 2026 rather than on 30 June 2026. (5 marks)

(c) Explain, with supporting calculations, which of the two alternatives for providing assistance with travel costs, will produce the lower overall cost for Dorian. (8 marks)

(d) State, with reasons, the due date for filing Taupe Ltd's corporation tax return for the year ended 30 April 2023, and the implications for Taupe Ltd in respect of filing it late. (3 marks)

Professional marks will be awarded for the demonstration of skill in analysis and evaluation, and commercial acumen in your answer. (5 marks)

(Total: 25 marks)

Section 6

ANSWERS TO SPECIMEN EXAM

1 REP LTD AND FREYA (ADAPTED) *Walk in the footsteps of a top tutor*

Key answer tips

This question covers ethics, establishing a company with overseas activities, controlled foreign companies, VAT on land and buildings, cessation of a sole trade and IHT on lifetime gifts. There is a lot to cover, so it is important that you allocate your time carefully between the different requirements to ensure that you don't run out of time.

The first part on ethics covers whether the firm is able to use knowledge acquired from working with other clients to assist this client. The key principle to identify here was confidentiality! Ethics will always offer some easy marks and this topic is tested on a reasonably regular basis.

Part (b) covers three main areas to do with establishing the new company. Part (i) requires explanations on corporate residency. Make sure you follow a logical approach covering UK residency issues and overseas residency issues separately. Part (ii) asks for a list of the implications of making an election to exempt profits of an overseas permanent establishment. This is a frequently examined topic and should provide easy marks. Finally, part (iii) requires an explanation of the purpose of the CFC rules and the CFC charge that can arise. Make sure that you only mention the relevant points and don't waste your time covering the CFC exemptions as this is not part of the requirement and will not score any marks. You need to manage your time efficiently, so that you have enough time to answer all three sub requirements.

You are also asked for explanations in part (c) about whether the input VAT suffered on the purchase of an investment property can be recovered. VAT on land and buildings is a common exam topic and should provide some easy marks. Make sure you remember to cover all of the basic points to score maximum marks.

Part (d)(i) requires a calculation of IT and NIC on the cessation of an individual's unincorporated business. This is really just knowledge from the TX exam put in to an ATX scenario.

Part (d)(ii) requires the calculation of lifetime inheritance tax on a gift into a trust. Make sure you set out your calculations in a clearly labelled pro forma. There are other lifetime gifts in the question but don't waste your time with any unnecessary calculations; the question asks for the lifetime IHT on just one of the gifts!

The highlighted words in the written sections are key phrases that markers are looking for in your answer.

Notes for meeting

Client REP Ltd and Freya

Purpose Discussion of corporate and personal matters

Prepared by Tax senior

Date 1 September 2024

(a) Knowledge obtained from advising other clients

– We have experience of advising clients trading from permanent establishments situated overseas.

We have also advised on trading in the country of Garia.

– We will be able to use this general experience and expertise for the benefit of REP Ltd.

– However, we must not use any confidential information obtained as a result of our professional and business relationships for the benefit of REP Ltd (or any other client).

Confidentiality is one of the fundamental principles of ethics within ACCA's Code of Ethics and Conduct.

– This principle of confidentiality applies to confidential information obtained in respect of both ex-clients and continuing clients.

Tutorial note

Candidates who mentioned the fundamental principle of professional competence and due care were also awarded credit

(b) Investment in JAY Ltd

(i) Residency of JAY Ltd

Taxation of profits

The profits of the business will be generated in Garia regardless of where JAY Ltd is resident.

Accordingly, the profits will always be subject to business tax at 13% in Garia.

Tutorial note

Companies suffer tax on their worldwide profits in the country in which they are resident, therefore if JAY Ltd is resident in Garia it will suffer Garian tax on the profits.

Profits of overseas permanent establishments are taxed in the country in which they are located. If JAY Ltd is not resident in Garia it will still have an overseas permanent establishment in Garia.

So either way Garian tax of 13% will be suffered on the profits.

If JAY Ltd is resident in the UK

The profits would be subject to UK corporation tax because the permanent establishment (PE) in Garia is not a separate legal entity and UK resident companies are subject to corporation tax on their worldwide profits.

UK corporation tax would be due at 25% as JAY Ltd's augmented profits exceed the reduced upper limit of £125,000 (£250,000 ÷ 2) for corporation tax.

However, double tax relief would be available in the UK: the amount payable in the UK would be 12% (25% – 13%) of the profits, as set out below:

	£
UK corporation tax (£135,000 × 25%)	33,750
Less: Double tax relief (£135,000 × 13%)	(17,550)
UK corporation tax payable	16,200

Tutorial note

JAY Ltd will have one associated company since CRO Ltd will own a controlling holding in the company. Therefore, the limits for determining the relevant rate of UK corporation tax would be divided by two.

Double tax relief is available at the lower of UK corporation tax due (£33,750) and overseas tax suffered (£17,550)

If JAY Ltd is resident in Garia

The profits will only be subject to tax in Garia at the rate of 13%, as noted above.

JAY Ltd would not have a UK corporation tax liability in respect of these profits.

Any dividends received by REP Ltd and CRO Ltd from JAY Ltd would be exempt from corporation tax.

Relief available in respect of trading loss

If JAY Ltd is resident in the UK

If REP Ltd owns 30% of JAY Ltd:

– JAY Ltd would be a consortium company because at least 75% of JAY Ltd would be owned by companies, each of which own at least 5%, and less than 75%, of the company.

– In these circumstances, REP Ltd would be able to offset up to 30% of JAY Ltd's trading loss against its taxable total profits.

Tutorial note

A consortium exists where two or more companies each own at least 5%, collectively own at least 75% but do not individually own at least 75% of the shares in a UK resident company.

Consortium relief allows the surrender of trading losses between the consortium company and the consortium members.

Where the loss is in the consortium company, the members (such as REP Ltd) can claim their proportionate ownership of the loss; so here REP Ltd can claim a maximum of 30% of the trading loss (restricted to the TTP in REP Ltd).

If REP Ltd owns 20% of JAY Ltd:

– No relief would be available to REP Ltd in respect of any trading loss of JAY Ltd because CRO Ltd would own more than 75% of JAY Ltd.

Tutorial note

There would be no consortium relief available if REP Ltd were to only own 20%. This is because CRO Ltd would own 80%, which is at least 75%, and therefore a normal 75% loss relief group would exist between JAY Ltd and CRO Ltd, which REP Ltd would not be part of.

If JAY Ltd is resident in Garia:

No relief would be available in the UK for REP Ltd in respect of any trading losses realised by JAY Ltd in Garia.

Tutorial note

Consortium relief and group relief are only available between UK resident companies.

(ii) Election to exempt the profits of JAY Ltd's overseas PE from UK tax

This election is available to UK resident companies which generate profits from PEs situated overseas. If JAY Ltd were to make this election:

- its profits in Garia would no longer be subject to corporation tax in the UK. If no election is made, UK corporation tax would be payable on the profits in Garia at the rate of 12% (25% – 13%) after double tax relief
- no relief would be available in the UK in respect of any losses generated by the activities in Garia
- it would be irrevocable
- it would apply to all future overseas PEs of JAY Ltd.

Tutorial note

The election to exempt the profits from overseas permanent establishments of UK resident companies is a blanket election. It therefore applies to all of a company's overseas permanent establishments that exist at the date of making the election and all of its overseas permanent establishments that may exist in the future.

(iii) Controlled foreign company (CFC) rules

The UK tax system charges corporation tax on the worldwide profits of UK resident companies. However, it does not charge corporation tax on the profits earned overseas by a non-UK resident company.

A UK resident company could seek to exploit the latter rule by establishing a non-UK resident subsidiary in which to generate its overseas profits. The CFC legislation is designed to prevent overseas subsidiaries being used to avoid tax in this way.

Where the rules apply (and no exemption is available), UK resident companies owning at least 25% of a CFC are charged UK corporation tax on their proportionate share of the CFC's chargeable profits.

(c) Purchase of investment property

Recovery of input value added tax (VAT) on the purchase

When REP Ltd grants a lease of the building to a tenant, it will be making an exempt supply.

Therefore, REP Ltd will not be able to recover any VAT in relation to the purchase of the building unless it makes an election opting to tax it.

Suggestion from Lamar's friend

This statement is not necessarily correct for the following reasons:

No impact on tenant

If REP Ltd opts to tax the building, it would be required to charge VAT on the monthly rental payments due from the tenant. This will not be a problem where the tenant is able to recover all of the VAT charged. The effect on the tenant will depend on the type of supplies being made for VAT purposes. If the potential tenant is not making fully taxable supplies, then it will not be able to recover all of the VAT charged. This will represent an additional cost which may impact on the tenant's decision to rent the building and, if so, at what price.

No impact on a future sale of the building

Whilst the option to tax remains in place, REP Ltd would be required to charge VAT on a sale of the building. This could impact on any eventual sales price achieved if a future purchaser were not able to recover some, or all, of the VAT charged.

Tutorial note

The sale of a new (less than three years old) commercial building is standard-rated for VAT. REP Ltd will therefore suffer input tax on the purchase price.

The input tax is only recoverable if REP Ltd uses the building to make taxable supplies. It is worth noting here that the capital goods scheme would not apply as the building did not cost at least £250,000 exclusive of VAT – the question also makes it clear that it does not apply!

Leasing of land and buildings is exempt from VAT unless the building is opted to tax. If the building is opted, then VAT must be charged on all future supplies of the building – including leasing and the eventual sale (if within 20 years). Leasing then becomes a taxable supply, therefore the input tax suffered on the purchase would be recoverable.

(d) Personal tax affairs

(i) Cessation of Freya's business on 31 March 2025

Liability to income tax and class 4 national insurance contributions (NIC): tax year 2024/25

Income tax

	£
Trading profit for the final period	94,000
Add: Balancing charge on sale of car (W)	1,560
Taxable trading profit	95,560
Less: Personal allowance	(12,570)
Taxable income	82,990

£	£
37,700 × 20%	7,540
45,290 × 40%	18,116
82,990	
Income tax liability	25,656
Class 4 NICs	
£37,700 (£50,270 – £12,570) × 9%	3,393
£45,290 (£95,560 – £50,270) × 2%	906
Class 4 NIC liability	4,299

Working: Capital allowances

	Private use car	B.U.	Allowances
	£	%	£
TWDV b/f	8,700		
Disposal:			
Market value	(11,100)		
	(2,400)		
Balancing charge	2,400	× 65%	(1,560)

Tutorial note

Freya's unincorporated business is ceasing to trade.

In the capital allowances computation cessation rules apply. There are no WDAs, FYAs or AIA available in the closing year. All pools will need to be bought down to nil with balancing adjustments.

(ii) Proposed gift of shares to trust on 1 November 2024

Inheritance tax (IHT) payable

	£	£	£
Transfer of value (W)			900,000
Less: Annual exemptions 2024/25 and 2023/24 (used by PET on 1 July 2024)			0
Chargeable amount			900,000
Nil rate band at gift		325,000	
Less: Gross chargeable transfers (CLTs only) in 7 years pre-gift (1.11.2017 – 1.11.2024)			
CLT 1 May 2020	170,000		
Less: Annual exemption 2020/21	(3,000)		
2019/20 (used by PET on 1 February 2020)	0		
		(167,000)	
			(158,000)
Taxable amount			742,000
IHT payable (£742,000 × 25%)			185,500

Since the transfer occurs in the second half of the tax year, the IHT will fall due six months after the end of the month of the transfer, i.e. by 31 May 2025.

Working: Transfer of value

	£
Value of shares held prior to the gift: (80,000 × £24 (80%))	1,920,000
Value of shares held after the gift: (60,000 × £17 (60%))	(1,020,000)
Transfer of value	900,000

Tutorial notes

1 Annual exemptions are allocated to lifetime gifts in a strict chronological order:

CLT 1 August 2014	*uses the annual exemptions for 2014/15 and 2013/14*
PET 1 February 2020	*uses the annual exemptions for 2019/20 and 2018/19*
CLT 1 May 2020	*uses the annual exemption for 2020/21; the annual exemption for 2019/20 has already been used by the PET on 1 February 2020*
PET July 2024	*uses the annual exemptions for 2024/25 and 2023/24*

2 *When calculating the lifetime tax on a CLT the nil rate band in force at the date of the gift is used, less the gross chargeable value of any CLTs that fall within the seven years prior to the date of the gift (PETS are ignored in nil rate band calculations for lifetime tax).*

3 *The rate of IHT use for lifetime gifts depends on who is paying the tax.*

If the donor pays, the rate is 25%.

If the trustees pay, the rate is 20%.

ACCA marking scheme

				Marks
(a)	One mark for each relevant point			5.0
				5.0
(b)	(i)	Taxation of profits		
		Subject to tax in Garia		1.0
		If JAY Ltd is UK resident		4.0
		If JAY Ltd is resident in Garia		2.0
		Relief for losses		
		If JAY Ltd is UK resident		4.0
		If JAY Ltd is resident in Garia		1.0
				12.0
			Maximum	10.0
	(ii)	One mark for each relevant point		4.0
			Maximum	3.0
	(iii)	One mark for each relevant point		4.0
			Maximum	3.0
(c)	Recovery on input VAT on purchase			2.0
	Implications for the tenant			2.0
	Implications for the future sale			2.0
				6.0
			Maximum	5.0
(d)	(i)	Capital allowances		2.5
		Other aspects of taxable income		1.5
		IT and class 4 NIC liability		2.0
				6.0
	(ii)	Taxable amount of transfer to trust		2.5
		Nil rate band		2.5
		IHT liability		1.0
		Payment date		2.0
				8.0
	Professional skills marks (see below)		**Maximum**	10.0
Total				**50.0**

Professional skills marks

Communication

- General format and structure of meeting notes (e.g. use of headings/sub-headings to make meeting notes easy to refer to).
- Style, language and clarity (tone of meeting notes, presentation of calculations, appropriate use of the tools, easy to follow and more than a negligible amount of content).
- Effectiveness of communication (answer is relevant, specific rather than general and focused to the requirement).
- Adherence to specific instructions made in the scenario (e.g. limiting explanation of controlled foreign company rules to what was required, attempt to consider differing levels of investment in JAY Ltd).

Analysis and evaluation

- Use of information to determine impact of JAY Ltd's residence status in part (b)(i).
- Demonstration of reasoned judgement when considering impact of level of investment by REP Ltd in part (b)(i).
- Appropriate use of the data to determine suitable calculations of inheritance tax payable on Lamar's proposed gift of shares into trust and income tax and class 4 national insurance contributions payable by Freya in part (d).

Scepticism

- Effective challenge of validity of advice provided to opt to tax the investment property in part (c).
- Demonstration of the ability to probe into the reasons for issues and problems with the advice to opt to tax the investment property, including the identification of uncertainty in respect of future tenant and purchaser in part (c).

Commercial acumen

- Recognition of external constraints and opportunities regarding the use of knowledge obtained from advising other clients in part (a).
- Recognition of possible consequences of potential future decision to elect to exempt the profits of a permanent establishment from UK tax in part (b)(ii).
- Demonstration of awareness of purpose behind the controlled foreign companies' legislation in part (b)(iii).

2 AMELIA

Key answer tips

This question looks at a sole trader whose business is currently loss making, is in the process of replacing a warehouse and is considering voluntarily deregistering for VAT.

Part (a)(i) requires a fairly generic answer just stating the different ways in which the loss could be offset. Make sure you provide precise answers detailing what the loss can be offset against and whether the use of the loss can be restricted.

Part (a)(ii) moves on from part (i) and asks you to explain and calculate the tax savings for each of the reliefs identified earlier. Your approach to the answer will require some thought and planning, and a logical approach dealing with each option in turn is advisable. Rather than preparing full tax computations, which are time consuming, try to work in the margins just considering the rate at which tax will be saved.

Part (b) is mostly about rollover relief. CGT reliefs are expected to be tested in the exam, so spend some time learning in detail the conditions for each relief as well as the detail of how they operate.

Part (c) requires an explanation of the immediate consequences of the individual deregistering for VAT. VAT will be tested at some point in the exam; registration and de-registration are frequently examined.

(a) (i) Reliefs available in respect of Amelia's trading loss of the year ending 31 March 2025

The loss of the year ending 31 March 2025 is a loss of the tax year 2024/25. Accordingly, Amelia can offset the loss against her total income of 2024/25 and/or 2023/24. If she chooses to offset the loss against her total income of 2024/25, she can then offset any remaining loss against her chargeable gains of that year.

Tutorial notes

Amelia can make a current year claim and/or a prior year claim against total income for both years, either year and in any order. After a claim has been made against total income it is then possible for Amelia to make a claim against chargeable gains in that same year.

(ii) Relief against income and chargeable gains in the tax year 2024/25

In the tax year 2024/25, Amelia's only income will be savings income of £6,000. This will be covered by her personal allowance, such that she will have no liability to income tax for this year. Accordingly, if she chooses to take relief for the loss against this income, there will be no income tax saving. However, the remaining loss of £8,000 (£14,000 – £6,000) could then be offset against her chargeable gains for the year.

Tutorial note

If Amelia wishes to make a claim against her chargeable gains in the tax year 2024/25, it is mandatory that an all or nothing claim must first be made against her total income.

Amelia's chargeable gains comprise total gains less the capital loss brought forward i.e. £62,300 (£45,000 + £28,000 – £10,700). Accordingly, the full £8,000 of trading loss could be offset.

Ignoring offset of the trading loss, Amelia would have taxable gains of £56,300 after deducting the annual exempt amount of £6,000. As Amelia will have no taxable income in 2024/25, £37,700 of her taxable gains will fall within her basic rate band, and the remaining £18,600 will be taxed at the higher rate.

The trading loss should therefore be offset against the gain on the UK rental property, as this will be taxed at the higher, residential property rates of 18%/28% (working). The capital gains tax (CGT) saving will be £2,240 (£8,000 × 28%).

Working: Offset of remaining trading loss against chargeable gains

	Residential property gain	**Other gain**	**Total gains**
	£	£	£
Gain on UK rental property	45,000		45,000
Gain on Swartz Ltd shares		28,000	28,000
Less: Trading loss converted to capital loss	(8,000)		(8,000)
Less: Annual exempt amount	(6,000)		(6,000)
Less: Capital loss brought forward	(10,700)		(10,700)
Gain remaining chargeable	20,300	28,000	48,300

Tutorial notes

After taking relief for the trading loss, only £10,600 (£48,300 – £37,700) of Amelia's taxable gains will be taxed at the higher rate, instead of £18,600.

The trading loss would be treated as a current year capital loss in the CGT computation, (i.e. it would be deducted from Amelia's chargeable gains before deducting the annual exempt amount and the capital loss brought forward), as shown above. However, candidates were awarded full credit regardless of the order in which they deducted the trading loss.

Relief against income in the tax year 2023/24

In the tax year 2023/24 Amelia's total income is £47,600 (£30,000 + £11,600 + £6,000), so the full amount of the loss of £14,000 can be offset. Amelia's taxable income was £35,030 (£47,600 – £12,570), such that she was a basic rate taxpayer. The loss offset (which is against her non-savings income of this year) would generate a tax saving of £2,800 (£14,000 × 20%).

Relief against income in the tax years 2024/25 then 2023/24

Amelia could offset the loss against her income of £6,000 in 2024/25, with the remaining £8,000 offset against her income in 2023/24. This would save no tax in 2024/25, and only £1,600 (£8,000 × 20%) in 2023/24.

(b) Capital gains tax and income tax implications of the sale of Warehouse 1 and the acquisition of Warehouse 2 and the forklift truck

The sale of Warehouse 1 will give rise to a chargeable gain of £32,000 (£118,000 – £86,000).

Rollover relief will be available to defer part of this gain because Amelia acquired a qualifying replacement asset, Warehouse 2, during the year prior to the sale.

The acquisition of the forklift truck does not qualify for rollover relief as it is a movable asset.

Tutorial note

Rollover relief is available to defer the gain arising on the disposal of a qualifying asset, where a replacement qualifying asset is purchased within a qualifying time period.

Qualifying assets include:
- *Land and buildings (used in the trade)*
- *Goodwill (individuals only – not companies)*
- *Fixed (not movable) plant and machinery*

The gain which is eligible for rollover relief is restricted to £24,000 (£32,000 × 3/4) because Amelia only occupied three of the four floors of Warehouse 1 for business purposes.

The rollover relief available will be further restricted because not all of the proceeds relating to the business use of Warehouse 1 have been used to acquire Warehouse 2:

	£
Proceeds of business element (£118,000 × 3/4)	88,500
Cost of replacement	(83,000)
Gain remaining chargeable	5,500

The balance of the eligible gain of £18,500 (£24,000 – £5,500) will be available for rollover relief. Amelia's chargeable gain in respect of the sale of Warehouse 1 will therefore be £13,500 (£32,000 – £18,500).

The gain of £18,500 will be rolled over and deducted from the base cost of Warehouse 2. The base cost of Warehouse 2 will be £64,500 (£83,000 – £18,500).

Tutorial note

Rollover relief is restricted where there is non-trade use of the qualifying asset being sold or replaced.

Rollover relief is also restricted where the proceeds received on the sale of the original asset are not fully re-invested into a replacement qualifying asset.

The cost of the forklift truck of £23,000 will be eligible for the annual investment allowance in AS Trading's year ending 31 March 2026.

(c) Deregistration for value added tax (VAT)

Amelia is able to apply to voluntarily deregister for VAT on 31 March 2025 as the value of her taxable supplies in the following year are not expected to exceed the deregistration limit of £83,000. Her registration will be cancelled from 31 March 2025, or from a later date agreed with HM Revenue and Customs (HMRC).

On deregistration, output VAT will be payable on all non-current assets and inventory held by Amelia, on which input VAT was previously reclaimed. If the total VAT payable does not exceed £1,000, no payment is needed.

As a result of deregistration, Amelia will not be able to reclaim input VAT on the acquisition of Warehouse 2 and the forklift truck.

Tutor's top tips

Don't forget you can find the VAT de-registration threshold in your tax rates and allowances.

ACCA marking scheme

				Marks
(a)	(i)	Reliefs available		3.5
			Maximum	3.0
	(ii)	Relief in 2024/25 – against income		1.5
		– against gains		5.0
		Relief in 2023/24		2.5
		Relief in 2024/25 and 2023/24		1.0
				10.0
			Maximum	8.0

(b)	Availability of rollover relief		2.5
	Calculation of rollover relief		3.5
	AIA on forklift truck		1.0
			7.0
		Maximum	6.0
(c)	Deregistration for VAT		4.0
		Maximum	3.0
	Professional skills marks (see below)	**Maximum**	5.0
Total			**25.0**

Professional skills marks

Analysis and evaluation

- Use of information to support impact of loss relief options by reference to Amelia's tax status in part (a)(ii).
- Appropriate use of the data to determine suitable calculations of tax savings associated with available trading loss relief options in part (a)(ii) and the tax implications of the proposed sale of Warehouse 1 and acquisition of Warehouse 2 and the forklift truck in part (b).
- Appropriate use of the data to support discussion and draw appropriate conclusions about the availability of rollover relief on the proposed sale of Warehouse 1 in part (b).
- Demonstration of ability to consider all relevant taxes specified in the requirements.

Commercial acumen

- Recognition of constraints and opportunities related to choice of trading loss relief, for example, trading loss offset may not be desirable, but allows offset against gains in part (a)(ii).
- Recognition of possible consequences of potential future decision to voluntarily deregister for value added tax in part (c).

3 DORIAN

Key answer tips

This question focuses on a close company, its transactions with one of the directors and the late filing of its corporation tax return.

In part (a), although the question states that the company is a close company, the requirement specifically asks for an explanation as to why the company is close. It is worth learning the definition as being able to identify a close company is a common requirement in the exam.

Part (b) moves on from the definition of a close company to the implications. Another expectation of the ATX exam is the ability to explain the consequences of close company status in respect of loans made, and benefits provided, to shareholders.

In part (c) a comparison is required of two alternative ways of the company providing assistance with travel costs to the employee, and then a determination of which of the two would be better for the employee. Here computations are required; remember to provide clear, professional looking and sufficiently labelled numerical answers with accompanying explanations. It would be useful to use the spreadsheet for this part of your answer.

Part (d) requires a brief explanation of the implications for a company of the late filing of its corporation tax return. Administration will be tested at some point in the exam, and learning the key areas should provide some easy marks.

(a) Reason for close company status

A company is a close company if it is controlled by:

– Any number of shareholders who are also directors, or

– The five largest shareholders in the company.

Control is exercised by shareholders who own more than half of the company's issued share capital.

For the purpose of determining control, a shareholder is regarded as owning any shares owned by their associates, in addition to the shares which they own personally. Associates include direct relatives, so Dorian is associated with his father.

Dorian is regarded as owning 28% of the shares (his own 5% plus his father's 23%). The remaining five directors own a total of 25%, so that overall the six directors own 53% of the issued share capital, and control the company.

Tutorial note

There are additional complexities when determining whether or not a company is a close company, but the above points were sufficient to score full marks.

(b) Tax implications for Dorian and Taupe Ltd of early repayment of Dorian's £7,500 loan

There will be no tax implications for Dorian. This will be the only loan outstanding in 2026/27, so there will be no loan interest benefit arising as it does not exceed £10,000.

As Taupe Ltd is a close company, it will have paid notional tax of £2,531 (£7,500 × 33.75%) to HM Revenue and Customs (HMRC) in respect of the loan to Dorian, who is a participator in the company.

HMRC will repay the £2,531 to Taupe Ltd nine months and one day after the end of the accounting period in which the loan is repaid.

Accordingly, if Dorian repays the loan on 30 April 2026, Taupe Ltd will receive the repayment by 1 February 2027, one year earlier than it would if the loan were repaid on 30 June 2026.

Tutorial note

Where the total loans to the employee do not exceed £10,000, at any point in the tax year, they are an exempt benefit, and therefore no preferential interest benefit will arise.

The company is exempt from paying notional tax where the loan satisfies three requirements:

- *The loan does not exceed £15,000, and*
- *The individual is a full-time working employee, and*
- *The individual (including associates' interests) owns 5% of the shares or less.*

Notional tax will have been payable in respect of the £7,500 loan made to Dorian, because Dorian (including his associate Basil) owns more than 5% of the shares in Taupe Ltd.

(c) The cost to Dorian of the two alternative travel assistance proposals

Alternative 1: Provision of an interest-free loan to purchase a season ticket

Dorian already has an existing interest-free loan from Taupe Ltd of £7,500. If he receives a further loan from Taupe Ltd of £4,800, the total amount outstanding will exceed £10,000, such that a taxable benefit will arise in respect of the whole of these loans.

Both of the loans are interest-free, so there will be a taxable benefit, calculated by reference to the official rate of interest, of £277 ((£7,500 + £4,800) × 2.25%). This will be subject to income tax at 40%, as Dorian will be a higher rate taxpayer in 2025/26, but the loans will not result in a liability to class 1 national insurance contributions (NICs) for Dorian. The income tax payable would be £111 (£277 × 40%).

When the loan is written off on 5 April 2026, the amount written off will be treated as a distribution, and therefore liable to income tax at the rate of 33.75%. As Dorian has no other dividend income, the dividend nil rate band would be available, such that Dorian would incur an income tax liability of £1,283 ((£4,800 – £1,000) × 33.75%)).

The cost to Dorian of this alternative will be £1,394 (£111 + £1,283).

Tutorial note

Where a close company makes a loan to a shareholder, and that loan (or part of it) is later written off, for IT purposes it will be treated as a distribution (a dividend) in the hands of the shareholder. This treatment is the same regardless of whether the shareholder is, or is not, an employee.

For the purposes of NIC, if the shareholder is also an employee, class 1 NIC will be due on the loan written off. Candidates who were aware of this were awarded credit in their answers.

Alternative 2: Payment of a mileage allowance and provision of a free car-parking space

The mileage allowance will be subject to income tax at 40% and class 1 NIC at 2%. This will give rise to a total tax cost of £1,512 (£3,600 × 42%).

Dorian will have additional travel costs, not covered by the mileage allowance of £300 ((£5,220 – £1,320) – £3,600).

Provision of a car parking space at, or near, an employee's normal place of work is an exempt benefit for income tax and NIC.

The total cost to Dorian of this alternative is therefore £1,812 (£1,512 + £300).

Provision of the interest-free loan to purchase a season ticket results in the lower overall cost for Dorian.

Tutorial note

The approved mileage rates are not relevant in this case as the driving costs are not related to journeys made in the course of Dorian carrying out his duties of employment.

(d) Implications for Taupe Ltd of the late filing of its corporation tax return

Taupe Ltd's corporation tax return for the year ended 30 April 2023 should have been filed by 30 April 2024 (12 months after the end of the period of account), as the notice requiring the filing of this return was issued before 1 February 2024.

As the return was filed more than three months late, a fixed late filing penalty of £200 will arise. Although the return for the year ended 30 April 2022 was also filed late, the penalty will not be increased to £1,000 as the return for the year ended 30 April 2021 was filed on time.

Tutorial note

Candidates were awarded equal marks for consideration of other valid implications of late filing, such as, the impact on the deadline by which HMRC can commence a compliance check, reputational damage, subsequent late returns etc.

ACCA marking scheme			
			Marks
(a)	General definition		2.0
	Associates		1.0
	Application to scenario		1.5
			4.5
		Maximum	4.0
(b)	Tax implications for Dorian		1.0
	Tax implications for Taupe Ltd		4.0
		Maximum	5.0
(c)	Interest benefit		3.5
	Loan written off		2.0
	Mileage allowance alternative		4.0
			9.5
		Maximum	8.0
(d)	Filing date		1.5
	Penalty		2.0
			3.5
		Maximum	3.0
	Professional skills marks (see below)	**Maximum**	5.0
Total			**25.0**

Analysis and evaluation

- Appropriate use of the data to arrive at conclusion regarding Taupe Ltd's close company status in part (a).
- Appropriate use of the data to determine suitable calculations of the overall cost to Dorian of Alternatives 1 and 2 and draw appropriate conclusions in part (c).
- Use of information to determine impact for Dorian and Taupe Ltd of early repayment of the loan in part (b).
- Demonstration of reasoned judgement regarding implications of late filing in part (d).

Commercial acumen

- Recognition of other possible consequences of late filing of corporation tax return in part (d).
- Other practical considerations related to the calculation of cost to Dorian of Alternative 2 (e.g. additional non-tax travel costs) in part (c).